Also by Antony Stockwell (A.S.)

'A Corrupt Tree'. Volume 1 – The Unholy Popes and the Debasement of Western Civilisation

Anti-Semitism of the Catholic Church

A History

Antony Stockwell

To order additional copies of this book, contact:
Xlibris
1-800-455-039
www.Xlibris.com.au
Orders@Xlibris.com.au
615573

Contents

Abbreviations

Bul Rom Pont	Bula Romanus Pontifex
BVP	Bayerische Volkspartei
CCC	Catechism of the Catholic Church
CCP	Catholic Centre Party (Deutsche Zentrumspartei)
CIA	Central Intelligence Agency
CIC	Counter Intelligence Corps
CRRJ	Commission for Religious Relations with the Jews
CSP	Christlichsoziale Partei
CSsR	Congregatio Sanctissimi Redemptoris
CTK	Česká tisková kancelář
CV	Cartellverband der katholischen deutschen Studentenverbindungen
DAIE	Delegación Argentina de Inmigración en Europa
DAP	Deutsche Arbeiterpartei
EK	Einsatzkommandos
ep	epistle
FCCH	The Fathers of the Church
Gestapo	Geheime Staatspolizei
HSL'S	Hlinka Slovenská ľudová strana
IMT	International Military Tribunal
JDC	American Jewish Joint Distribution Committee
KL	Konzentrationslager
Kripo	Kriminalpolizei
Ľudáks	Slovenská ľudová strana
MMC	Marsh & McLennan Companies
NDH	Nezavisna Država Hrvatska
NG	Nuremberg Government (NMT; concerning Nazi government agencies)
NMT	Nuremberg Military Tribunals
NOK	Nemzeti Összefogás Kormánya
NS	National Socialism
NSDAP	Nationalsozialistische Deutsche Arbeiterpartei
ODESSA	Organisation der Ehemaligen SS-Angehörigen
OSB	Order of Saint Benedict
OZON	Obóz Zjednoczenia Narodowego
PAC	*The Plot Against the Church*
PAN	Polska Akademia Nauk
PCA	Pontifical Commission of Assistance
PS	Paris-Storey (Col. R. Storey, Documentation Division, Paris; the principal US collection for the IMT)
PSF	Parti social français
RDL	Regio Decreto Legge

RGB	Reichsgesetzblatt
RSHA	Reichssicherheitshauptamt
SA	Sturmabteilung
SARE	Society in Argentina for the Reception of Europeans
SD	Sicherheitsdienst
SHO	Slovenské hnutie obrody
SiPo	Sicherheitspolizei
SJ	Society of Jesus
SND	Stronnictwo Narodowo-Demokratyczne
SNS	Slovenská národná strana
SS	Schutzstaffel
SSNJ	Strana slovenskej národnej jednoty
SSPX	Society of Saint Pius X (Fraternitas Sacerdotalis Sancti Pii X)
SS-WVHA	SS-Wirtschafts-Verwaltungshauptamt
Stasi	Staatssicherheit
T4	Tiergartenstrasse 4
USCCB	US Conference of Catholic Bishops

Tables

1 – Abysmal Hatred, Church Fathers, Saints, Popes

Consider mine enemies; for they are many; and they hate me with cruel hatred ... They compassed me about also with words of hatred; and fought against me without a cause. For my love they are my adversaries: but I give myself unto prayer. And they have rewarded me evil for good, and hatred for my love. Psalms 25:19, 109:3-5

One of the most common defences offered against the Church's responsibility for modern anti-Semitism is that, to the extent that Roman Catholic anti-Semitism did exist in the past, it was the product of apostates, reactionaries, or the ignorant and uneducated. In this refutation, the popes are alleged to have pursued a benevolent policy toward the Jews. There has been a very long history of specious Catholic attempts to portray the popes as both benefactors of the Jews and as their protectors against episodic outbreaks of violence whose antecedents have been said to lie outside the Church.[1] Typical of such efforts are the comments in the article 'Judaism' in the *Catholic Encyclopedia* – possibly one of the most self-exonerating, hypocritical, and mendacious articles in this entire enterprise:[2]

Judaism and early Christianity

> It is the Christian Church, which was able silently to leaven the Roman Empire, which has outlived the ruin of the Jewish Temple and its worship, and which, in the course of centuries, has extended to the confines of the world the knowledge and the worship of the God of Abraham, while *Judaism has remained the barren fig-tree which Jesus condemned during His mortal life* ...[3]

> Paul, now become an ardent Apostle of Christ ... The result of his consuming zeal for the salvation of souls redeemed by the blood of Christ was the formation of religious communities bound together by the same faith, hope, and charity[4] as the churches of Palestine, sharing in the same sacred mysteries, governed by pastors likewise vested with Christ's authority,[5] and forming a vast Church organism vivified by the same Holy Spirit and clearly distinct from Judaism. Thus the small mustard seed planted by Jesus in Judea had grown into a great tree fully able to near the storms of persecution and heresy.

Judaism since AD 70

> While Christianity thus asserted itself as the new Kingdom of God, the Jewish

---

[1] Kertzer, David I. *The Popes Against the Jews: The Vatican's Role in the Rise The Vatican's Role in ...* p18

[2] 'In the *Catholic Encyclopedia*,' wrote Joseph McCabe, a former professor of Catholic philosophy, 'we expect anything.' For more information on this subject, refer to: McCabe, Joseph. *The Myth of Catholic Scholarship: The Absurdities, Falsehoods and Distortions of the Catholic Encyclopedia.*

[3] Unless otherwise indicated, significant phrases in many quoted texts have been emphasised in this book with italics.

[4] The paucity of true Christian charity is one of the dominant features of the history of the Catholic Church.

[5] In his 2013 book *Why Priests?: A Failed Tradition*, Professor Gary Wills argues that 'the Catholic/Orthodox priesthood has been one long mistake.' (Review by *The Washington Post*. 15 February 2013)

theocracy, guided by leaders unable 'to know the signs of the times', was *hastening to its total destruction.*[1] ... The Romans came, and in AD 70 put an end forever to the Jewish Temple, priesthood, sacrifices, and nation, whereby it should have become clear to the Jews that their national worship *was rejected of God.*

Judaism and Church legislation

History proves indeed that Church authorities exercised at times considerable pressure upon the Jews to promote their conversion; but it also proves that the same authorities generally deprecated the use of violence for the purpose. It bears witness, in particular, to *the untiring and energetic efforts of the Roman pontiffs in behalf of the Jews* especially when, threatened or actually pressed by persecution, they appealed to the Holy See for protection. It chronicles the numerous protestations of the popes against mob violence against the Jewish race, and thus directs the attention of the student of history to the real cause of the Jewish persecutions, viz., the popular hatred against the children of Israel.[2]

There remains only to add a few remarks which will explain the *apparent* severity of certain measures enacted by either popes or councils concerning the Jews, or account for the fact that popular hatred of them so often defeated the *beneficent efforts of the Roman pontiffs* in their regard.

The obligation of wearing a distinguishing badge was of course obnoxious to the Jews. At the same time, Church authorities deemed its injunction necessary to *prevent effectively moral offences* between Jews and Christian women.[3]

It was for the laudable reason of protecting social morality and securing the maintenance of the Christian Faith, that canonical decrees were framed and repeatedly enforced *against free and constant intercourse* between Christians and Jews ...

History proves indeed that *Church authorities* exercised at times *considerable pressure* upon the Jews to promote their conversion ...

The article concludes magnificently, but mendaciously:

one can readily understand how the popular hatred[4] of the Jews has too often defeated *the beneficent efforts of the Church, and notably of its supreme pontiffs, in regard to them.*

In the following chapters, revealed history fully negates this supreme lie.

---

[1] Nevertheless, of the Jews it has been truly said: 'Their very persecution has preserved them from merging their individuality in that of other races, and *they remain to this day a monument of Christian ingratitude, falsity, and impotence.*'

[2] Whence did this hatred arise, if not from the Church?

[3] A vivid example of the consequences of the injunction is that of one Johannes Alardus (Jean Alard) who kept a Jewess in his house in Paris and had several children by her. He was convicted of sodomy on account of this relationship, and he and his partner were incinerated on behalf of the Catholic Church because 'coition with a Jewess is precisely the same as if a man should copulate with a dog.'

[4] *Hatred paralyzes life; love releases it. Hatred confuses life; love harmonizes it. Hatred darkens life; love illuminates it.* Martin Luther King, Jr

The Deity

The Roman Catholic 'God the Father' is the Jewish God of the *Torah*[1] (the Old Testament). There is no known evidence that he abandoned his Jewishness with the advent of Christianity.

The *Catholic Encyclopedia* ('the Blessed Trinity') states:

> "the Father is God, the Son is God, and the Holy Spirit is God, and yet there are not three Gods but one God." In this Trinity of Persons the Son is begotten of the Father by an eternal generation, and the Holy Spirit proceeds by an eternal procession from the Father and the Son. Yet, notwithstanding this difference as to origin, the Persons are co-eternal and co-equal: *all alike are uncreated.*

The Jewish *Book of Psalms* refers to the Jewish Holy Spirit (Holy Ghost):

> Create in me a clean heart, O God; and renew a right spirit within me. Cast me not away from thy presence; and take not thy holy spirit from me. (*Psalms* 51:10-11)

The *Catholic Encyclopedia* ('Holy Ghost') also states that 'The Holy Ghost is the Third Person of the Blessed Trinity.' 'Such is the belief the Catholic faith demands.' The Holy Ghost is therefore not only a person[2] 'consubstantial'(that is regarded as the same in substance or essence), 'co-eternal', and co-equal' with the Jewish God, he *is* that Jewish God.

Jesus is the Second Person of the Blessed Trinity. Such also 'is the belief the Catholic faith demands.' Jesus was born, lived and died a Jew. In the Christian faith, he is deemed to be the Son of God. He also is 'co-eternal' and 'uncreated' and 'consubstantial with' the Jewish God, he is, ipso facto, that same Jewish God. This is confirmed in the *Catholic Encyclopedia* ('The Blessed Virgin Mary') by the words: 'In general, the theology and history of Mary the Mother of God ...'

Hence, in the Roman Catholic faith, all three God persons are eternal. That is, they have always been so, and will remain so. It follows, therefore, that, in the Catholic faith, these three persons have always been, and always will be the Jewish God.

Accordingly, in the words of Moritz Güdemann, Chief Rabbi of Vienna, 1907:

> The Christian kneels before the image of the Jew, wrings his hands before the image of a Jewess; his Apostles, Festivals, and Psalms are Jewish. Only a few are able to come to terms with this contradiction – most free themselves by anti-Semitism. Obliged to revere a Jew as God, they wreak vengeance upon the rest of the Jews by treating them as devils.[3]

---

[1] The *Torah* is variously defined as either the first five books of the Hebrew Bible, or as the whole body of the Jewish sacred writings and tradition including the oral tradition.

[2] For an explanation of the Catholic Church's dogma of the 'Person', refer to the extensive article in the *Catholic Encyclopedia*. These persons are all said to be male – but there is no explanation of what this means.

[3] Dworkin, Andrea. *The Jews, Israel, and Women's Liberation*. p17

The Vast, Intense and Abysmal Christian Hatred of the Jews

The earliest Christians were Jews.[1] Jesus was born lived and died a Jew. His earthly father (Joseph), mother (Mary), brothers and sisters were all Jews.[2]

In its primal stages, Christianity comprised a Jewish messianic sect that claimed to be the true Israel, and which accused official Judaism of wickedness and perfidy. The resulting relationship between Christianity and anti-Semitism[3] has had a long history.

In the 'Foreword' to Father Flannery's book *The Anguish of the Jews*, Professor Philip Cunningham records that Flannery wrote the book 'to acquaint Christians generally with the immense sufferings of the Jews throughout the Christian era.'[4]

Anti-Semitism is a hatred. It has justifiably been described as the longest and deepest hatred of human history,[5,6] and as an unparalleled malignity.[7] It has also been universal, and the most obsessive, dangerous and chimerical hatred that has existed on earth. For Christians, the history of this longest hatred is 'a story that calls for repentance.' [8]

Throughout the Christian era, popes, saints, ecclesiastics, and Roman Catholics in civil authorities, as a necessary requirement of allegiance to their Church, took upon themselves the responsibility of constraining, punishing, and vilifying the Jew. With the dominating influence of Christianity on occidental society, culture and government, Christian anti-Semitism led to the marginalisation of the Jews and their institutionalised oppression.[9] Christian hatred and discrimination against Jews became systematic and universal.

In his work *The Devil and the Jews: The Medieval Conception of the Jew and Its Relation to Modern Anti-Semitism,* Joshua Trachtenberg reports that the most vivid impression that one acquires from reading Christian mediaeval references to the Jew is of a vast, intense and abysmal hatred. Such literature contains an endless array of vile adjectives, accusations and curses. It consistently represents the Jew as the paradigm of everything abominable and evil. The Jew was the recipient of fanatical, limitless scorn and vilification.[10]

Notwithstanding its claims to the contrary, history reveals that the Catholic Church has largely been responsible for this extended animosity. Some of the most virulent anti-

---

[1] Walls, Andrew. 'Christianity'. In: *A Handbook of Living Religions.* p56

[2] See, for example, *Mark* 6:3, 'Is not this the carpenter, the son of Mary, the brother of James, and Joseph, and Jude, and Simon? are not also his sisters here with us?' (Catholic *Douay-Rheims Bible*)

[3] In reviewing the literature, it is evident that the meanings attributed to the terms 'anti-Semitism', 'anti-Judaism' and 'anti-Jewish' are frequently: either unclear, refer to race alone, refer to culture alone, refer to religion alone, are integrated with respect to race and/or religion and/or culture, are conflicting, or are ambiguous. In this book, with the possible exception of quoted text, the term 'anti-Semitism' is used as an umbrella term denoting 'hostility and/or prejudice against Jews and/or their religion and/or their culture'.

[4] Foreword by Philip A Cunningham, to: Flannery, Edward H. *The Anguish of the Jews.* p vii

[5] Wistrich, Robert S. *Anti-Semitism: The Longest Hatred*

[6] Flannery, Edward H. *The Anguish of the Jews.* p284. Fr Flannery is considered a 'spiritual giant'.

[7] http://www.zionism-israel.com/his/judeophobia14.htm (2007)

[8] Foreword by Philip A Cunningham, to: Flannery, Edward H. *The Anguish of the Jews.* p xi

[9] Wistrich, Robert S. *Anti-Semitism: The Longest Hatred.* p xix

[10] Trachtenberg, Joshua. *The Devil and the Jews: The Medieval Conception of the Jew and its Relation ...* p12

Semites within the Church, were (and still are) revered as Saints.[1] Jews were maligned by the religion that was supposed to be compassionate;[2] discriminated against by the religion that was intended to manifest charity;[3] and segregated, massacred, and burned alive by the self-proclaimed 'apostolic' church that was supposedly centred upon love.[4]

Robert S Wistrich, in his book *Anti-Semitism: The Longest Hatred*, points out that by the thirteenth century, the Church's canon law had fully institutionalised the perverse status of the Jew and the doctrine of 'Servitus Judaeorum' ('Servitude of the Jews') that required Jews to be subordinate to Christians. Christian society had to be protected from Jewish 'contamination' via living, eating, and sexual relations.

Seven centuries later, Adolf Hitler, a Roman Catholic, confirmed that 'Hate is more lasting than dislike.'

Theologians insisted that persecution and seizure of property was a legitimate activity of Roman Catholic powers. Violence to the Jews was deemed legitimate, and they were put to the sword at the dictation of the Church. The Jew had no rights to be violated.[5]

John Jortin (1698-1770) was a church historian. In his *Remarks on Ecclesiastical History* he stated that:

> The account of the Jews who have been plundered, sent naked into banishment, starved, tortured, left to perish in prisons, hanged and burnt by Christians, would fill many volumes.[6]

The history of the Church's anti-Semitism has been summarised by G W Foote and J M Wheeler, in their book *Crimes of Christianity* (1887):

> The story of the crimes of Christianity against the people from whom it is derived, and to whom it owes its God and Savior, is one which lasts from the time when it first obtained civil power until the present day. Like an unnatural child, Christianity has turned against and pursued its parent with relentless malice. Pious Christians have fulfilled the prophecies by making the name of Jew a byword and a reproach, and have plundered and persecuted the chosen race until their lives became a curse. Yet, hounded from country to country, like beasts of the chase, visited with such atrocities that to escape them mothers have destroyed the children to whom they gave suck, they have not ceased to make their mute but unanswerable protest against the errors of Christianity. Their very persecution has preserved them from merging

---

[1] http://www.zionism-israel.cocornwm/his/judeophobia6.htm (2007). The *Catholic Encyclopedia* states that the Church sees the saints as 'friends and servants of God whose holy lives have made them worthy of His special love.' For many saints, this is a serious contradiction of the facts.

[2] 'Finally, be ye all of one mind, having compassion one of another ...' *1 Peter* 3:8-9

[3] 'Though I speak with the tongues of men and of angels, and have not charity, I am become as sounding brass, or a tinkling cymbal. And though I have the gift of prophecy, and understand all mysteries, and all knowledge; and though I have all faith, so that I could remove mountains, and have not charity, I am nothing.' *1 Corinthians* 13:1-2

[4] 'He that loveth not knoweth not God; for God is love.' *1 John* 4:8

[5] Russell, J B. *Witchcraft in the Middle Ages.* p148

[6] Source: Foote, G W & J M Wheeler. *Crimes of Christianity.* Vol I. Ch VIII. 'Persecution of the Jews'

their individuality in that of other races, and *they remain to this day a monument of Christian ingratitude, falsity, and impotence.*[1]

In his book *Pius XII: The Hound of Hitler*, Gerard Noel has confirmed that in the perception of the Church, because the Jews were guilty of deicide, by being party to Christ's crucifixion, they have been in some mysterious way damned throughout history. The ominous development[2] of this theological, anti-Semitic, 'historical fatalism', which lacks humanity and true Christianity, has led to deadly outcomes. While the Church has recently stated that it 'deplores' anti-Semitism, 'it has stopped short of condemning it.' And while it has, at last, exonerated Jews from the guilt of Jesus' crucifixion, it has failed to exculpate them of deicide.[3]

An example of the largely unconscious image that Roman Catholics continue to have of Jews is to be found in Catholicism's dominant place of pilgrimage, Lourdes. There, are depicted the Stations of the Cross in a series of epic tableaux portraying Jesus' progress towards Calvary. They portray the Roman soldiers protecting Jesus from the snarls and lewd gestures of the mob, who appear as hideous Jews with gaping mouths, hooked noses and gnarled accusing fingers. Jesus, a Jew, is portrayed as a god-like Aryan figure. Gerard Noel points out that the significant aspect of this parody is that its inappropriateness is scarcely ever, if at all, noticed by the myriads of pilgrims who stop to pray at each Station.[4]

In his *Les Prophètes d'Israel* (1892), James Darmesteter, the French author and antiquarian, confirmed that:

> The hatred of the people against the Jew is the work of the Church ...[5]

Christopher Hitchens, in his book *God is not Great: How Religion Poisons Everything*, points out to his readers that the Church did not claim that *some* Jews killed Christ, it insisted that *the* Jews were responsible for the crime.[6]

In *The Popes Against the Jews: The Vatican's Role in the Rise of Modern Anti-Semitism*, Professor David I Kertzer has reminded the world that the Church's anti-Semitism is an example of the age-old situation of a powerful religion that both credits itself as being the divinely appointed possessor of the truth, and as being the vicious opponent of a despised minority that is said to be the agent of the devil.[7]

One of the foremost problems of anti-Semitism today is that of bringing Catholics to a complete recognition of the enormity of the malign influence and the preponderant role played by Catholics and the Catholic Church.[8] 'There can be no quarter conceded to pious dissimulation or defensive minimizing of the magnitude of the crime committed

---

[1] Foote, G W & J M Wheeler. *Crimes of Christianity.* Vol I. Ch VIII. 'Persecution of the Jews'
[2] Flannery, Edward H. *The Anguish of the Jews.* p63
[3] Noel, Gerard. *Pius XII: The Hound of Hitler.* p198
[4] Ibid. pp198-99
[5] Source: http://www.zionism-israel.com/his/judeophobia14.htm (2007)
[6] Hitchens, Christopher. *God is not Great: How Religion Poisons Everything.* p210
[7] Kertzer, David I. *The Popes Against the Jews: The Vatican's Role in the Rise of Modern Anti-Semitism.* p21
[8] Flannery, Edward H. *The Anguish of the Jews.* p294

against the Jews'[1] by this asserted divinely appointed possessor of the truth. Undeniably:

> *most* Catholic writers, thinkers, theologians, politicians, and prelates have expressed a profound hostility towards the Jews, and their attitudes have incontestably influenced average Catholics.[2]

In all this, the Jewishness of the ancient Hebrew heroes was either systematically denied or subtly understated.[3] Even worse, the Church always ignored, and often denied, that Jesus was himself a Jew.[4] 'We call men dangerous whose minds are made differently from our own,' said Anatole France (1844-1942), the greatest French writer of his times, 'and immoral those who profess another standard of ethics.'[5] He also wrote a letter to the International Congress of Freethinkers in Paris in 1905, in which he stated:

> The thoughts of the gods are not more unchangeable than those of the men who interpret them. They advance – but they also lag behind the thoughts of men ... The Christian God was once a Jew. *Now he is an anti-Semite.*[6]

By the Middle Ages, Jews were perceived as the personification of evil, and were associated with demons. Sometimes they were depicted as the Devil himself; and in art, Jews were portrayed as agents of Lucifer with evil faces, horns and a tail. At other times, they were seen as intermediaries between the Devil and innocent humanity. This demonic Jew was specific to Christian Europe.

At other times Satan was portrayed as riding on the back of a Jew; on other occasions, he appeared in the semblance of a seductive woman to emphasise the lechery[7] that was traditionally ascribed to Jews. These portrayals symbolised the embodied forces of heresy and rebellion against the Christian God, and depicted the Jew as personifying the will of the Devil. Inexorably, this led to the dehumanisation of the Jew.[8]

Hence the Jew as a creature of the Devil was considered to be barely human, if at all. Peter the Venerable of Cluny declared 'Really I doubt whether a Jew can be human for he will neither yield to human reasoning, nor find satisfaction in authoritative utterances, alike divine and Jewish.'[9]

Having been burdened by such diabolical attributes, it followed that the Jews were butchered without remorse or guilt.[10]

Dr Gustavo Perednik has pointed out that the following characteristics make and have made anti-Semitism very different from the hatred of other groups:[11]

---

[1] Flannery, Edward H. *The Anguish of the Jews*. p294
[2] Michael, Robert. *A History of Catholic Antisemitism: The Dark Side of the Church*. p5
[3] Spong, John Shelby. *Liberating the Gospels: Reading the Bible with Jewish Eyes*. pp28-29
[4] See, for example: Callil, Carmen. *Bad Faith: A Forgotten History of Family & Fatherland*. p14
[5] France, Anatole. *The Garden of Epicurus*. p101
[6] McCabe, Joseph. *A Biographical Dictionary of Ancient, Medieval, and Modern Freethinkers*
[7] A modern example is a letter of Eugenio Pacelli (the future Pius XII) describing Jews: 'like all the rest of them … with lecherous demeanour and suggestive smiles.' Midlarsky, Manus I. *The Killing Trap ...* pp220-21
[8] Wistrich, Robert S. *Anti-Semitism: The Longest Hatred*. pp29-30
[9] Goldhagen, Daniel Jonah. *Hitler's Willing Executioners: Ordinary Germans and the Holocaust*. pp52-53
[10] Cohn-Sherbok, D. *The Crucified Jew: Twenty Centuries of Christian Anti-Semitism*. pp54-55
[11] http://www.zionism-israel.com/his/judeophobia.htm (2007)

It is the oldest hatred. There is no other hatred in the history of humankind that can be traced back two millennia.

It has existed in almost every country on earth, irrespective of whether it had had Jewish inhabitants, or how many lived there.

It is residual. Jews were despised and hated for decades and even centuries after they left their country of residence.

Negative stereotypes of the Jew are profoundly embedded. Anti-Semites have their own mental associations that are prejudicial to Jews.

It is based on fantasy. For example, it will be seen later that Jews have been accused: of killing Christians for their blood for ritual purposes; of desecration of the Host;[1] of being agents of the Devil; as possessing horns, tails, and the beard of a goat; and for producing a terrible odour.

It is obsessive, in that Jews are not just an enemy, they are *the* enemy.

Jews have been expelled from almost every country of the world in which they have lived.

It is dangerous because it has often been transformed into physical violence and murder.

The evidence of this and the following chapters amply substantiates these observations.

The Apostles were the Original Anti-Semites

Jesus was born, lived and died a Jew. His father, mother, brothers, sisters and first disciples were all Jews. According to Christian teaching and Christian theological interpretation of the Hebrew Scriptures, Jesus was also the Son of God and the glorious Messiah. But he died ingloriously on a cross, in the company of crucified malefactors, most probably as a troublesome Jewish agitator, at the hands of the Roman occupying power.

The original Apostles started the anti-Jewish propaganda – they transferred the guilt for the death of Jesus from the shoulders of the Roman authorities (who actually killed Jesus) to the Jewish leaders (who did not). They presented these Jews as the ones who led the suffering prophet – the Messiah depicted in the Old Testament – to his excruciating death. Jesus was perceived by these earliest Christians to be the Son of Man of whom this fate was written.

The narrative of the death of Jesus in the New Testament systematically transferred responsibility for his crucifixion from the Romans to the Jews.

The consequences of this deliberate Christian myth have been incalculable. On the one hand, by this alleged deicide, this killing of the Son of God, the Jews were seen to be a people damned, who were thenceforth condemned to permanent exile and

---

[1] In Roman Catholicism 'The bread destined to receive Eucharistic Consecration is commonly called the host'. *Catholic Encyclopedia* ('Host')

wandering; on the other hand, the Christian Church perceived itself as the new Israel and the recipient of the divine promises to Abraham.[1] Subsequently, through the centuries, when the Jews were incessantly blamed for killing Christ, not a single theologian ever called attention to the fact that the Jews never killed Christ – they simply handed him over to the Romans.[2]

The first gospel writers performed this fateful shift. In *Matthew*, for example, Pilate, the Roman governor of Palestine, is stated to have offered to release Jesus in exchange for a common criminal, but was unable to do so because the Jews were demanding Jesus' death. Matthew referred to these disbelieving Jews as blind fools, hypocrites and serpents.[3] He also added the well-known fictional statement of Pilate's washing his hands and his alleged affirmation of his own innocence:

> When Pilate saw that he could prevail nothing, but that rather a tumult was made, he took water, and washed his hands before the multitude, saying, I am innocent of the blood of this just person: see ye to it. (*Matthew* 27:24)

Furthermore, historical research has shown that Matthew also fabricated the infamous curse that thereafter saddled the Jews with the entire blame for the death of Jesus: 'Then answered all the people, and said, "His blood be on us, and on our children." ' (*Matthew* 27:25) The French historian Charles Guignebert wrote in 1935 about this and other passages of a similar kind in the New Testament: 'Few of the sayings of the Gospels have done more harm than these, and yet they are only the invention of a redactor.'[4,5]

Matthew also scribed:

> And I say unto you, That many shall come from the east and west, and shall sit down with Abraham, and Isaac, and Jacob, in the kingdom of heaven. But the children of the kingdom shall be cast out into outer darkness: there shall be weeping and gnashing of teeth. (*Matthew* 8:11-12)

Luke portrayed Pilate as making two attempts to free Jesus, and even introduced Herod to support him.

John's gospel, which was the last to be written, was also the one most hostile to the Jews,[6] being the pinnacle of anti-Semitism in the New Testament. In it, the term 'the Jews' became an embodiment of everything that resisted and rejected the light and expressed the malice that persistently sought to kill the Messiah. John insisted that Jesus was crucified by the Jews under Jewish Law and thereby affirmed the charge of deicide.

Over all, therefore, the Roman effectors of the Crucifixion were placed in the background, Pilate was totally acquitted of guilt, and the whole blame for the suffering and

---

[1] Wistrich, Robert S. *Anti-Semitism: The Longest Hatred.* pp13-15
[2] de Rosa, Peter. *Vicars of Christ: The Dark Side of the Papacy.* p177
[3] Cohn-Sherbok, D. *The Crucified Jew: Twenty Centuries of Christian Anti-Semitism.* pp13-15
[4] Guignebert, C. Quoted in: Bazes, Moses. *Jesus the Jew, the Historical Jesus*, p470. Source: Golding, Shmuel. 'Anti- Semitism in the New Testament', *Biblical Polemics*, 1 (May 1988): p12
[5] Redactor – someone who puts text into appropriate form for publication.
[6] Poliakov, Léon. *The History of Anti-Semitism.* Vol I. p24

death of Jesus was cast on his fellow Jews.[1]

✓ The Apostle Paul was extremely anti-Semitic and filled with missionary zeal. He was the person most responsible for separating Jesus from his Jewish background, for transferring the guilt for the Crucifixion from the Romans to the Jews, and for stigmatising the Jews as a God-rejected people.[2]

✓ In Paul's *Epistle to the Hebrews*, Jesus is conceptualised as the true eternal Temple who is opposed to the temporal cult of Jerusalem.[3] Paul also called to Christians to be 'blameless and innocent, children of God, without blemish, in the midst of a crooked and perverse generation, among whom you shine as lights in the world.' (*Philippians* 2:15) In proclaiming this Christian message, Paul stressed that God had rejected the Hebrews and the new covenant had replaced the old:

> the Jews: Who both killed the Lord Jesus, and their own prophets, and have persecuted us; and they please not God, and are contrary to all men: Forbidding us to speak to the Gentiles that they might be saved, to fill up their sins alway: for the wrath is come upon them to the uttermost. (*1 Thessalonians* 2:14-16)

✓ Hence Paul, who was later declared a Saint by the Church, was the true founder of anti-Semitic Christianity.[4,5] It was he, with his intense proselytisation, who ultimately changed the course of the history of the world,[6] and was the harbinger of all the sinister material recorded in this and the following chapters.

Accordingly, Rabbi Eliezer Berkovits has stated convincingly that 'without Christianity's *New Testament*, Hitler's *Mein Kampf* could never have been written.'[7]

During the 1960s, the philosopher Éliane Amado Levy-Valensi offered her interpretation, namely, that anti-Semitism is the consequence of the early Christians' theft of Jewish history for themselves. On the one hand, the Jews already had an ancient religion, possessed an outstanding historical literature embracing great heroes and sages, and were divinely promised an even more glorious future. On the other hand, Christianity had none of these. Therefore, from the very beginning, the Christians appropriated both the Hebraic Old Testament and the New Testament as being exclusively their own.[8,9]

The Role of the Crucifixion

The main source of later anti-Semitism is the account of the Crucifixion in the

[1] Trachtenberg, Joshua. *The Devil and the Jews: The Medieval Conception of the Jew and its ...* p20
[2] There have been recent claims that Paul was not anti-Semitic; that his doctrine was one of 'benevolence'. Refer: Flannery, Edward H. *The Anguish of the Jews.* p30.
[3] Cohn-Sherbok, D. *The Crucified Jew: Twenty Centuries of Christian Anti-Semitism.* p12
[4] Wistrich, Robert S. *Anti-Semitism: The Longest Hatred.* pp13-15
[5] See also: http://www.zionism-israel.com/his/judeophobia3.htm (2007)
[6] Poliakov, Léon. *The History of Anti-Semitism.* Vol I. p19. Source: Weitzman, Mark. *Antisemitism: A Historical Survey* (http://motlc.wiesenthal.com/resources/education/historicalsurvey/index.html)
[7] Source: Dietrich, Donald J. *God & Humanity in Auschwitz.* p47
[8] http://www.zionism-israel.com/his/judeophobia14.htm (2007)
[9] This theft was the precursor to the multitude of larcenies over the centuries, by the Catholic Church, of the religious sites and material of other Christian denominations and other religions.

Christian New Testament. It is replete with historical inaccuracies:

> The Sanhedrin was the supreme Jewish political, religious and judicial body in Judea during the Roman period. According to the New Testament narrative, the Sanhedrin tried Jesus and condemned him to death during Passover; then the Roman governor Pontius Pilate attempted to avoid implementing the death penalty, but he eventually acceded to an insistent Sanhedrin[1] and let Jesus be crucified by Roman soldiers. However, the Sanhedrin never met during festivals, and it seldom applied death penalties.[2]

> There were crimes that deserved capital punishment according to biblical law; but to claim to be the son of God appears nowhere in the Bible as a crime. Hence, there was alleged to have been a prompt death penalty decreed upon a Jew, Jesus, whose crime did not exist in Jewish law.

> ➤ Four methods of judicial capital punishment were stated in Talmudic law: stoning, burning, slaying and strangling. This was in contrast with crucifixion, which was a typical Roman method. Furthermore, the Sanhedrin could have carried out execution without any Roman intervention.

> The described role of Pilate is extremely unlikely. He was a man in charge of suppressing the Jews and had ordered the crucifixion of thousands of them. It is most improbable that he would strive to defend one of them.

> ◆ Pilate's means of expressing his defence of Jesus is also suspect. The custom of washing one's hands as a sign of purity, known as 'Netilat Yadaim', is an old Jewish one, which is still practised by Orthodox Jews. It is extremely unlikely that a Roman military man would resort to such a Jewish practice.[3]

Dr Gustavo Perednik believes that the reason why the Crucifixion was retold by the Gospel writers was to consolidate the new Christian religion. Accusing the mighty empire of having murdered God would have been perilous. However, by glossing over the Roman motivation and accusing the Jews, the evangelical Gospel sought to derive strength and acceptance.[4]

The Alleged Culpability of the Jews

These culpable, deicidal Jews were essential to Christian theology as the mythical projection of the arch-enemy. Hence Apostle John had Jesus saying of the Jews:

> Ye are of your father the devil, and the lusts of your father ye will do. He was a murderer from the beginning, and abode not in the truth, because there is no truth in

---

[1] The Sanhedrin ('sitting together', hence 'assembly' or 'council') was an assembly of twenty to twenty-three men appointed in every city in the biblical Land of Israel.

[2] The *Talmud* specifies that 'a Sanhedrin which puts a man to death once in seven years is called a murderous one.' (*Makkot* 1:10)

[3] http://www.zionism-israel.com/his/judeophobia4.htm (2007)

[4] Ibid.

him. When he speaketh a lie, he speaketh of his own: for he is a liar, and the father of it. (*John* 8:44)

Revelation (2:9) also associates the Jews to the Devil:

I know the blasphemy of them which say they are Jews, and are not, but are the synagogue of Satan.

Revelation (3:9) states as well:

Behold, I will make them of the synagogue of Satan, which say they are Jews, and are not, but do lie; behold, I will make them to come and worship before thy feet, and to know that I have loved thee.

Thereby making explicit a linked identity between the Devil and the Jews which continued for centuries.[1]

The consequence of this Christian myth's perception of the Devil and the Jew as being the inexorable enemies of Jesus was the establishment of a relationship between the two. This became ever more prominent over the coming centuries.

John also emphasised the contrast between the new believers (the true limb of God) and the old:

I am the vine, ye are the branches: He that abideth in me, and I in him, the same bringeth forth much fruit: for without me ye can do nothing. If a man abide not in me, he is cast forth as a branch, and is withered; and men gather them, and cast them into the fire, and they are burned. (*John* 15:5-6)[2]

The consequence of this intense anti-Semitism was that the new Church, having attributed a divine nature to Jesus, inevitably constructed his death as a deicide. Such killing was the sin of sins; and equally inevitably, the crime was on the heads of the non-Christian Jews who had denied him. There was no dispute. Their fall from grace was absolute.[3]

Classical Paganism and the Jews

The contrast between the almost incidental aversion of the pagans to Jews and the fundamental Catholic animosity is striking.[4]

No pagan attempts were made to restrict Jewish civil liberties or segregate them from the rest of society. They were not seen as murderers of a god, as they were by Catholic theology for centuries.

Posidonius believed the Jews to be atheists because they would not believe in the pagan gods; and Philostratus upbraided the Jews for keeping themselves apart. Apollonius claimed occasional cruelty of the Jews; but the Catholic Commodius averred the

---

[1] Wistrich, Robert S. *Anti-Semitism: The Longest Hatred.* p16

[2] The latter verse was the excuse for the Catholic Church's extensive incineration of innocent 'witches' during the Middle Ages.

[3] See, for example: Poliakov, Léon. *The History of Anti-Semitism.* Vol I. pp20-21

[4] Michael, Robert. *A History of Catholic Antisemitism: The Dark Side of the Church.* p10

Jews were possessed by a manic cruelty unique to them – the 'furor judaicus'. Apion deemed Jews to be politically seditious, but Saint John Chrysostom saw them as rebels against God and all that was holy. They were worthy of slaughter.[1]

The Jew as Usurer

Within Catholicism, the lending of money for interest has had a mixed history.

Because the Jews were ostracised from most professions by local rulers, by the Church, and by the guilds, they were pushed into marginal occupations considered socially inferior, such as tax and rent-collecting and money-lending. Accordingly, Jews were seen as insolent, greedy usurers. Natural tensions between creditors and debtors were added to social, political, religious, and economic strains:

> financial oppression of Jews tended to occur in areas where they were most disliked, and if Jews reacted by concentrating on moneylending to gentiles, the unpopularity – and so, of course, the pressure – would increase. Thus the Jews became an element in a vicious circle. The Christians, on the basis of the Biblical rulings, condemned interest-taking absolutely, and from 1179 those who practised it were excommunicated. But the Christians also imposed the harshest financial burdens on the Jews. The Jews reacted by engaging in the one business where Christian laws actually discriminated in their favour, and so became identified with the hated trade of moneylending.

> Peasants who were forced to pay their taxes to Jews could personify them as the people taking their earnings while remaining loyal to the lords on whose behalf the Jews worked. Gentile debtors may have been quick to lay charges of usury against Jewish moneylenders charging even nominal interest or fees. Thus, historically attacks on usury have often been linked to antisemitism.[2]

An expanding economy, which needed credit, was a major product of the First Crusade. The Jews provided this facility at a time when their relatively large-scale trade with the Orient was closed after the Crusade, and virtually all other avenues were closed to them due to the many restriction that were placed on their activities by the Church and secular authorities. Not being subject to usurious restriction, Jews dominated this business for a while.[3]

This situation was beneficial to the Jews, in that such an occupation was advantageous to them due to the insecurity of Jewish life. The need to keep their possessions in an easily negotiable and transportable state was a consequence of the perennial threats of constant extortions, expulsions and massacres. It was beneficial to temporal rulers who were thus able to exact a steady flow of tribute.[4] It was also beneficial to the hypocritical Church,[5] which borrowed money from Jews to build its cathedrals and churches.

---

[1] Michael, Robert. *A History of Catholic Antisemitism: The Dark Side of the Church*. p10
[2] http://en.wikipedia.org/wiki/Usury (2008)
[3] http://en.wikipedia.org/wiki/History_of_antisemitism (2007)
[4] Ibid.
[5] Hypocrisy is, and remains one of the central aspects of the Catholic Church.

This was a time of rudimentary capitalism. Trade was insecure, and non-productive enterprises such as wars or castle-building consumed funds without any financial returns. Thus, the usurer had to charge high interest rates, which became an intolerable burden on those who were unable to meet them, such as the lower and middle classes. Kings and nobles often resorted to force to avoid their financial obligations. The Jew, therefore, was in a vicious circle of being forced into usury and being a victim of the avarice of feudal masters. It was one from which there was no escape. The net result was that the usurer became one of the most despised and hated persons in mediaeval society. To the masses, he was perceived as grasping, avaricious, and an unmitigated evil.[1]

It was the fate of the Jew that the Church and civil authorities commenced a fierce campaign against usury at the time when almost all other economic activity was forbidden him. In the twelfth century usury was classed as a crime together with sorcery, sacrilege, fornication, and homicide. In 1179 Pope Alexander III decreed that all demonstrated usurers be excommunicated, and the state introduced legislation confiscating the property of usurers who died unrepentant.[2]

During the thirteenth century, contrary to the doctrine of the Church, Christians (including priests) began to take up money lending, perceiving it as a profitable enterprise. The Jew then lost his importance as a source of governmental revenue, and the state was no longer interested in protecting him. His funds were sequestered and he was expelled. During the thirteenth to the fifteenth centuries many expulsions occurred in England and Europe solely for reasons affecting the ruler's exchequer.[3]

During the Middle Ages, priests censured usurers as 'unnatural monsters' who were 'invented by the devil himself'. The Jew was the Devil's creature, and art portrayed Satan as a veritable participant in Jewish immoral financial operations. This theme was delivered repeatedly in poetry, legends, plays, and sermons. Joshua Trachtenberg gives the example of the title page of a sixteenth-century fulmination against Jewish usury and wealth that shows three devil-Jews each with claws, horns, tails, and Jew badge. Two seventeenth century examples are those of a copperplate that shows the Devil sharing in the profits of Jewish usury, and in the Arbogastkirche in Ruffach, Alsace, a statue of the Devil in the company of a Jew grasping a bulging money-bag.[4]

The pinnacle of Jewish usury was before the fifteenth century, after that, as cities grew in power and affluence, the development of banking squeezed the Jews out of money lending.

Over all – the Jew as a sole usurer was largely a myth. However, the fable of the grasping Jew persisted for hundreds of years. Centuries later the negative image of the Jewish money-lender was immortalised in Shakespeare's Shylock and Dickens' Fagin.

---

[1] http://en.wikipedia.org/wiki/History_of_antisemitism (2007)
[2] Ibid.
[3] Ibid.
[4] Ibid.

The Anti-Semitism of the Fathers of the Church

The Fathers of the Church and other Christian writers claimed that all the prerogatives of God's favoured people had been transferred to the Christian Church.[1] Accordingly, once Christians believed themselves to be God's chosen people, everyone else became God's unchosen people. As John Shelby Spong has pointed out, there is a very fine line between the vapid 'unchosen' and the antagonistic 'rejected'.[2] Consequently, because the claimed Christian God, it was asserted, had specifically not chosen the Jews, they were rejected, blamed and hated. Many of these Fathers and others wrote strongly against the Jews – their anti-Semitism was spread over many centuries.

Table 1. A Sample of Church Fathers and Others who wrote against the Jews

Abbé Barruel	Ferdinando Jabolot	Monk Rudolf
Abbé Pierre of Cluny	Fr Charles E Coughlin	Origen
Augustine of Hippo	Fra Bartolomeo Fumo	Pierre Abelard
Aurelius Prudentius	Friar Alonso de Espina	Sulpicius Severus
Barnabas	John Chrysostom	Tertullian
Bernardino of Feltro	Juliana of Norwich	Thomas de Chantimpré
Blaise Pascal	Maria Theresa	Vincenzo degli Antoni
Eusebius of Caesarea	Melito of Sardis	

This tradition of blame was expressed and amplified by such men in both the early Church and throughout most of its history. Many of the writings presented the Jews as the people who had been rejected and disowned by God. For example:

> The *Letter of Barnabas* (Barnabas was the surname given by the Apostles to Joseph, one of the members of the early Christian Church in Jerusalem).
>
> *Dialogue with the Jew Trypho* by St Justin the Martyr (c.100-c.165), a philosopher and theologian.
>
> The polemical treatise *Adversus Judaeos* (*Against the Jews*)[3] by Tertullian (c.160-c.220), the first important Christian ecclesiastical writer in Latin.
>
> *Expository Treatise against the Jews* by Hippolytus of Rome (c.170-c.235), the most important third-century theologian of the Roman Church.
>
> *Contra Celsum* (*Against Celsus*) by Origen (c.185-c.254), a celebrated Christian writer, teacher, and theologian.[4]
>
> *Three Books of Testimonies against the Jews* by St Cyprian (c.200-258).
>
> *De Civitate Dei* (*The City of God*) and *Contra Judaeos* (*Against the Jews*) by

---

[1] Kahl, Joachim. *The Misery of Christianity: A Plea for a Humanity without God.* p54
[2] Spong, John Shelby. *Living In Sin?* p28
[3] Not only did Tertullian write his much-quoted book *Adversus Judaeos*, but also Chrysostom, an early Church Father, wrote *Eight Homilies against the Jews* (*Adversus Judaeos*). Accordingly, a representative anti-Semitic argument in the early Church came to be known as an 'Adversus Judaeos'.
[4] Kahl, Joachim. *The Misery of Christianity: A Plea for a Humanity without God.* p54

St Augustine of Hippo (354-430), one of the most eminent Western Doctors of the Church and greatest of the Latin Fathers. He was strongly anti-Semitic.

Eight Orations (Homilies) against the Jews by St John Chrysostom (c.349-407).

De regimine Iudaeorum (On the Governance of the Jews) by St Thomas Aquinas (1225-1274), one of the leading Roman Catholic theologians, sometimes called the 'Angelic Doctor' and the 'Prince of Scholastics'.

The Saints

Many Saints[1] of the Catholic Church wrote strongly against the Jews; their anti-Semitism was spread over eighteen hundred years.

Table 2. A Sample of Saints who wrote strongly against the Jews

Justin Martyr (c.100-c.165)	John Chrysostom (c.349-407)
Irenaeus (c.140-202)	Augustine of Hippo (354-430)
Hippolytus (c.170-c.235)	Cyril of Alexandria (376-444)
Cyprian of Carthage (c.200-258)	Fulgentius of Ruspe (467-533)
Athanasius (c.293-373)	Felix of Toledo (694-700)
Ephraem (c.306-373)	Agobard (c.779-840)
Basil (c.329-379)	Pope Gregory VII (1073-85)
Amphilocius of Iconium (c.380)	Bernard of Clairvaux (1090-1153)
Gregory of Nyssa (c.335-394)	Thomas Aquinas (1225-1274)
Ambrose (c.340-397)	Vincent Ferrer (c.1350-1419)
Jerome (c.347-420)	Pope Pius V (1566-1572)
Aurelius Clemens (348-c.413)	Pope Pius X (1903-1914)

The Popes

Table 3. A Sample of Popes who wrote strongly against the Jews

Damasus I (d.384)	Gregory VII (1073-1085)	Paul IV (1555-1559)
Leo I (440-461)	Alexander III (1159-1181)	St Pius V (1566-1572)
Gregory I (590-604)	Innocent III (1198-1216)	Clement VIII (1592-1605)
Stephen III (768-72)	Gregory IX (1227-1241)	Benedict XIV (1740-1758)
Hadrian I (772-795)	Innocent IV (1243-1254)	Pius IX (1846-1878)
Stephen IV (816-17)	Honorius IV (1285-1287)	St Pius X (1903-1914)
Stephen V (885-891)	Nicholas IV (1288-1292)	Benedict XV (1914-1922)
Stephen VI (896-97)	Gregory XIII (1406-1415)	Paul VI (1963-1978)
Leo VII (936-939)	Martin V (1417-1431)	

---

[1] Saints are 'friends and servants of God whose holy lives have made them worthy of His special love.'

Thus, many popes[1] wrote against the Jews – their anti-Semitism was spread over at least sixteen hundred years, and was even expressed as late as the twentieth century.

Between the sixth and the twentieth centuries over one hundred anti-Semitic documents were published by the Church. During those fifteen centuries, there was never a single papal bull, encyclical, conciliar decree, or pastoral directive that intimated that Jesus' command, 'love your neighbour as yourself', applied to Jews.[2]

Consequently, it came about that the Holy Roman Catholic and Apostolic Church taught as doctrine that 'Jews are cursed for killing God'. Writing in 1988, the ex-Jesuit, Peter de Rosa, stated that this charge had still not been officially withdrawn.[3]

The Church, therefore, was the ultimate determinant of public opinion, of public behaviour, of judicial practice, and of commercial practice as it affected the Jew.[4]

It has been claimed that the papacy has never removed any official, or excommunicated any Catholic, for forcibly converting, torturing, or murdering a Jew.[5]

Synopsis

In all his three persons, the God worshipped by Roman Catholics is the Jewish God.

Jesus was born, lived and died a Jew. His father, mother, brothers, sisters and first disciples were all Jews.

The original Apostles started the anti-Jewish propaganda – they transferred the guilt for the death of Jesus from the shoulders of the Roman authorities, who killed Jesus, to the Jewish leaders, who did not.

The main source of later anti-Semitism is derived from the New Testament account of the Crucifixion, which is replete with historical inaccuracies.

Matthew fabricated the infamous curse that thereafter saddled the Jews with the entire blame for the death of Jesus: 'Then answered all the people, and said, "His blood be on us, and on our children." '

Subsequently, through the centuries when the Jews were blamed for killing Christ, not a single theologian ever called attention to the fact that the Jews never killed Christ, but simply handed him over to the Romans.[6]

Through their ancestral faith, the Jews have survived the two-millennial execrating barrage of Christian (largely Catholic) anti-Semitism. They 'remain to this day a monument of Christian ingratitude, falsity, and impotence.'

---

[1] The pope is 'the Vicar of Christ upon earth.' (*Catholic Encyclopedia*)

[2] de Rosa, Peter. *Vicars of Christ: The Dark Side of the Papacy.* p6

[3] Ibid. p5

[4] See, for example: Trachtenberg, Joshua. *The Devil and the Jews: The Medieval Conception of ...* p161

[5] Michael, Robert. *A History of Catholic Antisemitism: The Dark Side of the Church.* pp84-85

[6] de Rosa, Peter. *Vicars of Christ: The Dark Side of the Papacy.* p177

2 – Condemnation through the Centuries – 1st to 11th Century

Jesus is ideal and wonderful, but you Christians – you are not like him. Mahatma Gandhi

The Many Forms of Catholic Anti-Semitism

An examination of history reveals that Catholic anti-Jewish behaviour has extended from hostile words to mass murder:

Accusations – of deicide, ritual murder, desecration of the Host, conspiracies, corruption, greed, and others;

Odium – in sermons, writings, Passion plays, tales, jokes and pictures;

Prohibitions and Destructions – of Hebrew texts;

Restrictions – on religious practice, social interaction, trades and professions, civil and political rights, residence, and ownership;

Closures, Confiscations and Destructions of – places and articles of worship, and cemeteries;

Force – to make Jews pay higher taxes; and in child abduction, lootings, vandalism and expulsions;

Threats or coercions to – extort ransom money; drive from home; convert;

Violence – in beatings and torture;

Extermination – by means of hangings, burnings, inquisitions, slaughters, pogroms, Crusades, genocides and Holocausts.[1]

Christian Condemnations of the Jews through the Centuries

Even before it was a century old, the Christian church, as presented by the surviving writings of its leaders, began to produce a systematic anti-Jewish precept that resulted from its own theological assertions. By the second century, a consistent theological rationale had been developed for condemnation of the Jews and contempt for Judaism that set the course of occidental civilisation.[2]

For twenty centuries, a stream of Church writers, including Doctors, Fathers, popes, bishops and priests blamed and slandered the Jew. Many of these early defamers were declared to be Saints.[3]

Over the space of nearly two thousand years, the Christian image of the Jew was further developed in countless sermons, and in drama, art, literature, catechisms, lives of Jesus, and canticles.[4,5]

---

[1] See, for example: http://www.jcrelations.net/en/?id=836 (2007)

[2] http://motlc.wiesenthal.com/resources/books/genocide/chap03.html

[3] Saints – 'friends and servants of God whose *holy lives* have made them worthy of His special love.' (*Catholic Encyclopedia*, 'Beatification and Canonization'). Emphasis added.

[4] Wistrich, Robert S. *Anti-Semitism: The Longest Hatred.* p17

[5] Cohn-Sherbok, D. *The Crucified Jew: Twenty Centuries of Christian Anti-Semitism.* p236

During this time, theological 'logic' gradually extended the meaning of the Latin word 'perfidus' to its modern ecclesiastic significance of faithless, treacherous, false, deceitful, and cunning.[1]

The Church's liturgy, such as the Good Friday and Easter services, further increased feelings of hatred with the intercession 'Pro perfidis Iudaeis' ('For the perfidious/unbelieving/cunning Jew').[2] This practice was retained until as late as 1959.[3]

Innumerable treatises and legends of the Saints and all manner of Passion, mystery, miracle, and morality plays, chronicles, legends, poems, folk tales, folk songs, nursery tales, popular sermons, and other semi-religious diversions mocked and vilified the Jews.[4,5]

It mattered not whether there was any historical or factual authenticity to these tales. The Catholic accepted them as his and her principal source of entertainment and instruction. They had the official background of the all-knowledgeable Church. In the totalitarian ecclesiastic environment of those days, these notions were not only propagated by the Church, but also given added strength by secular and ecclesiastic legislation. The resulting conception of the Jew led, inevitably, to deep-seated and unreasoning hatred. Hence, mediaeval Christendom was so certain of the indisputable truth of its own 'knowledge' in these matters that any alternate truth was inconceivable.[6] Verification of this situation came from a twelfth-century chronicler:

> Whether what I am relating is true or not is no concern of mine, it is told thus, and thus must it be accepted.[7]

Irrational myths were added: the Jew was an agent of the Antichrist, a ritual murderer, a desecrator of the Host, a usurer, a sorcerer, and a vampire.[8] He was depicted, particularly in engravings and prints from popular books, as possessing horns, tails, and the beard of a goat.

It was a common Catholic belief that good spirits emitted a pronounced fragrance, while evil spirits were distinguished by an offensive stench. On the one hand, for example, when the coffin of the martyred St Stephen was opened, his body filled the air with fragrance – the 'odour of sanctity'. On the other hand, the Devil was associated with a malodour, often of brimstone (sulphur). By association, Jews also were said to produce a terrible odour (foetor judaïcus), hence, this stench was another distinctive sign of the demonic Jew. Naturally, any Jew lost this odour after receiving Catholic baptism. There is direct testimony that "the water of baptism carried off the Jews' odour" – the result was a fragrance "sweeter than that of ambrosia floating upon the heads touched

[1] *A Dictionary of Jewish-Christian Relations.* p171
[2] 'Let us pray for the perfidious Jews: that Our Lord and God may take away the veil from their hearts, that they may know Our Lord Jesus Christ.'
[3] Kahl, Joachim. *The Misery of Christianity: A Plea for a Humanity without God.* p56
[4] Ibid. p57
[5] Saperstein, Mark. 'Foreword', in: Trachtenberg, Joshua. *The Devil and the Jews: The Medieval ...* pp viii-ix
[6] Trachtenberg, Joshua. *The Devil and the Jews: The Medieval Conception of the Jew and ...* pp14-15
[7] http://www.academia.edu/4663813/The_Blood_Libel_Legend_Its_Longevity_And_Popularity (2013)
[8] Wistrich, Robert S. *Anti-Semitism: The Longest Hatred.* p xix

by the sanctified oil."[1] The eminent historian Henry Charles Lea recorded that:

> The Cistercian Caesarius of Heisterbach, in his dialogues for the moral instruction of his fellow monks, tells several stories which illustrate the utter contempt felt for the feelings and rights of Jews, and in one of them there is an allusion to the curious popular belief that the Jews had a vile odor, which they lost in baptism – a belief prolonged, at least in Spain, until the seventeenth century was well advanced.[2]

Caesarius also recorded that when 'the child sings, the Jews cannot endure this pure laudatory song, they cut off his tongue and hack him to pieces.'[3]

Jews were believed to have been born deformed and to have suffered from certain unique, secret afflictions that did not normally trouble Roman Catholics. The Jews needed Christian blood because it was the only effective therapeutic available to them. Most common of these ailments was that of menstruation (both males and females) and copious haemorrhages and haemorrhoids. Other maladies of the Jews included quinsy (peritonsillar abscess), scrofula (a form of tuberculosis), a distinct pallor, and a variety of mysterious skin diseases and sores that emitted a malodorous flux. These infirmities were generally believed to afflict all Jews.[4,5]

Jewish Magic & Catholic Magic – During the Middle Ages, non-Catholic magic became equated with heresy; this, in turn, engendered a crusade against sorcery. In the process, Jews as 'heretics' became sorcerers, who in turn became agents of the Devil. The Church fostered such 'bad' beliefs; and as offset, created its own 'sacred' magic by encouraging the recourse to not only the 'good' spirits of the Church's Saints and Martyrs, but also 'sacred' objects such as consecrated water, salt, candles, palms, flowers and herbs, holy fire, and relics. For example, in 1472 Pope Paul II extolled the magical virtue of the consecrated Agnus Dei, a figure of a lamb stamped in wax remaining from the paschal candles, as being effective 'in preserving from fire and shipwreck, in averting tempests and lightning and hail, and in assisting women in childbirth. '[6]

At the same time the Church promoted the belief in the figure of Satan, the Prince of Darkness, as the source of non-Catholic magic. The Devil was the author of disasters; he spied, schemed, and fought against humanity. From the thirteenth century there was a veritable cult of Satan in Christendom – to such an extent that disbelief in him and his demons was heretical.[7]

Hence, Jews were perceived as the incarnation of evil, and were associated with devils and demons. Sometimes they were depicted as the Devil himself, and in art, Jews were portrayed as agents of Lucifer with evil faces, horns and a tail. At other times, they were seen as intermediaries between the Devil and innocent humanity.

[1] Trachtenberg, Joshua. *The Devil and the Jews: The Medieval Conception of the Jew and its Relation ...* p48
[2] Lea, Henry Charles. *A History of the Inquisition of Spain.* Vol I. p82
[3] http://www.zionism-israel.com/his/judeophobia6.htm (2007)
[4] Cohn-Sherbok, D. *The Crucified Jew: Twenty Centuries of Christian Anti-Semitism.* pp54-55
[5] Trachtenberg, Joshua. *The Devil and the Jews: The Medieval Conception of the Jew and its Relation ...* p50
[6] Lea, Henry Charles. *A History of the Inquisition of the Middle Ages.* Vol 3. p410
[7] Ibid. pp196-99

No sin was too offensive to be claimed against the Jews. But the greatest offence was their assigned intention to destroy Christianity and Christendom.[1] Werner Heise, who had researched these matters, stated in 1932 that in spite of there being scarcely any objective truth in the accusations, nonetheless, all the common people and most of the educated laity believed them entirely.[2,3]

Catholic hatred and discrimination against Jews had become systematic and universal. Catholics at all levels constrained, punished, and reviled the Jew.

With the dominating influence of Roman Catholicism on western society, culture and government, Christian anti-Semitism led to the marginalisation of the Jews, their institutionalised oppression, their expulsion, destruction of the their religious books and places of worship, and frequent outbursts of murder.

Professor Richard E Sherwin confirmed that:

> Organized, institutionalized defamation of Jews and Judaism is shown to derive from the Christian Bible and its sainted interpreters, while *incitement to murder Jews begins with the Church Fathers, Popes, and holy men* and contaminates the Christian and Secular West.[4]

Professor Robert Michael wrote:

> Christianity's precise influence on the Holocaust cannot be determined and the Christian churches did not themselves perpetrate the Final Solution. But two millennia of Christian ideas and prejudices, their impact on Christian's behaviour, appear to be the major basis of antisemitism and of the apex of antisemitism, the Holocaust.[5]

He concluded that:

> Catholic theological and Catholic racist antisemitism prepared, conditioned, and encouraged Catholic antisemites and others to collaborate actively or passively with individual and institutional antisemitic behaviors – avoidance, discrimination, expropriation, antilocution, physical assault and torture, murder and mass murder. This *Catholic antisemitism* paved the long via dolorosa that led to Auschwitz and beyond.[6]

First and Second Centuries

Barnabas (d.61)

> Do not add to your sins and say that the covenant is both theirs and ours. Yes! It is ours; but they thus lost it forever.[7]

---

[1] Lea, Henry Charles. *A History of the Inquisition of the Middle Ages.* Vol 3. pp12-13
[2] Quoted in: Trachtenberg, Joshua. *The Devil and the Jews: The Medieval Conception of the Jew and ...* p14
[3] And, presumably, the Catholic hierarchy as well.
[4] Review of: Michael, Robert. *Holy Hatred: Christianity, Antisemitism, and the Holocaust.*
[5] Michael, Robert. *Holy Hatred: Christianity, Antisemitism, and the Holocaust.* p1
[6] Michael, Robert. *A History of Catholic Antisemitism: The Dark Side of the Church.* pp7-8
[7] *The Letter of Barnabas*, 4:6-7; FCCH, *Apostolic Fathers*, p195. Source: Flannery, Edward H. *The Anguish of*

St Justin Martyr (c.100-c.165)

> Jacob was hated for all time by his brother; and we now, and Our Lord Himself, are hated by you and all men. ... [The] tribulations were justly imposed upon you, for you have murdered the Just One.' (*Dialogue with Trypho the Jew*)[1]

Melito of Sardis (d.c.180) – Melito, the Bishop of Sardis near Smyrna, in a 167 CE sermon entitled 'Peri Pascha' ('On the Passover'), has been attributed with the first accusation against the Jews of deicide. This text blames the Jews for allowing King Herod and Caiaphas to execute Jesus, despite their calling as God's people. It says 'you did not know, O Israel, that this one was the firstborn of God.'[2]

St Irenaeus (c.140-202)

> For while they [the Jews] were thought to offer correctly so far as the outward appearance went, they had in themselves jealousy like unto Cain; therefore they slew the Just One, slighting the counsel of the Word, as did Cain ... But in Christ is every blessing, and therefore the latter people has snatched away the blessings of the former from the Father, just as Jacob took away the blessing of Esau. For which cause his brother suffered the plots and persecutions of a brother, just as the Church suffers this self-same thing from the Jews. (*Against the Heresies*)[3]

Third Century

Tertullian (c.160-c.220) – Tertullian, a prolific Christian apologist, maintained that there was 'no expiation possible, no indulgence, no pardon'; for their 'odious assassination of Christ'. (*Apologeticus*) He also wrote:

> For, withal, according to the memorial records of the divine Scriptures, the people of the Jews – that is, the more ancient – quite forsook God, and did degrading service to idols, and, abandoning the Divinity, was surrendered to images ...

> Since, therefore, the Jews were predicted as destined to suffer these calamities on Christ's account, and we find that they have suffered them, and see them sent into dispersion and abiding in it, it is manifest that it is on Christ's account that these things have befallen the Jews, the sense of the Scriptures harmonising with the issue of events and of the order of the times. (*An Answer to the Jews*; 13)[4]

St Hippolytus (c.170-c.235) – Hippolytus was the most important third-century theologian in the Christian Church in Rome. He was a presbyter of the Church. He reiterated the killing of Jesus by the Jews:

> Why was the Temple made desolate? Was it on account of the ancient fabrication of the calf? Or was it on account of the idolatry of the people? Was it for the blood of

the Jews: Twenty-Three Centuries of Antisemitism. p34
1   http://www.logoslibrary.org/justin/trypho/122.html (2012)
2   http://en.wikipedia.org/wiki/Jewish_deicide (2012)
3   http://www.christianforums.com/t3263001-11/ (2012)
4   http://books.google.com.au/books?isbn=3849621596 (2013)

the prophets? Was it for the adultery and fornication of Israel? [1] By no means, for in all these transgressions they always found pardon open to them. But it was because they killed the son of their Benefactor, for He is co-eternal with the Father ... And whereas thou didst pour out His blood in indignation, hear what thy recompense shall be: 'Pour out thy indignation upon them, and let thy wrathful anger take behold of them;' and, 'Let their habitation be desolate,' to wit, their celebrated temple ... But because thou didst cover the eyes of Christ when thou didst beat Him, for this reason, too, bend thou thy back for servitude always. (*Against the Jews*; 6,7)[2]

Origen (c.185-c.254) – Origen was an ecclesiastical writer and teacher, and the first Christian scholar to study Hebrew. He contributed to the early formation of Christian doctrines. For him, the Jews were a most wicked people:

On account of their unbelief, and the other insults which they heaped upon Jesus, the Jews will ... suffer more than others in that judgement which is believed to be impending over the world ... What nation is an exile from their own city, and from the place sacred to the worship of their fathers, save the Jews alone? And these calamities they have suffered, because they were a most wicked nation, which, although guilty of many other sins, yet has been punished so severely for none, as for those that were committed against our Jesus. (*Contra Celsum*; 2:8)[3]

St Cyprian of Carthage (c.200-258) – Cyprian was a famous orator. The *Catholic Encyclopedia* says: 'His gift of eloquence is evident in his writings. He was not a thinker, a philosopher, a theologian, but eminently a man of the world':

This name rebukes and condemns the Jews who not only spurned Christ faithlessly, but also cruelly executed Him Who was announced to them by the prophets, and sent first to their nation. No longer may they call God their Father, because the Lord confounds and refutes them, saying: 'your father is the devil' (*Saint John* 8:44). Oh sinful nation, Oh people weighed down with guilt, breed of evil-doers, lawless children, you have turned your backs on the Lord and have provoked the Holy One of Israel. (*The Lord's Prayer*)[4]

***

Christian vituperation then increased rapidly. By the end of the third century the image of the Jew was of one of a disbeliever and a competitor. A century later, the Jew had metamorphosed into a satanic figure who was cursed by God, and who was discriminated against by the state. During this early Christian era it was also argued that if Jesus were the Messiah, then the only person for whom the Jews were waiting would be the Antichrist.

---

[1] Adultery and fornication were frequent odious qualifiers applied by Catholics to the Jews.
[2] http://www.preteristarchive.com/StudyArchive/h/hippolytus.html (2013)
[3] http://www.ccel.org/ccel/schaff/anf04.vi.ix.ii.viii.html (2014)
[4] http://catholicforum.fisheaters.com/index.php?topic=3278706.5;wap2 (2013)

Fourth Century

Christian theological necessity developed the theories of prescribed Jewish miseries as divine punishment for Jesus' crucifixion. By the time Christianity became the dominant religion of the Empire in 323, the base of its anti-Semitism was already firmly established. The Church saw Judaism not as a distinct religion, but as a stubborn, perfidious rebellion against the only true religion, Christianity.[1]

⊳ This anti-Semitic theology was institutionalised in the fourth century when Constantine decreed Christianity to be the official religion of the Roman Empire. Ancient privileges that had been granted to Jews were withdrawn; jurisdiction of rabbis was abolished or restricted; Jews were excluded from military careers and high office; and Jewish proselytism and sexual relations with Christian women were punishable by death.[2]

The prohibition in the infamous Catholic *Canon 49*, against a Jew blessing standing crops, was due to the belief that Jews possessed the evil eye. It was intended to warn peasants that the harm thus done could not be undone later by the magic of a benediction of the Christian priest.[3]

Eusebius of Caesarea (c.260-c.340) – Eusebius was the Bishop of Caesarea. He blamed the calamities that befell the Jewish nation on the Jews' role in the death of Jesus:

> from that time seditions and wars and mischievous plots followed each other in quick succession, and never ceased in the city and in all Judea until finally the siege of Vespasian overwhelmed them. Thus the divine vengeance overtook the Jews for the crimes which they dared to commit against Christ. (*Church History*)[4]

St Athanasius (c.293-373) – Athanasius was Bishop of Alexandria, and a Confessor and Doctor of the Church. Even during his lifetime he earned the characteristic title of 'Father of Orthodoxy'. He repeated the death of Jesus as the cause of the ills of the Jews:

> [Jews] have no abiding place, but they wander everywhere ... But in every place they transgress the law, and as the judgments of God require; they keep days of grief instead of gladness. Now the cause of this to them was the slaying of the Lord, and that they did not reverence the Only Begotten ... Therefore the Lord cursed them under the figure of the fig tree. (*Letter 6*, Easter 334)[5]

St Ephraem (Ephraim) the Syriac (c.306-373) – Ephraem was a hymnographer who is venerated by Christians throughout the world. In a denunciatory hymn, he accused the Jews of idolatry, arguing that the persecution of Christ was foretold in earlier times:

> What is thine iniquity, O Daughter of Jacob, that thy chastisement is so severe? Thou hast dishonoured the King and the King's Son; thou shameless one and harlot! The King was dishonoured in the wilderness and the King's Son in Jerusalem. The

---

[1] http://www.zionism-israel.com/his/judeophobia3.htm (2007)
[2] Wistrich, Robert S. *Anti-Semitism: The Longest Hatred.* pp18-20
[3] Trachtenberg, Joshua. *The Devil and the Jews: The Medieval Conception of the Jew and its Relation to Modern Anti-Semitism.* p70
[4] http://www.sacred-texts.com/chr/ecf/201/2010048.htm (2013)
[5] http://www.newadvent.org/fathers/2806006.htm (2013)

Father was exchanged for the calf and for sundry similitudes, and the Son was exchanged for a thief and a blood-shedder. And the Spirit of the Lord they did vex among strange nations. (*Rhythm against the Jews*, Delivered on Palm Sunday)[1]

St Hilary of Poitiers (c.315-c.367) – Hilary referred to Jews as a murderous perverse people whom God has forever cursed. He wrote:

The Jews are always seething to slaughter the Christian people. (*Tractus Mysteriorum*)[2]

St Basil ('Basil the Great') (c.329-379) – Basil was Bishop of Caesarea, and one of the most distinguished Doctors of the Church.

And such are the prayers of the Jews, for when they stretch forth their hands in prayer, they only remind God-the-Father of their sin against His Son. And at every stretching-forth of their hands, they only make it obvious that they are stained with the blood of Christ. For they who persevere in their blindness inherit the blood-guiltiness of their fathers …' (*On Prayer*)

For, raging against the Gentiles as unclean, Israel became in very truth unclean themselves; while the Gentiles have become clean, the justice of Israel has become like the rag of a menstruous woman.[3]

St Amphilocius of Iconium (c.380)

It may be that the Jews, looking for another Christ, will laugh at our wisdom; for of them the prophet has rightly said: 'Their sepulchres shall be their houses forever' (*Psalm* 48:12). They laugh now, but they shall weep, for they shall weep when they look upon Him 'Whom they have pierced.' (*Zacharias* 12:10) (*Oration 5*)[4]

St Gregory of Nyssa (c.335-394) – Gregory was an erudite theologian who made significant contributions to the doctrine of the Trinity and the Nicene Creed. As a highly original and sophisticated thinker, Gregory is difficult to classify, and many aspects of his theology are contentious among both conservative Orthodox theologians and Western academic scholarship. His sophisticated Christian thinking carried vituperation of the Jews to a new high:

Jews are slayers of the Lord, murderers of the prophets, enemies of God, haters of God, adversaries of grace, enemies of their fathers' faith, advocates of the Devil, brood of vipers, slanderers, scoffers, men of darkened minds, leaven of the

---

[1] http://www.jewishencyclopedia.com/articles/5792-ephraem-syrus (2012)

[2] http://www.fatherfeeney.org/point/55-sep.html (2013). Father Feeney is a contemporary anti-Semitic preacher. For example, he states on his website: 'We American Catholics do not need that learned bishop and theologian, Saint Hilary of Poitiers, to warn us (as he does in his *Tractatus Mysteriorum*) that "The Jews are always seething to slaughter the Christian people." Every day we are coming to see more clearly for ourselves how the Jews are maneuvering to destroy all trace of what is Christian in our land.'

[3] http://www.romancatholicism.org/accursed-race.html (2015). This website by Mike Malone, entitled 'The Once-Chosen People Are Now The Accursed Race', is an excellent source of anti-Semitic quotations by notable Roman Catholics.

[4] http://www.romancatholicism.org/accursed-race.html (2013)

Pharisees, congregation of demons, sinners, wicked men, stoners and haters of goodness. (*Oration on the Resurrection of Christ*)[1]

St Ambrose (c.340-397) – Ambrose was one of the most celebrated Fathers of the Church and one of the four Doctors of the Church. He 'was one of the earliest to teach proscription when he reproved Theodosius the Great for the favor shown by him to Jews, who slew Christ and who deny God in denying his Son ...'[2] He defended a fellow bishop for burning a synagogue at Callinicum and asked: 'Who cares if a synagogue – a home of unbelief, a house of impiety, a receptacle of folly, which God himself has condemned – is burned?':

> The faithlessness of the Synagogue is an insult to the Saviour. Therefore, He chose the barque of Peter and deserted the boat of Moses; that is, He rejected the faithless Synagogue and adopted the believing Church ... Of these two ships, one is left at the shore, idle and empty; the other, loaded filled, is launched into the deep. For the Synagogue is left idle on the beach. Because of its own fault, it has lost Christ along with the warnings of the prophets. But the freighted Church is taken out into the deep, because it received the Lord together with the teaching of the Apostles. (*The Two Ships*)[3]

St Jerome (c.347-420) – In many ways Jerome was the epitome of the profoundly neurotic, monastic, intellectual Christian in whom commingle anti-Semitism and misogynism. Jesus was a man who is alleged to have lived without sexual intercourse; consequently, virginity became the Catholic ideal. In contrast, Judaism was linked to the sexual lusts of a wicked and carnal world. This persistent Catholic morbid fear of all sexuality[4] led to the projection of all the repressed Christian sexual impulses onto the 'carnal', sinful Jew.[5]

Jerome identified the Jews with Judas and with the immoral use of money, two themes that would bedevil Christian-Jewish relations for centuries. 'St Jerome associated materialism with Judas' sin, which, with his punishment, symbolized all Jewish behavior and the Jews' fate':[6]

Christ is saying: 'Judas betrayed Me, the Jews persecuted and crucified Me ... Judas,

---

[1] http://mynameisjoecortina.wordpress.com/2013/07/07/ye-are-of-your-father-the-devil-part-three-a-reminder-of-the-evil-nature-of-all-jews-a-must-read-for-all/ (2013). Joe's website is headed: '"YE ARE OF YOUR FATHER – THE DEVIL" PART THREE A REMINDER OF THE EVIL NATURE OF ALL JEWS. A MUST READ FOR ALL'.

[2] Lea, Henry Charles. *A History of the Inquisition* of Spain. Vol I. pp37-40

[3] http://thepowerofgod777.blogspot.com.au/2009/11/what-catholic-church-really-teaches.html (2013). This website, dated November 17, 2009, commences with the statement: 'What the Catholic Church Really Teaches Concerning the Jews. Unbalanced anti-Semitism is condemned by Traditional Church teaching, as it is sinful to hate a person for their race. Still, Catholic Tradition teaches it is incumbent on every Catholic to oppose with all their energy World Jewry. Pray that the wilful blindness of the Jews ceases and they will convert to the only means of salvation for all mankind, the Holy Roman Catholic Church.'

[4] 'Chastity – the most unnatural of all the sexual perversions.' Aldous Huxley

[5] Wistrich, Robert S. *Anti-Semitism: The Longest Hatred.* pp17-18

[6] Michael, Robert. *A Concise history of American anti-Semitism.* p19

in particular, was torn asunder by the demons – and the [Jewish] people as well ... Judas is cursed, that in Judas the Jews may be accursed.' ... From this Iscariot, they are called Judaeans ... Iscariot means money and price ... [The] Synagogue was divorced by the Saviour and became the wife of Judas the betrayer.'[1]

Aurelius Clemens Prudentius (348-c.413) – Prudentius was a Christian poet. He maintained that the Jew was the murderous brother who wandered the face of the earth:

> From place to place the homeless Jew wanders in ever-shifting exile, since the time when he was torn from the abode of his fathers and has been suffering the penalty for murder and having stained his hands with the blood of Christ whom he denied, paying the price of sin. See what has become of the virtue of his forefathers of olden times! The noble race that was heir to the faithful men of old has scattered away from them and is enslaved, no longer noble; it is in captivity under the younger faith. Such is the strength the new belief possesses; a race that formerly was unfaithful now confesses Christ and triumphs, but that which denied Christ is conquered and subdued and has fallen into the hands of masters who keep the faith. (*Apotheosis*)[2]

St John Chrysostom (c.349-407) – Chrysostom was Archbishop of Constantinople, an important early Church Father, and known for his eloquence in preaching and public speaking – hence his being labelled Χρυσόστομος (Chrysostomos), 'golden-mouthed'. He lifted literary anti-Semitism to its zenith. This significantly unsaintly Saint 'stands without peer or parallel in the entire literature' against the Jews.[3]

Chrysostom wrote eight sermons in the year 387 in which is to be found all the invective that has ever been used against the Jews. The Jew is a drunkard, sensual, obscene, lascivious, demonic, mercenary, accursed, and a criminal. He is a murderer of the prophets, of Christ, and of God. He worships the Devil.[4]

Chrysostom preached that Christians should hold no intercourse with Jews, whose souls were the habitations of demons and whose synagogues were their playgrounds.[5] His frequently quoted judgement of the synagogue states:

> Whatever name is given to the synagogue – whorehouse, den of iniquity, pandemonium, house of Satan, soul-destroying habitation, or yawning abyss of perdition – it cannot be described as it deserves to be described.[6]

Adversus Judaeos (*Against the Jews*) is a series of homilies by Chrysostom that has been circulated by many groups to foster anti-Semitism. Philosopher Steven Katz adduces Chrysostom's homilies as the decisive turning point in the history of Christian anti-Judaism, with the ultimate disfiguring consequence that 'was enacted in the political

[1] Michael, Robert. *A Concise History of American Anti-Semitism.* p19
[2] http://en.wikipedia.org/wiki/Wandering_Jew#cite_ref-Apotheosis_10-0 (2013)
[3] Flannery, Edward H. *The Anguish of the Jews.* p50
[4] Kahl, Joachim. *The Misery of Christianity: A Plea for a Humanity without God.* pp54-55
[5] Lea, Henry Charles. *A History* of the *Inquisition* of Spain. Vol I. pp37-40
[6] http://zingcreed.wordpress.com/2013/09/09/christian-atrocities-4-anti-semitism/ (2013)

antisemitism of Adolf Hitler.'[1] James Parkes called the writing on Jews 'the most horrible and violent denunciations of Judaism to be found in the writings of a Christian theologian.'[2] His sermons against Jews gave momentum to the idea that Jews are collectively responsible for the death of Jesus. Chrysostom used Jesus' words in *Luke* 19:27 to call for the murder of Jews:[3]

> The Jewish people were driven by their drunkenness and plumpness to the ultimate evil; they kicked about, they failed to accept the yoke of Christ, nor did they pull the plough of his teaching. Another prophet hinted at this when he said: 'Israel is as obstinate as a stubborn heifer ... Although such beasts are unfit for work, *they are fit for killing.*'[4]

Against the Jews also contained the words:

> The pitiful and miserable Jews ... Certainly it is the time for me to show that demons dwell in the synagogue, not only in the place itself but also in the souls of the Jews ... And this is what happened to the Jews: while they were making themselves unfit for work, they grew *fit for slaughter.*[5]

In his sermons in Antioch, Chrysostom said of the Jews that they were:

> lustful, rapacious, greedy, perfidious bandits, inveterate murders, destroyers, men possessed by the devil. They know only one thing, to satisfy their gullets, get drunk, to kill and maim one another ... They have surpassed the ferocity of wild beasts, for they murder their offspring and immolate them to the devil ...[6]

Chrysostom held Jews responsible for the murderous crucifixion of Jesus, and added that they continued to rejoice in Jesus' death.

He compared the synagogue to a pagan temple, representing it as the source of all vices and heresies. He described it as a place worse than a brothel and a drinking shop; it was a den of scoundrels, the repair of wild beasts, a temple of demons, the refuge of brigands and debauchees, the cavern of devils, and a criminal assembly of the assassins of Christ.[7]

***

Accordingly, by the end of the fourth century the revered Church Fathers had produced a demonic image of the Jew who combined extraordinary malevolence as a tool of Satan with total blindness to Christian 'truth'.

Thence, anti-Semitism became the Church's norm. The results were: discriminatory laws, contempt, defamations, animosity, segregation, forced baptisms, appropriation of

---

[1] Katz, Steven. 'Ideology, State Power, and Mass Murder/Genocide'. In: *Lessons and Legacies: The Meaning of the Holocaust in a Changing World.* Source http://en.wikipedia.org/wiki/Adversus_Judaeos (2012)

[2] Parkes, James. *Prelude to Dialogue.* p153

[3] http://en.wikipedia.org/wiki/Adversus_Judaeos (2012)

[4] http://en.wikipedia.org/wiki/Patristics (2013)

[5] http://www.tertullian.org/fathers/chrysostom_adversus_judaeos_01_homily1.htm (2013)

[6] http://www.zionism-israel.com/his/judeophobia3.htm (2013)

[7] http://en.wikipedia.org/wiki/Adversus_Judaeos (2012)

children, restrictions on living and profession, unjust trials, pogroms, exiles, systematic persecution, rapine, social degradation, destruction of Hebrew literature, and destruction and appropriation of synagogues and cemeteries.

Fifth Century

In the year 438 the *Codex Theodosianus* (*Theodosian Code*) of the Roman Emperor Theodosius II was decreed. It was the first official collection of imperial statutes relating to the Jews. It sanctioned the civil inferiority of the Jews, defined them as 'enemies of the Roman laws and of the supreme majesty', reflected the intentions of Church councils in denigrating Judaism as a 'wicked sect' and Jews as 'abominable' people, and ruled that no Jew might occupy a position of authority over a Christian.[1]

The *Codex* stated that the Jews were, inter alia: 'contaminated with Jewish sacraments', 'insulters of the Christian faith', 'abominable and vile', 'blindly senseless' and 'monstrous heretics'.[2]

The Visigoths:

> who dominated southern Gaul and Spain, when adapting the Roman law to suit their needs, had contented themselves with punishing by confiscation the Christian who turned Jew, with liberating Christian slaves held by Jews, and with inflicting the death penalty on Jewish masters who should force Christian slaves to conversion, besides preserving the law of Theodosius II prohibiting Jews from holding office or building new synagogues. This was by no means full toleration, but *it was merciful in comparison with what followed the conversion of the Goths to Catholicism.*[3]

St Augustine of Hippo (354-430) – The constructs that Paul bequeathed to the Church reached their culmination in the writings of Augustine, the greatest of the Latin Fathers and one of the most eminent Western Doctors of the Church. His teachings were of enormous influence on the policy of the popes and Catholic secular rulers of the Middle Ages. He contributed a veritable arsenal of anti-Semitic texts. He reinforced the concept of the Jew as a wandering, dispossessed, rejected and execrated person. He equated the Jew to Cain, the first killer recorded in biblical history. The *Torah* became the mark of Cain of these Jewish killers who remained blind and lived in error.[4] Rather than being eliminated for their crime, Augustine preferred that the Jews be preserved until the end of time as 'witnesses' to Christian truth. They would then turn to Christ at the Last Judgement.

This Catholic myth of the 'Wandering Jew' developed throughout the Middle Ages. 'As with so many other Catholic myths about Jews, this Wandering Jew fantasy affirmed a positive identity for Catholics at the same time as it confirmed the pariahship of the Jews.'[5]

[1] Wistrich, Robert S. *Anti-Semitism: The Longest Hatred.* pp18-20
[2] Michael, Robert. *A History of Catholic Antisemitism: The Dark Side of the Church.* pp36-37
[3] Lea, Henry Charles. *A History* of the *Inquisition* of *Spain.* Vol I. pp37-40
[4] Wistrich, Robert S. *Anti-Semitism: The Longest Hatred.* pp18-20
[5] Michael, Robert. *A History of Catholic Antisemitism: The Dark Side of the Church.* p51

Augustine urged the Church to promote fear as a weapon. He claimed the Antichrist would most probably be a Jew, and if this were so, all Jews would become committed supporters of the Antichrist:[1]

> Judaism, since Christ, is a corruption; indeed, Judas is the image of the Jewish people: their understanding of Scripture is carnal; they bear the guilt for the death of the Saviour, for through their fathers they have killed Christ... (*Contra Judaeos*)[2]

> So the unbelieving people of the Jews is cursed from the earth, that is, from the Church, which in the confession of sins has opened its mouth to receive the blood shed for the remission of sins by the hand of the people who would not be under grace, but under the law. And this murderer is cursed by the Church; that is, the Church admits and avows the curse pronounced by the Apostle: 'whoever are of the works of the law are under the curse of the law.' (*Reply to Faustinus the Manichaean*)[3]

> Two nations are in thy womb, and two manner of people shall be separated from thy bowels; and the one people shall overcome the other people, and the elder shall serve the younger. (*City of God*)[4]

The resulting calumny of the 'perfidious', 'obscene', 'lascivious' Jew in this early Christian literature led to the creation of an inhuman fabricated stereotype completely divorced from reality, to which were attributed all of the Jews' alleged wrongdoings.

The *Catholic Encyclopedia* makes no mention of either 'Jew' or '*Contra Judaeos*' in its three articles on Augustine, one of which is specifically devoted to his works.

Sulpicius Severus (c.360-c.425)

> Jews ... have been punished for no other reason than for the impious hands they laid on Christ. (*The Chronicle*, II)[5]

St Cyril of Alexandria (376-444)

> And from what they afterwards dared to do, it is plain to see that the Jews have swallowed their vomit and turned again to wallow in their ancient mire and relapsed into the errors of Egypt, for the Evil Spirit has again entered into them, and their last state has become worse than their first.[6]

St Maximus of Turin (c.380-c.465) – bishop and theological writer:

> Whence the Gospel says: 'Two women shall be grinding at the mill; one shall be taken and the other left' (*Matthew* 24:42). The Holy Church shall be taken up into eternal rest: she who has ground the food of holiness unto the Lord. The Synagogue,

---

[1] James, Alexander. *The Myth of Christianity*. pp182-83
[2] http://www.theapricity.com/forum/archive/index.php/t-54938.html (2013)
[3] http://www.newadvent.org/fathers/140612.htm (2013)
[4] http://www.clerus.org/bibliaclerusonline/en/b4c.htm (2013)
[5] http://www.romancatholicism.org/accursed-race.html (2013)
[6] http://www.stsimonoftrent.com/ (2013)

stained with blood, shall be left at the mill, to endure its own unfaithfulness forever. (*Christ our Leaven*)[1]

St Theodoret (c.393-c.457) – Theodoret was an influential author, theologian, and Bishop of Cyrrhus, Syria:

> O most wretched man! You know very well that on the Day of Judgement the crucified God Whom you blaspheme will send you to Hell.[2]

A gradual claim, that Semitic moral failure was the cause of Jewish 'blindness' to Christ, was promoted from patristic times. St Leo I ('the Great') (440-61), for example, repeatedly accused the Jews of this blindness.[3] Leo also stated: 'O Jews! Your impiety has served our salvation. The death of Christ liberates us; it accuses you. You alone, by right, lack that which should be lost to everyone.'[4]

Sixth Century

In the sixth century the Byzantine emperor Justinian I issued the enormous *Corpus Juris Civilis* (*Body of Civil Law*), otherwise known as the *Justinian Code*, which eroded Jewish rights still further. It virtually stripped any legal protection from Judaism, banned the *Mishnah*,[5] closed synagogues in North Africa, and ruled that anyone who rejected the Resurrection or the Last Judgement be put to death.[6]

Additionally, by the sixth century, 'Jews were forbidden to have Christian wives or concubines or servants, and all children sprung from such unions were to be baptized; any Christian slave circumcised or polluted with Jewish rites was to be set free; no Jew was to hold an office in which he could inflict punishment on a Christian, and this action was followed by some further disabilities decreed by the council of Narbonne ...'[7]

St Fulgentius of Ruspe (467-533):

> Hold most firmly and doubt not that all the pagans, but also all the Jews, heretics and schismatics who depart from the present life outside the Catholic Church, are about to go into eternal fire prepared for the devil and his angels. (*Writings*)[8]

Pope St Gregory I (590-604) – Many of this saint's writings were dominated by stigmatising images of Jews and Judaism. This latter was 'vomit', 'perdition', a 'stone of darkness', 'treachery', and a 'shadow of death'; the former as 'enemies of Christ', 'wild asses', 'dragons of poisonous ideas', 'wicked', 'people of Satan', 'of the Devil'.[9]

---

[1] http://www.romancatholicism.org/accursed-race.html (2013)
[2] http://thepowerofgod777.blogspot.com.au/2009/11/what-catholic-church-really-teaches.html (2013)
[3] Sermons 52.5 & 70. Source: *A Dictionary of Jewish-Christian Relations.* p171
[4] http://www.romancatholicism.org/accursed-race.html (2013)
[5] *Mishnah* – the first part of the *Talmud.*
[6] Wistrich, Robert S. *Anti-Semitism: The Longest Hatred.* pp18-20
[7] Lea, Henry Charles. *A History of the Inquisition of Spain.* Vol I. p37-40
[8] http://www.orthodoxchristianity.net/forum/index.php?topic=7766.0;wap2 (2013)
[9] Michael, Robert. *A History of Catholic Antisemitism: The Dark Side of the Church.* p77

Seventh Century

Sixteenth Council of Toledo – This Council met in 693. It was important in the long legal history of the Visigoths in suppressing Judaism in Spain. Penalties were even enacted against Christians who transacted with unconverted or unproven Jews (*Canon 1*):

> There are innumerable judgments of the ancient Fathers concerning the falsehood of the Jews ... According to the prophetic forecast concerning their stiffneckedness, theirs is the sin of Judas who, in their blindness and stiffneckedness, are harder than a stone. ('In the Face of Jewish Falsehood')[1]

St Felix of Toledo (694-700):

> It is known that the Jewish people are polluted with wickedness, blasphemy, and the shedding of the blood of Jesus Christ so that their wickedness has no limit. (*On the Condemnation of the Jews*) – Council XVII of Toledo (694), *Canon 8*; PAC, p376[2]

Eighth Century

Pope Stephen III (768-772):

> With great sorrow and mortal anxiety, We have heard that the Jews have in a Christian land the same rights as Christians, that Christian men and women live under the same roof with these traitors and defile their souls day and night with blasphemies. (*Epistle to the Bishop of Narbonne*)[3]

St Agobard (c.779-840) – Agobard, Archbishop of Lyons, has been called 'the most enlightened man of his age'. He wrote a number of anti-Jewish epistles in which he expressed alarm about Christian contact with those of the Jewish faith:[4]

> No matter how kindly we treat them, we do not succeed in drawing them to the purity of our spiritual faith.[5]

He also emphasised their multi-cursed status:

> Jews are cursed and covered with malediction as by a cloak. The curse has penetrated them like water in their bowels and oil in their bones. They are cursed in the city and cursed in the country, cursed in their coming in and in their going out. Cursed are the fruits of their loins, of their lands, of their flocks; cursed are their cellars, their granaries, their shops, their food, the very crumbs off their tables. (*Letter to the Bishop of Narbonne*)[6]

In his book *The Anguish of the Jews: Twenty Three Centuries of Antisemitism*, 'a respected work on this topic,'[7] Edward H Flannery, a Catholic priest, considered that 'Agobard has few equals in anti-Judaic literature.' As with St Chrysostom, his anti-

---

[1] http://www.romancatholicism.org/accursed-race.html (2013)
[2] Ibid.
[3] http://www.romancatholicism.org/popes-jews.html (2013)
[4] Poliakov, Léon. *The History of Anti-Semitism.* p29
[5] Cohn-Sherbok, D. *The Crucified Jew: Twenty Centuries of Christian Anti-Semitism.* p39
[6] http://www.theapricity.com/forum/archive/index.php/t-54938.html (2013)
[7] So states *Catholic Answers.*

Semitism was uncharitable and uncivil; it 'contributed substantially to the growth of Christian antisemitism.'[1]

Ninth Century

Pope Stephen V (VI) (885-891) – Historian H C Lea wrote: 'The privileges accorded to the Jews and the social equality to which they were admitted under the Carlovingians provoked the severest animadversions of the churchmen. About 890, Stephen VI writes to the archbishop of Narbonne that he has heard with mortal anxiety that these enemies of God are allowed to hold land and that Christians dealt with these dogs and even rendered service to them.'[2]

The Roman Liturgy – From the ninth century onwards, certain sacramentaries of the liturgy directed: 'Pro Iudaeis non flectant' ('Do not genuflect[3] to the Jews').[4]

Tenth Century

Pope Leo VII (936-939) decided: 'Let the Gospels be preached unto them and, if they remain obstinate, let them be expelled.'[5]

Eleventh Century

By the eleventh century, Christians accused the Jews of murdering young, innocent Christian children, of poisoning wells, of engaging in satanic worship with limitless powers for doing evil, and of being experts in black magic.[6]

Pope St Gregory VII (1073-1085) – The *Catholic Encyclopedia* refers to Gregory as: 'One of the greatest of the Roman pontiffs and one of the most remarkable men of all times'.

> We exhort you not to tolerate that Jews rule Christians and have power over them. For, to allow Christians to be subjected to Jews and to be delivered to their whims means to oppress the Church of God and to revile Christ Himself. (*Epistle to King Alphonsus of Castile*)[7]

The Crusaders of Rouen (c.1098) – Chronicler Guibert of Nogent (1053-1124) reported the Crusaders as saying:

> We desire to combat the enemies of God in the East; but we have under our eyes the Jews, a race more inimical to God than all the others.[8]

---

[1] Flannery, Edward H. *The anguish of the Jews: twenty three centuries of antisemitism.* pp84-85
[2] Lea, Henry Charles. *A History* of the *Inquisition of Spain.* Vol I. p81
[3] The source of Catholicism's practice of genuflection was the early adoption by the Church of many of the pagan structures and ceremonies of Imperial Rome.
[4] Poliakov, Léon. *The History of Anti-Semitism.* Vol I. p24
[5] See also: *Catholic Encyclopedia* 'Pope Leo VII'
[6] James, Alexander. *The Myth of Christianity.* pp167-83
[7] http://www.romancatholicism.org/accursed-race.html (2013)
[8] Evangelical Sisterhood of Mary. *The Guilt of Christianity towards the Jewish People*

3 – Condemnation through the Centuries – 12th Century onwards

Hatred is the vice of narrow souls. Honoré de Balzac

Twelfth Century

Cistercian Monk Rudolf (c.1140): 'First avenge the Crucified upon His enemies living here among us, and then go off to fight against the Turks.'[1]

Pierre Abelard (Petrus Abelardus) (1079-c.1142) – This philosopher and theologian had a Jew speak these poignant words in a Dialogue between a philosopher, a Jew, and a Christian: 'To mistreat the Jews is considered a deed pleasing to God. Such imprisonment as is endured by the Jews can be conceived by the Christians only as a sign of God's utter wrath ...' (*Dialogus inter Philosophum, Judaeum, et Christianum*)[2]

Venerable Abbé Pierre of Cluny (c.1145):

> What is the good of going to the end of the world, at great loss of men and money, to fight the Saracens, when we permit among us other infidels who are a thousand times more guilty toward Christ than the Mohammedans?[3]

> Really I doubt whether a Jew can be human for he will neither yield to human reasoning, nor find satisfaction in authoritative utterances ...[4]

St Bernard of Clairvaux (1090-1153) – Bernard was an outspoken French abbot, and the primary builder of the reforming Cistercian Order. He wrote:

> Jews ... are dispersed all over the world, so that, by expiating their crime, they may everywhere be the living witnesses of our redemption. ... Wherefore, the Church says: 'Scatter them by Thy power and bring them down, O Lord.' These words have been fulfilled literally: the Jews are dispersed, humbled, and reduced to hard servitude.[5]

Bernard declared that the Jews were 'a race who had not God for their father, but were of the devil.'[6] Opposing a papal aspirant of Jewish ancestry, Bernard wrote: 'It would be an insult to Christ if the offspring of a Jew occupied the throne of Peter.'[7]

Pope Alexander III (1159-1181):[8]

> They on being admitted to our acquaintance in a spirit of mercy, repay us, the

---

[1] Poliakov, Léon. *The History of Anti-Semitism.* Vol I. p48

[2] http://www.wgcjr.unitingchurch.org.au/page20/page21/page21.html (2015)

[3] Poliakov, Léon. *The History of Anti-Semitism.* Vol I. p48

[4] Trachtenberg, Joshua. *The Devil and the Jews: The Medieval Conception of the Jew and its Relation ...* p18

[5] Quoted in: Sparks, Thomas. *The Curse of Cain and Theologically Correct Social Policy toward the Jews*

[6] Brown, Michael L. *Our Hands are stained with Blood: The Tragic Story of the 'Church' and the ...* p12

[7] *Encyclopaedia Britannica* (3rd edn, 1970) 'Bernard'. Source: http://wiccanhistorian.home.att.net/histories/persecutionJews.html (2007)

[8] The *Catholic Encyclopedia* states that 'Alexander III's epitaph expresses the truth, when it calls him "the Light of the Clergy, the Ornament of the Church, the Father of his City and of the World." ' This, notwithstanding that Alexander also commended King Henry II of England as 'the most beloved son in Christ' for his invasion of Ireland which was 'so praiseworthy begun'.

popular proverb says, as the mouse in the wallet, the snake in the lap and fire in the bosom usually repay their host. (*Ad Haec de Judaeis*)[1]

Let not the sons of the free woman be servants of the sons of the handmaid; but as servants rejected by their lord for whose death they evilly conspired, let them realize that the result of this deed is to make them servants of those whom Christ's death made free. (*Etsi Judaeos*)[2]

Third Lateran Council (1179):

Jews and Saracens are not to be allowed to have Christian servants in their houses, either under pretence of nourishing their children or for service or any other reason. We declare that the evidence of Christians is to be accepted against Jews in every case, since Jews employ their own witnesses against Christians – and that those who prefer Jews to Christians in this matter are to lie under anathema, since Jews ought to be subject to Christians ...[3]

Thirteenth Century

The thirteenth century was particularly prolific in its outpourings of anti-Semitism.

The Jews were typically portrayed in obscene contact with unclean animals such as sows, or as representing a devil. Such representations appeared on cathedral and church ceilings, pillars, utensils, etchings, and the like; and many of these still exist.

Additionally, there developed a series of beliefs that Jews were actually a sub-human race[4] of pig-like monsters. Christian Poles believed that Jewish women had vaginas like sows, and that their pregnancies were only six months. Some parts of Germany charged a 'cloven foot' tax on all Jews; others were required to swear an oath in court "on their mother's body" while standing on the skin of a sow. If found guilty, they were hung by their ankles as a mimicry of the way pigs are slaughtered.[5]

Around the thirteenth century, the Judensau (German for "Jews' sow") appeared. This was the derogatory and dehumanising imagery of Jews that was presented in Germany and some other European countries.

A typical 'Judensau' portrayed the mother sow feeding her Jewish offspring, with the Devil supervising the operation. The development of printing made the Judensau a forceful stereotyping image.

The Catholic popularity of the Judensau lasted for over 600 years.

The Nazis revived the term as 'Saujuden'; and in Germany, schoolchildren were sent to see images of this in churches and similar places.

Pope Innocent III (1198-1216) – 'one of the greatest popes of the Middle Ages,'

---

[1] *A Quo Primum*. Encyclical of Pope Benedict XIV 'ON JEWS AND CHRISTIANS LIVING IN THE SAME PLACE'. Source: http://www.papalencyclicals.net/Ben14/b14aquo.htm (2013)

[2] http://www.fisheaters.com/aquoprimum.html (2010)

[3] http://www.ewtn.com/library/COUNCILS/LATERAN3.HTM (2013)

[4] Following the lead of the Catholic Church, the Nazis described the Jews as 'untermenschen' ('sub-human beings').

[5] Allen, Stewart Lee. *In the Devil's Garden: A Sinful History of Forbidden Food*

wrote to the Count of Nevers that the Jews:

> against whom the blood of Jesus Christ cries aloud, are not to be slain, lest Christians should forget the divine law, yet are they to be scattered as wanderers over the earth, that their faces may be filled with ignominy and they may seek the name of Jesus Christ. Blasphemers of the Christian name are not to be cherished by princes, in oppression of the servants of the Lord, but are rather to be repressed with servitude ...[1]

Innocent's writings variously described the Jews:

> When Jews are admitted out of pity into familiar intercourse with Christians, they repay their hosts, according to the popular proverb, after the fashion of the rat hidden in the sack, or the snake in the bosom, or of the burning brand in one's lap.[2]

> The Jews, by their own guilt, are consigned to perpetual servitude because they crucified the Lord ... As slaves rejected by God, in whose death they wickedly conspire, they shall by the effect of this very action, recognise themselves as the slaves of those whom Christ's death set free ... (*Epistle to the archbishops of Sens and Paris*)[3]

Thomas de Chantimpré (1201-272) – Thomas was a writer, preacher and theologian. In his *The Accursed Talmud*, he recounted:

> [St] Louis King of France, devoutest of princes, commanded about the year 1239, at the persuasion of Brother Henry of Cologne, of the Order of Friars Preachers, that men should gather together at Paris, under pain of death, all copies of that most abominable Jewish book called the Talmud[4] ... wherefore divers copies of this book were brought to Paris to be burned. The Jews therefore came in tears to the Archbishop ... and offered him untold gold for the preservation of those books ...

But, miraculously, the Catholic God intervened:

> The Jews, having recovered their books, ordained a solemn yearly day of thanksgiving; but in vain, since the Spirit of God had ordered otherwise: for at the year's end, on the same day and at that very place where these execrable books had been rendered back ... the Archbishop aforesaid was seized with intolerable inward pains on his way to the King's council, and died that same day amidst cries and lamentations. The King with all his train fled from the spot, fearing sore lest he also should be struck by God's hand;[5] and within a short space, at the persuasion of Brother

---

[1] Lea, Henry Charles. *History of the Inquisition of Spain*. Vol 1. p82

[2] http://www.romancatholicism.org/accursed-race.htm (2007)

[3] http://jewishroots.net/library/anti-semitism/a-brief-history-of-anti-semitism-2.html (2013)

[4] The *Talmud* is a record of rabbinic discussions pertaining to Jewish law, ethics, customs, and history. It has two components: the *Mishnah* (c.200 CE), the first written compendium of Judaism's Oral Law; and the *Gemara* (c.500 CE), a discussion of the *Mishnah* and related Tannaitic writings that often ventures onto other subjects and expounds broadly on the *Tanakh*. The *Tanakh* is the Hebrew name of the Bible. (*Wikipedia*)

[5] A prime example of the naïve mediaeval credulity of the Catholic Church.

Henry as before, the Jews' books were gathered together under pain of death and burned.[1]

Pope Gregory IX (1227-1241):

They ought to know the yoke of perpetual enslavement because of their guilt. See to it that the perfidious Jews never in the future become insolent, but that they always suffer publicly the shame of their sin in servile fear ... Ungrateful for favours and forgetful of benefits, the Jews return insult for kindness and impious contempt for goodness. (*Epistle to the Hierarchy of Germany*)[2]

The bishop of Lisbon, Dom Soeiro, complained to Gregory IX in Rome that the King of Portugal gave preference to the Jews in public governmental jobs. The Pope censured King Sancho I.[3]

Pope Innocent IV (1243-1254):[4]

The wicked perfidy[5] of the Jews, from whose hearts Our Saviour did not remove the veil because of their enormous crimes but caused them justly to continue in their blindness, commit acts of shame which engender astonishment in those who hear, and terror in those who discover it... (*The Wicked Perfidy of the Jews*)[6]

St Thomas Aquinas (1225-1274) – Aquinas was one of the leading Roman Catholic theologians – sometimes called the 'Angelic Doctor' and the 'Prince of Scholastics':

Jews, in consequence of their sin, are or were destined to perpetual slavery; so that sovereigns of states may treat their goods as their own property; with the sole proviso that they do not deprive them of all that is necessary to sustain life ... It would be licit to hold Jews, because of the crimes, in perpetual servitude, and therefore the princes may regard the possessions of Jews as belonging to the state. (*De Regimine Judaeorum – On the Governance of the Jews*)[7]

Pope Honorius IV (1285-1287) – Honorius called the *Talmud* 'that damnable book' and urged the Archbishops of Canterbury and York 'vehemently to see that it be not read by anyone, since all evils flow from it.'[8]

Pope Nicholas IV (1288-1292):[9]

With troubled heart, We are reminded that many of those converted from the error of Jewish blindness to the light of the Christian Faith have fallen back into their former falsehood. Proceed with intensity against all who make themselves guilty of

---

[1] *Life In The Middle Ages*. Vol I. p121 (*The accursed Talmud*. Chantimpré, Thomas de (Lib. i, c. iii, p. 14))
[2] http://www.romancatholicism.org/accursed-race.html (2013)
[3] de Mello, Alfredo. *'The Jews in Portugal'*
[4] The word 'Jew' is not mentioned in the *Catholic Encyclopedia* under 'Pope Innocent IV'.
[5] By the Middle Ages, the term 'perfidus' attracted the connotations of 'stubborn, blind, intentionally disbelieving, maliciously unfaithful, malevolent, and treacherous.' Michael, Robert. *A History of Catholic Antisemitism: The Dark Side of the Church*. p18
[6] http://www.romancatholicism.org/popes-jews.html (2013)
[7] http://www.fatherfeeney.org/point/55-feb.html (2013)
[8] Ibid.
[9] The *Catholic Encyclopedia* states that 'Nicholas was pious and learned'.

this crime, against heretics, and against those who support, protect, and defend them. (*Turbato corde*)[1]

Fourteenth Century

The Cortes of Toro[2] – In 1371 the Cortes described why the kingdom was suffering:

for whatever reason, the Jews, evil and rash men, enemies of God and of all of Christianity, cause numerous evils and sow corruption with impunity, so that the greater part of our kingdom is tyrannised and ruined by the Jews, in contempt of the Christians and our Catholic faith.[3]

Fifteenth Century

Father Bernardino of Feltro – Bernardino was a fierce enemy of the Jews:

Jewish usurers bleed the poor to death and grow fat on their substance, and I who live on alms, who feed on the bread of the poor, shall I then be mute before outraged charity? Dogs bark to protect those who feed them, and I, who am fed by the poor, shall I see them robbed of what belongs to them and keep silent?[4]

St Vincent Ferrer (c.1350-1419) – Ferrer was a Dominican professor of theology:

Since His spouse, the Synagogue, refused to receive Him, Christ answered: 'This is a harlot!' And He gave her a bill of divorce, as we read in *Isaias* (50:1): 'Thus says the Lord: Behold, you are sold for your iniquities; and for your evil deeds have I put your mother away. Because I came and there was not a man; I called and there was no one who would hear.' And so the Jews, the sons of the harlot, were repudiated.[5]

One who dies a Jew will be damned.[6]

Blessed Juliana of Norwich (1342-1423):

I knew in my faith that the Jews were accursed and condemned without end, except those who were converted. (*Sixteen Revelations of Divine Love*)[7]

Pope Martin V (1417-1431):[8]

The Jews, whom Holy Church tolerates in diverse parts of the world in testimony

---

[1] http://www.romancatholicism.org/accursed-race.html (2103)
[2] Toro is currently a town and municipality in the autonomous community of Castile-León, Spain. Cortes is the Spanish and Portuguese term for a court
[3] Quoted in: Cohn-Sherbok, D. *The Crucified Jew: Twenty Centuries of Christian* ... pp77-78
[4] Refer: Flornoy, E. *Le Bienheureux Bernardin de Feltre*. Quoted in: Sparks, Thomas. *The Curse of Cain and Theologically Correct Social Policy toward the Jews*
[5] http://www.romancatholicism.org/accursed-race.html (2013)
[6] Ibid.
[7] Ibid.
[8] Pope Martin was not only an anti-Semite but also a genocidal maniac. In 1429 he commanded the King of Poland to kill all Christian Hussites: 'Know that the interests of the Holy See, and those of your crown, make it a duty to exterminate the Hussites [who] dare proclaim principles of equality ... Turn your forces against Bohemia; burn, massacre ... nothing could be more agreeable to God, or more useful to the cause of kings, than the extermination of the Hussites.' Refer to Volume 1, Chapter II-6, of '*A Corrupt Tree*' for more details of this most unholy pope.

to Jesus Christ, wish to persevere in their hardness and blindness rather than acknowledge the words of the prophets and the mysteries of the Holy Scriptures, and
to come to the knowledge of the Christian faith and salvation.[1]

Council of Ferrara-Florence (1438-1445):

The most holy Roman Church firmly believes, professes, and teaches that the
Mosaic Law ... cannot be observed without the loss of eternal salvation ... Everyone,
therefore, who observes circumcision and the Sabbath and the other requirements
of the Law, the Church declares not in the least fit ... to participate in eternal
salvation.[2]

Friar Alonso de Espina (c.1460) – This notable Franciscan published his *Fortalitium
fidei contra Judaeos*, which stirred up hatred against Jews and conversos.[3] The work
contained deliberate distortions and fabrications; the Jews were: homosexuals, blas-
phemers, traitors, child murderers, murdering doctors, and poisoners.[4]

Sixteenth Century

. It was well established that the Jews were agents of the Devil. One series of sixteenth-
century prints shows the Devil assisting the Jews in the procedures of the bathhouse,
while a century later, a print depicts the Devil participating in the Jewish ritual of the
synagogue. Satan himself is often featured with grotesque exaggeration of Semitic
features.[5] William Shakespeare (1564-1616) portrayed the popular conception of the
Jew in the *Merchant of Venice*: "Let me say 'Amen' betimes lest the devil cross my
prayer, for here he comes in the likeness of a Jew," and "Certainly the Jew is the very
devil incarnal!"

· *Martin Luther* – As an Augustinian monk before he left the Catholic Church, Luther
wrote antagonistically about Jews in his book *On the Jews and their Lies*. It describes
the Jews in extremely harsh terms, excoriates them, and provides detailed recommendations for a pogrom against them and their permanent oppression and/or expulsion.[6]

∕ *Fra Bartolomeo Fumo* – Fra Fumo, Inquisitor-General for the Duchies of Parma and
Piacenza (c.1542), concluded that:

To judaise, namely to observe Saturday, or other Jewish ceremonies, is mortal [sin]
... If however one observes Saturday, not for the purposes of a Jewish rite, but for
some other pious reason, such as to venerate the Blessed Virgin Mary, he would not
sin mortally. To converse with Jews is forbidden at Canon Law... and especially in
ten cases is it forbidden: First, to live with them; Second, to eat with them; Third, to

---

[1] http://www.romancatholicism.org/accursed-race.html (2013)
[2] Ibid.
[3] Converso – a Jew or Moor in mediaeval Spain or Portugal who converted, or professed conversion to
Christianity to avoid persecution or expulsion.
[4] Kamen, Henry. *The Spanish Inquisition: An Historical Revision.* pp33-34
[5] Trachtenberg, Joshua. *The Devil and the Jews: The Medieval Conception of the Jew and its Relation ...* p26
[6] http://en.wikipedia.org/wiki/Martin_Luther#Indulgences_controversy_and_the_start_of_the_Reformation
(2007)

bathe with them; Fourth, to call upon them for medical care; Fifth, to accept their medicine; Sixth, to feed their children in their houses; Seven, to serve them, as employees; Eight, to be their slaves; Nine, for them to hold public office amongst Christians; Ten, to eat their azyme [matzah].[1] To tolerate them in public office is mortal, because this disparages the dignity of the Christian Faith, and for that reason is it forbidden. (Citation from the mediaeval Inquisitors' manual – based on the canonical legislation promulgated by Gregory IX in 1234 in the capitular *De Judaeis* (*Of the Jews*).[2]

⊢ *Pope Paul IV (1555-1559)* – Paul IV promulgated the Bull *Cum nimis absurdum* in 1555. It was a landmark in the history of anti-Semitism, and is recognised as the most devastating Christian anti-Jewish document ever written. It placed both economic and religious restrictions on Jews in Rome and the Papal States. It renewed anti-Jewish legislation, and subjected Jews to various degradations and restrictions on their personal freedom.[3,4]

⸰ *Pope St Pius V (1566-1572)* – Saint Pius V[5] was one of the most anti-Semitic popes:

> We have carefully investigated how this revolting sect abuses the name of Christ and how harmful they are to those whose life is threatened by their deceit.

> We order that, within 90 days, *all Jews* in our entire earthly realm of justice – in all towns, districts, and places – *must depart these regions.* (*Hebraeorum gens*)[6]

⸰ *Pope Gregory XIII (1572-1585)* – Gregory stated that the guilt of Jews in rejecting and crucifying Christ only grows deeper with successive generations, entailing perpetual slavery.[7]

Seventeenth Century

Pope Clement VIII (1592-1605)[8]

> All the world suffers from the usury of the Jews, their monopolies and deceit. They have brought many unfortunate people into a state of poverty, especially the farmers, working class people and the very poor. Then as now Jews have to be reminded intermittently anew that they were enjoying rights in any country since they left Palestine and the Arabian Desert, and subsequently their ethical and moral doctrines

---

[1] Matzah – unleavened bread eaten at Passover.
[2] http://www.stsimonoftrent.com/ (2013)
[3] http://www.jcrelations.net/A_Short_Review_of_a_Troubled_History.2267.0.html?L=8&page=6 (2013)
[4] This bull is excluded from the article 'Pope Paul IV' in the *Catholic Encyclopedia*; as is the word 'Jew'.
[5] There is no mention of 'Jew' or of *Hebraeorum gens* in the *Catholic Encyclopedia* under 'Pope St. Pius V'.
[6] http://jewishcurrents.org/tag/papacy (2013)
[7] See, for example: http://www.zionism-israel.com/hdoc/Papal_Bulls_Jews.htm (2013)
[8] The *Catholic Encyclopedia* reports that Clement was 'Blameless in morals from childhood', and that he gave 'his attention to the more important spiritual interests of the Church.'

as well as their deeds rightly deserve to be exposed to criticism in whatever country they happen to live. (*Caeca et obdurata*)[1]

– *French King Henri IV* – Henri appointed Pierre de l'Ancre as Grand-Inquisitor to clean out witchcraft. This 'bigoted Catholic' was a 'gleeful executioner' who 'gloried in his Jesuit education.'[2] He recorded that 'filth [is] the attribute common to Jews and pigs … the Jews deserve every execration, as destroyers of all divine and human majesty …' He had hundreds of 'witches' burned.

Eighteenth Century

· Even as late as the eighteenth century, the situation had not improved for the Jews. The French Revolution (1789-1799) led to the Age of Enlightenment, but this illumination did not enter the conservative Holy See. A sequence of popes continued to reinforce the Church's prejudices against Jews. For example, if a Jew left Rome without permission of the Inquisitor he was fined. If a Christian doctor was requested to treat a patient in the ghetto, he had first to try to convert him to Catholicism – if he failed, the doctor was required to leave immediately. Jewish children were taken for baptism and turned into Christians – if the parents objected they were sent before the Inquisition. Death was the penalty if two Catholics testified that a Jew had insulted a Catholic priest or the 'true religion'.[3]

Pope Benedict XIV (1740-1758) – The *Catholic Encyclopedia* reports that "Benedict's claim to immortality rests principally on his admirable ecclesiastical writings." In his encyclical *A Quo Primum* 'On Jews and Christians living in the same place',[4] Benedict wrote:

> To the Primate, Archbishops and Bishops, of the Kingdom of Poland ...
>
> 3. … some households of the great have employed a Jew as 'Superintendent-of-the-Household'; in this capacity, they not only administer domestic and economic matters, but they also ceaselessly exhibit and flaunt authority over the Christians they are living with ...
>
> 6. But if it is asked what matters the Apostolic See forbids to Jews living in the same cities as Christians, We will say that all those activities which are now allowed in Poland are forbidden ...
>
> 7. … To you then, Venerable Brothers, passes the task of renewing those sanctions ... You will be able to give these orders and commands easily and confidently, in that neither your property nor your privileges are hired to Jews; furthermore you do no business with them and you neither lend them money nor borrow from them. Thus,

---

[1] http://www.romancatholicism.org/popes-jews.html (2013)

[2] Michael, Robert. *A History of Catholic Antisemitism: The Dark Side of the Church.* p119

[3] de Rosa, Peter. *Vicars of Chris: The Dark Side of the Papacy.* p195

[4] The Nazi Holocaust in Poland was a sequel to the Pope's views expressed in this encyclical. See later chapters.

you will be free from and unaffected by all dealings with them.[1]

St Alphonsus Maria Liguori (1696-1787):

> Poor Jews! You invoked a dreadful curse upon your own heads in saying: 'His blood be on us and on our children'; and that curse miserable race, you carry upon you to this day, and to the end of time you shall endure the chastisement of that innocent blood. (*The Passion and Death of Jesus Christ*)[2]

Maria Theresa, Catholic Queen of Hungary and Bohemia (1717-1780):

> I know of no other troublesome pest within the state than this race, which impoverishes the people by their fraud, usury and money-lending and commits all deeds which an honourable man despises.[3]

- *Voltaire* – Voltaire saw Jews as having permanently evil traits. His traditional Catholic anti-Jewishness ran 'like a sewer through his writings.' He told the Jews 'Your priests have always sacrificed human victims with their sacred hands.' Of the 118 articles in his famous *Dictionnaire Philosophique*, more than 30 attack Jews.[4]

- *Charles Fourier* – Fourier 'was a utopian socialist and radical antisemite whose charges against the Jews ran the gamut from parasitism to usury.' He was concerned that if France had many more Jews it 'would have become one huge synagogue.'[5]

Nineteenth Century

- *Abbé Barruel* – This French Jesuit priest wrote a treatise in 1806 blaming the Masonic Order for the French Revolution. He later issued a letter claiming it was the Jews, not the Masons, who were responsible. This was the source of a belief in an international conspiracy for Jews to control the world.[6]

Vincenzo Berni degli Antoni – degli Antoni, a professor at the University of Bologna, and the city's most distinguished expert in civil law, published a document in 1827 in which he stated that:

> Judaism was a vicious religion. Jews as a people were condemned by God to wander homeless across the earth. Jews were an object of scorn among God-fearing peoples. Jews in the Papal States were simply slaves. Jews had no right to share with Christians in the intestate inheritance of a Christian relative. Jews had no rights of citizenship. Judaism had an implacable hatred of Christians. Jews used trickery, treachery and torture, to work ceaselessly to reduce Christians to perpetual slavery. The Christian restrictions on Jews were definitely necessary to avoid the deadly effects of their religion.[7]

---

[1] http://www.papalencyclicals.net/Ben14/b14aquo.htm (2012)
[2] http://www.romancatholicism.org/accursed-race.html (2013)
[3] Quoted in: Sparks, Thomas. *The Curse of Cain and Theologically Correct Social Policy ...*
[4] Michael, Robert. *A History of Catholic Antisemitism: The Dark Side of the Church*. pp121-23
[5] Ibid. p127
[6] *The Scandal of Roman Catholicism*
[7] Kertzer, David I. *The Kidnapping of Edgardo Mortara*. pp19-20

Ferdinando Jabolot pronounced the Jews to be:

> the plague of humanity, a bunch of filthy usurers and lawless ruffians, richly deserving of the divine punishment that had been meted out to them.[1]

Deputy Hermida – During 1813, when Spanish 'racial purity' was still an issue, Hermida declared in the Cadiz Cortes (parliament):

> The continuous complaints that the Catholic Monarchs heard ... they were forced to find a remedy in the establishment of the Inquisition ... the hate of Christ's enemies was terrible ... it was necessary to purge the Spanish domains of this race of enemies, throwing them out of Spain.[2]

León Carbonero y Sol – Carbonero y Sol, an influential professor from Sevilla, published an article in the well-known Catholic magazine *La Cruz* (*The Cross*):

> The Jews are deceiving themselves very much if they believe that the Spaniards have forgotten their old betrayals and treacheries, their insurrections and their deceits, their swindles and their racketeering, their iniquities and their wild ferocity ... The Jewish race that despises and reviles Jesus Christ, that insults his most Saintly Mother with sacrilegious words, the Mother of the Spaniards ... The coming of the Jews to Spain, would be the beginning of new evils ... they are Our Lord Jesus Christ's crucifiers, scornful to his most Sacred Mother ... usurious, swindlers, and pirates of peoples.[3]

Henri-Roger Gougenot des Mousseaux – His book, *Le Juif, Le Judaïsm et la judaïsation des peuples Chrétiens* (*The Jew, Judaism, and the Judaisation of the Christian people*), was called by Norman Cohn 'the Bible of modern antisemitism'. An ultramontane Catholic, he believed the Jews to be 'the representatives on earth of the spirit of darkness.'[4]

Pius IX (1846-1878) – Pius blessed the *Le Juif, Le Judaïsm et la judaïsation des peuples Chrétiens* of Gougenot des Mousseaux.[5]

He also issued stricter laws against the Jews – for example, there was a case of a Jew of good reputation being sent to prison for employing a Christian lady to look after his linen.[6]

In 1871, addressing a group of Catholic women, Pius said of the Jews that:

> owing to their obstinacy and their failure to believe, they have become dogs. We

[1] Kertzer, David I. *The Kidnapping of Edgardo Mortara.* pp18-19
[2] http://www.jcpa.org/phas/phas-perednik-f03.htm (2007)
[3] Carbonero y Sol, Leon. 'Claims of the Jews for their Establishment in Spain'. *La Cruz.* Vol 2. (Sevilla, 1854) pp 623-27. (*La Cruz*, the Roman Catholic magazine of Spain, was published until 1915) Source: http://www.jcpa.org/phas/phas-perednik-f03.htm (2007)
[4] Michael, Robert. *A History of Catholic Antisemitism: The Dark Side of the Church.* p128
[5] Ibid.
[6] de Rosa, Peter. *Vicars of Christ: The Dark Side of the Papacy.* p195

have today in Rome unfortunately too many of these dogs, and we hear them barking in all the streets, and going around molesting people everywhere.[1]

- *G K Chesterton (1874-1936)* – Chesterton, a Catholic author, is said to have expressed his regret 'that the Crusaders who slaughtered Jewish men, women and children could not be canonised.'[2,3]

Twentieth Century

- 'You killed Christ' was a common invective used by Catholic children against Jewish children. An example of such vilification is that of Martin Hellman. He was born in 1946 in a Jewish neighbourhood in the Bronx, but at the age of four his family moved to a predominantly Irish Catholic neighbourhood. According to Hellman, this permanently changed his attitude to life. He found that the other children went to church and learned that 'the Jews killed Christ,' so he got called 'Christ killer', and was beaten up.[4]

Another example is that of Mike Gold whose childhood was in a New York City ghetto. One day he wandered beyond the ghetto's limit, whereupon he was accosted: 'So you are a Christ-Killer. Well you're in Christian territory and we are Christians. We're going to teach you to stay where you belong!' And they beat him up and tore his clothes, jeering: 'We are Christians and you killed Christ! Stay where you belong! We are Christians, and you killed Christ ...'[5]

- *Pope St Pius X (1903-1914)* – The *Catholic Encyclopedia* states that 'his greatest care always turned to the direct interests of the Church.' Consequently, in an interview with Zionist leader Benjamin Ze'ev (Theodor) Hertzl in 1904, Pius said:

> We are unable to favour this movement [Zionism]. We cannot prevent the Jews from going to Jerusalem – but we could never sanction it. The ground of Jerusalem, if it were not always sacred, has been sanctified by the life of Jesus Christ. As the head of the Church, I cannot answer you otherwise. The Jews have not recognised our Lord, therefore we cannot recognise the Jewish people. Jerusalem cannot be placed in Jewish hands.[6]

Herzl then asked the Pope if he had any problem with the Holy Land being under the control of the Muslims. Pius replied:

> I know it is disagreeable to see the Turks in possession of our Holy Places. But we simply have to put up with it. But to sanction the Jewish wish to occupy these sites that we cannot do.[7] ... The Jews have not recognised our Lord, therefore we cannot

---

[1] http://en.wikipedia.org/wiki/Timeline_of_antisemitism (2007)

[2] Hagee, John. http://www.mosquitonet.com/~prewett/hag1016.html (2010)

[3] *The Independent* reports that: 'The Bishop of Northampton has taken a first step towards making the writer GK Chesterton a saint, by appointing a priest to make initial investigations into the claims of an American literary society that he is worthy.'

[4] Singh, Simon. *The Code Book*

[5] Source: http://michaeldalycj.wordpress.com/2010/09/23/what-sort-of-christ-do-we-preach/ (2010). See also: http://www.kingsolomon.com/literary/essays/passion/buchwald.html (2010)

[6] http://catholicforum.fisheaters.com/index.php?topic=3455259.20;wap2 (2013), and several other websites.

[7] http://ziomania.com/herzl/Theodore%20Herzl%20and%20the%20Pope.htm (2010)

recognise the Jewish people ... If you go to Palestine and your people settle there, you will find us clergy and churches ready to baptise you all.[1]

Pius X was declared a Saint in 1954.

Benedict XV (1914-1922) – Benedict, speaking through a Vatican spokesman, informed representatives of the Zionist Movement in 1921 that the Church did not wish to assist 'the Jewish race, which is permeated with a revolutionary and rebellious spirit, to gain control over the Holy Land.'[2]

The Holy Office – In the early 1920s the Catholic missionary organisation Society of Friends of Israel requested that the phrase 'perfidious Jews' be removed from the Catholic liturgy. The movement was banned by the Holy Office.[3]

L'Osservatore Romano – As late as 1961, this paper claimed that the Jewish people 'had stained themselves with a horrible crime deserving of expiation.'[4]

Padre St Pio of Pietrelcina (1887-1968):

> The Jews are enemies of God and foes of our Holy Religion.[5,6]

Father Charles E Coughlin – Fr Coughlin was one of the best known Catholic priests in America in the 1930s. In radio programmes he railed against the threat of Jews to the American economy and defended Hitler's treatment of the Jews.[7]

Paul VI (1963-1978):

> Jews were predestined to receive the Messiah and had been waiting for him for thousands of years. When Christ comes, the Jewish people not only do not recognise him, they oppose him, slander him and finally kill him.[8]

Twenty-first Century

Slaves of the Immaculate Heart of Mary – This Congregation, which was founded by Jesuit Father Leonard Feeney (1897-1978), comprises a congregation of religious brothers and sisters committed to a Crusade consisting of, firstly, the propagation and defence of Roman Catholic dogma (especially 'extra ecclesiam nulla salus'[9]), and, secondly, the conversion of America to the 'one, true Church'.[10,11]

Thomas Sparks (Br. Benedict Mary MICM Tert.)[12] – A contemporary view (c.2000) of the culpability of the Jews is lucidly presented by Thomas Sparks in *The Curse of*

---

[1] http://www.catholicapologetics.info/apologetics/judaism/rabbi.htm (2010)

[2] http://www.sullivan-county.com/id2/timeline.htm (2007)

[3] Cymet, David. *History vs. Apologetics: The Holocaust, the Third Reich, and the Catholic Church*. p446

[4] Ibid. p445

[5] Quoted in: Sparks, Thomas. *The Curse of Cain and Theologically Correct Social Policy ...*

[6] Source of quotation: Pagnossin, Joseph. *The Calvary of Padre Pio*. p91. Source: http://mauricepinay. blogspot.com.au/2011/10/rabbis-demand-pope-condemn-bishop.html (2015), et al.

[7] *The Scandal of Roman Catholicism'*. http://www.liberalslikechrist.org/Catholic/RCscandal-1.html (2007)

[8] de Rosa, Peter. *Vicars of Christ: The Dark Side of the Papacy.* p201

[9] 'extra ecclesiam nulla salus' – 'there is no salvation outside the Church'.

[10] http://www.catholicism.org/micm-apostolate-overview.html (2010)

[11] http://en.wikipedia.org/wiki/Feeneyism (2010)

[12] https://groups.yahoo.com/neo/groups/aquinas/conversations/messages/5807 (2015)

Cain and Theologically Correct Social Policy toward the Jews.[1] It asserts that the Jews corporately murdered Christ, and all bear the guilt of his murder, which is deicide. Therefore all Jews are cursed with the curse of Cain. This document also claims that the Jews are perpetually genocidal, that the *Talmud* teaches genocide, and that the Jews brought about the French Revolution, World Wars I and II, and the Russian Revolution.

Sparks' solution to the current world problems created by the Jews is simple: the multitude must again learn to fear Cain, and the Jew must be justly segregated, subjugated, and expelled in conformity with 'his cursed perfidy'.

Condemnatory Words used against the Jews

Almost every conceivable derogatory word in the language has been used by Catholics to denigrate the Jews.

Table 4. A Sample of Condemnatory Words used against the Jews

abominable	despotic	haters	parasites	sinful
accursed	destroyers	haughty	perfidious	sinister
adulterous	destructive	heretics	pernicious	slanderers
argumentative	detestable	horned	perverse	slayers
blasphemous	diabolical	idolatrous	perverted	sorcerers
blind	disbelievers	immoral	pestiferous	soulless
blood-shedders	dishonest	impetuous	pests	speculators
bloodthirsty	drunken	impious	pig-like	stench
capitalists	enemies	implacable	pirates	stiff-necked
carnal	evil	inhuman	plotters	stubborn
cheaters	execrable	insatiable	poisonous	sub-human
Christ-killers	executioners	irreverent	polluted	swindlers
cloven footed	exploiters	lascivious	predators	thieves
condemned	faithless	lawless	rapacious	treacherous
corrupt	false	liberal	rash	tricksters
corrupting	fat	lustful	revolting	troublesome
criminals	fornicators	malodorous	robbers	tyrannical
cruel	fraudulent	manipulators	ruffians	unbelievers
cunning	free thinkers	materialistic	satanic	unclean
cursed	fremdkörper	monsters	scoffers	unfaithful
dangerous	greedy	murderers	scrofulous	usurious
deceitful	guilty	obscene	seducers	vampires
degrading	harlots	obstinate	sensual	vipers
demons	harmful	oppressors	shameless	wicked

---

[1] http://www.stormfront.org/posterity/ci/curseofcain.html (2013)

Synopsis

Even before it was a century old, the Christian church began to produce a systematic anti-Jewish precept. By the second century, a consistent theological rationale had been developed for condemnation of the Jews and contempt for Judaism that set the course of occidental civilisation.

Christian anti-Semitism has justifiably been described as the longest and deepest hatred, and as an unparalleled malignity. It has also been universal, and the deepest, most obsessive, dangerous and chimerical hatred ever.

The Catholic Church has been largely responsible for this extended animosity. Some of the most virulent anti-Semites were (and are) revered as saints.

St Augustine of Hippo had enormous influence on the policy of the popes and Catholic secular rulers of the Middle Ages. He contributed a veritable arsenal of anti-Semitic texts. He reinforced the concept of the Jew as a dispossessed, rejected and execrated person. He equated the Jew to Cain.

Anti-Semitism is based on fantasy. Jews have been accused: of killing Christians for their blood for ritual purposes; of desecration of the host, of being agents of the Devil; as possessing horns, tails, and the beard of a goat; and for producing a terrible odour. The fable of the grasping Jew persisted for hundreds of years. The Christian myth perceived the Devil and the Jew as being the inexorable enemies of Jesus. This became ever more prominent over the centuries.

Many popes, also, wrote strongly against the Jews. The worst was Paul IV, whose Bull *Cum nimis absurdum* was a landmark in the history of anti-Semitism, and is recognised as the most devastating Christian anti-Jewish document ever written.

Historical evidence reveals conclusively that the vast majority of Nazi ideologists developed their malevolent attitude to Jews from the institutional Church's extended, extensive, and active anti-Semitic teachings and legislations.

Conclusion

Jules Isaac was a French Jewish historian, whose wife, son, daughter, and son-in-law were deported to the Nazi death camps. While in hiding during the War, Jules pondered the question of what made the Holocaust happen in Christian Europe. He reached the conclusion that the ultimate responsibility lay with the Christian Church whose millennia of anti-Semitism had incubated the Nazi devil:

> Christian anti-Semitism is the powerful, millennial tree, with many and strong roots, onto which all the other varieties of anti-Semitism – even the most antagonistic by nature, even anti-Christian – have come to be grafted in the Christian world.[1]

---

[1] Quoted in: Cymet, David. *History vs. Apologetics: The Holocaust, the Third Reich, and the Catholic Church.* p445

In confirmation, in his *A History of Catholic Antisemitism*, Professor Robert Michael concluded that:

> Many lay Catholics and widely respected Catholic writers still hesitate to come to grips with the two millennia of Catholic antisemitism that not only prepared Catholics to perceive Jews in a negative way but also primed them to accept the anti-Jewish aspects of secular ideas – and to take action on them.[1]

He referred to:

> the history of Catholic antisemitism and the set of beliefs that created a climate of opinion that led to untold suffering, and millions of Jewish deaths before the Holocaust, and not only made the Holocaust possible, but likely.[2]

Continual organisational propaganda was the culprit.[3] Historian Walter Zwi Bacharach pointed out that 'no human being gets up one fine morning and sets out to kill Jews, just because he is ordered to do so.'[4]

In 1998 the Holy See[5] issued *We Remember: A Reflection on the Shoah*. Father John T Pawlikowski is a Servite priest and Professor of Social Ethics at the Catholic Theological Union. He received a Distinguished Service Award from the American Jewish Committee (Chicago). He pointed out and concluded:

> *We Remember* leaves the strong impression that there was no inherent connection between Nazi ideology and classical Christian anti-Judaism and anti-Semitism. This is basically inaccurate. Among Europe's Christian population, Christian anti-Judaism and anti-Semitism had *everything to do* with widespread acquiescence and even collaboration with the Nazi policy devoted to the destruction of the Jews.

> I like to speak of classical Christian anti-Judaism and anti-Semitism as providing an *indispensable* 'seedbed' for Nazism.[6]

Father Pawlikowski also pointed out that it is known from many studies, that anti-Semitism permeated Roman Catholic catechesis and preaching and the popular culture created thereby.[7] Consequently:

> the 'sons and daughters' of the church who fell into the sin of anti-Semitism did so because of what they had learned from teachers, theologians (including the very important patristic writings), and preachers sanctioned by the *institutional* church[8]

---

[1] Michael, Robert. *A History of Catholic Antisemitism: The Dark Side of the Church*. p1

[2] Ibid. p7

[3] See also: Paley, Susan and Koesters, Adrian Gibbons, eds. 'A Viewer's Guide to Contemporary Passion Plays'. Source: https://en.wikipedia.org/wiki/Criticism_of_the_Catholic_Church (2015)

[4] Ibid.

[5] 'Holy See' is an ecclesiastic euphemism for 'Holy Seat', from the original Latin title 'Sancta sedes'. The term 'Holy Seat' was perceived as not suiting the status of the operational centre of the organisation.

[6] Quoted in: Cymet, David. *History vs. Apologetics: The Holocaust, the Third Reich, and the Catholic ...* p451

[7] Ibid. p452

[8] Quoted in: Cymet, David. *History vs. Apologetics: The Holocaust, the Third Reich, and the Catholic Church*.

4 – Dictates, Bulls, Forceful Conversions

The Church held the Jew to be a being deprived, by the guilt of his ancestors, of all natural rights save that of existence. Henry Charles Lea[1]

It was a doctrine of Christendom that the Jews were the violators of the moral order of the world. This conception was embedded in the Christian collective psyche from the formative period of Christianity to the activities of World War II, and possibly beyond.[2]

Consequently, the discrimination against, and the malevolent treatment of Jews were ongoing practices of the Catholic Church for twenty long centuries. No religious group was so singled out for vituperation, vilification, harassment, denigration, conversion, restriction, and extermination as were the Jews. The popular doctrine of the Church was that anyone who persecuted, tortured or massacred Jews had acted as an instrument of Divine wrath against them.[3]

The *First Council of Nicaea* was convoked in 325 by Emperor Constantine I. It was the first oecumenical conference of bishops of the early Christian Church. It was historically significant because it was the first effort to attain consensus in the Church through an assembly representing all Christians.[4] It decided to separate the date of Christian Easter from the Jewish Passover:

> We desire, dearest brethren, to separate ourselves from the detestable company of the Jews ... How, then, could we follow these Jews, who are almost certainly blinded.[5]

Significantly, Church theologians converted the joyous Jewish Passover celebrating liberation and freedom into a tragic Good Friday commemorating the alleged Jewish crime of deicide.[6]

For two millennia, the Church has promulgated the concept of this alleged Jewish deicide of Jesus as being *evil*, while, by contrast, it states in its *Catechism of the Catholic Church*:

> 599 Jesus' violent death was not the result of chance in an unfortunate coincidence of circumstances, but is part of the mystery of *God's plan*, as St Peter explains to the Jews of Jerusalem in his first sermon on Pentecost: "This Jesus [was] delivered up according to the *definite plan and foreknowledge of God*."[7]

The *Catechism*, with linguistic circumspection and elegant periphrasis, continues to state that although this was *God's definite plan*: 'This Biblical language does not mean that those who handed him over were merely passive players in a scenario written in advance by God.' No, indeed:

[1] Lea, Henry Charles. *A History of the Inquisition of Spain*. Vol I. pp81-82
[2] See, for example: Goldhagen, Daniel Jonah. *Hitler's Willing Executioners: Ordinary Germans and ...* p52
[3] Sister Pista. Evangelical Sisterhood of Mary, Darmstadt
[4] http://en.wikipedia.org/wiki/First_Council_of_Nicaea (2007)
[5] http://www.atheistresource.co.uk/christjew.html (2007)
[6] Michael, Robert. *A History of Catholic Antisemitism: The Dark Side of the Church*. p19
[7] http://www.scborromeo.org/ccc/p122a4p2.htm#599 (2015)

To God, all moments of time are present in their immediacy. When therefore he establishes his eternal plan of 'predestination', he includes in it each person's free response to his grace … For the sake of accomplishing *his plan* of salvation, God *permitted* the acts that flowed from their ['Herod and Pontius Pilate, with the Gentiles and the peoples of Israel'] blindness.

Ergo, without the 'permitted' acts that flowed from the 'blindness' of these people, the 'angry' Judeo-Catholic God's mysterious and *definite plan of salvation* would not have been effected. The fundamental question then arises: are not the Jews, in the context of the Catholic Church's constructs of the deity's design, the unfeigned benefactors of humankind?

***

Raul Hilberg, in his book *The Destruction of the European Jews*, reminds his readers that since the fourth century there have been three major ecclesiastical anti-Semitic policies, namely, conversion, expulsion, and annihilation. Each later one appeared as an alternative to the former.[1]

An initial sample of accusations and negative actions against the Jews is presented below – a second sample is presented in the following chapter.

Detrimental Roman Imperial Dictates

Constantine the Great (306-337)

Constantine was the first Roman ruler to be converted to Christianity. St Chrysostom stated that when the Jews assembled to rebuild their holy city, Jerusalem, Constantine cut off their ears and dispersed them as fugitive slaves throughout the provinces of the empire. Eutychius (876-940), the Melchite Patriarch of Alexandria and author of a history of the world, recorded that Constantine obliged them all to be baptised and to eat pork at Easter.[2]

Constantine's law of 18 October 329 made it a criminal offence to become a Jew. Exile or death were to be the lot of Jews who tried to prevent other Jews from converting to Christianity or who encouraged conversion to Judaism.[3]

Emperor Theodosius II (401-450)

Theodosius' *Codex Theodosianus* (438-9) was concerned with the imposition of Roman orthodoxy within the Christian religion. It denied Jews numerous rights, such as prohibitions on holding any public office or function, and on building new synagogues.

Justinian I (527 to 565)

The *Codex* was followed by the *Corpus Juris Civilis* (*Body of Civil Law*) (529-534),

---

[1] Hilberg, Raul. *The Destruction of the European Jews.* Vol I. p8. Quoted in: Weitzman, Mark. *Antisemitism: A Historical Survey.* http://motlc.wiesenthal.com/resources/education/historicalsurvey/index.html (2007)

[2] Foote, G W & J M Wheeler. *Crimes of Christianity.* Vol I. Ch VIII. 'Persecution of the Jews'. Source: http://www.ftarchives.net/foote/crimes/c8.htm (2007)

[3] Michael, Robert. *A History of Catholic Antisemitism: The Dark Side of the Church.* p36

a collection of fundamental works in jurisprudence, issued by order of Emperor Justinian. It denied Jews many rights:

> This code compiled all of the existing imperial *constitutiones* (imperial pronouncements having the force of law), back to the time of Hadrian. It used both the *Codex Theodosianus* and the fourth-century private collections embodied in the *Codex Gregorianus* and [*Codex*] *Hermogenianus* ...
>
> The provisions of the *Corpus Juris Civilis* also influenced the Canon Law of the church since it was said that ecclesia vivit lege romana – the church lives under Roman law.
>
> The principle of 'Servitus Judaeorum' ('Servitude of the Jews') established by the new laws determined the status of Jews throughout the Empire for hundreds of years ahead. The Jews were disadvantaged in a number of ways. The emperor became an arbiter in internal Jewish affairs and Jews could not testify against Christians and were disqualified from holding a public office. Jewish civil and religious rights were restricted: 'they shall enjoy no honours'. The use of the Hebrew language in worship was forbidden. *Shema Yisrael*, sometimes considered the most important prayer in Judaism ('Hear, O Israel, the Lord is one') was banned, as a denial of the Trinity.[1,2]

Detrimental Papal Bulls and the Like through the Centuries

Numerous mediaeval bulls and the like were openly anti-Semitic. For example:[3]

Sixth Century

Sicut judaeis non (598) of Gregory I forbade Jews from having Christian slaves, and encouraged conversions.

Twelfth Century

Post miserabile (1198) of Innocent III suspended payment of interest and principal to Jewish lenders for crusaders. Since many did not return, the debt was effectively cancelled.[4]

Thirteenth Century

Etsi non displiceat (1205) of Innocent III requested kings to put an end to 'Jewish evils' such as arrogance, usury and murder.

In generali concilio (1218) of Honorius III compelled Jews to wear special clothing.

Bul. Rom. Pont., III, 497 of Gregory IX (1227-1241) commanded the archbishops of Germany with the following words:

---

[1] http://en.wikipedia.org/wiki/Corpus_juris_civilis (2007)

[2] In Christianity, the doctrine of the Trinity states that God is one being who exists simultaneously as three male persons: Father, Son, and Holy Spirit. An explanation of this concept is given in the long article 'Person' in the *Catholic Encyclopedia*.

[3] Many of the details of these Bulls are from: http://www.zionism-israel.com/hdoc/Papal_Bulls_Jews.htm

[4] http://www.zionism-israel.com/hdoc/Papal_Bulls_Jews.htm (2010)

The Jews, who are admitted to our acquaintance only through our mercy, should never forget their yoke of perpetual slavery, which they bear through their own fault. In the Council of Toledo it was decreed that Jews of both sexes, and for all time, should be distinguished from others by their mode of dress. We therefore command that each and every one of you to have all the excesses of the Jews completely repressed, lest they should presume to raise their necks from the yoke of servitude in contumely of the Redeemer; forbidding them to discuss in any way concerning their faith or rites with Christians. In this matter calling to your aid the help of the civil power, inflicting upon Christians, who offer opposition, due ecclesiastical punishment.[1]

Sufficere debuerat perfidioe judeorum perida (1233) of Gregory IX stated that Jews were forbidden to employ Christian servants.

Si vera sunt (1239) of Gregory IX ordered the seizure and examination of Talmudic and Jewish literature, leading to their eventual incineration.

Bul. Rom. Pont., IV, 509 (1240), also of Gregory IX, exhorted King Louis IX of France to 'continue with due severity' 'to prosecute those who perpetuate these detestable excesses'.

Impia judaeorum perfidia (1244) of Innocent IV: the French King was ordered to burn the *Talmud*. Jews were forbidden to employ Christian nurses.

Impia gens (1244) of Innocent IV ordered the *Talmud* to be burned.

Turbato corde (1267) of Clement IV, and in 1274 of Gregory X: Christians were forbidden to embrace Judaism.

Vineam sorce (1278) of Nicholas III ordered the selection of schooled men to preach Christianity to the Jews.

Turbato corde (1288) of Nicholas IV forbade Christians to convert to the Jewish faith.

Fourteenth Century

John XXII (1316-1334) 'published violent bulls against the poor persecuted Hebrews, and commanded the bishops to destroy the source of their detestable blasphemies, to burn their Talmuds.'[2]

The historian Henry Hart Milman recorded that:

The Papal sanction was thus given to the atrocities which followed. In many provinces, says a chronicler, especially in Aquitaine, the Jews were burned without distinction. At Chinon a deep ditch was dug, an enormous pile raised, and one hundred and sixty of both sexes burned together.[3] Many of them plunged into the ditch of their own accord, singing hymns, as though they were going to a wedding. Many women, with their children, threw themselves in to escape forcible baptism.

---

[1] See, for example: http://www.stormfront.org/forum/t326994/ (2010)

[2] http://www.ftarchives.net/foote/crimes/c8.htm (2013)

[3] Foote, G W & J M Wheeler. *Crimes of Christianity*. Vol I. Ch VIII. 'Persecution of the Jews'. So similar to the methods of the Nazis.

Fifteenth Century

Etsi doctoribus genium (1415) was a collection of anti-Jewish laws issued by Benedict XIII and ratified by Martin V:

> in which were virtually embodied the *Ordenamiento de doña Catalina,*[1] thus giving to its *system of terrible repression* the sanction of church as well as of state. He further forbade the possession of the Talmud or of any books contrary to the Christian faith, ordering the bishops and inquisitors to make semi-annual inquests of the aljamas[2] and to proceed against all found in possession of such books. No Jew should even bind a book in which the name of Christ or the Virgin appeared.

> Princes were exhorted to grant them no favors or privileges and the faithful at large were commanded not to rent or sell houses to them or to hold companionship or conversation with them. Moreover they were prohibited to exercise usury and thrice a year they were to be preached to and warned to abandon their errors.

> The bishops in general were ordered to see to the strict enforcement of all these provisions ... as the utterance of the anti-pope Benedict, this searching and cruel legislation, designed to reduce the Jews to the lowest depths of poverty and despair, was current only in the lands of his obedience, but when his triumphant rival, Martin V, confirmed the charge confided to the bishop of Sigüenza he accepted and ratified the act of Benedict.[3]

Sedes apostolica (1425) of Martin V obliged Jews to wear a distinctive badge.

Dudum ad nostram audientiam (1442) of Eugenius IV contained a host of restrictions on the Jews:

> We decree and order that from now on, and for all time, Christians shall not eat or drink with Jews; nor admit them to feasts, nor cohabit with them, nor bathe with them. Christians shall not allow Jews to hold civil honours over Christians, or to exercise public offices in the State. Jews cannot be merchants, Tax Collectors, or agents in the buying and selling of the produce and goods of Christians, nor their Procurators, Computers or Lawyers in matrimonial matters, nor Obstetricians; nor can they have association or partnership with Christians. No Christian can leave or bequeath anything in his last Will and Testament to Jews or their congregations. Jews are prohibited from erecting new synagogues. They are obliged to pay annually a tenth part of their goods and holdings. Against them Christians can testify, but the testimony of Jews against Christians in no case is of any value. All and every single Jew, of whatever sex and age, must everywhere wear the distinct dress and known marks by which they can be evidently distinguished from Christians. They

---

[1] 'The *Ordenamiento* was a compilation of all the existing laws against Jews enacted by the Bishop of Burgos, Pablo de Santa María, aimed at not giving them other alternative but conversion.' http://www.netanya.ac.il/ResearchCen/IntInstitute/Activities/Documents/Bonninpape.pdf (2015)

[2] Aljama – a Spanish-language term of Arabic origin used in old official documents to designate the self-governing communities of Moors and Jews living under Spanish Christian rule.

[3] Lea, Henry Charles. *History of the Inquisition of Spain.* Vol 1. pp118-19

cannot live among Christians, but in a certain street, separated and segregated from Christians, and outside which they cannot under any pretext have houses.[1]

Super Gregem Dominicum (1442) of Eugenius IV revoked the privileges of the Castilian Jews and imposed severe restrictions on them. It forbad Castilian Christians to eat, drink, live or bathe with Jews or Muslims, and declared invalid the testimony of Jews or Muslims against Christians.

Eugenius IV (1443) – issued a bull prohibiting the Jews from studying the *Talmud.*

Super Gregem Dominicum was re-issued by Nicholas V in 1447, and again in 1451.

Nicholas V (1451) issued a bull confirming the old exclusions of Jews from Christian society and all honourable walks of life.

Super Gregem Dominicum (1455) of Nicholas V made it illegal for Jews and Muslims to interact with Catholics.

Si ad reprimendos (1456) of Callixtus III confirmed the restrictions of *Dudum ad nostram audientiam.*

St Pius V (1458-1464) issued a bull against the Jews, accusing them of magic, of hating the Christians, and of ruining the ecclesiastical state. Finally he expelled them from all places in his dominions except Rome and Ancona.[2]

Numquam dubitavimus (1482) of Sixtus IV instructed Ferdinand of Aragón to appoint inquisitors to extirpate heresy and investigate backsliding of Jewish converts to Christianity. The Spanish Inquisition and expulsion of the Jews from Spain followed.

Sixteenth Century

• *Paul IV*, in July 1555, 'issued a decree which, for ferocious anti-Jewishness, was not equalled until the coming of Hitler to modern Germany.'[3] Paul's *Cum nimis absurdum* was a landmark in the history of anti-Semitism, and is recognised as the most devastating Christian anti-Jewish document ever written. It confirmed all the more severe bulls against the Jews issued up to that time, and added others still more oppressive and containing all manner of prohibitions, which condemned the Jews to the most abject misery, deprived them of the means of sustenance, and denied to them the exercise of all professions. It established the Roman Ghetto and forbade contact between Jews and Christians. 'They were finally forced to labor at the restoration of the walls of Rome without any compensation whatsoever.' It ordained:

> Laws and ordinances to be followed by Jews living in the Holy See decreed by the Bishop Paul, servant of the servants of God, for future recollection.
>
> As it is completely absurd and improper in the utmost that the Jews, who through their own fault were condemned by God to eternal servitude, can under the pretext that pious Christians must accept them and sustain their habitation, are so ungrateful to Christians, as, instead of thanks for gracious treatment, they return contumely,

---

[1] http://www.talmudunmasked.com/appendix.htm (2010)
[2] Foote, G W & J M Wheeler. *Crimes of Christianity.* Vol I. Ch VIII. 'Persecution of the Jews'
[3] http://jloughnan.tripod.com/chistory.htm (2010)

and among themselves, instead of the slavery, which they deserve, they manage to claim superiority: we, who newly learned that these very Jews have insolently invaded our City Rome and a number of the Papal States, territories and domains their impudence increased so much that they dare not only to live amongst the Christian people, but also in the vicinity of the churches without any difference of dressing, and even that they rent houses in the main streets and squares, buy and hold immovable property, engage maids, nurses and other Christian servants, and commit other and numerous misdeeds with shame and contempt of the Christian name.

It contained evidence of Paul IV's sanctimony:

Considering that the Church of Rome tolerates these very Jews [is] evidence of the true Christian faith and to this end [we declare]: that they, won over by the piety and kindness of the See, should at long last recognise their erroneous ways, and should lose no time in seeing the true light of the catholic faith, and thus to agree that while they persist in their errors, realising that they are slaves because of their deeds, whereas Christians have been freed through our Lord God Jesus Christ, and that it is iniquitous for it to appear that the sons of free women serve the sons of maids.

It confined Jews to ghettos:

Desiring firstly, as much as we can with God, to beneficially provide, by this that will forever be in force, we ordain that *for the rest of time*, in the City as well as in other states, territories and domains of the Church of Rome itself, all Jews are to live in one and if there is not that capacity in two or three or however many quarters may be enough; they should reside entirely side by side in designated streets and be thoroughly separate from the residences of Christians, by our authority in the City and by that of our representatives in other states, lands and domains noted above, and that there must be only one entrance and exit from this quarter.

Only one synagogue was to be allowed. The rest were to be destroyed:

Furthermore, in each and every state, territory and domain in which they are living, they will have only one synagogue, in its customary location, and they will construct no other new ones, nor can they own buildings. Furthermore, all of their synagogues, besides the one allowed, *are to be destroyed and demolished.* And the properties, which they currently own, they must sell to Christians within a period of time to be determined by the magistrates themselves.

Compulsory emblems were to be worn:

Moreover, so that Jews should be distinguishable everywhere: men must wear a hat, women, indeed, some other evident sign, yellow in colour, that must not be concealed or covered by any means, and must be tightly affixed; and furthermore, they can not be absolved or excused from the obligation to wear the hat or other emblem of this type to any extent whatever and under any pretext whatsoever of their rank or prominence or of their ability to tolerate this adversity, either by a chamberlain of the Church, clerics of an Apostolic court, or their superiors, or by legates of the Holy See or their immediate subordinates.

Social restrictions were applied:

> Also, they may not have nurses or maids or any other Christian domestic or service by Christian women in wet-nursing or feeding their children.

> They may not work or have work done on Sundays or on other public feast days declared by the Church.

> Nor may they incriminate Christians in any way, or promulgate false or forged agreements.

> And they may not presume in any way to play, eat or fraternise with Christians.

Commercial and other restrictions were imposed:

> And they cannot use other than Latin or Italian words in short-term account books that they hold with Christians, and, if they should use them, such records would not be binding on Christians.

> Moreover, these Jews are *to be limited to the trade of rag-picking*, or 'cencinariae' (as it is said in the vernacular), and they cannot trade in grain, barley or any other commodity essential to human welfare.

> And those among them who are physicians, even if summoned and inquired after, cannot attend or take part in the care of Christians.

> And they are not to be addressed as superiors [even] by poor Christians.

Financial restrictions were also imposed:

> they are prohibited from selling collateral, put up as temporary security for their money, unless [such goods were] put up a full eighteen months prior to the day on which such [collateral] would be forfeit; at the expiration of the aforementioned number of months, if Jews have sold a security deposit of this sort, they must sign over all money in excess of the principal of the loan to the owner of the collateral.

> And the statutes of states, territories and domains wherever they presently live, concerning primacy of Christians, are to be adhered to and followed without exception.

Jews were to be treated as criminals:

> And, should they, in any manner whatsoever, be deficient in the foregoing, it would be treated as a crime: in Rome, by us or by our clergy, or by others authorised by us, and in the aforementioned states, territories and domains by their respective magistrates, *just as if they were rebels and criminals* by the jurisdiction in which the offence takes place, they would be accused by all Christian people, by us and by our clergy, and could be punished at the discretion of the proper authorities and judges.

Notwithstanding other decisions:

> Not to be confuted by conflicting decrees and apostolic rules, and regardless of any tolerance whatever or special rights and dispensation for these Jews of any Roman

Pontiff prior to us and of the aforementioned See or of their legates, or by the courts of the Church of Rome and the clergy of the Apostolic courts, or by other of their officials, no matter their import and form, and with whatever, even with repeated derogations, and with other legally valid sub-clauses, and erasures and other decrees, even those that are 'motu proprio'[1] and from 'certain knowledge' and have been repeatedly approved and renewed.

Therefore:

By this document, even if, instead of their sufficient derogation, concerning them and their entire import, special, specific, expressed and individual, even word for word, moreover, not by means of general, even important passages, mention, or whatever other expression was favoured, or whatever exquisite form had to be retained, matters of such import, and, if word for word, with nothing deleted, would be inserted into them in original form in the present document holding that rather than being sufficiently expressed, those things that would stay in effect in full force by this change alone, we specially and expressly derogate, as well as any others contrary to them.[2]

Cum Nos nuper (1567) of St Pius V prohibited Jews from owning real estate.

Hebraeorum gens sola (1569) of Pius V, a Saint, stated:

The Jewish people fell from the heights because of their faithlessness and condemned their Redeemer to a shameful death. Their godlessness has assumed such forms that, for the salvation of our own people, it becomes necessary to prevent their disease. Besides usury, through which Jews everywhere have sucked dry the property of impoverished Christians, they are accomplices of thieves and robbers; and the most damaging aspect of the matter is that they allure the unsuspecting through magical incantations, superstition, and witchcraft to the Synagogue of Satan and boast of being able to predict the future. We have carefully investigated how this revolting sect abuses the name of Christ and how harmful they are to those whose life is threatened by their deceit. On account of these and other serious matters, and because of the gravity of their crimes which increase day to day more and more, We order that, within 90 days, *all Jews* in our entire earthly realm of justice – in all towns, districts, and places – *must depart these regions*. After this time limit shall all at the present or in the future, who dwell or wander into that city or other already mentioned, be affected, their property confiscated and handed over to the Siscus, and *they shall become slaves of the Roman Church, live in perpetual servitude* and the Roman Church shall have the same rights over them as the remaining [worldly] lords over slaves and property.

Gregory XIII (1572-1585) promulgated a bull that 'was published and suspended at the gate of the Jews' quarter, prohibiting the reading of the *Talmud*, blasphemies against Christ, or ridiculing the ceremonies of the Church. All Jews above twelve years were

---

[1] A motu proprio ('on his own impulse') is a document issued and signed by the Pope on his own initiative.

[2] http://www.zionism-israel.com/hdoc/cum_nimis_absurdum.htm (2009)

bound to attend in turn the weekly sermons preached for their conversion. Special preachers were appointed to expound the alleged prophecies of Jesus as the Messiah who had abolished the Law; and to dilate upon the long misery the Jews had suffered from adhering to a different interpretation.'[1]

Vices eius nos (1577) of Gregory XIII ordered obligatory preaching of Christian sermons to Jews; and the creation of a college of neophytes.

Antiqua judaeorum improbitas (1581) of Gregory XIII authorised the Inquisition to directly handle cases involving Jews, especially those concerning blasphemies against Jesus or Mary, incitement to heresy or assistance to heretics, possession of forbidden books, or the employment of Christian wet nurses.

Multos adhuc ex Christianis (1581), also of Gregory XIII, renewed Church law against Jewish physicians.

Sancta mater ecclesia (1584) of Gregory XIII decreed that each Saturday (the Shabbat) one hundred Jewish men and fifty Jewish women had to come to church to receive sermons on conversion to Roman Catholicism.

A Bull of Clement VIII (1591) prohibited the owning, reading, buying, or circulating of the Talmudic and Cabbalistic books and other 'godless writings' that contained heresies or assaults upon Christian doctrines or upon the practices of the Church.[2]

Cum saepe accidere (1592) of Clement VIII stated that the Jews of Avignon were forbidden to sell new goods.

Caeca et Obdurata Hebraeorum perfidia (*The blind and obdurate perfidy of the Hebrews*) was promulgated by Clement VIII in 1593. It expelled the Jews from the Papal States, effectively revoking the bull *Christiana pietas*[3] (1586) of his predecessor Sixtus V. Clement's edict restored the previous oppressive situation – this revocation remained in force till the 19th century.[4]

Three days later, Clement promulgated *Cum Hebraeorum malitia*, decreeing that the *Talmud* should be burned along with cabalistic works and commentaries. It gave the owners of such works ten days to turn them over to the Inquisition of Rome and subsequently two months to hand them over to local inquisitors.

Seventeenth Century

Cum allias piae (1636) of Urban VIII specified that synagogues of the Duchies of Ferarri and Urban were required to pay a tax of 10 ecus.

Eighteenth Century

Beatus Andreas (1755) of Benedict XIV reviewed the cases of alleged ritual murder by Jews, which it explicitly upheld as fact.

Editto sopra gli Ebrei (*Edict over the Jews*) was a severe 44-clause decree issued in

---

[1] Foote, G W & J M Wheeler. *Crimes of Christianity.* Vol I. Ch VIII. 'Persecution of the Jews'
[2] Cabbala (Cabbalah, Kabbalah) is an esoteric theosophy of rabbinical origin based on the Hebrew Scriptures.
[3] *Christiana pietas* relieved the Jews of many oppressive restrictions imposed on them by Paul IV and Pius V.
[4] http://www.jewishvirtuallibrary.org/jsource/judaica/ejud_0002_0004_0_03728.html (2012)

1775 by Pius VI. It returned the status of the Jews of the Papal States to those of the 1500s. Pius ordered its rigorous enforcement through the supervision of the Inquisitors. To this end, Jews were no longer to 'infect' the Christian population, and were, once again, to be confined to ghettos. They were prohibited from owning any real estate and from pursuing any occupation other than selling rags. The *Edict* included prohibitions against the possession of Talmudic writings and the erection of grave stones. It also prohibited Jews from passing the night outside the ghetto under pain of death. The regulations were valid until the arrival of Napoléon's army 25 years later.[1]

Proselytism, Forced Child Abductions, Forced Baptism, Forced Sermons, and Forced Conversions through the Centuries

During the fifth, sixth and seventh centuries, Church and Imperial officials repeatedly warned against the pernicious influence of the Jews, and at times attempted to convert them by force.[2] There follows a selection of these obnoxious actions:

Fifth Century

As Christianity became the dominant religion in the Roman Empire, so large numbers of Jews were forcibly baptised. The first record of Jews being forced to convert or face expulsion occurred in the year 418. Severus, the Bishop of Minorca, on conquering the island, claimed to have forced 540 Jews to accept Christianity.[3]

425 – Jews were required by law to observe Catholic feasts and fasts and to listen to sermons persuading them to convert.[4]

Other major campaigns of forced conversions spread through Europe. For example, Emperor Justinian I ('The Great') (483-565) made the mass baptism of all Jews compulsory.[5]

In his book *A History of Catholic Antisemitism*, Professor Robert Michael provides extensive details of the changed baptismal rites of the conversion of Jews to Catholicism at this time. Included are such requirements as that converts curse themselves, the Jewish people and their history. The Jew had to state 'I will never return to the vomit of Jewish superstition, the vomit of my former error ...', and had to acknowledge 'If I wander from the straight path ... I shall be handed over to the eternal fire, in the company of the Devil ...'[6]

Sixth Century

576 – After a Christian mob had destroyed the synagogue in Clermont-Ferrand, France, the Bishop said to the Jews: 'If you are ready to believe as I do, be one flock

---

[1] http://www.jewishhistory.org.il/history.php?startyear=1770&endyear=1779 (2007)
[2] Cohn-Sherbok, D. *The Crucified Jew: Twenty Centuries of Christian Anti-Semitism.* pp38-39
[3] http://en.wikipedia.org/wiki/Timeline_of_antisemitism (2007)
[4] http://www.sullivan-county.com/id2/timeline.htm (2007)
[5] Kahl, Joachim. *The Misery of Christianity: A Plea for a Humanity without God.* p55
[6] Michael, Robert. *A History of Catholic Antisemitism: The Dark Side of the Church.* p21

with us, and I shall be your pastor; but if you are not ready, depart from this place.' About 500 Jews converted – the rest left for Marseilles.

Pope St Gregory I ('The Great') (590-604) decided that baptism should be accepted willingly and not imposed by force. But this was subject to interpretation. He overcame this hurdle by bribing Jews into baptism – any Jew in Rome who converted to Catholicism had his rent reduced by a third. Gregory wrote:

> For even if they themselves come with little faith, there will certainly be more faith in their children who are baptised, so that if we do not gain the parents, we shall gain the children. Therefore, any reduction of rent for Christ's sake is not to be considered a loss.[1]

The Visigoths invaded Spain in 415, and found a small Jewish settlement there. In general, these Jews enjoyed a peaceful life until Visigothic King Reccared converted from Arianism to Roman Catholicism in 586.

589 – The Third Synod of Toledo proclaimed the first anti-Jewish laws. Thence, persecutions, forced conversions, and expulsions constituted anti-Jewish policy.[2] Reccared ordered children born of mixed marriages to be forcibly baptised.

Seventh Century

612-621 – Spanish King Sisebut severely restricted the rights of Jews in his kingdom. They were not allowed to own or work the land or to practice certain trades. Later he issued the first edicts against the Jews of expulsion from Spain. Following his 613 decree that the Jews either convert or be expelled, some fled to Gaul and North Africa, while as many as 90,000 converted.[3]

614 – The Fifth Council of Paris decreed that all Jews holding military or civil positions must accept baptism, together with their families.

628-629 – Emperor Heraclius ordered the forced conversion of all Jews in his empire and renewed the Hadrian and Constantine codes that barred Jews from Jerusalem.

633 – The Fourth Council of Toledo produced the severest anti-Semitic legislation.[4] It decreed that Jewish children baptised as Catholics were to be separated from their parents. It issued laws demanding the removal of Jewish children from their families, and forbidding Jews and Christians of Jewish origin from holding office.[5]

638 – The Sixth Council of Toledo ordered the baptism of all Jews living in Spain.

Holy-Cross Day[6] (14 September) – "in memory of the exaltation of the Saviour's cross") was adopted by the Church. On this day Jews were forced to attend an annual Catholic sermon in Rome. This practice was not abolished until twelve centuries later during the reign of Gregory XVI (1831-1846).

---

[1] de Rosa, Peter. *Vicars of Christ: The Dark Side of the Papacy.* p191
[2] *Dictionary of the Middle Ages.* Vol 7. p79
[3] http://en.wikipedia.org/wiki/History_of_the_Jews_in_Spain (2008)
[4] *Dictionary of the Middle Ages.* Vol 7. p79
[5] http://www.atheistresource.co.uk/christjew.html (2007)
[6] Since 1970, Holy-Cross Day has been officially called the 'Triumph of the Cross' in the Latin Church.

653 – The Eighth Council of Toledo required Jews to sign an oath (placitum) that made the practice of Judaism almost impossible. Further measures at this time included the forbidding of all Jewish rites (including circumcision and the observation of the Shabbat), and all converted Jews had to promise to put to death, either by burning or by stoning, any of their brethren known to have relapsed to Judaism.

655 – The Ninth Council of Toledo ordered converted Jews to spend all Jewish and Catholic holy days in the presence of a bishop so as to prove the veracity of the faith. Lack of compliance with this last rule resulted in flogging or forced fasting, depending on the age of the offender.

681 – The Twelfth Council of Toledo 'implemented diverse measures against the Jews, enacting against them twenty eight laws.' The bishops ordered the reading in all the churches of the canons against the Jews and conserved all acts of abjuration and conversion of Jews, prohibiting conversos from returning to Judaism. The Council decreed the burning of the *Talmud* and other Jewish literature. In the same year, King Erwig of Spain forbade practising Jews from entering seaports. All Jews were ordered to be baptised.

694 – The Seventeenth Council of Toledo ordered that Jewish children were to be taken away from their parents when they reached the age of seven years, and that they were later to be married to Catholics.[1]

Eighth Century

722 – Judaism was outlawed in the domain of Byzantine Emperor Leo III, and Jews were forcibly baptised. Some were burned to death in their synagogues.[2]

Ninth Century

820 – The first recorded cases of sermons directed at Jews were those of Archbishop Agobard (canonised as 'the most enlightened man of his age').[3,4] His *Epistola de baptizandis Hebraeis* stated that, following his instruction, the clergy of Lyon went to preach in synagogues every Saturday (the Shabbat).

Tenth Century

938 –Leo VII told the Archbishop of Mainz that he should expel local Jews if they refused to willingly convert.

Thirteenth Century

In a letter of 1201, Innocent III stated that a Jew who bowed to baptism under threat of force, evinced a conditional willingness to accept the sacrament, and consequently was not allowed to renounce it thenceforth. In enlightened mediaeval Catholicism the relapsing of faith was heretical and punishable by death

---

[1] Kahl, Joachim. *The Misery of Christianity: A Plea for a Humanity without God.* p56
[2] http://www.jcrelations.net/en/?id=836 (2007)
[3] Poliakov, Léon. *The History of Anti-semitism: From the time of Christ to the court Jews*
[4] Friedman, Saul S. *Jews and the American Slave Trade.* p265

Later there were waves of forced baptisms. One swept through the kingdom of Naples in the thirteenth century, and one in Spain from 1391.

Fourteenth Century

The treatment of Jews in Catholic Spain was described by Henry Charles Lea:

> the Spanish prelates returned from the council of Vienne in 1312 and the proscriptive legislation enacted by them in the council of Zamora in 1313 and its successors. Everything favored the development of this *spirit of intolerance*, and at the Cortes of Burgos, in 1315, the regents of the young Alfonso XI [King of León and Castile] conceded that the Clementine canon, abrogating all laws that permitted usury, should be enforced, that all mixed actions, civil and criminal, should be tried by the royal judges, that the evidence of a Jew should not be received against a Christian while that of a Christian was good against a Jew, that Jews were not to assume Christian names, Christian nurses were not to suckle Jews and sumptuary [restrictive] laws were directed against the luxury of Jewish vestments. This may be said to mark the commencement of the long struggle which, in spite of their wonderful powers of resistance, was to end in the destruction of the Spanish Jews.[1]

Alfonso, King of Aragón introduced a code which included the death penalty:

> in his systematic code known as the *Partidas*, which was not confirmed by the Cortes until 1348, allowed himself to be influenced by the teachings of the Church and the maxims of the imperial jurisprudence. He accepted the doctrine of the canons that the Jew was merely suffered to live in captivity among Christians; he was forbidden to speak ill of the Christian faith, and any attempt at proselytism was punished with death and confiscation. The murder rite[2] was alluded to as a rumor, but in case it was practised it was a capital offence and the culprits were to be tried before the king himself. Jews were ineligible to any office in which they could oppress Christians; they were forbidden to have Christian servants, and the purchase of a Christian slave involved the death punishment. They were not to associate with Christians in eating, drinking, and bathing and the amour of a Jew with a Christian woman *incurred death*. While Jewish physicians might prescribe for Christian patients, the medicine must be compounded by a Christian, and the wearing of the hateful distinctive badge was ordered under penalty of ten gold maravedís or of ten lashes.[3]

Fifteenth Century

Thousands of Jews settled in Portugal, having been expelled from Spain by the *Alhambra Decree*[4] in 1492. King Manuel of Portugal found that in order to purge his

---

[1] Lea, Henry Charles. *A History of the Inquisition of Spain.* Vol I. pp95-96

[2] Ritual Murder and the 'Blood Libel' – refer to Chapter 8 for details.

[3] Lea, Henry Charles. *A History of the Inquisition of Spain.* Vol I. pp89-90

[4] See below.

realm of heresy it was unnecessary to expel his Jewish subjects, who were valuable economic assets. Instead, he set out on a systematic campaign of forced conversion which was initially directed against the children. They were seized from their parents in the hope that the adults would follow suit. Later he enforced conversion on the entire population. By the end of 1497, not a single professing Jew remained in Portugal.[1]

Henry Charles Lea recorded of Aragón:

> Jaime[2] had issued an edict, confirmed by Innocent IV in 1245, empowering the mendicant friars to have free access to juderías and morerías,[3] to assemble the inhabitants and compel them to listen to sermons intended for their conversion. The Dominicans now availed themselves of this with such vigor and excited such hostility to the Jews that Jaime was obliged to step forward for their protection.[4]

1421 – Persecutions of Jews occurred in Vienna. Known as the *Wiener Gesera* (*Vienna Edict*), their possessions were confiscated, and forced conversion was imposed on Jewish children.

1431-1443 – The Ecclesiastical Council of Basel required Jews to attend Church sermons.[5]

Peter Arbues (de Arbués) (Pedro d'Arbus) was a fifteenth-century Spanish inquisitor famed for his forcible conversion of Jews. He was canonised in 1867 by Pius IX, who stated in the canonisation document:

> The divine wisdom has arranged that in these sad days, when Jews help the enemies of the church with their books and money, this decree of sanctity has been brought to fulfilment.[6]

• Isabel (Isabella la Católica) became Queen regnant of Castile and León. She and her husband Ferdinand (Fernando) II of Aragón became, in the words of Pope Alexander VI, the 'Catholic Monarchs' ('Los Reyes Católicos'). Don Emanuel, Catholic King of Portugal, sought the hand of the eldest daughter of Ferdinand and Isabella. It was made a condition of his marriage that he should banish from his dominions all Muslims and Jews. In December 1496, Emanuel issued a proclamation ordering that all non-converted Jews leave Portugal within ten months under pain of confiscation of property. On the following Passover, when all the Jews who had chosen exile rather than conversion were assembled, it was ordered that all their children under fourteen should be forcibly taken from the parents and brought up in 'the saving knowledge of the Christian faith.' A contemporary historian wrote of the unchristian Catholics:

---

[1] http://www.zionism-israel.com/his/judeophobia4.htm (2007)
[2] James I the Conqueror (Jaime el Conquistador) was King of Aragón, Count of Barcelona, and Lord of Montpellier from 1213 to 1276.
[3] Juderías – Jewish quarters; Morerías – Muslim quarters.
[4] Lea, Henry Charles. *A History of the Inquisition of Spain.* Vol I. p91
[5] Poliakov, Léon. *The History of Anti-Semitism.* Vol I. p121
[6] Wills, Garry, review of 'The Popes Against the Jews: Before the Holocaust'. *New York Times.* 23 September 2001. http://online.sfsu.edu/~rone/Religion/popesagainstjews.html (2007)

It was a horrid and wretched spectacle to see tender children torn from the arms and breasts of their distressed mothers; fathers, who fondly held them in their embrace, dragged about to force them from their arms. To hear the cries, sighs, groans, lamentations, and female shrieks that filled the air was dreadful. Some were so distracted that they destroyed their children by casting them into wells; others, in fits of despair, made away with themselves.[1]

Don Emanuel suddenly revoked the order for the Jews' embarkation at Oporto and Setubal, causing many to go to Lisbon, but the delay made them liable to the law. More than twenty thousand Jews were lodged in a vast barrack, called the Estáos, 'where every means of fair promise and foul intimidation was used to make them renounce Judaism.' Those more unshakable in their faith were shipped off as slaves, but most of them were broken in spirit.[2]

But the unchristian Christians persisted in their bigotry:

A fresh edict now went forth, that all children between fourteen and twenty should also be taken from their parents and baptised, and multitudes were dragged forcibly by their hair and by their arms into the churches, and compelled to receive the waters of baptism, together with new names, being afterwards given over to those who undertook to instruct them in the Catholic faith. Next, the parents themselves were seized, and were offered to have their children restored to them if they would consent to be converted; in case of their refusal, they were to be *placed in confinement for three days without food or drink.* It is indeed wonderful that any mortals could be proof against so terrible and fiendish an ordeal; yet, t*o the glory of the Hebrew race*, very many still remained unmoved. Resistance was, however, not to be tolerated, and it was therefore decreed that the same fate was to be meted out to the adults and to the aged, as had already been the portion of the younger members of the race of Israel. Amid the most heart-rending cries and the most determined resistance, men and women in the flower of their days, or the decrepitude of age, were dragged into the churches and forcibly baptised, amid *the mocking and exultation of an excited populace.*[3]

Sixteenth Century

A catechumen, derived from the ecclesiastical Latin 'catechumenus' ('one being instructed'), was a convert to Christianity who had not yet been baptised and was undergoing instruction in the Roman Catholic faith. In the early Church, catechumens were taught according to a syllabus which they memorised in the form of a Creed. In 1543 a new stage in forced baptism arose with the establishment of the House of Catechumens in Rome. Soon, similar enterprises opened in other cities.

Any person who, by whatever Catholic casuistry, had been deemed to have shown any inclination towards Christianity could be incarcerated in the House 'to explore his

---

[1] Source: Foote, G W & J M Wheeler. *Crimes of Christianity.* Vol I. Ch VIII. 'Persecution of the Jews'
[2] Foote, G W & J M Wheeler. *Crimes of Christianity.* Vol I. Ch VIII. 'Persecution of the Jews'
[3] Source: Ibid.

intention'. During such period, he or she was submitted to unremitting pressure. A popular Catholic superstition claimed that any person who secured the baptism of an unbeliever was assured of an entry to paradise. This led to a spate of such procedures throughout the Roman Catholic world.[1] By the mid-eighteenth century the main enforcers of this practice were the Jesuits.[2] In that century, the House of the Catechumens, although a religious institution, did not allow its residents to come and go at will. The regulations specified that no resident, whether baptised or not, could go out without the permission of the rector. The papal police were involved, and anyone found outside at night was subject to a month in prison, in shackles.[3]

⌐ As an aside: Pius XII, in his 1958 encyclical *Ad Apostolorum Principis* ('Encyclical of Pope Pius XII On Communism and the Church in China'),[4] complained of the treatment of Christians in China. There is a striking similarity between the methods of the Chinese, of which Pius complained, and those of the Catholic Church towards Jews, heretics, and schismatics. Pius wrote:[5]

> 6. ... We declared that the Catholic Church is a stranger to no people on earth, much less hostile to any. With a mother's anxiety, she embraces all peoples in impartial charity. She seeks no earthly advantage but *employs what powers she possesses* to attract the souls of all men to seek what is eternal.

> 10. For by particularly subtle activity an association has been created among you to which has been attached the title of "patriotic," and Catholics are being forced by every means to take part in it ...

> 11. For under an appearance of patriotism, which in reality is just a fraud, this association aims primarily at making Catholics gradually embrace the tenets of atheistic materialism ...

⌐ In common with the horrendous methods of the Portuguese Inquisition in Goa against Hindus and Jews, for example:

> 14. Hence all its members are forced to approve those unjust prescriptions by which missionaries are cast into exile, and by which bishops, priests, religious men, nuns, and the faithful in considerable numbers are thrust into prison; to consent to those measures by which the jurisdiction of many legitimate pastors is persistently obstructed; to defend wicked principles totally opposed to the unity, universality, and hierarchical constitution of the Church; to admit those first steps by which the

---

[1] http://www.zionism-israel.com/his/judeophobia4.htm (2007)

[2] Ibid.

[3] Kertzer, David I. *The Popes Against the Jews: The Vatican's Role in the Rise The Vatican's Role in the Rise of Modern Anti-Semitism.* p43

[4] http://w2.vatican.va/content/pius-xii/en/encyclicals/documents/hf_p-xii_enc_29061958_ad-apostolorum-principis.html (2015)

[5] Of particular interest also were the methods of forced conversion of Serbian Orthodox Christians to the Catholic faith during the Church's Croatian Holocaust during World War II.

clergy and faithful are undermined in the obedience due to legitimate bishops; and to separate Catholic communities from the Apostolic See.

15. In order to spread these wicked principles more efficiently and to fix them in everyone's mind, this association – which, as We have said, boasts of its patriotism – uses a variety of means including violence and oppression, numerous lengthy publications, and group meetings and congresses.

16. In these meetings, the unwilling are forced to take part by incitement, threats, and deceit. If any bold spirit strives to defend truth, his voice is easily smothered and overcome and he is branded with a mark of infamy as an enemy of his native land and of the new society.

The similarity to Catholic forced conversions over the centuries is evident:

17. There should also be noted those courses of instruction by which pupils are forced to imbibe and embrace this false doctrine. Priests, religious men and women, ecclesiastical students, and faithful of all ages are forced to attend these courses. An almost endless series of lectures and discussions, lasting for weeks and months, so weaken and benumb the strength of mind and will that by a kind of psychic coercion an assent is extracted which contains almost no human element, an assent which is not freely asked for as should be the case.

18. In addition to these there are the methods by which minds are upset – by every device, in private and in public, by traps, deceits, grave fear, by so-called forced confessions, by custody in a place where citizens are forcibly "re-educated", and those "Peoples' Courts" to which even venerable bishops are ignominiously dragged for trial.

19. Against methods of acting such as these, *which violate the principal rights of the human person* and trample on the sacred liberty of the sons of God, all Christians from every part of the world, indeed all men of good sense cannot refrain from raising their voices with Us in real horror and from uttering a protest deploring the deranged conscience of their fellow men.

Seventeenth Century

The Counter-Reformation was a movement within the Church in the sixteenth and seventeenth centuries that attempted the revitalisation of the Church and its opposition to Protestantism. During this period the sermon became a regular way of indoctrination against Jewish beliefs. The situation was worst in Rome, where, every Saturday afternoon (the Jewish Shabbat), groups of Jews were required to march to a nearby church or hall, during which they were taunted by the surrounding Catholic population.[1] They were required to listen to an hour-long denouncement of their spiritual leaders, their beliefs, and their practices, while beadles armed with rods ensured their attention and examined their ears for plugs. The preacher was generally a Dominican, known for both

---

[1] Kertzer, David I. *The Popes Against the Jews: The Vatican's Role in the Rise of Modern Anti-Semitism.* p59

zeal and learning.[1] These sermons were not abolished until the mid-nineteenth century.

One Catholic superstition was that whoever baptised an infidel (Jew or other) gained free passage to heaven. Hooligans roamed the city, pouncing on Jewish children and christening them with rainwater. In the eighteenth century, Benedict XIV decided that any child baptised against his or her parents' wishes and contrary to the procedures of canon law was nevertheless a Christian and was required to live as such. If not, he or she was labelled a heretic, with consequent dire penalties.[2]

Nineteenth Century

These forced baptisms continued into the nineteenth century. The answer of the Vatican officials to the anguished pleas for mercy from parents whose babies had been stolen by papal police was the same as that which the popes had issued for centuries. Even in cases where it was illegal, a baptism, once performed, was valid – the alleged Catholic (Jewish, in fact) Holy Ghost had entered the child and its soul was regenerated by the spirit of Christ. This act of the deity could not be reversed by humans, hence the child was now forever a Catholic and could no longer be raised by Jewish parents.[3]

The *Catholic Encyclopedia* records that certain Church departments have been organised by the Holy See at various times to assist it in the transaction of those affairs which canonical discipline and the individual interests of the faithful bring to Rome. Of these, the most important are the Roman Congregations (Sacrae Cardinalium Congregationes). Their membership consists of cardinals who are officially the chief collaborators of the sovereign pontiff in the administration of the affairs of the Universal Church.[4] Some of these congregations were exclusively aimed at converting Jews. Many Roman Catholic saints were noted specifically because of their missionary zeal in Jewish conversion – such as the Dominican Vincent Ferrer, who has been said to have been responsible for converting many Jews, allegedly under duress or persecution.[5]

Several cases of forced child abduction became infamous. In 1762 the son of the rabbi of Carpentras was seized and baptised in mythically-powered ditch water, and was consequently lost to his family thereafter. In 1783 the kidnapping for baptism of children from Terracina caused a revolt in the Roman ghetto.

Pius VII (1800-1823) adopted forced baptisms with a vengeance. The frequent nocturnal visits of the papal police and the seizure of women and children continued until the demise of the Papal States. These stolen women and children were confined to the House of the Catechumens. Some of the women returned, but never the small children.[6]

An atrocious case of forced baptism which gained international notoriety was that of Edgardo Mortaro in 1858. He was a six-year-old Jewish boy who was kidnapped by

---

[1] Kertzer, David I. *The Popes Against the Jews: The Vatican's Role in the Rise of Modern Anti-Semitism.* p63
[2] *The Scandal of Roman Catholicism.* http://www.liberalslikechrist.org/Catholic/RCscandal-1.html (2007)
[3] See, for example: Kertzer, David I. *The Popes Against the Jews: The Vatican's Role in the Rise ...* pp49-50
[4] *Catholic Encyclopedia* 'The Roman Congregations'
[5] http://en.wikipedia.org/wiki/Vincent_Ferrer (2007)
[6] Kertzer, David I. *The Popes Against the Jews: The Vatican's Role in the Rise of Modern Anti-Semitism.* p59

papal police in Bologna on the excuse that he had been baptised 'in extremis' (near to death) by a servant girl six years earlier. Edgardo was placed in the House of Catechumens and forcibly instructed in the Roman Catholic faith. Pius IX adopted the child as a Christian. When Edgardo's parents pleaded in person with the Pope for the return of their son, he replied that they could have their son back immediately, once they had converted to Roman Catholicism. The world was outraged, but to no avail.[1] This case caused international condemnation.[2] Partly in reaction, was the founding of the Alliance Israélite Universelle in 1860 'to defend the civil rights of the Jews'.[3]

Twentieth Century

*   After the Second Vatican Council, many missionary orders that had aimed at converting Jews to Christianity no longer actively sought such proselytism. However, traditionalist Roman Catholic groups, congregations and clergymen continue to support the proselytising of Jews according to traditional patterns.[4]

Synopsis

It was a doctrine of Christendom that the Jews were the violators of the moral order of the world. This conception was embedded in the Christian collective psyche from the formative period of Christianity until beyond World War II.

A number of Roman Imperial anti-Semitic dictates followed the action of Emperor Constantine 'the Great' against the Jews of Jerusalem.

There has been a very long history of Roman Catholic attempts to portray the popes as both benefactors of the Jews and as their protectors against episodic outbreaks of violence whose antecedents lay outside the Church. By contrast, history reveals that many popes proclaimed numerous bulls and the like that were extremely hostile to the Jews – some even enforcing the death penalty.

The Councils of Toledo passed increasingly destructive legislations against Jews.

Over the centuries, the church Catholic exerted ceaseless pressure on Jews, old and young, to convert to the 'One True Faith'.

As Catholicism became the dominant religion in the Roman Empire, so large numbers of Jews were forcibly baptised. The frequent nocturnal visits of the papal police and the seizure of women and children continued until the demise of the Papal States. These stolen women and children were confined to the House of the Catechumens. The small children were never returned.

———

[1] *The Scandal of Roman Catholicism.* http://www.liberalslikechrist.org/Catholic/RCscandal-1.html (2007)
[2] A book has been devoted entirely to the case: *The Kidnapping of Edgardo Mortara*, by David Kertzer.
[3] http://www.zionism-israel.com/his/judeophobia4.htm (2007)
[4] http://en.wikipedia.org/wiki/Christianity_and_antisemitism (2007)

5 – Restrictions on Living, Denial of Rights, Denial of Citizenship

General prohibitions of maltreatment availed little when prelate and priest were busy in inflaming popular aversion and popes were found to threaten any prince hardy enough to interpose and protect the unfortunate race. Henry Charles Lea

A small sample of these impositions is presented here.

Marital Relations

306 – The Synod of Elvira prohibited intermarriage and sexual intercourse between Christians and Jews, and prohibited them from eating together.[1,2] Early in the fourth century the [Church] Council of Elvira, held under the head of the uncompromising Hosius of Córdoba, forbade marriage between Christians and Jews, because there could be no society common to the faithful and the infidel.'[3]

All the resulting canons that pertained to Jews served to maintain a separation between the two communities: *Canon 15* prohibited marriage with pagans, while *Canon 16* prohibited marriage of Christians with Jews. *Canon 78* threatened ostracism of Christians who committed adultery with Jews.

1179 – The Third Lateran Council threatened all Christians with excommunication who lived with Jews.[4]

, 1350 – In Orvieto, a decree was issued that required that when a man and a woman became involved in a love affair in which one of them was Christian and the other Jewish, then the woman, of whichever faith, must be either beheaded or burned alive.[5] Such a case was cited by Nicholas Boer in which one Johannes Alardus (Jean Alard) kept a Jewess in his house in Paris and had several children by her. He was convicted of sodomy on account of this relationship, and he and his partner were incinerated because:

coition with a Jewess is precisely the same as if a man should copulate with a dog.[6]

▾ 1752 – Maria Theresa, Archduchess of Austria introduced a law limiting each Jewish family to one son.[7]

Social Relations

c.300 – In the Iberian Peninsula, Jews became the objects of restrictive legislation by the Council of Elvira. It is noteworthy that Jews had resided in Spain during the first centuries CE, well before Constantine made Christianity the official religion of the

---

[1] http://www.remember.org/History.root.classical.html (2007)

[2] http://astro.temple.edu/~hfreiden/Antisemitism/timeline.htm (2007)

[3] Lea, Henry Charles. *A History* of the *Inquisition* of *Spain.* Vol I. p37-40

[4] http://en.wikipedia.org/wiki/Timeline_of_antisemitism (2007)

[5] Tuchman, Barbara. *A Distant Mirror.* p118. Source: http://wiccanhistorian.home.att.net/histories/persecution Jews.html (2007)

[6] Trachtenberg, Joshua. *The Devil and the Jews: The Medieval Conception of the Jew and its Relation* ... p187

[7] Ibid.

Roman Empire in the year 313. However, Judaism had competed strongly with Christianity for believers among the native pagans. The Council, therefore, proclaimed the first piece of legislation that restricted the relations between Jews and Christians. This was the foundation for a process that climaxed in the extinction of the Jews in Spain more than a thousand years later.[1]

Canon 48 of the Council forbade the blessing of Christian crops by Jews, and *Canon 50* forbade the sharing of meals by Christians and Jews:

> Indeed, if anyone of the clergy or faithful has taken a meal with the Jews, it is determined that, as a corrective punishment, he is to abstain from Communion so that he may be reformed.[2]

Things worsened substantially for Iberian Jews at the end of the sixth century when King Reccared of the Visigoths became a Roman Catholic.

589 – The Third Council of Toledo reiterated in more vigorous form the original restrictions of the Council of Elvira. It prohibited Jews from taking Christian wives or concubines and prescribed baptism of the resulting children. Jews could not have Christian slaves in domestic service. Such legislation became progressively more explicit and severe in the later Councils of Toledo.[3]

692 – The Trulanic (Quinisext) Synod forbade Christians from attending Jewish religious feasts, or having friendly relations with Jews:

> Let no one in the priestly order nor any layman eat the unleavened bread of the Jews, nor have any familiar doings with them, nor summon them in illness, nor receive medicines from them, nor bathe with them; but if anyone shall take in hand to do so, if he is a cleric, let him be deposed, but if a layman, let him be cut off.[4]

Amolon, Archbishop of Lyon ruled in the ninth century:

> I have twice publicly asked that our faithful draw aside from them, that no Christian serve them either in the cities or in the villages, letting them perform their labour with the help of their pagan slaves; I have also forbidden the eating of their food and the drinking of their liquors.[5]

1050 – The Synod of Narbonne prohibited Christians from living in Jewish homes.
1050 – The Council of Coyanza held in the Diocese of Oviedo[6] stated:

> no Christian shall live in the same house with Jews or eat with them; if anyone infringes our constitution, they shall do penance for seven days, and if not willing to do it, being a noble person, they shall be deprived of communion for a full year,

---

[1] Markman, Sidney David. *Jewish Remnants in Spain: Wanderings in a Lost World.* p6
[2] Lea, Henry Charles. *A History of the Inquisition of Spain.* Vol I. pp37-40
[3] Markman, Sidney David. *Jewish Remnants in Spain: Wanderings in a Lost World.* p6
[4] Quoted in: Sparks, Thomas. *The Curse of Cain and Theologically Correct Social Policy toward the Jews.* http://www.stormfront.org/posterity/ci/curseofcain.html (2006)
[5] Cohn-Sherbok, D. *The Crucified Jew: Twenty Centuries of Christian Anti-Semitism.* p39
[6] Oviedo – capital of the autonomous region of Asturias, Spain.

and if an inferior person they will receive a hundred lashes.'[1]

1451 – In a bull, Pope Nicholas V confirmed the old exclusions of Jews from Christian society and all honourable walks of life.

1456 –Callistus III banned all social communication between Christians and Jews.

1733 – Cardinal Lambertini, Archbishop of Bologna, issued an edict on the Jews which warned that 'the Jews may not play, nor eat, nor drink, nor have any other familiarity or conversation with Christians.' It also reiterated the evil of allowing Christians to work in the homes of Jews, and stated that any father who allowed his child to do so would be punished severely, and his child imprisoned.[2]

Slaves and Servants

Emperor Constantine the Great (306-337) enacted that Jews were not allowed to own Christian slaves or to circumcise their slaves; however, Christians were allowed to own slaves. Conversion of Christians to Judaism was outlawed. Congregations for religious services were restricted.[3] If a Christian converted to Judaism, Constantine's sons seized his entire property; and mixed marriages between Jews and Christians were punished by death.[4]

Christian rulers of the Roman Empire forbade Jews during the fifth century acquiring Christian servants.[5]

The Tenth Council of Toledo (656) authorised expulsion from the Church of all clerics of all ranks who were caught trading Christian slaves with Jews.

Occupational and Business Restrictions

535 – The First Council of Clermont prohibited Jews from holding public office.

633 – The Fourth Council of Toledo issued laws forbidding Jews and Christians of Jewish origin from holding office.[6]

1078 – The Council of Rome renewed the old prohibitions against functions that placed Jews in command of Christians.

1215 – The Fourth Lateran Council ordained that Jews could not work on Sundays, and enacted that:

> We therefore renew in this canon, on account of the boldness of the offenders, what the Council of Toledo providently decreed in this matter: we forbid Jews to be appointed to public offices, since under cover of them they are very hostile to Christians.[7]

1499 – The *Sentencia-Estatuto* was written by a fanatical Spanish Catholic, Pedro

[1] http://www.sefarad-asturias.org/home.html (2010)
[2] Kertzer, David I. *The Popes Against the Jews: The Vatican's Role in the Rise The Vatican's Role* ... pp37-38
[3] http://www.atheistresource.co.uk/christjew.html (2007)
[4] Kahl, Joachim. *The Misery of Christianity: A Plea for a Humanity without God.* p55
[5] Kertzer, David I. *The Popes Against the Jews: The Vatican's Role in the Rise of Modern Anti-Semitism.* p37
[6] http://www.atheistresource.co.uk/christjew.html (2007)
[7] Quoted in: Sparks, Thomas. *The Curse of Cain and Theologically Correct Social Policy* ...

Sarmiento; it was an anti-Semitic statute that prohibited conversos from holding public or ecclesiastical offices; it also prohibited conversos from bearing witness against Spanish Christians in courts of law.[1]

Financial Impositions

429 – Theodosius II, Roman Emperor of the East, ordered that all funds raised by Jews to support their schools be turned over to his treasury.[2]

King Egica (687-702) increased taxes and the forced sale, at a fixed price, of all property ever acquired from Christians. This effectively ended all agricultural activity for the Jews of Spain. Furthermore, Jews were not to engage in commerce with the Christians of the kingdom nor conduct business with Christians overseas.[3]

King Charles III (898-929) confiscated Jewish-owned property in Narbonne and donated it to the Church.

1078 – The Synod of Gerona required Jews to pay taxes to support the Church.

1095-1096 – The Duke of Lorraine gathered an army for the First Crusade which had been preached by Urban II. To aid his finances, he spread the rumour that he would kill the Jews to avenge the death of Christ. The Jews of the Rhineland paid him 500 pieces of silver as ransom.[4]

Urban II, in turn, had told the Crusaders that sins would be forgiven in advance to any man who 'answered the call of the Crusade', such person could also consider all his financial debts to any Jewish creditor cancelled.[5]

1179 – The Third Lateran Council prohibited Jews from withholding inheritance from descendants who had accepted Christianity.[6]

Philip Augustus, King of France (1180-1223), was one of the most powerful European monarchs of the Middle Ages. After only four months in power, he imprisoned all the Jews in his lands and demanded a ransom for their release. A year later, he annulled all loans made by Jews to Christians and took a percentage for himself. A year later again, he confiscated all Jewish property and expelled the Jews from Paris.[7]

King Richard I of England ('the Lion Heart') returning from the Third Crusade was captured en route by Leopold V, the Duke of Austria. He was then handed over to Holy Roman Emperor Henry IV. He was released in 1194 only after the payment of a heavy ransom. The Jews of London had to pay three times the amount that Christians had to pay toward this ransom.[8]

1215 – The Fourth Lateran Council headed by Innocent III enacted that:

The more the Christian religion is restrained from usurious practices, so much the

[1] *Encyclopaedia Britannica* 'Converso'
[2] http://en.wikipedia.org/wiki/Timeline_of_antisemitism (2007)
[3] http://en.wikipedia.org/wiki/History_of_the_Jews_in_Spain (2008)
[4] http://www.jcrelations.net/en/?id=836 (2007)
[5] http://www.mosquitonet.com/~prewett/hag1016.html
[6] http://en.wikipedia.org/wiki/Timeline_of_antisemitism (2007)
[7] Ibid.
[8] http://www.jcrelations.net/en/?id=836 (2007)

more does the perfidy of the Jews grow in these matters, so that within a short time they are exhausting the resources of the Christians. Wishing therefore to see that Christians are not savagely oppressed by Jews in this matter, we ordain by this synodal decree that if Jews in the future, on any pretext, extort oppressive and excessive interest from Christians, then they are to be removed from contact with Christians until they have made adequate satisfaction for the immoderate burden. Christians too, if need be, shall be compelled by ecclesiastical censure, without the possibility of an appeal, to abstain from commerce with them. We enjoin upon princes, not to be hostile to Christians on this account, but rather to be zealous in restraining Jews from so great oppression.[1,2]

In cases where Jews had bought land from Catholics, they were enjoined by the Fourth Lateran Council to pay tithes to the Catholic Church:

And under the threat of the same penalty [social and economic boycott by the Church] we decree that Jews should be compelled to make good the tithes and dues owed to the churches which the churches have been accustomed to receive from the houses and other possessions of the Christians before they came into possession of the Jews, regardless of the circumstances, so that the church be preserved against loss.[3,4]

Economic motives lay behind some of the massacre of Jews. At the time of the Third Crusade (1189–1192) one of the most tragic anti-Jewish riots in England occurred in York. There, before setting out, the Crusaders, many of whom were deeply in debt to Jews, plundered Jewish possessions and then slaughtered the Jews. The attackers then burned all records of financial obligations to them.[5]

Innocent III (1198-1216) – 'Holy Scripture', and a treatise by St Thomas Aquinas in his *De regimine Iudaeorum ad Ducissam Brabantae* enabled Innocent to describe the Jews as 'damned slaves'. Thereafter, popes, kings and princes were allowed to dispose of property belonging to Jews as though it were their own.[6] Innocent wrote to the King of France that he must crush the insolence of the Jews residing in his kingdom:

And at times, when they to whom Jews have loaned money with usury produce Christian witnesses about the facts of payment, the deed which the Christian debtor through negligence indiscreetly left with them is believed rather than the witnesses whom they bring forward.

Consequently, in 1230, Jews in France were forbidden to lend money at interest.

1241 – There occurred the first of a series of royal levies in England which forced

---

[1] Quoted in: Sparks, Thomas. *The Curse of Cain and Theologically Correct Social Policy ...*

[2] See also: Kahl, Joachim. *The Misery of Christianity: A Plea for a Humanity without God.* p56

[3] http://www.mosquitonet.com/~prewett/hag1016.html (2006)

[4] The ever avaricious Church of Rome. Catholic institutional greed persists to this day.

[5] Sister Pista. Evangelical Sisterhood of Mary, Darmstadt. http://www.cdn-friends-icej.ca/antiholo/guilt.html (2007)

[6] Kahl, Joachim. *The Misery of Christianity: A Plea for a Humanity without God.* p56

the Jews to sell their debts to non-Jews to the disadvantage of the former

Clement IV (1265-68) 'addressed King Jaime [of Aragón] in wrathful mood, blaming him for the favor shown to Jews and ordering him to deprive them of office and to depress and trample on them.'[1]

1271 – The City of London prohibited Jews from acquiring any more property there, and in 1275, Jews in England were forbidden to lend money at interest.

1279 – The Synod of Ofen, Hungary, ordained that Christians could not sell or rent real estate to Jews.

After the bloody excesses of 1391, the popular hatred of the Jews in Spain continued unabated. The Cortes of Madrid and that of Valladolid (1405) mainly busied themselves with complaints against the Jews, so that King Enrique III found it necessary to prohibit the latter from practising usury and to limit the commercial intercourse between Jews and Catholics; he also reduced by one-half the claims held by Jewish creditors against Catholics.

1498 – Prince Alexander of Lithuania forced most of the Jews to either forfeit their property or convert. The main motivation was to cancel the debts which the nobles owed to them.

1744 – Maria Theresa, Archduchess of Austria, ordered that 'no Jew is to be tolerated in our inherited duchy of Bohemia.' In 1748 she reversed her position, on condition that Jews paid for re-admission every ten years. This extortion was known as malke-geld (queen's money).[2]

Public Appearance

Councils of Orléans, during the period 533 to 541: prohibited Jews from appearing in the streets during Easter because 'their appearance is an insult to Christianity;'[3] forbade marriages between Christians and Jews; and prohibited the conversion to Judaism of Christians.[4]

In the thirteenth century Jews were forbidden to visit Catholic inns and baths, and even to appear on the streets during Catholic feasts.[5]

The Fourth Lateran Council (1215) headed by Innocent III enacted that:

> They [the Jews] shall not appear in public at all on the days of lamentation and on passion Sunday; because some of them on such days, as we have heard, do not blush to parade in very ornate dress and are not afraid to mock Christians who are presenting a memorial of the most sacred passion and are displaying signs of grief. What we most strictly forbid however, is that they dare in any way to break out in derision of the Redeemer.[6]

---

[1] Lea, Henry Charles. *A History of the Inquisition of Spain*. Vol I. p91
[2] http://en.wikipedia.org/wiki/Timeline_of_antisemitism (2007)
[3] http://www.atheistresource.co.uk/christjew.html (2007)
[4] Ibid.
[5] Kahl, Joachim. *The Misery of Christianity: A Plea for a Humanity without God.* p56
[6] Quoted in: Sparks, Thomas. *The Curse of Cain and Theologically Correct Social Policy* ...

During the Counter-Reformation (sixteenth and seventeenth centuries), Roman Jews were pelted with mud by the crowds 'as the faithless deserve', and made to run naked through the streets of the Carnival in the freezing cold and rain.[1]

In the seventeenth century, Jews were humiliated and made to stand barefoot on reviled pigskins while making oaths before Catholic authorities.[2]

Legal Restrictions

- The earliest referral to the *Juramentum Judaeorum* (*Jewish Oath*) occurred in Italy in the year 615. This ruling stated that no heretic (including a Jew) could be believed in court against a Christian. The oath became standardised throughout Europe in 1555.[3]
- The Third Lateran Council (1179) declared:

> the evidence of Christians is to be accepted against Jews in every case, since Jews employ their own witnesses against Christians – and that those who prefer Jews to Christians in this matter are to lie under anathema, since Jews ought to be subject to Christians and to be supported by them on the grounds of humanity alone.[4]

- It also prohibited Jews from being plaintiffs or witnesses against Catholics.[5]

The Ecclesiastical Council of Basel of 1431-1443 forbade Jews from certain contractual arrangements between Catholics.[6]

Medical Restrictions

- 692 – The Trulanic (Quinisext) Synod forbade Catholics from going to Jewish doctors. This was a forerunner of the *Nürnberger Gesetze* (*Nuremberg Laws*)[7] of Nazi Germany, which prohibited people going to Jewish doctors.[8]

1179 – The Third Lateran Council prohibited certain medical care by Catholics of Jews.[9]

1212 – A Church Council of Paris:

> forbade, under pain of excommunication, Christian midwives to attend a Jewess in labor, it shows that they were authoritatively regarded as less entitled than beasts to human sympathy.[10]

The Jew-Devil was perceived as stalking Europe and seeking Christians as his prey. In particular, Jewish doctors were seen as satanic agents and magicians who practised sorcery – hence, they were condemned by the Church. Consequently, in the thirteenth

---

[1] Kühner, Hans. *Der Antisemitismus der Kirche*. p166. Source: http://christianactionforisrael.org/antiholo/guilt.html (2010)

[2] http://www.atheistresource.co.uk/christjew.html (2007)

[3] http://en.wikipedia.org/wiki/Timeline_of_antisemitism (2007)

[4] http://www.stormfront.org/posterity/ci/curseofcain.html (2007)

[5] http://en.wikipedia.org/wiki/Timeline_of_antisemitism (2007)

[6] Poliakov, Léon. *The History of Anti-Semitism*. Vol I. p121

[7] These were anti-Semitic laws in Germany introduced at the annual Nuremberg Rally of the Nazi Party.

[8] Refer to the section 'The Nazi Holocaust and the Catholic Church', below.

[9] http://en.wikipedia.org/wiki/Timeline_of_antisemitism (2007)

[10] Lea, Henry Charles. *A History of the Inquisition of Spain*. Vol I. p81

century the Council of Béziers forbade Catholics from obtaining care from Jews. This proscription was repeated by the Councils of Albi, Vienna, and the University of Paris. In defence, for example, the Vienna Faculty of Medicine stated that Jewish physicians were required by private code to kill one patient in ten.[1] In Spain, however 'While Jewish physicians might prescribe for Christian patients, the medicine must be compounded by a Christian.'[2]

In spite of the increasing obstacles erected by ecclesiastic and secular legislation, Jewish medical skills were recognised by members of the upper classes, such as princes and ecclesiastics right up to the pope himself. These people held themselves above the restrictions that they had imposed upon the masses. For example, Pope Martin V, in a bull of 1421, granted to Spanish royalty the explicit privilege of employing Jewish physicians. And, while Jews were forbidden to reside in England after 1290, Edward II granted a Jewish physician the right to enter the country in 1310. A century later, Henry IV summoned two Jewish physicians from Italy, and a third from France.[3]

As late as 1852, Pius IX persuaded Tuscany to forbid Jewish doctors from practising medicine.[4]

Academic Restrictions

The Council of Basel in 1434 prohibited Jews from attending universities.[5]

Multiple Restrictions

438 – The *Codex Theodosianus* denied Jews numerous rights, including prohibitions on holding any public office or function, or building new synagogues.

529-534 – The *Corpus Juris Civilis* also denied Jews numerous rights.

694 – At the Seventeenth Council of Toledo, King Egica forced Jews to give all their land, slaves and buildings bought from Catholics, to his treasury.[6] The Council again severely restricted the rights of Jews and charged them with undermining the Church, of the massacre of Roman Catholics, and of destruction of the country.

1275 – The *Statutum Judeismo* was passed in England under King Edward I. The law forbade Jews from charging interest, restricted the areas where they could live, ordered all Jews from the age of seven to wear the badge, and required those above the age of twelve to pay an annual poll tax at Easter. Three years later Edward charged Jews with coin clipping. House-to-house searches took place throughout England and 680 Jews were thrown into the Tower of London. Many were hanged and their property seized by the King.

1447 – Casimir IV (King of Poland and Grand Duke of Lithuania) renewed all the rights of Jews of Poland and made his charter one of the most liberal in Europe. Eight

---

[1] Cohn-Sherbok, D. *The Crucified Jew: Twenty Centuries of Christian Anti-Semitism.* pp62-63
[2] Lea, Henry Charles. *A History of the Inquisition of Spain.* Vol I. pp89-90
[3] Trachtenberg, Joshua. *The Devil and the Jews: The Medieval Conception of the Jew and its Relation ...* p95
[4] de Rosa, Peter. *Vicars of Chris: The Dark Side of the Papacy.* p247
[5] Poliakov, Léon. *The History of Anti ...* Vol I. p121. Many other restrictions appear in this encyclopaedia.
[6] http://en.wikipedia.org/wiki/Timeline_of_antisemitism (2007)

years later he revoked it at the insistence of Bishop Zbigniew Oleśnicki, a high-ranking Catholic clergyman and an influential Polish statesman and diplomat.

- In Spain and Portugal, around this time, conversos were viewed with suspicion within the Church. Opprobrious terms were applied to them, most commonly that of 'marrano' (pig). Although they were no longer non-converted Jews in their religion, nonetheless, the conversos continued to suffer from anti-Semitism.[1] In 1449 the officials of Toledo proclaimed:

> We declare that all the said conversos, descendants of the perverse line of the Jews ... in reason of the above-mentioned heresies and other offences, insults, seditions, and crimes committed by them up to this time, should therefore be held as disgraceful, unfit, inept, and unworthy of holding any office and public and private benefit in said city or public notaries or as witnesses ... to have domain over Old Christians in the holy Catholic faith.[2]

King Ferdinand II of Aragón showed the greatest intolerance to Jews, whether converted or otherwise, commanding all conversos to reconcile themselves with the Inquisition by the end of 1484, and obtaining a bull from Innocent VIII ordering all Christian princes to restore all fugitive conversos to the Inquisition.[3]

- 1555 – Paul IV's Bull *Cum nimis absurdum* was a landmark in the history of anti-Semitism, and is recognised as the most devastating Christian anti-Jewish document ever written.[4]

- 1566 – Pius V confirmed the harsh anti-Jewish laws of Paul IV.

1775 – Pius VI issued a severe 44 clause *Editto sopra gli ebrei* (*Edict over the Jews*).

Purity of Blood

- During the sixteenth century in Spain, the 1499 *Sentencia-Estatuto* was followed by the laws of Limpieza de sangre (Purity of blood). This strengthened further the legislation against those of Jewish ancestry. For example, every candidate for the priesthood had to produce a certificate proving that he had Limpieza de sangre going back to the fourth generation.[5] Some of this legalised prejudice against Jews in Spain was not modified until the late nineteenth and early twentieth centuries.[6]

- These many Roman Catholic regulations were precursors of the Nazi *Arierparagraph* (*Aryan Paragraph*) that forbade Jews from being members in German political parties, economic groups and social and student clubs. It became official German legislation when the *Nuremberg Laws*, finally separating the Jews from the German Volk, were passed in 1935.

---

[1] Kamen, Henry. *The Spanish Inquisition: An Historical Revision.* p11
[2] Cohn-Sherbok, D. *The Crucified Jew: Twenty Centuries of Christian Anti-Semitism.* p84
[3] http://en.wikipedia.org/wiki/History_of_the_Jews_in_Spain (2008)
[4] Refer to Chapter 4 for more details.
[5] Kahl, Joachim. *The Misery of Christianity: A Plea for a Humanity without God.* p58
[6] *Encyclopaedia Britannica* 'Converso'

—A similar precursor to the Nazi *Arierparagraph* existed in the Jesuit Order's *Aryan paragraph*. Its Constitutions contain six impediments against reception into the Order – the first of which is Jewish ancestry up to the fourth generation. This *Aryan paragraph* first appeared in the Orders' statutes in 1593; it was confirmed in 1608, and occurred in the official edition published in Florence in 1893. General councils of the Jesuit order have often promulgated that Jewish descent must be considered as 'an impurity, scandal, dishonour and infamy.'[1]

Denial of Citizenship

It was nearly eighteen centuries after the outset of Christianity that European Jews were finally given the right of citizenship:

Table 5. The Years in which Right of Citizenship was granted to Jews in European states[2]

France	1791
Holland	1796
Belgium	1815
Denmark	1849
England	1858
Switzerland	1865
Austria-Hungary	1867
Germany	1870
Russia	1917
The Papal States	Never

In 1870 the Church's Papal States were finally abolished and Italy was united as a nation under King Victor Emanuel II.[3] He gave the Jews full citizenship.[4]

Synopsis

For centuries, numerous restrictions and impositions: social, legal, financial, professional, business, medical, marital, and academic were placed on Jews by the Catholic Church.

———

[1] Lehmann, L H. *Behind the Dictators: A Factual Analysis of the Relationship ...* p25

[2] Fr Leonard Feeney, SJ. *The Point,* April 1956. Quoted in: Sparks, Thomas. *The Curse of Cain and Theologically Correct Social Policy toward the Jews*

[3] In 1860, through local plebiscites, Tuscany, Modena, Parma and Romagna decided to side with Sardinia-Piedmont. Victor Emanuel then marched victoriously into Marche and Umbria after the victorious battle of Castelfidardo (1860) over the Papal Forces, after which he gained a papal excommunication (in contrast to the Nazis of the Catholic faith who were never excommunicated).

[4] http://en.wikipedia.org/wiki/Papal_States#Italian_nationalism_and_the_end_of_the_Papal_States (2007)

6 – Desecration of Synagogues, Prohibition and Destruction of Hebrew Texts, Restrictions on Worship, Distinguishing Apparel

The oppression of any people for opinion's sake has rarely had any other effect than to fix those opinions deeper.   Hosea Ballou

Table 6. A Sample of Places and Dates where Synagogues were closed, stolen or destroyed by the Church[1]

Date	Place	Building	Outcome
415	Alexandria	the synagogue	stolen
c.415	Constantinople	the great synagogue	stolen
c.500	Rome	the synagogue	burned
6th C	North Africa	many	closed
c.6th C	Orléans	one	destroyed
c.600	Palermo	many	stolen
1180	Toledo	Ibn Shushan Synagogue	stolen[2]
1181	France	many	stolen
1189	London	many	destroyed
1307	France	many	sold or gifted[3]
1349	Vienna	the synagogue	unspecified
1419	Segovia	Old Main Synagogue	stolen, never returned
1473	Mainz	the synagogue	stolen
1482	Sevilla	a large synagogue	stolen
1492	Spain	all synagogues	stolen
1492	Toledo	Synagogue, El Transito	turned into a museum
1492?	Híjar	Híjar Synagogue	stolen, never returned
15th C	Spain	a large number	stolen, never returned
1519	Regensburg	the synagogue	demolished
1555[4]	many places	a large number	destroyed
c.1670	Vienna	the synagogue	demolished
1899	Segovia	the old synagogue	burned/stolen
1938	Reichkristallnacht[5]	1000+ synagogues	destroyed
1933-45	Nazi Holocaust[5]	many	destroyed
1983	Banská Bystrica	synagogue built in 1867	destroyed

---

[1] A major source of information is http://www.jewishencyclopedia.com/articles/14160-synagogue (2015)

[2] This famous synagogue has never been returned to the Jews; it is owned and preserved as a museum by the Catholic Church.

[3] French King Philippe the Fair presented one to his coachman.

[4] Following the issuing of the Bull *Cum nimis absurdum* by Pope Paul IV.

[5] While not destructions by the Church itself, nevertheless very many Catholics participated, and 'the bishops of Germany said nothing at all.' Refer to Chapter 15.

Location of Synagogues

Canon law forbad synagogues from being situated so that they might be seen from the street. Consequently, the building was often set back in a forecourt surrounded by a high wall shielding the main façade from Catholic view.[1]

Closure, Appropriation and Destruction of Synagogues, Jewish Cemeteries and Other Buildings through the Centuries

Fourth Century

388 – At the instigation of the local bishop, a mob of Christians looted and burned the synagogue in Callinicum, a town on the Euphrates.[2]

399 – The Western Roman Emperor Honorius called Judaism 'superstitio indigna' and confiscated gold and silver collected by the synagogues for Jerusalem.[3]

413 – A group of monks traversed Palestine, destroying synagogues and massacring Jews at the Western Wall.[4]

Fifth Century

415 – Bishop Severus burned the synagogue in the village of Magona. Christians confiscated synagogues in Antioch.[5]

419 – The monk Barsauma (who became the Bishop of Nisibis) gathered a group of followers, and for the next three years destroyed synagogues throughout Palestine.[6]

Cyril (376-444) succeeded to the See of Alexandria. He is one of the Church Fathers and a Doctor of the Church. One of his first acts was to attack the Jews, who numbered forty thousand:

> Without any legal sentence, without any royal mandate, the patriarch, at the dawn of day, led a seditious multitude to the attack of the synagogues. Unarmed and unprepared, the Jews were incapable of resistance; their houses of prayer were levelled with the ground, and the episcopal warrior, after rewarding his troops with the plunder of their goods, expelled from the city the remnant of the unbelieving nation.[7]

For efforts such as this, Cyril was declared a Saint.

442 – The synagogue in Constantinople was turned into a church.[8]

---

[1] Markman, Sidney David. *Jewish Remnants in Spain: Wanderings in a Lost World.* p63

[2] http://en.wikipedia.org/wiki/Timeline_of_antisemitism (2007)

[3] Ibid.

[4] http://www.sullivan-county.com/id2/timeline.htm (2007)

[5] http://astro.temple.edu/~hfreiden/Antisemitism/timeline.htm (2007)

[6] http://en.wikipedia.org/wiki/Timeline_of_antisemitism (2007)

[7] Foote, G W & J M Wheeler. *Crimes of Christianity.* Vol I. Ch II. 'Athanasius to Hypatia'. Source: http://www.ftarchives.net/foote/crimes/c2.htm (2007)

[8] http://www.liberalslikechrist.org/Catholic/ChurchvsJews.html (2010). As it was to do so many times over the centuries, the Catholic Church purloined the religious building of a different faith. The *Catholic Encyclopedia* records: 'Not only the taking, but the keeping or the use unjustly of what belongs to another against his will, is to be considered theft ... The sin of theft is of itself grievous, because it violates the great virtues of justice

Emperor Justinian I ('The Great') (483-565) outlawed the Jews, and synagogues were seized by the state and converted into churches. Justinian also legalised the burning and plundering of synagogues by Christian bishops and monks. He also made the mass baptism of all Jews compulsory.[1]

Sixth Century

519 – The synagogues in Ravenna, Italy, were burned down by a local mob.[2]

582 – John of Ephesus turned seven synagogues into churches.

A certain Dr Hemen stated that:

> At this time, Bishops did not hesitate to resort to acts of violence to compel the Jews to become Christians. Bishop Avitus, of Clermont-Ferrand, having preached to the Jews without any results, the Christians destroyed the synagogues.[3]

Twelfth Century

In France, King Philip II (Philippe Auguste) commanded in his *Edict of Expulsion*, dated 1182, that all synagogues be transformed into churches.

Thirteenth Century

1215 – The Fourth Lateran Council enacted that synagogues must remain lowly and miserable buildings.

1222 – The Council of Oxford prohibited the construction of new synagogues.

1250 – A papal bull halted construction of a large synagogue in Córdoba, Spain. The site became known as 'Plazas de las Bulas' ('Plaza of the Papal Bulls').[4]

1254 – King Louis IX expelled the Jews from France – their property and synagogues were confiscated.

1282 – The Archbishop of Canterbury closed all synagogues in his diocese. A year later, Archbishop Peckham of London closed all synagogues in his diocese also.

Spain: Catholic princes, the counts of Castile and the first kings of León, treated the Jews as mercilessly as did the Almohades. In their operations against the Moors they did not spare the Jews, destroying their synagogues and killing their teachers and scholars.[5]

Fourteenth Century

1390 – In Spain, Ferrant Martinez[6] ordered the destruction of the synagogues in Écija, Alcalá de Guadaira, Coria del Río, and Cantillana del Río.[7]

1391 – Sevilla is said to have contained 7000 Jewish families. Of the three large synagogues existing in the city two were transformed into churches.

---

and charity.'

[1] Kahl, Joachim. *The Misery of Christianity: A Plea for a Humanity without God.* p55
[2] http://en.wikipedia.org/wiki/Timeline_of_antisemitism (2007)
[3] Foote, G W & J M Wheeler. *Crimes of Christianity.* Vol I. Ch VIII. 'Persecution of the Jews'
[4] Markman, Sidney David. *Jewish Remnants in Spain: Wanderings in a Lost World.* p81
[5] http://en.wikipedia.org/wiki/History_of_the_Jews_in_Spain (2008)
[6] The evil Martinez is described in detail in Chapter 10, below.
[7] Markman, Sidney David. *Jewish Remnants in Spain: Wanderings in a Lost World.* p92

1395 – After mass slaughters and forced conversions, a new synagogue in the aljama[1] of Barcelona 'was converted into a church or monastery of Trinitarian monks and the wealthy aljama of Barcelona, with its memories of so many centuries, ceased to exist.'[2]

In Liegnitz and Breslau, Poland, King John authorised the destruction of Jewish cemeteries so that the tombstones could be used to repair the city walls.[3]

Fifteenth Century

In Spain, both for some while before, and during the fifteenth century, Jews were forbidden to build new houses of worship.[4] Large numbers of synagogues were stolen by the Church and converted to churches. The process of purloining often followed the sequence of: expelling the Jewish worshippers, removing the *Torah* scrolls from the Ark, and substituting an altar for the immediate celebration of the Mass.[5] Such appropriated buildings still remain in the hands of the Catholic Church. Seventeen of these stolen Jewish holy places are mentioned in Sidney Markman's book *Jewish Remnants in Spain: Wanderings in a Lost World.*

One of these is the Old Main Synagogue in Segovia which was converted in 1419 into the church of Corpus Christi – an annual procession still commemorates the event.[6] It was later transformed into a convent for the inappropriately named 'Sisters of Penitence'. It has never been returned to the Jews. The brazen Roman Catholic altar is situated where the Jewish Ark of the *Torah* was originally located.[7]

Another remarkable example is the Ibn Shushan Synagogue in Toledo, built in 1180 – 'the largest and most beautiful synagogue in Spain'. In the fifteenth century the Jews of Toledo were massacred and the synagogue was appropriated by the Catholic Church and renamed the Church of Santa María la Blanca.[8,9] It is disputably considered the oldest synagogue building in Europe that is still standing. It also has never been returned to the Jews.

Sixteenth Century

1555 – The Roman Ghetto was established by the Bull *Cum nimis absurdum* promulgated by Paul IV. The Jews were allowed only one synagogue in each city. Within days, there was a ghetto in Venice and another in Bologna called 'the Inferno'. In Rome seven out of eight synagogues were destroyed, and eighteen out of nineteen in the

---

[1] As mentioned above, 'Aljama' is a Spanish word of Arabic origin designating the self-governing communities of Moors and Jews living under Spanish Catholic rule.

[2] Lea, Henry Charles. *History of the Inquisition of Spain.* Vol 1. p110

[3] http://en.wikipedia.org/wiki/Timeline_of_antisemitism (2007)

[4] Markman, Sidney David. *Jewish Remnants in Spain: Wanderings in a Lost World.* p18

[5] Ibid. p63

[6] Lea, Henry Charles. *History of the Inquisition of Spain.* Vol 1. p116

[7] Markman, Sidney David. *Jewish Remnants in Spain: Wanderings in a Lost World.* p52

[8] Source: http://wiccanhistorian.home.att.net/histories/persecutionJews.html (2007)

[9] http://en.wikipedia.org/wiki/History_of_the_Jews_in_Spain#Forced_conversions (2010)

Campania.[1] It was said of Pope Paul 'His arm is dyed in blood to the elbow.'[2]

1593 – Clement VIII, after expelling all Jews from the city of Bologna and its surrounding territories, offered the Jewish cemetery as a gift to the nuns of the convent of Saint Peter the Martyr. He told them:

> to destroy all graves ... of the Jews ... and to take the inscriptions, the memorials, the marble grave-stones, destroying them completely, demolishing them ... and to ex-hume the cadavers, the bones and the fragments of the dead and to move them wherever they please ...[3]

Twentieth Century

Amongst other claims against the Croatian Ustaše and the Franciscans in the Roman Catholic Independent State of Croatia during World War II, were instances of mass rape, torture, mutilations, burnings, destruction and requisition of Orthodox churches and Jewish synagogues.[4]

In Catholic moral theology wrongful possession of another's goods has always required restitution. In the light of the history of these, and other stolen synagogues, it is valid to ask how moral is Catholic moral theology?

Prohibition and Destruction of Hebrew Texts through the Centuries

The *Talmud* is one of the foundations of Judaism.[5]

It has two components. The first is the *Mishnah*, the written compendium of Judaism's Oral *Torah*. The second is the *Gemara*, an elucidation of the *Mishnah* and related Tannaitic writings that often ventures onto other subjects and expounds broadly on the Hebrew Bible.[6] The term *Talmud* can be used to mean either the *Gemara* alone, or the *Mishnah* and *Gemara* as printed together.

In the centuries preceding the institution of the Church's multiplicity of Indexes of Forbidden Books and the like,[7] the *Talmud* and the other doctrinal texts of the Hebrews came repeatedly under the prohibitions of the Church.[8]

681 – The Synod of Toledo ordered the burning of the *Talmud* and other books.[9]

Thirteenth Century

1239-1320 – Beginning with Gregory IX, a series of orders was issued by successive popes for the destruction of copies of the *Talmud*, which was seen as a symbol of Jewish

---

[1] de Rosa, Peter. *Vicars of Chris: The Dark Side of the* Papacy. pp191-92

[2] *The Scandal of Roman Catholicism*. http://www.liberalslikechrist.org/Catholic/RCscandal-1.html (2007)

[3] Kertzer, David I. *The Kidnapping of Edgardo Mortara*. pp13-14

[4] http://www.remnantofgod.org/ustashe.htm (2005)

[5] Michael, Robert. *A History of Catholic Antisemitism: The Dark Side of the Church*. p90

[6] The Hebrew Bible is a term used by biblical scholars to refer to the *Tanakh*, the canonical collection of Jewish texts, which is the common textual source of the several canonical editions of the Christian Old Testament.

[7] For specific instances, refer to Volume 1 of *'A Corrupt Tree'*, Chapter IV-1 – Censorship – Introduction.

[8] Putnam, George Haven. *The Censorship of the Church of Rome, and its Influence* ... Vol I. pp72-76

[9] http://www.sullivan-county.com/id2/timeline.htm (2007)

blasphemy against the Christian faith.[1] In letters to the kings and archbishops of France, England, Spain and Portugal, Gregory ordered that, on a specified day, all copies of these books were to be delivered to the Dominicans and the Minorites[2], and if they were found to contain certain heresies they were to be burned. Thereafter, the Talmudic Jew was seen as plotting and blaspheming against Christianity. This perspective was widespread and persisted into the twentieth century.[3]

1242 – Twenty-four cart-loads of hand-written Talmudic manuscripts were burned in the streets of Paris. Two years later, Innocent IV exhorted King Louis IX of France to burn all copies of the Talmudic texts to be found in his kingdom:

> Our dear Son, the Chancellor of Paris, and the Doctors, before the clergy and people, publicly burned by fire the aforesaid books [the *Talmud*] with all their appendices. We beg and beseech your Celestial Majesty in the Lord Jesus, that, having begun laudably and piously to prosecute those who perpetuate these detestable excesses, that you continue with due severity. And that you command throughout your whole kingdom that the aforesaid books with all their glossaries, already condemned by the Doctors, be committed to the flames. (*Bul. Rom. Pont. IV, 509*)[4]

Thereafter, during the next two hundred years, the Inquisition launched repeated attacks on all forms of Jewish literature. The secular authorities, influenced by the Church, joined the attack. This 'violent war against the Talmud' continued unabated for centuries. The *Talmud* was perceived as not only the source of Jewish blindness and obstinacy, but also as a source of blasphemous attacks on Christians and Christianity. It was seen as being filled with foul iniquities and anti-Christian ploys, and with superstition and magic.[5]

1248 – Cardinal Odo ordered the destruction of such books.

1254 – Louis IX issued renewed orders for the burning of copies of the *Talmud* and of other Hebrew books containing blasphemies.

1267 – Clement IV ordered the Archbishop of Tarragona, Spain, to destroy the books of the Jews, and especially the *Talmud*.

1320 – The Inquisition in Toulouse and in Perpignan burned the *Talmud* under orders of Pope John XXII, 'a man of serious character, of austere and simple habits, broadly cultivated,'[6] who asserted that:

> The Jewish religion is a plague and deadly diseased weed and must be pulled out by its roots.[7]

---

[1] Putnam, George Haven. *The Censorship of the Church of Rome, and its Influence* ... Vol I. p25
[2] Minorite – a Franciscan friar.
[3] Wistrich, Robert S. *Anti-Semitism: The Longest Hatred.* pp24-26
[4] http://www.talmudunmasked.com/appendix.htm (2014)
[5] Trachtenberg, Joshua. *The Devil and the Jews: The Medieval Conception of the Jew and its Relation to Modern Anti-Semitism.* p179
[6] *Catholic Encyclopedia* ('Pope John XXII')
[7] Michael, Robert. *A History of Catholic Antisemitism: The Dark Side of the Church.* p75

Fifteenth Century

1443 – Eugenius IV issued a bull prohibiting the Jews from studying the *Talmud*.

In the fifteenth century Benedict XIII ordered all copies of the Talmudic books to be delivered to the bishop of the diocese. The Jews were forbidden to possess copies of any works that contained assaults on the Christian faith.

* 1490 – The Inquisitor Tomás de Torquemada burned 6000 volumes of Jewish manuscripts in Salamanca.

Sixteenth Century

During the sixteenth century Hebrew texts suffered extensively.

1509 – Emperor Maximilian authorised the destruction of everything that was blasphemous or hostile to Christianity. In Frankfurt, alone, Jewish homes and synagogues were searched, and more than 1500 manuscripts were confiscated.

1553 – Hebrew books including hundreds of copies of the *Talmud* were publicly burned in Rome on Rosh Hashanah[1] and elsewhere in Italy by order of Pope Julius III and the Inquisition. About 12,000 copies were destroyed.[2]

In the same year Julius III published an edict directing all princes, bishops, and inquisitors to confiscate and destroy by fire all copies of the 'Talmuds' of Jerusalem and of Babylon. Catholics were forbidden, under pain of excommunication, to possess or to read these books, or to aid the Jews in producing copies by script or by printing.

* 1555 – The *Roman Index*, under Paul IV, included among prohibited books the *Talmud* of the Jews, with all commentaries, glosses, and interpretations. In that year also, the Inquisitor-General, Antonio Ghislieri (who subsequently became Pius V) ordered the burning of all copies.

Sixtus of Siena was sent to Cremona where there was a magnificent Hebrew school and where was kept in store a supply of copies of the Talmudic books. Sixtus reported that he had destroyed 12,000 volumes of these religious works.

1564 – Pius IV, for a substantial consideration in money, issued a bull permitting the printing and the circulation of an expurgated *Talmud*. A year later, the Inquisition of Rome condemned and ordered destroyed all books having to do with the 'Cabbala'.

1591 – Clement VIII issued a bull prohibiting both Christians and Jews from owning, reading, buying, or circulating the Talmudic and Cabbalistic books and other 'godless writings', whether written or printed, in Hebrew or in other languages, that contained heresies or assaults upon Christian doctrines or upon the practices of the Church. The substance of this bull was printed in the *Index of Clement* issued in 1596.

1586 –Sixtus V forbade printing of the *Talmud*.

Eighteenth Century

* 1711 – Johann Andreas Eisenmenger, having collected citations from 193 Hebrew books and rabbinical tracts, published his *Entdecktes Judenthum* (*Judaism Unmasked*),

---

[1] Rosh Hashanah (רֹאשׁ הַשָּׁנָה) – Jewish New Year.
[2] http://en.wikipedia.org/wiki/Timeline_of_antisemitism (2007)

which has remained the arsenal for detractors of Talmudic literature down to the present day.[1,2]

1733 – An *Edict on the Jews* was issued in Bologna signed by Cardinal Lambertini, Archbishop of Bologna. It stated that Jews must not read the *Talmud* or any other prohibited book.

1775 – Clement XIV issued an edict in 1775 in which rabbis and Jews generally were forbidden to possess copies of the Talmudic and Cabbalistic books or of any others that contained heresies or utterances against the Catholic faith. No Hebrew books were to be bought or sold until they had been examined and approved by the Magister Palatii[3] in Rome, or, outside of Rome, by the bishop or inquisitor. The penalty included seven years' imprisonment.[4]

Restrictions on Worship and Other Matters

529-534 – The *Corpus Juris Civilis* denied Jews numerous rights. The use of the Hebrew language in worship was banned as a denial of the Trinity.

589 – The Council of Narbonne forbad Jews from chanting psalms while burying their dead.

616 – Sisebut, king of the Visigoths in Hispania, ordered that those Jews who refused to convert to Christianity be punished with the lash.[5] Four years later, after many of his anti-Jewish edicts were ignored, he prohibited Judaism. Those not baptised fled. This was the first incidence where a prohibition of Judaism affected an entire country.[6]

682 – Erwig, Catholic king of the Visigoths in Hispania, began his reign by enacting twenty eight anti-Jewish laws. He pressed for the 'utter extirpation of the pest of the Jews' and decreed that all converts had to be registered by a parish priest. All holidays, Christian and Jewish, had to be spent in the presence of a priest to ensure piety and to prevent regression.[7]

1215 – The Fourth Lateran Council enacted that Jews could not enter churches or walk in the streets on holy days, and that synagogues must remain lowly and miserable buildings.

Gregory IX (1227-41) dictated:

> We order all our brother bishops absolutely to suppress the blasphemy of Jews in your dioceses, churches, and communities, so that they do not dare raise their necks, bent under eternal slavery, to revile the Redeemer.

---

[1] http://en.wikipedia.org/wiki/Johann_Andreas_Eisenmenger (2007)
[2] http://en.wikipedia.org/wiki/Timeline_of_antisemitism (2007)
[3] Magister Sacri Palatii (Master of the Sacred Palace) is a Roman Curial office which has always been entrusted to a Friar Preacher of the Dominican Order and may be described as the pope's theologian.
[4] Putnam, George Haven. *The Censorship of the Church of Rome, and its Influence* ... Vol I. pp72-76
[5] http://en.wikipedia.org/wiki/Sisebur (2010)
[6] http://en.wikipedia.org/wiki/Timeline_of_antisemitism (2007)
[7] Ibid.

1267 – The Synod of Vienna decreed that Christians could not attend Jewish ceremonies, and Jews could not dispute with the Catholic laity about the Roman Catholic religion.

1325 – The Council of Lérida in Aragón issued a canon forbidding Catholics from attending Jewish weddings and circumcisions.[1]

Vincent Ferrer (c.1350-1419), a Dominican friar and professor of theology, journeyed throughout Spain and France attempting conversion. He was the leader of bands of flagellants. He travelled about Castile urging the Jews to embrace Catholicism, appearing with a Cross in one hand and the *Torah* in the other, but with the force of the law behind him. He entered synagogues and required of worshippers that they accept Christianity. Also persecuted were Jewish communities in Zaragoza, Valencia and Tortosa.[2] For his efforts on behalf of the Church he was declared a Saint.

1436 – In Norway, Archbishop Aslak Bolt forbade the practice of Shabbat in a Jewish manner.[3]

Seventeenth Century – The Jesuits denied membership to any man with Jewish ancestry as far back as five generations. This rule was not changed until 1946.[4]

1919 – Poland passed a law making Sunday a compulsory day of rest throughout the country. It was intended to force Jews to observe the Catholic Sabbath in addition to their own (Saturday).

Distinguishing Apparel through the Centuries

Over the ages, Jews were singled out by laws which compelled them to wear badges, hats, or other items of clothing that distinguished them from the surrounding population. The identification varied from one country to another, and from period to period. Belts, headgear, shoes, armbands and/or cloth patches were used. In particular, the 'yellow badge' ('yellow patch') ('Jewish badge'[5]) was a cloth patch that Jews were required to sew on their outer garments. The shape of the patch varied. The yellow badge was compulsory in the Middle Ages in Christendom, and was revived by the Nazis. In the Middle Ages also, Jews were often required to wear the 'pileus cornutus' a cone-shaped hat, also known as the Judenhut.[6] (People actually believed that Jews had horns that they were hiding under these hats.)[7] The consequence of these distinctive appurtenances was to make the Jews more visible and expose them to both physical and verbal abuse.[8]

---

[1] Lea, Henry Charles. *A History of the Inquisition of Spain.* Vol I. p100

[2] Cohn-Sherbok, D. *The Crucified Jew: Twenty Centuries of Christian Anti-Semitism.* p61

[3] Uriely, Erez. 'Jew-hatred in contemporary Norwegian caricatures'. Jerusalem Center for Public Affairs. http://www.jcpa.org/phas/phas-050-uriely.htm (2015)

[4] Hardy, Rob. *What Role did the Vatican Play in Fostering Anti-*Semitism? (http://www.nonfictionreviews. com/article1273.html) (2006)

[5] Jew Badge – Normally a yellow disc sewn onto the clothing. Its colour symbolised the betrayal of Christ by Judas for pieces of gold.

[6] http://en.wikipedia.org/wiki/Yellow_badge (2007)

[7] http://www.jcrelations.net/en/?id=836 (2007)

[8] Wistrich, Robert S. *Anti-Semitism: The Longest Hatred.* pp24-26

The Jew-Devil was perceived as stalking Europe and seeking Christians as his prey. In particular, Jewish doctors were seen as satanic agents and magicians who practised sorcery. Accordingly, they were condemned by the Church; so that, in the thirteenth century in Spain, the wearing of the hateful distinctive badge was ordered under penalty of ten gold maravedís or of ten lashes.[1]

Thirteenth Century

The thirteenth century was particularly active in this field.

1215 – The Fourth Lateran Council, headed by Innocent III, enacted that:

> In the countries where Christians do not distinguish themselves from Jews ... it is decreed that henceforth Jews of both sexes will be distinguished from other peoples by their garments, as moreover has been prescribed unto them by Moses.[2] They will not show themselves in public during Holy Week, for some among them on these days wear their finest garments and mock the Christians clad in mourning. Trespassers will be duly punished by the secular powers, in order that they no longer dare flout Christ in the presence of Christians.[3,4]

1218 – King Henry II made the above conciliar decree into a secular one, and ordered all Jews in England to wear a badge on their outer clothing at all times to distinguish them from Christians.

1222 – The Archbishop of Canterbury, Stephen Langton, ordered English Jews to wear a white band, two fingers broad and four long.

1223 – King Jaime I of Aragón ordered the Jews to wear the distinguishing badge.

1227 – The Synod of Narbonne ruled:

> That Jews may be distinguished from others, we decree and emphatically command that in the centre of the breast [of their garments] they shall wear an oval badge, the measure of one finger in width and one half a palm in height.

1234 – The Council of Arles ordered Jews to wear a round patch; the Council of Béziers ordered likewise in 1246, as did the Council of Albi in 1254.

1265 – King Alfonso X of Castile enacted the legal code *Siete Partidas*. It included a requirement for Jews to wear distinguishing marks; but was not implemented until many years later.

1267 – The Vienna City Council forced Jews to wear the pileus cornutus in addition to a yellow badge which they were already forced to wear.

---

[1] Lea, Henry Charles. *A History of the Inquisition of Spain.* Vol I. pp89-90

[2] 'And the LORD spake unto Moses, saying, Speak unto the children of Israel, and bid them that they make them fringes in the borders of their garments throughout their generations, and that they put upon the fringe of the borders a ribband of blue: And it shall be unto you for a fringe, that ye may look upon it, and remember all the commandments of the LORD, and do them; and that ye seek not after your own heart and your own eyes, after which ye use to go a whoring: That ye may remember, and do all my commandments, and be holy unto your God.' (*Numbers* 15:37-9)

[3] Cohn-Sherbok, D. *The Crucified Jew: Twenty Centuries of Christian Anti-Semitism.* p45

[4] Poliakov, Léon. *The History of Anti-Semitism.* Vol I. p64

1269 – Louis IX, King of France, ordered all Jews found in public without a badge to be fined ten livres of silver. This regulation was repeated by local councils at Arles 1234 and 1260, Béziers 1246, Albi 1254, Nîmes 1284 and 1365, Avignon 1326 and 1337, Rodez 1336, and Vanves 1368.

1274 – King Edward I of England enacted the *Statute of Jewry* which required that:

> Each Jew, after he is seven years old, shall wear a distinguishing mark on his outer garment, that is to say, in the form of two Tables joined, of yellow felt of the length of six inches and of the breadth of three inches.[1]

1289 – The Council of Vienna ordered Jews to wear a round patch.

1294 – The earliest mention of the Jew badge in Erfurt, Germany.

Fourteenth Century

King Henry II of Castile forced the Jews to wear the yellow badge.

1326 – The Council of Avignon prescribed Jews to wear a round patch.

1378 – The Cortes of Toro demanded that Jews should be: neither officials nor tax-collectors; required to wear a distinctive badge; prohibited from riding on horseback, and dressing extravagantly.

Fifteenth Century

1415 – Benedict XIII, in a bull, ordered the Jews to wear a yellow and red badge, the men on their breast, the women on their forehead; and Emperor Sigismund I reintroduced the Jew badge at Augsburg (Holy Roman Empire) in 1434.

1435 – King Alfonso ordered the Jews of Sicily to attach a round patch to their clothing and also over their shops.

1443 – Jews in Venice had to wear the yellow badge.

Sixteenth Century

Paul IV (1555-1559) required Jews to wear distinctive headgear.

King Sigismund II passed a law in 1566 requiring Lithuanian Jews to wear yellow hats and head coverings.

Eighteenth Century

An *Edict on the Jews* was issued in Bologna in 1733, signed by Cardinal Lambertini, Archbishop of Bologna. It stated that Jews must 'wear the sign of yellow colour, by which they are distinguished from others, and they must always wear it in every time and place, both within the ghetto and outside it.'

Nineteenth Century

Following the fall of Napoléon in 1815, the Congress of Vienna (1815) restored the Papal States to the papacy, and thereby umbral papal power was restored to Rome. Accordingly, the city's rabbis were again forced to make their demeaning appearance at

---

[1] http://en.wikipedia.org/wiki/Yellow_badge (2007)

Carnival. They were required to dress in grotesque black outfits, with short pants and a small cloak. They had to march through the streets serving as a target for rotten food and other projectiles hurled by the jeering mobs.[1]

Twentieth Century

From 1933 to 1945, the Nazi regimes in the occupied countries of Europe forced Jews to wear an identifying mark under threat of death. There were no consistent requirements as to colour and shape: it varied from a white armband to a yellow Star of David badge. The requirement to wear the Star of David with the German word 'Jude' ('Jew') inscribed was then extended to all Jews over the age of six in the Reich and the Protectorate of Bohemia and Moravia, and was gradually introduced in other German-occupied areas, where local words were used (for example, 'Juif' in French, 'Jood' in Dutch).[2]

Synopsis

Religious restrictions imposed by Catholics have been particularly heavy on the Jews.

Synagogues, other buildings, and Jewish cemeteries were closed, stolen, and destroyed. Appropriated synagogues have rarely been returned to their rightful owners – examples of the immorality of Catholic moral theology.

Hebrew texts were prohibited and destroyed, often in vast numbers, on a multitude of occasions.

Restrictions were placed on the practice of Jewish worship.

The Church compelled Jews to wear badges, hats or other items of clothing to distinguish them from the surrounding population. This practice was adopted by Adolf Hitler for his Third Reich.

––––

[1] Kertzer, David I. *The Kidnapping of Edgardo Mortara.* pp15-16
[2] http://en.wikipedia.org/wiki/Yellow_badge (2007)

7 – Enslavement, Ghettos, Expulsions, The Black Death Holocaust

If liberty and equality, as is thought by some are chiefly to be found in democracy, they will be best attained when all persons alike share in the government to the utmost. Aristotle

Raul Hilberg, in his book *The Destruction of the European Jews*, reminds his readers that since the fourth century, there have been three major Christian ecclesiastical anti-Semitic policies, namely, conversion, expulsion, and annihilation. Each later one appeared as an alternative to the former.[1]

Enslavement

633 – St Isidore of Sevilla, during the Fourth Council of Toledo, condemned Jews as the killers of Christ, he believed that the Jews should be exiled and persecuted. He gave instruction that the Jews who persisted in the faith should be enslaved and later executed.[2]

694 – The Seventeenth Council of Toledo defined Jews as the serfs of the prince. It declared all Jews to be slaves, and ordered all their possessions to be confiscated.[3]

1179 – The Third Lateran Council confirmed the doctrine of Augustine, a Saint, that 'the Jew is the slave of the Christian'. This was soon embedded in canon law.[4]

1205 – Innocent III laid down the principle that Jews were doomed to perpetual servitude because they had crucified Jesus.

1255 – King Henry III of England sold his rights to the Jews (who were regarded as royal 'chattels') to his brother Richard for 5000 marks.[5]

1535 – All the local Jews were sold into slavery after Spanish troops captured Tunis.

During World War II, millions of Jews, Roma, Poles, other Eastern Europeans, and people of other nationalities and religions were forced to work under inhuman conditions in Nazi industries as slave labourers. Many did not survive.[6]

Ghettos through the Centuries

A ghetto was a street or part of a city set apart as a legally imposed residential area for Jews. The name 'ghetto' was first used in 1516 in Venice, when an area, guarded by Catholics, was set aside for Jews. During the previous two centuries, no Jew had been allowed to live anywhere in the city of Venice for more than 15 days per year.[7] Other names for ghetto were 'Carrière' in France, 'Judenviertel' in Germany, 'Judería' in Spain, and 'Judiaria' in Portugal.

[1] Hilberg, Raul. *The Destruction of the European Jews.* Vol I. p8. Quoted in: Weitzman, Mark. *Antisemitism: A Historical Survey* (http://motlc.wiesenthal.com/resources/education/historicalsurvey/index.html)
[2] Ibid.
[3] Kahl, Joachim. *The Misery of Christianity: A Plea for a Humanity without God.* p56
[4] Wistrich, Robert S. *Anti-Semitism: The Longest Hatred.* pp24-26
[5] http://en.wikipedia.org/wiki/Timeline_of_antisemitism (2007)
[6] http://www.religioustolerance.org/fin_nazi.htm (2007). Many other references to servitude occur in this book.
[7] http://en.wikipedia.org/wiki/Ghetto (2007)

- Ghettos were usually enclosed with high walls and gates that were kept locked at night, and during certain Church festivals. Catholic gatekeepers guarded the entrance, for whom the Jews within had to pay.[1] Lateral expansion was not allowed, so that buildings were often crammed together, resulting in unsanitary conditions and fire hazards. The popes' own Roman Ghetto, for example, held 110,000 inhabitants in an area of less than one square kilometre.[2]

The Jewish quarter, 'Judaeorum habitacula', is mentioned as early as the beginning of the eleventh century (1006-28), and is the oldest German ghetto to which there is any reference in historical sources. The Jews were granted their first privileges there in a charter of 1182.[3]

- 'By the end of the twelfth century, a walled ghetto marked most of Catholic Europe's towns.'[4]

- Ultimately, these confined areas became the unhealthy and humiliating elements of the papacy's policy of Judaic degradation.[5]

Thirteenth Century

1267 – The Synod of Breslau decreed that there be compulsory ghettos for Jews.

1294 – Jews in France were restricted to special quarters of the cities.

In England, ghettos were established at the end of the thirteenth century to segregate the Jews prior to their expulsion from the country. They were deemed to be living in England by special consent of the king and not by common right, and were, therefore, not subject to common law but to special regulations.[6]

Fourteenth to Eighteenth Centuries

Forced segregation of Jews spread throughout Europe during the fourteenth and fifteenth centuries.

1413 – The anti-Semitic Ferdinand of Aragón issued a decree against the Jews of Majorca by which they were compelled to dwell exclusively in the Jewish quarter, and were forbidden to: eat or drink with Christians; employ Christian nurses or other servants; attend Christian marriages or funerals; hold any public office; carry weapons, such as swords or daggers; use any costly material for their clothes; wear silk, fur, or any ornaments; sell any foodstuffs to Christians; make them gifts of pastry, meats, or drinks; be physicians to them, or to give them any medicine.

Moreover, they had to wear the badge that marked the Jew. Christian women, whether married or unmarried, and courtesans, were strictly prohibited from visiting the

---

[1] Flannery, Edward H. *The Anguish of the Jews*. p146
[2] Ibid.
[3] http://www.jewishencyclopedia.com/view.jsp?artid=126&letter=R (2007)
[4] Michael, Robert. *A History of Catholic Antisemitism: The Dark Side of the Church*. p49
[5] Ibid. p96
[6] Cheyney, Edward P. *A Short History of England*. Quoted in: Sparks, Thomas. *The Curse of Cain and Theologically Correct Social Policy toward the Jews*.

Jews' quarter by day or night. Jews who wished to be baptised were not to be deterred by any one from their resolve; and the officers of the king were ordered to prevent Jewish women who had converted to Christianity from emigrating to Africa, since they were reported to revert to Judaism when there and then send for their children to follow them.[1]

1480 – At the Cortes of Toledo, all Jews were ordered to be separated in special 'barrios' ('quarters'), and this was also ordered at the Cortes of Fraga, Aragón, two years later. The same law was enforced in Navarre, where they were ordered to be confined to the Juderías at night.[2]

. The Castilian *Ghetto Edict* was passed in 1412, the Venetian Ghetto was established in 1516, while the Roman Ghetto was established in 1555 by the Bull *Cum nimis absurdum* promulgated by Paul IV. This bull segregated the Jews, who had lived freely in Rome since antiquity, in a walled quarter with three gates that were locked at night, and subjected them to various restrictions on their personal freedom (such as limits to the allowed professions), and degradations (like compulsory Catholic sermons on the Jewish Shabbat). During the next three centuries, similar ghettos were established in most of the countries of Europe. The Jews were allowed only one synagogue in each city. In the Papal States, Jews were forced to live exclusively in ghettos.

The Roman Ghetto:

> The area of Rome chosen for the ghetto was the most undesirable quarter of the city, owing to constant flooding by the River Tiber. [It was malarial.] At the time of its founding, the four-block area was designated to contain roughly 2,000 inhabitants. However, over the years, the Jewish community grew, which caused severe overcrowding. Since the area could not expand horizontally (the ghetto was surrounded by high walls), the Jews built vertical additions to their houses, which blocked the sun from reaching the already dank and narrow streets. Life in the Roman Ghetto was one of crushing poverty, due to the severe restrictions placed upon the professions that Jews were allowed to perform ...

> In 1798, during the Roman Republic, the Ghetto was legally abolished, and the Tree of Freedom was planted in Piazza delle Scole, but [the Ghetto] *was reinstated as soon as the Papacy regained control.* In 1848, during the brief revolution, the Ghetto was abolished once more, again temporarily. The Jews had to petition annually for permission to live there, and were disabled from owning any property even in the Ghetto. They paid a yearly tax for the privilege; formality and tax survived until 1850. They had to swear yearly loyalty to the Pope by the Arch of Titus (it celebrates the Roman sack of Jerusalem).[3,4]

---

[1] http://en.wikipedia.org/wiki/History_of_the_Jews_in_the_Baleric_Islands (2010)
[2] http://en.wikipedia.org/wiki/History_of_the_Jews_in_Spain (2008)
[3] http://en.wikipedia.org/wiki/Ghetto (2007)
[4] http://en.wikipedia.org/wiki/Roman_Ghetto (2007)

A ghetto was established in 1624 in Ferrara, Italy. An *Edict on the Jews* was issued in Bologna in 1733 signed by Cardinal Lambertini, Archbishop of Bologna; it stated that Jews were to remain in the ghetto every night.[1]

'A Jewish ghetto is a better proof of the truth of the religion of Jesus Christ than a whole school of theologians,' said the 18th century Catholic publicist G B Roberti.[2,3]

Nineteenth Century

Leo XII (1823-1829) confined the Jews living in the Papal States to the old ghettoes, reinstated the old restrictions on their movements and on their interaction with Christians, subjected them to the Inquisition, and ordered that their property be confiscated. In 1825 the Cardinal Vicar of Rome recorded the new determination:

> The Jews living in Rome, having obtained an expansion of the ancient ghetto, by which any reasonable pretext they had of overcrowding and unhealthiness has been removed, have received the last, formal order to separate themselves totally from the Christians. They must close themselves once again in the Ghetto with all of their possessions within the fixed time of one month.

The next year, the Cardinal Vicar issued another proclamation:

> His Holiness after having over the past year given the opportune orders for the return of all the Jews to the Ghetto ... has recently prescribed the following further orders so that the Jews ... not leave the Ghettoes and go wandering about without any licence as they had been doing before.

> Beginning this August 20, no Jew living in the Rome Ghetto will be able to leave, even for a single day, if he does not have a written permit ... from our Criminal Tribunal which gives legitimate grounds for his absence. ... while they are away from the Ghetto, the Jews shall not be allowed to live or converse in a familiar way with Christians.[4,5]

The papacy continued exhorting other Italian states to follow its own subjugation.

In the early nineteenth century, successive waves of cholera swept through Europe. Accordingly, in 1836 the Pope established a new public health commission, which asked one of its members, Prince Pietro Odescalchi, to examine conditions in the Roman Ghetto. The Prince commenced by reading all the documents on the Ghetto that had been gathered by a former commission. This led him to write:

> If the reading of those materials moved me to a deep commiseration for the unhappy fate of the inhabitants of that part of Rome, that commiseration, I must confess, grew

---

[1] Kertzer, David I. *The Kidnapping of Edgardo Mortara.* pp37-38
[2] Wistrich, Robert S. *Anti-Semitism: The Longest Hatred.* p23
[3] http://www.therefinersfire.org/christian_antisemitism.htm (2013)
[4] Kertzer, David I. *The Popes Against the Jews: The Vatican's Role in the Rise of Modern ...* pp66-67
[5] Of such were 'the untiring and energetic efforts of the Roman pontiffs in behalf of the Jews'.

a thousand times as great when, just last week, I decided to go in person ... to walk the ghetto streets, and to go into some of those hovels which I would be going beyond the bounds of truth to call dwellings.

He observed one case in which 'in three miserable rooms seven families were enclosed.' Over all, the crowded residents, he reported:

languish in the clutches of untold misery. Tiny, foetid rooms house eight or twelve people, built in such a way that they lack any air, and light shines in only from the door ... and only a little fireplace allows those miserable souls a glimmer of light at night.[1]

Fr Giuseppe Oreglia di Santo Stefano, one of the founders of *La Civiltà Cattolica*, proposed a return to the old laws separating Jews from Christian society. He likened the Jews to wolves alongside the Christian sheep.[2]

⊱ The Church's ghettos were largely abolished in Europe as a consequence of the French Revolution and the liberal movements of the nineteenth century. The Venetian Ghetto was abolished after the fall of the Republic of Venice to Napoléon in 1797. The requirement that Jews live within the Pope's Roman Ghetto, the last legally compulsory ghetto in Europe, was abolished when the final remnant of the Papal States was overthrown in 1870. The City of Rome tore down the Ghetto's walls in 1888 and demolished it almost completely – the area was then reconstructed around a new synagogue.

Expulsions through the Centuries

Jews have been expelled from nearly every town, city and country in which they have resided.

Thomas Sparks, in *The Curse of Cain and Theologically Correct Social Policy toward the Jews*,[3] provides a revealing list of places, many of which were predominantly Roman Catholic, from which the Jews were expelled. Most of them are listed below. In several places there were repeated expulsions. This usually arose because the economy of the locality was found to be dependent on the business activities of the Jews, hence they were re-admitted for economic reasons, and then later expelled again.

The fourteenth and fifteenth centuries appear to have been the worst in this regard.

Table 7, below, summarises the situation by providing a vivid picture of the enormity of the extent of these expulsions of Jews from Christian territory. It comprises only a sample of such places and dates.

---

[1] Kertzer, David I. *The Popes Against the Jews: The Vatican's Role in the Rise of Modern Anti-Semitism*. pp72-73
[2] Ibid. p138
[3] http://www.stormfront.org/posterity/ci/curseofcain.html (2007)

Table 7. A Sample of Dates and Places of Expulsion of the Jews

250 Carthage	1439 Augsburg	1590 Lombardy
415 Alexandria	1446 Bavaria	1593 Bologna
554 Diocese of Clement	1453 Breslau	1593 Brandenburg
561 Diocese of Uzès	1453 Franconia	1593 Papal States
576 Clermont	1454 Würzburg	1597 Cremona
613 Visigoth Spain	1483 Lithuania	1597 Lodi
629 Kingdom of Franks	1483 Portugal	1597 Pavia
855 Italy	1483 Sicily	1614 Frankfort
876 Sens	1485 Vicenza	1615 France
1010 France	1485 Warsaw, etc.	1615 Worms
1012 Mainz	1492 Spain	1619 Kiev
1026 Limoges, etc.	1493 Sicily	1649 Ukraine
1181 France	1495 Lithuania	1656 Lithuania
1240 Brittany	1497 Portugal	1670 Vienna
1275 Cambridge, etc.	1499 Germany	1682 Southern France
1289 Gascony & Anjou	1510 Prussia	1712 Sandomierz
1290 England	1514 Strasbourg	1738 Württemberg
1290 Southern Italy	1519 Regensburg	1744 Bohemia
1294 Berne	1540 Naples	1744 Livonia
1306 France	1540 Prague	1745 Moravia
1348 Switzerland	1542 Bohemia	1753 Kovad
1349 Heilbronn	1550 Genova	1761 Bordeaux
1350 much of Germany	1551 Bavaria, etc.	1775 Warsaw
1360 Hungary	1555 Pesaro	1789 Alsace
1386 Swabian League	1557 Prague	1815 Bavaria
1388 Strasbourg	1558 Recanati	1815 Bremen
1394 France	1559 Austria	1815 Franconia
1394 Germany	1561 Prague	1815 Lübeck
1420 Lyon	1565 Prague	1815 Swabia
1422 Austria	1567 Genoese Republic	1820 Bremen
1424 Fribourg	1567 Würzburg	1843 Austria
1424 Zurich	1569 Papal States	1843 Prussia
1426 Cologne	1571 Brandenburg	1866 Galatz (Galaţi)
1432 Saxony	1582 Hungary	1919 Bavaria
1438 Mainz	1582 Netherlands	1938-45 Nazi areas

Fifth Century

415 – The bishop of Alexandria, St Cyril, expelled Jews from Alexandria and gave the mob Jewish property:

> The antagonism thus stimulated found its natural expression, in 415, in the turbulent city of Alexandria, where quarrels arose resulting in the shedding of Christian blood, when St Cyril took advantage of the excitement by leading a mob to the synagogues, of which he took possession, and then abandoned the property of the Jews to pillage and expelled them from the city, which they had inhabited since its foundation by Alexander.[1]

Seventh Century

612 – In the Iberian Peninsula, when Sisebut became king of the Visigoths, matters became bad for the Jews. They were accused, inter alia, of violating the laws of the Third Council of Toledo. Accordingly, Sisebut ordered that the Jews be expelled from Spain. Many Jews overtly converted to Christianity, but many also left Spain and settled in France. Sisebut died in 621, whereupon many of the forcibly baptised Jews returned openly to Judaism.

629 – The Frankish King Dagobert I, encouraged by Byzantine Emperor Heraclius, expelled all Jews from the kingdom.

633 – Under the driving force of Bishop Isidor of Sevilla, the civil authorities enacted new and harsher legislation against the Jews.

The Jewish population in Spain remained sufficiently sizeable to prompt King Wamba (672-680) to issue limited expulsion orders against them.

Eleventh Century

1010 – The Bishop of Limoges ordered the expulsion of Jews from France for refusing to convert to Christianity. Some Jews fled the persecution, others were put to death, and others killed themselves.[2]

1012 – Emperor Henry II of Germany expelled Jews from Mainz; this was the beginning of general persecutions against Jews in Germany.

1026 – The French chronicler Raoul Glaber blamed the Jews for the destruction of the Church of the Holy Sepulchre, which was destroyed in 1009 by (Muslim) Caliph Al-Hakim. As a result, Jews were expelled from Limoges and other French towns.[3]

Twelfth Century

1181-1182 – Jews were expelled from France by King Philippe Auguste, all their property was confiscated, and Catholics' debts to them were cancelled with the payment of one-fifth of their value going to the treasury.

---

[1] Lea, Henry Charles. *A History* of the *Inquisition* of *Spain.* Vol I. pp37-40
[2] http://www.atheistresource.co.uk/christjew.html (2007)
[3] http://en.wikipedia.org/wiki/Timeline_of_antisemitism (2007)

Thirteenth Century

1240 – Duke Jean le Roux expelled Jews from Brittany.
Innocent IV (1243-54) wrote:

> We who long with all our hearts for the salvation of souls, grant you full authority by these present letters to banish the Jews, either in your own person or through the agency of others, especially since, as we have been informed, they do not abide by the regulations drawn up for them by this Holy See. (*To the King of France*)[1]

1254 – Louis IX expelled the Jews from France. Their property and synagogues were confiscated.

1289 – Jews were expelled from Gascony and Anjou.

As commerce in Europe grew in the late Middle Ages, some Jews became prominent in trade and banking. The resultant Jewish economic and cultural successes tended to arouse the envy of the public. This resentment, combined with traditional Catholic prejudice, incited the forced expulsion of Jews from several countries or regions, including England (1290), Germany (1350s), Spain (1492), Portugal (1496), Provence (1512), and the Papal States (1569). The outcome of these mass expulsions was that the centres of Jewish life shifted to Turkey and then to Poland and Russia.[2]

Fourteenth Century

1306 – King Philippe IV ('Philippe the Fair')[3] of France, imprisoned all 100,000 Jews of his realm. They were told to leave the country within one month. They could only take the clothes on their backs and provisions for one day. The property they left behind was used by Philippe to replenish the royal treasury.

1322 – King Charles IV expelled the Jews from France.

The Black Death Holocaust

In 1348 the devastating bacterial disease 'the Black Death' ('the Plague') arrived in Europe. It lasted until 1351. It is estimated to have killed between 25 to 60 percent of all Europeans. Because the biology of the disease was not understood, many Christians believed that it was a form of divine punishment – retribution for sins such as blasphemy and heresy. Ergo, the only way to overcome the plague was to win God's forgiveness by purging the community of heretics and the like. For this reason many thousands of Jews were massacred in 1348 and 1349.

Additionally, the largely illiterate Catholic population[4] credulously blamed the Jews for directly causing the plague. Charges were that they poisoned the wells with a powder

---

[1] http://www.romancatholicism.org/popes-jews.html (2014)
[2] *Encyclopaedia Britannica*
[3] King Philippe was also a partner of Pope Clement V in the purposeful destruction of the Knights Templar, solely for the financial gain of both parties.
[4] Refer to Volume 1 of *'A Corrupt Tree'* to discover why the Church kept the laity ignorant.

derived from portions of the Basilisk.[1,2] 'Christians everywhere in Europe went on a murderous rampage against Jews, burning them alive wherever they found them.'[3] The massacres spread throughout Spain, France, Germany and Austria. In excess of 200 Jewish communities were destroyed. Many communities were expelled. For example, in 1349, in Basel, 600 Jews were burned at the stake, 140 children were forcibly baptised; the remaining Jews were expelled.

Late Fourteenth Century

1386 – Holy Roman Emperor Wenceslaus, nicknamed 'der Faule' ('the Idle'), expelled the Jews from the Swabian League and Strasbourg, and confiscated their property.

During the fourteenth century, the Jews in Catholic Spain lost their legal rights, their prosperity, and the level of culture which they had acquired. All of these disappeared through the endemic religious hatred, which had persisted since Visigothic times. The rate of baptisms greatly accelerated. Persecutions and massacres were frequent, the severest taking place in 1391. Jews were removed from public office permanently; they were also prohibited from engaging in commerce, from working at a trade, and ultimately were forced to live within walled ghettos, known as juderías, where they were often massacred. In May 1355, for example, in the Judería of Toledo 1200 men, women and children were slaughtered.[4] This long, tragic history finally resulted in the literal destruction of Spanish Jewry in the fifteenth century via the *Edict of Expulsion* of 1492.

Fifteenth Century

1474 – Isabel (Isabella la Católica) became Queen regnant of Castile and León. She and her husband Ferdinand (Fernando II of Aragón) became, in the words of Pope Alexander VI, 'the Catholic Kings' ('Los Reyes Católicos'). In 1492 they conquered Granada, the last Muslim stronghold in Europe. Later, after having lived there for 800 years, Muslims were expelled from the Iberian Peninsula. This was fatal for the Jews, because the Spanish Muslims had given Jews the best homeland they had ever had since the Diaspora.

The Spanish Holocaust

1492 – The *Alhambra Decree* (*Edict of Expulsion*) (*Decreto de la Alhambra, Edicto*

---

[1] The lethal Basilisk, the king of serpents, was one of the many creatures adopted by Catholic mythology ('faith') from the pagans. Saint Isidore, Archbishop of Sevilla, defined it as the king of snakes, due to its lethal glare and its poisonous breath. The Venerable Bede, a Doctor of the Church, was the first to attest to the legend of the birth of a basilisk from an egg by an old cockerel. The theologian Alexander Neckam claimed that not the glare, but the 'air corruption', was the killing tool of the Basilisk, a theory developed one century later by Pietro d'Abano, a professor of medicine. In his *De animalibus*, Saint Albertus Magnus, 'the wonder and the miracle of his age' (*Catholic Encyclopedia*) wrote about the Basilisk's killing gaze.

[2] Michael, Robert. *A History of Catholic Antisemitism: The Dark Side of the Church.* p72

[3] http://www.sixmillioncrucifixions.com/Blaming_the_Jews_for_the_Black_Death_plague.html (2015)

[4] Markman, Sidney David. *Jewish Remnants in Spain: Wanderings in a Lost World.* p60

de Granada) was an edict issued on 31 March by the joint Catholic Monarchs of Spain Isabel I[1] and Ferdinand II ordering the expulsion of Jews from the Kingdom of Spain and its territories and possessions by 31 July of that year. The Jews were permitted to take their property provided it was not in gold, silver, or money. The *Edict* and its fateful consequences are examined in greater detail in Chapter 10.

For hundreds of years after the expulsion, the conversos were seen as being alien to the 'purity' of Spanish society. This obsession with racial purity anticipated that of the Nazis, and the racist fervour helped bring about the decline of Spain through impoverishment of the population, and contempt for the productive and commercial occupations.[2] Rafael Cansinos Assens, one of the most important modern Spanish authors, wrote that the consequence of the edict of expulsion was that the Jews disappeared from Spain and from its literature. The Jew was thereby erased from the consciousness of Spaniards.[3]

Those Jews who were fortunate enough to reach the Ottoman Empire had a better fate, the Sultan Bayezid II was known to have sarcastically thanked Ferdinand for sending him some of his best subjects – thus impoverishing Ferdinand's own lands while enriching Bayezid's.[4] In fact, Constantinople became the site of the largest Jewish community in Europe during the sixteenth century.

In his *A Short History of Christianity*, John Mackinnon Robertson summed up the consequences of the Church's evangelism:

> And centuries after the barbarian heathenism of Europe was ostensibly drowned in blood, Christian Spain, having overthrown the Moslem Moors, proceeded in the same fashion to dragoon Moslems and Jews into the true faith, baptising in droves those who yielded or dissembled, and driving out of the country myriads more who would not submit. *The misery and the butchery wrought from first to last are unimaginable.*[5]

Henry Charles Lea gave a poignant description of the Church's gross barbarity to the Jews and conversos of Spain:

> while the object of the inquisition was to secure the unity of faith, its founding destroyed the hope that ultimately the Jews would all be gathered into the fold of Christ. This had been the justification of the inhuman laws designed to render existence outside of the church so intolerable that baptism would be sought as a relief from endless injustice, but the awful spectacle of the autos da fé and the miseries attendant on wholesale confiscations *led the Jew to cherish more resolutely than ever the ancestral faith* which served him as shield from the terrors of the holy office

---

[1] Within the Church, there exists a lobby to canonise Queen Isabella. See, for example: http://www.prayfor spain.com/comment/index9.html (2008). The Holy See recognises Queen Isabella as a 'Servant of God' – http://www.queenisabel.com (2008) – the inference being that the Catholic God favoured the expulsion of the Jews.
[2] Wistrich, Robert S. *Anti-Semitism: The Longest Hatred.* pp36-37
[3] *Los judios en la literatura espanola.* p31
[4] http://en.wikipedia.org/wiki/History_of_the_Jews_in_Spain (2008)
[5] Robertson, John Mackinnon. *A Short History of Christianity.* p101

and the dreadful fate ever impending over the conversos.[1]

Late Fifteenth Century

1492 – The Jews of Mecklenburg were accused of stabbing a consecrated wafer – twenty seven were burned. All the Jews were expelled from the Duchy.

1493 – The Jews were expelled from Sicily.

Sixteenth Century

1540 – All Jews were banished from Prague.

1550 – Dr Joseph Hacohen was chased out of Genoa for practising medicine; soon all Jews were expelled.

1558 – The Jews were expelled from Recanati, Italy.

1569 – Pius V expelled from the Papal States all Jews dwelling outside of the ghettos of Rome, Ancona, and Avignon.

1593 – Clement VIII expelled all 900 Jews from the city of Bologna and its surrounding territories.[2]

Seventeenth and Eighteenth Centuries

King Louis XIII of France decreed in 1615 that all Jews must leave the country within one month on pain of death.

Maria Theresa, Catholic Queen of Hungary and Bohemia[3] (1717-1780):

> Henceforth no Jew, no matter under what name, will be allowed to remain here without my written permission. I know of no other troublesome pest within the state than this race, which impoverishes the people by their fraud, usury and money-lending and commits all deeds which an honourable man despises. Subsequently they have to be removed and excluded from here as much as possible.[4]

Synopsis

The Church was a prominent slaver. It approved general slavery of the Jews.

Ghettoisation spread throughout Europe. Ghettos became one of the unhealthy and humiliating elements of the papacy's policy of Judaic degradation. The conditions in the pope's own Roman Ghetto was appalling.

Jews have been expelled by Catholics from almost every country of the world in which they have lived.

The Black Death Holocaust followed the eruption of the disease in 1348. In excess of 200 Jewish communities were destroyed by credulous Catholics.

————

[1] Lea, Henry Charles. *History of the Inquisition of Spain*. Vol 1. p131. Further details are given in Chapter 10.

[2] Kertzer, David I. *The Kidnapping of Edgardo Mortara*. p x 'Prologue'

[3] Bohemia – a kingdom constituting approximately the westernmost two-thirds of what is now the Czech Republic.

[4] Quoted in: Sparks, Thomas. *The Curse of Cain and Theologically Correct Social Policy toward the Jews*. http://www.stormfront.org/posterity/ci/curseofcain.html (2006)

8 – Misapplied Catholic Credulity – Ritual Murder, Blood Libel, Desecration of the Host

I don't think anyone has been slandered more than the Jews. Fidel Castro

Accusations of Ritual Murder and the Blood Libel, and their Consequences through the Centuries

One of the most potent themes in the popular Catholic perception of the Jew throughout the Middle Ages and into early modern times was that of a sorcerer and a magician. This conception underlay the multitude of accusations that Jews were: spreaders of disease, poisoners of wells, desecrators of the Host, and murderers of Christian children. These perceived forms of magic bore no relation to the actual magic practices of Jews.[1]

One of the most bizarre, tenacious, notorious and disastrous Christian myths was that of 'Ritual murder'. In its popular version it claimed that Jews murdered Christian children and used their blood in the preparation of their Passover (Pesach) unleavened bread (matzah). The Jews were said to kidnap Christian children and whip them and crown them with thorns before drawing off their blood for mixing into the unleavened bread.[2] This was the infamous 'Blood Libel'.[3] It rendered the Jew a figure of sinister horror, whom the common people came to despise, fear and hate with fanatical intensity.[4]

In those times, thanks to the efforts of the Church, very few people doubted that Jewish ceremonies, such as the Passover service, Purim[5], circumcisions, and weddings, needed the use of this Christian blood.[6] Today, its absurdity has been established conclusively.[7]

This Jewish use of human blood was a *fact* of mediaeval Catholicism. Such blood was notoriously known, for example, to be employed in the sorcery and rituals of witches. The use of blood to write a compact with the Devil, which became characteristic of the Church's later 'knowledge' of witchcraft, is mentioned as early as the thirteenth century.[8]

Consequently, Blood Libels became a common form of anti-Semitism during the Middle Ages. The pattern was generally that:

a corpse was found, usually of a Christian child, and often close to Easter;

Jews were accused of having committed the murder to obtain the blood for use in their rituals;

---

[1] Saperstein, Mark. 'Foreword' to: Trachtenberg, Joshua. *The Devil and the Jews: The Medieval ...* p viii-ix
[2] http://en.wikipedia.org/wiki/Ritual_murder (2007)
[3] See, for example: http://remember.org/guide/History.root.classical.html (2015)
[4] Trachtenberg, Joshua. *The Devil and the Jews: The Medieval Conception of the Jew and its Relation ...* p124
[5] Purim (פּוּרִים) – a Jewish holy day commemorating the Jews' deliverance from massacre by Haman.
[6] Trachtenberg, Joshua. *The Devil and the Jews: The Medieval Conception of the Jew and its Relation ...* p31
[7] Ibid. p124
[8] Ibid. p140

the principal rabbis and/or community leaders were detained and tortured until they confessed their guilt;

finally, either the whole community was expelled, or most of its members were tortured, or the community was exterminated. This sequence was repeated generation after generation.

• More than 150 charges of ritual murder are listed in the *Jewish Encyclopedia*; but these are believed in all probability to be no more than a fraction of the whole.[1]

' In some cases the alleged victim of this human sacrifice became venerated as a martyr. A few have been beatified and some have even been canonised as saints. Most of the accusations arose from the clergy, who profited from the martyr and his shrine bringing credulous pilgrims and offerings in the propagandised belief of spiritual benefits.[2]

- Joshua Trachtenberg, in his book *The Devil and the Jews*, quotes a German publication which states that the Jewish unleavened bread, baked with Christian blood, 'has' (in the twentieth century), according to Christian belief, peculiar magical virtues among Christians. In particular, there is widespread belief throughout rural sections of Germany and Eastern Europe that a piece of Judenmatz 'has' the power to: extinguish fires and prevent house fire; protect houses, men, and animals against lightning and hail; protect clothing against moths; and prevent the paralysis of bodily organs which witches can produce.[3]

Twelfth Century

William of Norwich (1144) – The first recorded instance of such a Blood Libel in Europe occurred in the twelfth-century legend surrounding William of Norwich. This was turned into a cult; with William acquiring the status of martyr, and crowds of pilgrims bringing wealth to the local church. The libel was encouraged by an account, *The Life and Miracles of William of Norwich*, a multi-volume work by Thomas of Monmouth, a monk in the Norwich Benedictine monastery. In it, the Jews declared their intention 'to kill the Christian as we killed Christ;' and an informant apostate Jew named Theobald was declared to have reported:

> It was laid down by [the Jews] in ancient times that every year they must sacrifice a Christian in some part of the world to the Most High God in scorn and contempt of Christ ... Wherefore the leaders and Rabbis of the Jews who dwell in Spain assemble together at Narbonne ... and they cast lots for all the countries which the Jews inhabit ... and the place whose lot is drawn has to fulfil the duty imposed by authority.[4]

This, the earliest recorded account of Jewish ritual murder, is ornamented with the proposition of an international Jewish conspiracy against Christians that was allegedly

---

[1] See, for example: Trachtenberg, Joshua. *The Devil and the Jews: The Medieval Conception of the Jew and its Relation to Modern Anti-Semitism.* p125
[2] Ibid. p124
[3] Ibid. p147
[4] http://www.fordham.edu/halsall/source/1173williamnorwich.asp (2012)

sanctioned by ancient Hebrew texts.[1] It led to the killing of Jewish leaders.

1171 – Blois, France, was the site of a Blood Libel accusation against its Jewish community which led to at least 31 Jews being burned to death.

1181 – A ritual murder charge was made at Bury St Edmunds, England. In 1183 the same charge was made in Bristol, and in 1192 in Winchester.

Thirteenth Century

1230s – Gregory IX placed the responsibility for rooting out heretics with members of the Franciscan and Dominican orders. These friars soon came to be seen by the Jews as their worst enemies, for it was they, who for many centuries, oversaw virtually all the anti-Semitic activities of the clergy.[2]

1235 – Fulda, Germany, a blood-libel charge was laid that on Christmas Day, while their parents were at church, five boys were killed and their blood was collected in bags smeared with wax. Thirty-four Jews were then burned to death.[3]

1244 – Jews in London were accused of ritual murder and were assessed a large amount of money as punishment.

c.1250 – Thomas of Cantimpré[4] wrote:

> It is quite certain that the Jews of every province annually decide by lot which congregation or city is to send Christian blood to the other congregations.

Thomas also believed that since the time when the Jews called out to Pilate, 'His blood be on us, and on our children' (*Matthew* 27:25), they have been afflicted with haemorrhages:

> A very learned Jew, who in our day has been converted to the [Catholic] faith, informs us that one enjoying the reputation of a prophet among them, toward the close of his life, made the following prediction: 'Be assured that relief from this secret ailment, to which you are exposed, can only be obtained through Christian blood ("solo sanguine Christiano").' This suggestion was followed by the ever-blind and impious Jews, who instituted the custom of annually shedding Christian blood in every province, in order that they might recover from their malady.[5]

Dominguito del Val (1250) – A famous case of alleged ritual murder occurred in 1250, in Zaragoza, Spain. The alleged victim was a choirboy, Dominguito del Val. It was claimed that the Jews of Zaragoza plotted to kill every Christian in the town. To accomplish this, they needed a Christian heart. They captured the innocent Dominguito on Good Friday, re-enacted Jesus' trial by Pilate and Caiaphas in celebration – with Dominguito as Jesus – then ritually murdered him by crucifixion. Fortunately for the Christians, the henchman sent to complete the ritual stopped by a church for reasons

---

[1] Carroll, James. *Constantine's Sword: The Church and the Jews.* p273
[2] Kertzer, David I. *The Popes Against the Jews: The Vatican's Role in the Rise of Modern Anti-Semitism.* p153
[3] Trachtenberg, Joshua. *The Devil and the Jews: The Medieval Conception of the Jew and its ...* pp135-37
[4] Cantimpré is a monastery near Cambrai – in what is now northern France.
[5] http://en.wikipedia.org/wiki/Blood_libel (2013)

unclear and was found with the boy's heart. He confessed, and all the Jews of Zaragoza were put to the gallows. King Alfonso 'the Wise' allegedly wrote the original version of the story in 1250, saying 'We have heard it said that some very cruel Jews, in memory of the Passion of Our Lord on Good Friday, kidnapped a Christian boy and crucified him.'[1] Dominguito was canonised, and became the patron saint of altar boys, acolytes and choirboys.[2]

Dominguito remained a saint for around seven hundred years. However, Saint Dominguito is no longer included in the official Roman Catholic liturgical calendar. Nevertheless, there is still a chapel dedicated to him in the cathedral of Zaragoza. The *Catholic Encyclopedia* records that the relics of Saint Dominguito del Val 'a boy of seven who was crucified[3] by the Jews' are preserved in the chapel.[4] In the Church of St Nicholas in Sevilla there is an altar devoted to Dominguito who was 'murdered by Jews in 1250.'[5]

In Spain the ritual murder myth was incorporated in the law: 'We have heard it said that in certain places on Good Friday the Jews do steal children and set them on the cross in a mocking manner.' (*Siete Partidas*, Code, 1263).[6]

Little Saint Hugh of Lincoln (1255) – The case of Little Saint Hugh of Lincoln, England, is mentioned by Geoffrey Chaucer, and thus also became well known. A child of eight years, named Hugh, disappeared in 1255. His body was discovered later, covered with filth, in a pit or well belonging to a Jewish man named Copin or Koppin. On being promised by a judge that his life would be spared, Copin is said to have confessed that the boy had been crucified by the Jews, who had assembled at Lincoln for that purpose. The chronicler Matthew Paris related 'the Child was first fattened for ten days with white bread and milk and then ... almost all the Jews of England were invited to the crucifixion.'[7] King Henry III, on reaching Lincoln some five weeks later, refused to honour the promise, and had Copin executed, and had 91 of the Jews of Lincoln seized and sent up to London, where 18 of them were also executed.[8]

Meanwhile, the Cathedral in Lincoln was beginning to benefit from the event, as Hugh was seen as a Christian martyr; and sites associated with his life became objects of pilgrimage.

The legend surrounding Hugh that emerged became part of popular culture, and his story became the subject of poetry and folk songs. An English Benedictine monk, Matthew Paris, compiled *Historia Anglorum*, a diary of events, anecdotes and the like

---

[1] The legend is described in detail at http://en.wikipedia.org/wiki/Saint_Dominguito_del_Val (2013)

[2] http://en.wikipedia.org/wiki/Saint_Dominguito_del_Val (2007)

[3] The *Catholic Encyclopedia* states categorically that the boy 'was crucified'. There is no admission that he 'is alleged to have been crucified'.

[4] *Catholic Encyclopedia* 'Saragossa'

[5] http://www.jcpa.org/phas/phas-perednik-f03.htm (2007)

[6] http://www.zionism-israel.com/his/judeophobia6.htm (2007)

[7] Ibid.

[8] http://en.wikipedia.org/wiki/Blood_libel_against_Jews#Actual_Jewish_practices_regarding_blood_and_sacrifice (2007)

from 1236 to 1259. In it, he reported about some Jews in Norwich who were charged with circumcising a Christian boy, intending to crucify him:

> Four of the Jews, therefore, having been found guilty of the aforesaid crime, were first dragged at the tails of horses, and afterwards hung on a gibbet, where they breathed forth the wretched remains of life.[1]

1263 – In Spain the *Code of the Seven Parties* stated: 'We have heard that in certain places during Holy Friday the Jews kidnap children and they mockingly put them on the cross.'[2]

1267 – Pforzheim, Germany – the corpse of a seven-year-old girl was found in the river by fishermen. The Jews were suspected, and when they were led to the corpse, blood allegedly began to flow from the wounds, the face of the child became flushed, and both arms were raised. In addition to these alleged miracles, there was the testimony of the daughter of the woman who had allegedly sold the child to the Jews. In reprisal, a judicial murder was committed against the Jews.[3]

1270 – Weissenburg in Alsace – The body of a child was found in the Lauter River. The Jews were accused of suspending him by the feet, and of opening every artery in his body in order to obtain all the blood. The wounds were said to have bled for five days.

1285 – A Blood Libel in Munich resulted in the death of 68 Jews. 180 more Jews were burned alive at the synagogue.[4]

At Oberwesel, Germany, the corpse of a child was said to have floated up the Rhine (against the current) emitting radiance and being invested with healing powers. Accordingly, local Jews and those of other adjacent localities were severely persecuted during the years 1286 to 1289.

The statement was made, in the *Chronicle* of one Konrad Justinger of 1423, that in 1294, at Bern, Switzerland, the Jews had tortured and murdered a boy called Rudolph. The historical impossibility of this widely credited story has been demonstrated.

Blood Libel myths were repeated in both literature and the arts throughout Christendom. About a century after the expulsion of the Jews from England in the thirteenth century, the cultural theme is found in James Joyce's *Ulysses* and was the plot of the *Prioress' Tale* by Geoffrey Chaucer, in which Jews obey their demonic master and kill a child: 'likewise murdered so by cursed Jews ...'[5]

Fifteenth Century

1431 – A ritual murder charge led to the destruction of the southern German Jewish communities of Ravensburg, Uberlingen and Lindau.

---

[1] Burl, Aubrey. *God's Heretics: The Albigensian Crusade.* p181
[2] http://www.jcpa.org/phas/phas-perednik-f03.htm (2007)
[3] http://en.wikipedia.org/wiki/Blood_libel_against_Jews#Actual_Jewish_practices_regarding_blood_and_
     sacrifice (2007)
[4] http://en.wikipedia.org/wiki/Timeline_of_antisemitism (2007)
[5] See, for example: Michael, Robert. *A History of Catholic Antisemitism: The Dark Side of the Church.* p43

c.1451 – San Giovanni da Capestrano (St John of Capistrano) was appointed by Pope Nicholas V to the office of Papal Inquisitor against the Jews. He was a great orator, and in his sermons he repeated the charges of ritual murder and Host desecration that led to Jewish persecutions in Breslau under King Władysław of Silesia,[1] where many Jews were tortured and burned alive, and many committed suicide. Additionally, 36 Jews were burned in the Berlin marketplace, and the entire Jewish community of Liegnitz (Legnica) was burned to death because of John's incitement of mobs. He also instigated the abolition of Jewish rights in Naples and other towns, while in Bavaria, he forced the authorities to require that Jews wear a badge, to expel them from several villages, and to have their Christian debts cancelled. Additionally, he manoeuvred Kazimierz IV, King of Poland, to abolish Jewish rights in that country. This set off a train of anti-Jewish violence. San Giovanni was also responsible for a papal edict that prohibited the transportation of Jews to the Land of Israel. He was known as 'the scourge of the Jews'.[2]

For his 'good' works, Giovanni was later canonised. He is still venerated and has a feast day of 28 March.[3] There is an extant ornate pulpit of San Giovanni da Capestrano at the Stefansdom (St Stephen's Cathedral) in Vienna.[4]

1462 – At Rinn, near Innsbruck, a boy was said to have been bought by Jewish merchants and cruelly murdered by them in a forest near the city; his blood being carefully collected in vessels. The accusation of drawing off the blood (without murder) was not made until the beginning of the seventeenth century, when the cult was founded. This cult continued until it was officially prohibited in 1994.

Simon of Trentino (1475) – The case of Simon of Trentino, Italy, was particularly infamous. In 1475 the friar Bernardino da Feltre announced that 'the sins of the Jews were to be soon manifested to all.' A few days later, Simon, aged two, disappeared and his corpse was soon found near the house of the head of the Jewish community. His father alleged that he had been kidnapped and murdered by the Jews. The whole Jewish community was arrested, including women and children. Seventeen of them were tortured until they 'confessed', some dying from the treatment. The few who converted to Christianity were strangled, and the rest were burned at the stake. Their property was confiscated. In 1476 a papal court of inquiry justified the libel. Sixtus IV endorsed the 'legality' of the trial, and Simon was beatified, and has been venerated as a martyr ever since. In 1588 Simon was declared to be a Saint by Sixtus V. His feast day was 24 March. His entry in the *Roman Martyrology*[5] for March 24 reads:

> At Trent, the martyrdom of the boy St. Simeon, who was barbarously murdered by the Jews, but who was afterwards glorified by many miracles.[6]

---

[1] Silesia – a region of central Europe, mostly in what is now Poland.
[2] http://www.zionism-israel.com/his/judeophobia6.htm (2007)
[3] Ibid.
[4] http://en.wikipedia.org/wiki/Giovanni_da_Capistrano (2007)
[5] Refer to the *Catholic Encyclopedia* 'Martyrs' for details of the various martyrologies.
[6] *Roman Martyrology*, March 24. http://www.boston-catholic-journal.com/roman-martrylogy-in-english/roman-martrylogy-march-in-english.htm#March_24th (2015)

However, nearly 400 years after his canonisation, Simon was removed from the calendar and veneration was forbidden by the Sacred Congregation of Rites in 1965.[1] A conservative Catholic website states that this prohibition of the cult was a sacrilegious attempt at suppression by the Racist Zionist Mafia and Marranos ('pigs')[2] in the Vatican.[3]

 There is a website displaying: *'The Talmud Unmasked: The Secret Rabbinical Teachings Concerning Christians* by Rev I B Pranaitis (Roman Catholic Priest) – With Ecclesiastical Imprimatur'. It has a 'Note from the Webmaster: This unchanged, online version of Father Pranaitis scholarly book, *The Talmud Unmasked*, is dedicated to the Holy Infant Martyr St. Simon of Trent, who was mercilessly slayed by the Jews in Trent, Italy on the 21st March, 1475 A.D.'[4]

After his Trentino success, friar da Feltre fabricated similar scenarios at Reggio, Bassano and Mantua. He was responsible for the expulsion of the Jews from Peruggia, Gubbio, Ravenna, Campo San Pietro, and Brescia. The friar was beatified shortly after his death in 1494. Five centuries later, in 1965, he was downgraded, and is no longer 'Blessed'.[5]

 Christopher of La Guardia (1490) – Christopher of La Guardia or 'the Holy Child of La Guardia' (el Santo Niño de La Guardia) was an alleged four-year-old Christian boy supposedly murdered by a small band of Jews and conversos in 1490. Eight men were executed in retaliation. It is now believed that this case was fabricated by the Spanish Inquisition to facilitate the expulsion of Jews from Spain. Certainly, his alleged death greatly assisted the Inquisition and its Inquisitor-General, Tomás de Torquemada, in their campaign against heresy and crypto-Judaism.[6] It was one of the main factors, if not the decisive one, in the decision of King Ferdinand and Queen Isabella to expel the Jews from Spain.[7]

Henry Charles Lea gave a vivid description of this case:

> the most effective device, however, was a cruel one, carried out by Torquemada unshrinkingly to the end. In June, 1490, a Converso named Benito Garcia, on his return from a pilgrimage to Compostella, was arrested at Astorga on the charge of having a consecrated wafer [Host] in his knapsack. The episcopal vicar, Dr Pedro de Villada, tortured him repeatedly till he obtained a confession implicating five other conversos and six Jews in a plot to effect a conjuration with a human heart and a consecrated Host, whereby to cause the madness and death of all Christians, the

[1] http://en.wikipedia.org/wiki/Simon_of_Trent (2007)
[2] To demonstrate that a Jew had truly converted to Christianity, he or she would eat pork publicly. To eat the meat of the pig was the definitive proof of the acceptance of Christianity. (Markman, Sidney David. *Jewish Remnants in Spain: Wanderings in a Lost World.* p59)
[3] 'The torture and death of Saint Simon of Trent'. http://www.stsimonoftrent.com (2007)
[4] http://www.talmudunmasked.com/index.htm (2010)
[5] http://www.zionism-israel.com/his/judeophobia6.htm (2007)
[6] http://en.wikipedia.org/wiki/Blood_libel_against_Jews#Actual_Jewish_practices_regarding_blood_and_sacrifice (2007)
[7] http://www.stsimonoftrent.com/ (2007)

destruction of Christianity and the triumph of Judaism. Three of the implicated Jews were dead, but the rest of those named were promptly arrested and the trial was carried on by the inquisition. After another year spent in torturing the accused, there emerged the story of the crucifixion at La Guardia of a Christian child, whose heart was cut out for the purpose of the conjuration. The whole issue was so evidently the creation of the torture-chamber that it was impossible to reconcile the discrepancies in the confessions of the accused, although the very unusual recourse of confronting them was tried several times; no child had anywhere been missed and no remains were found on the spot where it was said to have been buried.[1]

The consequences were that:

the inquisitors finally abandoned the attempt to frame a consistent narrative and, on November 16, 1491, the accused were executed at Avila; the three deceased Jews were burned in effigy, *the two living ones were torn with red-hot pincers* and the conversos were 'reconciled' and strangled before burning. The underlying purpose was revealed in the sentence read at the auto-da-fé, which was framed so as to bring into especial prominence the proselyting efforts of the Jews and the Judaizing propensities of the Conversos and no effort was spared to produce the widest impression on the people.

The cult was then engendered by the deceitful Church:

We happen to know that the sentence was sent to La Guardia, to be read from the pulpit, and that it was translated into Catalan and similarly published in Barcelona, showing that it was thus brought before the whole population – a thing without parallel in the history of the inquisition. The cult of the Saint-Child of La Guardia – *El santo niño de la Guardia* – was promptly started with miracles and has been kept up to the present day ...[2]

Over the years, details were added to the La Guardia fabrication, which acquired epic proportions. Each century, Spain produced a literary masterpiece that reiterated the topic. For example:

In 1583 Fray Rodrigo de Yepes wrote the *Story of the Death and Glorious Martyrdom of the Innocent Saint called de La Guardia*.[3]

In the following century, de Yepes' work formed the basis for *The Innocent Child of La Guardia* by Félix Arturo Lope de Vega y Carpio.[4]

During the eighteenth century, José de Cañizares y Suárez adapted it in *La imagen de Cristo (The Very Image of Christ)*.

In the nineteenth century Gustavo Adolfo Bécquer used it in his story, *La Rosa de Pasión (The Rose of Passion)*.

---

[1] Lea, Henry Charles. *History of the Inquisition of Spain*. Vol 1. pp133-34
[2] Ibid.
[3] *Historia de la muerte y glorioso martirio del santo inocente que llaman de Laguardia*
[4] *El niño inocente de La Guardia*

☞ In 1943 Manuel Romero de Castilla published the story as *A Unique Event during the Kingdom of the Catholic Monarchs*.[1,2]

☞ The alleged Christopher, the alleged child, allegedly a martyr, was canonised by Pius VII in 1805. The cult is still celebrated in La Guardia.

Sixteenth Century

1505 – In České Budějovice, a town in what is now the Czech Republic, 10 Jews were tortured and executed after accusations of killing a Christian girl. Later, a dying shepherd confessed to fabricating the accusation.[3]

☞ 1529 – At Bösing, Hungary, it was charged that a nine-year-old boy had been bled to death, suffering cruel torture. Thirty Jews confessed to the crime and were publicly burned. It was disclosed later, when the child was found alive, that he had been stolen by the accuser, Count Wolf of Bazin, as an easy means of ridding himself of his Jewish creditors.

Eighteenth Century

1712 – A blood libel claim in Sandomierz led to the expulsion of the town's Jews.[4]

1790 – Eleazer Solomon was quartered for the alleged murder of a Christian girl in Grodno.[5]

Nineteenth Century

1882 – The Jews of the village of Tiszaeszlár, Hungary, were accused of the ritual murder of a fourteen-year-old Christian girl. Although the accused were eventually acquitted, the case was one of the main causes of the rise of anti-Semitism in that country.

1899 – There arose the Hilsner case against a 22-year old Jewish drifter. The founder and first President of modern Czechoslovakia, Tomáš Garrigue Masaryk, took a stand 'not to defend Hilsner but to defend the Christians against superstition.' The affair led to an anti-Semitic campaign throughout Europe which was conducted by the Vienna Blood Libel 'specialist' Ernst Schneider.[6]

☞ *The Roman Catholic Press*

In the nineteenth century a dramatic change of focus occurred with respect to ritual murder charges that was pertinent to the anti-Semitic ethos of the Nazi Holocaust. Whereas previously these charges had been treated as local events, now they became identified with the publications closest to the Vatican itself.[7] This new campaign, with

---

[1] *de Singular suceso en el Reinado de los Reyes Católicos*
[2] Perednik, Gustavo D. *Jewish Political Studies Review* 15:3-4 (Fall 2003) Source: http://www.jcpa.org/phas/phas-perednik-f03.htm (2007). See also: http://www.conocereisdeverdad.org/website/index.php?id=3113 (2015)
[3] http://en.wikipedia.org/wiki/Timeline_of_antisemitism (2007)
[4] Ibid. (2012)
[5] Ibid.
[6] http://www.zionism-israel.com/his/judeophobia6.htm (2007)
[7] For example, *La Civiltà Cattolica* was founded in 1850 by the Jesuits 'as an organ of Papal sentiment'.

its obsessive reporting of Jewish ritual murder, assisted in the demonisation of European Jews at a time when the modern mass anti-Semitic movement was developing into a distinctive entity.[1]

⸙ This medium enabled the traditional Catholic hostility toward the Jews to be transformed into modern anti-Semitism. Particularly prominent were accusations of contemporary 'blood libel' that appeared in thousands of newspaper accounts. For example:

La Civiltà Cattolica. 'Contemporaneous Reports – Florence, the 23rd of June, 1881':

> Rome (Our Correspondence) ... the Jewish race's evil action against all peoples, especially Christian ones, among whom such race is forced to live scattered, is not only a religious and political reaction in the sense explained in our previous correspondence.

> It is an especially criminal one that exercises itself by means of *prescribed murders* which are considered by Jews as religious duties, precepts of the law and externalizations of piety and devotion ...

⸙ *La Civiltà Cattolica.* 'Contemporaneous Reports – Florence, the 10th of November, 1881':

> Rome (Our Correspondence) - The Jew Vitale confirms what the Jew Israel revealed about the bloody Passover rite. He reveals the bloody Passover rites celebrated by him and his uncle Solomon that took place in Monza and Milan. He describes St. Little Simon's dreadful martyrdom and talks about his purpose and motivations.

> By means of the interrogations reported in previous correspondence, the Jew Israel revealed all he knew about St. Little Simon's murder and the reasons for it ...

⸙ The press claimed that the need for Christian children's blood by Jews was insatiable. Accordingly, at that time there was an upsurge in legal charges against European Jews that led to a multitude of trials, which in turn were reported in sensational detail by the Roman Catholic press.[2]

Twentieth Century

Unità Cattolica – Even as late as 1913, the Florentine newspaper *Unità Cattolica* published an article by its editor in which he stated that as a consequence of the trial of the murderers of Simon of Trentino and his subsequent canonisation, belief in ritual murder by the Jews 'cannot escape the conscience of Catholics.' He went on: 'As is well known, little Saint Simon was honoured on the altars not because he was murdered, but because it was proven through numerous confessions that it was a case of a crime committed for ritual ends.'[3]

⸙ Reporting on a notorious trial in Kiev, in which the accused was found not guilty, Father Silva summed up:

---

[1] Kertzer, David I. *The Popes Against the Jews: The Vatican's Role in the Rise of Modern Anti-Semitism.* p156
[2] Ibid. pp13-14
[3] Ibid. pp232-33

A boy goes missing on the grounds of a Jewish factory and his body is found riddled with wounds. Science has established the time and the method; it has measured the systematic blows and the agony suffered by the victim. It has indicated the goal ... the murder was committed by people who wanted to extract the blood. Now of such people one race alone is known.[1]

Shortly after, Father Silva reported in *La Civiltà Cattolica* that the Kiev case had shown that the Jew continually drinks blood, and that he has to ensure the Christian child dies in the most painful manner possible.[2]

These continual allegations against the Jews prompted an approach to the Holy See by English Jews about the reporting of alleged ritual murder in the Roman Catholic press. This approach was made through the person of Lord Rothschild. In response, two extensive articles, which once again denigrated the morality and ethics of the Jews, were published in *La Civiltà Cattolica* by Jesuit Father Paolo Silva. These articles had been screened by the Cardinal Secretary of State, Rafael Merry del Val (a 'Servant of God'). The articles stated:

Among the authorities consulted ... to demonstrate the nonexistence of ritual murder, there is one to which the synagogue attributes more value than to all the rallies and all the newspapers in the world. It is one that merits our own special attention as well, for it is the authority of the Holy See. [It is curious] to see the haste with which these eternal haters of the Christian name have sought to call on papal testimony to escape this capital charge ...

We confess that we cannot see why a man [Lord Rothschild] speaks on behalf of his people when, essentially, he is nothing but a rich trafficker, a banker ... [This demonstrates that] the entire Jewish religion has been reduced to the cult of the golden calf.[3]

After World War II, blood Libels continued in the twentieth century, with the Kielce Pogrom of 4 July 1946 against the survivors of the Nazi Holocaust in Catholic Poland.[4] This was triggered by a Blood Libel. The key motivation for the Kielce Pogrom, however, was that Jewish survivors had returned to reclaim their land and property, which their Polish neighbours had stolen. The Poles would not relinquish their stolen goods, and instead murdered the Jews.[5]

The Kielce Pogrom was a major factor in the flight of Jews from Eastern Europe.[6,7] A memorial plaque was dedicated by Lech Wałęsa in 1990. A monument by New York-based artist Jack Sal entitled *White/Wash II* commemorating the victims was dedicated

---

[1] http://www.clevelandjewishnews.com/topic/?q=holocaust&l=25&sd=asc (2013)

[2] Kertzer, David I. *The Popes Against the Jews: The Vatican's Role in the Rise of Modern* ... pp235-36

[3] Ibid.

[4] http://en.wikipedia.org/wiki/Blood_libel_against_Jews (2007)

[5] Ibid.

[6] http://en.wikipedia.org/wiki/Pogroms (2007)

[7] Further details of the anti-Semitic actions of both the laity and ecclesiastics are given in: Cymet, David. *History vs. Apologetics: The Holocaust, the Third Reich, and the Catholic Church.* Chapter 12.

on 4 July 2006 in Kielce, on the 60th anniversary of the pogrom. At the dedication ceremony, a statement from the President of the Republic of Poland, Lech Kaczyński, condemned the events as a 'crime and a great shame for the Poles and tragedy for the Polish Jews'.[1]

Summary

·   Over all, there were about 130 reported cases of Blood Libel. They spread from England to Italy and Spain, and then Eastwards. In the last few centuries the Libel occurred mainly in Russia and Poland. Germany was the most active – one third of all Blood Libels took place there, most recently under Nazi rule (Memel, 1936; Bamberg, 1937). The 1 May 1934 special issue of the magazine *Der Stürmer*, a Nazi publication notorious for its fanatical anti-Semitism, was entirely devoted to the myth.[2]

Allegations of Desecration of the Host, and their Consequences through the Centuries

·   The Catholic dogma of Transubstantiation, whereby the wafer (Host[3]) consecrated in the ceremony of the Eucharist is believed to become the actual body of Jesus,[4] was established by Innocent III at the Fourth Lateran Council in 1215. Thereafter, the consecrated Host was publicly worshipped and the masses believed it, although with some initial qualms. The great popular preacher of the thirteenth century, Berthold of Regensburg, explained, by analogy, why Christ, though present in the wafer, does not let himself be seen in it:

> Who would like to bite off the little head, or the little hands, or the little feet of a little child?[5]

·   This dogma[6] soon precipitated the myth of the Jewish 'Desecration of the Host', which persisted intransigently until the Reformation. The legend was that Jews stole the Host, or acquired it by purchase or bribery. They were then alleged to have secretly either stabbed or transfixed it (whereupon it began to bleed), or to have burned it. Jews were charged with buying consecrated wafers from Christians and torturing them in ways that re-enacted Jesus' torture at the Crucifixion – such as driving nails through them, hammering them on an anvil, or trampling them under foot. As a result, the Host would begin

---

[1] http://en.wikipedia.org/wiki/Kielce_pogrom (2013)

[2] Source: http://www.zionism-israel.com/his/judeophobia6.htm (2007)

[3] The *Catholic Encyclopedia* states: 'The valid material of the Eucharistic host is unadulterated wheat reduced to flour, diluted with natural water, and baked with fire …we may say that theologians agree upon the rejection of buckwheat, barley, oats, etc.'

[4] Protestants consider the wafer to be only a *symbol* of the body of Jesus, thus avoiding the accusation of cannibalism. See, for example: *Church History: A Biblical View*. http://www.bible.ca/history/eubanks/history-eubanks-6.htm (2008)

[5] Trachtenberg, Joshua. *The Devil and the Jews: The Medieval Conception of the Jew and its Relation to Modern Anti-Semitism*. pp109-10

[6] In general usage, dogma has been defined as a religious doctrine that is proclaimed as true without any proof whatsoever. The *Catholic Encyclopedia* ('Dogma') confirmingly states: 'It might be described briefly as a revealed truth *defined* by the Church …'

to haemorrhage.

- Although it was most unlikely in reality, stories of physical attack upon processions bearing the Host in public became common. Accordingly, steps were taken to protect the Host and its bearers from these audacious Jews.

- As early as the second half of the eleventh century, rumours of such profanation led to the slaughter of Jews across France.[1]

- In 1267 the Council of Vienna decreed that Jews must immediately withdraw to their homes the moment that they heard the bell announce the bearing of the Host through the streets. This directive was frequently repeated and strictly enforced.[2]

- Because Christ resided literally and physically in the Host, he was also present in the crucifixes and other physical representations of him[3] that decorated Christian homes and churches. The saints, martyrs and the like were also believed by the laity to be literally and physically present in their images and paintings. Consequently, parallel with the myth of Host desecration, there were innumerable legends of Jewish ill-treatment of such images and pictures: the Jews threw stones and refuse at the images, they spat on them, insulted, pierced, slashed and shattered them. These tales soon migrated into folklore.[4]

- The accusation of Host desecration gradually ceased after the Reformation, when first Martin Luther in 1523 and then Sigismund August of Poland in 1558 were among those who repudiated the accusation. Nevertheless, even in the twentieth century, Julius Steicher, publisher of the popular Nazi journal *Der Stürmer*, maintained that there had to be a factual basis for these accusations.[5]

Thirteenth Century

- The first recorded case of retaliation against Jewish desecration of the Host was in 1243 at Belitz, near Berlin, where Jewish men and women were burned at the stake on the spot, later known as the Judenberg ("Jews' hill"). To conceal their crime, it was alleged that the Jews would throw the Host into a fiery furnace, but it would not be consumed. In desperation, they might throw the sacred object into a well or stream, that would immediately turn to blood. Their crime could not be hidden. Soon it would be discovered and avenged through a pogrom.

- Even when such an accusation was supported only by the testimony of a disreputable person such as a thief, the alleged perpetrators were put on trial, and, on evidence that was often absurd, or after a confession that had been exacted by torture, were condemned and burned, sometimes with all the other Jews of the neighbourhood. The resulting charge brought further persecutions and massacres. Forty of these infamous cases took place in Germany and Austria.

[1] Michael, Robert. *A History of Catholic Antisemitism: The Dark Side of the Church.* p71
[2] Ibid. p114
[3] So contrary to God's second commandment (*Deuteronomy* 5:8)
[4] Michael, Robert. *A History of Catholic Antisemitism: The Dark Side of the Church.* p118
[5] See, for example: Ibid. pp71-72

Fourteenth Century

Massacres of Jews were particularly prominent in Germany, where possibly 100,000 of them, in 146 communities, were obliterated by Roman Catholics during this time.[1]

1308 – The Bishop of Strasbourg, John of Dirpheim, accused the Jews of Sulzmatt and Rufach of the charge of Host desecration. They were burned alive.[2]

1338 – In Deggendorf, Bavaria, local burghers and members of the gentry set fire to the houses of the Jewish quarter and slaughtered the inhabitants. Duke Henry sanctioned the massacre by presenting the perpetrators with the Jews' properties. As a consequence, the killings spread to 21 other places. The slaughter of the Jews greatly benefited the impoverished townspeople, and a magnificent church was erected in place of the synagogue.[3] Only later, was the allegation of Host desecration made to justify the massacre. From the fifteenth century, relics of the supposed desecration were venerated in the church, and Deggendorf developed into a major place of pilgrimage. The last mass pilgrimage took place in 1843; the pictures in the church depicting the affair were covered up in 1967. The pilgrimage was finally abolished in 1992.[4]

In the Church of Sainte-Gudule, Brussels, are several Goblin tapestries containing representations of the supposed desecration of the Host in 1370.[5] In the same year, the accusation at Enghien led to the extermination of Belgian Jewry.

1399 – In Posen, Poland, a rabbi and 13 elders of the Jewish community were slowly burned to death on the charge of stabbing the Host and throwing it into a pit. Rumours had circulated that the Host had bled, which confirmed the dogma of transubstantiation of the Eucharist.

This myth of bleeding was enhanced by the belief that this spurting blood was especially useful to the Jews, particularly to counteract the foetor judaïcus and to cure the secret ills from which they supposedly suffered.[6]

Pilgrimages were made to places that justified and celebrated the persecution of the Jews. Myth about Host-desecration was the dominant explanation for these cults. These myths increased during the mid-fourteenth and late-fifteenth centuries, and were promoted as a basis for crusades against this increasingly marginalised group. Particularly in Bavaria, sites of these alleged crimes grew to be enormously successful pilgrimage shrines.[7]

Fifteenth Century

According to a story still current, the Jews committed a flagitious sacrilege in 1410.

[1] See, for example: Michael, Robert. *A History of Catholic Antisemitism: The Dark Side of the Church*. p71
[2] http://www.jcrelations.net/en/?id=836 (2007)
[3] Yet another of an almost limitless number of thefts of religious sites of other faiths by the Catholic Church.
[4] http://www.jewishvirtuallibrary.org/jsource/judaica/ejud_0002_0005_0_05033.html (2012)
[5] http://www.jewishencyclopedia.com/articles/7906-host-desecration-of (2015)
[6] Trachtenberg, Joshua. *The Devil and the Jew: The Medieval Conception of the Jew and its Relation* ... p116
[7] 'Spiritual Medicine for Heretical Poison', Pilgrimage and Propaganda in the Early Counter-Reformation. Source: http://content.cdlib.org/xtf/view?docId=ft738nb4fn&doc.view=content&chunk.id=d0e5654&toc.depth=1&anchor.id=0&brand=eschol (2007)

The fable states that a Jew stole the Host from the monastery of Santa Cruz in Segovia and took it to a synagogue, where the rabbis threw it into a cauldron of boiling water. The Host rose up in the air and shook the synagogue as if an earthquake had occurred. It was so strong that some of the walls were cracked. In fear, the rabbis returned the Host to the prior of the monastery. In a subsequent Communion, the prior administered the Host to a novice, who died three days later. The Jews who were guilty of this irremissible sacrilege were hanged and their broken bodies were later dragged through the streets of Segovia. The Church then sequestered the synagogue and converted it into the church of Corpus Christi. The building has never been returned to the Jews, and is still in use by the Roman Church.[1]

In 1496 in the Gothic church in Sternberg, Germany, a stone was mortared into the wall of a chapel. It has deeply embedded in it large prints of two bare feet. The stone is one on which the wife of the Jew Eleazar is claimed to have stood when she tried to sink a desecrated Host in the nearby brook. Unable to do so she purportedly sank into the stone.[2]

Later Occurrences

1520 – In Brandenburg, 38 Jews were executed and the rest were expelled.

The accusations gradually ceased after the Reformation. The last Jew burned for stealing a Host died in 1631.[3] The last accusation of desecration was in 1836.[4]

***

It was shown in 1848 that the phenomenon of the bloody Host was exactly similar to the red microscopic infusoria, later termed 'Micrococcus prodigiosus', which settle on bread and other food, especially on wafers, kept in the dark for any length of time.[5]

Centenaries or jubilees were also held in commemoration of past Host desecrations. For instance, the Jubilee of 1799 in commemoration of the desecration of the Host in Posen 400 years earlier. As late as 1820, a Great Jubilee was celebrated at Brabant in commemoration of the desecration at Enghien 450 years previously. Sixteen Hosts studded with diamonds were borne in solemn procession through the streets in this festival which lasted eight days.[6]

Summary

Through re-enactment, in Host tragedies or miracle plays, Catholic devotions mem-

[1] Markman, Sidney David. *Jewish Remnants in Spain: Wanderings in a Lost World.* pp50-51
[2] Bynum, Caroline Walker. 'The Presence of Objects: Medieval Anti-Judaism in Modern Germany', *Common Knowledge* (Vol 10, Issue 1, Winter 2004) pp1-32. Source: http://muse.jhu.edu/login?uri=/journals/common_knowledge/v010/10.1bynum.html (2007)
[3] http://www.jewishencyclopedia.com/articles/7906-host-desecration-of (2015)
[4] http://www.zionism-israel.com/his/judeophobia6.htm (2007)
[5] http://www.jewishencyclopedia.com/view.jsp?artid=938&letter=H (2007)
[6] Ibid.

orialised the Host's desecration, its miraculous discovery, and the subsequent punishment of the perpetrators. The resulting expulsions of Jews have been celebrated every year, for example, at Segovia in Spain, since 1415.[1]

· One of the most bizarre, tenacious, notorious, and disastrous Catholic myths was that of 'Ritual Murder'. In its popular version it claimed that Jews murdered Christian children and used their blood in the preparation of their Passover unleavened bread. This was the infamous 'Blood Libel'. It made the Jew a figure of sinister horror, whom the common people came to despise, fear and hate. In some cases, the alleged victim of this alleged human sacrifice became venerated as a martyr. A few have been beatified and some have even been declared saints. Most of the accusations arose from the clergy, who profited from the martyr and his shrine bringing pilgrims and offerings.

· The Catholic dogma of Transubstantiation states that the wafer (Host) consecrated in the Eucharist becomes the actual body of Jesus. This tenet soon precipitated the fiction of the Jewish 'Desecration of the Host', which persisted intransigently until the Reformation. The legend was that Jews stole the Host or acquired it by purchase or bribery. They were then alleged to either have secretly stabbed or transfixed it, whereupon it began to bleed, or to have burned it. Vicious reprisals against the Jews followed. The following table lists some of the many places where desecration charges resulted in persecutions of the Jews.

Table 8. A Sample of Places where Desecration Charges resulted in Persecutions of the Jews

1243	Belitz	1325	Cracow	1420	Ems
1290	Paris	1330	Güstrow	1453	Breslau
1294	Laa	1337	Deggendorf	1478	Passau
1298	Röttingen	1338	Pulka	1492	Sternberg
1298	Korneuburg	1370	Enghien	1510	Berlin
1299	Regensburg	1388	Prague	1514	Mittelberg
1306	Saint-Pälten	1399	Posen	1520	Brandenburg
1308	Rufach	1401	Glogau	1558	Sochaczew
1308	Sulzmatt	1410	Segovia	1631	unknown[2]

General ignorance,[3] and credulity of the laity in these bizarre fabricated phenomena, both so ably fostered by the institutional Church, had untold disastrous effects on the innocent Jews.

———

[1] http://www.zionism-israel.com/his/judeophobia6.htm (2007)

[2] The last Jew burned for stealing a host died in 1631. http://www.jewishencyclopedia.com/articles/7906-host-desecration-of (2015)

[3] For details of the Church's ruthless stranglehold on knowledge and learning for most of Christian history, refer to Volume 1 of 'A Corrupt Tree'.

9 – Executions, Pogroms, Massacres, The Crusades Holocaust

Such evil deeds could religion prompt. Lucretius

The historian Dagobert D Rune estimated that 3,500,000 Jews were killed during the Catholic Church's seven Holy Wars.[1,2] A multitude also lost their lives from other diverse calumnious activities of the Church. In all, the historical evidence suggests that the Catholic Church ('a divine society')[3] has been directly responsible for the annihilation of at least as many Jews as were killed by the Nazis.

Outbreaks of violence against Jews occurred as early as the first centuries CE, and occasionally Jews were massacred. Several synagogues were destroyed or converted into churches.[4] That such acts of violence were common then, is shown:

> by the frequent repetition of imperial edicts forbidding the maltreatment of Jews and the spoiling and burning of their synagogues; they were not allowed to erect new ones but were to be maintained in possession of those existing. At the same time the commencement of legal disabilities is manifested in the reiterated prohibitions of the holding of Christian slaves by Jews, while confiscation and perpetual exile or death were threatened against Jews who should convert or circumcise Christians or marry Christian wives. The Church held it to be a burning disgrace that a Jew should occupy a position of authority over Christians ...[5]

A pogrom is a form of riot directed against a particular group, whether ethnic, religious or other, and characterised by destruction of their homes, businesses and religious centres. Usually pogroms are accompanied by physical violence against the targeted people, and may include murder or massacre. The term has historically been used to denote extensive violence, either spontaneous or premeditated, against Jews, but has also been applied to similar incidents against other, mostly minority, groups.[6]

Eleventh Century – the Major Crusades: the First Catholic Holocaust

Soon after the year 1000, rumours began to circulate in Christian lands about the 'Prince of Babylon' who had caused the destruction of the Holy Sepulchre in Jerusalem and the persecution of Christians at the behest of the Jews. In response, princes, bishops and townspeople took revenge against the Jews in Rouen, Orléans, Limoges, Mainz and elsewhere. Jews were either converted by force or massacred.[7]

1021 – Pope Benedict VIII had Jews executed, blaming them for a hurricane and an earthquake.[8]

---

[1] Sinton, D Christie, 'Arnoume'. *Christian Terrorism* Also: http://www.buckcash.com/opinions/temp/Christian _Crimeline.htm (2006)

[2] http://www.atheistresource.co.uk/christjew.html (2007)

[3] *Catholic Encyclopedia* 'The Church'

[4] Wistrich, Robert S. *Anti-Semitism: The Longest Hatred.* pp18-20

[5] Ibid.

[6] http://en.wikipedia.org/wiki/Pogroms (2007)

[7] Cohn-Sherbok, D. *The Crucified Jew: Twenty Centuries of Christian Anti-Semitism.* p39

[8] Kühner, Hans. *Der Antisemitismus der Kirche.* p108. Source: Evangelical Sisterhood of Mary. *The Guilt of Christianity towards the Jewish People.* 1997 (http://www.kanaan.org/israel1.htm) (2007)

1065 – A Crusade was started against the Moors of Spain; the Crusaders killed all Jews in France whom they met en route.[1] Then, from 1096 to 1272, the Church launched a series of Holy Crusades. The purpose of these wars was to liberate the Holy Land (Palestine) from Moslem 'infidels'. The First Crusade was the turning point in popular anti-Semitism;[2] it ushered in a period of viciously cruel harassment which, in terms of duration, was unique in Jewish history:[3]

> When religious exaltation culminated in the crusades, it seemed to those who assumed the cross a folly to redeem Palestine while leaving behind the impious race that had crucified the Lord, and everywhere, in 1096, the assembling of crusaders was the signal for Jewish massacre.[4]

- Thousands of Jews were massacred in communities of Worms, Mainz, Cologne and other cities. A chronicler reported: 'The enemies stripped them naked and dragged them off, granting quarter to none, save those few who accepted baptism. The number of the slain was eight hundred in these two days.'[5]
- Thus began the first Catholic Holocaust.
- Half of the Jews of Worms were slaughtered,[6] while overall, approximately a quarter to one-third of the entire Jewish population in Germany and northern France was murdered during the First Crusade alone.[7] An annalist of Würzburg in Bavaria recorded:

> An enormous host, coming from all regions and all nations, went in arms unto Jerusalem and obliged the Jews to be baptized, massacring by thousands those who refused. Near Mainz, 1014 Jews, men, women, and children, were slaughtered, and the greatest part of the city burned.[8]

Chronicler Richard of Poitiers referred to the brutalities of the crusading mobs:

> they [the Crusaders] exterminated by many massacres the Jews of almost all Gaul, with the exception of those who accepted conversion. They said in effect that it was unjust to permit enemies of Christ to remain alive in their own country, when they had taken up arms to drive out the infidels abroad.[9]

The chronicler Fruitolf wrote:

> In the villages they traversed, the latter [the Crusaders] killed or forced baptism upon what remained of those impious Jews, who are truly enemies which the Church

[1] http://www.atheistresource.co.uk/christjew.html (2007)
[2] Poliakov, Léon. *The History of Anti-Semitism.* Vol I. p41
[3] Sister Pista. Evangelical Sisterhood of Mary, Darmstadt. http://www.cdn-friends-icej.ca/antiholo/guilt.html (2007)
[4] Lea, Henry Charles. *A History of the Inquisition of Spain.* Vol I. p83
[5] http://www.shc.edu/theolibrary/resources/01Teaching.htm (2014)
[6] de Rosa, Peter. *Vicars of Christ: The Dark Side of the* Papacy. p157
[7] Flannery, Edward H. *The Anguish of the Jews: Twenty-Three Centuries of Antisemitism.* Source: (http://www.kanaan.org/israel1.htm) (2007)
[8] Poliakov, Léon. *The History of Anti-Semitism.* Vol I. pp50-51
[9] Ibid. p42

tolerates in its bosom. Of these there was a certain number that returned to Judaism, even as dogs to their own vomit ...[1]

Chronicler, Guibert of Nogent reported the Crusaders of Rouen as having said:

> We desire to combat the enemies of God in the East; but we have under our eyes the Jews, a race more inimical to God than all the others. We are doing this whole thing backwards.[2]

☞ When the Crusaders reached Jerusalem, the Jews fled from them and locked themselves in the main synagogue, where all 969 were burnt to death. Chronicler Raymond of Aguilers, who was there at the time, quoted *Psalm* 118:24:

> This is the day which the Lord has made; let us rejoice and be glad in it.[3]

During the first two Crusades, German Jews appealed to the crown for protection. In return for protection they were made 'serfs of the Imperial Chamber'. As the king's property, they were bought, loaned and sold to pay off creditors. This custom spread to other countries. The Church justified this practice through earlier ecclesiastic teaching that the Jews were doomed to perpetual servitude for having crucified Christ.[4,5]

Wikipedia, in a section devoted to the legacy of the Crusades, records:

> Though the Muslims in power at the time tried to protect the Jews in The Holy Land, the Crusaders' atrocities against them in the German and Hungarian towns, later also in those of France, England, and in the massacres of Jews in Palestine and Syria have become a significant part of the history of anti-Semitism, although no Crusade was ever declared against Jews. These attacks left behind for centuries strong feelings of ill will on both sides. The social position of the Jews in western Europe was distinctly worsened, and legal restrictions increased during and after the Crusades. They prepared the way for the anti-Jewish legislation of Innocent III and formed the turning-point in medieval anti-Semitism.[6]

Twelfth Century

‣ 1100 – The first pogroms occurred against the Jews in Kiev.

1143 – 150 Jews were killed in Ham, northern France.

These first massacres of Jews were directly instigated by Catholic clerical preaching, and the murderous mobs were sometimes led by priests. For example, William of Newbury, described an attack on the Jews of York in 1190:

---

[1] Poliakov, Léon. *The History of Anti-Semitism.* Vol I. pp50-51

[2] Sister Pista. Evangelical Sisterhood of Mary, Darmstadt. http://www.cdn-friends-icej.ca/antiholo/guilt.html (2007)

[3] Rausch, David. *A Legacy of Hatred: Why Christians must not Forget the Holocaust.* p 27. Source: Evangelical Sisterhood of Mary. *The Guilt of Christianity towards the Jewish People* (1997) (http://www.kanaan.org/israel1.htm) (2007)

[4] Flannery, Edward H. *The Anguish of the Jews: Twenty-Three Centuries of Antisemitism.* p.95

[5] Brown, Michael L. *Our Hands Are Stained with Blood: The Tragic Story of the 'Church' and the Jewish People.* p13. Source: http://www.kanaan.org/israel1.htm (2007)

[6] http://en.wikipedia.org/wiki/Crusades#Legacy (2007)

And there were not lacking among the mob many clergymen, among whom a certain hermit seemed more vehement than the rest ... The deadly work was urged on before the others by that hermit from the Premonstratensian[1] canonry ... who ... was busily occupied with the besiegers, standing in his white garment and frequently repeating with a loud voice that Christ's enemies ought to be crushed.[2]

The Jewish quarters of the Port of Lynn in Norfolk were also burned and the Jews were slaughtered. Norwich Jews took refuge in the royal castle. The Jewish community at Stanford was pillaged and those who did not reach the castle were killed.[3]

1147 – Historian Dr Karlheinz Deschner estimates that several hundred Jews were slain at Ham, Sully, Carentan, and Rameru in France.[4]

1171 – Around fifty Jews in Blois, France, were burned to death in a locked wooden shed for refusing to convert to Christianity.[5]

1183 – Great massacres of Jews occurred in England. Crusaders en route to the Third Crusade plundered Jewish possessions and forced the Jews to flee to a castle where they were besieged – between 500 and 1500 died as a consequence. The attackers then burned all the records of financial obligations to the Jews.[6,7]

1189 – At the coronation of King Richard I of England, a Jewish delegation that had brought gifts and pledges of allegiance to the new king was driven from the palace, accused of casting spells on the king, and was set upon by the crowds. This onslaught was followed by numerous attacks on Jewish communities throughout the country.[8]

Thirteenth Century

1209 – The inhabitants of Béziers, France, were massacred during the Albigensian Crusade. 20,000 people including the Jewish community were slaughtered.

Henry Charles Lea wrote of the Crusaders in Spain in 1210:

the legate Arnaud of Narbonne led his crusading hosts to the assistance of Alfonso IX [King of León]. Although their zeal for the faith was exhausted by the capture of Calatrava and few of them remained to share in the crowning glories of Las Navas de Tolosa, their ardor was sufficient to prompt an onslaught on the unoffending Jews. The native nobles sought in vain to protect the victims, who were *massacred without mercy*, so that Abravanel declares this to have been one of the bloodiest

[1] 'Premonstratensians' constituted a Christian religious order of Augustinian canons, known in England as the 'White Canons'.
[2] Trachtenberg, Joshua. *The Devil and the Jews: The Medieval Conception of the Jew and its Relation to Modern Anti-Semitism.* p166
[3] http://www.jcrelations.net/en/?id=836 (2007)
[4] http://apocalisselaica.net/en/varie/eventi-storici/vittime-della-fede-cristiana (2013)
[5] Ibid.
[6] Flannery, Edward H. *The Anguish of the Jews: Twenty-Three Centuries of Antisemitism.* p119
[7] Poliakov, Léon. *The History of Anti-Semitism.* Vol I. p49
[8] Cohn-Sherbok, D. *The Crucified Jew: Twenty Centuries of Christian Anti-Semitism.* p55

persecutions that they had suffered and that *more Jews fled from Spain than Moses led out of Egypt*.[1]

1235 – Thirty-four Jews were burned to death in Fulda, Germany, on a blood-libel charge.

1236 – Crusaders attacked the Jewish communities of Anjou and Poitou and attempted to baptise all the Jews. Those who resisted, around 3000, were slaughtered.

1261-1264 – Students, priests and monks in Canterbury attacked the Jewish quarter. Mobs sacked the Jewish section of London in 1262 and 1264.

1270 – Jews were massacred in Germany: at Magdeburg, Sinzig, Erfurt, Weissenberg and other cities. In Sinzig the community was locked in the synagogue on the Sabbath and burned alive.

1283-1285 – Germany: 10 Jews were murdered by a mob in Mainz after they had been charged with ritual murder. 26 Jews were killed likewise in Bacharach, and forty were murdered in Oberwellel. 180 Jews were burned in Munich after a rumour was spread that a Christian child was bled to death in a synagogue

1287 – King Edward I of England had the Jews thrown into prison.

1290 – Dr Deschner estimates that 10,000 Jews were slaughtered in Bohemia by predatory Catholics.

1294 – All the Jews in Berne, Switzerland were killed or expelled amidst claims that they had ritually sacrificed Christian children.

1298 – The *Rintfleisch Pogrom* was a pogrom against Jews. The Jews of the Franconian town of Röttingen were accused of having obtained and desecrated a consecrated host. A 'Lord Rintfleisch' pretended to have received a mandate from heaven to exterminate 'the accursed race of the Jews'. He gathered a mob around him and burned the Jews of Röttingen on April 20. After this, he and his mob went from town to town and killed all Jews that fell under their control, destroying the Jewish communities at Rothenburg ob der Tauber, Würzburg, Nördlingen, and Bamberg. In Nuremberg the Jews sought refuge in the fortress and were assisted by the Christian citizens, but Rintfleisch overcame the defenders and butchered the Jews on 1 August. In all, the persecutors destroyed 146 communities, and about 20,000 Jews were killed.[2,3]

Fourteenth Century

Popular fanaticism against Jews continued into the fourteenth century, with massacres in Cologne, Estella, the Low Countries, Bordeaux, Toulouse, Albi, and Spain.[4]

1320 – A teenage shepherd claimed to have been visited by the Holy Spirit which instructed him to fight the Moors in Spain. This "Shepherds' Crusade" included mostly young men, women, and children. They marched south to Aquitaine, attacking castles,

---

[1] Lea, Henry Charles. *A History of the Inquisition of Spain.* Vol I. p88
[2] Sinton, D Christie, 'Arnoume'. *Christian Terrorism*
[3] http://www.atheistresource.co.uk/christjew.html (2007)
[4] Poliakov, Léon. *The History of Anti-Semitism.* Vol I. p50

royal officials, priests, and lepers along the way – however, their main targets were Jews. They eventually crossed into Spain, where, at the fortress of Montclus, over 300 Jews were killed.

A Christian chronicler recorded:

> The shepherds laid siege to all the Jews who had come from all sides to take refuge ... the Jews defended themselves heroically ... but their resistance served no purpose, for the shepherds slaughtered a great number of the besieged Jews by smoke and by fire ... The Jews, realising that they would not escape alive, preferred to kill themselves ... They chose one of their number [and] this man put some five hundred of them to death, with their consent. He then descended from the castle tower with the few Jewish children who still remained alive ... They killed him by quartering. They spared the children, whom they made Catholics by baptism.[1]

1321 – King Philip fined those communities in which Jews had been killed by the Crusade. This resulted in more attacks on Jews.[2]

· 1336-1339 – There was a series of persecutions by bands of marauders who massacred a large number of Jews. Also in 1336, a nobleman of Franconia, pretending that an angel had commissioned him, gathered a band of thugs, and pillaged and murdered the Jews. They styled themselves 'Judenschläger' (Jewbeaters). John Zimberlin, an innkeeper of Upper Alsace, who 'received a call to avenge the death of Christ by murdering the Jews', led 5000 followers armed with crude weapons and wearing leather armbands. This practice gave rise to the name 'Armleder' – Zimberlin himself was called 'King Armleder'. They slaughtered Jews from Alsace through the Rhineland, besieging the city of Colmar and devastating the surrounding country.[3]

1337 – The entire Jewish population of Deggendorf, Germany, was burned after stories were spread that they had defiled communion hosts. Persecution also spread to Austria and Poland where 51 Jewish towns were attacked.

1338 – Bishop John of Dirpheim caused the massacre of Jews in Strasbourg on the anniversary of the Conversion of St Paul.

Henry Charles Lea recorded of the Kingdom of Navarre:

> Navarre had the earliest foretaste of the wrath to come. It was then under its French princes and, when Charles le Bel died, February 1, 1328, a zealous Franciscan,[4] Fray Pedro Olligoyen, apparently taking advantage of the interregnum, stirred, with his eloquent preaching, the people to rise against the Jews, and led them to pillage and slaughter. The storm burst on the Aljama of Estella, March 1st, and rapidly spread throughout the kingdom. Neither age nor sex was spared and the number of victims is variously estimated at from six to ten thousand.[5]

---

[1] http://www.sullivan-county.com/id2/timeline.htm (2007)

[2] http://en.wikipedia.org/wiki/Shepherds'_Crusade (2007)

[3] 'Armleder Persecutions'. http://www.jewishencyclopedia.com/view.jsp?artid=1790&letter=A

[4] The Franciscans – so evident throughout this encyclopaedia for their homicidal tendencies.

[5] Lea, Henry Charles. *A History of the Inquisition of Spain.* Vol I. p100

1347 – 600 Jews of Brussels were massacred by a Catholic mob, while in Bavaria, 10,000 Jews were slaughtered after Catholic mobs rampaged through 80 Jewish communities.

The Second Catholic Holocaust

• The Black Death (c.1347-1351) was the start of another series of bloody murders. The Jews, it was claimed, had caused the Plague by poisoning the wells and springs. Consequently, in southern France, northern Spain, Switzerland, Bavaria, Rhineland, eastern Germany, Belgium, Poland and Austria over 200 Jewish communities were destroyed. The first case occurred in 1348 near Lake Geneva. The Jews 'confessed' that the disease was spread by a Jew on the instructions of a rabbi who had prepared the poison.

. Over all, more Jews were murdered by Catholics, mostly burned alive, in a single year in Germany than all the Christians who were persecuted by the Romans over a period of 200 years.[1] This fourteenth-century epidemic of extermination has been claimed by Dr Joachim Kahl, in his book *Das Elend des Christentums oder Plädoyer für eine Humanität ohne Gott* (*The Misery of Christianity: A Plea for a Humanity without God*), as comparable to the pogroms that took place under Hitler.[2] At the end, only a few impecunious and vagabond Jews remained in northern Europe.[3]

In Basel 600 Jews were burned at the stake for allegedly poisoning the wells, 140 children were forcibly baptised, and the remaining Jews were expelled. The city's synagogue was turned into a church and the Jewish cemetery was destroyed.[4] In Poland 10,000 casualties were reported; and considerably more than 10,000 were killed in the three German towns of Erfurt, Mainz and Breslau alone.[5] 2000 Jews in Strasbourg were herded into a large wooden barn and burned alive after Catholics accused them of starting the Bubonic Plague. In Frankfurt dozens of Jews were slaughtered after Catholic mobs marched through the town. In many places Jews were killed even before the plague had reached the locality. Holy Roman Emperor Charles IV, who originally defended the victims, finally granted 'forgiveness for every transgression involving the slaying and destruction of the Jews.'

• After the Black Death, the legal status of the Jews deteriorated throughout almost all of Europe.

Mid-Fourteenth Century onwards

Around the middle of the fourteenth century, Catholic forces moved into the free city of Cologne where Jewish merchants, weavers, and other commercial enterprises flourished. The result: the Jewish merchants were incinerated alive with their wives and

---

[1] Sinton, D Christie, 'Arnoume'. *Christian Terrorism*
[2] Kahl, Joachim. *The Misery of Christianity: A Plea for a Humanity without God.* p58
[3] Poliakov, Léon. *The History of Anti-Semitism.* Vol I. p100
[4] http://www.atheistresource.co.uk/christjew.html (2007). Yet again, theft of religious real estate by the Church.
[5] Ibid.

children; those who escaped were banished. Their property went to the Catholics, with fifty percent going to the triumphant archbishop.[1]

1355 – A civil war erupted in Spain. A rapacious mob invaded that part of the Judería of Toledo called the Alcaná; they plundered the warehouses and murdered about 12,000 Jews. The friendlier King Pedro showed himself toward the Jews, and the more he protected them, the more antagonistic became the attitude of his illegitimate half-brother, who, when he invaded Castile in 1360, murdered all the Jews living in Najera and exposed those of Miranda de Ebro to robbery and butchery.[2] Historian Lea described some of the massacres:

> When, in 1355, Henry of Trastamara and his brother, the master of Santiago, entered Toledo to liberate Queen Blanche, who was confined in the Aleazar[3], they sacked the smaller Judería and slew its twelve hundred [Jewish] inmates without sparing sex or age. ... Five years later when, in 1360, Henry of Trastamara invaded Castile with the aid of Pedro IV of Aragon, on reaching Najara he ordered a massacre of the Jews and, as Ayala states that this was done to win popularity, it may be assumed that free license for pillage was granted. Apparently stimulated by this example the people of Miranda del Ebro, led by Pero Martinez, son of the Precentor and by Pedro Sanchez de Bafluelas, fell upon the Jews of their town.[4]

Jewish sufferings were often a highlight of pre-Lenten carnivals in mediaeval Rome. For example, a weak member of the Jewish community would be forced naked into a nail-spiked barrel and rolled down a hill to his death.[5]

1366-1369 – While the Castilian civil war raged between King Pedro and Henry of Trastamara, many Jews were killed by mercenaries employed by both sides.[6]

1370 – One hundred Jews were burned and 500 'mutilated until dead' in Brussels, after claims that a Jew broke a communion wafer.[7] In another incident, Jews were also accused of profaning the Host, and in consequence, twenty were burned at the stake.[8]

1384 – The Jews in Nördlingen were attacked and massacred.

1389 – Mobs attacked and murdered thousands of Jews in Prague.

1390 – King John (Juan) I of Castile died; and was succeeded by his eleven-year-old son. The council-regent appointed by the king in his testament, consisting of prelates, grandees, and six citizens from Burgos, Toledo, León, Sevilla, Córdoba, and Murcia, was powerless; every vestige of respect for law and justice had disappeared.

[1] Agrippa, Henry Cornelius. *The Philosophy of Natural Magic.* p19. Source: http://wiccanhistorian.home. att.net/ histories/persecutionJews.html (2007)

[2] http://en.wikipedia.org/wiki/History_of_the_Jews_in_Spain (2008)

[3] Aleazar – royal palace.

[4] Lea, Henry Charles. *A History of the Inquisition of Spain.* Vol I. p102

[5] Sister Pista. Evangelical Sisterhood of Mary, Darmstadt. http://www.cdn-friends-icej.ca/antiholo/guilt.html (2007)

[6] http://www.jcrelations.net/en/?id=836 (2007)

[7] Sinton, D Christie, 'Arnoume'. *Christian Terrorism*

[8] Cohn-Sherbok, D. *The Crucified Jew: Twenty Centuries of Christian Anti-Semitism.* p45

～1391 – This year was a turning-point in the history of the Spanish Jews. The persecution then was the immediate forerunner of the Inquisition, which, ninety years later, was introduced as a means of spying on the converted Jews.[1] Don Fernando Martinez (Ferrant Martinez), the archdeacon of Écija and pious Queen Leonora's confessor, one of the most inveterate enemies of the Jewish people,[2] preached anti-Semitic sermons in which he encouraged Catholics to expel Jews from the cities and to either demolish or take over their synagogues. This was his 'Guerra Sacra Contra Los Judios' ('Holy War against the Jews').[3,4] The result, over 10,000 Jews were murdered.[5] In Sevilla hundreds of Jews were murdered and the aljama was destroyed. Within days, the violence spread across the Iberian Peninsula: in Valencia, 250 Jews were assassinated, and in Barcelona 400 likewise. The major aljamas of Spain were destroyed.[6] Most of the Jews of Écija were forcibly baptised. Almost a century later, there was another riot when the Marranos of Écija suffered a pogrom. Judaism there was extinguished forever.[7,8]

These massacres, in the words of Historian Henry Charles Lea 'form a turning-point in Spanish history. In the relations between the races of the Peninsula the old order of things was closed and the new order, which was to prove so benumbing to material and intellectual development, was about to open ...'[9] Lea continued:

> The most deplorable result of the massacres was that they rendered inevitable this further progress in the same direction. *The church had at last succeeded in opening the long-desired chasm between the races.* It had looked on in silence while the archdeacon of Écija was bringing about the catastrophe and pope and prelate uttered no word to stay the long tragedy of murder and spoliation,[10] which they regarded as an act of God to bring the stubborn Hebrew into the fold of Christ. Henceforth the old friendliness between Jew and Christian was, for the most part, a thing of the past. Fanaticism and intolerance were fairly aroused, to grow stronger with each generation as fresh wrongs and oppression widened the abyss between believer and unbeliever and as new preachers of discord arose *to teach the masses that kindness to the Jew was a sin against God.* Thus gradually the Spanish character changed until it was prepared to accept the inquisition, which, by a necessary reaction, stimulated the development of bigotry until Spain became what we shall see it in the sixteenth and seventeenth centuries ...

> While the massacres, doubtless, were largely owing to the attractions of disorder and pillage, the religious element in them was indicated by the fact that everywhere

---

[1] http://en.wikipedia.org/wiki/History_of_the_Jews_in_Spain (2008)
[2] http://www.jewishencyclopedia.com/view.jsp?artid=223&letter=M (2007)
[3] Cohn-Sherbok, D. *The Crucified Jew: Twenty Centuries of Christian Anti-Semitism.* pp77-78
[4] *Dictionary of the Middle Ages.* Vol 7. p82
[5] http://www.atheistresource.co.uk/christjew.html (2007)
[6] Kamen, Henry. *The Spanish Inquisition: An Historical Revision.* p10
[7] Markman, Sidney David. *Jewish Remnants in Spain: Wanderings in a Lost World.* p94
[8] Cohn-Sherbok, D. *The Crucified Jew: Twenty Centuries of Christian Anti-Semitism.* pp77-78
[9] Lea, Henry Charles. *History of the Inquisition of Spain.* Vol I. pp106-11
[10] A prelude to the extended and much criticised silence of Pius XII during the Nazi Holocaust.

the Jews were offered the alternative of baptism and that where willingness was shown to embrace Christianity, slaughter was at once suspended. The pressure was so fierce and overwhelming that whole communities were baptized.[1]

Lea also stated that Ferrant Martinez, was by his actions, in reality the remote founder of the Spanish Inquisition.[2]

1382 – Rioters looted and vandalised the Jewish quarter in Paris after a wave of the Plague.[3]

1389 – In Prague a priest carrying a wafer host was accidentally sprayed with sand by Jewish children at play. This led to 3000 Jews being massacred.[4]

Towards the end of the Middle Ages, legislations were filled with degrading decrees. For example, by the end of the fourteenth century it was an established custom, in cases of capital punishment, to hang a Jew by the feet and sometimes to hang a fierce wolf-dog beside him also.[5]

Fifteenth Century

1421 – Persecutions of Jews occurred in Vienna following the *Wiener Gesera* (*Vienna Edict*) of Albert V, in which he ordered the annihilation of the city's Jews. 270 were burned at the stake.

1435 – There was a massacre and forced conversion of Majorcan Jews.

Giovanni da Capestrano (John Capistrano) (1386-1456) was an Italian friar, theologian and inquisitor. In 1451 he visited all parts of the Holy Roman Empire. As legate or inquisitor he persecuted the Jews of Sicily, Moldavia and Poland. His renowned oratory was not only used to inspire religious faith but to incite mobs to conduct the mass murders of Jews in different cities. For example, 41 Jews were burned in the city of Breslau, Germany, while 36 Jews were burned in the Berlin marketplace, and the entire Jewish community of Liegnitz, Poland was incinerated.[6] He also led a campaign in Italy against the Jews. He initiated a series of trials for ritual murder that resulted in a number of autos-da-fé.[7] He was later canonised for his efforts on behalf of the Church.

1457 – Polish troops on the march to the Crusade against the Turks attacked the Jews of Kraków and killed about thirty.

Spain – By the mid-15th century, hatred toward the conversos exceeded that toward the professed Jews. In Toledo a bloody uprising against these 'Marranos' ('Pigs') took place in July 1467, many being killed. In March 1473 an outbreak occurred at Córdoba, the houses of the conversos being invaded, plundered, and burned, and many of their inmates horribly butchered.

[1] Lea, Henry Charles. *History of the Inquisition of Spain* Vol I. pp106-11
[2] Ibid. p111
[3] Tuchman, Barbara. *A Distant Mirror.* p380. Source: http://wiccanhistorian.home.att.net/histories/persecution Jews.html
[4] Flannery, Edward H. *The Anguish of the Jews: Twenty-Three Centuries of Antisemitism.* p112
[5] Poliakov, Léon. *The History of Anti-Semitism.* Vol I. p121
[6] http://en.wikipedia.org/wiki/Giovanni_da_Capestrano (2007)
[7] Cohn-Sherbok, D. *The Crucified Jew: Twenty Centuries of Christian Anti-Semitism.* p61

1473 – Jews were accused of ritual murder in the Tyrol. Nine were tortured and executed. Later, several trials with the same accusation took place in Austria and Italy 'followed by expulsions and autos-da-fé'.[1]

1475 – In Trent, Italy, nearly all the Jews were tortured, tried and burned amid unproven claims that they had ritually sacrificed a Christian child named Simon.[2,3]

1462 – Alfonso de Oropesa, Prior-General of the Order of St Jerome, urged King Henry IV to establish the Castilian Inquisition. A bull of the corrupt and unscrupulous Sixtus IV did just that in 1478. He appointed the notorious Inquisitor-General, Tomás de Torquemada. The majority of Jews who appeared before the Inquisition accepted reconciliation with the Catholic Church, and were sentenced to imprisonment after receiving various humiliations and having their property confiscated.[4]

1469 – The marriage of Isabella I of Castile and Ferdinand V of Aragón made them joint rulers of Castile in 1474 and of Aragón in 1479. These pious monarchs, who took the title 'Catholic Monarchs', established the Spanish Inquisition in 1478 to enforce purity of the faith. Although it only had authority over Christians, Converso Jews soon found themselves in its line of fire and all their worst sufferings began.[5] The Inquisition burned its first victims in 1481.[6] Between 1481 and 1488 seven hundred and fifty men and women were burned at the stake.[7] Thence, over the years an estimated 30,000 conversos were incinerated.[8] Luis de Santangel, a baptised Jew, was the treasurer of Queen Isabella and a supporter of Columbus' enterprise. His family was persecuted during the Spanish Inquisition – his older cousin was beheaded – he himself has been said to have been incinerated alive in 1491.[9]

Conversos of Jewish origin constituted 99 percent of those tried by the Barcelona tribunal between 1488 and 1505, and 92 percent of those tried by the Valencia tribunal between 1484 and 1530. The prisons of Sevilla were inundated with conversos waiting to be interrogated. The Toledo tribunal 'reconciled' 2400 repentant conversos during the year 1486 alone. Henry Kamen, in his work *The Spanish Inquisition: An Historical Revision*, recorded that fear was their sole motivation for conversion.[10]

1490 – A number of Jews and conversos were charged by the Spanish Inquisition with attempting to destroy Christendom through black magic. After the victims confessed they were all burned. The imaginative accusation against one of them stated:

[1] Cohn-Sherbok, D. *The Crucified Jew: Twenty Centuries of Christian Anti-Semitism.* p61

[2] http://www.atheistresource.co.uk/christjew.html (2007)

[3] See also Chapter 8.

[4] Cohn-Sherbok, D. *The Crucified Jew: Twenty Centuries of Christian Anti-Semitism.* p85

[5] Kamen, Henry. *The Spanish Inquisition: An Historical Revision.* p17

[6] Flannery, Edward H. *The Anguish of the Jews: Twenty-Three Centuries of Antisemitism.* p137

[7] Markman, Sidney David. *Jewish Remnants in Spain: Wanderings in a Lost World.* pp136-38

[8] Brown, Michael L. *Our Hands are Stained with Blood: The Tragic Story of the 'Church' and the Jewish People.* p78. Source: http://www.kanaan.org/israel1.htm

[9] Markman, Sidney David. *Jewish Remnants in Spain: Wanderings in a Lost World.* pp136-38

[10] Kamen, Henry. *The Spanish Inquisition: An Historical Revision.* pp56-57

His soul embittered and depraved, he went in good company with several others to crucify a Christian child on a Good Friday in the same fashion, with the same animosity and cruelty as his forefathers had for our Saviour Jesus Christ, tearing his flesh, beating him and spitting in his face, covering him with wounds, crushing him with blows, and turning to ridicule our holy Faith ... He mixed its heart with a consecrated host. With this mixture, Yuce Franco and the others expected that the Christian religion would be overturned and destroyed, so that the Jews would possess all the property which belongs to the Catholics, that their race would grow and multiply while that of the faithful Christians would be extirpated forever.[1]

1492 – Jews in Mecklenburg, Germany were accused of Eucharistic sabotage. Twenty seven were annihilated, including two women. The site of their destruction is still called the Judenberg. All the remaining Jews were expelled from the Duchy.[2]

Sixteenth Century

1506 – In Lisbon, 4000 conversos were thrown from windows to street mobs below.[3] Four years later, 40 Jews in Brandenburg were executed for allegedly desecrating the Host; the rest were expelled. Thirty eight Jews in Berlin were burned in the same year.

1528 – Three Judaisers were burned at the stake in Mexico City's first auto-da-fé.[4]

The Goan Holocaust

ᶜ 'A notable Jewish population once existed in Goa [India]. The Jews had their own synagogues and enjoyed freedom. They had been settled in Goa before the Portuguese arrived.'[5]

⁺ In 1536, the Portuguese Inquisition was established. It held its first auto-da-fé in 1540. Like the Spanish Inquisition, it concentrated its efforts on rooting out converts from other faiths who did not adhere to the strictures of Catholic orthodoxy, particularly the Jewish 'New Christians' ('Conversos', or 'Marranos'). The Portuguese Inquisition expanded its scope of operations from Portugal to the Portuguese Empire, including Brazil and Cape Verde.

ᵓ In 1552, Francis Xavier's evil Inquisition was established in Goa.[6]

ᵣ While its ostensible aim was to preserve the Catholic faith, the Inquisition was also used as an instrument of social control, as well as a method of confiscating property and enriching the Inquisitors.

ᵣ Its malign activities are covered in detail in Volume 3 of this encyclopaedia. In essence, it had a long programme to convert the native population (Hindus and Muslims) by torture to Catholicism. It was much larger and endured for a longer period than the

[1] Cohn-Sherbok, D. *The Crucified Jew: Twenty Centuries of Christian Anti-Semitism.* pp86-87
[2] http://www.atheistresource.co.uk/christjew.html (2007)
[3] http://astro.temple.edu/~hfreiden/Antisemitism/timeline.htm (2007)
[4] auto-da-fé, or auto-de-fé, is the Spanish equivalent of the Portuguese auto da fé.
[5] https://en.wikipedia.org/wiki/Sephardic_Jews_in_India (2015)
[6] See, for example: https://agniveerfan.wordpress.com/2013/04/04/portuguese-inquisition-in-goa-ordered-by-francis-xavier/ (2015)

Spanish Inquisition. Thousands of citizens suffered horrors and execution.

⚖ The Goan Inquisition is regarded by all contemporary portrayals as the most violent and horrendous inquisition ever executed by the Catholic Church. Certainly, it was one of the most violent institutions in the history of Goa. 'The inquisitors in Goa became the most fanatic and violent of the Portuguese Catholic Church.' Dr P P Shirodkar, in his article 'Evangelisation and its Harsh Realities in Portuguese India', justifiably described:

> the criminal acts of the [Goan] Inquisition which surpassed those of the Nazis in horror.[1]

- This Inquisition also massacred South Indian Jewry. Eventually, the Jews sought refuge with the Hindu King of Cochin. The Portuguese wrote to the King seeking permission to exterminate them. They then destroyed the Jewish settlement in Cochin and also the remnants of the Jewish population, the synagogue, and Jewish historical documents in Kodungallore.[2] The Inquisition also persecuted the large population of Jews in the Konkan region. They were accused of 'crimes' of different kinds, such as blasphemies, impiety, sodomy, necromancy and witchcraft. Participation in the Jewish Shabbat ('superstitious assemblies') resulted in the victim being burnt at the stake. If he confessed at the last moment, and was 'truly sorry', he was condemned to the garrotte for capital punishment, and then burned. Otherwise he was combusted alive. The Goan Inquisition resulted in a massive depopulation of Indian Jewry in that region of the country.[3,4]

- In spite of the Church, the Portuguese Inquisition was extinguished in 1821 by the 'General Extraordinary and Constituent Courts of the Portuguese Nation'.[5]

- For worthy efforts such as this on behalf of the church Catholic, Xavier was declared a Saint.

Seventeenth Century

1614 – Vincent Fettmilch, the 'new Haman of the Jews'[6], led a raid on a Frankfurt synagogue. It turned into an attack that destroyed the whole community.

1664 – About 100 Jews of the Lviv (Lvov) Ghetto were killed.

Eighteenth Century

1723 – Hundreds of Polish Jews were beaten to death after the Bishop of Gdańsk roused mobs to invade ghettoes and provinces.[7] A year later, 20,000 Jews were killed.

---

[1] In: *Discoveries, Missionary Expansion and Asian Cultures*. p80
[2] http://en.wikipedia.org/wiki/Goa_Inquisition (2007)
[3] http://en.wikipedia.org/wiki/Christianity_and_antisemitism (2007)
[4] http://en.wikipedia.org/wiki/Portuguese_India (2007)
[5] http://en.wikipedia.org/wiki/History_of_the_Jews_in_Portugal (2012)
[6] In Rabbinical tradition, Haman (also known as Haman the Agagite ro המן האגגי, Haman the evil (המן הרשע) is considered an archetype of evil and a persecutor of the Jews.
[7] Sinton, D Christie, 'Arnoume'. *Christian Terrorism*

Nineteenth Century

1819 – A series of anti-Jewish pogroms occurred in Germany which spread to several neighbouring countries including Denmark, Poland, Latvia and Bohemia. They were known as 'Hep-Hep' riots, from the derogatory rallying cry against the Jews in Germany. Many Jews were killed, and much Jewish property was destroyed.[1]

Twentieth Century

1913 – Pius X refused to intervene in a trial of a Jew in Kiev on the charge of ritual murder, and his administration allowed it to continue.[2]

1918 and during the Polish-Bolshevik War of 1920, there were sporadic pogroms.

1919 – In Hungary 3000 Jews were killed in pogroms. And in Argentina there was a pogrom during the 'Tragic Week'.

The Croatian Holocaust in Catholic Croatia, under dictator Ante Pavelić, destroyed 32,000 Jews. The Slovakian Holocaust in Slovakia, under Msgr Jozef Tiso, resulted in the loss of more than 110,000 Jewish lives. These genocides are covered in Chapter 14.

The Nazi Holocaust lasted from 30 January 1933 to 8 May 1945. 6,000,000 European Jews were targeted and methodically murdered in the largest genocide in history.

Synopsis

For nearly two thousand years there have been extensive imprisonments, executions, attacks, pogroms and massacres of Jews by and for the Catholic Church.

Approximately a quarter to one-third of the entire Jewish population in Germany and northern France was murdered during the First Crusade alone.

The genocides of Jews during the Major Crusades constituted the First Catholic Holocaust.

The Second Catholic Holocaust comprised retributions for perceived influences by the Jews in causing the ravages of the Black Death in Europe.

Saint Francis Xavier's evil Portuguese Inquisition was established in the province of Goa. It resulted in a massive depopulation of Jewry in the region.

The Slovakian and Croatian Catholic Holocausts during World War II devastated the Jewish populations in those countries.

The Nazi Holocaust was the largest genocide in history.

Over the centuries, hatred of Jews has been a particular and enduring obsession of the Catholic Church. The resultant sufferings and murders of these peoples have been astronomic.

———

[1] http://en.wikipedia.org/wiki/Hep-Hep_riots (2007)
[2] Hardy, Rob. *What Role did the Vatican Play in Fostering Anti-Semitism?* (http://www.nonfictionreviews. com/article1273.html) (2006)

10 – Anti-Semitism in Iberia, The Spanish Holocaust

Homophobia is like racism and anti-Semitism and other forms of bigotry in that it seeks to dehumanize a large group of people, to deny their humanity, their dignity and personhood. Coretta Scott King

The most certain test by which we judge whether a country is really free is the amount of security enjoyed by minorities. Lord Acton

Early History and the Council of Elvira

Hispania came under Roman control with the fall of Carthage after the Second Punic War (218-202 BCE).[1]

As citizens of the Roman Empire, the Jews of Spain engaged in a variety of occupations. Until the adoption of Christianity in the Empire, Jews had close relations with non-Jewish populations, and played an active role in the social and economic life of the province.

The Synod of Elvira (Concilio de Elvira)[2] was an ecclesiastical synod held during the years 305 and 306 in Elvira, in what was then the Roman province of Hispania Baetica, now Granada. It ranks among the more important provincial synods for the breadth of its canons.

All the canons that pertained to Jews served to maintain a separation between the two communities: *Canon 15* prohibited marriage with pagans, while *Canon 16* prohibited marriage of Christians with Jews. *Canon 78* threatened Christians who committed adultery with Jews with ostracism. *Canon 48* forbade the blessing of Christian crops by Jews, and *Canon 50* forbade the sharing of meals by Christians and Jews.

Visigothic Rule (5th century to 711) and the Councils of Toledo

Barbaric invasions brought most of the Iberian Peninsula under Visigothic[3] rule by the early fifth century. Other than their contempt for Catholics, who reminded them of the Romans, the Visigoths took little interest in the religious creeds within their kingdom.

587 – The tide turned following the conversion of the Visigothic royal family under King Reccared (Recared) (586–601) from Arianism to Roman Catholicism. In consolidating the realm under Christianity, the Visigoths adopted an aggressive policy towards the Jews, leading to repeated persecutions.[4]

From the sixth to the seventh century, about thirty synods (councils), variously counted, were held at Toledo in what would become part of Spain.[5] The seventh century

---

[1] Principal source: http://en.wikipedia.org/wiki/History_of_the_Jews_in_Spain (2008)
[2] Principal source: http://en.wikipedia.org/wiki/Council_of_Toledo (2010)
[3] The Visigoths were one of two main branches of the Goths, the Ostrogoths being the other. These Germanic tribes spread through the late Roman Empire during the Migration Period. The Visigoths defeated the Romans at the Battle of Adrianople in 378, and under Alaric I eventually moved into Italy and famously sacked Rome in 410.
[4] Will Durant. *Age of Faith*
[5] The following material is based on http://en.wikipedia.org/wiki/Visigoths (2012)

is sometimes called by Spanish historians the 'Siglo de Concilios', or 'Century of Councils'

Because nearly one hundred early canons of Toledo found a place in the *Decretum Gratiani*,[1] they exerted an important influence on the development of Catholic ecclesiastical law.

589 – The Third Council of Toledo convened. It marked the formal entry of Catholic Christianity into the rule of Visigothic Spain. It also enacted restrictions on Jews and reiterated in more vigorous form the original restrictions of the Council of Elvira. It prohibited Jews from taking Christian wives or concubines, and prescribed baptism of the resulting children. Jews could not have Christian slaves in domestic service. Such legislation became progressively more explicit and severe in the later Councils of Toledo.[2] King Reccared approved the decisions of the Council.

King Liuva II, who ruled from 601 to 603, was a youthful son of Reccared. King Witteric succeeded Liuva from 603 to 610. He tried to re-establish Arianism in the kingdom. In April 610 a faction of Catholic nobles assassinated him during a banquet, and had his body dragged ignominiously through the streets. The nobles then proclaimed Gundemar, Duke of Narbonne, king. King Gundemar died a natural death in 612. He was succeeded by Sisebut.

King Sisebut (612-620) embarked on Reccared's course against the Jews with renewed vigour. Soon after upholding the edict of compulsory baptism for children of mixed marriages, he instituted what was to become a recurring phenomenon in Spain, by issuing the first edict of expulsion from the country against the Jews.

613 – Following Sisebut's decree that the Jews either convert or be expelled, some fled to Gaul and North Africa, while as many as 90,000 converted. Many of these conversos, as did those of later periods, maintained their Jewish identities in secret.

During the more tolerant reign of King Suintila (621-631), most of the conversos returned to Judaism, and a number of those exiled returned to Spain.

King Sisenand (631-636) overthrew Suintila with the aid of the devout Catholic, Dagobert I, King of all the Franks.

633 – The Fourth Council of Toledo produced the severest anti-Semitic legislation.[3] It issued laws demanding the removal of Jewish children from their families, and forbidding Jews and Christians of Jewish origin from holding office.[4] It took stringent measures against baptised Jews who had relapsed into their former faith, and decreed that Jewish children baptised as Christians were to be separated from their parents. Saint Isidore of Sevilla (c.560-636)[5] (patron saint of children) condemned Jews as the killers

---

[1] In 1503, the legist Jean Chappuis printed and published in Paris, under the title *Corpus Iuris Canonici*, the *Decretum of Gratian* and the three official and two private collections of decretals. The *Corpus*, along with the decrees of the Council of Trent (1545-1563), remained the fundamental law of the Roman Catholic Church until the new *Codex Iuris Canonici* appeared in 1917.

[2] Markman, Sidney David. *Jewish Remnants in Spain: Wanderings in a Lost World.* p6

[3] *Dictionary of the Middle Ages.* Vol 7. p79

[4] http://www.atheistresource.co.uk/christjew.html (2007)

[5] Isidore's *De fide catholica contra Iudaeos* exceeded the anti-rabbinic polemics of earlier theologians by

of Christ; he believed that the Jews should be exiled and persecuted. He gave instruction that the Jews who persisted in the faith should be enslaved and later executed.[1] He contributed *Canon 60* calling for the forced removal of Jewish children from their parents and for their education by Christians, and *Canon 65* forbidding Jews and Christians of Jewish origin from holding public office.[2]

With the ascent of King Chintila (636-639) the trend towards intolerance continued.

638 – The Sixth Council of Toledo was held. Four of the nineteen canons of the council were specifically political, the rest covered Jews, monks, penitents, freedmen, holy orders, benefices, and ecclesiastical property. Certain measures, including the order that all Jews living in Spain be baptised, were first taken against the Jews to please Honorius I, who, it seems, had demanded them in a letter. King Chintila directed the Sixth Council to order that only Catholics could remain in the kingdom. Again, many Jews converted, while others chose exile.

King Recceswinth ruled jointly with his father Chindaswinth from 649 and as sole king from 653 to 672. At this time, the church councils in the capital became the most powerful force in the government, and the bishops the primary support of the monarchy. Will Durant wrote in *The Age of Faith*: 'By their superior education and organization they dominated the nobles who sat with them in the ruling councils of Toledo; and though the king's authority was theoretically absolute, and he chose the bishops, these councils elected him, and exacted pledges of policy in advance.'

653 – The Eighth Council of Toledo again tackled the issue of Jews. In his general law code of 654, King Recceswinth outlawed a set of essential Jewish practices, including circumcision of males, dietary laws (kashrut), marriage laws and ceremonies, and the celebration of Passover. It required Jews to sign an oath (placitum) that made the practice of Judaism almost impossible. Violations were punished by burning or stoning.

655 – The Ninth Council of Toledo ordered conversos to spend all Jewish and Christian holy days in the presence of a bishop. The synod declared that all conversos had to pass Christian festivals in the presence of their bishop to prove the acceptance of their new faith. Lack of compliance with this last rule resulted in flogging or forced fasting, depending on the age of the offender.

656 – The Tenth Council of Toledo ordered the expulsion from the family of the Church all clerics of all ranks who, in the future, would be caught trading Christian slaves with Jews.

The Jewish population remained sufficiently sizeable to prompt King Wamba (672-680) to issue limited expulsion orders against them; and the reign of King Erwig (680-687) was vexed by the matter.

681 – The Twelfth Council of Toledo implemented diverse measures against the Jews, enacting against them twenty eight laws. The bishops ordered the reading in all

criticising Jewish practice as deliberately disingenuous.

[1] http://www.atheistresource.co.uk/christjew.html (2007)
[2] Bar-Shava, Albert. (1990). 'Isidore of Seville: His attitude towards Judaism and his impact on early Medieval Canonical law'. *The Jewish Quarterly Review* XXX. 3,4. http://www.jstor.org/pss/1454969

the churches of the canons against the Jews and conserved all acts of abjuration and conversion of Jews, prohibiting conversos from returning to Judaism. The Council decreed the burning of the *Talmud* and other Jewish literature

King Egica (687-702), recognising the wrongfulness of forced baptism, relaxed the pressure on the conversos, but kept it up on practising Jews. Economic hardships for the Jews included increased taxes and the forced sale, at a fixed price, of all property ever acquired from Christians. This effectively ended all agricultural activity for the Jews of Spain. Furthermore, Jews were not to engage in commerce with the Christians of the kingdom nor conduct business with Christians overseas. Egica's measures were upheld by the Sixteenth Council of Toledo.

693 – The Sixteenth Council of Toledo was important in the long legal history of the Visigoths in suppressing Judaism. A Converso was allowed to trade with Catholics, but not until he had proved himself by recitation of Catholic creeds and eating non-kosher food. Penalties were enacted against Catholics who transacted with unconverted or unproven Jews.

694 – The Seventeenth Council of Toledo was primarily directed, as was the Sixteenth, against the Jews, of whom King Egica appears to have had a profound distrust and dislike. The King opened the synod by claiming that he had heard news of Jews overthrowing their Christian rulers overseas and that Iberian Jews were conspiring with these cousins to end the Christian religion once and for all. The Council therefore decreed in its eight canons that all Jews, except those in Narbonensis,[1] were to be deprived of their property, which was to be given to their Christian slaves. Their slave-keepers were chosen by the king and were to be contractually obligated to never allow the practice of the Jewish religion again. The Council also defined Jews as serfs of the prince. It declared all Jews to be slaves, and ordered all their possessions to be confiscated.[2] The Council charged the Jews with undermining the Church, of the massacre of Catholics, and of destruction of the country. All Jewish children over the age of seven were to be taken from their homes and raised as Catholics.[3]

Thus, under the Catholic Visigoths, the trend was one of increasing persecutions of the Jews. By the time of the Muslim invasion in 711, the Jews of Spain had been utterly embittered and alienated by Catholic rule.

Moorish Spain – 711 to the Twelfth Century

The Almoravids comprised a Berber dynasty of Morocco who formed an empire that by the 11th-century stretched over the western Maghreb and Al-Andalus.[4]

---

[1] Gallia Narbonensis was a Roman province located in what is now Languedoc and Provence, in southern France.

[2] Kahl, Joachim. *The Misery of Christianity: A Plea for a Humanity without God.* p56

[3] http://en.wikipedia.org/wiki/Timeline_of_antisemitism (2007)

[4] Al-Andalus also known as Moorish Iberia, was a mediaeval Muslim state and territorial region occupying parts of what is today Spain and Portugal, and small parts of modern France. Its precise extent varied over time. The name more generally describes parts of the Iberian Peninsula and Septimania governed by Moors, at various times in the period between 711 and 1492, although the territorial boundaries underwent constant

The Almoravids were crucial in avoiding a precipitated fall of Al-Andalus to the Iberian Catholic kingdoms, when they decisively beat a coalition of the Castilian and Aragónese armies at the Battle of Sagrajas. This enabled them to control an empire that stretched 3000 kilometres from north to south.

711 – With the victory of the Almoravid Tariq ibn Ziyad, the lives of the Sephardic Jews changed dramatically.[1] To them, the Moors were perceived as, and indeed were, a liberating force. Wherever they went, the Muslims were greeted by Jews eager to aid them in administering the country. In many conquered towns the garrison was left in the hands of the Jews before the Muslims proceeded further north. Thus was initiated the period that became known as 'the Golden Age' for Spanish Jews.[2]

In spite of the restrictions placed upon the Jews, life under Muslim rule was one of great opportunity in comparison with that under the previous Catholic Visigoths. To Jews throughout the Catholic and Muslim worlds, Iberia was seen as a land of relative tolerance and opportunity. Following initial Arab victories, and especially with the establishment of Umayyad rule by Abd-ar-Rahman I in 755, the native Jewish community was joined by Jews from the rest of Europe, as well as from Arab territories from Morocco to Babylon. Thus the Sephardim found themselves enriched culturally, intellectually and religiously by the commingling of diverse Jewish traditions.

Arabic culture also made a lasting impact on Sephardic cultural development. In adopting the Arabic language, not only were the cultural and intellectual achievements of Arabic culture opened up to the educated Jew, but also much of the scientific and philosophical speculation of Greek culture, which had generally been lost under Catholicism, but best preserved by Arab scholars.

The first approximately two centuries that preceded 'the Golden Age' were marked by increased activity by Jews in a variety of professions, including medicine, commerce, finance, and agriculture.

The first period of exceptional prosperity took place under the reign of Abd ar-Rahman III (882-942), the first independent Caliph of Córdoba. The inauguration of the Golden Age is closely identified with the career of his Jewish councillor, Hasdai ibn Shaprut (882-942).

Abd ar-Rahman III's support for Arabic scholasticism had made Iberia the centre of Arabic philological research. It was within this context of cultural patronage that interest in Hebrew studies developed and flourished. With Hasdai as its leading patron, Córdoba became the 'Mecca of Jewish scholars who could be assured of a hospitable welcome from Jewish courtiers and men of means.'[3]

'In its time,' writes Professor Sidney David Markman in his *Jewish Remnants in Spain: Wanderings in a Lost World*, 'Córdoba was the most important city in the Western

changes due to wars with the Catholic kingdoms.
[1] Much of what follows is taken from http://en.wikipedia.org/wiki/History_of_the_Jews_in_Spain (2012)
[2] See, for example: Flannery, Edward H. *The Anguish of the Jews*. p63
[3] http://en.wikipedia.org/wiki/History_of_the_Jews_in_Spain (2012)

world and the setting of a glorious epoch in Jewish History.'[1]

Comparing the town of Córdoba as it was under the Islamic Moors with its subsequent decline under Roman Catholicism, Joseph McCabe wrote circa 1929:

> A few years ago I stood on the bridge at Córdoba and contemplated the melancholy spectacle. Some guide-book assured me that Córdoba was 'a vivacious over-grown village,' which I could only take to be a reference to its goats and asses. Gautier, who once stood where I was standing, imagined it as the 'whitened skeleton' of a once beautiful maid; but I could not find the whiteness. Garbage-laden bullocks and impoverished Spaniards wander along its narrow dirty streets; which were paved in the ninth century and have never since been mended, says one ironic writer. Its river-edges are ragged and squalid. Less than a hundred thousand people struggle for life in its decaying frame. Yet *a thousand years ago it was the greatest city on earth,* with near a million prosperous and happy people in it, with a wealth that could have bought up the whole of European Christendom many times, with miles of glorious marble mansions shining out of superb gardens along that river-front, with art and learning that drew men from every part of the world where art and learning were still appreciated.[2]
>
> Spain, like Britain, Gaul, South Germany, Italy and North Africa, had been civilized by the Romans. *Those uninspired, materialistic, sensual, immoral Romans had made of its primitive inhabitants a happy cultured folk immeasurably higher than any section of Christendom was a thousand years later.*
>
> We have to see how in Spain itself they developed a policy which makes the rest of Europe look like savagery. But note, before we pass on, that the brilliance and refinement of the Moors made a lasting impression on the people of southern France, and for centuries these people remained culturally in contact with the Moors. The passes of the Pyrenees were the real source of the first inspiration of barbaric Europe; and the south of France soon became the most prosperous and most skeptical or heretical region in Europe. It is not merely the warm sun that has made Provence the proverbial land of song and gaiety.
>
> Let us turn back to Spain. Representatives of an already civilized race and acting under constant instructions from the Khalif of Damascus, the Moorish governors at once took over and remodeled the civic and political administration and the agricultural system ... But the basis of the Moorish civilization which was now developed in Spain was the solid economic life of the country itself.[3]

[1] Markman, Sidney David. *Jewish Remnants in Spain: Wanderings in a Lost World.* p77

[2] In *'A Corrupt Tree'*, Volume 1, 'Chapter V-2 – Repression, Regression & Retardation of Western Civilisation – Mathematics, Science & Knowledge' provides a broad picture of this enlightened time under the Moors.

[3] McCabe, Joseph. *The Story of Religious Controversy.* Ch XXV 'The Moorish Civilization in Spain'. Source: http:// http://www.infidels.org/library/historical/joseph_mccabe/religious_controversy/chapter_25.html (2006)

The intellectual achievements of the Sephardim of al-Andalus under the Moors enriched the lives of non-Jews as well. Jews were also active in such fields as astronomy, medicine, logic, and mathematics. Al-Andalus also became a major centre of Jewish philosophy during Hasdai's time. Following in the tradition of the *Talmud* and the *Midrash*, many of the most notable Jewish philosophers were dedicated to the field of ethics.

In addition to contributions of original work, the Sephardim were active as translators. Greek texts were rendered into Arabic, Arabic into Hebrew, Hebrew and Arabic into Latin, and all combinations. In contrast to the centuries of the repression of knowledge, philosophy and science under Roman Catholicism, the translation of the great works of Arabic, Hebrew and Greek into Latin by Iberian Jews was instrumental in bringing these fields into Catholic Europe, and formed much of the basis of Renaissance learning.

In the early eleventh century, centralised authority based at Córdoba broke down following the Berber invasion and the ousting of the Umayyads.

The Golden Age ended before the completion of the Catholic Reconquista.[1] The Granada massacre of Jews in 1066 was one of the earliest signs of a decline in the status of Jews, which resulted largely from the penetration and influence of increasingly bigoted Islamic sects from North Africa. Wars in North Africa with Muslim tribes eventually forced the Almoravids to withdraw their forces from Iberia. The Islamic Almohads, who had taken control of much of Islamic Iberia by 1172, treated Jews and Christians harshly, and many persons were expelled from Morocco and Islamic Spain. Faced with the choice of either death or conversion, many Jews emigrated.

Meanwhile the Reconquista continued in the north. By the early twelfth century, conditions for some Jews in the emerging Christian kingdoms became increasingly favourable. The services of Jews were employed by the Christian leaders who were increasingly emerging victorious during the later Reconquista. The necessity of having colonisers settle in reclaimed territories also outweighed the prejudices of anti-Semitism, at least while the Muslim threat was imminent. Thus, as conditions in Islamic Iberia worsened, immigration to Christian principalities increased.

Many of the newly-arrived Jews of the north prospered during the late eleventh and early twelfth centuries. As conditions became more oppressive in the areas under Muslim rule during the twelfth and thirteenth centuries, Jews again looked to an outside culture for relief. Christian leaders of reconquered cities granted them extensive autonomy, so that Jewish scholarship recovered and developed as communities grew in size and importance.

Catholic Spain – 974 to 1249

Catholic princes, the counts of Castile, and the first kings of León, treated the Jews

---

[1] Reconquista ('Reconquest') – campaigns waged by the Christian realms of mediaeval Spain and Portugal to recover territory from the Muslim Moors who had conquered most of the Iberian Peninsula between 711 and 718.

as mercilessly as had the Almohads. In their operations against the Moors they did not spare the Jews, destroying their synagogues and killing their teachers and scholars.

Only gradually did the rulers come to realise that, surrounded as they were by powerful enemies, they could not afford to turn the Jews against themselves. In León, the metropolis of Catholic Spain until the conquest of Toledo, many Jews owned real estate and engaged in agriculture and viticulture as well as in the handicrafts; and there, as in other towns, they lived on friendly terms with the Christian population.

Nonetheless, the Council of Coyanza in 1050 issued a decree limiting the interaction of Christians and Jews.

King Alfonso VI, the conqueror of Toledo (1085), was tolerant and benevolent in his attitude toward the Jews. To estrange the wealthy and industrious Jews from the Moors he offered the former various privileges. To show their gratitude to the King for the rights granted them, the Jews willingly placed themselves at his and the country's service. Alfonso's army contained 40,000 Jews, who were distinguished from the other combatants by their black-and-yellow turbans; for the sake of this Jewish contingent the Battle of Zallaka was not begun until after the Shabbat had passed.

The King's favouritism toward the Jews roused the hatred and envy of the Catholics. Consequently, in 1108 an anti-Jewish riot broke out in Toledo; many Jews were slain, and their houses and synagogues were burned. The following year the inhabitants of Carrión fell upon the Jews; many were slain, others were imprisoned, and their houses were pillaged.

Alfonso VII became the King of Galicia in 1111, and King of León and Castile in 1126. In the beginning of his reign he curtailed the rights and liberties that his father had granted the Jews. He ordered that neither a Jew nor a convert might exercise legal authority over Christians. Soon, however, he became more friendly, confirming the Jews in all their former privileges and even granting them additional ones, by which they were placed on an equality with Christians. He died in 1157.

During the reign of Alfonso VIII (1166-1214), the Jews gained still greater influence. The King was defeated at the Battle of Alarcos by the Almohades. After the victory, the emir Mohammed al-Nasir ravaged Castile with a powerful army and threatened to overrun the whole of Christian Spain. The Archbishop of Toledo called a crusade to aid Alfonso. In this war against the Arabs the King was greatly aided by the wealthy Jews of Toledo. Notwithstanding, the Crusaders began the 'Holy War' in Toledo (1212) by robbing and butchering the Jews. Shortly before his death in 1214, the King issued the *fuero de Cuenca*, settling the legal position of the Jews in a manner favourable to them.

Catholic Spain – 1250 to 1390

1250 – A bull issued by Innocent IV stipulated that Jews might not build a new synagogue without special permission, and proselytisation was forbidden to the Jews under pain of death and confiscation of property. Jews might not associate with Catholics, live under the same roof with them, eat and drink with them, or use the same bath; neither might a Catholic partake of wine that had been prepared by a Jew. The Jews might not employ Catholic nurses or servants, and Catholics might use only medicinal remedies that had been prepared by competent Catholic apothecaries. Every Jew had to wear the distinguishing badge; anyone not doing so was liable to a fine or to the infliction of ten stripes. The Jews were forbidden to appear in public on Good Friday.

1252 – Innocent also issued the infamous Bull *Ad extirpanda* that explicitly authorised the use of torture by the Inquisition for eliciting confessions from heretics.

The Jews of Spain lived almost solely in the Juderías – various enactments being issued from time to time preventing them from living elsewhere.

During the early fourteenth century the position of Jews became precarious throughout Spain. As anti-Semitism increased, many Jews emigrated from Castile and Aragón. It was not until the reigns of Alfonso IV and Pedro IV of Aragón, and of the young and active Alfonso XI of Castile, León and Galicia (1325), that an improvement set in.

Pedro I, the son and successor of Alfonso XI, was King of Castile and León from 1350 to 1369. He was favourably disposed toward the Jews, who under him reached the zenith of their influence. During the (First) Castilian Civil War (1366 to 1369), a rapacious mob invaded that part of the Judería of Toledo called the Alcana; they plundered the warehouses and murdered about 1200 Jews.

When Enrique de Trastámara (Henry II) became king, after killing his half-brother Pedro I, there began for the Castilian Jews an era of suffering and persecution, culminating in their expulsion. Prolonged warfare had devastated the land; the people had become accustomed to lawlessness, and the Jews had been reduced to poverty.

As a result of an accusation that the Jewish prayers contained clauses cursing the Christians, the King ordered that within two months, on pain of a fine, they should remove from their prayer-books the objectionable passages. Whoever caused the conversion to Judaism of a Muslim or of anyone confessing another faith, or performed the rite of circumcision upon him, became a slave and the property of the treasury. Jews no longer dared show themselves in public without the badge, and in consequence of the ever-growing hatred toward them they were no longer sure of life or limb; they were attacked and robbed and murdered in the public streets. A resolution adopted by the Council of Palencia ordered the complete separation of Jews and Christians and the prevention of any association between them.

The Massacre of 1391

Ferrant Martinez was the archdeacon of Écija and confessor to pious Queen Leonora. He was one of the most inveterate enemies of the Jewish people. His sermons delivered in Sevilla soon increased the hatred of the Catholics against the Jews.

King Juan I of Castile died in 1390, and was succeeded by his eleven-year-old son. The appointed council-regent was powerless; 'every vestige of respect for law and justice had disappeared.' Martinez continued to incite the mob against the Jews and encourage it to acts of violence. In consequence, a revolt broke out in Sevilla in 1391. Martinez continued his inflammatory appeals to the rabble to kill the Jews or baptise them. On 6 June, the mob attacked the Judería in Sevilla and killed 4000 Jews; the rest submitted to baptism as the only means of escaping death.

At that time Sevilla was said to have contained 7000 Jewish families. Of the three large synagogues, two were transformed into churches.[1]

The Jews were robbed and slain in all the towns throughout the archbishopric.

In Córdoba the butchery was repeated; the entire Judería was burned down; factories and ware-houses were destroyed. Everyone was ruthlessly slain. From Córdoba the murder spread to Jaen, and then to Toledo. Most of the Jewish communities in Castile, Aragón, Catalonia, and Majorca were attacked.

In July an outbreak of violence occurred in Valencia. More than 200 persons were killed, and most of the Jews of that city were baptised.

In August the wave of murder visited Palma in Majorca; 300 Jews were killed, and 800 sailed to North Africa; but many submitted to baptism.

Three days later, a riot began in Barcelona. On the first day, 100 Jews were killed; on the following day the mob invaded the Judería and began pillaging. Then, the citadel was stormed and more than 300 Jews were murdered. The riot raged in Barcelona, and many Jews were baptised. The last town visited was Lérida, where seventy-five were slain, and the rest were baptised.

> The year 1391 forms a turning-point in the history of the Spanish Jews. The per-
> secution was the immediate forerunner of the Inquisition, which, ninety years later,
> was introduced as a means of checking on the converted Jews.[2]

Catholic Spain – 1392 to 1468

After the bloody excesses of 1391, the popular hatred of the Jews continued unabated. The Cortes of Madrid and that of Valladolid mainly dealt with complaints against the Jews, so that King Enrique III found it necessary to prohibit the latter from practising usury and to limit the commercial intercourse between Jews and Christians; he also reduced by one-half the claims held by Jewish creditors against Christians.

During the fourteenth century, the Jews in Catholic Spain lost their legal rights, their prosperity, and the level of culture that they had acquired. All of these disappeared through the endemic religious hatred of the Catholics. The rate of Christian baptisms greatly accelerated. Jews were removed from public office permanently; they were also prohibited from engaging in commerce, from working at a trade, and ultimately were forced to live within walled ghettos, known as juderías, where they were often massacred.

This long, tragic history finally resulted in the literal destruction of Spanish Jewry in the fifteenth century via the *Edict of Expulsion* of 1492.

Renewed sufferings were inflicted upon the Jews as a result of the mission of the

---

[1] As an example of such theft, the Old Main Synagogue of Segovia was constructed around the mid-14th century. It was stolen by the Catholics and converted into a church in 1419. It was later transformed into a convent for the Sisters of Penitence. Typically, it has never been returned to the Jews. Refer to Chapter 6, and below.

[2] *The Jewish Encyclopedia.* Quoted in: http://en.wikipedia.org/wiki/History_of_the_Jews_in_Spain (2012)

Dominican Vicente Ferrer. He travelled about Castile urging the Jews to embrace Christianity, appearing with a cross in one hand and the *Torah* in the other, but with the force of the law behind him. He spent the month of July 1411 in Toledo where he invaded the large Ibn Shushan Synagogue, which he transformed into the Church of Santa Maria la Blanca.[1]

1412 – At Ferrer's request a law consisting of twenty-four clauses was issued in the name of the child-king Juan II of Castile. The object of these Valladolid Laws was to reduce the Jews to poverty and to further humiliate them:

> Christian women, married or unmarried, were forbidden to enter the Judería either by day or by night.

> Jewesses were required to wear plain, long mantles of coarse material reaching to the feet; and it was strictly forbidden for Jews as well as Jewesses to wear garments made of better material.

> Jews might not engage in handicrafts or trades of any kind, nor might they fill public offices, nor act as money-brokers or agents.

> Jews were allowed no self-jurisdiction whatever, nor might they, without royal permission, levy taxes for communal purposes; they might not assume the title 'Don', nor carry arms, nor trim beard nor hair.

> Jews were not allowed to hire Christian servants, farm-hands, lamplighters, or grave-diggers; nor might they eat, drink, or bathe with Christians, or hold intimate conversation with them, or visit them, or give them presents.

> Jews were ordered to live by themselves, in enclosed juderías, and they were to repair, within eight days after the publication of the order, to the quarters assigned to them under penalty of loss of property.

> Jews were prohibited from practising medicine, surgery or chemistry, and from dealing in bread, wine, flour, meat, and the like.

> On pain of loss of property and even of slavery, Jews were forbidden to leave the country, and any grandee or knight who protected or sheltered a fugitive Jew was punished with a fine of 150,000 maravedís for the first offence.

These laws, which were rigidly enforced, any violation of them being punished with a fine of from 300 to 2000 maravedís and flagellation, were calculated to compel the Jews to embrace Christianity.[2] Thereby the persecution of the Jews was pursued systematically.

1415 – Anti-Pope Benedict XIII issued a bull by which Jews:

---

[1] Santa María la Blanca (originally known as the 'Ibn Shushan Synagogue', or commonly 'The Congregational Synagogue of Toledo') is a museum and former synagogue. It is disputably considered the oldest synagogue building in Europe which is still standing. It is now owned by the Catholic Church. It is yet another synagogue that has never been returned to the Jews.

[2] http://en.wikipedia.org/wiki/History_of_the_Jews_in_Spain (2012)

might have no intercourse with Christians, nor might they disinherit their baptised children;

might hold no public offices, nor might they follow any handicrafts, nor act as brokers, matrimonial agents, physicians, or apothecaries;

might not dispose of meat that they were prohibited from eating;

of both sexes over the age of twelve were required to listen to a Christian sermon on the Messiah;

were denied all rights of self-jurisdiction, nor might they proceed against accusers;

were forbidden to bake or sell matzah, or to give it away;

were forbidden to build new synagogues or ornament old ones; and each community was allowed only one synagogue;

were forbidden to study the *Talmud*, to read anti-Christian writings, and to pronounce the names of Jesus (a Jew), Mary (a Jewess), or the Catholic saints;

were required to wear the Jew badge at all times.

The persecutions, the laws of exclusion, the humiliation inflicted upon them, and the many conversions among them had greatly injured the Jews, but with them suffered the whole kingdom of Spain. Commerce and industry came to a standstill, the soil was not cultivated, and the finances were disturbed. In Aragón entire communities had been destroyed; many had been reduced to poverty and had lost more than half of their members.

In order to restore commerce and industry Queen Maria, consort of Alfonso V and temporary regent, endeavoured to draw Jews to the country by offering them privileges, while she made emigration difficult by imposing higher taxes. After the persecutions of 1391, there were in Aragón and Castile many conversos. On account of their talent and wealth, and through intermarriage with noble families, they gained considerable influence and filled important government offices.

By the mid-fifteenth century, hatred toward the conversos exceeded that toward the professed Jews. In Toledo a bloody uprising against them took place in 1467, many being killed. In 1473 an outbreak occurred at Córdoba, the houses of the conversos being invaded, plundered, and burned, and many of their inmates horribly butchered.

As soon as the Catholic monarchs Ferdinand and Isabella ascended their respective thrones, steps were taken to segregate the Jews both from the conversos and from their fellow countrymen. At the Cortes of Toledo in 1480, all Jews were ordered to be separated in special 'barrios' ('quarters'), and at the Cortes of Fraga two years later the same law was enforced in Navarre, where they were ordered to be confined to the juderías at night.

Catholic Spain – 1469 to 1491

Ferdinand ('el Católico') was King of Aragón (1479–1516), as Fernando II de

Aragón, of Sicily (1468–1516), of Naples (1504–1516), of Valencia, Sardinia, and Navarre, Count of Barcelona, and jure uxoris King Ferdinand V of Castile (1474–1504), in right of his wife, Isabella I (Isabel I) ('la Católica'), Queen of Castile and León.

They married in 1469. The marriage resulted in the unification of the two principal Spanish kingdoms, Aragón and Castile. The results were both a single royal state – the precursor of the modern state of Spain – and a bringing of the hostility of the Jews to a climax.

Ferdinand and Isabella took seriously the reports that some crypto-Jews were not only privately practising their former faith, but were secretly trying to draw other conversos back into the Jewish fold. Accordingly:

> In the year 1479, Ferdinand and Isabella obtained the privilege from Sixtus IV of creating inquisitors, and six years afterwards the work of devastation began.[1]

Thus, began the infamous Spanish Inquisition.

Ferdinand, although he was the grandson of a Jew, showed the greatest intolerance to them, whether converted or otherwise – commanding all conversos to reconcile themselves with the Inquisition by the end of 1484, and obtaining a bull from Innocent VIII ordering all Christian princes to restore all fugitive conversos to the Inquisition. Under the authority of this new institution, thousands of converted Jews were killed within twelve years. It is not known how many, if any, had lapsed from their new Christianity, or were trying to convince others to do the same.[2]

The Confiscation of the Great Mosque of Córdoba

The site of the Great Mosque of Córdoba was originally a pagan temple; then the building was begun around the year 600 as the Christian Visigothic church of St Vincent.

After the Islamic conquest of the Visigothic kingdom, the church was divided between the Muslims and the Christians. When the exiled Umayyad prince Abd ar-Rahman I escaped to Spain and defeated the Andalusian governor Yusuf al-Fihri, he allowed the Christians to rebuild their ruined churches, and purchased the Christian half of the church of St Vincent.

Starting in 784, Abd ar-Rahman I and his descendants reworked the building over two centuries to refashion it as a mosque. Additionally, he used the mosque (originally called Aljama Mosque) as an adjunct to his palace and named it to honour his wife.

The mosque underwent many subsequent changes: Abd ar-Rahman III ordered a new minaret, while Al-Hakam II, in 961, enlarged the building and enriched the mihrab.[3] The last of the reforms was carried out by Al-Mansur Ibn Abi Aamir ('Almanzor') in 987. It was connected to the Caliph's palace by a raised walk-way – mosques within the palaces being the tradition for the Islamic rulers of all times. The Mezquita (Mosque)

---

[1] *A History of the Catholic Inquisition, compiled from various authors.* p42
[2] http://answers.yahoo.com/question/index?qid=20090205183757AAIGRYK (2012)
[3] Mihrab – a niche in the wall of a mosque that indicates the direction of Mecca.

reached its current dimensions in 987 with the completion of the outer naves and court-yard. It is regarded as the one of the most accomplished monuments of Islamic architecture. It was described by the poet Muhammad Iqbal: 'Sacred for lovers of art, you are the glory of faith, you have made Andalusia pure as a holy land!'

After the Spanish Reconquista, the Mosque was taken over by the Catholic Church and converted to a church, with a plateresque[1] cathedral – the 'Catedral de Nuestra Señora de la Asunción' ('Cathedral of Our Lady of the Assumption') – later inserted into the centre of the large Moorish building. The Mosque has never been returned to the Muslims.[2]

The Cathedral and former Great Mosque of Córdoba, known by the inhabitants of Córdoba as the Mezquita-Catedral (Mosque–Cathedral), is today a World Heritage Site and the cathedral of the Catholic Diocese of Córdoba.

Since the early 2000s, Spanish Muslims have lobbied the Catholic Church to allow them to pray in the Mezquita-Catedral. The Muslim campaign has been rejected on many occasions, by both Spanish Catholic authorities, and the Holy See.[3]

The Reconquista

The Islamic conquest of the Christian Visigothic Kingdom in the eighth century extended over almost the entire Iberian Peninsula.

The Reconquista ('Reconquest') was a period of almost 800 years (539 years in Portugal) during which several Christian kingdoms succeeded in retaking the Muslim-controlled areas of the Peninsula broadly known as Al-Andalus. It began soon after the Islamic conquest. The victory over the Moors at the Battle of Covadonga in 722 was the first major formative event.

The last remaining Moorish government in the Kingdom of Granada was defeated in 1492. The entire Iberian Peninsula was thus brought back under Christian rule, completing the Reconquista.

Catholic Spain, the 1492 Edict of Expulsion, the Spanish Holocaust

· On 2 January 1492, after the final battle of the Granada War, the last Muslim ruler in Iberia, Emir Muhammad XII, surrendered complete control of the Emirate of Granada to 'Los Reyes Católicos' Ferdinand and Isabella. It is one of the most significant events in Granada's history because it marks the completion of the Reconquista of Al-Andalus.

· Less than three months after the fall of Granada, an *Edict of Expulsion* (*The Alhambra Decree*) was issued against the Jews of Spain by Isabella and Ferdinand. In it, Jews were accused of trying 'to subvert our holy Catholic faith and trying to draw faithful Christians away from their beliefs.' It ordered the expulsion of Jews from the

---

[1] Plateresque – from the Spanish plataresco, in the manner of a silversmith. Thus, pertaining to an ornate style of architecture of 16th century Spain suggestive of silver plate.

[2] As is mentioned in many places in this encyclopaedia, the theft of sacred property of other religions and denominations has been a recurrent world-wide activity of the Catholic Church.

[3] http://en.wikipedia.org/wiki/Great_Mosque_of_C%C3%B3rdoba (2012)

Kingdom of Spain and its territories and possessions by 'the end of July of this year.' They were permitted to take their belongings with them, except 'gold or silver or minted money'. The punishment for a Jew who did not leave by the deadline was death. The penalty for a non-Jew who sheltered or hid a Jew was the confiscation of all belongings and hereditary privileges.

The *Edict* resulted in the Spanish Holocaust.

It included the words:

> We have been informed by the Inquisitors, and by other persons, that the mingling of Jews with Christians leads to the worst evils. The Jews try their best to seduce the Christians, and their children, bringing them books of Jewish prayers, telling them of the days of Jewish holidays, procuring unleavened bread for them at Passover, instructing them on the dietary prohibitions, and persuading them to follow the Law of Moses. In consequence, our holy Catholic faith is debased and humbled. We have thus arrived at the conclusion that the only efficacious means to put an end to these evils consists in the definitive breaking of all relations between Jews and Christians, and this can only be obtained by their expulsion from our kingdom.[1]

Expulsion or death were the only two options:

> Therefore, we, with the counsel and advice of prelates, great noblemen of our kingdoms, and other persons of learning and wisdom of our Council, having taken deliberation about this matter, resolve to order the said Jews and Jewesses of our kingdoms *to depart and never to return ...*

> And concerning this we command this our charter to be given, by which we order all Jews and Jewesses of whatever age they may be, who live, reside, and exist in our said kingdoms and lordships, as much those who are natives as those who are not, who by whatever manner or whatever cause have come to live and reside therein, that by the end of the month of July next of the present year, they depart from all of these our said realms and lordships, along with their sons and daughters, menservants and maidservants, Jewish familiars, those who are great as well as the lesser folk, of whatever age they may be, and they shall not dare to return to those places, nor to reside in them, nor to live in any part of them, neither temporarily on the way to somewhere else nor in any other manner, under pain that if they do not perform and comply with this command and should be found in our said kingdom and lordships and should in any manner live in them, *they incur the penalty of death* and the confiscation of all their possessions by our Chamber of Finance, incurring these penalties by the act itself, without further trial, sentence, or declaration.

No one was to assist or protect them:

> And we command and forbid that any person or persons of the said kingdoms, of whatever estate, condition, or dignity that they may be, shall dare to receive, protect, defend, or hold publicly or secretly any Jew or Jewess beyond the date of the end of July and from henceforth forever, in their lands, houses, or in other parts of any of

---

[1] Cohn-Sherbok, D. *The Crucified Jew: Twenty Centuries of Christian Anti-Semitism.* p88

our said kingdoms and lordships, under pain of losing all their possessions, vassals, fortified places, and other inheritances, and beyond this of losing whatever financial grants they hold from us by our Chamber of Finance.[1]

The declared role of the Inquisition in this affair was stated:

The Holy Office of the Inquisition, seeing how some Christians are endangered by contact and communication with the Jews, has provided that the Jews be expelled from all our realms and territories, and has persuaded us to give our support and agreement to this, which we now do, because of our debts and obligations to the said Holy Office: and we do so despite the great harm to ourselves, seeking and preferring the salvation of souls above our own profit and that of individuals.[2,3,4]

Historian Henry Charles Lea recorded that:

The terror and distress of the exodus, we are told, were greatly increased by an edict issued by Torquemada, as Inquisitor-General, in April, forbidding any Christian, after August 9th, from holding any communication with Jews, or giving them food or shelter, or aiding them in any way.[5]

The fate of these exiles was described by one of their number:

Some travelled through the ocean but God's hand was against them, and many were seized and sold as slaves, while many others drowned in the sea. Others were burned alive as the ships on which they were sailing were engulfed by flames. In the end, all suffered: some by the sword and some by captivity and some by disease, until but a few remained of the many.[6]

Lea summarised:

Whatever may have been the number, the sum of human misery was incomputable.[7]

Yet such were the convictions of the period, in the fifteenth century after Christ had died for man, that *this crime against humanity met with nothing but applause among contemporaries*. Men might admit that it was unwise from the point of view of statesmanship and damaging to the prosperity of the land, but this only enhanced the credit due to the sovereigns whose piety was equal to the sacrifice. When, in 1495, [Pope] Alexander VI granted to them the proud title of 'Catholic Kings' the expulsion of the Jews was enumerated among the services to the faith entitling them to this distinction ...

so far, indeed, was it from being a cruelty, in the eyes of the theologians of the period,

---

[1] http://www.sephardicstudies.org/decree.html (2006) See also: Cohn-Sherbok, D. *The Crucified Jew: Twenty Centuries of Christian Anti-Semitism.* p236

[2] Kamen, Henry. *The Spanish Inquisition: An Historical Revision.* p21

[3] See also: Cohn-Sherbok, D. *The Crucified Jew: Twenty Centuries of Christian Anti-Semitism.* p88

[4] Saving souls – a recurrent exculpation of the Catholic Church for its infliction of harm on innocents.

[5] Lea, Henry Charles. *History of the Inquisition of Spain.* Vol 1. p137

[6] Kamen, Henry. *The Spanish Inquisition: An Historical Revision.* p24

[7] Lea, Henry Charles. *History of the Inquisition of Spain.* Vol 1. p143

that Ferdinand was held to have exercised his power mercifully, for Arnaldo Albertino proved by the canon law[1] that he would have been fully justified in putting them all to the sword and seizing their property.[2]

Scholars disagree about how many Jews left Spain as a result of the decree; the numbers vary between 130,000 and 800,000. Many (probably more than half) went to Portugal, where they only eluded persecution for a few years.[3] The Jews in Portugal were then declared Christian by Royal decree unless they left, but since their departure was severely hindered by the King (who needed their expertise for Portugal's overseas enterprises), the vast majority were forced to stay as nominal Christians.

As a result of the expulsion, Spanish Jews also dispersed throughout the region of North Africa known as the Maghreb. They also fled to Europe and England. Thousands of the more fortunate reached the Ottoman Empire. There, the Sultan Bayezid II, was known to sarcastically send his gratitude to Ferdinand for sending him some of his best subjects, thus 'impoverishing his own lands while enriching his [Bayezid's]'. These Jews were mostly resettled in a country that preserved the Islamic policy of toleration; and thereby Constantinople became the site of the largest Jewish community in Europe during the sixteenth century.

Other Spanish Jews (estimates range between 50,000 and 70,000) chose to convert to Christianity and thereby escape expulsion. Their conversion served as poor protection from Catholic hostility after the Spanish Inquisition came into full effect – persecutions and expulsions were common.[4,5] The Spanish town of Ávila, for example, flourished during mediaeval times. After the expulsion of the Jews and Moslems it receded into permanent decline.[6]

Those who stayed pretended to be, or became, converts ('conversos'). Indelicately, the *Catholic Dictionary* recorded that 'This gave employment to the inquisition for centuries'.[7] Jews everywhere felt the subsequent obliteration of Spanish Jewry by the Church as being the greatest disaster to have befallen them since the demolition of the Temple in the year 70.[8] According to contemporary theologians 'no illegitimate violence was being done to the Jews, infidels, and heretics put to the sword at the behest of the Church: these people had no rights to be violated.'[9] For hundreds of years after the expulsion, the conversos were seen as being alien to the 'purity' of Spanish society. This obsession with racial purity anticipated that of the Nazis, and the racist fervour helped

---

[1] Proving, once again, Martin Luther's claim that the Catholic Church's Canon Law has nothing to do with Christ.

[2] Lea, Henry Charles. *History of the Inquisition of Spain.* Vol 1. pp143-44

[3] See below.

[4] http://en.wikipedia.org/wiki/Alhambra_Decree (2012)

[5] See also: Brown, Michael L. *Our Hands are Stained with Blood: The Tragic Story of the ...* p11. Quoted in: Evangelical Sisterhood of Mary, 1997. Source: http://www.cdn-friends-icej.ca/antiholo/guilt.html

[6] Markman, Sidney David. *Jewish Remnants in Spain: Wanderings in a Lost World.* p38

[7] de Rosa, Peter. *Vicars of Christ: The Dark Side of the Papacy.* p103

[8] Armstrong, Karen. *A History of God.* p296

[9] Russell, J B. *Witchcraft in the Middle Ages.* p148. Source: http://wiccanhistorian.home.att.net/histories/persecutionJews.html (2007)

bring about the decline of Spain through impoverishment of the population, and contempt for the productive and commercial occupations.[1]

Rafael Cansinos-Asséns, one of the most important modern Spanish authors, wrote that the consequence of the *Edict of Expulsion* of 1492 was that the Jews disappeared from Spain and from its literature. The Jew was thereby erased from the consciousness of Spaniards.[2,3]

Catholic Spain – The Theft of Synagogues by the Catholic Church

The theft of religious sites and buildings from other religious faiths, and their conversion to Catholic ecclesiastic properties, has been a worldwide characteristic of the Catholic Church.

In Spain, both for some while before, and during the fifteenth century, Jews were forbidden to build new houses of worship.[4] A large number of synagogues were stolen by the Church and converted to churches. The process of purloining often followed the sequence of: expelling the Jewish worshippers, removing the *Torah* scrolls from the Ark, and substituting an altar for the immediate celebration of the Mass.[5] Such appropriated buildings still remain in the hands of the Catholic Church. Seventeen of these stolen Jewish holy places are mentioned in Professor Sidney Markman's book *Jewish Remnants in Spain: Wanderings in a Lost World.*

Santa María la Blanca – Toledo

The Ibn Shushan Synagogue in Toledo built in 1180 was 'the largest and most beautiful synagogue in Spain'. In the fifteenth century the Jews of Toledo were massacred and the synagogue was appropriated by the Catholic Church, and renamed the Church of Santa María la Blanca.[6,7] It is disputably considered the oldest synagogue building in Europe that is still standing. It has never been returned to the Jews.

The Synagogue of El Tránsito – Toledo

The Synagogue of El Transito (Sinagoga del Tránsito) is a historical building in Toledo, founded by Samuel ha-Levi in 1356. He was a diplomat and treasurer at the court of Peter of Castile.

After the expulsion of the city's Jews in 1492, the Synagogue was requisitioned for the order of Calatrava[8] and was transformed into a hospital of the Priorate of Saint Benito. In the sixteenth century it became a church of Saint Benito. Later, in the seventeenth

---

[1] Wistrich, Robert S. *Anti-Semitism: The Longest Hatred.* pp36-37

[2] *Los judios en la literatura espanola.* p31. Source: http://www.jcpa.org/phas/phas-perednik-f03.htm (2007)

[3] A similar situation exists in modern Croatia with respect to the eradicated Serbs.

[4] Markman, Sidney David. *Jewish Remnants in Spain: Wanderings in a Lost World.* p18

[5] Ibid. p63

[6] Source: http://wiccanhistorian.home.att.net/histories/persecutionJews.html (2007)

[7] http://en.wikipedia.org/wiki/History_of_the_Jews_in_Spain#Forced_conversions (2010)

[8] The Order of Calatrava (Orden de Calatrava) was the first military order founded in Castile. The papal bull confirming the Order of Calatrava as a Militia was given by Pope Alexander III on 26 September 1164. It was founded at Calatrava la Vieja in Castile, by a Saint, Raymond of Fitero, as *a military branch* of the Cistercian

century the name changed into the Church of Nuestra Senora del Transito. The synagogue was also used as military headquarters during the Napoleonic Wars. In 1877 the building became a national monument. Today it forms part of the Sephardi Museum, exploring the Jewish culture of Mediaeval Toledo.

The Old Main Synagogue – Segovia

The Old Main Synagogue in Segovia was constructed around the mid-14th century. In 1419 it was confiscated and converted into a church dedicated to Corpus Christi. It was later transformed into a convent for the Sisters of Penitence. It has never been returned to the Jews.

The Híjar Synagogue – Híjar

This synagogue in the city of Híjar, Aragón, was purloined by the Church and converted to the Church of San Antón Híjar. It has never been returned to the Jews.

Catholic Portugal

Jewish populations existed in the Roman era long before the country of Portugal was established. With the fall of the Roman Empire, Jews were persecuted by the Visigoths and other European Christian kingdoms who controlled the Iberian region from then on.

In 711 the Moorish invasion of the Iberian Peninsula was seen by many in the Jewish population as a liberation, and marked the beginning of the Golden age of Jewish culture in there.

In the eight century the Christian kingdoms of the northern mountainous areas of the Iberian Peninsula (Kingdom of Asturias) started a long military campaign, the 'Reconquista', against the Muslim invaders. The Jews, since many knew the Arabic language, were used by the Christians as both spies and diplomats on this campaign that took centuries.

1095 – Portugal separated almost completely from the Kingdom of Galicia. At the end of the eleventh century, the Burgundian knight Afonso Henriques became count of Portugal and defended his independence. He merged the County of Portucale and the County of Coimbra. Afonso declared independence for Portugal while a civil war raged between León and Castile.

1128 – The Battle of São Mamede took place. Portuguese forces led by Afonso defeated forces led by his mother, Teresa of León, and her lover Fernão Peres de Trava. Following his victory, Afonso styled himself 'Prince of Portugal' and later became known as 'King of Portugal'. He is also known as Afonso I.

1249-1250 – The Algarve, the southernmost region, was finally re-conquered by Portugal from the Moors. In 1255 the capital moved to Lisbon.

Until the fifteenth century, some Jews occupied prominent places in Portuguese political and economic life. Many also had an active role in the Portuguese culture. By this time, Lisbon and Évora were home to important Jewish communities.

family.

1492 onwards – Following the *Edict of Expulsion*, many Jews emigrated to Portugal.

In December 1496 it was decreed that any Jew who did not convert to Christianity would be expelled from Portugal. However, those expelled could only leave the country in ships specified by the king. When those who chose expulsion arrived at the port in Lisbon, they were met by clerics and soldiers who used force, coercion, and promises in order to baptise them and prevent them from leaving the country. Nevertheless, most Portuguese Jews, eventually left the country.

This expulsion and the conversions technically ended the presence of Jews in Portugal. Afterwards, all converted Jews and their descendants were referred to as 'New Christians', and they were given a grace period of thirty years in which no inquiries into their faith would be allowed; this was later extended until 1534.

Hard times followed for the unconverted Portuguese Jews. A popular riot in 1504 ended in the death of 2000 individuals; and a massacre of 5000 in Lisbon in 1506.

The Catholic Confiscation of the Synagogue of Tomar

The Synagogue of Tomar is the best preserved of the mediaeval synagogues of Portugal. It is located in the historic centre of the city of Tomar.

With the expulsion and forced conversions of Portuguese Jews in 1496, the Tomar synagogue was appropriated by the Catholic Church, it then served as jail, church, and later as storage house. In the 1930s the old synagogue was bought by the Polish scholar Samuel Schwarz, who restored the building and donated it to the Portuguese government with the condition that it should be turned into a museum. Since 1939 it has functioned as the small 'Jewish Museum Abraham Zacuto' (Abraão Zacuto), named after the Sephardi astronomer, astrologer, mathematician, rabbi and historian who served as Royal Astronomer in the 15th century to King João II.

Portuguese Inquisition

The Portuguese Inquisition (Inquisição Portuguesa) was formally established in Portugal in 1536 at the request of King John III. Manuel I had asked for the installation of the Inquisition in 1515 to fulfil the commitment of marriage with Maria of Aragon, but it was only after his death that Pope Paul III acquiesced.

One offshoot of this inquisition was the establishment, at the request of Francis Xavier, of the Portuguese Inquisition in Goa – the horrendously evil Goan Inquisition.

Synopsis

Restrictions on the Jews of Spain commenced as early as the year 305.

Barbaric invasions brought most of the Iberian Peninsula under Visigothic rule by the early fifth century. In 587 the Visigoths adopted Roman Catholicism. They practised an aggressive policy towards the Jews, leading to repeated persecutions.

From the sixth to the seventh century, about thirty councils, were held at Toledo. Many of them placed further restrictions on the Jews.

The Islamic conquest of the Visigothic Kingdom in the eighth century extended over almost the entire Iberian Peninsula. To the Jews, the Moors were a liberating force. Thus was initiated the period that became known as 'the Golden Age' for Spanish Jews. Córdoba became the Mecca of Jewish scholars.

A decline in the status of Jews resulted largely from the penetration and influence of the bigoted Islamic Almohads from North Africa. Faced with the choice of either death or conversion, many Jews emigrated.

The Reconquista ('Reconquest') was a period of almost 800 years (539 years in Portugal) during which several Christian kingdoms succeeded in retaking the Muslim-controlled areas of the Peninsula. The last remaining Moorish government was defeated in 1492.

Archdeacon Ferrand Martinez was one of the most inveterate enemies of the Jewish people. His sermons soon increased the hatred of Catholics against the Jews. The result was a series of massacres. The persecutions were the immediate forerunner of the Inquisition.

After the massacres, the popular hatred of the Jews continued unabated. They lost their legal rights, their prosperity, and the level of culture that they had acquired. All of these disappeared through the endemic religious hatred of the Catholics. Ultimately they were forced to live within walled ghettos, known as juderías, where they were often butchered.

'In the year 1479, Ferdinand and Isabella obtained the privilege from Sixtus IV of creating inquisitors, and six years afterwards the work of devastation began.' Under the authority of this new institution, thousands of converted Jews were killed. The infamous Spanish Inquisition was not extinguished until 1834.

The long, tragic history of the Jews finally resulted in the literal destruction of Spanish Jewry via the *Edict of Expulsion* of 1492. It ordered the expulsion of Jews from the Kingdom of Spain and its territories and possessions. This was the Spanish Holocaust. 'Whatever may have been the number [expelled], the sum of human misery was incomputable.'

Over the years, a large number of synagogues were stolen by the Catholic Church and converted to churches. Most of such appropriated buildings still remain in the hands of the Church.

Following the Spanish *Edict of Expulsion*, many Jews emigrated to Portugal. However, four years later, it was decreed that any Jew who did not convert to Christianity would be expelled from Portugal. This expulsion and the conversions technically ended the presence of Jews in Portugal.

The Portuguese Inquisition was established in 1536. It held its first auto-da-fé in 1540. Like the Spanish Inquisition, it concentrated its efforts on rooting out converts from other faiths who did not adhere to the strictures of Catholic orthodoxy, particularly the Jewish 'New Christians'. It was extinguished in 1821.

Final Summation

Under the enlightened Moors, the Jews of Iberia enjoyed a Golden Age. Under Roman Catholicism, they suffered repression, exploitation, expulsion and murder for nearly 1500 years.

———

11 – The Catholic Press

Through clever and constant application of propaganda, people can be made to see paradise as hell, and also the other way round, to consider the most wretched sort of life as paradise. Adolf Hitler

Introduction

Christian anti-Semitism and anti-Judaism made the Holocaust possible. In the words of Arieh Doobov,[1] 'Modern anti-Semitism's thorough dehumanization of the Jews, which facilitated their mass murder, drew upon centuries of theologically encouraged disdain.'

Behind Hitler's anti-Semitism there is a long and well-documented history of hatred of the Jews developed and nurtured by the Catholic Church.[2] The vast majority of Christian writers have reached a consensus that 'to argue that there was no connection between nearly 2,000 years of church-inspired anti-Semitism and the Nazi assault on European Jewry is utterly fallacious and offensive.'[3]

Professor of Jewish Studies, Peter J Haas, has affirmed that 'by the sixteenth century it was absolutely normal in Europe to think about evil and the Jews together and in utterly mythic terms'. 'These views were taken out of theological discourse and placed into scientific discourse of nineteenth- and twentieth-century theories of race'.[4]

A few days after the signing of the 1929 *Lateran Treaty* between the Kingdom of Italy and the Holy See, Adolf Hitler wrote an article for the Nazi party's official newspaper, *Völkischer Beobachter* (*People's Observer*), warmly welcoming the Treaty. He confidently asserted:

> The fact that the Curia is now making its peace with Fascism shows that the Vatican trusts the new political realities far more than did the former Liberal democracy, with which it could not come to terms.

> The fact that the Catholic Church has come to an agreement with fascist Italy proves beyond doubt that the fascist world of ideas is closer to Christianity than those of Jewish Liberalism or even atheistic Marxism, to which the so-called Catholic Centre Party sees itself so closely bound, to the detriment of Christianity today and our German people.[5]

Italian socialist, L Segni, found that 'Fascism is an epiphenomenon in keeping with the evolution of the Catholic Church as directed by the tactics of the Jesuits.'[6]

---

[1] Doobov, Arieh. *The Vatican and the Shoah: Purified Memory or Reincarnated Responsibility?*

[2] See, for example: Paul, Gregory S. 'The Great Scandal: Christianity's Role in the Rise of the Nazis'. *Free Inquiry*, Vol 23, No 4

[3] Editorial in *Commonweal* (10 April 1998) p6. Source: http://www.shc.edu/theolibrary/resources/03Connection.htm (2014)

[4] Haas, Peter J. *Morality after Auschwitz: The Radical Challenge of the Nazi Ethic.*

[5] Noel, Gerard. *Pius XII: The Hound of Hitler.* p53

[6] Segni, L. *L'Esprit du Fascisme.* p15 et seq. Source: Lehmann, L H. *Behind the Dictators.* p59

ᵉ In his book *History vs. Apologetics: The Holocaust, the Third Reich, and the Catholic Church*, Dr David Cymet noted that in modern times, the Church:

> systematically accused the Jews of being responsible for freemasonry, secularism, Liberalism, industrialism, capitalism, urbanisation, and parliamentary democracy.[1]

He also discussed the Catholic Church's frontline participation in the adoption of anti-Semitic legislation in almost every country in fascist Europe, and its very active role in Hitler's rise to power and his conquest of Europe.[2]

It is a fact that many of the laws passed by the Nazis against the Jews had direct antecedents in Catholic laws through the centuries.[3]

For hundreds of years, on every continent, the Church fought against all rights for Jews. In many of the countries where the Holocaust was implemented, in particular Austria, Poland, France and Italy, Catholicism had for some considerable while been actively anti-Semitic.[4]

In particular, the German participants in the Nazi genocide were ordinary Germans from all walks of life. Their actions resulted from a universal, undisputed, and venomous Catholic anti-Semitism and anti-Judaism. The Nazis' barbarous attack on the Jews occurred in a climate of popular opinion that had been fostered by centuries of Christian hostility to both the Jewish *religion* and the Jewish *people*.[5] This prior environment had led the people to believe that the Jew was a demonic enemy whose liquidation was both necessary and just.[6] Accordingly, many serious historians find that the teachings of the popes facilitated the Nazis' extermination of the Jews.[7]

Insightfully, Émile Zola wrote in 1897:

> The Jews such as they are today are our work, the work of our 1,800 years of idiotic persecution.[8]

Hans Küng, a leading Catholic theologian who taught at the University of Tübingen, wrote that the anti-Judaism of the Nazis was the work of godless criminals, and that it would not have been possible without the previous almost two thousand years of Christian anti-Semitism.[9] Confirmingly, James Carroll in his monumental work *Constantine's Sword: The Church and the Jews* showed how the seeds that produced the Holocaust had been sown by the Church in its earliest days, and nurtured for at least seventeen centuries.[10] And, the French Jewish scholar, Jules Isaac, wrote that without

---

[1] Cymet, David. *History vs. Apologetics: The Holocaust, the Third Reich, and the Catholic Church.* p6
[2] Ibid. Preface, p xiv
[3] http://blogs.setonhill.edu/ncche/015098.php (2008)
[4] See, for example: Kertzer, David I. *The Popes Against the Jews: The Vatican's Role in the Rise of ...* pp17-18
[5] See, for example: Lewy, Guenter. *The Catholic Church & Nazi Germany.* p269
[6] See, for example: Goldhagen, Daniel Jonah. *Hitler's Willing Executioners: Ordinary Germans ...* dustcover
[7] Mannion, Michael. *Book Reviews: The Catholic Church and Nazi Germany.* http://www.mindshiftinstitute. org/Article_Catholic_Nazi.htm (2007)
[8] http://www.zionism-israel.com/his/judeophobia7c.htm (2014)
[9] Küng, Hans. *On Being a Christian.* p169
[10] *The Scandal of Roman Catholicism.* http://www.liberalslikechrist.org/Catholic/RCscandal-1.html (2007)

the centuries of Christian catechism, preaching, and invective, the precepts, propaganda and vituperation of Hitler would have been impossible.[1]

Daniel J Goldhagen has pointed out that the underlying German perception of 'the Jew' comprised three notions. He was: different from the German; the direct opposite of the German; malevolent and vitriolic.[2]

It mattered not whether the Jews were conceived from the viewpoint of religion, nationality, political group, or race, they constituted an alien body – a 'Fremdkörper'. Accordingly, Germans generally perceived any problems in society (economic, political, or social) as the product of the Jew.[3] After the inauguration of the Third Reich on 30 January 1933, no public institution supported any view of Jews other than this general perception and its Nazi elaboration.

The German Catholic Church generally accepted it and taught it. The February 1936 official guidelines for religious instruction of the German episcopate stated:

> Race, soil, blood and people are precious natural values which God the Lord has created and the care of which he has entrusted to us Germans.[4]

Throughout the 1930s, as attacks on the Jews increased, a few priests voiced objections, but the institutional Church itself said virtually nothing. At the time of the boycott of Jewish businesses on 1 April 1933, Cardinal Bertram told the archbishops that the Church should not comment on 'measures directed against an interest group which has no very close bond with the church'; and, he added, 'the Press, which is overwhelmingly in Jewish hands, has remained consistently silent about the persecution of Catholics in various countries.'[5]

In the first half of the twentieth century, the Church was willing to accept the loss of political liberties that followed the accession to power of fascist movements, so long as they served as a bulwark against Communism. Both Pius XI and Pius XII courted and showed considerable benevolence to both fascist Italy and Nazi Germany, and in 1939 Pius XII supported the fascist movement Action Française.[6]

The Catholic Conference of Dutch Bishops of 1995 stated very bluntly that there was a direct road from New Testament theology to Auschwitz.[7] The work of Professor David Kertzer has demonstrated convincingly how the Church's demonisation of the Jews was a preparation for the Holocaust.[8]

The Catholic press was a key element in this process.

---

[1] Isaac, Jules. *Jésus et Israël.* p508. Quoted in: *The Scandal of Roman Catholicism.* http://www.liberalslike christ.org/Catholic/RCscandal-1.html (2007)

[2] Goldhagen, Daniel Jonah. *Hitler's Willing Executioners: Ordinary Germans and the Holocaust.* p55

[3] Ibid.

[4] Ibid. p106

[5] http://www.shc.edu/theolibrary/resources/04German.htm (2014)

[6] Lewy, Guenter. *The Catholic Church & Nazi Germany.* pp328-29

[7] http://www.zionism-israel.com/his/judeophobia6.htm (2007)

[8] Mannion, Michael. *Book Reviews: The Catholic Church and Nazi Germany.* http://www.mindshiftinstitute. org/Article_Catholic_Nazi.htm (2007)

The Catholic Press

Guenter Lewy, in his book *The Catholic Church & Nazi Germany*, pointed out that at the time when the Third Reich was established, Roman Catholicism in German had over 400 daily newspapers constituting a press that was dedicated to the defence of the Church's privileges. This compared with only 120 National Socialist newspapers.[1]

At the adoption of the *Reichskonkordat*[2] in 1933, Hitler explained to his cabinet that the main reason for signing the accord with the Holy See was to involve the Catholic Church in 'the struggle against World Jewry.' Hitler was not disappointed. The Church fully cooperated with him in his anti-Semitic campaign during the twelve years of his regime.[3]

Throughout Europe, before and during the Nazi era, Roman Catholic publications of all classes defamed and denigrated Jews in a manner that was often indistinguishable from that of the Nazis. They justified the need for elimination of the Jewish Fremdkörper from Germany. Such action was 'justifiable self-defence to prevent the harmful characteristics and influences of the Jewish race.'[4]

For the general public there was little difference between the hate campaigns against Jews conducted in the Catholic press and the campaign the Nazis were carrying out in their publications. David Kertzer has pointed out that the Church and the Nazis, were vying with each other during the 1930s to keep or gain new followers by trying to prove who was a superior anti-Semite.[5]

David Cymet has stated that researchers studying the periodicals available in world libraries, as Ronald Modras did so carefully in the case of pre-war Poland:

> are astonished and overwhelmed by the virulence and magnitude of the daily anti-Semitic attacks in the Catholic press at the time.

Ronald Modras has also shown that there was Catholic violence against Jews in Poland during the 1930s, and the Catholic hierarchy looked the other way.[6]

All over Europe, these Catholic periodicals and publications were full of ceaseless anti-Jewish libels and malice. In Austria, France, Hungary, Italy, Poland, Romania, and the rest of continental Europe, the Roman Catholic press conducted an unremitting campaign to besmirch the imaginary Jewish enemy menacing Christian Europe. The word

---

[1] Lewy, Guenter. *The Catholic Church & Nazi Germany.* pp133-34

[2] A concordat is an agreement between the Holy See and a government or sovereign on religious and political matters. This often includes both recognition of, and privileges for the Catholic Church in a particular country. The *Reichskonkordat* was one of the most immoral, corrupt, duplicitous, and parlous agreements ever formulated between two authoritarian powers. It integrated the Catholics, their episcopate and their clergy into the Nazi system. Refer to Chapter 20.

[3] Cymet, David. *History vs. Apologetics: The Holocaust, the Third Reich, and the Catholic Church.* p145

[4] Goldhagen, Daniel Jonah. *Hitler's Willing Executioners: Ordinary Germans and the Holocaust.* p109

[5] Cymet, David. *History vs. Apologetics: The Holocaust, the Third Reich, and the Catholic Church.* p145

[6] Modras, Ronald. 'The Catholic Church in Poland and Antisemitism 1935-39: Responses to Violence at the Universities and in the Streets'. In: *Remembering for the Future: Working Papers and Addenda.* Vol 1. pp183-96

Jew was used as a synonym of Bolshevik, Freemason, Liberalism, and international capitalism.[1]

This systematic campaign conditioned the public to accept the Nazi persecution as morally justified, and prepared Europe for the Final Solution. Additionally, the European clergy informed the people that the persecution of the Jews was warranted – it was right to eliminate them as an alien body.

Even in America, the Catholic priest Father Charles E Coughlin was spreading hate against Jews to tens of millions of listeners from his radio station. He was protected by his superior, Bishop Michael James Gallagher, and was never disciplined by the hierarchy until America entered the war. His methods were confirmed by Adolf Hitler in *Mein Kampf*:

> But the power which has always started the greatest religious and political avalanches in history rolling has from time immemorial been the magic of power of the spoken word, and that alone.

> Particularly the broad masses of the people can be moved only by the power of speech.[2]

The German Catholic Press

'There was really no reason for Hitler to doubt his good standing as a Catholic. The Catholic press in Germany was eager to curry his favor, and the princes of the Catholic Church never asked for his excommunication.'[3] In June 1933 the Association of Catholic Newspapers in Bavaria adopted a resolution to place the Catholic press at the service of the Nazi state and support its policies:

> To support the policy of national liberation by the present government, the strengthening of the authority of the state ... the struggle against Liberalism, Marxism, and above all Bolshevism and for a peaceful understanding between Church and State.[4]

Following the annexation of the Sudetenland to the Third Reich in 1938, the Munich diocesan Sunday newspaper reminded the faithful to remember in gratitude their Führer who had made possible the achievement:

> We did not forget to thank the man who has preserved the peace for us and yet at the same time has achieved the freedom of our German brothers in Bohemia. Together with the German Cardinals the entire Catholic community in the Greater German Reich thanks the Führer for the act of peace.[5]

The principal official Catholic publication in Germany, *Klerusblatt*, rejoiced on 12 April 1939:

---

[1] Cymet, David. *History vs. Apologetics: The Holocaust, the Third Reich, and the Catholic Church.* p145
[2] http://www.nobeliefs.com/hitler.htm (2012)
[3] http://ffrf.org/legacy/fttoday/back/hitler.html (2011)
[4] Cymet, David. *History vs. Apologetics: The Holocaust, the Third Reich, and the Catholic Church.* p59
[5] Ibid. p134

The frontiers imposed upon us by the 'hate-peace' of Versailles are broken; the Lebensraum of the German people has been widened. Multitudes of unemployed again have work. God's holy providence has provided that in a decisive hour, Hitler is entrusted with the leadership of the German people.[1]

Later, the Bavarian Catholic press gave blind support to the War. Bamberg's diocesan newspaper, the *St Heinricksblatt*, justified a war for Lebensraum.[2] The Augsburg *Katholisches Kirchenblatt* of 20 April 1941, endorsed Hitler's wars for Lebensraum. It concluded that 'the person of the Führer contains the strength, greatness and future of the German people.[3]

The Italian and Vatican Catholic Press

In Italy, Catholic papers had railed against the influence of Jews for many decades.

. *La Civiltà Cattolica* – Pius IX (1846-1878) founded the most influential Catholic periodical anywhere in the world – the Jesuit biweekly, *La Civiltà Cattolica*. Its main task was to defend the Pope and help spread his message. It was intended to provide an authoritative Church voice on current affairs which would influence popular opinion. By the turn of the century its influence was great, and its articles were constantly quoted by the worldwide network of Catholic newspapers. In Italy, it worked 'on the Vatican's behalf to legitimate Fascism in the eyes of all good Catholics, in Italy and beyond.'[4]

- Two significant principles were to determine the approval by the Papal Secretary of State of *La Civiltà Cattolica*'s text before publication: firstly, the articles must conform to the Church's official teachings in matters of faith and morals; and secondly, the timing of publishing the article must be opportune.

In formulating his anti-Jewish laws, Mussolini's legal experts examined the many Church edicts that had plagued the Jews of Rome since at least 1555, and which had persisted until 1870. In 1938 to establish that these new proposed laws were soundly based on Church tradition, the fascist newspaper *II Regime Fascista* cited a famous series of fanatical anti-Semitic articles on 'the Jewish Question' published in 1890 by *La Civiltà Cattolica*. These articles favoured the repealing of Jewish emancipation, and stripping citizenship and civil equality from the Jews, because 'as long as governments remained faithful to the principles of the French Revolution, they would suffer under the Jewish yoke.' The newspaper exhorted acceptance of the Jesuit recommendations of 1895:

> Italy has much to learn from the Fathers of the Company of Jesus ...

To which the editors of the Jesuit journal concluded only days after the racial laws were introduced in Italy:

---

[1] Cymet, David. *History vs. Apologetics: The Holocaust, the Third Reich, and the Catholic Church.* p135

[2] Lebensraum: Space sought for occupation by a nation whose population is expanding – in this case by Nazi Germany, eastwards.

[3] Phayer, Michael. *The Catholic Church and the Holocaust, 1930-1965.* p72

[4] Kertzer, David I. *The Pope and Mussolini: The Secret History of Pius XI and the Rise of Fascism in Europe* p48

[The Catholic battle against the Jews] is to be understood as a struggle inspired solely by the need for the legitimate defense of Christian people against a foreign nation in the nations where they live and against the sworn enemy of their well-being. This suggests measures to render such people harmless.[1]

La Civiltà 'unceasingly attacked, vilified, and defamed the Jewish people for over a century.'[2]

In the last two decades of the nineteenth century and the first decades of the twentieth century, it published many anti-Semitic articles, which, coming at this time, proved crucial to the rise of Nazi anti-Semitism.[3] It published such statements as:

[Jewish society] lives and grows fat with the products of the nations that give it refuge ... It reigns unopposed ... [Judaism] calls on Jews to treat Christians as if they were animals, and do all they can to rob and cheat them ... We seek to sound an alarm for Italians so that they defend themselves against those who, in order to impoverish them, dominate them, and make them their slaves, interfere with their faith, corrupt their morals, and suck their blood.[4]

A series of savage articles drafted by Father Giuseppe Oreglia di Santo Stefano was published also at this time. In these he claimed that the *Talmud* commands the 'Jewish race' to kill Christians. By way of proof, he quoted cases that included vivid passages from the trial of the alleged murderers of Simon of Trentino[5] in 1475. He also wrote long reports focussing on the Jewish need for Christian blood for both Purim and Passover. Concerning Purim, he wrote, 'the Jews are busy capturing all the Christians they can, especially children. On this night, however, they only kill one (a child or adult), pretending to kill Haman.' With regard to Passover, Father Oreglia explained that the reason some matzah[6] is labelled kosher is because it contains a Christian child's blood.[7]

During the 1890s, Father Oreglia's work was continued by other Jesuit writers. Father Rondina wrote an article in which he claimed that Jews were fraudulent bankers, held many countries' economies in their hands, and were bent on world domination. The basis of their evil was the *Talmud*. Claims of ritual murder again were brought before the public:

For the blood of a Christian child to be appropriate for the rite and good for the health of the Jewish soul it is necessary for the little child to die amidst torments.

[1] Kertzer, David I. *The Popes Against the Jews: The Vatican's Role in the Rise of Modern Anti-Semitism.* p287
[2] Ibid. p146
[3] Ibid. p135
[4] Hardy, Rob. *What Role did the Vatican Play in Fostering Anti-Semitism?* Quoted in: http://www.nonfiction reviews.com/article1273.html (2006)
[5] See Chapter 8 for details of this case.
[6] Matzah – brittle flat bread eaten at Passover.
[7] Kertzer, David I. *The Popes Against the Jews: The Vatican's Role in the Rise of Modern Anti-Semitism.* pp159-60

This is what happened to the innocent little Simon and to so many others who were killed by needles stuck into them, or who were cut up piece by piece, or crucified.[1,2]

In 1897 *La Civiltà Cattolica* stated categorically: 'The Jew remains always in every place immutably a Jew.'[3]

In 1921 the paper's correspondent reported that in Vienna it was:

the common opinion among Catholics ... that behind Bolshevism and Communism is none other than Jewish Masonry which, by means of the total confiscation of Christians' wealth, is moving towards Judaism's absolute rule.[4]

A year later, the correspondent warned that if the Jews were allowed their way:

Vienna will be nothing but a Judaic city; property and houses will all be theirs, the Jews will be the bosses and the gentlemen, the Christians their servants. This is what the Jews want for the future of Vienna, and the socialists' ceaseless violence, carried out by a credulous crowd under the Jews' cunning direction, serves this goal alone. ... Austria will be absolutely the subject, tributary, and slave of the Jews, or it will not exist at all. This, in short, is the guiding idea of our Judeo-Masonic socialist leaders.[5]

Susan Zuccotti is an American historian specialising in studies of the Holocaust. She has emphasised the authoritative position held by *La Civiltà Cattolica*:

Of the journal in the 1920s and 1930s, one prominent Church historian has written that it was 'extremely authoritative because of its tight ties with the Vatican secretary of state.' Another respected scholar has observed, 'As always, the views of La Civiltà Cattolica were in accord with those of the Pontiff.'[6]

Jews and Freemasons have frequently been linked as conspirators by the Church. David Cymet confirmed that every conceivable fabrication, particularly the accusation of a Jewish-Masonic conspiracy of world domination, was expressed in the pages of *La Civiltà Cattolica*.

Jews allegedly aspired to rule the world through capitalist financial domination and revolutionary Communism; they were in control of international banking, finance, politics, and the press; the Freemasons were mere pawns of the Jews, doing their bidding. The preposterous accusation was made that 'Jews use Masonry as a means to rule the world, to prepare the way for their Messiah.' According to the journal, none others but the Jews stood behind religious persecutions against Catholics and the clergy; they were the source of 'the anti-Christian struggle that is the sorry end product of the entire Liberal and Masonic movement.' All the modern political developments that the Church

---

[1] Kertzer, David I. *The Popes Against the Jews: The Vatican's Role in the Rise of Modern ...* pp160-61
[2] These alleged tortures were very similar to the actual tortures inflicted by the horrendous Portuguese Inquisition in Goa.
[3] Atkin, Nicholas & Frank Tallet. *Priests, Prelates & People.* p165
[4] Kertzer, David I. *The Popes Against the Jews: The Vatican's Role in the Rise of Modern Anti-Semitism.* p272
[5] Ibid. p273
[6] Cymet, David. *History vs. Apologetics: The Holocaust, the Third Reich, and the Catholic Church.* p146

disliked at the time were ascribed to the Jews by *La Civiltà Cattolica*, whether Liberalism, Socialism, Communism, Constitutionalism, democracy, and even Rationalism, and atheism.[1]

On 25 March 1928, Pius XI published a papal decree disbanding a Catholic organisation, the Friends of Israel, which had tried to discontinue the Church's charge of deicide.[2] With the sole exception of Cardinal Ildefonso Schuster, who expressed sympathy for the petition of this group and opined that such expressions as 'perfidious Jews' exemplified a practice that was 'late and superstitious', all the other members of the Holy Office rejected the petition. Pius XI vented his wrath on Cardinal Schuster for having called the liturgical expressions 'late and superstitious'. He ordered Cardinal-Secretary of the Holy Office Rafael Merry del Val to question Schuster why he articulated opinions 'so grave and offensive to the Church.'[3]

Accordingly, the Holy Office decided to issue a ban against the Friends of Israel and to order its dissolution. It added a warning that 'no one in the future write or publish books that in any way favour such erroneous initiatives.' To protect itself against charges of conspicuous anti-Semitism, it added a duplicitous caveat 'which became a standard formula in all Church pronouncements concerning Jews':

> Hatred against the people whom God once chose, that hatred that it is today known as anti-Semitism is unacceptable.[4]

Nonetheless, Merry del Val launched the accusation that beyond the Friends of Israel stood 'the hand and the inspiration of the Jews':

> Today, the Jews were attempting more than ever to reconstruct the Kingdom of Israel. They penetrated modern society, seeking to hide their history and win the confidence of Christians while forming alliances with Masonry and practising usury.[5]

In 1928 Father Enrico Rosa, director of *La Civiltà Cattolica*, explained the ban in an article entitled 'The Jewish Danger and the Friends of Israel':

> The Church has always sought to protect even its most bitter enemies and persecutors, which is what the Jews are ... We have tried in these pages to demonstrate how much the Jews are to blame for the Soviet Revolution ... as they were previously in the French Revolution and as they have been in the more recent one in Hungary ... In the short time Jews had been given equal rights they have established their hegemony in many sectors of public life, especially in the economy and industry, as well in high finance, where they are indeed said to have dictatorial power. They can dictate laws to states and governments, in political as well as in financial matters, without fear of having any rivals ... They are first in the large businesses, occupying

---

[1] Cymet, David. *History vs. Apologetics: The Holocaust, the Third Reich, and the Catholic Church.*
[2] http://www.haaretz.com/culture/books/the-silence-was-deafening-1.312003 (2011)
[3] Cymet, David. *History vs. Apologetics: The Holocaust, the Third Reich, and the Catholic Church.* p7
[4] Ibid.
[5] Ibid.

the highest posts, especially in industry, in the large banks, in diplomacy, and even more predominant in the occult sects, scheming to achieve their world hegemony.[1]

By comparison with these claims of Jewish wealth by the Church, it is worthy of note that the popes in the fifteenth and sixteenth centuries were the wealthiest men in the world.[2] And currently, the Catholic Church is the biggest financial power, wealth accumulator and property owner in existence. It is 'the biggest possessor of material riches than any other single institution, corporation, bank, giant trust, government or state of the whole globe. The pope, as the visible ruler of this immense amassment of wealth, is consequently the richest individual of the twentieth century. No one can realistically assess how much he is worth in terms of billions of dollars ...'[3]

An article published in *La Civiltà Cattolica* on 19 June 1937 suggested another final solution:

> Even when the Zionist state becomes a reality, there will still be several million sons of Israel in the world, who will not be very different from what they are today: speculators who soak up gold, Messianic and revolutionaries ... The tragic aspect of the Jewish question is that Israel everlastingly tries to assimilate itself but never succeeds. The Jewish question is insoluble and it therefore was useless to try and find a solution ... There is only one hope left to the Christians, the conversion of Israel. That would be the final solution.[4]

In 1934 *La Civiltà Cattolica* recognised the Nazi's contribution in exposing the evil nature of the *Talmud.* During the mid-1930s, the journal stressed that as the Jews were a serious, permanent danger to society, Jewish civil rights should be rescinded and the Jews be placed in ghettos. Shortly after, Catholic governments in most of the countries of Europe revoked Jewish rights.

Another Jesuit article in *La Civiltà Cattolica*, 'Concerning the Question of Zionism', depicted Judaism as sinister, and Jews as plotting to seize the world with the Devil as their lord. 'Judaism is a deeply malevolent religion, inasmuch as it pertains to a nation which presumes itself elect, and ... is the religion of corrupt messianism [which] renders Jewry a tinderbox of disorders and a standing menace to the world.'[5]

In 1941 and 1942, at the apex of the Holocaust, when millions of Jews were being annihilated, *La Civiltà Cattolica* published two articles in which the Jews were accused of ritual murder. Sam Waagenaar[6] has pointed out that such declarations vanished opportunistically from Catholic publications after the War. Very different assertions, of having helped and defended the Jews, replaced them after the defeat of the Axis:

> Such sentiments and opinions would, after the war, disappear from the variously

---

[1] Cymet, David. *History vs. Apologetics: The Holocaust, the Third Reich, and the Catholic Church.*

[2] Manchester, William. *A World Lit only by Fire* ... p132

[3] http://www.knowledgeoftoday.org/2012/05/vatican-banks-corporations-knights.html (2014)

[4] Cymet, David. *History vs. Apologetics: The Holocaust, the Third Reich, and the Catholic Church.* pp146-47

[5] Source: Michael, Robert. *A History of Catholic Antisemitism: The Dark Side of the Church.* p176

[6] Author of *The Pope's Jews.*

repeated texts about how much the Vatican had done for the Jews of Rome conveniently forgetting what some of its highest dignitaries had done against them and against Jews in general.[1]

L'Osservatore Romano – The only publication closer to the Pope and the Holy See's hierarchy than *La Civiltà Cattolica* is *L'Osservatore Romano*. In 1870 it became the Holy See's official daily newspaper, and by the 1890s the Cardinal Secretary of State regularly contributed to it. It covers all the Pope's public activities, publishes editorials by important churchmen, and prints official documents after their release.

It also promoted the Jews-and-their-ritual-murder campaign. One article claimed that ritual murder was a fact, and the reason that recent trials had all ended with acquittals was that the Jews had resorted to bribery of the judiciary:

> The trial against a Jew accused of the ritual murder of a Christian boy has barely begun, and it has already been established by many unimpeachable witnesses that Jews practice ritual homicides so that they can use Christian blood in making their Passover matzah.

> It only confirms the conviction that the Jews truly do murder Christians to use their blood in their detestable Talmudic and rabbinical rites, and that to help them conceal these crimes, as well as for others no less atrocious, the judiciary is entirely in the synagogues.[2]

These ritual murder campaigns persisted throughout the 1890s.

In an ominous premonition on 23 August 1892, *L'Osservatore Romano* warned the Jews that:

> they had better beware, for ... God would inevitably grow intolerant of their behaviour and *then people's patience would be at an end*. Then disturbances and horrible crimes could result, but who will be responsible [if not the Jews themselves]?[3]

During this same period, the Apostolic Nuncio to France made an equally disturbing threat, when he wrote:

> the Jewish danger is everywhere, it threatens all of Christianity ... and *all means should be used to crush it. ... The Catholic Church has reserved special indulgences for those who, when the good cause demands it, spill the blood of Jews* and pagans.[4]

In 1898 *L'Osservatore Romano* attacked the Jews as being vampires who sought Christian blood and conspired to destroy the Catholic Church.

In 1924, in support of Benito Mussolini, *L'Osservatore Romano* reminded Catholics of the teaching by the Church to obey civil authority, *La Civiltà Cattolica* also reminded its readers to obey government authority.[5]

---

[1] Quoted in: Michael, Robert. *A History of Catholic Antisemitism: The Dark Side of the Church.* p147
[2] Kertzer, David I. *The Popes Against the Jews: The Vatican's Role in the Rise of Modern ...* pp160-61
[3] Michael, Robert. *A History of Catholic Antisemitism: The Dark Side of the Church.* p170
[4] Ibid.
[5] Michael, Robert. *A History of Catholic Antisemitism: The Dark Side of the Church.*

On 9 July 1940, *L'Osservatore Romano* published an article in praise of Marshal Pétain. It told of the 'good Marshal who more than any other man seems to personify the best traditions of his race,' and ended up by speaking of the 'dawn of a new radiant day, not only for France but for Europe and the world.'[1] Cardinal Hinsley published:

> that Vatican circles will sustain and strengthen Marshal Pétain in his work to Catholicise France and *win the sanction of Hitler to that end* is also clear.[2]

During the last decades of the nineteenth century, the Holy See's crusade against the Jews involved not only these two central publications but also a large and growing network of other Catholic newspapers.

Towards the end of World War II *L'Osservatore Romano*, grossly distorted news details to the disadvantage of the Soviet Union, even though Nazi atrocities in western Poland against Roman Catholics far exceeded those of the Soviet army in the east.[3]

L'Osservatore Cattolico – A Milanese Catholic daily paper, *L'Osservatore Cattolico*, was closely identified with the Vatican. During the 1880s and the 1890s it contributed significantly to the rising German and Austrian anti-Semitic movement.

It was obsessive about Jewish ritual murder, with its publication of 'such good scientific material.' In 1891 it offered 10,000 francs to anyone who could establish the innocence of the Jews in this regard. This campaign intensified, and in two months in 1892, forty four articles were published on this subject from which extracts were published in Catholic papers in Austria, Germany, Italy and France. During this period, the director of *L'Osservatore Cattolico*, Father Davide Albertario, was granted a private audience with Leo XIII at which the Pope praised the journal's good work.[4] German Catholics, in particular, followed this audience with interest.

La Corrispondenza – This official daily international bulletin of the Holy See came out on 13 March 1933 with a statement that there was a need to reassess the previous negative attitude towards Hitler's movement because 'no one could fail to recognize certain nobility in the National Socialist movement.'[5]

Piccolo Monitore delle Associazioni cattoliche dell'Umbria – This newspaper was an organ of Comitati cattolici delle regione.[6] Umberto Benigni was a talented priest who climbed rapidly through the ecclesiastical hierarchy in Rome. He became a head of Pius X's secret spy service, and was a former superordinate member of the Vatican Secretariat of State. In 1902 he was appointed to the chair in ecclesiastical history at the Roman Pontifical Seminary. He was a keen journalist and wrote an article in *Piccolo Monitore*. His attitudes to the Jews were in harmony with those of other conservative clerics closest

---

[1] Moore, Edith. *No Friend of Democracy: A study of Roman Catholic politics – their influence on the course of the present War and the growth of Fascism* Source: http://www.iterasi.net/openviewer.aspx?sqrlitid= z3mvttwmhk61bd_zubmgqq (2009)

[2] Ibid.

[3] Phayer, Michael. *Pius XII, the Holocaust, and the Cold War*. p56

[4] Kertzer, David I. *The Popes Against the Jews: The Vatican's Role in the Rise of Modern Anti-Semitism*. p163

[5] Cymet, David. *History vs. Apologetics: The Holocaust, the Third Reich, and the Catholic Church*. p44

[6] De Rosa, Gabriele. *I tempi della 'Rerum Novara'*. p505

to the Pope. In 1890, he began publishing ardent attacks on the Jews as ritual murderers. For example:

> If we keep up the way things have been going, within a few years the property and the businesses of all countries will be divided among a dozen exploitative Cyclops. Of these, eleven will belong to that worthy rabbinical race that still today in 1891 slits the throats of little Christians for the Synagogue's Passover.[1]

Bollettino antisemita – Monsignor Benigni, began to focus heavily on the Jewish threat. To this end he published his own *Bollettino antisemita* from 1920 to 1921.[2]

⌃ *Fede e Ragione (Faith and Reason)* – In 1921 Benigni published the first Italian edition of the *Програма завоевания мира евреями (Protocols of the Elders of Zion)*[3] – already recognised worldwide as an anti-Semitic forgery – as a series of supplements to the Florentine periodical *Fede e Ragione*. Initially a bimonthly publication, by 1923, *Fede e Ragione* was issued weekly. A year later, *Fede e Ragione* published a small supplement, *I Documenti della conquista ebraica del Mondo (The Documents of the Jewish Conquest of the World)*.[4] Another major publisher of the *Protocols* in Italy was Giovanni Preziosi, a fascist politician, who had joined the Catholic priesthood after completing his studies. He and Benigni became incessant campaigners for the importance of the *Protocols*.

Giornale d'Italia – This paper that had first published the racial manifesto, recalled the Church's teaching that the Jews were 'perfidious'.

Il Tevere – a notoriously ant-Semitic paper, reminded its readers that 'In every era, the popes have sought to erect barriers around the Jews' activities, to isolate them as one does an epidemic.'[5]

La Difesa della razza (The Defence of the Race) – was a glossy, colour, twice-monthly publication. It published many anti-Semitic articles. For instance, the feature 'The Eternal Enemies of Rome' told its readers that the Church had always treated Jews as second-class citizens to protect Roman Catholics from the Jews' predation. The enemy was the French Revolution – the work of a Masonic, Jewish conspiracy.[6]

The Austrian Catholic Press

According to Simon Wiesenthal, nearly half the crimes associated with the Holocaust were committed by Austrians, who comprised just 8.5 percent of the population of Hitler's Greater German Reich.[7]

---

[1] Kertzer, David I. *The Pope Against the Jews: The Vatican's Role in the Rise of Modern ...* pp226-27
[2] Ibid. p266
[3] *Protocols of the Learned Elders of Zion* was a forged document containing alleged plans for Jewish world conquest. It was supposed to have been submitted by the Zionist writer Theodor Herzl and others to the first Zionist Congress at Basel in Switzerland in 1897. It was published in Russia in 1905.
[4] Kertzer, David I. *The Popes Against the Jews: The Vatican's Role in the Rise of Modern Anti-Semitism.* p266
[5] Kertzer, David I. *The Pope and Mussolini: The Secret History of Pius XI and the Rise of Fascism in Europe.* p313
[6] Ibid. p389
[7] Pauley, Bruce F. *From Prejudice to Persecution: A History of Austrian Anti-Semitism.* back cover

Grazer Volksblatt, Salzburger Volksblatt, Der Bauernbündler, Kleines Kirchenblatt, Klerus Zeitschrift für soziale Arbeit,[1] *Reichsport,*[2] *Schönere Zukunft, and Kikiriki* were Catholic publications that commonly contained articles demonising Jews.

Schönere Zukunft (Brighter Future) – During the 1920s and 1930s, this prestigious Austrian Catholic weekly carried frequent attacks on the pestilential influence of Jews on Austrian society.[3]

Kikiriki – The pages of the Austrian Catholic satirical magazine *Kikiriki* were filled with virulent caricatures of Orthodox Jews. It 'specialised in attacks on "stock-market Jews" and carried inflammatory caricatures of Orthodox Ostjuden with sidelocks.'[4] It has been described as a precursor of the Nazi weekly *Der Stürmer*, notorious for its rabid anti-Semitism.[5]

Klerusblatt – This newspaper justified the *Nürnberger Gesetze* (*Nuremberg Laws*) as an 'indispensable safeguard for the qualitative make-up of the German people.'[6,7]

The question whether the Church should lend its help to the Nazi state in sorting out people of Jewish descent via its parochial records was never debated. On the contrary, a priest wrote in the *Klerusblatt* in September 1935: 'We have always unselfishly worked for the people without regard to gratitude or ingratitude. We shall also do our best to help in this service to the people.'[8]

Monsignor Johannes Maria Gföllner – A pastoral letter published in 1935 by the Bishop of Linz, Monsignor Gföllner, is representative of the views of the Catholic Church on anti-Semitism, at a time when the Jews were already subject to savage persecution in Germany. He wrote:

> It is beyond any doubt that many Jews, unrelated to any religious concern, exercise an extremely pernicious influence on almost all sectors of modern civilisation. The economy and business ... law and medicine, society and politics are all being infiltrated and polluted by materialistic and liberal principles that derive primarily from Judaism. Newspapers and leaflets, the theatre and cinema, are full of frivolous and immoral elements that deeply poison the Christian soul, and it is in fact Judaism that, for the most part, inspires them and spreads them ... Not only is it legitimate to combat to end Judaism's pernicious influence, it is indeed the strict duty of conscience of every informed Christian. One can only hope that Aryans and Christians will increasingly come to recognise the dangers and troubles created by the Jewish spirit and to *fight them more tenaciously*.[9]

[1] Pauley, Bruce F. *From Prejudice to Persecution: A History of Austrian Anti-Semitism.* p153
[2] *Why Didn't the Press Shout?: American and International Journalism During the Holocaust.* pp270-71
[3] Kertzer, David I. *The Popes Against the Jews: The Vatican's Role in the Rise of Modern Anti-Semitism.* p274
[4] Pauley, Bruce F. *From Prejudice to Persecution: A History of Austrian Anti-Semitism.* p153
[5] Kertzer, David I. *The Popes Against the Jews: The Vatican's Role in the Rise of Modern Anti-Semitism.* p274
[6] Phayer, Michael. *The Catholic Church and the Holocaust, 1930-1965.* p16
[7] Cymet, David. *History vs. Apologetics: The Holocaust, the Third Reich, and the Catholic Church.* p375
[8] Ibid. p83
[9] Quoted in ibid. p3

The French Catholic Press

Le Flambeau – The French far right league Croix-de-Feu (Cross of Fire) was founded in 1927 by Maurice d'Hartoy; but for most of its life it was led by Colonel François de la Rocque. In 1929 it acquired its own newspaper, *Le Flambeau* (*The Flame*). It was subsidised by wealthy perfumer François Coty, who supported Mussolini. It also had the support of the Jesuits; and many conservative Catholics became members. As one of the most important paramilitary associations, and because of its nationalist position, the organisation was considered to be among the most dangerous of the imitators of Mussolini and Hitler.[1,2]

La Croix (*The Cross*) – In 1933 *La Croix* expressed satisfaction that 'the German concordat [*Reichskonkordat*] of 20 July is the most important religious event since the Reformation'; *La Croix* 'rejoices that the new German education regulations require the complete exclusion of secularism from the school.'[3] In 1942 Pius XII extended his blessing to *La Croix* and described it as: 'an organ of pontifical thought'.[4]

L'Univers – One article in this the oldest, most respected, and ultramontane Catholic paper in France, stated:

> We French Christians are all, in effect, vanquished, conquered, expropriated from our own country and our own faith, by a race of cosmopolites, of cunning intelligence, of greedy soul ... The Jew is master of all.[5]

La Libre Parole (*Free Speech*) – This virulently anti-Semitic daily was founded by Jesuit money, and its treasury was constantly replenished by the Jesuits.[6]

Le Pèlerin (*The Pilgrim*) – A newspaper that poured forth anti-Semitic obloquy at the end of the nineteenth century was the Catholic *Le Pèlerin*.[7]

La Défense – From 1897, this virulent Catholic weekly was sold to devout parishioners after Mass. The faithful were directed to oppose the French Republic, to disapprove of Socialism, and to be tolerant of extreme right-wing parties.[8]

The Polish Catholic Press

After World War I, the countries of Eastern Europe 'vibrated with a national Catholic identity that excluded Jews.'[9] This was particularly evident in Poland. The Church's print media published a list of grievances against Jews. The word 'Jew' was equated with 'Bolshevik', 'Freemason', and 'international capitalist'. Consequently, Jews took the blame for whatever woes beset the country.

---

[1] http://en.wikipedia.org/wiki/Croix_de_Feu (2007)
[2] Lehmann, L H. *Behind the Dictators: A Factual Analysis of the Relationship* ... p7
[3] Marshal Pétain's marriage of convenience with the Catholic Church. http://www.concordatwatch.eu/showkb. php?org_id=867&kb_header_id=850&kb_id=1527&order=kb_rank%20ASC (2007)
[4] Ibid.
[5] Kertzer, David I. *The Popes Against the Jews: The Vatican's Role in the Rise of Modern Anti-Semitism.* p178
[6] Lehmann, L H. *Behind the Dictators: A Factual Analysis of the Relationship of Nazi-Fascism and* ... p7
[7] Callil, Carmen. *Bad Faith: A Forgotten History of Family & Fatherland.* p15
[8] Ibid. p17
[9] Phayer, Michael. *The Catholic Church and the Holocaust, 1930-1965.* pp7-8

- The Franciscan, Saint Maximilian Kolbe, edited several Catholic newspapers, which in the 1920s associated the Jews with Freemasonry and Communism, and in the 1930s supported economic discrimination against the Jews.[1]

This press, such as that of the Knights of the Immaculata publishing house, was riddled with warnings of the dangers posed by the Jews. In the late 1930s a Christian Democratic newspaper stated that the Jewish problem would remain while the Jews had equal rights with true Poles. One Jesuit editor advised his readers that Poland had a Jewish problem that was 'a hundred times more severe than anywhere else,' and it would be best if Catholic Poland were to become 'asemitic'.[2]

At that time, the Catholic press accounted for 27 per cent of the total output of periodicals in Poland, and therefore exercised considerable influence on the thinking of the populace.

Professor at the Institute of History PAN, Anna Landau-Czajka did an extensive study of the image of the Jew in the Polish Catholic press between the Wars, and demonstrated that 'the Jews were presented to the reader as the slayers of Christ, a tool in the hand of Satan, a people cursed by God who had been in conflict with the Catholic Church and its faithful from the dawn of Christianity.'[3]

- The anti-Semitism presented in the Polish Catholic Church in the 1930s infected all levels of the Church, and was publicly expressed in the 1936 pastoral letter issued by the Polish Primate, Cardinal August Hlond:

> It is a fact that Jews oppose the Catholic Church, are steeped in free-thinking, and represent the avant-garde of the atheist movement, the Bolshevik movement, and subversive action. The Jews have a disastrous effect on morality and their publishing houses dispense pornography. It is true that Jews commit fraud, usury, and are *involved in trade in human beings.* It is also true that the influence of Jewish young people on their Catholic peers is generally, on the religious and ethical level, a negative one. But we must be fair. Not all Jews are like this. There are very many Jewish faithful who are honest, just, compassionate, and charitable.[4]

Mały Dziennik (Little Daily) – In May 1935 the Franciscans at Niepokalanów commenced publishing *Mały Dziennik*. It was an enormous success, becoming Poland's largest circulating daily newspaper. It ceaselessly disparaged Jews and Judaism,[5] and identified Jews with communists.

The primary goal in Catholic Poland was to isolate the Jews from the main body of society.[6] Thus, a few days after Kristallnacht, Father Stanisław Trzeciak wrote:

> Jews should not elect or be elected to the Sejm, the Senate, and local government

[1] Michael, Robert. *A History of Catholic Antisemitism: The Dark Side of the Church.* p154

[2] Kertzer, David I. *The Popes Against the Jews: The Vatican's Role in the Rise of Modern Anti-Semitism.* p275

[3] Landau-Czajka, Anna. *The Image of the Jew in the Catholic Press during the Second Republic.* p157

[4] Landau-Czajka, Anna. 'The Jewish Question in Poland: Views Expressed in the Catholic Press between the Two World Wars', *POLIN: Studies in Polish Jewry*, 11 (1998) pp263-78

[5] http://www.shc.edu/theolibrary/resources/05Polish.htm#_ftnref1 (2014)

[6] Source: http://www.shc.edu/theolibrary/resources/05Polish.htm (2014)

bodies; they should not be state or local government officials; they should not serve in the army ... They should not be teachers in schools or universities, they should not be journalists or editors of newspapers intended for the Polish population; they should not purchase land or real estate.[1]

A 1938 headline in *Mały Dziennik* stated:

If we don't *declare war on them*, the Jewish rope will strangle us.

Pro Christo – The most extreme and brazen expressions of anti-Semitism in the Polish Catholic press 'regularly came from *Pro Christo*, a [Marist] monthly published for "young Catholics".' Here were 'justifications for Catholic totalitarianism and hatred for Jews in the name of love.' As late as the 1930s, the ritual murder accusations were taken seriously. *Pro Christo* reminded its readers of a series of articles in *Civiltà Cattolica* which attributed their deaths to Jewish 'hatred of the faith'.[2] It also issued such statements as 'Remove the Jews. Remove them from the areas of culture, economy, and politics'.

Father Marian Wisniewski wrote:

If anyone is allowed to shoot a thief who touches his property, and if anyone can use a sword or a rifle to defend his life, and if anyone is allowed to kill to defend his dignity and honor, in the same way a whole nation can defend its spirit and traditions; and it can use to that end the [necessary] means.[3]

We do not condemn everything the Nazis do, least of all their vigorous self-defense against the Jewish plague.[4]

Sodalis Marianus – A writer for this monthly avowed in February 1939:

We should implement the dictates of justice, which demands the establishment of ghettos, and not withdraw from those dictates in the name of any love whatsoever.[5]

The same issue warned its readers that:

It is not permissible to belittle the danger [presented by Jews] in the name of pretending to be Catholic; it is not permissible to temper our watchfulness; it is not permissible to prevent the forging of effective arms.

Ruch Katolicki (*Catholic Movement*) – Father S Kowalski wrote in this monthly of July 1936:

The Jewish soul, the Talmudic soul, obstinately spurns each hand which is stretched

[1] Landau-Czajka, Anna. 'The Jewish Question in Poland: Views Expressed in the Catholic Press between the Two World Wars'. In: *Studies in Polish Jewry*, 11 (1998) p271. *Source*: http://www.shc.edu/theolibrary/resources/05Polish.htm (2014)
[2] Modras, Ronald. *The Catholic Church and Antisemitism: Poland, 1933-1939*
[3] http://www.shc.edu/theolibrary/resources/05Polish.htm (2014)
[4] http://www.shc.edu/theolibrary/resources/03Connection.htm (2014)
[5] Landau-Czajka, Anna. 'The Jewish Question in Poland: Views Expressed in the Catholic Press between the Two World Wars', *Studies in Polish Jewry*, 8 (1994) p151. Source: http://www.shc.edu/theolibrary/resources/05Polish.htm (2014)

out towards it in friendship. For the Christian peoples *there remains only armed struggle* against fanatical Jewry.

Kultura – This literary-political magazine was published by the Central Institute of Catholic Action. Fr Paul Kuczka wrote in *Kultura*, 'Christian ethics allows you to defend yourself against an aggressor, even if the aggressor should thereby lose his life.'[1]

Kultura published an article in September 1936 asserting:

> Jews are so terribly alien to us, alien and unpleasant, that they are a race apart. They irritate us and all their traits grate against our sensibilities. Their oriental impetuosity, argumentativeness, specific mode of thought, the set of their eyes, the shape of their ears, the winking of their eyelids, the line of their lips, everything.[2]

The Hungarian Catholic Press

In Hungary the Jews were identified with Marxists and Liberals. Newspapers such as the *National Journal* and the *New Generation* blamed them for Hungary's misfortunes during World War I.[3]

The Croatian Catholic Press

The Croatian Catholic press was consistently anti-Semitic:

Katolički Tjednik, a Catholic Action publication, published an anti-Semitic and anti-Serb hate speech in the 25 May 1941 issue, written by Franjo Kralik, a priest subordinate to Archbishop Ivan Šarić (the 'Hangman of the Serbs'). It was part of a campaign to explain to the masses why the Jews around them were being 'disappeared':

> In order to maintain a correct point of view in evaluating the Jewish movement in the world, it is necessary to keep in mind a number of important facts. It is an undeniable truth that the Jews, a small people, scattered throughout the world and pursued by God's curse, are an object of ridicule and scorn on the part of all other peoples. They succeeded through their commercial talents in forcing themselves upon governments and rulers either as financiers or as secret manipulators and occasionally as open, bloody dictators ...

> The descendants of those who hated Jesus, who condemned him to death, who crucified him and immediately persecuted his disciples, are guilty of greater excesses than those of their forefathers ... The Jews who led Europe and the entire world to disaster – morally, culturally and economically – developed an appetite which nothing less than the world as a whole could satisfy ...

> As soon as a revolution is engineered by them, they slaughter mercilessly the intelligentsia. Satan helped them to invent Socialism and Communism. And they invented them and directed this liberal world movement of the workers – they, the

---

[1] http://www.shc.edu/theolibrary/resources/05Polish.htm (2014)

[2] Landau-Czajka, 'The Jewish Question in Poland: Views Expressed in the Catholic Press between the Two World Wars'. pp165-166. Source: http://www.shc.edu/theolibrary/resources/05Polish.htm (2014)

[3] Phayer, Michael. *The Catholic Church and the Holocaust, 1930-1965.* p8

most cruel and soulless of men, the most awful capitalists, the Jews ...

And did the Socialists and Communists not begin to defend them and praise these Jews who are the greatest criminals in the world? ... The movement for freeing the world from Jews is a movement for the renaissance of human dignity. The all-wise and Almighty God is behind this movement. [1,2]

Hrvatska Straža (Croatian Guard) of 24 August 1940, published an article under the title 'The Jewish Question in the Near Future'. The article approved the anti-Jewish measures in the Axis countries and put special emphasis on the proposal that Jews from all parts of the world be sent to the island of Madagascar. The article concluded with the statement that the Jewish question existed in many other countries and that 'Final solutions' should be put into effect everywhere.[3]

Nedelja (Sunday) – This paper of the Catholic Crusaders approved the Nazi racist theories and published an article about 'Jewish Atavism':

Up to the birth of Christ, Jewish atavism proved its sinful inclinations toward knavery, its lack of gratitude to God, its ruthless selfishness, its disobedience toward the heads of the state, its anarchism, its love of profit-making through the accumulation of worldly goods by means of corruption, bloodthirstiness, despotism, lasciviousness and homosexuality, incorrigible stubbornness and haughtiness ... Having realised all this, we dare to conclude that the Jews have always been destructive regardless of whether they governed themselves or were governed by others. The Jews will never change, because according to the laws of psychology their national soul cannot change for the better as long as the human race continues to exist.[4]

Glasnik Sv. Ante (Voice of St Anthony), Nos. 7 and 8, 1942, published:

The 'Talmud' is a work which the Jews created through the centuries. That type of work, however, must also come to an end. The struggling peoples' movements have uncovered the work of the Jews among the nations and have warned of its dangers, which threatened to ruin the best and most positive forces in all nations. The Croatian people have also had an accounting with such Jewish activity and have shown, under the leadership of the Ustaša[5] movement, how deceitful and ruinous is the activity carried on by the Jews among the Croatian people.[6]

Narodne Novine (Official Gazette) – In February 1942 the Interior Minister, Andrija Artuković, made an important policy speech to the Sabor (parliament) that dealt with

---

[1] See http://www.jasenovac-info.com/cd/biblioteka/Pavelićpapers/Šarić/is0003.html (2008).

[2] *Exterminate the Jews*

[3] Ibid.

[4] Ibid.

[5] Ustaša was a Catholic Croatian Revolutionary Movement whose members were known collectively as Ustaše – which have sometimes been anglicised as Ustashas or Ustashi. The word Ustaša derives from the Croatian 'ustati' – 'to rise up'.

[6] http://www.inarchive.com/com/h/hartford-hwp.com/7299/2011-11-06-description/156/The_Women_39_s_Ad_Hoc_Coalition_39_97_to_influence_and_monitor_the_elections_in_Croatia/ (2016)

'the Jewish Question'. A transcript of the speech was published in *Narodne Novine* of the Pavelić government:

> In the life of Yugoslavia, it was the Jews – who worked for and prepared the world for revolution – alongside their two most important international allies – the Communists and the Freemasons, who especially distinguished themselves. These three national groups have attempted with all their might to destroy everything Croatian they could find ...

> They tried through different organizations and offices to estrange the Croatian youth from the religion of their fathers and from the family hearth ...

> They tried to impoverish and humiliate the peasant, in a state of financial dependence and beggary, in political chaos and cultural darkness, in order to be able, at any given moment, to trade him away, to barter on his sentiments like he was a bale on the exchange.

> All this was done by the Jews, one of the most dangerous international syndicates, in order to achieve the goals of World Jewry, readying the world for the revolution by which the Jews will gain full mastery over all material possessions of the world and all the power in the world, when other nations will serve as a means to their dirty profits and their insatiable greed and ravenous thirst for control ...[1]

> The Croatian people, having re-established the Independent State of Croatia, could do nothing else but to clean off the poisonous and insatiable parasites – Jews, Communists and Freemasons – from their national and state body ...

> The Independent State of Croatia, led by the Ustaše, finding itself in a state of siege and self-defence against these insatiable and poisonous parasites, has indeed settled the so-called Jewish Question through resolute and sound actions.[2]

Synopsis

Before and during the Nazi era, Catholic publications of all classes propagated an anti-Semitism that was often indistinguishable from that of the later Nazis. They expressed the need for elimination of the Jewish Fremdkörper as 'justifiable self-defence to prevent the harmful characteristics and influences of the Jewish race.'

La Civiltà Cattolica published many anti-Semitic articles in the last two decades of the nineteenth century, which, coming at this time, proved crucial to the rise of modern anti-Semitism. *L'Osservatore Romano* also promoted the Jews-and-their-ritual-murder campaign.

The multitude of anti-Semitic publications and homilies of the Catholic press, directly engendered Nazi anti-Semitism and the Holocausts in Catholic Europe.

———

[1] By substituting the words 'Catholic Church' for 'Jews', and 'the Holy See' for 'Jewry' one has a most apposite description of Roman Catholicism.

[2] http://www.jasenovac-info.com/cd/biblioteka/pavelicpapers/artukovic/aa0013.html (2009)

12 – Catholic Action, The Jesuits

The broad mass of a nation ... will more easily fall victim to a big lie than to a small one. Adolf Hitler

Catholic Action was the name of many groups of lay Catholics which were attempting to foster a Catholic influence on society. They were especially active in the Catholic states of Spain, Italy, Bavaria, France, Belgium, and Poland.

These organisations were particularly prominent in the Nazi political strategy for the War. They were key to the Nazi occupation in Vichy France and Belgium, and provided many of the shock troops used for persecution there.

The Jesuits and their Followers

Ex-Catholic priest L H Lehmann, in his book *Behind the Dictators: A Factual Analysis of the Relationship of Nazi-Fascism and Roman Catholicism*, found that Nazi-Fascism had its origin in the Society of Jesus.

The Jesuit Oath includes the following:

> Go ye, then, into all the world and take possession of all lands in the name of the Pope. He who will not accept him as the Vicar of Jesus and his Vice-Regent on earth, *let him be accursed and exterminated.*
>
> I furthermore promise and declare that I will, when opportunity presents, make and *wage relentless war,* secretly or openly, against all heretics, Protestants and Liberals, as I am directed to do, to extirpate and *exterminate them from the face of the whole earth*; and that I will spare neither age, sex or condition; and that I will hang, waste, boil, flay, strangle and bury alive these infamous heretics, rip up the stomachs and wombs of their women and crush their infants' heads against the walls, in order to annihilate forever their execrable race. That when the same cannot be done openly, I will secretly use the poisoned cup, the strangulating cord, the steel of the poniard or the leaden bullet, regardless of the honor, rank, dignity, or authority of the person or persons, whatever may be their condition in life, either public or private, as I at any time may be directed so to do by any agent of the Pope or Superior of the Brotherhood of the Holy Faith, of the Society of Jesus.[1]

Włodzimierz Ledóchowski, SJ

Włodzimierz (Wlodimir) Ledóchowski (1866-1942) was the 26th Superior-General of the Society of Jesus ('the Black Pope'). He was a 'virulent anti-Semite, kindly disposed toward Fascism, he was a man Mussolini looked to for help.'[2] It has been stated that Eugenio Pacelli, later Pius XII, and the Jesuit Order under Ledóchowski, helped mould the Deutsche Arbeiterpartei (DAP) (German Workers' Party), into the National Socialist German Workers' Party (NSDAP), also known as the Nazi Party. It has also been stated that there was formed a secret agreement by Ledóchowski, and later

---

[1] http://www.biblebelievers.org.au/jesuits.htm (2014)
[2] Kertzer, David I. *The Pope and Mussolini: The Secret History of Pius XI and the Rise of Fascism* ... p xix

confirmed by Pius XII, that SS officers were given the spiritual powers of Jesuit priests.[1]

Jesuit Fathers Du Lac, Overmanns, Hugger, Loffler, Muckermann, Pachtler, Bangha, and Bresciana

For many years before the arrival of Mussolini and Hitler, the Jesuits fought against Judaism and Freemasonry in Belgium, France, Germany, Hungary, Italy, Poland, and Spain. In each of these countries a Catholic priest led attacks on both the Jew and the Freemason. For example in:

France – Jesuit Father Du Lac, with his 'Ligue Nationale Anti-semitique de France'.

Germany – Jesuit Fathers Overmanns, Hugger, Loffler, Muckermann and Pachtler. These latter two proclaimed the fascist doctrines of Nazism before Hitler rose to prominence; while Father Muckermann wrote prolifically in favour of racial eugenics and sterilisation.

Hungary – Father Adalbert Bangha.

Italy – Father Bresciana.[2]

In 1911 Father Overmanns wrote in the Jesuit bi-monthly magazine *Stimmen aus Maria Laach* (*Voices from Maria Laach*):[3]

It is impossible to deny the harmful influence of the Jews on the ideal which we desire in our literature ... The Jews make use of the great scope of their influence to spread corrupt and obscene principles and thus cause immense damage to the spiritual life ... Everyone can see that they create many literary works which are inspired by vile and worldly ideas ... the books of these writers are filled with the base pleasures of life, a vile sensuality and pure naturalism. The commercial sense of the Jews is not offended by the worst obscenities, white slavery, prostitution and immorality of all kinds ...

Shortly after the establishment of the Weimar Republic in 1919, Father Hugger wrote in *Stimmen der Zeit* (*Voices of the Times*) (the renamed *Stimmen aus Maria Laach*):

We are facing a ruinous state of affairs. Once again the work of restoration will have to be accomplished by youth. Will the Congregations of Mary not go forth for the third time as the instrument of reconstruction chosen by Divine Providence?[4]

The German historian Wilhelm Herzog (1884-1960) stressed that those who directed the anti-Semitism at the time of the Dreyfus Affair (Die Affäre Dreyfus)[5] depended upon

---

[1] http://vaticanassassinsarchive.com/ledochowski.htm (2013)

[2] Lehmann, L H. *Behind the Dictators: A Factual Analysis of the Relationship* ... p5

[3] Maria Laach Abbey is a Benedictine abbey in the Eifel region of Germany. It appears again in a later chapter.

[4] *Stimmen der Zeit* (June 1919) p171. Source: Lehmann, L H. *Behind the Dictators: A Factual Analysis of the Relationship of Nazi-Fascism and Roman Catholicism.* p6

[5] The Dreyfus Affair is described in the following chapter.

the instructions and, above all, upon the financial support of the Jesuits.[1,2]

Jesuit Father Gustav Gundlach

An authoritative formulation of the Church's view on anti-Semitism was published in 1930by a long-life close associate of Eugenio Pacelli, namely, the Jesuit theologian Gustav Gundlach (1892-1963), under the title 'Anti-Semitismus' in the *Lexicon für Theologie und Kirche*. Gundlach approved anti-Semitism being promoted for general political, economic, and cultural reasons. He alleged that 'global plutocracy and Bolshevism' manifest 'dark aspects of the Jewish soul expelled from its homeland which are destructive of human society.' He fully subscribed to the measures against the Jews advocated by the Nazis. Thus, anti-Semitism:

> is permissible when it combats, by moral and legal means, a truly harmful influence of the Jewish segment of the population in the areas of economy, politics, theatre, cinema, the press, science ... The Church has ... inspired and supported measures opposing unjust and harmful influence of economic and intellectual Judaism.[3]

Gundlach's approval to fight the 'harmful' influence of the Jews in these areas is indistinguishable, in a practical sense, from the position of Nazism. David Cymet concluded that effectively, 'Gundlach and the Church were on the same wavelength as the Nazis.' Their attacks against the artistic and intellectual Jewish elite in Austria and Germany 'is permeated with the same mean-spirited envy and jealousy that inspired Hitler and his followers.'[4]

Eugenio Pacelli

Eugenio Pacelli, later as Pius XII, was a great friend and promoter of the Jesuits. In the years preceding World War II, the Jesuit Party in Germany 'was instrumental in tying up the Vatican's policy to that of Hitler.' It 'Nazified' the Catholic Church in Germany and made it the willing collaborator with Hitler.[5] Walter Montano, a former Catholic priest, states in his book *Vatican Policy and World Affairs*:

> There is now no doubt that the idea of 'totalitarianising' the entire body of a nation by the ruthless intolerance of a controlling organism within the greater organisation was taken from the Jesuit set-up in the Catholic Church.[6,7]

---

[1] *Stimmen der Zeit* (June 1919) p171. Source: Lehmann, L H. *Behind the Dictators: A Factual Analysis of the Relationship of Nazi-Fascism and Roman Catholicism.* p6

[2] Michael, Robert. *A History of Catholic Antisemitism: The Dark Side of the Church.* p200

[3] Cymet, David. *History vs. Apologetics: The Holocaust, the Third Reich, and the Catholic Church.* pp1-2

[4] Ibid.

[5] A whole chapter in *'A Corrupt Tree'* is devoted to the darker side of Eugenio Pacelli. Refer also to Antony Stockwell. *Pius XII: The Dark Side.* Pacelli had a strong and abiding affinity for Germany He demonstrated his special appreciation for Germany and the Nazi Führer by sending his first official letter to Adolf Hitler, before any other head of state. He never publicly stated the word 'Jews'.

[6] http://www.xanga.com/home.aspx?user=ReligionStinks&nextdate=8%2f30%2f2002+8%3a22%3a57.0 (2009)

[7] http://www.ianpaisley.org/article.asp?ArtKey=jesuits (2010)

Pacelli was trained by the Jesuits. His close associate, Giovanni Montini (the future Paul VI) had a Jesuit education. Pius' inner circle was dominated by Jesuits: Robert Leiber was his closest advisor; Gustav Gundlach drafted many of his statements on social issues; Wilhelm Hendrich was his librarian; and August Bea was his confessor.

During the time of the mass murders of the Jews, Pacelli was responsible for the content of *La Civiltà Cattolica*, which published anti-Semitic material including the Jews' mythic sins such as deicide.[1]

Jesuit Father Bea

Shortly after the revolution in Germany, Father Bea wrote:

> The part played by many Jews at the time of the revolution ... the Zionist movement ... all this should be a lesson to those who take their religion and their country seriously to put themselves resolutely on the defensive. The increase of anti-Semitic literature and anti-Semitic organisations is evidence that *the people are ready for the fight against Judaism.*[2]

Adolf Hitler

Adolf Hitler's *Mein Kampf* repeated the precepts of the Jesuits against Judaism. Everything that he said against the Jews, about Zionism, about Jewish exploitation of indecency and obscenity in literature, films, theatre and the press, about the Jewish part in the organisation of vice, prostitution and white slavery, was taken almost word for word from the official writings of the Jesuits.[3]

He also stated in *Mein Kampf* that he was so impressed by the ruthlessness of the Church down the centuries that he both admired and modelled his tactics on the Jesuits:

> Above all, I have learned from the Jesuits. And so did Lenin too, so far as I recall. The world has never known anything quite so splendid as the hierarchical structure of the Catholic Church. *There were quite a few things that I simply appropriated from the Jesuits for the use of the [Nazi] Party.*[4,5]

Additionally, Hitler's atrocious operations were perceived by him as merely manifestations of what the Church had inflicted on innocent humanity over the centuries in the name of Christianity.[6] His use of brute force against all opposing convictions and philosophical opinions is the consequence of the fact that:

> I made a rigorous analysis of analogous cases which are to be met with in history, especially in the domain of religion.[7]

---

[1] See, for example: Michael, Robert. *A History of Catholic Antisemitism: The Dark Side of the Church.* p188
[2] Lehmann, L H. *Behind the Dictators: A Factual Analysis of the Relationship of Nazi-Fascism and ...* p8
[3] Ibid. ... p7
[4] http://www.ianpaisley.org/article.asp?ArtKey=jesuits (2010)
[5] Rauschning, Hermann. *Hitler said to Me.* pp266-67. Source: http://liberalslikechrist.org/Catholic/Hitlers Faith.html (2007)
[6] See, for example: Lockhart, D. *The Dark Side of God: A Quest for the Lost Heart ...* p21
[7] Lehmann, L H. *Behind the Dictators: A Factual Analysis of the Relationship of Nazi-Fascism and ...* p39

Article 24 of Hitler's National Social Party Programme stated: 'the Party as such starts from the standpoint of a Positive Christianity.' This is a specifically Jesuit principle of action, with the ultimate objective of making all forms of Christianity unite under the Catholic Church for a 'Christian reform of states' which would be entirely devoid of Jewish, Masonic and Protestant influence.[1]

Synopsis

Christian anti-Semitism made the Nazi Holocaust possible. The Nazis' barbarous attack on the Jews occurred in a climate of popular opinion that had been fostered by centuries of well-documented Catholic hostility to both the Jewish religion and the Jewish people. This prior environment had led the laity to believe that the Jew was a demonic enemy whose liquidation was both necessary and just.

Accordingly, many serious historians find that the teachings of the Church facilitated the ascent of Adolf Hitler and his National Socialist Party, and in the implementation of the 'Final Solution to the Jewish Question'.

Nazi-Fascism had its origin in the Society of Jesus. For many years before the arrival of Mussolini and Hitler, the Jesuits fought against Judaism in Belgium, France, Germany, Hungary, Italy, Poland, and Spain. In each of these countries a Catholic priest led attacks on the Jew.

Eugenio Pacelli (later Pope Pius XII) was a great friend and promoter of the Jesuits. In the years preceding World War II, the Jesuit Party in Germany 'was instrumental in tying up the Vatican's policy to that of Hitler.' It 'Nazified' the Catholic Church in Germany and made it the willing collaborator with Hitler.

Many of the laws passed by the Nazis against the Jews had direct antecedents in Catholic anti-Semitic laws issued through the centuries.

As Catholic Nazis later proudly commented, some factors of German Catholicism during the nineteenth century shared in the growth of a new anti-Semitism.

Völkischer Beobachter was the Nazi Party's newspaper from 1920. For twenty-five years it formed part of its official public face. Catholic politician and Papal Knight, Franz von Papen, declared in its issue of 14 January 1934: '*The Third Reich* is the first power which not only recognises, but which *puts into practice the high principles of the Papacy.*'

Final Summation

The activities of Catholic Action and the Jesuits ('Rome's caterpillars') directly engendered both Nazi anti-Semitism and the Holocausts in Catholic Europe.

———

[1] Lehmann, L H. *Behind the Dictators: A Factual Analysis of the Relationship of Nazi-Fascism and Roman Catholicism.* p21

13 – Catholicism of European Nations

By means of shrewd lies, unremittingly repeated, it is possible to make people believe that heaven is hell – and hell heaven. The greater the lie, the more readily it will be believed. Adolph Hitler

... the political opinion of the masses represents nothing but the final result of an incredibly tenacious and thorough manipulation of their mind and soul. Adolf Hitler

Austrian Catholicism

Father Sebastian Brunner

Modern anti-Semitism in Austria began in 1848, when a Catholic priest, Father Sebastian Brunner, published the Catholic federalist newspaper, *Wiener Kirchenzeitung* (*The Vienna Journal of the Church*). Brunner was obsessed with the Jewish threat to society and blamed the Jews for Austria's reduced Christianity. This paper became the leading Austrian anti-Semitic publication.[1]

The prelude to this publication was, according to the *Catholic Encyclopedia*, Liberalism, which had guided Austria from rule by the aristocracy to democracy. But the downside of this new orientation was the:

> economic advancement for the capitalist at the cost of the small tradesman, the capitalist being usually a Jew. The result was an appalling material moral degradation and a regime of political corruption focussed at Vienna … The Jewish Liberalism ruled supreme in city and country, public opinion was moulded by a press almost entirely Jewish ...[2]

Karl Lueger

Karl Lueger, the mayor of Vienna from 1897 until his death in 1910, helped in this pioneering political anti-Semitism in Austria. He was, says the *Catholic Encyclopedia*, 'a fearless outspoken Catholic',[3] who propagandised the physical annihilation of both the Jews and the Serbs.[4] He formed the Christian Social Party (Christlichsoziale Partei) (CSP). The populist and anti-Semitic politics of his CSP are sometimes viewed as a model for Hitler's Nazism.[5] The CSP was soon joined by the Reform and the German National organisations, to constitute the Anti-Semitic Party (Antisemitische Partei). This union developed later into the dominant party in Austria: the Christian Socialists.[6] In 1885 Lueger was elected to the Reichsrat (Parliament). He was the first politician to be elected to office in Europe on an explicitly anti-Semitic platform.

---

[1] Dowe, Dieter. *Europe in 1848: revolution and reform.* p601
[2] *Catholic Encyclopedia* 'Karl Lueger'
[3] Ibid.
[4] Dedijer, Vladimir. *The Yugoslav Auschwitz and the Vatican: The Croatian Massacre ...* p39
[5] Zacharia, Fareed. *The Future of Freedom: Illiberal Democracy at Home and Abroad.* p60. Source: http://en.wikipedia.org/wiki/Karl_Lueger (2010)
[6] *Catholic Encyclopedia* 'Karl Lueger'

During his adolescence, Adolf Hitler spent six years in Vienna, and adopted Lueger as his role model.[1] Lueger himself showed Hitler the popularity of anti-Semitism, which used pseudo-scientific sanction to create an environment where nothing that Jews could do, including conversion, could change their essence.[2] Hitler wrote in *Mein Kampf*:

> I soon realized that the correct use of propaganda is a true art which has remained practically unknown to the bourgeois parties. Only the Christian-Social movement, especially in Lueger's time achieved a certain virtuosity on this instrument, to which it owed many of its successes.[3]

Leo XIII and his Secretary of State, Cardinal Rampolla

Consequent to this Jewish 'moral degradation', the Holy See pursued a strategy in Austria of encouraging the growth of a Catholic political movement. Leo XIII and Cardinal Rampolla believed that such a movement was needed to oppose a variety of forces that threatened the role of the Church in Austria. They saw anti-Semitism as a powerful tool for activating the Catholic populace.

In 1889 Cardinal Rampolla reported the results of the recent Viennese municipal elections, namely, the 'triumph of the Catholics ... against the Judaic candidates'. These results showed 'a strong shift in public opinion and a return to Christian principles of civil order.'

Professor David Kertzer found that the Vatican Secret Archives provide striking evidence of the active role played by Leo XIII and his secretary of state in fostering the anti-Semitic campaign of the CSP.[4] For example, Leo sent a letter to Lueger in which he expressed his firm sympathy for the party's efforts, and added his personal blessings for the man himself.[5]

Father August Rohling

In 1871 the Kulturkampf had started, and Father Rohling, priest and professor of theology, published *Der Talmudjude* (*The Talmud Jew*).[6] It is a faulty abstract of the *Entdecktes Judenthum* (*Judaism Unmasked*) of Johann Andreas Eisenmenger, which has served as a source for detractors of Talmudic literature down to the present day.[7]

Der Talmudjude claimed that the religion of the Jews required them to murder Christian children for their blood. Rohling was summoned as an expert witness in several Ritual Murder trials. He also wrote and spoke widely on the 'Jewish threat'. His work was seen as one of the main causes of the anti-Semitic unrest that was beginning to spread through the Austrian empire in the 1880s.[8]

---

[1] See: Hitler, Adolf. *Mein Kampf*. pp55, 121. Source: Weitzman, Mark. *Antisemitism: A Historical Survey*
[2] Weitzman, Mark. *Antisemitism: A Historical Survey*
[3] http://www.mondopolitico.com/library/meinkampf/v1c6.htm (2015)
[4] Kertzer, David I. *The Popes Against the Jews: The Vatican's Role in the Rise of Modern* ... pp186-89
[5] Ibid. p193
[6] Flannery, Edward H. *The Anguish of the Jews*. p180
[7] http://en.wikipedia.org/wiki/Johann_Andreas_Eisenmenger (2010)
[8] See, for example: Kertzer, David I. *The Popes Against the Jews: The Vatican's Role in the Rise* ... p136

Fürst Cardinal Schwarzenberg

David Kertzer points out that in 1883, the governor of Bohemia wrote to Cardinal Schwarzenberg requesting him to stop Father Rohling from pursuing his anti-Semitic fermentation. Schwarzenberg refused, and advised that in reality it was the Jews who were causing the problems by using their newspapers to besmirch the Church – the Catholics were merely defending themselves. 'I believe,' he said, 'that it is time to counteract the defamation of the Church ... and to carefully investigate ... the blood ritual of the Jews, and to take appropriate measures depending on the result.'[1]

Monsignor Antonio Agliardi

Nuncio Monsignor Agliardi was uncompromisingly conservative. He also supported the anti-Semitism movement, and met Lueger frequently.[2]

Professor Kertzer has drawn attention to a debate in the Austrian Lower Parliament in which Deputy Schneider had, 'to the applause of the anti-Semites ... unrolled a Hebrew parchment, reading a passage in Hebrew which he then explained. It contains the command of ritual murder on Passover.' The liberals made a big commotion and tried to drown the man out with raucous laughter. 'But,' asked *L'Osservatore Cattolico,* 'do these cynical and petulant bursts of laughter do anything to detract from the truth that Schneider spoke?' The criticisms of this and other like acts in the Austrian parliament were stated by the paper as being most likely due to a fear of Jewish retribution and a love of their gold.[3]

The United Christians

This group preached social reform and identified the Jews as the enemy. Its first programme called for the exclusion of the Jews from the army, the civil service, the judiciary, retail trade, medicine, and the teaching of non-Jewish students.

Karl, Freiherr von Vogelsang

Freiherr von Vogelsang was one of the founders of the Austrian Christian Social Party, and the founder of the Austrian Christian Social Movement. In 1875 he became editor of the Catholic newspaper *Das Vaterland (The Fatherland)*. As a social reformer, he was a precursor of the Austrian authoritarian state of the 1930s, and was quoted in the regime's propaganda by its leader, Chancellor Engelbert Dollfuss.[4]

Eugen Kogon

Some of von Vogelsang's decidedly unfavourable remarks about Jews were included by his admirer, the Austrian fascist Eugen Kogon, in a volume entitled *Katholisch-konservatives Erbgut (Catholic-conservatives Heritage)* which called for the establishment of a Catholic Third Reich. This book was edited in 1934 by the Benedictine abbot

---

[1] Kertzer, David I. *The Popes Against the Jews: The Vatican's Role in the Rise of Modern ...* pp158-59
[2] Ibid. p192
[3] Ibid. p164
[4] http://en.wikipedia.org/wiki/Karl_Freiherr_von_Vogelsang (2010)

of the Abbey Maria Laach in Germany, to be distributed to a large proportion of Catholic households in Germany, Austria and Switzerland.[1]

The Pius Association for Promoting the Catholic Press of Austria

This association was named after Pius X, with the motto 'protection of the German people, internally and externally, from Jewish penetration, from the destructive work of the Jews.' It was founded in Vienna in 1905.

Father Victor Kolb

Kolb presented a convincing report 'to offset the demoralising Liberal Daily Press with an equally able Christian Press.'[2] This widely distributed lecture reflected the perception of Jews by Austrian Catholicism: 'Wherever you look, you always see Judaism's work, a conscious work, backed by unlimited means, always aimed at supremacy in every form.' The speech was translated into Italian and distributed throughout the Vatican.[3]

Bishop Sigismund Waitz

At a 1925 conference of Catholic academicians in Innsbruck, Bishop Waitz called the Jews an 'alien people' who had corrupted England, France, Italy, and especially America.[4]

Bishop Johannes Maria Gföllner

Bishop Gföllner of Linz, warned his countrymen in the early 1930s that:

> One can only hope that Aryans and Christians will increasingly come to recognise the dangers and troubles created by the Jewish spirit and to fight them more tenaciously.[5]

Bishop Alois Hudal ('the Brown Bishop')

Hudal was ordained Titular Bishop of Aela by Eugenio Cardinal Pacelli in 1933. From then on he publicly embraced pan-Germanic nationalism, proclaiming that he always wished to be a 'servant and herald' of 'the total German cause'. He became Rector of the Collegio Teutonico in Rome and was one of the consultants of the Holy See on German and Austrian affairs. He confirmed the role of the Catholic hierarchy in strongly supporting Hitler's programme from the beginning.

In the 1930s he became an honorary member of the Nazi Party. He also became increasingly anti-Semitic, linking the so-called 'Semitic race', which he alleged 'sought to set itself apart and dominate' with the nefarious movements of democracy and

---

[1] http://en.wikipedia.org/wiki/Karl_Freiherr_von_Vogelsang (2010).
[2] *Catholic Encyclopedia* 'Piusverein'
[3] Kertzer, David I. *The Popes Against the Jews: The Vatican's Role in the Rise of Modern Anti-Semitism.* pp273-74
[4] http://www.sullivan-county.com/id2/timeline.htm (2007)
[5] Kertzer, David I. *The Popes Against the Jews: The Vatican's Role in the Rise of Modern Anti-Semitism.* pp274-75

Cosmopolitanism,[1] and even denouncing an alleged Jewish conspiracy to become 'the financial masters of the Eternal City'.

Bishop Hudal is famous for his 1937 book *Die Grundlagen des Nationalsozialismus* (*The Fundamentals of National Socialism*), in which he praised Hitler and some of his policies, and rightly pointed out the common identity of the fundamentals of National Socialism and Catholicism.[2] The book defended Nazi racial ideology, supported laws preventing a flood of Jewish immigrants, and criticised the 'Jewish' press for pitting Austrians against Germans. Archbishop (later Cardinal) Theodor Innitzer of Vienna provided an imprimatur of the book. Hudal sent Hitler a copy with a handwritten dedication praising him as 'the new Siegfried of Germany's greatness'.[3] An example from the book reveals:

> Let us see, for example, how interesting are some of the objectives of the National Socialist programme: popular unity as opposed to everything that can disrupt; language as the nation's spiritual bond; consciousness of Germany's historical destiny; the sentiment of race consciousness; the attempt to solve the Jewish question; assurance of pure German breeding; destruction of parties; culture of the family, and the ideal of the large family considered as a matter of honour and national pride; the militarisation of the nation ...; a new system of instruction and education; the corporative idea; the aristocratic principle of government by a Leader ... Above all, the German people are indebted to this spiritual movement for *the slow destruction of the ideology of the Rights of Man*, upon which the edifice of Weimar was founded, as well as for destruction of faith in formal juridical constitutions, of the dialectics of parliamentary procedures ... and *of democracy*.[4]

Hudal boasted a Golden Nazi Party membership badge and, until the liberation of Rome, drove around the Vatican with a Greater Germany flag flying on his official car.[5] His long-term goals also included 'the reunification of Rome with the Eastern Orthodox Church and the conversion of the Balkans from the Serbian Orthodox Church to Catholicism'.[6]

Hudal's subsequent efforts, in assisting Nazi war criminals to escape justice, is detailed in a later chapter.

The Austrian Concordat and Engelbert Dollfuss (Dollfuß)

Engelbert Dollfuss was a devoted son of the Church, and Chancellor of Austria from 1932 to 1934. Once appointed, he allied himself with the Heimwehr (Home Guard), an armed Austrian fascist group supported by Benito Mussolini. In March 1933, shortly

---

[1] 'Cosmopolitanism' is the idea that all of humanity belongs to a single moral community. This is in contrast to communitarian theories, in particular the ideologies of patriotism and nationalism.

[2] Lehmann, L H. *Behind the Dictators: A Factual Analysis of the Relationship of Nazi-Fascism and Roman Catholicism.* p21

[3] http://en.wikipedia.org/wiki/Alois_Hudal (2007)

[4] Lehmann, L H. *Behind the Dictators: A Factual Analysis of the Relationship* ... p33

[5] Goñi, Uki. *The Real ODESSA: How Perón Brought the Nazi War Criminals* ... pp230-32

[6] http://en.wikipedia.org/wiki/Alois_Hudal (2007)

/ after Adolf Hitler came to power in Germany, Dollfuss dissolved the parliament, abolished freedom of speech, the press, and assembly. On 5 July 1933 he signed a concordat between the Holy See (represented by Eugenio Pacelli) and the Republic of Austria. It stated:

> His Holiness Pope Pius XI and the Republic of Austria, united in the common desire to newly regulate in an enduring fashion the legal position of the Catholic Church in the Republic of Austria to the advantage of ecclesiastical and religious life, have resolved to enter into a solemn accord.

Within a year, significant parts of the concordat were incorporated into the new Austro-Fascist Constitution. It began with the words: 'In the name of God, the Almighty, from Whom all law proceeds, the Austrian people receive this Constitution for their Christian German Federal State.'[1]

The country's Christian leaders resolved to use fascist methods not only to defend economic privilege, but to expand and safeguard the power of their Church. Catholicism increased its influence by various decrees such as:

> applying an ecclesiastical test to the civil service;

> the allocation of 58 out of the 60 seats in the State Cultural Council to the Catholic community, thus giving the Church a monopoly in all cultural matters;

> the compulsory attendance at religious instruction for all children in primary and secondary schools;

> the suppression of the powerful Austrian Freethought Union.

Accordingly, the Austrian Fascist State bore a close resemblance to the Christian conditions laid down by successive papal encyclicals dealing with the Social Order. In September 1933 prominent Catholic publicist C F Melville wrote of this fascist state:

> Economically it will resemble to a great extent the Fascist Corporate State of Signor Mussolini. Its spirit will derive from the interpretation of Pope Pius XI, in his Encyclical of May, 1931, *Quadragesimo anno*,[2] in which the principle of private ownership is acknowledged, but the right of the State to intervene 'for the common good' is also admitted. *Liberal parliamentarism is to disappear for good*; industrial disputes prevented by the substitution of corporations for the existing trade unions and the employers' federations; and *all political parties are eventually to be suppressed* ... Above all, the Austrian Corporative State will be integrally and essentially a Catholic State.[3]

---

[1] http://www.concordatwatch.eu/showtopic.php?org_id=921&kb_header_id=1811 (2007)

[2] *Quadragesimo anno* describes in considerable detail a desired tripartist corporatist social structure in which government, industry, and labour work together in concert as part of a third way between capitalism and communism. Corporatism was widely adopted in the fascist nations of Catholic Europe, including the regimes of António Salazar in Portugal, Benito Mussolini in Italy, Francisco Franco in Spain, and Engelbert Dollfuss in Austria

[3] *New Britain*, 20 September 1933. Source: *Moore, Edith. No Friend of Democracy: A study of Roman*

⁃ *Theodor Cardinal Innitzer*

Theodor Innizer, Primate of Austria, was involved in politics and cooperation with the Austro-fascist government of Engelbert Dollfuss and Kurt Schuschnigg from 1934 to 1938.[1] Additionally, Hitler's conquest of Austria in March 1938 was well prepared by Artur Seyss-Inquart – a Catholic Minister of the Interior, and a Nazi leader.

Hitler's troops entered Vienna to the pealing of Church bells that had been ordered by Archbishop Innitzer, who hastened to assure the Nazis of his fidelity and that of his Church. He issued a declaration stating that Catholics must support without hesitation the Great German State and its Führer 'whose struggle against Bolshevism and for power and for the honour and unity of Germany corresponds to the voice of Divine Providence.'[2]

Austrians were confronted with large posters everywhere, with an address 'To the Catholic people of Austria!' endorsing the Anschluss. It was signed by all archbishops and bishops of the country headed by the name of Cardinal Innitzer who signed it with 'Heil Hitler!'. The clerics stated that they had considered the political situation deeply and had decided that Adolf Hitler had proved himself to be the protector of German rights and culture. They further entreated the people to trustfully follow the Führer.[3]

Also in 1938, in honour of Hitler's birthday (20 April), Innitzer ordered all Austrian churches to fly the swastika flag, ring their bells, and pray for the Nazi dictator.[4]

German Catholicism

At this time, the influence of German priests on their parishioners 'was as considerable as was their hatred of Jews.' They denied the value of Jewish scripture and the Shabbat, accused Jews of being Cains, called Jews poisonous 'weeds' and 'snakes', denigrated the *Torah*, and regarded the synagogue as 'an assembly [of] beasts, in their lust for corporal things.'[5]

Professor Bacharach has shown that, in the century before the Holocaust, Catholic anti-Semitism was as forceful as ever.[6]

As Catholic Nazis later proudly commented, some factors of German Catholicism during the nineteenth century shared in the growth of a new anti-Semitism.[7]

Joseph Edmund Jörg

Jörg (1819-1901), who had studied theology and history, promoted the breaking of

---

Catholic politics – their influence on the course of the present War and the growth of Fascism

[1] http://en.wikipedia.org/wiki/Cardinal_Innitzer (2008)

[2] Moore, Edith. *No Friend of Democracy (1941): A study of Roman Catholic politics ...*

[3] See, for example: Mannanberg, Leopold. *A Vital Condition for Lasting Peace.* Appendix to: Lehmann, L H. *Behind the Dictators: A Factual Analysis of the Relationship of Nazi-Fascism and Roman Catholicism.* p102

[4] http://en.wikipedia.org/wiki/Cardinal_Innitzer (2008). See also: Read, Anthony. *The Devil's Disciples: Hitler's Inner Circle.* p475

[5] Michael, Robert. *A History of Catholic Antisemitism: The Dark Side of the Church.* p109

[6] Ibid.

[7] Lewy, Guenter. *The Catholic Church & Nazi Germany.* pp270-71

the yoke of economic exploitation under which the Christian nations were suffering. In the magazine *Historisch-Politische Blätter für das katholische Deutschland* (*Historical-political pages for Catholic Germany*) of 1860, Jörg warned ominously: 'The people have their irrepressible instinct and woe unto the Jewish outrages when once it flares up.' The *Catholic Encyclopedia* ('Joseph Edmund Jörg') describes him as 'A man of stainless honour, a Catholic of firm faith, a prominent politician, a sound political writer and thorough scholar'.

Bishop Martin of Paderborn and Bishop Keppler of Rottenburg

These two Catholic bishops also preached an anti-Semitic message. Paderborn (1812-1879) exposed Jewish wickedness in the *Talmud* and concluded that the accounts of Jewish ritual murder of Christian children at Eastertide were true. Bishop Keppler (1852-1926) wrote of that perverted part of the Jewish people which outside of Palestine constitutes:

> a thorn in the side of Christian peoples, reduces them to servitude with the golden chains of millions and with pens saturated with poison, contaminates the public wells of education and morality by throwing into them sickening and purulent substances.[1]

Father Erhard Schlund

Father Schlund, a Franciscan, agreed with the Nazis on the importance of fighting 'hegemony in finance' of the Jews, and 'the destructive influence of the Jews in religion, morality, literature and art, and political and social life.'

Curate Roth

Roth was an early supporter of the Hitler movement. He later became an official in the Nazi Ministry of Ecclesiastical Affairs. He viewed the Jews as a morally inferior race who would have to be removed from public life.[2]

Dr Haeuser and Father Senn

Dr Haeuser, whose 1923 book carried the Imprimatur of the diocese of Regensburg, described the Jews as "Germany's cross, a people disowned by God and under their own curse." He claimed that the Jews bore much of the blame for Germany having lost World War I, and that they had been dominant in the 1918 revolution. Father Senn called the Hitler movement 'the last big opportunity to throw off the Jewish yoke.'[3]

Ecclesiastic Rituals and Commemorations

These systems maintained the German perception of the malignant Jew

For example, in 1337 the entire Jewish population of Deggendorf in Catholic Bavaria was burned after stories were spread that they had defiled a communion Host.

---

[1] Paldiel, Mordecai. *Churches and the Holocaust: Unholy Teaching, Good Samaritans, and ...* p46
[2] Hunt, Dave. http://www.keithhunt.com/Whore8.html (2016)
[3] Ibid.

Persecution also spread to Austria and Poland where 51 Jewish towns were attacked. Following the 'torture' of the Host, 'a lovely little child' had emerged from it. For many years, the people of Deggendorf had commemorated this miracle.[1] A picture in one of the town's churches had the inscription 'God grant that our fatherland be forever free from this hellish scum.' A Benedictine monk composed a play which was performed every year during the week-long celebrations. The Jews were called 'brood of Judas', 'hordes of the devil', 'poison mixers' and other derogatory phrases. 10,000 visitors attended the commemoration every year.[2] This local annual celebration, known as 'Deggendorfer Gnad', celebrated the defilement of the Host by Jews up until the 1980s.[3]

The Federation of German Catholic Student Societies

In 1923 the Federation required all its members to produce a certificate proving that they had Aryan grandparents.[4]

Franz von Papen and Alfred Hugenberg

Franz Joseph Hermann Michael Maria von Papen (1879-1969) was a German noble-man, a Catholic politician, a Papal Knight, and a diplomat. He was a Catholic Centre Party member of the Prussian diet from 1921 to 1932. He served briefly as Chancellor of Germany (Reichskanzler) in 1932. To many historians, von Papen was also a key member in the small clique of right-wing politicians who manipulated Adolf Hitler into power by furtive intrigue. He has been called a 'stirrup holder' (Steigbügelhalter) for Hitler.[5] Evidence suggests that without von Papen's aid, Hitler would not have become the leader of Germany.

It is significant that ten years of ruthless strategy had not brought electoral victory to the Nazi party. By 1932 the tide began to turn against Nazism; Hitler lost ground in several elections, and his funds began to run low. He realised that his campaign was lost. At this critical moment powerful assistance came to the Nazis via Franz von Papen and the German nationalist Alfred Hugenberg. Both men were 'notorious henchmen of the Vatican'.[6]

In Germany during 1918, the Second Reich of Kaiser Wilhelm II was replaced by the democratic Weimar Republic. Paul von Hindenburg was the second president of the Weimar Republic. Hugenberg, von Papen, the ultra-clerical Bavarian People's Party, and the Catholic Centre Party persuaded von Hindenburg to make Hitler the Reich chan-cellor. The Weimar Republic was supplanted in January 1933 by this Third Reich, and Adolf Hitler achieved supreme power. Thus, the era of the Nazi regime was initiated,

---

[1] Refer to Chapter 8 for further details.
[2] Lewy, Guenter. *The Catholic Church & Nazi Germany.* pp272-73
[3] http://en.wikipedia.org/wiki/Host_desecration (2007). https://en.wikipedia.org/wiki/Deggendorf#The_course_of_the_.22Deggendorfer_Gnad.22 (2015)
[4] Kahl, Joachim. *The Misery of Christianity: A Plea for a Humanity without God.* p59
[5] http://en.wikipedia.org/wiki/Franz_von_Papen (2007)
[6] Mannanberg, Leopold. A Vital Condition for Lasting Peace. Appendix to: Lehmann, L H. *Behind the Dictators: A Factual Analysis of the Relationship of Nazi-Fascism and Roman Catholicism.* p91

and the future of Europe was changed forever. The manipulative Catholic Church congratulated Hitler.[1]

Von Papen declared in the issue of 14 January 1934 of the *Völkischer Beobachter*:

> The Third Reich is the first power which not only recognises, but which puts into
> practice the high principles of the Papacy.[2]

Kreuz und Adler (Cross and Eagle)

In 1933 an organisation of Catholic intellectuals and leaders who wanted to 'work
with' the Nazis was founded. At the first public meeting of the Kreuz und Adler in
Berlin, von Papen characterised the Third Reich as a Christian counter-revolution to the
French (liberal) Revolution of 1789.[3]

Joseph Lortz

Joseph Lortz decided in his teens to prepare for the priesthood, and began the study
of theology and philosophy in Rome. In 1935 he was appointed to the Catholic Faculty
at the University of Münster. Professor Lortz came to see a logical connection between
his perception of the redemptive role of Catholicism and the social and political reforms
sought by National Socialism. Nazism was compatible with Catholicism in its attack on
both liberal principles and subjective relativism, and it promised to restore a social
framework more conducive to the work of the Church. Thus there was a strong connection between National Socialist views of social unity and equality (including the
affirmation of the priority of the community over the rights of the individual) and the
corporatist principles of Pius XI's 1931 encyclical *Quadragesimo anno*. Lortz found in
earlier times the renewed vision that had been lost:

> A comparison of the conclusions of our analysis of the nineteenth century until our
> time with the fundamental thought and emphases of National Socialism shows to
> what an extraordinary degree and sense the Nazi movement has become the fulfil-
> ment of our time.[4]

Lortz showed in his *Geschichte der Kirche* (*History of the Church*) (1934) that
Roman Catholicism and Nazi-Socialism agreed on the following points:

> 1. Both are mortal enemies of Liberalism, Relativism, and Bolshevism, that is to
> say, of the three deadly maladies from which our age is suffering, and which fiercely
> attack the work of the Church. The essential ideas of Nazi Socialism, together with
> the principle of liberty bound to authority, correspond exactly to the ideas that Popes
> Gregory and Pius IX endeavoured to *impose upon the 19th century*, in face of a

[1] Paul, Gregory S. *The Great Scandal: Christianity's Role in the Rise of the Nazis*. Source: http://www.
secularhumanism.org/index.php?section=library&page=paul_23_4 (2007)

[2] Lehmann, L H. *Behind the Dictators: A Factual Analysis of the Relationship of Nazi-Fascism and ...* p35

[3] Lewy, Guenter. Quoted in: *The Scandal of Roman Catholicism*. Sec 1. 'How "the one true Church" helped
bring about the Jewish Holocaust'. http://www.liberalslikechrist.org/Catholic/RCscandal-1.html (2007)

[4] Lukens, Michael B. 'Joseph Lortz and a Catholic Accommodation with National Socialism' in: *Betrayal:
German Churches and the Holocaust*. p164

world which called itself progressive, and which received their teachings with sarcastic smiles. To this is added their common fight against Freemasonry.

2. Their common fight against the Godless movement; against public immorality; *against the stupid doctrine of equality*, which is destructive of life; their fight for a rational and fertile structure of human society as desired by God, and for the corporative structure of the state as proposed by Popes Leo XIII and Pius XI.

3. By its principle of authority and government by a Leader, a principle upon which all national life rests, *National Socialism combines the German and the Roman Catholic attitude towards human life.*

4. Most important of all: *National Socialism is a confession of faith*; opposing, as it does, unbelief and destructive doubt it has convinced all classes of society that the outlook of the believer is not, as liberalism has taught, an attitude of inferiority, but one that carries man towards the total accomplishment of his destiny. And although the Roman Catholic Church should never identify itself with any movement, it cannot afford to miss the opportunity of gratefully accepting the help of this powerful ally in the fight which she is carrying on against atheistic rationalism.[1]

5. It [Nazism] was born originally out of the most profound tendencies of the epoch, of which it is the crowning act. Undoubtedly, we now have the right to speak of an essential transformation, of the birth of a veritable new era, the accomplishments of which will remain. A new epoch has opened which *will serve religion and the Church*, and which will be extraordinarily well armed to carry on the fight against atheism.[2]

Lortz was seen as the most pivotal figure of the time, both because of the scope of his argument and because of its persuasive appeal to the Catholic intellectual community.[3] He and other Catholic theologians gave a theological and intellectual legitimacy to National Socialism at exactly the time when the question of popular acceptance of Nazism hung in a delicate balance. They built upon the practice and intellectual authority that Church academic figures had in the minds of the laity. The evidence shows that from the laity upwards to the conferences of German bishops there was a growing acceptance of and, in some circles, great enthusiasm for the Nazi cause. These theologians thereby played an effective intellectual role in creating total political control by the Nazis and 'a total social and spiritual disaster for the Church.'[4]

ˉ *The Bishops of Speyer and Trier*

Saarland is a state in south-western Germany. Consequent to the Treaty of Versailles, a plebiscite was held in 1935 to determine the territory's future status. An appeal to

[1] Notwithstanding, not one of the top Nazi leaders was raised in a liberal or atheistic family.
[2] Lehmann, L H. *Behind the Dictators: A Factual Analysis of the Relationship of Nazi-Fascism and Roman Catholicism.* pp34-35
[3] Lukens, Michael B. 'Joseph Lortz and a Catholic Accommodation with National Socialism' in *Betrayal: German Churches and the Holocaust.* p155
[4] Ibid. p167

Catholic voters was issued by, and read from the pulpits of the churches under the bishops' control:

> Dear diocesans, – On Sunday, January 13th next, the plebiscite will be held in the Saar to decide whether this German country and its inhabitants shall or shall not remain in that state of separation from Germany which was forced upon them by the dictated peace of Versailles. No Germans can regard with indifference a decision which will fall due in a few days and which will have such important consequences for the future of the Fatherland. As German Catholics it is our duty to uphold the greatness, the welfare, and the peace of our Fatherland. Our most important means to this end is prayer. We therefore ordain that on the given Sunday, after the usual services, Pater Noster and Ave Maria be said thrice in all the churches with the participation of the congregation, in order to pray that the Saar Plebiscite may have a blessed result for our German people.[1]

More than 90 per cent of the electorate voted for reunification with Germany. The Saar subsequently re-joined Germany. A few days later, *The Catholic Times* (18 January 1935) stated of Hitler:

> He owes this triumph, this vindication of Germany to the Catholics ...[2]

The Benedictine Abbey, Maria Laach

Maria Laach became a focal point in the Weimar Republic for right-wing Catholics. Here the Benedictines attracted members of the Catholic aristocracy who were more receptive to the right-wing nationalist movements of the time.

The monks, politicians, businessmen, theologians and students who gathered there were strongly influenced by the idea of a coming 'Reich', hoping to build a third Holy Roman Empire.

Many at Maria Laach embraced Hitler's regime and even chided other Catholics for failing to work with the new state. The rise of the Third Reich was seen to be part of the workings and designs of God. Hitler's promise to build Germany on a Christian foundation on 21 March 1933 led several monks to hang a picture of Hitler in the abbey.

French Catholicism

Parti social français (PSF)

François de la Rocque formed the PSF. Moderate estimates place its membership at half a million in the build-up to World War II, making it the first French right-wing mass party. Its slogan 'Travail, Famille, Patrie' ('Work, Family, Fatherland') was later used by Vichy France to replace the Republican slogan 'Liberté, Egalité, Fraternité' ('Liberty, Equality, Brotherhood'). The PSF was supported by the Jesuits.[3]

---

[1] Source: *The Times* (London), 18 January 1935
[2] Moore, Edith. *No Friend of Democracy: A study of Roman Catholic politics – their influence on the course of the present War and the growth of Fascism*
[3] Ibid.

Joseph Arthur, Comte de Gobineau

Gobineau (1816-1882) was a devout Catholic French diplomat and social philosopher. He became famous for developing the theory of the Aryan master race in his book *Essai sur l'inégalité des races humaines* (*An Essay on the Inequality of the Human Races*). In it, he affirmed the superiority of the white race over others, and classed the Aryans as representing the pinnacle of civilisation.

This racial theory, permeated with anti-Semitism, was a potent philosophical justification for later Nazi racism.

Father E A Chabauty

Father Chabauty published *Les Juifs, nos maitres!* (*The Jews, our Masters!*) in 1882. It claimed that Christian nations were being attacked by a Jewish conspiracy.[1]

Father Henri Delassus

Delassus, a French priest, directed for forty-nine years one of the better-known Catholic weekly papers, *La Semaine religieuse de Cambrai*. He was one of the fiercest campaigners against the Jews. For example, he wrote in his weekly: 'Anti-Semitism and Catholicism are one and the same thing.' In 1911 Pope St Pius X honoured Delassus by appointing him an apostolic prothonotary.[2] The next year, the Pope sent Delassus a personal, signed letter congratulating him on his golden anniversary as a priest.[3]

Édouard Adolphe Drumont

Édouard Drumont represented Catholic anti-Semitism at its worst. This French journalist and writer founded the Ligue antisémitique de France (Anti-Semitic League of France) in 1889. His 1886 book *La France Juive* (*Jewish France*) attacked the role of Jews in France and argued for their exclusion from society. The book promoted the idea that Jews controlled every aspect of French commercial life – hence France was an enthralled nation.[4] It relied heavily on previous Catholic authors, including Father Oreglia of *La Civiltà Cattolica*, and was checked by a priest to ensure that it contained no theological errors.[5] It has been called the first work to introduce racial anti-Semitism into France and the most influential anti-Semitic work published in nineteenth-century Europe. It was commended by *Revue du Monde Catholique* – an uncompromising ultramontane[6] journal – which praised Drumont for defending the Church against those 'insatiable vampires' the Jews. The journal concluded: 'Monsieur Drumont's devoted wish to serve, and the virtue of his having served the cause of Christ, cannot be denied.'[7]

La France Juive was also reviewed most favourably by the Church's publications

---

[1] http://www.jcrelations.net/en/?id=836 (2007)

[2] Prothonotary – a member of the highest college of prelates in the Roman Curia, or an honorary prelate on whom the pope has conferred this title and its special privileges.

[3] Kertzer, David I. *The Popes Against the Jews: The Vatican's Role in the Rise of Modern Anti-Semitism.* p226

[4] Callil, Carmen. *Bad Faith: A Forgotten History of Family & Fatherland.* p17

[5] Kertzer, David I. *The Popes Against the Jews: The Vatican's Role in the Rise of Modern Anti-Semitism.* p178

[6] Ultramontanism – the policy that the absolute authority of the church should be vested in the pope.

[7] Kertzer, David I. *The Popes Against the Jews: The Vatican's Role in the Rise of Modern Anti-Semitism.* p178

such as *La Civiltà Cattolica*, *La Croix*, and in France by *L'Univers*. A study by Jeannine Vèrdes-Leroux of the French diocesan bulletins published during this period showed that they highly praised Drumont and *La France Juive*.[1]

In 1892 Drumont founded the newspaper *La Libre Parole* (*Free Speech*) which became a platform for virulent anti-Semitism.[2] At the turn of the century, this journal had as many as 30,000 priests among its subscribers. When the newspaper ran a contest in 1895 for the best essay on dealing with the Jewish threat, priests took both top prizes.[3]

Drumont's classic phrase was 'Everything comes from the Jew, everything returns to the Jew'.[4] His book *Testament d'un antisémite* (*An Anti-Semite's Testament*) included such statements as 'The murder of Christian children by Jews is a fact as clear as day.' The Vatican, he reported, after punctilious investigations, had elevated various child martyrs to sainthood based on their authenticated deaths by Jews.[5]

Drumont attracted many supporters and was one of the primary sources of anti-Semitic ideas that were later embraced by Nazism. For example, *L'Osservatore Cattolico* praised the efforts of this 'indomitable adversary of the Jews, Édouard Drumont.' Notwithstanding, to defend themselves against accusations of bias, its writers stated that their negativity towards the Jews was not based in unchristian hatred:

> Drumont fights the Jews, as we fight them, not out of any caste or personal hatred, but rather because they are the vampires of humanity, monopolizers, usurers, speculators; they are dishonest, implacable, destroyers and slanderers, exploiters of Christian blood. It is a [matter of] defense ... an act of patriotism, of charity, of religion.[6]

Drumont reached the peak of his notoriety during the Dreyfus Affair, in which he was the most strident of Alfred Dreyfus' accusers. He has been called the Father of French anti-Semitism. He popularised the belief that in France Jews controlled banks, property, universities, letters, theatre, media, and prostitution.[7]

' The Dreyfus Affair

Alfred Dreyfus was an obscure Jewish captain in the French army who was accused in 1894 of providing secret information to the German government. Despite his protests of innocence he was found guilty of treason in a secret court-martial, during which he was refused the right to examine the evidence against him. He was condemned to life imprisonment.[8]

In 1898 the novelist Émile Zola published his denunciation of the army cover-up,

---

[1] Source: Kertzer, David I. *The Popes Against the Jews: The Vatican's Role in the Rise of Modern Anti-Semitism.* p178

[2] http://en.wikipedia.org/wiki/Edouard_Drumont (2007)

[3] Kertzer, David I. *The Popes Against the Jews: The Vatican's Role in the Rise of Modern Anti-Semitism.* p178

[4] Callil, Carmen. *Bad Faith: A Forgotten History of Family & Fatherland.* p482

[5] Kertzer, David I. *The Popes Against the Jews: The Vatican's Role in the Rise of Modern Anti-Semitism.* p179

[6] Ibid. p165

[7] Callil, Carmen. *Bad Faith: A Forgotten History of Family & Fatherland.* p17

[8] See, for example: Flannery, Edward H. *The Anguish of the Jews.* pp185-89

J'accuse! It indicted not only the country's political and military leaders for their involvement in the miscarriage of justice, but also France's Catholic ethos and its identification with the military.[1]

French society became polarised. The political right and the leadership of the Catholic Church, both of which were openly antagonistic to the liberal French Republic, claimed the pro-Dreyfus case to be a conspiracy of Jews and Freemasons contriving to damage the prestige of the army and thus destroy France.[2,3]

'The Affair' ('l'affaire Dreyfus'), as it was known, aroused virulent passions due to the existence of widespread anti-Semitism in France. This prejudice was due to: firstly, the failure in 1885 of the Union Générale, a Catholic banking establishment that had aimed at replacing Jewish finance and whose collapse was blamed on the Jews;[4] and secondly, to the publication of *La France Juive*.

'The Affair' strengthened the French Republic, largely as a reaction to its enemies, principally the army and the Catholic hierarchy.[5] Consequently, in 1905 the Radical Party, emphasising the role of the Catholic leadership in the Dreyfus case, enabled the passing of legislation separating church and state.[6]

Over all, the explosion of hatred of the Jews in France was enkindled and fuelled by Catholicism. Hundreds of Catholic priests attended anti-Semitic congresses and stirred up congregations throughout France via speeches and sermons. The Jew was a revolutionary, a usurer, a traitor, a killer of Christ, and a ritual murderer. The Church hierarchy never reprimanded them. Indeed, one Catholic Dreyfusard commented:

> No authorised voice was raised in the Church of France against their judicial monstrosities. The universal silence of the French episcopate appeared as a crime ... The Church ... did not protest, it did not wax indignant, when *forgery, collusion and perjury combined in broad daylight to mislead the conscience of Christians*.[7]

The Congregation of the Augustinians of the Assumption, known as the 'Assumptionist Fathers' or the 'Assumptionists', was founded by the Venerable Emmanuel d'Alzon in 1850 at the College of the Assumption in Nîmes, France. The Assumptionists were established, inter alia, to support and strengthen the Church, its values and its principles.[8] In France they published the daily newspaper *La Croix*, which openly claimed to be 'the most anti-Jewish newspaper in France'.[9] It was enormously popular, with 104 separate editions published throughout France. Its readership numbered

---

[1] Michael, Robert. *A History of Catholic Antisemitism: The Dark Side of the Church*. p134
[2] Sinclair, Michael. *The Affair - The Case of Alfred Dreyfus*. http://www.jewishvirtuallibrary.org/jsource/anti-semitism/Dreyfus.html (2010)
[3] http://www.wordiq.com/definition/Dreyfus_affair (2010)
[4] http://www.jewishvirtuallibrary.org/jsource/vjw/France.html (2010)
[5] See, for example: Callil, Carmen. *Bad Faith: A Forgotten History of Family* ... inside cover
[6] http://www.Jewishvirtuallibrary.org/jsource/anti-Semitism/Dreyfus.html (2006)
[7] Carroll, James. *Constantine's Sword: The Church & the Jews*. pp457-58
[8] http://www.hitchin-rc.org.uk/order.html (2007)
[9] Ibid.

hundreds of thousands including 25,000 clergy. The editor stressed: 'With our eye fixed on the Vatican, we want to be and to remain simply Catholic, apostolic, and Roman.'[1]

La Croix especially criticised the attempts to reverse Dreyfus' false conviction.[2] Pope Leo XII never objected to the anti-Dreyfus campaign of *La Croix.* In fact, his official newspaper *L'Osservatore Romano,* the 'moral and political' voice of the Holy See, insisted on the guilt of Dreyfus and defended the anti-Semitism of the mobs.[3] Dreyfus' guilt should come as no surprise, the paper declared, as he was a Jew:

> The Jewish race, the deicide people, wandering throughout the world, brings with it everywhere the pestiferous breath of treason. And so too in the Dreyfus case ... it is hardly surprising if we again find the Jew in the front ranks, or if we find that the betrayal of one's country has been Jewishly conspired and Jewishly executed.[4]

At this time anti-Semitic demonstrations were spreading throughout France. They were praised by *L'Osservatore Romano:*

> The agitation that is now developing from one end of France to the other as a result of the truly detestable provocations of Judaism ... attempting to rehabilitate a traitor ... of the French nation, has neither the look nor the nature of those popular disorders motivated only by sentiments of disorder ... These demonstrations are becoming ever more anti-Semitic ... out of *a natural weariness of Jewish oppression* ...[5]

In 1899, a retrial of Dreyfus was ordered, and he was brought back to France. *L'Unità Cattolica* reported that Jewry was taking over France and using its gold to purchase a judgement of 'not guilty' for the traitor. 'Israel won a victory today: Israel is the victor and France the vanquished.'[6] However, the second court-martial again found Dreyfus guilty. Later that year, the president of France pardoned Dreyfus and made him a knight in the Legion of Honour.

In spite of the pardon, *La Civiltà Cattolica* was still arguing his guilt a year later. The editor, Father Raffaele Ballerini, SJ, claimed that in order to acquit Dreyfus the Jews 'had bought all the newspapers and consciences in Europe'.[7]

Friar R P Constant

Around this time also, there was a bombardment of books and pamphlets on the Blood Ritual subject, many of which were written by ecclesiastics.[8] For example, in 1897 a French Dominican, J P Constant, published a virulently anti-Semitic book *Les Juifs devant L'Église et l'Histoire* (*The Jews Before the Church and History*). The book

[1] Kertzer, David I. *The Popes Against the Jews: The Vatican's Role in the Rise of Modern Anti-Semitism.* p171
[2] Hardy, Rob. *What Role did the Vatican Play in Fostering Anti-Semitism?* (http://www.nonfictionreviews.com /article1273.html) (2006)
[3] Ibid.
[4] Kertzer, David I. *The Pope Against the Jews: The Vatican's Role in the Rise of Modern Anti-Semitism.* p184
[5] Ibid.
[6] Ibid.
[7] Cornwell, John. *Hitler's Pope: The Secret History of Pius XII.* p24
[8] Kertzer, David I. *The Popes Against the Jews: The Vatican's Role in the Rise of Modern Anti-Semitism.* p165

reiterated the claims of Jewish treachery, disloyalty, voracity, and malevolence. It recorded that the *Talmud* commanded Jews to slaughter Christian children for their blood; and praised Édouard Drumont as 'one of the best informed men on the [Jewish] question.'[1] Two years later, *L'Osservatore Romano* published an article on Judaic ritual murder.

The 1896 National Christian Democratic Conference

In 1896 a six-day National Christian Democratic Conference was held in Lyon. One major part was devoted to an anti-Semitism 'congress'. Two of the official sponsors of this congress were the directors of the two most important Catholic newspapers in France, Eugène Veuillot of *L'Univers* and Father Bailly of *La Croix*. Soon after the conference, an unprecedented wave of anti-Semitism began to sweep over France.[2]

Action Française (French Action)

Action Française was an influential pro-Church anti-Republican group, founded in 1899 and later led by Charles Maurras, of whom Pius X said 'I bless his work.' It campaigned for the abolition of the Republic, restoration of the monarchy, and, after the 1905 law on the separation of church and state, the restoration of Catholicism as the state religion. It was supported by many Catholics who constituted the vast majority of its members, and was the most important ally of the French Catholic Church which gave Maurras and his movement active support. It published an anti-Semitic and anti-democratic newspaper, *Action française*, from which the Church reproduced articles for dissemination to the laity and used such material in its sermons.[3] In 1926 Pius XI condemned *Action française*, but in 1939, following the Spanish Civil War and a revival of anti-communism in the Church, the anti-Semitic Pius XII (Eugenio Pacelli) ended the condemnation.[4] Thereafter, *Action française* claimed that the condemnation was decided for political purposes. Significantly, *Action française* greeted the appearance of the Spanish self-proclaimed dictator General Francisco Franco ('the Spanish Butcher') with delight, and supported him during the Spanish Civil War (1936-39).[5]

Monsignor Ernest Jouin

In 1912 Father Jouin initiated the *Revue Internationale des Sociétés Secrètes* (*International Review of Secret Societies*). A year later, he founded the Ligue catholique française (French-Catholic League), of which he remained president for the rest of his life. He stated that he assayed only to follow the Pope's requirement that the clergy fight against the forces that were aiming at destroying Christianity.[6]

In 1918 Jouin was given the ecclesiastic title 'Prelate of His Holiness Benedict XV' in recognition of his work on behalf of the Church – 'We know that you have conducted

---

[1] Kertzer, David I. *The Popes Against the Jews: The Vatican's Role in the Rise of Modern Anti-Semitism.* p165
[2] Ibid. pp180-82
[3] Callil, Carmen. *Bad Faith: A Forgotten History of Family & Fatherland.* pp18-19
[4] Michael, Robert. *A History of Catholic Antisemitism: The Dark Side of the Church.* p183
[5] http://en.wikipedia.org/wiki/Action_Fran%C3%A7aise (2008)
[6] Kertzer, David I. *The Popes Against the Jews: The Vatican's Role in the Rise of Modern Anti-Semitism.* p267

your sacred ministry in an exemplary manner.' Next year, the Vatican Secretary of State sent Jouin a note of papal appreciation for his anti-Masonic work:

> His Holiness is thus pleased to congratulate you and to encourage you in your work, whose influence is so important in warning the faithful and helping them to struggle effectively against the forces aimed at destroying not only religion but the whole social order.[1]

In the 1920s, Jouin was the familiar exponent of Catholic anti-Semitism. He was the principal protagonist for the *Protocols of the Elders of Zion.*

He devoted his life to warning of the Jewish threat, following the Pope's injunction that the clergy fight the forces that were aiming to destroy Christendom. His particular fixation was the Jewish-Masonic conspiracy for which he invented the term 'Judeo-Masonic'. He declared:

> Israel is king, the Mason is his helper, the Bolshevik his executioner. The Jew believes in the world domination of his race.

In 1925, Jouin praised Mussolini for saving Italy from the Judeo-Masonics, and also praised Germany that had 'better than we, recognised the Jewish peril'. Pius XI complimented Jouin in a private audience because he was 'combating our mortal enemy.' Eventually, Pius increased Jouin's ecclesiastical status by appointing him apostolic prothonotary.[2]

Canon Viguié

Viguié, editor of the virulent French Catholic weekly *La Défense,* described Léon Blum, three times Prime Minister of France during the period 1936 to 1947, as:

> a sinister Jew ... hideous métèque[3] who is preparing new massacres to establish his tyranny on our corpses.[4]

At that time also, although the Church directed Catholics to pray for the perfidious Jew and to pardon him for the murder of Jesus, yet, said Viguié, 'the Jewish race can never efface that stain'.[5]

Belgian Catholicism

Parti Rexiste

Rexism was a Belgian fascist political movement. It was the ideology of the Parti Rexiste (Rexist Party), officially called Christus Rex (Christ the King), founded in 1930 by Léon Degrelle (the Belgian peasants nicknamed him 'Adolf' Degrelle). Degrelle was won over to this political orientation by Monsignor Picard when he was a student at the University of Louvain. He and all his assistants were the products of Jesuit training –

---

[1] Kertzer, David I. *The Popes Against the Jews: The Vatican's Role in the Rise of Modern ...* pp268-69
[2] Ibid. pp267-68
[3] Métèque – a description of all foreigners living in France; similar to 'dago', 'wog', 'wop', and the like.
[4] Callil, Carmen. *Bad Faith: A Forgotten History of Family & Fatherland.* p134
[5] Ibid. p184

part of the Jesuit drive to align the Church with Nazi-Fascist plans for the 'new order' in Europe after the anticipated destruction of Liberalism and democracy.[1]

Rexism soon began to ally itself with the interests of Nazi Germany, and it incorporated Nazi-style anti-Semitism into its platform after Hitler's rise to power. Consequently, in October 1940, the Catholic bishops of Belgium instructed the laity: 'It is doubtless necessary to recognize the occupying power as a de facto power and to obey it within the limits of international conventions.'[2] After the German occupation of Belgium most Rexists proudly supported the occupiers.[3]

Hungarian Catholicism

'The complicity of the Hungarian Christian church in the mass extermination of Hungarian Jews by the Nazis is a largely forgotten episode in the history of the Holocaust.'[4]

The Kingdom of Hungary was the first Catholic country in Europe outside Germany to officially adopt anti-Jewish legislation. On 29 May 1938, the *Bill for a More Effective Guarantee of a Balanced Social and Economic Life*[5] was passed in the parliament. The preamble to the Bill links it with the Clerical People's Party, which had struggled at the close of the nineteenth century against granting recognition to the Jewish religion.[6] It imposed quotas on Jewish participation in free professions, particularly in journalism.

Cardinal Serédi

The highest echelons of the Hungarian Catholic clergy were in the forefront of the campaign to promote anti-Semitic legislation. The Latin and Greek Catholic Churches convened at the residence of the Primate of Hungary, Jusztinián Cardinal Serédi, himself also a member of the Upper House of Parliament, and unanimously adopted a resolution expressing their support for the law:

> The synod registers with satisfaction the fact that the Royal Government of Hungary strives to defend the interests of the Christian public in face of Jewish spiritual domination.[7]

Cardinal Serédi advocated a much broader body of legislation against the Jews; as he explained in his address to Parliament:

---

[1] Callil, Carmen. *Bad Faith: A Forgotten History of Family & Fatherland.* p60
[2] Quoted from the Jesuit magazine *America*, February 22, 1941. Source: Lehmann, L H. *Behind the Dictators: A Factual Analysis of the Relationship* ... p61
[3] http://en.wikipedia.org/wiki/Rexism (2007)
[4] https://books.google.com.au/books/about/Christianity_and_the_Holocaust_of_Hungar.html?id=0dcugBs WTYEC&hl=en (2015)
[5] *Első zsidótörvény 'a társadalmi és a gazdasági élet egyensúlyának hatályosabb biztosításáról'*. Source: http://regi.sofar.hu/hu/node/13267 (2015)
[6] Herczl, Moshe Y. *Christianity and the Holocaust of Hungarian Jews.* p85
[7] Ibid. p98

Nevertheless, it is necessary to take additional measures against the Jews. We must uproot decisively all those phenomena that Judaism has introduced into our economic, our social, and our public lives, as well as into our legal system. The reasons for this struggle are the same that led the Church in our homeland to oppose bitterly the liberal outlook ever since the granting of full recognition to the Jewish religion.[1]

Synod of Catholic Bishops

On 15 April 1939, Cardinal Serédi spoke officially in the Parliament in the name of the Synod of Catholic Bishops to express their support for further discriminatory legislation:

I declare that in our treatment of the Jewish question I perceive an act of justifiable self-defense ... The concept of imposing limitations on the Jews is acceptable to all. Part of the Jewish population – disguised as the press, art, literature, poetry, and music – has cast doubt upon values sacred to Christians. They have done so with the acquiescence of the other Jews and despite the constant protests of Catholics ... The influence of the Jews must be curtailed, for they have sinned much against Christian-Hungary ... We must ascribe the responsibility to the liberal regime that facilitated the Jewish tricks, despite the constant protest of Catholic Hungarians.[2]

A second, more harmful law was passed on 4 May 1939, under the title *Law to Limit the Expansion of Jews in the Public and Economic Domain*. It abolished the political rights of Jews and excluded Jews completely from all participation in Hungarian cultural life. Employment of Jews in commerce, industry, banking, and trade was severely limited. Jews were forbidden to acquire land, and they could be compelled to sell or lease their lands. One-quarter of Hungarian Jewry lost its livelihood overnight, while many were reduced to near starvation.[3]

Hungarian Catholic Action

Hungarian Catholic Action, which had a membership of 250,000, proclaimed a programme in the 1930s:

The Jews ... do not have the right to influence the intellectual life of the country, nor the press, nor literature, nor artistic life. This same principle should be applied against all those Hungarians who show solidarity with the Jews.[4]

National Socialist Arrow Cross Party

Ferenc Szálasi was the Catholic founder and leader of the 'National Socialist Arrow Cross Party – Hungarist Movement', and both Head of State and Prime Minister of the

[1] Herczl, Moshe Y. *Christianity and the Holocaust of Hungarian Jews.* p99
[2] Ibid. p111
[3] Cymet, David. *History vs. Apologetics: The Holocaust, the Third Reich, and the Catholic Church.* p160
[4] Kertzer, David I. *The Popes Against the Jews: The Vatican's Role in the Rise of Modern Anti-Semitism.* p279

Kingdom of Hungary's 'Government of National Unity' (Nemzeti Összefogás Kormánya)[1] (NOK) for the final three months of Hungary's participation in World War II.[2]

The NOK turned the Kingdom of Hungary into a client state of Nazi Germany after Regent Miklós Horthy was removed from power during Operation Panzerfaust.

During the Party's short rule, ten to fifteen thousand people (many of whom were Jews) were murdered outright, and 80,000 people were deported from Hungary to their deaths in the Auschwitz Concentration Camp. After the war, Szálasi and other Arrow Cross leaders were tried as war criminals by Soviet courts. Szálasi was executed.[3]

Italian Catholicism

Catholicism is by far the largest religious group in Italy (approximately 81% of the population). In 2014 only 0.05% of the population was Jewish.

David Cymet[4] has pointed out that exactly one year before World War II broke out in September 1938, Italy commenced introducing anti-Semitic legislation against the ancient Jewish community of only 57,000 persons, whose presence in Italy pre-dated that of Christianity.

With Benito Mussolini in power, the Italian government promulgated its first set of anti-Jewish 'Racial laws'. This brought about: the dismissal of all Jewish teachers from public schools; the separation of Jewish children from Catholics in elementary schools; the expulsion of Jewish children from secondary schools; the prohibition of marriage between Catholics and Jews; the dismissal of Jews from the public service and the army; restrictions on Jewish business.[5] All Jewish literature was forbidden, and no book by a foreign Jew could be translated into Italian, nor could a play by a foreign Jew be produced. No Jew was allowed to broadcast over the radio. Jewish professors were barred from Italian universities, and very many textbooks by Jewish writers were withdrawn from schools. Jews were expelled from all administrative posts.[6]

Pope Pius XI, on 13 February 1929, called Mussolini 'the man providence has sent unto us ...'[7]

Roberto Farinacci

Farinacci, a member of the Fascist Grand Council, spoke at the Institute for Fascist Culture in Milan on the topic of 'The Church and the Jews':

> For over twenty years, I have been denouncing the Judaic peril and the need to free the nerve centres of our country from the Jews, who, through diabolical means, have succeeded in extending their tentacles everywhere.

[1] http://lexikon.katolikus.hu/N/Nemzeti%20%C3%96sszefog%C3%A1s%20Korm%C3%A1nya.html (2015)
[2] http://en.wikipedia.org/wiki/Ferenc_Sz%C3%A1lasi (2012)
[3] http://en.wikipedia.org/wiki/Arrow_Cross_Party (2012)
[4] Much of this section on Italy is abstracted from: Cymet, David. *History vs. Apologetics: The Holocaust, the Third Reich, and the Catholic Church.* pp154-9
[5] Cymet, David. *History vs. Apologetics: The Holocaust, the Third Reich, and the Catholic Church.* p282
[6] http://www.talmudunmasked.com/appendix.htm (2007)
[7] http://www.biblebelievers.org.au/bb931015.htm (2010)

We fascist Catholics consider the Jewish problem from a strictly political point of view ... But it comforts our souls to know that if, as Catholics, *we became anti-Semites, we owe it to the teachings that the Church has promulgated over the past twenty centuries.*[1]

Farinacci reminded his listeners that the constitution of the Jesuit Order prohibited its acceptance of:

anyone descended from the Jewish race ... up to the fifth generation. ... The Aryan racism of the Jesuits is thus more severe than that of Germany itself.

The Jesuits were therefore the:

constant precursors and masters in the Jewish question ... And if we can be faulted for anything, it is for not having applied all of their intransigence in our dealings with the Jews.[2]

Alfredo Romanini

Alfredo Romanini reprinted his strongly anti-Judaic pamphlet *Ebrei-Cristianesimo-Fascismo* (*Jews-Christianity-Fascism*). It contained sentiments such as these:

Jews aspired to dominate Europe first, to be followed by the enslavement of the world: Banks, industries, newspapers, film studios, railroads and steamship lines were in the hands of Jews ... high Jewish finance had been dominating European politics for over half a century ... Mussolini is the chief who raises himself powerfully and majestically against this malicious Israel, which thirsts after a Christian-Aryan vendetta, and which desires world domination with its gold, corruption, Masonic thirst and international organizations of various names and colors, having as its goal the brutalization of the masses.[3]

The publication received the enthusiastic imprimatur of the upper echelons of the Italian Catholic Church. Adeodato Cardinal Piazza blessed the author with 'all my heart, for this work is most opportune to make known the grave danger that hangs over the world.' Other Cardinals praised the work as 'excellent, and of unquestionable usefulness in the understanding of the Jewish problem.'

Monsignor Francesco Borgoncini-Duca

During 1938, Italian Foreign Minister Galeazzo Ciano met the Papal Nuncio to Italy, Monsignor Borgoncini-Duca. He was delighted to pen in his diary:

He [the Nuncio] seems fairly convinced ... I want to add that he personally revealed himself as very anti-Semitic.[4]

---

[1] http://www.amazon.com/The-Popes-Against-Jews-Anti-Semitism/product-reviews/037540 6239 (2014)

[2] Kertzer, David I. *The Popes Against the Jews: The Vatican's Role in the Rise of Modern Anti-Semitism.* p284

[3] Cymet, David. *History vs. Apologetics: The Holocaust, the Third Reich, and the Catholic Church.* p158

[4] Ibid. p156

Monsignor Agostino Gemelli

Monsignor Gemelli was president of the Pontifical Academy of Science, rector of the Catholic University of Milan, and a frequent visitor to the Vatican:

> In politics we have only one Chief, Il Duce – whom a great and august voice [the Pope] has called incomparable![1]

Adeodato Giovanni Cardinal Piazza

The patriarch of Venice, Cardinal Piazza, a member of the Roman Curia, denied that the Church intended to protect the Jews:

> To say simply *that the Church protects the Jews, is to assert what is not true;*[2] for the Church, properly speaking, protects by divine mandate only the freedom of its universal mission, which is to communicate its supernatural good to each and all ... It is true that it had to defend itself as well as its faithful, and not rarely, with the means it had at its disposition, against dangerous contacts and the Jewish invasion, which seems in truth the hereditary mark of this people.[3]

Niccolò Giani

Niccolò Giani, Professor of Fascist History at the University of Pavia, compiled a booklet in 1939: *Perche siamo antisemiti* (*Why We are Anti-Semites*). In it, he confirmed the role of the Church in anti-Semitism, for example, that the *Talmud* instructs Jews to kill Christians, who should be treated as animals.[4]

The Bishop of Cremona

The bishop preached in favour of the new Racial Laws:

> The Church has never denied the state's right to limit or to impede the economic, social, and moral influence of the Jews, when this has been harmful to the nation's tranquillity and welfare. *The Church has never said or done anything to defend the Jews, the Judaics, or Judaism.*[5]

> The Church has always regarded living side by side with Jews, as long as they remain Jews, as dangerous to the faith and tranquillity of Christian people. It is for this reason that *you should find an old and long tradition of ecclesiastical legislation and discipline*, intended to brake and limit the action and influence of the Jews on Christians, and the contact of Christians with them, isolating the Jews and not allowing them the exercise of those offices and professions in which they could dominate or influence the spirit, the education, the customs of Christians.[6]

---

[1] Cymet, David. *History vs. Apologetics: The Holocaust, the Third Reich, and the Catholic Church.* p158

[2] Contrast this statement with that of the *Catholic Encyclopedia*: 'the untiring and energetic efforts of the Roman pontiffs in behalf of the Jews ...'. Refer to page 2, above.

[3] Cymet, David. *History vs. Apologetics: The Holocaust, the Third Reich, and the Catholic Church.* p156

[4] Ibid.

[5] Ibid. pp160-61

[6] Ibid. p157

The Archbishop of Florence

Elia Dalla Costa was a Cardinal, Archbishop of Florence, and ultimately a 'Servant of God'. He supported the anti-Jewish legislation. He wrote in his archdiocesan bulletin:

> As for the Jews no one can forget the ruinous work that they have often undertaken not only against the spirit of the Church, but also in detriment of civil coexistence. One needs to recall that, with the outbreak of the First World War, Italian Jewry succeeded in seeing that the Vicar of the Prince of Peace, the Holy Father, was excluded from the future peace conference.[1] Above all, however, the Church has in every epoch judged living together with the Jews to be dangerous to the Faith and to the tranquillity of the Christian people. Hence the laws promulgated by the Church for centuries aimed at isolating the Jews. The Church has never changed its policy of forbidding Christians from work in Jewish homes, or forbidding Christian children from being taught by Jews.[2]

The Anti-Jewish Decrees

The first anti-Jewish decree, *RDL 1390, Provvidimenti per la difesa della razza nella scuola fascita* (*Provisions for the Defence of the Race in the Fascist School*) was adopted on 5 September 1938. It ordered the immediate dismissal of all Jewish teachers in public schools, the exclusion of Jewish children from elementary and secondary public schools, and banned matriculation to newly entering Jewish students in universities. This was followed two days later by *RDL 1381, Provvidimenti nei confronti degli ebrei stranieri* (*Provisions Regarding Foreign Jews*) that terminated the right of residence for foreign-born Jews and Jews who had become naturalised after 1 January 1919. They were given a maximum of six months to voluntarily leave the country or face forced expulsion.

The so-called 'November Laws' of 1938 were far more severe and comprehensive. They prohibited the employment of Jews in the civil service at all levels, as well as in banks and private insurance companies, the armed forces, and the Fascist Party. Jews were forbidden to own land, factories, or businesses above a certain value. They could not employ Aryan domestic servants. The laws prohibited mixed marriages between baptised Jewish converts and Christians. A Jew was defined by race rather than by religion. This followed Hitler's paradigm.

The anti-Semitic decrees were strengthened by the passing of an anti-Jewish Code on 29 June. Addenda to the laws 'prohibited Jews from publishing books, holding public conferences, owning radios, being listed in telephone directories, using popular vacation resorts, and even placing any type of advertisements in the newspapers, including death notices.' It also proscribed Jews practising their professions among Christians. Neither

---

[1] The Paris Peace Conference was the meeting of the Allied victors of World War I to set the peace terms for Germany and other defeated nations. It took place in Paris in 1919 and involved diplomats from more than 30 countries. L H Lehmann states that 'it is not generally known that the reasons which led the Allies to exclude the pope [Benedict XV] from the Peace Conference after the First World War were connected with the activities of Monsignor Eugenio Pacelli, later Pope Pius XII.' For further details, refer to *'A Corrupt Tree'*, and to Stockwell, Antony. *Pius XII: The Dark Side*, Chapter 1.

[2] Cymet, David. *History vs. Apologetics: The Holocaust, the Third Reich, and the Catholic Church.* p157

could Jews be judges, notaries, or journalists.[1]

These laws were devastating for the Jewish community.

Professor David Kertzer summed up the situation:

> Anyone should not find it surprising that in response to these measures against the Jews *neither the Pope nor the Vatican hierarchy uttered a single word of protest.* The explanation for this fact is simple: Mussolini's new laws embodied measures and views long championed by the Church itself.[2]

Polish Catholicism

Poland has had a mixed history of religious tolerance and intolerance.

Ever since the country officially adopted Latin Christianity in 966, the Catholic Church has played an important religious, cultural and political role in the country. Today, approximately 90% of the population is Catholic.[3]

From the beginning of its statehood, rulers of Poland supported religious minorities. The *Edict of Wieluń* was a 1424 law issued in Wieluń by the King of Poland, Władysław II Jagiełło, under pressure from the Catholic Church. The edict outlawed Hussitism and represented a temporary regression for the Kingdom of Poland, which had a long tradition of religious toleration.

In the 16th and 17th centuries Poland was famous for its unique religious tolerance. However in the 15th and 18th century, pressure from the Catholic Church caused tensions to rise between Catholics and Protestants after the Edict of Wieluń, and later, the Tumult of Toruń.[4]

The Tumult of Thorn (Toruń), also called 'Blood-Bath of Thorn', refers to executions ordered in 1724 by the Polish Supreme Court under Augustus II 'The Strong' of Saxony. During a religious conflict between Protestant townsfolk represented by the mayor, and the Roman Catholic students of the Jesuit College in the city of Toruń, the college was vandalised by a crowd of German Protestants. The mayor and nine other Lutheran officials were blamed for neglect of duty, sentenced to death, and executed. Voltaire called the Tumult an example 'of the religious intolerance of the Poles'.

The last remaining Protestant church, Saint Mary's, Gdańsk, was made Catholic and given to Franciscan monks who celebrated a mass there on the day of the execution – a date which is now observed in remembrance of the Protestant martyrs. In addition, the majority of the town council was required to be Catholic from then on. A Protestant school, chapel, and printing press were required to be handed over to Catholic control. This is yet one more case of religious sites being stolen by the Catholic Church.

---

[1] Cymet, David. *History vs. Apologetics: The Holocaust, the Third Reich, and the Catholic Church.* p158

[2] Kertzer, David I. *The Popes Against the Jews: The Vatican's Role in the Rise of Modern Anti-Semitism.* p287

[3] Much of this Section on Poland has been abstracted from: Cymet, David. *History vs. Apologetics: The Holocaust, the Third Reich, and the Catholic Church.* pp150-4

[4] http://en.wikipedia.org/wiki/Religion_in_Poland (2012)

During the nineteenth century, the vision of a pan-national state (państwo narodowo-ściowe) inspired the struggle for an independent Poland, giving everyone, including Jews, a rightful place.

However, by the twentieth century, the leaders of the Polish Church were certain that they followed the same path as the Holy See with respect to their opposition to modern Jewish values.[1]

  Inter-war Poland was 'the leading antisemitic country in Europe, second only to Germany alone.'[2]

  In 1939 on the eve of World War II, there were 3.5 million Jews in Poland. By the end of the War, over 3 million of them had been murdered or perished in the Holocaust. Poland is now overwhelmingly Roman Catholic.[3,4]

Roman Stanisław Dmowski

After World War I, the ideal of a pan-national state was discarded, particularly under the influence of the Stronnictwo Narodowo-Demokratyczne (SND) (The National-Democratic Party)[5] of Roman Dmowski. It was replaced by 'an exclusionary xenophobic vision of a Catholic, monocultural and homogeneous Poland in which Jews had no place.' By the simple phrase 'the Pole is a Catholic', Polish Jews, whose presence dated back to the beginnings of the country's history, became personae non gratae.

  The minority rights clause of the Versailles Treaty became the source of acrimonious resentment. The interpreters of the new Poland did everything in their power to propagandise the deadly notion that there were too many Jews in Poland. Everywhere and in the media, Jews were abused and told to go to Palestine: 'Żydzi do Palestyny'.

Józef Klemens Piłsudski

Piłsudski was a Polish statesman: Chief of State (1918–22), 'First Marshal' (from 1920), and authoritarian leader (1926–35) of the Second Polish Republic. In 1934, with the developing rapprochement between Poland and the Third Reich, he signed a ten-year non-aggression pact and trade agreement with Hitler. The pact allowed Hitler time for re-armament and acted as an incentive to Poland to join Hitler's war against the Jews.

Edward Rydz-Śmigły

  Marshall Rydz-Śmigły succeeded Józef Piłsudski in May 1935. The government and the Church drew closer, and a clear anti-Semitic policy developed. The Jews were seen as an element that weakened the normal development of national strength in Poland. Legislative and economic policies were designed to undermine Jewish enterprises and 'induce the emigration of as many Jews as fast as possible.' Jewish access to higher

---

[1] See, for example: Michael, Robert. *A History of Catholic Antisemitism: The Dark Side of the Church.* p153
[2] Source: Ibid. p157
[3] http://en.wikipedia.org/wiki/Poland#Religion (2012)
[4] So similar to Croatia with respect to Jews, Serbs, and Roma.
[5] The National-Democratic Party was a political opponent of the Polish Socialist Party.

education was restricted. Jews, who constituted around 10 percent of the population, were forced to pay 40 percent of the taxes. Jews, who had lived for centuries in the small towns and villages of rural Poland, were pressured economically by the government to enable the peasants to take over their businesses and homes. These policies advocated the forced mass emigration of 3.5 million Jews. The economist Lord Keynes referred to Poland as:

> an economic impossibility whose only industry is Jew-baiting.

Józef Beck

Józef Beck detested the Minorities Treaty, guaranteeing the rights of Poland's Jewish, Ukrainian, Belarusian, Lithuanian and German minorities, which the Allies had forced on Central European states under the 1919 Versailles Treaty. On 13 September 1934, he unilaterally revoked the Treaty before the League of Nations in Geneva.

Felicjan Sławoj Składkowski

In June 1936, Prime Minister Składkowski declared his support for an escalation of the economic war against the Jews.

The Polish Parliament

The Deputy-President of the parliament, Bogusław Miedziński, declared that in a country of 35 million people there was no room for more than 50,000 Jews; while on 16 June 1937, General Lucjan Żeligowski stated in the Senate 'There is *no* place in Poland for the Jews.'

In December 1938 moves were made in the parliament to declare Jews temporary citizens. Shortly after, a resolution was introduced demanding 'a radical and immediate solution of the Jewish question in Poland through emigration.'

Since 1923, anti-Semitic politicians allied with Catholic priests tried to outlaw kosher slaughtering in Poland to eliminate Jewish competition in the meat-packing business. Laws restricting and banning kosher slaughtering were introduced in 1923, 1936, and 1939.

Obóz Zjednoczenia Narodowego

In February 1937 the anti-Semitic Obóz Zjednoczenia Narodowego (OZN; OZON) (Camp of National Unity) was organised to tighten control on the government. OZON was open to everyone except Jews. Historian Davies has pointed out:

> After Pilsudski's death, the OZON leadership saw little place for the Jews in their vision of Polish national unity ... Polish Jews in the 1930s were indeed subjected to a number of ugly threats and denigrations, and to a mounting campaign of economic hardship and emotional insecurity.

The OZON programme demanded that Jews be forced to emigrate from Poland:

Until their expulsion will be carried out, it is necessary as a first step to abolish their civic rights and confiscate their properties. All the large industries will have to be nationalized.[1]

Polish Students

In the early 1930s Polish students began a systematic anti-Semitic campaign throughout Poland, physically attacking Jewish students, and demanding restrictions on the entry of Jews to universities. The students also joined others in preventing customers entering Jewish-owned stores; 'they distributed anti-Semitic literature, organized riots, attacked Jewish shopkeepers, and threw Jews down from moving trains.'

Polish Jesuits

The Jesuits declared that 'Jews should be expelled from Christian societies'; but to do this in a humane way, the Catholic paper *Mały Dziennik* suggested:

> Jews must be compelled to emigrate, not by Nazi methods but by withdrawing their citizenship and reorganizing our national economy according to the needs of the Polish people. There is no other way.[2]

Aleksander Cardinal Kakowski

In the entire inter-war years the Catholic Church was at the centre of Polish anti-Semitism:

> The Catholic clergy were not innocent bystanders or passive observers of the wave of anti-Semitism encompassing Poland in the late half of the 1930s.[3]

To try and stop the physical and social attacks against Jews, a delegation of prominent rabbis pleaded in June 1934 with his Eminence Aleksander Kakowski, Cardinal Archbishop of Warsaw. They entreated him to use his moral authority and to issue a pastoral letter to the laity to stop the attacks:

> In the name of the Rabbis and Jews of this illustrious Republic, we entreat you, Cardinal, to issue a pastoral about this to all Polish Catholics.[4]

The Cardinal refused. He told them that, although as a Christian he *might* condemn such attacks, as a Pole he could not.

Cardinal Hlond

His Eminence August Cardinal Hlond, the primate of Poland and Archbishop of Poznań and Gniezno, issued a pastoral letter in 1936, calling for the elimination and separation of the Jews, to protect the Catholic Poles from dangerous Jewish influences:

> There will be a Jewish problem as long as the Jews remain ... It is a fact that the Jews

[1] Cymet, David. *History vs. Apologetics: The Holocaust, the Third Reich, and the Catholic Church.* p153
[2] Kertzer, David I. *The Popes Against the Jews: The Vatican's Role in the Rise of Modern Anti-Semitism.* p276
[3] Modras, Ronald. *Catholic Church and Antisemitism: Poland, 1933-1939.* p396. Quoted in: Cymet, David. *History vs. Apologetics: The Holocaust, the Third Reich, and the Catholic Church.* p151
[4] Ibid.

are fighting against the Catholic Church, *persisting in free thinking*, and are the vanguard of godlessness, Bolshevism and subversion.

In commercial relations it is right to favour one's own people, to avoid Jewish shops and Jewish stalls on the market.

It is true that in the schools the influence of Jewish youth upon the Catholic is in general negative from the religious and moral viewpoint ... It is necessary to find protection from the harmful moral influence of the Jews, to keep away from their anti-Christian culture, and in particular to boycott the Jewish press and demoralizing Jewish publications.[1]

Hlond urged Catholics to boycott Jewish businesses, because the Jews were waging a war against the Church.[2] He and other Catholic spokesmen:

conformed exactly to the ancient witness theology, launching a torrent of anti-Jewish vituperation but calling of restraint and charity in action, telling the faithful that they should not follow the logic of the antisemitic assertions they have just launched into the air.[3]

Polish Bishops

In December 1937 the Synod of Polish Bishops adopted a resolution calling for the legal segregation of Jewish children in elementary schools. Thus began a growing campaign to segregate Jews in every walk of life: education, railways, housing districts, markets, and taxis. Catholic lawyers started to demand separate benches in the courts for their Jewish counterparts.

Slovakian Catholicism

Chapter 14 gives details of Slovakia's extensive anti-Semitism.

Croatian Catholicism

Volume 2 provides details of Croatia's virulent and barbaric anti-Semitism.

Synopsis

Catholic anti-Semitism and anti-Judaism made the Nazi Holocaust not only possible but engendered it. The Nazis' barbarous attack on the Jews occurred in a climate of popular opinion that had been fostered by centuries of well-documented Catholic hostility to both the Jewish religion and the Jewish people.

Austria – The Vatican Secret Archives provide striking evidence of the active role played by Leo XII and his Secretary of State in fostering the anti-Semitic campaign of the Christian Social party in Hitler's home country.

---

[1] Modras, Ronald. *Catholic Church and Antisemitism: Poland, 1933-1939.* p396. Quoted in: Cymet, David. *History vs. Apologetics: The Holocaust, the Third Reich, and the Catholic Church.* p152

[2] Kertzer, David I. *The Popes Against the Jews: The Vatican's Role in the Rise of Modern Anti-Semitism.* p275

[3] Source: Michael, Robert. *A History of Catholic Antisemitism: The Dark Side of the Church.* p152

Germany – The influence of German priests on their parishioners 'was as considerable as was their hatred of Jews.' They denied the value of Jewish scripture and the Shabbat, accused Jews of being Cains, called Jews poisonous 'weeds' and 'snakes', denigrated the *Torah*, and regarded the synagogue as 'an assembly [of] beasts, in their lust for corporal things.'

Belgium – Rexism was a Belgian fascist political movement. It was product of Jesuit training – part of the Jesuit drive to align the Catholic Church with Nazi-Fascist plans for the 'new order' in Europe, after the anticipated destruction of Liberalism and democracy. Rexism soon began to ally itself with the interests of Nazi Germany, and it incorporated Nazi-style anti-Semitism into its platform after Hitler's rise to power.

Hungary – The highest echelons of the Hungarian Catholic clergy were in the forefront of the campaign to promote anti-Semitic legislation. Consequently, Hungary was the first Catholic country in Europe outside Germany to officially adopt such legislation.

France – Édouard Drumont founded the newspaper *La Libre Parole* which became a platform for virulent anti-Semitism. At the beginning of the twentieth century, it had as many as 30,000 priests among its subscribers. Monsignor Ernest Jouin founded the French-Catholic League in 1913, of which he remained president for the rest of his life. He devoted his life to warning of the Jewish threat, following the Pope's injunction that the clergy fight the forces that were aiming to destroy Christendom. Pius XI complimented him in a private audience because he was 'combating our mortal enemy.'

Italy – For many years, Catholic papers railed against the influence of Jews in Italy. Accordingly, with Mussolini in power, the Italian government promulgated its first set of anti-Jewish 'Racial laws' in 1938. The Bishop of Cremona preached in favour of these new Laws, and the Archbishop of Florence wrote: 'Above all, however, the Church has in every epoch judged living together with the Jews to be dangerous to the Faith and to the tranquillity of Christian people. Hence the laws promulgated by the Church for centuries aimed at isolating the Jews.'

Poland – The Polish Catholic press was riddled with warnings of the dangers posed by the Jews. In the late 1930s a Christian Democratic newspaper stated that the Jewish problem would remain while the Jews had equal rights with true Poles.

Final Summation

Decades of blatantly anti-Semitic and anti-Judaic preachings by the Catholic Church, its ecclesiastics, and its many organisations throughout Catholic Europe, brought forth the Nazi's 'Final Solution to the Jewish Question'.

14 – Croatian and Slovakian Catholic Holocausts

Who will rise up for me against the evildoers, or who will stand up for me against the workers of iniquity? Psalm 96:16

Catholic Croatia

The Croatian Holocaust during World War II is presented in considerable detail in Volume 2.

 Briefly: dictator Ante Pavelić, 'the Butcher of the Balkans', proclaimed the newly created (1941) Independent State of Croatia (NDH) to be a 'Pure Catholic State'. The consequence was disaster. Croatia became a state of atrocious ruin and evil. After reviewing the history of the NDH, Dr Lazo M Kostich stated in his scholarly book *The Holocaust in the 'Independent State of Croatia'*:

> The Independent State of Croatia was a travesty of a state.[1]

 Principally, the resulting genocide by Catholics was that of Serbian Orthodox Christians. Nevertheless, some of the most horrific Holocaust atrocities against Jews were also perpetrated by Catholics in the NDH. 'The tragic history of the Jewish communities in that country has yet to be told because there are literally no survivors.'[2]

 The Franciscans were particularly active in the field of torture and murder. Miroslav Filipović became the infamous camp commandant of the notorious Jasenovac death camp ('the Balkan Auschwitz'), where he was nicknamed 'Father Satan' by inmates.

 Avi Yaffe of IsraCast[3] has revealed documented evidence of how the institutional Catholic Church collaborated in this annihilation of the Jewish communities of Croatia. As example, Ivan Šarić, Bishop of Sarajevo, stated:

> The movement of liberation of the world from the Jews is a movement for the renewal of human dignity. Omniscient and omnipotent God stands behind this movement.[4]

 After the War, dictator Pavelić escaped justice through the efforts of various Catholic organisations, including the Holy See. He also received special blessings from Pius XII.

Catholic Slovakia

In 1938 the population of Slovakia was three-quarters Catholic.

This account commences with the rise of the Catholic priest Jozef Tiso to become President of the clerical-fascist state of Slovakia during World War II.

In May 1939 Tiso declared that 'the building of the State will be completed on the

---

[1] Kostich, Lazo M. *The Holocaust in the 'Independent State of Croatia'.* p68

[2] http://www.isracast.com/article.aspx?ID=544 (2010)

[3] IsraCast is a non-profit, independent, multimedia broadcast and distribution network that focuses on Israeli foreign affairs and defence issues.

[4] Menachem Shelah, "The Catholic Church in Croatia, the Vatican and the Murder of the Croatian Jews," *Holocaust and Genocide Studies*, 4:3 (1989) p327

guidelines laid down in the Encyclical *Quadragesimo anno.*'

Under Tiso, Slovakian Jews and dissidents were sent to concentration camps in Poland, where most of them were eliminated.

During and after World War II, the Holy See's ever-running political machinations centred on both Croatia and Czechoslovakia as part of its active plan to re-evangelise secular Europe from the east.

Post-War, there have been attempts by members of the Slovakian Church to rehabilitate Tiso's tarnished image and to glorify the Church's clerical-fascist state. Behind all the Church's whitewashing, lies its mission for a new Catholic clerical Slovakia.

- *Konrad Ernst Eduard Henlein*

Othmar Spann (1878-1950) was a conservative Austrian philosopher, sociologist and economist with radical anti-liberal and anti-Socialist views. He was the theoretician of the Corporative State, and a protégé of the Jesuits.

Konrad Henlein (1898-1945) was the most important pro-Nazi politician in Czechoslovakia and leader of Sudeten[1] German separatists. His party preached the doctrines of Othmar Spann. Henlein aligned himself with the Third Reich, thus calling for the predominantly (typically more than 80%) German-speaking Sudetenland to be a part of Germany.

In September 1938 he helped organise hundreds of terrorist attacks and two coup attempts in the Sudetenland, and inspired Adolf Hitler's frenetic speech in Nuremberg. After the secession of the Sudetenland, Henlein's party merged with Hitler's National-sozialistische Deutsche Arbeiterpartei (Nazi Party) in 1938.

In 1939 Henlein joined the SS and was appointed Reichsstatthalter of the Sudetenland, a position he held until the end of the War.[2]

- *Monsignor Jozef Tiso ('the Jew Vendor')*

In 1886 a Catholic priest, Father Andrej Hlinka, founded the clerical Slovak People's Party (Slovenská ľudová strana) (SĽS), otherwise known as the Ľudáks. It was a right-wing party with a strong Catholic orientation, and had an anti-liberal and anti-Semitic platform.

Slovak nationalists admired the growth of fascist regimes in post-World War I Europe, and, by 1924, a paramilitary organisation, Rodobrana, the forerunner of the Hlinka Guard, had been established.[3]

Jozef Tiso was born in 1887 in Veľká Bytča in the Austro-Hungarian Empire. He studied for the priesthood, and graduated in 1911 from the prestigious Pázmáneum in Vienna. His early ministry was spent as an assistant priest. He taught religion at the girls' secondary school in Nitra, and, despite accusations by parents of misconduct, he was

---

[1] Sudeten – general name for a frontier region of the Czech Republic. Before their expulsion in 1945 more than 3 million Sudeten Germans inhabited the region.
[2] http://en.wikipedia.org/wiki/Konrad_Henlein (2007)
[3] http://www.deathcamps.org/Reinhard/slovakia%20transports.html (2009)

steadily promoted.[1] In 1915 he was appointed Spiritual Director of the Nitra Seminary. Tiso eventually became a Monsignor.

With the collapse of Austria-Hungary and the creation of Czechoslovakia in 1918, Tiso suddenly embraced politics as a career, and declared himself to be a Slovak. Within a few weeks, he had joined the Ľudáks. From 1921 to 1923, he served as the secretary to the Slovak Bishop of Nitra. During that period, Tiso was convicted twice for inciting political agitation, the second of which resulted in his imprisonment.

After 1925, the Ľudáks was the largest party in Catholic Slovakia. Tiso claimed a parliamentary seat in 1925. The Ľudáks' inter-war platform demanded the autonomy of Slovakia within a Czechoslovak framework.

In Slovakia, Adolf Hitler found allies among the Slovak clerical-fascist separatists and their leader Father Andrej Hlinka. 'The Vatican was an important player in the Czechoslovak political game. It supported Hlinka and his clerical Slovak separatist movement.' From 1934, 'the Vatican began to work for the disintegration of the Czechoslovak Republic, in parallel to the Nazis.'[2]

In due course, Tiso succeeded Father Hlinka as the leader of the Ľudáks, which stressed Slovak nationalism and Roman Catholic issues.[3]

The Hlinka Guard and Hlinka Youth were copies of the Nazi SS and the Hitler Youth. Using slogans such as, 'First to go are the Czech bosses, to be followed by Jews and Protestants,' they organised pogroms, and plundered Jewish property long before the War.[4]

Under Hitler's directives the Hlinkas turned their claims for autonomy into a demand for secession and complete independence of Slovakia.

Until 1938, Tiso was a fixture in the Czechoslovak parliament in Prague. In 1938 he emerged as de facto leader of the party. He quickly consolidated his control of the Ľudáks, becoming its undisputed chairman in 1939.

During 1938, regions of Czechoslovakia were annexed to the German Reich, and Slovakia was declared an autonomous region. Then, parts of Slovakia were annexed to Hungary.

Finally, Slovakia fell under the control of the one-party totalitarian regime, the Ľudáks, under the leadership of Monsignor Jozef Tiso, 'a loyal son of the Church'[5] – 'a man of undeniable loyalty to the Church.'[6]

By a decree of 29 October 1938, the Hlinka Guard was designated the only body that was authorised to give its members paramilitary training, and it was this decree which

[1] http://www.absoluteastronomy.com/topics/Jozef_Tiso (2009)
[2] Cymet, David. *History vs. Apologetics: The Holocaust, the Third Reich, and the Catholic Church.* p132
[3] Kopanic, Michael J Jr. *Central Europe Review*, 13 March 2000. http://www.ce-review.org/00/11/kopanic11.html (2009)
[4] Cymet, David. *History vs. Apologetics: The Holocaust, the Third Reich, and the Catholic Church.* p132
[5] Ibid. p320
[6] Vatican historian Father P Blet. Quoted in: Ibid. p332

established its formal status in the country.[1] Soon after, the Guard, similar in character to the SS, had begun terrorising and killing Jews.

Of the 63 representatives elected to the Slovak Diet in December 1938, 58 were Catholics, of whom 12 were priests.

On 14 March 1939, the Slovak parliament unanimously declared the independence of Slovakia, and the next day, Germany invaded the remaining Czech lands.

Despite its close ties to Nazi Germany, the new Slovak state was proud of its Catholic character, and in May 1939 Tiso declared that 'the building of the State will be completed on the guidelines laid down in the Papal Encyclical *Quadragesimo anno*.'[2] Roman Catholicism was declared the official religion of the country, and Slovakia became what was probably at the time the most clerically oriented state in the world.[3]

The government immediately aligned itself with Nazi Germany and signed a Treaty of Protection that effectively permitted Germany to interfere in Slovak internal affairs and to dictate Slovak foreign policy.

In October 1939 Tiso became the president of the Ľudáks. On 26 October 1939, Pius XII ('the neutral pope') sent him his blessings on his appointment and addressed him as 'My dear son'. Tiso solemnly pledged to turn Slovakia into a 'model Catholic State'.[4]

From 1942, Tiso was the self-styled 'Vodca' ('Führer') of the country. He 'presided over a shabby state' that was maintained in power by means of the Hlinka Guard. This obnoxious body was responsible for all manner of atrocities. In 1944 Tiso invited the Wehrmacht to help suppress an uprising that hoped to link up with the advancing Red Army. Later, he used a church ceremony of thanksgiving to give medals to SS officers. He 'had committed that unpardonable offence of employing Nazi military successes to pursue his own ends.'[5]

Tiso and the Catholic Corporate State

At that time, much space in the Catholic press was devoted to praising the 'Corporate State', in which Catholic clergy played a dominant role. Included, were frequent reports and articles about the achievements of the clerical dictatorship under Monsignor Jozef Tiso in the 'Independent State of Slovakia', and about the influence of the Church in Hungary, in Vichy France and Franco's Spain.

Tiso's Slovak national corporatism, under which all political power was concentrated in the hands of Catholic priests, was praised as the ideal corporate state.

In January 1940 *Katolički List*, the organ of Croatian primate Alojzije Stepinac,[6] carried an article 'Catholicism and Slovakian National Socialism', in part it read:

---

[1] See, for example: http://www.holocaustresearchproject.org/nazioccupation/hlinka.html (2009)

[2] Darring, Gerald. 'Central European Churches and the Holocaust'

[3] Cymet, David. *History vs. Apologetics: The Holocaust, the Third Reich, and the Catholic Church.* pp134-35

[4] Ibid. p135

[5] Atkin, Nicholas & Frank Tallet. *Priests, Prelates & People.* p270

[6] Alojzije Stepinac, later a cardinal, features prominently and negatively in the barbaric Catholic Croatian Holocaust.

In a modern state, which placed the interests of the people above all other consider-ations, the church and the state must cooperate in order to avoid all conflicts and misunderstandings. Thus, in accordance with the teachings of Christ, the Church in Slovakia had already exerted itself to arrange a new life for the Slovakian people.

The views of Dr Tuka[1] are fulfilled by the formation of a people's Slovakia, which has the approval of the President of the Republic, Monsignor Dr Josip Tiso. In the National-Socialist system in Slovakia, the Church will not be persecuted. Persecu-tions will be used against the opponents of National-Socialism.[2]

In Croatia, the Catholic daily *Hrvatska Straža* of 1 July 1940 stated that in the Independent State of Slovakia the people became sovereign citizens after they were freed from their political oppressors. The same paper in its issue of 6 August 1940, praised the Slovak Minister of Internal Affairs, Alexander Mach (a sort of Himmler) as 'a man of action' and added: 'We need such men today, only they can create a new world and a new order.'[3]

Not only was Slovakia thoroughly clerical, it was also unequivocally fascist and racist. The totalitarian regime persecuted not only political dissidents, but also those who did not stem from the same 'tribal clan' ('genus'). This notion of 'genus' in the L'udáks' understanding was extremely close to the Catholic and the Nazi's notion of 'race'.[4] The affinity between the Catholic Church and the Slovak state was based on their shared anti-Semitism and their common belief in authority.[5]

A Vatican Radio broadcast in June revealed conclusively that Catholic policy was to manoeuvre, bargain and negotiate with Fascism until Tiso's Catholic Government won sufficient freedom for its own reforms:

The announcement by Monsignor Tiso, head of the Slovak State, of his intention to reconstruct Slovakia on a Christian plan, is greatly welcomed by the Holy See. The new organisation of the State is to be based on the Corporate system, on Christian lines and modelled on the system which has proved so successful in Portugal[6] ... This, coming so soon after Marshal Pétain's statement that he intended to recon-struct France on a Christian basis, is doubly welcome ... we have great hopes in the fledgling reforms of Tiso and Pétain,[7] and trust that they will win sufficient freedom

[1] See below.
[2] http://www.tenc.net/croatia/stepinac1.htm (2009)
[3] Ibid.
[4] Professors Mešťan, Pavol and Alexander Rehák. *Catholic Church of Slovakia involved in attempts to exculpate Fascism.*
[5] Neumann, Johann. 'The churches in Germany before and after 1945'
[6] One of the key factors in the establishment and operations of several modern wars, genocides and holocausts, was that of Roman Catholic clerical fascism. This form of fascism was the basis or a major component of the twentieth-century dictatorships in Italy, Portugal, Spain, Nazi Germany-Austria, Hungary, Poland, Romania, Slovakia, Croatia, and Vichy France.
[7] Marshall Pétain, a French Catholic, notoriously signed Vichy's first *Statut des Juifs* (*Statute on the Jews*), under which Jews were banned from teaching, journalism, radio, film, theatre, and the civil service, to prevent them from influencing the French people. This was followed by a second decree for which Pétain, 'as a loyal Catholic, sought the approval of the Holy See.'

to permit them to carry through these plans.[1]

The Sufferings of the Romany People under Tiso

The Romany people of Slovakia were persecuted by the Tiso regime as early as March 1939. Hlinka Guardsmen killed suspect Roma rebels in front of their wives and children, then murdered the whole family. The Hlinka guard massacred the entire Roma communities of Ilija, Slatina and Kresnice in November 1944. Mass shootings of Roma families occurred in the Vydrovo Valley. In Lierny Balog, a Hlinka Guard unit rounded up 65 Roma men, forced them into a barn, then set the building on fire, killing all within.[2]

Tiso's Anti-Semitism and Anti-Judaism

There had been Jews in Slovakia since at least the twelfth century, and, by the early 1930s around 137,000 Slovakians were Jews – about 50% of the doctors and 60% of lawyers were Jewish. 'Intensive Jewish life pulsated in Slovakia during countless generations. Cities like Bratislava, Nitra, Surany, Galanta, and Tymau were important Jewish centers. The preeminent yeshiva of central Europe flourished for many generations in Bratislava.'[3]

During the 1930s the clerical Ľudáks conducted a campaign against Jewish capital and members of the liberal professions.

'One of the first actions undertaken by the new independent Slovak state under the leadership of Father Tiso after its secession from Czechoslovakia in 1939 was to adopt anti-Semitic legislation.' On 18 April, hardly one month after its declaration of independence, Slovakia passed its first anti-Semitic laws to 'defend itself against the Jews and eliminate Jewish influence from Slovakian life.[4] Progressively harsher anti-Jewish legislation was approved between April 1939 and May 1942.

There were about 89,000 Slovakian Jews in 1939, and the new state began to impose restrictions on their participation in economic life.

As early as the beginning of the 1940s, Tiso openly stated his intention to act against Jews in Slovakia. Accordingly, the Slovak People's Party under his leadership aligned itself with Nazi policy on anti-Semitism; and stringent anti-Jewish laws were introduced in the country. There was held a conference in Salzburg on 28 July 1940, which was attended by Adolf Hitler and the Catholic Slovak leaders Jozef Tiso (President), Vojtech Tuka (Prime Minister), Alexander Mach (head of the Hlinka Guard, later to become Minister of the Interior), and Franz Karmasin (head of the local German minority). There, it was resolved to set up a National Socialist (fascist) regime in Slovakia, with an increased and more systematic policy of anti-Semitism. There were to be two state agencies created to deal with 'Jewish affairs'.[5]

[1] http://www.iterasi.net/openviewer.aspx?sqrlitid=z3mvttwmhk61bd_zubmgqq (2010)
[2] http://www.holocaustresearchproject.org/nazioccupation/hlinka.html (2009)
[3] Cymet, David. *History vs. Apologetics: The Holocaust, the Third Reich, and the Catholic Church.* p161
[4] Ibid.
[5] http://en.wikipedia.org/wiki/Vojtech_Tuka (2011)

This process of identifying and isolating the Jews culminated with the implementation of the so-called *Zidovsky kodex* (*Jewish Code*) on 9 September 1941. The *kodex* comprised 270 articles. Jews had to wear a yellow armband bearing a Star of David. The star had to be affixed to every letter sent by a Jew. The police were empowered to open such letters and destroy them. Based closely upon the *Nürnberger Gesetze* (*Nuremberg Laws*), the legislation imposed a host of restrictions on Slovak Jews, including a ban on intermarriage. Additionally, Jews in Slovakia could no longer own real estate or luxury goods, and could not participate in sport or cultural events. They were also excluded from secondary schools and universities.[1] Jews required special permits to travel from one city to another. They were only allowed to shop at certain hours and were forbidden to employ non-Jewish maids. Jews could not teach in institutions of higher education, hold civil service jobs, or serve in the army. The licenses of Jewish physicians, pharmacists, and lawyers were revoked.[2]

In his report to Cardinal Maglione, the new apostolic delegate, Giuseppe Burzio, who had only recently arrived, expressed his approval of this infamous legislation:

> Some or all of these measures are justified given the preponderant influence of Jews in business.[3]

For Tiso, Jews were merely 'Pests'. In his Holíč speech of 1942 on Slovak policy towards the Jews, he said:

> in accordance with God's order: Slovak, go and get rid of your pests!

He is also recorded as having said:

> It is a Christian action to expel the Jews, because it is for the good of the people, which is thus getting rid of its pests.[4]

Thus, when Himmler proposed that Slovakia be made free of Jews, 'The Slovak government enthusiastically embraced the idea of deporting their Jews.'[5] An intensive propaganda campaign was launched against them. The newspaper *Gränzbote* published articles praising the facilities and conditions of the Lublin region of Poland, where so many deported Jews were destined to go.

Tiso is also reported to have said:

> God forbid that the Germans should lose the war. All the Jews and other such types would return.[6]

---

[1] http://en.wikipedia.org/wiki/Tiso (2009)
[2] Cymet, David. *History vs. Apologetics: The Holocaust, the Third Reich, and the Catholic Church.* p161
[3] Ibid.
[4] Rothkirchen, Livia. "Vatican Policy and the 'Jewish Problem' in 'Independent' Slovakia (1939-1945)", *The Nazi Holocaust*. 3. pp1306-32. See also: *Yad Vashem Studies*, Vol 6.
[5] http://www.deathcamps.org/Reinhard/slovakia%20transports.html (2009)
[6] Source: Darring, Gerald. 'Central European Churches and the Holocaust'. http://www.shc.edu/theolibrary/resources/07Central.htm#_edn5 (2009)

Consequently, as president, Tiso was directly responsible for the deportation to concentration camps of 58,000 Jews, and of another 30,000 people whom the clerical-fascist state regarded as 'suspect'. Only a few hundred ever returned.[1] 'Ultimately, most of Slovakia's Jews perished in the gas chambers at Auschwitz and other death camps. This has left a bitter legacy.'[2]

'Most of the Catholic population of Slovakia reacted to the persecution of Jews with indifference, and most of the bishops supported the government's anti-Jewish policies.'[3]

Historian Professor Michael Phayer sees Tiso as the leader of the party that persecuted Jews, and he records, for example, that when Tiso was approached by Jews for protection from impending deportations, he responded by launching an investigation into how the Jews had received their information.[4]

With the prospect of acquiring the properties left behind by the Jews, Slovakia was even willing to pay the Germans for every Jew deported. Post-War, Adolf Eichmann commented in Jerusalem:[5]

> They offered us their Jews like discarded beer cans.

Accordingly, in February 1942, Monsignor Tiso proposed paying Germany 500 Reichsmarks (US$200) for every deported person. The Slovak State paid the German state 100 million Slovak crowns in advance.[6]

After the announcement of the deportations was made, Monsignor Burzio wrote to Prime Minister Tuka on February 1942 that the Jews sent to eastern Poland would be taken to be killed and not to work. Burzio also informed the Vatican in his reports of 9 and 11 March, and warned:

> The deportation of 80,000 persons to Poland at the mercy of the Germans is the equivalent of condemning a great part of them to certain death.

The warning made no impression on the Holy See under Pius XII.[7,8]
The deportations began on 25 March 1942. Significantly, Slovakia was the only country that paid Nazi Germany to deport its Jews.

> The first Slovak Jews that arrived in Auschwitz from Nitra and Tyrnau were employed in building the crematoria that subsequently turned them into ashes.[9]

After meeting Interior Minister Alexander Mach, Monsignor Burzio informed the

[1] *The Slovak Spectator*. http://www.spectator.sk/articles/view/31550/2/archbishop_prays_for_tiso.html (2009)
[2] Kopanic, Michael J Jr. *Central Europe Review*, 13 March 2000. http://www.ce-review.org/00/11/kopanic11.html (2009)
[3] http://www.shc.edu/theolibrary/resources/07Central.htm (2014)
[4] Phayer, Michael. '*Slovakia,' The Catholic Church and the Holocaust, 1930-1965*. pp 86-91. Source: http://www.shc.edu/theolibrary/resources/07Central.htm#_edn5 (2009)
[5] Cymet, David. *History vs. Apologetics: The Holocaust, the Third Reich, and the Catholic Church.* p312
[6] *The Slovak Spectator*. http://www.spectator.sk/articles/view/31550/2/archbishop_prays_for_tiso.html (2009)
[7] Cymet, David. *History vs. Apologetics: The Holocaust, the Third Reich, and the Catholic Church.* p322
[8] See below. Refer also to Stockwell, Antony. *Pius XII: The Dark Side* for an in depth examination of the wartime notorious inactions and glacial silence on the Holocaust atrocities of the aloof Pius XII.
[9] Cymet, David. *History vs. Apologetics: The Holocaust, the Third Reich, and the Catholic Church.* p325

Vatican Secretary of State on 31 March 1942 that several convoys of deportees had already left for the German border. Mach insisted that the Slovakian Church hierarchy was in total agreement with the government on the deportations.[1]

After escaping from deportation to Auschwitz in the autumn of 1944, Rabbi Michael Dov-Ber Weissmandel approached the papal nuncio to plead for help for the Jews. The Nuncio replied:

> This, being a Sunday, is a holy day for us. Neither I nor Father Tiso occupy ourselves with profane matters on this day.[2]

He explained:

> There is no innocent blood of Jewish children in the world. All Jewish blood is guilty. You have to die. This is the punishment that has been awaiting you because of that sin [the deicide of Jesus].[3]

Tiso made his attitude to the Jews quite clear, when, on 8 August 1942, he made a speech in which he stated:

> I think that no one has to be convinced that the Jewish element posed a threat to the life of the Slovak State ... *We acted according to the law of God*: Slovakia, dispose of your enemies! In this sense we establish order and will continue to do so.[4]

By the end of the war, of more than 58,000 Slovak Jews deported to Poland in 1942, only about 700 were alive.

Opinions differ widely on Tiso's role in the Jewish deportations from Slovakia, but it is known that he adhered to the Nazi line to a considerable extent. Documents concerning the Holocaust in Slovakia[5] prove that the Slovak government consentingly cooperated with the Nazis and helped coordinate the deportations. In fact, at a meeting with Tiso in April 1942, Hitler praised the policy concerning the Jews of Slovakia.

Still serving as the priest of Bánovce, President Tiso spoke from the pulpit in Holíč on 15 August 1942:

> As regards the Jewish question, people ask if what we do is Christian and humane. I ask that too: is it Christian if the Slovaks want to rid themselves, of their eternal enemies the Jews? Love for oneself is God's command, and this love makes it imperative for me to remove anything harming me.[6]

[1] Cymet, David. *History vs. Apologetics: The Holocaust, the Third Reich, and the Catholic Church.* p325
[2] http://www.iclnet.org/pub/resources/text/m.sion/shul53-4.htm (2014)
[3] See also: Berkovits, Eliezer. *Faith After the Holocaust.* pp16-17. Source: http://www.geocities.com/pharsea/Perfidy.html (2007)
[4] Hoppenbrouwers, Frans. 'Nationalistic Tendencies in the Slovak Roman Catholic Church'. *Occasional Papers on Religion in Eastern Europe*, Vol XVIII, No 6, December 1998. Source: http://www.concordatwatch.eu/kb-1216.843 (2009)
[5] See, for example: Niznansky, E, et al (eds), *Holokaust na Slovensku*, Vols 1-5
[6] Cymet, David. *History vs. Apologetics: The Holocaust, the Third Reich, and the Catholic Church.* pp327-28

Tiso lost power when the Soviet Army conquered the last parts of western Slovakia in April 1945. He was sentenced to death for 'internal treason, treason of the Slovak National Uprising[1] and collaboration with Nazism'. Wearing his clerical outfit, Monsignor Jozef Tiso was hanged in Bratislava on 18 April 1947.[2]

The Slovakian Bishops

On 26 April 1942, the bishops of Slovakia issued a pastoral letter approving the deportations of the Jews:

> The greatest tragedy of the Jewish nation lies in the fact of not having recognised the redeemer and of having prepared a terrible and ignominious death for him on the cross ... Also in our eyes has the influence of the Jews been pernicious. In a short time they have taken control of almost all the economic and financial life of the country to the detriment of our people. Not only economically, but also in the cultural and moral spheres, they have harmed our people. The Church cannot be opposed, therefore, if the state with legal regulations hinders the dangerous influence of the Jews.[3]

Rabbi Unger approached the senior archbishop of Nitra, Dr Karol Kmetko, a rabid anti-Semite, to plead with him for assistance in stopping the deportations. The archbishop replied:

> These are not expulsions, there you will not die from hunger and epidemics, there you will be slaughtered all together, old and young, children and women, all at once. This is the punishment you deserve for the death of our saviour. Your only salvation is to accept our religion, only then will I intervene for the decree to be repealed.[4]

Pius XII and the Holy See

On 11 March 1942, several days before the first transport of Slovakian Jews were to be sent to concentration camps, the Slovakian chargé d'affaires in Bratislava told Pius XII:

> I have been assured that this atrocious plan is the handwork of ... Prime Minister (Tuka), who confirmed the plan ... he dared to tell me – he who makes such a show of his Catholicism – that he saw nothing inhuman or un-Christian in it ... the deportation of 80,000 persons to Poland, is equivalent to condemning a great number of them to certain death.[5]

Characteristically, Pius did not intervene.

On 13 March 1943, Pius 'received in a personal audience Hungarian nun Margit

---

[1] The Slovak National Uprising was an armed insurrection organised by the Slovak resistance movement. It was launched on 29 August 1944 from Banská Bystrica in an attempt to oust the collaborationist government of Jozef Tiso. Although the rebel forces were defeated by Germany, guerrilla warfare continued until 1945.

[2] See, for example: Niznansky, E, et al (eds), *Holokaust na Slovensku*, Vols 1-5

[3] Cymet, David. *History vs. Apologetics: The Holocaust, the Third Reich, and the Catholic Church.* pp325-26

[4] Ibid. p326

[5] http://www.astrotheme.fr/en/portraits/HD5ErVtDrzha.htm (2008)

Slachta, who came to tell him that the last 20,000 Jews of Slovakia were in imminent danger of being deported to their death. Sister Slachta left Rome empty-handed, and was not able to elicit any verbal comment from Pius XII on the terrible crime that a Catholic government led by a Catholic priest was on its way to bring to its final conclusion:

> Pius listened to me all the way through [and] expressed his shock ... He listened to me but said very little.[1]

On 4 November 1944, Monsignor Burzio went to convey, in the name of the Pope, his sorrow for the suffering inflicted on so many people because of their 'nationality or race' and to remind Tiso that 'his opinions and decisions are to conform to his dignity and his sacerdotal integrity.' The Vatican worried, said Michael Phayer, that its loyal servants in Slovakia should not implicate the Church and the Pope in mass murder because, 'in Slovakia the Church's fingerprints were undeniably on the trigger.'[2]

Five days later, Tiso sent a letter to the Holy See. He justified his collaboration with the Germans, which, he said, recognised and protected Slovakia's independence. He defended his actions against the Czechs and the Jews – which were designed to eliminate their pernicious influence. 'The dignity of the priesthood was always before my eyes, it was pharisaic on the part of Slovakia's enemies to express concern for the reputation of the clergy.' He had not acted on his own, but 'had consulted the best advisors within the Church.'[3]

Professor Michael Phayer has pointed out that at no time did the Holy See publicly protest the murder of the Jews of Slovakia, who were the first and the last victims of the Holocaust.[4]

Subsequently, Fr John Morley wrote of the dismissive role of the Holy See. Slovakia was a model Catholic state with a priest as president and a prime minister 'who prided himself of being a practicing Catholic.' Anti-Semitism was rampant. 'It was also a country proud of its dedication and loyalty to the Pope.' Consequently, the Holy See did nothing; issuing neither threats of excommunication nor interdict against the president, the prime minister, or the laity. 'The failure of Vatican diplomacy in Slovakia must be attributed as much to its own indifference to the deportation of the Jews as to any other factor.'[5] It was another example of Pius XII's general unconcern for the fate of the Jews.

Other Prominent Catholics

Vojtech 'Béla' Tuka

Vojtech Tuka prided himself on attending Mass daily and of periodically going to confession.[6]

---

[1] Cymet, David. *History vs. Apologetics: The Holocaust, the Third Reich, and the Catholic Church.* p330
[2] Ibid. p332
[3] Ibid.
[4] Ibid.
[5] Quoted in: Cymet, David. *History vs. Apologetics: The Holocaust, the Third Reich, and the Catholic Church.*
[6] Ibid. p135

He was the leader of the radical wing of the Slovak People's Party, and in 1910 he was elected to the Presidium of the Countrywide Christian Socialist Party.

After the founding of Czechoslovakia in 1918, Tuka joined the autonomist Hlinka Slovak People's Party (Hlinka Slovenská ľudová strana) (HSL'S). He served as the secretary of the Party, and edited its periodical, *Slovák*. The party argued that the 1920 constitution had not included the provision for Slovak autonomy alluded to in the *Pittsburgh Declaration*. Acting on this, the HSL'S introduced a Slovak-autonomy bill in the Czechoslovak parliament in 1922. The bill was rejected, but the HSL'S had established that autonomy was the core of its program. This growing separatist sentiment later enabled Tuka's rise to power.

In 1923 Tuka founded the organisation Rodobrana ('Home Guard'), an armed militia.

Tuka was a deputy to the Czechoslovak parliament from 1925 to 1929.

In 1938 the Slovak members of Czech political parties in Slovakia merged with the HSL'S and formed Hlinkova slovenska ľudova strana - Strana slovenskej národnej jednoty (HSL'S-SSNJ). The Slovak National Party then joined the HSL'S-SSNJ. This new party quickly developed clear authoritarian characteristics. It immediately subjected the leftist and Jewish parties to considerable harassment.

Tuka was Prime Minister and Minister of Foreign Affairs of the Slovak Republic between 1940 and 1945.

He was one the main forces behind the deportation of Slovak Jews to Nazi concentration camps in Poland. On 3 September 1940, he convinced the Slovak assembly to enact *Constitutional Law 210*, authorising the government to do everything necessary to exclude Jews from the economic and social life of the country. Previous laws had already stripped them of political participation.

On 24 November 1940, Vojtech Tuka and von Ribbentrop signed a protocol entering Slovakia into alliance with Germany, Japan, and Italy.[1]

Tuka, together with Dieter Wisliceny, an SS hauptsturmführer, composed the *Codex Judaicus*, or *Jewish Code*, which comprehensively denied rights to Slovak Jews. Section 225 of the *Code* gave the President the right to exempt individuals of his choosing from the Code's provisions. Jews who had converted to Christianity were given letters of amnesty.[2]

Negotiations to deport Jews from Slovakia to Poland, to clear the country of Jews, began towards the end of 1941. President Tiso and Interior Minister Alexander Mach met Hitler and Himmler to discuss the deportations. The *Codex Judaicus* provided the legal base for such an action, 'which was looked upon with favor by the secular and clerical Catholic leadership.'[3] The scheme began under the guise of an operation to provide 20,000 Jewish workers for the Axis war industries.

---

[1] http://www.jewishvirtuallibrary.org/jsource/vjw/slovakia.html (2009)
[2] http://en.wikipedia.org/wiki/Vojtech_Tuka (2011)
[3] Cymet, David. *History vs. Apologetics: The Holocaust, the Third Reich, and the Catholic Church.* p320

In 1942 Tuka strongly advocated the deportation of Slovakia's Jewish population to the eastern Nazi concentration camps. Together with Internal Affairs Minister Alexander Mach, Tuka became the leader of the pro-Nazi wing within the Slovak People's Party.

The date for the commencement of the deportations was set for 26 March. Tiso had already been told by his chief general at the Soviet front that 18,000 Jews from Slovak Ruthenia deported to Kamenetz Podolsk had been mass murdered by the Einsatzgruppen and the Hungarian military. Tiso did not intervene.

Monsignor Burzio was also well-informed of the massacre by the Slovak chief military chaplain, who was an eyewitness to the massacre. He thus already knew the real meaning of 'resettlement' and 'labour mobilisation'.[1] Burzio did not intervene either.

Between 25 March and 20 October 1942, Slovakia sent about 57,700 Jews to Nazi concentration camps. By the end of the war in April 1945, another 13,500 Jews had been deported.[2]

Adolf Eichmann personally visited Slovakia several times to make sure the deportations were running smoothly.

After World War II, following a brief trial, Vojtech Tuka was executed.[3]

Ferdinand Ďurčanský

Ferdinand Ďurčanský was a Slovak nationalist leader who for a time served with the collaborationist government of Jozef Tiso. His followers, who came to be known as the 'Young Generation', held a number of posts in the Ľudáks' administration, with Ďurčanský himself serving as Minister for Home and Foreign Affairs. He was responsible for the murder of tens of thousands of Jews.

His public speech in Topolčany at the beginning of the war is well-known:

> Look around you. All these are Jewish shops. Jews are living all around you. All this will be yours.[4]

Ďurčanský remained a strong supporter of Tiso. The United Nations War Crimes Commission accepted Czechoslovakian charges that he had been paid by the Nazi secret service and had been complicit in the deaths of Jews. Condemned to death in absentia, Ďurčanský nevertheless escaped to Austria in 1945. Later that year, he moved to the Vatican. In 1947 he escaped to Argentina with the help of the Catholic Church.[5]

Ďurčanský became an informant for Perón's secret service and a founding member of the SARE (Society in Argentina for the Reception of Europeans) Nazi rescue organisation.[6]

---

[1] Cymet, David. *History vs. Apologetics: The Holocaust, the Third Reich, and the Catholic Church.* p321
[2] http://en.wikipedia.org/wiki/Vojtech_Tuka (2011)
[3] Ibid.
[4] http://www.delet.sk/en/news-and-politics/slovakia/the-guardsman-durcansky-will-have-a-bust-unveiled-in-rajec (2011)
[5] Refer to Chapter 23 – Catholic Assistance to War Criminals, for additional details of the Holy See's assistance to escaping war criminals.
[6] Goñi, Uki. *The Real ODESSA: How Perón Brought the Nazi War Criminals to Argentina.* pp xi-xv

Reports in 2011 reveal that the town of Rajec, Slovakia, plans to unveil a statue in honour of Ďurčanský. His bust has been placed in front of the town museum. The mayor, Ján Rybárik defends him.[1]

Jan Ďurčanský

Jan Ďurčanský was a Slovak war criminal who escaped to Argentina with his brother Ferdinand. He was appointed by Perón to the Immigration Office. He helped fellow fugitives obtain Argentinian identification and citizenship.[2]

In July 1960 an Argentinian court decided to dismiss, on a technical legal argument, the application for the extradition of Ďurčanský who was wanted by Czechoslovakia as a war criminal.

Slovakian Labour and Transit Camps

Sered' Labour Camp

Sered' (Szered) is a town in southern Slovakia. It was utilised as a detention centre and as a staging ground for deportations to Poland. The Hlinka Guard oversaw the camp. During 1944 and 1945, 13,500 Jews were deported from Sered' to Theresienstadt and Auschwitz.

The Sered' camp was liberated by the Red Army in 1945.

Žilina Transit Camp

The Slovak government also established a transit camp at Žilina where many thousands of Jews passed through this 'anteroom to hell' on their journey to the death camps.[3]

Rudolf Vrba, born Walter Rosenberg, the son of a sawmill owner, was born in Slovakia in 1924. At the age of fifteen he was expelled from his high school in Bratislava under the Slovak state's anti-Semitic laws. In 1942 like other Jews, he was rounded up and sent to the concentration camp at Auschwitz. Vrba and a friend, Alfréd Wetzler, escaped with the help of the Communist party in Auschwitz. They came to public attention in 1944, when, in April that year, they passed information to the Allies about the mass murder that was taking place at Auschwitz. The 32 pages of information which the men dictated became known as the *Vrba-Wetzler Report*. In September 1944 Vrba joined the Czechoslovak partisans and was later decorated for bravery. In 1967 he became Professor of Pharmacology at the University of British Columbia.

As a young Slovak Jew, Vrba described his realisation on the journey to Auschwitz of the un-Christianity of Monsignor Tiso:

> Up and down the train the officers began to shout: 'All men between sixteen and forty-five out!' At first nobody moved because they could not believe their ears. This was against the rules, contrary to the principles which Monsignor Tiso, President of

---

[1] http://www.delet.sk/en/news-and-politics/slovakia/the-guardsman-durcansky-will-have-a-bust-unveiled-in-rajec (2011)

[2] Goñi, Uki. *The Real ODESSA: How Perón Brought the Nazi War Criminals to Argentina.* pp xi-xv

[3] http://www.deathcamps.org/Reinhard/slovakia%20transports.html (2009)

Slovakia, had expounded over and over again. In the newspapers, on the radio, he had never tired of saying: 'It is a basic principle of the Christian faith that families should not be separated. That principle will be observed when the Jews are sent to their new settlements'.

The men were herded out of the car and as their mothers, wives and daughters stretched their arms through the narrow barred windows, the men tried to spring forward for one last touch. But the guards beat them back and they beat the women's hands, too. As the train slowly moved away and the young man heard the anguished cries of women and children, whose wrists were bruised and broken, he finally realised that they had been betrayed.[1]

Nováky Labour Camp

Nováky is a town in the Trenčín Region in western Slovakia.

In 1942, nearby barracks were used for the assembly and detention of Slovak Jews from all over the country pending their deportation to Nazi death camps in German occupied Poland. The camp was guarded by the Slovak Hlinka Guard militia.[2]

Stropkov Deportations

Stropkov is a town in the Prešov Region of Slovakia. Before the Slovakian Holocaust, approximately 2000 Jews lived there. The first transport of Jews left Stropkov on 24 March 1942, carrying hundreds of them to Auschwitz. By 1945, only 100 Stropkov Jews remained. *Today, not a single Jew remains in Stropkov.*[3]

Post-War Catholic Apologetics

In 1990, Bishop (now Cardinal) Ján Chryzostom Korec formally unveiled Jozef Tiso's memorial board at the secondary grammar school in Tiso's birthplace, Bánovce nad Bebravou. In 1997, on the 50th anniversary of Tiso's execution for 'internal treason, treason of the Slovak National Uprising and collaboration with Nazism', Korec celebrated a requiem mass for him in Nitra.[4]

In 2007, an urn containing remains from the Bratislava grave of Jozef Tiso was brought to St Andrew Abbey, Cleveland, Ohio, for permanent keeping at the Slovak Institute and Reference Library. The urn was received at a public Mass at which the Right Reverend Clement Zeleznik, OSB, 'eloquently spoke of the difficult period in which Monsignor Tiso was asked to serve as President. How he literally saved his country and actually saved many lives.'[5] 'The occasion also marked the 60th anniversary of the *martyrdom* of Msgr. Tiso ...'

For Tiso as a priest, God was not on the back burner but was the centre of his life ...
The proof is that in his entire reign of five years, no opponents were thrown into jail,

[1] Vrba, Rudolf. *Escape from Auschwitz: I cannot forgive.* pp56-57
[2] http://en.wikipedia.org/wiki/Nov%C3%A1ky (2012)
[3] http://www.jewishvirtuallibrary.org/jsource/vjw/slovakia.html (2015)
[4] *The Slovak Spectator.* http://www.spectator.sk/articles/view/31550/2/archbishop_prays_for_tiso.html (2009)
[5] http://blog.cleveland.com/slovakia/2007/12/tiso_ashes_received_in_clevela.html (2009)

hanged, or died for being opposed to him.[1]

In 2008 Tiso was honoured by the Catholic Archbishop of Trnava, Ján Sokol, who celebrated a requiem mass for Tiso on the 61st anniversary of his execution. The mass took place in the Blumental Church in Bratislava, and, behind the altar was a portrait of Tiso, the presidential standard of the wartime Slovakia, and the Lorraine-cross emblem used by the fascist Hlinka Guard during the War. Sokol prayed 'For the redemption of the soul of our departed brother, priest, President Jozef Tiso'. Later, Sokol stated:

> I respect President Tiso, I respect him very much ...

The organisers of the 'We do not want to stand by' civic initiative consider these symbols proof that the mass was misused for political purposes.[2] A petition by 'We do not want to stand by' has been signed by hundreds of people. Representatives of the initiative, including university educator Miroslav Kocúr, lecturer Dušan Jaura, and the ethnologist Monika Vrzgulová, stressed at a press conference:

> The religious service, despite being allegedly private, had all the signs of a public festive mass: it was held on the site of a publicly accessible parish church, in the presence of numerous guests and a big crowd of people.[3]

The Jewish religious community also reacted against the issue. A spokesman, Jaroslav Franek, stated that as President of the fascist Slovak state, Tiso bore full responsibility for the actions of that state. He told the daily paper *Sme* (*We Are*):

> We have expressed several times amazement and pity that representatives of the Catholic Church do not treat politicians of the [wartime] Slovak state as convicted criminals, but rather as people who deserve acknowledgement.[4]

The spokesman of the Conference of Bishops of Slovakia, Jozef Kováčik, told *The Slovak Spectator* that the Convention of Bishops of Slovakia regarded Tiso primarily as a priest:

> we simply cannot blame him for everything, when others also bore responsibility. It would *probably* be very irresponsible to *definitely* close the historical debate on this personality.[5,6]

---

[1] http://www.outdoorsunlimited.net/~j.martin/Tiso1.html (2011)

[2] *The Slovak Spectator*. http://www.spectator.sk/articles/view/31763/2/activists_launch_petition_against_tiso_mass.html (2009)

[3] Ibid.

[4] Ibid.

[5] Ibid.

[6] Such apologetics are reminiscent of the disavowal by the Catholic Bishop of Aberdeen of the responsibility of the Church for its abuse of girls at Nazareth House homes in Scotland during the 1960s and 1970s. He stated that child disciplinary practices had changed drastically over the last 30 years and that *some* practices (cleverly evading the *actual* practices) which rightly today seem excessive and even cruel would *not necessarily* have been viewed in this light *many* years ago. A somewhat similar tactic was used by the Church's 'Commission for religious relations with the Jews' – refer to Chapter 24.

Notwithstanding, Katarína Zavacká, a lawyer for the Institute of Law and State of the Slovak Academy of Sciences, emphasised that Jozef Tiso's personality is sufficiently understood from ample archive documents. Documents from the Nuremberg Trials indicate that the wartime Slovak state was regarded as a satellite of fascist Germany, and that full responsibility for this status rested with Jozef Tiso as President. Additionally, as a consequence of the Nuremberg Trials, fascist groups in Slovakia, such as the HSĽS, Hlinkova garda (Hlinka Guard) and Hlinkova mládež (Hlinka Youth) were banned.[1]

Katarína Zavacká also pointed out that during the Nuremberg Trials, it was agreed that states would incorporate the promotion of Fascism as a crime into their Penal Codes. She thought the requiem mass for Jozef Tiso could be deemed promotion of Fascism.

Miroslav Kocúr stated that the Church's ambiguous evaluation of Tiso is wrong:

> Historians, politicians or religious representatives in positions of responsibility who do not take a clear stand on this issue make it possible for people with minimal information and romantic ideals to maintain the opinion that the things that happened here during the wartime Slovak state were right.[2]

He confirmed that:

> We are religious people, who understand religious symbolism. We wanted to protest against this mass, which we consider misused for political goals.

The representatives of the initiative stressed at a press conference:

> We want a completely different opinion to that of Archbishop Ján Sokol to be heard from citizens, especially believers. We do not want to stand by and just watch sympathy towards the fascist Slovak State, led by a Catholic priest, being *expressed by bishops through false professional solidarity*.

> This state imposed humiliating, inhumane treatment on the people whom it was supposed to protect.[3]

Miroslav Kocúr's initiative was supported by such personalities as Catholic priest Anton Srholec, chairman of the Convention of Political Prisoners of Slovakia, and Professor Igor Kišš, theologian of the Protestant Theology Faculty of Comenius University.[4]

The Holy See's ever Continuing Battle for Dominance

After World War I the Holy See was determined, as were its fascist partners Italy and Germany, to reconstitute in that region the power and influence which the papacy had lost with the collapse of the Austro-Hungarian Empire in 1918. This determination was reinforced by the fact that the Holy See, firstly, was no longer the supreme religious

---

[1] *The Slovak Spectator*. http://www.spectator.sk/articles/view/31550/2/archbishop_prays_ for_tiso.html (2009)

[2] A similar comment is applicable to Catholic apologetic attitudes to the Church's Croatian Holocaust.

[3] *The Slovak Spectator*. http://www.spectator.sk/articles/view/31763/2/activists_launch_petition_against_ tiso_mass.html (2009)

[4] Ibid.

authority in Central and Eastern Europe, and secondly, it had lost the foundations on which citizens owed a dual allegiance to the Latin Church and the state. This had resulted in a sharp decline in its power and influence in the region.

Consequently, in the twentieth century the shared vision of the Church and the fascist states was that of a reconstituted Catholic confederation of nations along the Danube River basin, from Croatia to Austria, Slovakia and Germany. In effect, a reconstructed Holy Roman Empire.

Accordingly, during and after World War II, the Holy See's ever-running political machinations centred on both Croatia and Czechoslovakia as part of its active plan to re-evangelise secular Europe from the east. It has been called the Vatican's 'battle for the soul of Europe'.[1]

Right-wing Slovak nationalism was therefore being encouraged by the Church for its own ends.[2] The Vatican recently attempted to push through an unprecedented 'conscience concordat'[3] and has drawn up an audacious five-year plan for 'evangelising' the whole country.[4]

This is not the freedom that some Slovaks had hoped for:

> Two decades after the end to Communism in Czechoslovakia, many Slovak democrats have begun to wonder if their country is still being steered from abroad – not from Moscow – but from the Vatican.[5]

Just a few months after the bloodless liberation from Communism, John Paul II made his first trip to Czechoslovakia. Three years later, the president of the new Slovak Republic thanked him for encouraging the breakup of Czechoslovakia.[6] During this period, the chairman of the Czechoslovak Bishops' Conference, as well as the Slovak bishops, propagandised the 'right' to Slovak self-determination and did not call for the referendum which, in the words of Franciscus Hoppenbrouwers, Catholic Church historian and secretary of studies of the Dutch Catholic relief organisation, 'Communicantes', 'would have prevented the splitting up of Czechoslovakia'.[7]

The Holy See is also constantly attempting to link Catholicism with Slovak nationalism. Hence, the Church, the Christian political parties, and a group of revisionist historians are all promoting and praising the wartime Slovak state as a golden era, as 'an ideal

---

[1] Allen, John L Jr. "Pope's health status competes with message: In Slovakia, he honors martyrs under communism, stresses right to life", *National Catholic Reporter*, 26 September 2003. Source: http://www.concordatwatch.eu/kb-1216.843 (2009)

[2] In a manner similar to that current in Croatia.

[3] Concordats are one of the Church's favourite means of stamping its interests on to its targeted states. A prime example was the *Reichskonkordat* with Nazi Germany that legitimised Adolf Hitler's fascist state.

[4] http://www.concordatwatch.eu/kb-1216.843 (2009)

[5] http://www.secularism.org.uk/whyslovakia.html?CPID=f87c5ae23900628406273799d2ad6a c5 (2011)

[6] Hoppenbrouwers, Frans. 'Nationalistic Tendencies in the Slovak Roman Catholic Church'. *Religion in Eastern Europe*, Vol XVIII, No 6, December 1998. Source: http://www.concordatwatch.eu/kb-1216.843 (2009)

[7] Ibid.

society, where Roman Catholic social doctrine prevailed'.[1] In fact, the country was then so tightly controlled by Tiso's totalitarian regime and the Church, that it was known as 'the parish republic' – hence the title of the Slovak writer and journalist Dominik Tatarka's major work, *Farská Republika*.[2] Slovakia was indeed a prime example of Catholic Clerico-fascism. Its genocides and treatment of dissidents compares with those of the Independent State of Croatia, which 'was an example of the Roman Catholic Church's ideal society. It serves as a warning to all freedom loving peoples.'[3]

The Church's whitewashing the Past

Today, the Catholic Church is busily whitewashing Slovakia's clerical-fascist past. Cardinal Korec has stated that Jozef Tiso opposed the establishment of a Nazi-dominated Slovak state and never signed a single death sentence.[4] What Korec failed to mention is that Monsignor Tiso 'simply let the Germans do the job.' In fact, as mentioned above, in February 1942, Tiso offered to pay Germany 500 Reichsmarks for every deported person. Accordingly, the Slovak State paid the German state 100 million Slovak crowns in advance.

The Church now attempts to dissociate itself from the fascist wartime Slovak state, even though priests were in firm control of the country at all levels. The Church has fallen back on the excuse that although the clerics wielded power they were still helpless, and that their hands are not stained with the blood of all those they were, so sadly, obliged to hand over.[5] In fact, a revisionist Slovakian historian has gone so far as to declare that Tiso dared to do something the like of which 'no other statesman in Europe dared – he saved Jews, not liquidated them'.[6]

Prominent among Tiso's admirers is Jan Slota, leader of the far-right Slovenská národná strana (SNS) (Slovak National Party) that was a partner in former Prime Minister Vladimír Mečiar's coalition. The Czech news agency Česká tisková kancelář (CTK) quoted Slota as telling a rally commemorating the birth of the first Slovak state:

> We bow before Jozef Tiso, and we are glad that he lives and will continue to live in the Slovak nation for a long time.[7]

---

[1] Hoppenbrouwers, Frans. 'Nationalistic Tendencies in the Slovak Roman Catholic Church'. *Religion in Eastern Europe*, Vol XVIII, No 6, December 1998. Source: http://www.concordatwatch.eu/kb-1216.843 (2009)

[2] Mestan, Pavol. 'New interpretations and deliberate misinterpretations of the Jewish question in Slovakia: some remarks', *South-East Europe Review* 2/2000, pp173-79. Source: http://www.concordatwatch.eu/kb-1216.843 (2009)

[3] Manhattan, Avro. *The Vatican's Holocaust: The Sensational Account of the Most ...* p9

[4] Kantz, Matt. 'Slovak cardinal defends record of president', *National Catholic Reporter*, 22 October 1999. Source: http://www.concordatwatch.eu/kb-1216.843 (2009)

[5] Hoppenbrouwers, Frans. 'Nationalistic Tendencies in the Slovak Roman Catholic Church'. *Religion in Eastern Europe*, Vol XVIII, No 6, December 1998. See the section: 'President Jozef Tiso: an innocent bystander?'. Source: http://www.concordatwatch.eu/kb-1216.843 (2009)

[6] Quoted by Mestan, Pavol. 'New interpretations and deliberate misinterpretations of the Jewish question in Slovakia: some remarks', *South-East Europe Review* 2/2000, p177

[7] http://www.nizkor.org/ftp.cgi/people/ftp.py?people//t/tiso.jozef/press/jozef-tiso (2009)

Even Tiso's execution at the War's end as a traitor and war criminal has been given a nationalistic and religious gloss. In a manner akin to the whitewashing of Ante Pavelić (the despotic 'Führer' of the Roman Catholic state of Croatia), Tiso is increasingly being portrayed as 'the saviour of the Slovak nation during World War II and a martyr for Slovak independence.'[1] This was an actual description of an exhibit in April 1995 sponsored by Matica slovenská (Slovakia's public-law cultural and scientific institution). Matica recently started publishing its newspaper *Matičné zvesti* as an annex of a newspaper published by Slovenské hnutie obrody (SHO) (Slovak Revival Movement), an association whose chairman is Monsignor Róbert Švec, praising both the World War II Slovak Republic and Jozef Tiso.[2,3]

Again, in a manner similar to that performed by Franjo Tuđman, the late Catholic President of post-War Croatia, the Slovakian landscape is now being 'rewritten' to remove discordant evidence of massacres on Slovak soil, of resistance to Tiso's authoritarian state, and of the final liberation by the Red Army. Thus, streets have been renamed and statues taken down.

Monuments destroyed include the one marking the mass graves in Kremnička of more than 700 Slovaks murdered by the Germans on suspicion of aiding the resistance, and the one marking the graves in Zvolen of the Red Army troops who finally liberated Slovakia in 1945.

Monuments have also disappeared from Prešov. Prešov is a town, which, before World War II had a large Jewish population and housed a major Jewish museum. Under the Tiso government 6400 Jews were deported from the town. The 2001 census recorded that 67% of the population was Catholic, but *there was no mention of Jews*.[4]

Monuments have also disappeared from Banská Bystrica, a key city in central Slovakia. During World War II, Banská Bystrica became the centre of anti-Nazi opposition when the Slovak National Uprising, one of the largest anti-Nazi resistance events in Europe, was launched from the city on 29 August 1944. The insurgents were defeated, however, and Banská Bystrica was briefly occupied by the German forces before it was liberated by Soviet and Romanian troops on 26 March 1945. According to the 2001 census, 47% of the city's population were Catholics, but again there is no mention of Jews. Before World War II, the population of the city included significant Jewish minorities. The Jews resided for a long time in Radvaň[5] because they were prohibited from entering the city itself. Built in 1867, the synagogue in Banská Bystrica was demolished in 1983.[6]

---

[1] See, for example: *Jozef Tiso, Martyr pro Deo et Patria.* https://www.facebook.com/pages/Jozef-Tiso-Martyr-pro-Deo-et-Patria-multilingual/853704468010682 (2015)

[2] http://en.wikipedia.org/wiki/Matica_slovensk%C3%A1#Controversy (2009)

[3] US Department of State. 'Slovak Republic Human Rights Practices, 1995', March 1966

[4] http://en.wikipedia.org/wiki/Pre%C5%A1ov#History (2009)

[5] Radvaň was a village located south-west of the centre of Banská Bystrica.

[6] http://en.wikipedia.org/wiki/Bansk%C3%A1_Bystrica (2009)

The Church's Plans for a New Roman Catholic State of Slovakia

Behind all the Church's whitewashing, lies its mission for a new clerical Slovakia. In 1995 on his second trip to the state, John Paul II hinted to the Prime Minister about his political plans:

> A new model can be instituted in Slovakia with establishment of a society respectful of Christian values. This model could considerably influence the future of the world.[1]

In 1997 on the eve of elections, the Holy See judged that the Slovak government would be most vulnerable to political pressure from the Church. Accordingly, the Vatican Foreign Minister, Tauran, an expert on concordats was sent to instruct the Slovakian bishops on their negotiations with the government.[2]

In the year 2000, the Slovak bishops recruited 'more than fifty professionals' to help them draw up a plan for this 'new model' Slovakia. The result is a blueprint for a Church-saturated society. Eight years later, the next pope, Benedict XVI, repeated the political message claiming that:

> Slovakia holds great potential for revitalising the soul of the European continent.[3]

The result has been three concordats, with the Holy See pressing for another two.[4] One of these is about Catholic conscientious objection, which was temporarily halted due to criticism by European Union legal experts. The other is the finance concordat whose original aim was to introduce a 'church tax'; however, the Church (probably the richest organisation in the world) is now pressing to maintain an annual subsidy to it according to its 'present needs'.[5]

Renewed Jewish Concerns

Under Tiso's rule, the Nazi-trained Hlinka Guard was formed and assisted Hitler's plan to wipe out European Jewry. About 60,000 Slovakian Jews were deported to Auschwitz alone. Slovakia's Jewish community has shrunk from 120,000 before World War II to just 3000 members today.[6]

---

[1] Quoted by: Hubenak, Ladislav. 'Secular Humanism in Slovakia', *International Humanist News*, 4 December 1995. Source: http://www.concordatwatch.eu/kb-1216.843 (2009)

[2] Hoppenbrouwers, Frans. 'Nationalistic Tendencies in the Slovak Roman Catholic Church'. *Religion in Eastern Europe*, Vol XVIII, No 6, December 1998. See the section, 'President Jozef Tiso: an innocent bystander?'. Source: http://www.concordatwatch.eu/kb-1216.843 (2009)

[3] 'Society Should Aid Young Families, Says Pontiff', *ZENIT*, 14 September 2007. http://www.zenit.org/article-20505?l =english

[4] Ibid.

[5] Hoppenbrouwers, Frans. 'Nationalistic Tendencies in the Slovak Roman Catholic Church'. *Religion in Eastern Europe*, Vol XVIII, No 6, December 1998. See the section, 'President Jozef Tiso: an innocent bystander?'. Source: http://www.concordatwatch.eu/kb-1216.843 (2009)

[6] http://www.nizkor.org/ftp.cgi/people/ftp.py?people//t/tiso.jozef/press/jozef-tiso (2009)

Jewish scholarship is universal in its condemnation of Tiso. The *Encyclopedia of the Holocaust* states:

> Even after the Slovak National Uprising in 1944, in which thousands of Slovaks rebelled against the Nazis, Tiso stayed loyal to Hitler and his murderous activities. He had the ability to exempt people from deportations, but he only used this to help some 1100 wealthy Jews or Jews-turned-Catholics.[1]

Jewish leaders in Slovakia are alarmed by the praise being lavished on Tiso. In an open letter to leading politicians, the Slovak Jewish Community Union said:

> Despite declared support for democratic traditions, our concern is growing over the campaign to rehabilitate exponents of Fascism.
>
> There are some groups here which want to rehabilitate Jozef Tiso, whose rehabilitation is impossible to separate from the rehabilitation of Slovak Fascism ... This campaign is organised, enduring and aggressive.[2]

Jaroslav Franek recorded that 'We're still waiting for a clear statement from the church on anti-Semitism.' He emphasised that the Tiso years and the legacy of the deportations remain very sore topics between Jews and Christians in Slovakia. 'We had hoped for a more constructive, conciliatory position from certain cardinals and the archbishop.'[3]

Overt expressions of anti-Semitism and Neo-fascism were rare under Communism, but since 1989 there have been at least 10 incidents of vandalism at Slovak Jewish cemeteries. Recently, an American rabbi was assaulted in Bratislava and hooligans have also attacked Romany citizens.

The *National Catholic Reporter* stated that the Church in Slovakia has been conspicuously silent about the resurgence of anti-Semitism, the desecration of Jewish cemeteries, and the legacy of Slovakia's fascist past.[4]

Synopsis

A Catholic priest, Fr Hlinka, founded the clerical People's Party in Slovakia on an anti-Semitic platform. By 1924, a paramilitary organisation, Rodobrana, the forerunner of the Hlinka Guard, had been established.

Jozef Tiso studied for the priesthood, and after graduation was steadily promoted within the Church. With the collapse of Austria-Hungary, and the creation of Czechoslovakia in 1918, Tiso suddenly embraced politics as a career, and joined the Slovak People's Party. He claimed a parliamentary seat in 1925. In 1938 he emerged as de facto leader of the party, and in 1939, became its chairman.

---

[1] Source: Darring, Gerald. 'Central European Churches and the Holocaust'. http://www.shc.edu/theolibrary/resources/07Central.htm#_edn5 (2009)

[2] http://www.nizkor.org/ftp.cgi/people/ftp.py?people//t/tiso.jozef/press/jozef-tiso (2009)

[3] http://findarticles.com/p/articles/mi_m1141/is_n35_v30/ai_15687062/pg_2/ (2011)

[4] Ibid.

During 1938, regions of Czechoslovakia were annexed to the German Reich, and Slovakia was declared an autonomous region. In May 1939 Tiso declared that 'the building of the State will be completed on the guidelines laid down in *Quadragesimo anno.*' Slovakia then became clerical, fascist and racist.

Soon after, the Hlinka Guard, a paramilitary body similar in character to the Nazi SS, had begun terrorising and killing Roma and Jews. Stringent anti-Jewish laws were introduced. Slovakia paid Nazi Germany to accept its deported Jews.

The Holy See's ever-running political machinations are centred on both Croatia and Slovakia as part of its active plan to re-evangelise secular Europe from the east. Right-wing Slovak nationalism is, therefore, being encouraged by the Church for its own ends. Consequently, Tiso's and Slovakia's sordid wartime pasts are being whitewashed for the Church's political ends.

Jewish scholarship is universal in its condemnation of Tiso. Under his rule, of the 137,000 Jews in pre-war Slovakia, 72,000 perished in death camps and another 40,000 perished in the deportations.[1] Only a few hundred ever returned.[2]

The Importance of the Slovakian Holocaust to the Present and the Future

The Slovakian Holocaust is an example in the modern world of the Catholic Church's:

> callous indifference to, and total absence of remorse for the sufferings that it caused;
>
> ceaseless pursuit of its ambitions for religious dominance;
>
> chronic involvement in international politics;
>
> continuing mendacity and falsification of the facts;
>
> encouraging and praising the formation of the clerico-fascist 'Corporate State';
>
> pervasive habit of denying its involvement in atrocities;
>
> persistent denial of its moral obligations resulting from its involvement in evil;
>
> whitewashing its involvement in atrocities.

The Church's Exculpation of Jozef Tiso

In spite of his overt anti-Semitism and its appalling consequences, and notwithstanding the deaths of dissidents and Roma during his time in power, Jozef Tiso was never condemned or excommunicated by the Holy See.[3,4] The Catholic Church now praises him.

---

[1] http://www.axt.org.uk/antisem/archive/archive4/slovakrep/slovakrep.htm (2011)

[2] *The Slovak Spectator.* http://www.spectator.sk/articles/view/31550/2/archbishop_prays_for_tiso.html (2009)

[3] Darring, Gerald. 'Central European Churches and the Holocaust'. http://www.shc.edu/theolibrary/resources/07Central.htm#_edn5 (2009)

[4] A similar situation applies to the diabolical Catholic, Ante Pavelić, the World War II leader of the Roman

The Self-serving Holy See

- Historian Claude-Carloman de Rulhière in his *Eclaircissements historiques sur les causes de la révocation de l'édit de Nantes* (*Historical Elucidations of the Causes of the Revocation of the Edict of Nantes*) recorded that:

> the dogma that THE END JUSTIFIES THE MEANS, was tolerated from an early period in the councils of the church Catholic, – was formally stated and defended in the decretal epistles of Pope Innocent III. at the commencement of the thirteenth century, – and was *universally* received by the papal clergy as an established and familiar doctrine at the times of the Reformation ... Pope Innocent III., by stating it formally *ex cathedra*, gave it the sanction of papal infallibility ...[1]

This perpetual, infallible dogma of the Holy See and its Church was, and is, exemplified in the history of the Croatian and Slovakian Holocausts. Pius XII and the Holy See allowed these genocides to continue to their conclusion, unabated and uncondemned, because they served the ends so strongly pursued by the Church.

Of the hundreds of thousands of human beings who died during these mass murders, not one, so far as is known, was from the Vatican.

Yet again, the political Holy See remains 'the great unpunished.'[2]

———

Catholic 'Independent State of Croatia'.
[1] De Rulhiere. 'Historical Elucidations of the Causes of the Revocation of the Edict of Nantes' (trans David Scott). *The Churchman's Monthly Review*, 1844. p269.
[2] See, for example: Callil, Carmen. *Bad Faith: A Forgotten History of Family & Fatherland.* p442

15 – Anti-Semitism and the War in European Countries

No trace of a Jew is to remain. We should erase them from the face of the earth. From the sermon of a priest in Kowel, 1942[1]

The total number of human casualties during World War II has been estimated at approximately 60 million. In Axis-occupied Europe there occurred the slaughter of:

6,000,000 Jews of Polish, French, German, Hungarian, Croatian, Slovakian, Rumanian, Italian, and other nationalities;

More than 3,000,000 Russian prisoners of war;

500,000-700,000 Christian Orthodox Serbs;

Roma (gypsies) – variously estimated at between 220,000 and 1,500,000;

200,000 incurably ill Germans who were sacrificed via euthanasia.

Additionally, tens of millions of peaceful people suffered death, injury, forced labour, homelessness, famine, and other casualties.

While all levels of the Roman Church were active in the Holocaust, more than 50% of the Nazi Elite in Germany were practising Catholics.[2] 'German Catholics were strongly supportive of Hitler's aggressive assertion of German power.'[3]

Of the sixteen European Nazi and fascist dictators, puppets and quislings, twelve were Catholics.

A measure of Catholic support for Adolf Hitler may be gauged by the fact that in the entire German Greater Reich, only seven Catholics refused military service – and the Church brought pressure on all of them to conform to the official line. A parish priest who called the war 'stupid' was forced by his diocesan chancery to send a formal apology to the army. Another priest, who objected to the War, was refused communion on the basis that he had violated his Christian duty by refusing to take the military oath of allegiance to Hitler.[4]

The Holy See and Pius XII (who had fostered Hitler's rise to power) had a superficial semblance of a diplomatic approach of neutrality, but nonetheless put pressure on the German Bishops to maintain a working relationship with the Nazi regime.[5]

Reichkristallnacht

Kristallnacht, also known as 'the Night of Broken Glass', was a pogrom against Jews

---

[1] Quoted in Yitzhak Arad, 'The Christian Churches and the Persecution of Jews in the Occupied Territories of the USSR', in *The Holocaust and the Christian World: Reflections on the Past, Challenges for the Future.* p110

[2] http://alistaport.org/en/articles/dark-ages-of-roman-catholicism (2009)

[3] http://www.shc.edu/theolibrary/resources/04German.htm (2014)

[4] Ibid.

[5] Source: http://www.shc.edu/theolibrary/resources/04German.htm (2014) See, for example: Braham, Randolph L. 'Remembering and Forgetting: The Vatican, the German Catholic Hierarchy, and the Holocaust', *Holocaust and Genocide Studies*, 13:2 (1999) pp222-51.

throughout Nazi Germany and parts of Austria on 9-10 November 1938, carried out by the SA[1] and non-Jewish civilians. German authorities looked on without intervening. The name derives from the shards of broken glass that littered the streets after Jewish-owned stores, buildings, and synagogues had had their windows smashed.

At least 91 Jews were killed in the attacks, and 30,000 were arrested and incarcerated in concentration camps. Jewish homes, hospitals, and schools were ransacked. More than 1000 synagogues were burned, and over 7000 Jewish businesses were destroyed or damaged. The accounts from foreign journalists working in Germany sent shock waves around the world.[2]

Effectively Kristallnacht was the beginning of the Jewish Holocaust. It 'marked a new phase in Nazi antisemitism – and a point of no return.'[3]

But 'the bishops of Germany said nothing at all.'[4]

Catholicism, Nazism, and 'the Final Solution to the Jewish Question' ('Die Endlösung der Judenfrage')

Adolf Hitler's Holocaust was the worst military genocide in history. Its object was the systematic elimination of all European Jews. It was a major part of the most terrible war of all time, resulting in the destruction of a people without example in history.[5,6]

Although not a genocide by the Catholic Church as such, nevertheless the Holocaust had its origins in the anti-Semitic diatribes and pejoratives of the Church that had extended over two millennia, and in the Church's more recent recurrent, virulent anti-Judaic propaganda. It occurred throughout Europe, where well over 90% of Europeans identified themselves as Christians. In Germany particularly, Christianity was pervasive. More than 95% of Germans were baptised members of an established Christian church. Accordingly, Germany was one of the most Christian nations in the world.[7] In 1933 approximately 32% of Germans were Catholics. Austria was a largely Catholic state – for example, pre-War, 87% of Vienna's population were Catholic. A quarter of the Nazi's military elite SS was also Catholic.[8]

Some of the worst atrocities occurred in such devout Catholic countries as Austria and Poland.[9]

---

[1] The Sturmabteilung (SA) (Storm Detachment, or Assault Division) functioned as the original paramilitary wing of the Nazi Party. It played a key role in Hitler's rise to power in the 1920s and 1930s.
[2] http://en.wikipedia.org/wiki/Krystallnacht (2014)
[3] Flannery, Edward H. *The Anguish of the Jews*. p216
[4] http://www.shc.edu/theolibrary/resources/04German.htm (2014)
[5] *The Catholic Worker*. Source: The Notre Dame Press (www3.undpress.nd.edu/exec/dispatch.php?s=title, P00153) (2007)
[6] But, refer to the Catholic Church's own Albigensian Holocaust – the first case of total genocide in Europe.
[7] *Journal of Religion & Science*. Supplement Series. 'The Contexts of Religion and Violence'. James E Waller 'Deliver Us From Evil. Genocide and the Christian World'. http://moses.creighton.edu/JRS/2007/2007-10.html (2008)
[8] Noel, Gerard. *Pius XI: The Hound of Hitler.* p100
[9] http://www.mindshiftinstitute.org/Article_Catholic_Nazi.htm (2007)

The Anschluss between Germany and Austria was implemented in 1938. It resulted in a:

> decree authorising local authorities to bar Jews from the streets on certain days; decree empowering the justice Ministry to void wills offending the 'sound judgment of the people'; decree providing for compulsory sale of Jewish real estate; decree providing for liquidation of Jewish real estate agencies, brokerage agencies, and marriage agencies catering to non-Jews; directive providing for the concentration of Jews in houses.

Einsatzgruppen

Einsatzgruppen were mobile SS paramilitary death squads that were responsible for mass killings, typically by shooting, of Jews in particular, but also significant numbers of other population groups and political categories. They constituted a key component in Hitler's expansionist plans.

The Einsatzgruppen operated throughout the territory occupied by the Nazi forces following the German invasions along the Eastern Front. They carried out operations ranging from the murder of a few people to operations that lasted several days, such as the massacres at Babi Yar and Rumbula. They were the first Nazi organisations to commence mass killing of Jews as an organised policy. For example, an SS Standartführer reported:

> Today I can confirm that our objective to solve the Jewish problem for Lithuania, has been achieved by EK 3. In Lithuania there are no more Jews, apart from Jewish workers and their families.[1]

The Einsatzgruppen followed the German armies into Poland in 1939 and the Soviet Union in June 1941. They were to kill all Jews, communist officials, the handicapped, institutionalised psychiatric patients, Romany people, and other undesirables.

They had a leading role in the implementation of the Final Solution in territories conquered by Nazi Germany. Almost all of the people they killed were civilians, beginning with the Polish intelligentsia and swiftly progressing to Soviet political commissars, Jews, and Roma throughout Eastern Europe.[2]

They were composed primarily of German SS and police personnel, and were under the command of the German Security Police and Security Service officers.

The German army provided logistical support to the Einsatzgruppen. At first the Einsatzgruppen shot primarily Jewish men. By late summer 1941, however, they shot Jewish men, women, and children without regard of age or sex. Often with the help of local informants, Jews were identified and taken to collection points. Thereafter they were marched or transported by truck to the execution sites, where trenches had been prepared. In some cases the victims had to dig their own graves. After the victims had handed over their valuables and undressed, men, women and children were shot, either

---

[1] Cymet, David. *History vs. Apologetics: The Holocaust, the Third Reich, and the Catholic Church.* p218
[2] https://en.wikipedia.org/wiki/Einsatzgruppen (2015)

standing before the open trench, or lying face down in the prepared pit.[1]

Shooting was the most common form of execution. However, in the summer of 1941, Himmler, noting the psychological burden that mass shootings produced on his men, requested that a more convenient mode of killing be developed. The result was the gas van, a mobile gas chamber mounted on the chassis of a truck which used the carbon oxides from the truck's exhaust to kill its victims. Gas vans made their first appearance on the Eastern Front in the autumn of 1941.

Historian Raul Hilberg estimates that between 1941 and 1945 the Einsatzgruppen and related troops killed more than two million people, including 1.3 million Jews.[2]

The final judgment at the trial of the Einsatzgruppen commanders during 1947 and 1948 before the Nuremberg International Tribunal reads:

> Only the fact that the reports from which we have quoted came from the pens of men within the accused organizations can the human mind be assured that all this actually happened. The reports and the statements of the defendants themselves verify what otherwise would be dismissed as the product of a disordered imagination ... A crime of such unprecedented brutality and of such inconceivable savagery that the mind rebels against its own thought image and the imagination staggers in the contemplation of a human degradation beyond the power of language to adequately portray ... *One cannot grasp the full cumulative terror of murder one million times repeated.*[3]

The Actions of the Nazis against the Jews

The role of Catholicism. In her book *Holy War: The Crusades and their Impact on Today's World*, Karen Armstrong found that 'one of the passions that crusading would bequeath to the Western World was a long and shameful tradition of hatred for the Jewish people'. Additionally, 'Hitler's attempted destruction of the Jewish people was fuelled by many submerged crusading myths.'[4]

Synagogues

Synagogues were burned in Austria and Germany throughout 1938. During the same year, Hitler reintroduced the Church's laws requiring all Jews to wear a yellow Star of David as identification.

Ghettos

The Nazis established at least fifty ghettos.[5] The situation in the ghettos was brutal. In Warsaw, thirty percent of the population were forced to live in less than three percent of the city's area – a density of 9.2 people per room. In the ghetto of Odrzywół, 700 people lived in an area previously occupied by 5 families. As the Jews were not allowed

---

[1] http://www.ushmm.org/wlc/en/article.php?ModuleId=10005130 (2015)

[2] Hilberg, Raul. *The Destruction of the European Jews.* pp342-43

[3] Cymet, David. *History vs. Apologetics: The Holocaust, the Third Reich, and the Catholic Church.* p219

[4] Armstrong, Karen. *Holy War: The Crusades and their Impact on Today's World.* p71

[5] Pope Paul IV established the first legal Jewish ghetto in Rome in 1555. 'It was the anteroom to Auschwitz.' Refer within *'A Corrupt Tree'*, Chapter II-9 – Rome & the Papal States – Dominions of Papal Unholiness'.

out of the ghetto they had to rely on food supplied by the Nazis. With crowded living conditions, starvation diets, and little sanitation, hundreds of thousands of Jews died of disease and starvation.[1]

Pogroms

A number of deadly pogroms occurred during the Holocaust at the hands of non-Germans, for example the Jedwabne Pogrom of 1941 in predominantly Catholic Poland, in which Polish citizens killed between 400 and 1600 Jews with little or no German assistance.[2] In Lithuania, nationalists engaged in anti-Jewish pogroms killing about 3800 Jews, and burning synagogues and Jewish shops.

Concentration Camps

During the 1930s and 1940s, the Nazis established many concentration camps where Jews, along with Roma, homosexuals, Communists, Slavs, and others judged undesirable, were imprisoned. Many prisoners were worked to death, shot, gassed, or given lethal injections. Other such camps were established by Catholics in Catholic Croatia.

The *Encyclopedia of Camps and Ghettos, 1933–1945* of the United States Holocaust Memorial Museum[3] catalogues around 42,500 Nazi ghettos and camps throughout Europe operating from 1933 to 1945. It estimates that 15 million to 20 million people died or were imprisoned in the sites.

Exterminations

During 1940, gassing and shootings occurred in Polish ghettos. Hungarian Jews were exterminated in 1944. The Kaunas Pogrom was a massacre of Jewish people living in Kaunas, Lithuania, which commenced on 25 June 1941. By 28 June, 3800 people were killed in Kaunas and further 1200 in other towns of the region.[4]

Ukraine's Jewish population was devastated during the Holocaust in which some 1.5 million Ukrainian Jews are believed to have been killed.

At Babi Yar outside the capital of Kiev the Nazis slaughtered 34,000 Jewish civilians over two days in September 1941. The Babi Yar Massacre is considered to be the largest single massacre in the history of the Holocaust.[5]

About 240,000 Jews were killed by the Nazis in the Odessa region, which was occupied by the Romanians in alliance with the Germans. Anatoly Podolsky, director of the Ukrainian Centre for Holocaust Studies, has said that there are believed to be 250 to 350 mass graves dating from the Nazi occupation.

The Rumbula Massacre is a collective term for incidents during November and

---

[1] http://en.wikipedia.org/wiki/Ghetto#Second_World_War (2007)
[2] *Encarta Encyclopedia* 'Kwaśniewski, Aleksander'
[3] http://www.ushmm.org/research/publications/encyclopedia-camps-ghettos (2015)
[4] http://en.wikipedia.org/wiki/Kaunas_pogrom (2007)
[5] Lower, Wendy Morgan. 'From Berlin to Babi Yar: The Nazi War Against the Jews, 1941-1944' (Towson University) *Journal of Religion & Society*, Vol 9 (2007). Source: http://en.wikipedia.org/wiki/Babi_Yar (2007)

December 1941 in which about 25,000 Jews were killed in or near Rumbula forest near Riga, Latvia.[1]

In 1942 the Nazis began 'Operation Reinhard' ('Aktion Reinhard'/'Einsatz Reinhard'), the systematic deportation to extermination camps.[2] The authorities deported Jews from everywhere in Europe to the ghettos of the East, or directly to the extermination camps. Almost 300,000 people were deported from the Warsaw Ghetto alone to Treblinka over the course of 52 days.

Mobile Gas Vans

According to several credible witnesses Catholic Bishop Alois Hudal was a very close friend of Walter Rauff the SS officer who oversaw the development of the Nazi's mobile gas vans. These vans, known as 'Black Ravens', annihilated around 100,000 Jews, mostly women and children, by pumping exhaust fumes into the back of sealed vans. Rauff was later involved in the persecution of Jews in North Africa. He rapidly gained a reputation for total ruthlessness. He is thought to be responsible for nearly 100,000 deaths.[3] The friendship of Bishop Hudal and Rauff began around 1943, and many believe their friendship remained until Rauff's death.[4]

Euthanasia Programmes

In 1933 the Nazis passed the *Law for the Prevention of Progeny of Sufferers from Hereditary Diseases*. This formed the basis for the Euthanasia Programme 'Aktion T4' which began in force after the invasion of Poland. This programme ran in Nazi Germany, officially between 1939 and 1941, during which it systematically killed between 75,000 to 250,000 people with intellectual or physical disabilities. The codename T4 was an abbreviation of "Tiergartenstrasse 4", the address of a villa in the Berlin borough of Tiergarten which was the headquarters of the General Foundation for Welfare and Institutional Care (Gemeinnützige Stiftung für Heil- und Anstaltspflege).[5]

Other killing centres were located in Brandenburg Euthanasia Centre; Grafeneck Castle in Baden-Württemberg; Schloss Hartheim near Linz in Austria; Sonnenstein Euthanasia Clinic in Saxony; Bernburg in Saxony-Anhalt; and Hadamar Clinic in Hesse.

The Eastern Front

The Eastern Front was a theatre of conflict between the Axis powers and Finland against the Soviet Union, Poland and other allies. It encompassed Northern, Southern, Central, and Eastern Europe from 22 June 1941 to 9 May 1945. It has been known as the Great Patriotic War in the former Soviet Union, and in modern Russia.[6]

---

[1] https://en.wikipedia.org/wiki/Rumbula_massacre (2015)
[2] Aktion Reinhard marked the beginning of the most deadly phase of the Holocaust – the use of extermination camps. During this operation, as many as two million people were murdered in Bełżec, Sobibór, Treblinka and Majdanek – almost all of them Jews.
[3] http://en.wikipedia.org/wiki/Walter_Rauff (2007)
[4] http://hist.academic.claremontmckenna.edu/jpetropoulos/holocaust/aftermathintro.htm (2007)
[5] http://en.wikipedia.org/wiki/Aktion_T4 (2007)
[6] https://en.wikipedia.org/wiki/Eastern_Front_%28World_War_II%29 (2015)

It was decisive in determining the outcome of World War II, ultimately serving as the main reason for Germany's defeat.

The battles on the Eastern Front constituted the largest military confrontation in history. They were characterised by unprecedented ferocity, wholesale destruction, mass deportations, and immense loss of life. The Eastern Front, as the site of nearly all extermination camps, death marches, ghettos, and the majority of pogroms, was central to the Holocaust. Of the estimated 70 million deaths attributed to World War II, over 30 million, many of them civilian, occurred on the Eastern Front.

Significantly, Pius XII showed great jubilation as Hitler's armies crossed the Russian frontier. He said joyful prayers and asked God to intercede for the Nazis' total victory in Russia.[1]

Anti-Semitism during the War in Catholic Poland

As a lead up to the Second World War, the Polish Catholic Church found itself fighting the effects of Socialism, Communism, Modernism, Liberalism, atheism, secularism, and feminism. 'Most of these "isms" it associated with the Jews.'[2]

Until the War, Poland was a religiously diverse society, in which substantial Jewish, Protestant and Christian Orthodox minorities coexisted with a Catholic majority. As a result of the Holocaust and the post-War flight and expulsion of German and Ukrainian populations, Poland has become overwhelmingly Roman Catholic. In 2011, approximately 91 percent of the population belonged to the Catholic Church.

During the Holocaust, many priests admired the Jewish policies of the Nazis, seized Jewish property, discouraged the laity from assisting the Jews, and denounced them from the pulpit.[3]

'Polish society, staunchly Catholic, witnessed the Holocaust up close. The death camps were all on Polish soil, and the largest concentrations of Jews were in Poland. Many Poles were happy to witness the misfortune of the Jews; many others commiserated with the Jews, but from a distance, as it were, caring but not caring enough to do anything about it. There were many Polish collaborators, people who turned in Jews to the Gestapo or even helped in the killing process'.[4]

During World War II, under this Catholic majority, the Jews suffered extreme intolerance – more than 2 million of them were herded into ghettos.

By 1941, almost all the Jews in the Generalgouvernement were enclosed in more than 400 ghettos. These ghettos and the labour camps were used, not only as a means of isolating the Jews and using them as slave labourers, but also for gathering them for deportation for annihilation.[5]

Poland became the locus of most of the mass murders of the Holocaust.

[1] Refer to Chapter 21 for further details.
[2] Michael, Robert. *A History of Catholic Antisemitism: The Dark Side of the Church.* p148
[3] Ibid. p155
[4] http://www.shc.edu/theolibrary/resources/05Polish.htm (2014)
[5] Michael, Robert. *A History of Catholic Antisemitism: The Dark Side of the Church.* pp184-85

Jedwabne Pogrom

During June-July of 1941, Catholic Poles actively participated in several massacres of the Jews. The most notable were at Jedwabne, where Poles violently murdered about one thousand Jews. The Church did not actively oppose these events.[1,2]

The Kraków Ghetto

The Kraków Ghetto was one of five major metropolitan Jewish ghettos in the Generalgouvernement established for the purpose of persecution, terror, and exploitation of Polish Jews. It was a staging point for the division of 'able workers' from those who would later be deemed unworthy of life. The Ghetto was liquidated between June 1942 and March 1943, with most of its inhabitants being sent to Bełżec and Płaszów, and exterminated at Auschwitz Concentration Camp.[3]

This treatment occurred without any protest or opposition from the Catholic bishops or the general population – in Warsaw they actively collaborated. After the War, Gerald Reitlinger stated that the forced separation of Jews in ghettos could not have been possible had the Polish Catholic Church or the people objected.[4]

Zamość Ghetto

Shortly before World War II approximately 12,000 Jews lived in the city of Zamość. In 1942 the Nazis set up a ghetto there. From April to September 1942, around 4000 Jews were deported to the Bełżec Extermination Camp. In October 1942 the Germans shot dead 500 people, and the remaining 4000 were deported to Bełżec. In 2012, only three Jews lived in Zamość.[5]

Chełmno Extermination Camp

Chełmno Extermination Camp was situated 50 kilometres from Łódź, near the small village of Chełmno nad Nerem. After annexation by Germany, it was included in Reichsgau Wartheland.

At least 152,000 people were killed in the camp, mainly Poles, Jews from the Łódź Ghetto and the surrounding area, Romani from Greater Poland, some Hungarian Jews, Czechs, and Soviet prisoners of war. Most of the victims were killed by the use of gas vans, and the camp served the purpose of early experimentation and development of methods of mass murder, some of which were applied in later phases of the Holocaust.

Only 2 or 3 people are known to have survived the camp.

Auschwitz Concentration Camp

Auschwitz Concentration Camp was a network of concentration and extermination camps built and operated by the Third Reich in Polish areas annexed by Nazi Germany during World War II. It was the largest of the German concentration camps, consisting

---

[1] http://en.wikipedia.org/wiki/Jedwabne (2014)
[2] Michael, Robert. *A History of Catholic Antisemitism: The Dark Side of the Church.* p156
[3] http://en.wikipedia.org/wiki/Krak%C3%B3w_Ghetto (2012)
[4] Reitlinger, Gerald. *The Final Solution*
[5] http://en.wikipedia.org/wiki/Zamosc (2012)

of Auschwitz I; Auschwitz II-Birkenau; Auschwitz III-Monowitz; and 45 satellite camps.

Auschwitz was the German name for Oświęcim, the town in and around which the camps were located.

Auschwitz II–Birkenau was designated by Reichsführer-SS Heinrich Himmler as the place of 'the final solution of the Jewish question in Europe'. From early 1942 until late 1944, transport trains delivered Jews to the camp's gas chambers from all over Nazi-occupied Europe. Around 1.3 million people, approximately 90 percent of them Jews, died there. Those not killed in the gas chambers died of starvation, forced labour, infectious disease, individual executions, and medical experiments.

David Cymet records that the prospect of taking over the towns and Jewish homes, possessions, and businesses was a major incentive that lured the largely Catholic Poles to cooperate willingly with the Germans. Their greed and envy of the Jews converted 'many of them into willing informers and active Nazi collaborators.'[1]

On 27 January 1945, Auschwitz was liberated by Soviet troops – a day commemorated around the world as International Holocaust Remembrance Day.[2,3]

Sobibór Extermination Camp

Sobibór Extermination Camp was located on the outskirts of the town of Sobibór in occupied Poland. It was part of Operation Reinhard. Jews from Czechoslovakia, France, Poland, Germany, and Holland, as well as Soviet prisoners of war (many of them Jewish), were transported to Sobibór by rail, and suffocated in gas chambers that were fed with the exhaust from petrol engines. Estimates of the number of people killed range from 200,000 to more than 250,000.

The camp was split into four sections:

Garrison Area: This included the main entrance gates and the railway platform where the victims were taken off the trains.

Camp I – was built directly west and behind the Garrison Area. It was made escape proof by extra barbed wire fences and a deep trench filled with water. The only opening was a gate leading into the area.

Camp II – was a larger section and included an assortment of vital services for both the killing process and the everyday operation of the camp. 400 prisoners, including women, worked here. Camp II contained the warehouses used for storing the objects taken from the dead victims, including hair, clothes, food, gold and all other valuables. It also housed the main administration office. Here,

---

[1] Cymet, David. *History vs. Apologetics: The Holocaust, the Third Reich, and the Catholic Church.* p185
[2] http://en.wikipedia.org/wiki/Auschwitz (2012)
[3] International Holocaust Remembrance Day commemorates the genocide that resulted in the death of an estimated 6 million Jews, 1 million Roma, 250,000 mentally and physically disabled people, and 9000 homosexual men by the Nazi regime and its collaborators. It was designated by the United Nations General Assembly resolution 60/7 on 1 November 2005 during the 42nd plenary session. https://en.wikipedia.org/wiki/International_Holocaust_Remembrance_Day (2015)

Jews were prepared for their death. Here they undressed, women's hair was shaved, clothing searched and sorted, and documents destroyed in the nearby furnace. The victims' final steps were taken on a path framed by barbed wire. It was called 'the Road to Heaven' and led directly to the gas chambers.

Camp III – was where the victims met their end. The entrance for the victims descended immediately into the gas chambers and was decorated with flowers and a Star of David.[1]

Majdanek Concentration Camp or KL Lublin

This camp, also known to the SS as Konzentrationslager Lublin (KL Lublin), was established on the outskirts of the city of Lublin. It was used to kill people on an industrial scale during Operation Reinhard, the German plan to murder all Jews within their own Generalgouvernement territory of Poland. It operated from 1 October 1941 until 22 July 1944, and was captured nearly intact by the Soviet Red Army during Operation Bagration. Estimates of the number of people exterminated in Majdanek vary widely – from around 79,000 to 360,000.

Trawniki Concentration Camp

This camp was set up by Nazi Germany in the village of Trawniki about 40 kilometres southeast of Lublin. The camp first opened after the outbreak of war with the USSR, intended to hold Russian POWs, with rail lines in all major directions in the Generalgouvernement territory. Between 1941 and 1944, it was an SS training camp for collaborationist auxiliary police, mainly Ukrainian. In 1942 it became the forced-labour camp for thousands of Jews within the KL Lublin system of sub-camps. It provided slave labourers for the nearby industrial plants of SS Ostindustrie to work in appalling conditions with little food. The Jews were all massacred in Operation Harvest Festival on 3 November 1943.

Treblinka Extermination Camp

This camp was situated in occupied Poland near the village of Treblinka. It was constructed as part of Operation Reinhard. Approximately 850,000 men, women and children were killed at Treblinka. This included more than 800,000 Jews, as well as an undetermined number of Romani people.[2]

The camp, which was operated by the SS and Eastern European Trawnikis,[3] consisted of Treblinka I and II.

Treblinka II was designed as a death factory. More than 99% of all arrivals at this site were sent immediately to its gas chambers where they were killed by exhaust fumes.

---

[1] http://en.wikipedia.org/wiki/Sobibór_extermination_camp (2012)

[2] http://en.wikipedia.org/wiki/Treblinka (2012)

[3] Although the majority of Trawniki men came from among prisoners of war, there were also Volksdeutsche from Eastern Europe among them, valued because of their ability to speak many languages of the occupied territories. All the officers at Trawniki were ethnic Germans, and most of the squad commanders were Volksdeutsche.

The small number who were not killed immediately became members of the Sonder-kommandos. These slave labour groups were forced to bury the bodies in mass graves. Later, corpses were burned on massive open-air pyres.

The Catholic Church in Poland

The Catholic Church in Poland sent a report to the Polish government in exile during the summer of 1941. It had significant praise for the Germans for their handling of the Jewish question. It stated that in spite of the evil that the Germans had perpetrated, they had been proven to possess a realistic attitude in 'liberating Polish society from the Jewish plague.'[1]

Polish nuns were especially active in rescuing Jewish children. Certainly this help, which endangered the lives of the nuns, was praiseworthy, nevertheless, many times the nuns baptised the children and trained them to be Catholics, 'revealing a self-serving motivation for their actions.'[2]

The clergy of Kraków provided assistance to Catholic converts from Judaism, and Archbishop Adam Sapieha of Lvov intervened on their behalf, but little or nothing was done to help the Jews per se.

As a whole, the Polish hierarchy remained silent in the face of the Holocaust. No less than three councils were held by the Polish bishops during the Nazi occupation, yet not one of them mentioned the mass murder of Jews that was taking place on their territory. Jesuit Pierre Blet has documented the flow of correspondence between the Polish bishops and the Holy See, and there is little expression of concern for the plight of the Jews.[3]

An impartial examination of these events in Poland confirm that 'the Polish Liberals, Communists, socialists, and Freemasons, "were much more Christian and Catholic than the leadership of the Roman Catholic Church." '[4]

Anti-Semitism during the War in the Catholic Independent State of Croatia

Some of the most horrific Holocaust atrocities against Jews were perpetrated in the Roman Catholic Independent State of Croatia (Nezavisna Država Hrvatska) (NDH) by Ante Pavelić's Ustaša regime. 'The tragic history of the Jewish communities in that country has yet to be told because there are literally no survivors.'[5]

The Pavelić regime offered Croatian Jews conversion to Catholicism plus contribution of their personal property, in return for not being deported to death camps. However, evidence has been uncovered that even these Jews and their families were later executed by the Ustaša. Documented evidence has revealed how the Catholic Church collaborated in the annihilation of the Jewish communities of Croatia. The town of Vukovar is but an example of what transpired when the Ustaše were unleashed with the

---

[1] Cymet, David. *History vs. Apologetics: The Holocaust, the Third Reich, and the Catholic Church.* pp184-85
[2] http://www.shc.edu/theolibrary/resources/05Polish.htm (2014)
[3] Blet, Pierre. 'The Church in Occupied Poland', in: *Pius XI and the Second World War: According to the Archives of the Vatican* (Mahwah: Paulist Press, 1999) pp69-92
[4] Michael, Robert. *A History of Catholic Antisemitism: The Dark Side of the Church.* p158
[5] http://www.isracast.com/article.aspx?ID=544 (2010)

support of the Holy See to launch a ferocious campaign of murder and torture against Serbs, Jews and Gypsies.[1]

The Holy See is pushing for the sainthood of Pius XII, yet:

> While Pius can be legitimately criticized for his tepid condemnations of the Nazi Holocaust there is no question he was complicit in the deaths of at least 500,000 Orthodox Christian Serbs, Jews and Roma murdered in Croatia, Bosnia, and Krajina during the Second World War by the Axis allied Croatian regime.[2]

Although the Orthodox Serbs were the primary target of the Ustaša's ethnic cleansing campaign, they were not the only targets. In line with Hitler's directives, and a substantial amount of indigenous anti-Semitism and racism, the Ustaša also rounded up and exterminated the vast majority of the Jews and Gypsies in the country.

In complete contrast to the actions of the Catholic Croats, a Jewish physician attested to the fact that the Orthodox Serbs supported the Jews:

> Thanks to the Serbs, the Yugoslav Jews had succeeded in saving and rescuing many of their compatriots from Germany and German-occupied countries ... *In Serbia ... anti-Semitic feeling has never had any root.* No German measures in Belgrade were able to upset the friendly relations between the Serbs and Jews ... during the period when Serbian students and peasants were hung in the main square in Belgrade, the Serbs of the capital had sufficient courage to protest publicly their indignation at the treatment of the Jews.[3]

Roman Catholic Propaganda against the Jews

Before the War, the Roman Catholic University Society 'Domagoj' distributed a brochure which approved Hitler's actions against the Jews, entitled *Why Jews are Persecuted in Germany*:

> There are measures which the Germans can and must undertake for their own protection ... Let us remember that people with weak or incorrect Christian concepts opened the doors to domination by Jews in Germany. What was spoiled by some is now being put right by others. [4,5]

Croatian Archbishop Alojzije Stepinac, on the positive side, is reported to have defended *converted* Jews – thus, the Bishops' Synod of November 1941 intervened exclusively on behalf of converted Jews. Later, it has been claimed, Stepinac extended his defence to include all Jews. Notwithstanding, his alleged efforts failed totally to prevent the deportations of 1942 and 1943.[6] On the other hand, in May 1943, Stepinac

---

[1] Ibid.

[2] Dr Jonathan Levy. Co-counsel for Plaintiffs. *Alperin v. Vatican Bank and Franciscan Order*. United States District Court for Northern California, Case No. C-99-04941 MMC. http://www.remnantofgod.org/ustashe. htm (2015)

[3] Mitchell, Ruth. *The Serbs choose war.* pp260-64

[4] *Exterminate the Jews*

[5] http://emperors-clothes.com/croatia/stepinac2.htm (2015)

[6] Shelah, Menachem, 'The Catholic Church in Croatia, the Vatican and the Murder of the Croatian Jews', *Holocaust and Genocide Studies*, 4:3 (1989) pp323-39

visited the Vatican, and, according to the Ustašan ambassador to the Holy See, Stepinac:

> mentioned our laws on abortion, a point very well received in the Vatican. Basing his arguments on these laws, the Archbishop justified in part the measures used against the Jews ... [1]

Croatian Legislation against the Jews

The Ustaša government began seizing Jewish property with the promulgation of the so-called *Aryan Law* of 18 April 1941. At the beginning of June, a series of legal regulations followed, which materially ruined Croatian Jews. The law of 4 June 1941, referring to 'the protection of the national and Aryan culture of the Croatian people', excluded Jews from all institutions and professions of a cultural character. That same day, an order was decreed that Jews and Jewish stores must be marked by the Star of David. Four further decrees of 5 June 1941 required the registration of Jewish properties and the expulsion of Jews from the civil service and academic professions. By September 1941, Jewish property was being expropriated without compensation – industrial concerns especially.

Deportation and Massacre of Jews

Concurrently, 'undesirable' Jews were deported to concentration camps and forced labour brigades, which in many cases resulted in their physical liquidation by the Ustaše guards. In the spring of 1945 a great number of the Jews who had been in the camps were deported to Auschwitz.[2]

The savagery of the anti-Semitic activities of the Ustaše was reported in a document entitled *The Extermination of the Jews under Tri-partite Rule*:

> Particularly ferocious was the persecution of the Jews in occupied Serbia and in the so-called Independent Croatia, where it was carried out by the Ustashi bands.[3]

A Vatican document has revealed that Dr Ivan Šarić, Archbishop of Sarajevo, personally expropriated property belonging to Jews in Bosnia.[4]

Menachem Shelah, of the University of Haifa, found that the Church remained unperturbed at the persecution of the Jews, the seizure of their property, the annulment of their rights, and their banishment to camps where they were eliminated. It was only towards the end of the war that the heads of the Latin Church in Croatia protested against the murder of the Jews – but Croatian Jewry had by then been almost totally destroyed. Consequently, on 18 April 1944, Siegfried Kasche, the German consul in Zagreb, and police attaché Hans Helm reported to Berlin that:

---

[1] http://pavelic-papers.com/timeline/ndhtimeline.html (2009)
[2] Hory, Ladislaus & Martin Broszat. *Der Kroatische Ustascha-Staat,, 1941-1945.* p94. Source: Kostich, Lazo M. *The Holocaust in the 'Independent State of Croatia'.* p127
[3] 'The Extermination of the Jews under Tri-partite Rule'. *Report of the Inter-Allied Information Committee in London.* Source: Kostich, Lazo M. *The Holocaust in the 'Independent ...* p239
[4] Falconi, Carlo. *The Silence of Pius XII.* pp294-96. Source: Lituchy, Barry. *What Is The Vatican Hiding? The Vatican's Complicity in Genocide in Fascist Croatia: The Suppressed Chapter of Holocaust History*

Croatia is one of the countries in which the Jewish problem has been solved.[1]

Over all, the Simon Wiesenthal Center estimates that Ustašan terrorists murdered 30,000 Jews (75 percent) in the Independent State of Croatia.

· Anti-Semitism during the War in Catholic Hungary

Roman Catholicism was the major religion of Hungary.

Historically, Hungary was home to a significant Jewish community. The census of January 1941 found that 846,000 people were considered Jewish according to the racial laws of that time.

Hungarian Catholics based their hostility towards Jews in terms of the centuries-old Church's teaching of contempt.[2] This attitude of the Hungarian Catholic Church was reflected in the statement of Dr Jozsef Trikal, Rector of the Catholic University of Sciences at Budapest:

> By erecting the barriers of economic limitation before the unrestrained jealousy of the Jews, we are protecting our dear nation and the pure bride of Jesus the Nazarene: the church.

· The destruction of Hungarian Jewry is one of the worst components of the Holocaust. In only two months, half a million Hungarian Jews either were deported to concentration camps, from which the majority did not return, or were murdered by the Hungarian Arrow Cross fascists.[3] This 'kept Auschwitz's crematoria burning night and day.' It was the consequence of the killing machine 'masterfully operated by Adolf Eichmann'.[4]

· The ultimate basis of this massive annihilation was the deep-rooted anti-Semitism of the Hungarian people. In the first six weeks following German occupation, the Hungarian people made around thirty-five thousand denouncements against the Jews.

· This popular hostility toward the Jews had been fed by the lower Catholic clergy. For example, in an editorial in a January 1939 edition of the daily newspaper of the anti-Semitic Arrow-Cross Party, a priest expressed his view of Jews:

> In places where priests are murdered, the educated are slaughtered, and churches are burnt – that's where the Jew is to be found. Even if no Jew is actually there in a physical sense, his presence is represented there by his venomous literary works. Like naked spirits they drift all over the world, and by means of their filthy moral concepts, their distorted philosophy, and their base artistic schools, they spread their revolting ideas. Their sullied views corrupt the world.[5]

On the day of the first Jewish deportation, 15 May 1044, Hungary's Undersecretary of State, Laszlo Endre, declared in a speech:

> The popes, as well as our own ancient and saintly kings, legislated draconian laws

[1] http://www.jewishvirtuallibrary.org/jsource/judaica/ejud_0002_0021_0_21336.html (2009)
[2] http://www.shc.edu/theolibrary/resources/07Central.htm (2014)
[3] http://en.wikipedia.org/wiki/Hungary#Religion (2012)
[4] http://www.shc.edu/theolibrary/resources/07Central.htm (2014)
[5] http://www.shc.edu/theolibrary/resources/07Central.htm (2014)

and imposed severe decrees upon this parasitic race. Thus, no one can complain that we are not acting in accordance with the spirit of Christianity when we enact draconian regulations against the Jews so as to protect our nation.[1]

At the height of the killings, a priest, wrote that:

> Ever since the Jews crucified Jesus, they have been the foes of Christianity. May the Jews be expelled from Hungary, and then the church, too, will be able to breathe more freely.[2]

Anti-Semitism was not limited to the lower clergy. When the government was passing anti-Jewish laws in the late 1930s, Justinian Cardinal Serédi, the Primate of Hungary, voiced no objection to them. When the deportations were under way in 1944, Serédi's only concern was for those had-been Jews who had converted to Catholicism. Professor of history at Marquette University, Michael Phayer, characterised Serédi as 'callously anti-Semitic.' Most of the bishops were also hostile or indifferent to the fate of the Jews. For example, when Serédi was considering making a statement on behalf of Jews during the mass deportations, Archbishop Gyula Czapik of Eger advised against it, asserting that: the bishops should not make public what they knew was happening to the Jews, that the Jews were receiving appropriate historical punishment, and that the Church should not endanger its good relations with the government.[3]

As a finale, after the last Jew had been deported from the town of Veszprém, the residents were invited to a thanksgiving ceremony that took place in the Franciscan Church.[4]

- *The Arrow Cross Party*

The Arrow Cross Party (Nyilaskeresztes Párt-Hungarista Mozgalom) was a national socialist party led by Szálasi Ferenc (Ferenc Szálasi), which formed a government known as the Government of National Unity from 15 October 1944 to 28 March 1945. The party was pro-Catholic and its anti-Semitism had its origins in Christian belief.[5] It was supported by individual priests, and bishops such as József Grősz, who was promoted in 1943 by Pius XII[6] to the important bishopric of Kalocsa.

The Hungarian government introduced a 'campaign of systematic robbery seldom witnessed' as they prepared for the Jewish deportations. A moratorium was declared on all debts owed to Jews by Christians. Every Jew was required to declare all his properties and to immediately hand over to the banks his jewellery and gold. Jewish bank accounts were frozen and the banks' safes were closed.

When the deportation trains reached the borders, the Hungarian border police robbed

---

[1] Source: http://www.shc.edu/theolibrary/resources/07Central.htm (2014)
[2] Source: ibid. Similar to the thoughts of Archbishop Stepinac with respect to the Orthodox Serbs in Croatia.
[3] http://www.shc.edu/theolibrary/resources/07Central.htm (2014)
[4] Ibid. So typical of the Franciscans.
[5] http://en.wikipedia.org/wiki/Arrow_Cross_Party (2012)
[6] The role of Pius XII in the Holocaust is revealed in '*A Corrupt Tree*', Chapter II-7. See also Stockwell, Antony. *Pius XII: the Dark Side*.

the Jews of the food they were taking along for the journey to Auschwitz.

Three days after the deportations had begun, Interior Minister Jaross spoke to the Hungarian people:

> I make it clear that all property and valuables which Jewish greed managed to accumulate during the liberal period has ceased to be their property. All this belongs to the Hungarian nation ...[1]

The Arrow Cross conducted a campaign of deadly terror in Budapest. Between October 1944 and January 1945 approximately 100,000 Hungarian Jews were murdered by the German and Hungarian Nazis. Additionally, a death march to the camps in Austria was implemented in November 1944. Approximately 20,000 Jews were forced to march to the Austrian border. Thousands died from starvation, hypothermia, and being shot during the march. The survivors were taken to various concentration camps, such as Mauthausen and Dachau.[2]

Moshe Y Herczl, in his book *Christianity and the Holocaust of Hungarian Jews*, commented:

> Thus the voice of Christianity reached the ears of the Hungarians from the mouths of such government ministers as Endre [see above] and his colleagues. They spoke in the name of Christianity, and no priest voiced other opinions.[3]

Herczl has presented a contemporary Catholic statement which reflects the depth of Hungarian Catholic anti-Semitism:

> Why must we suffer, in that by virtue of the invasion of all these new Christians our churches will turn into inferior, stinking synagogues? ... The priests must not allow these bloodsucking peddlers to manage their business at the expense of the priests in the sacred temples of God.[4]

Between December 1944 and the end of January 1945, the Arrow Cross seized about 20,000 Jews from the ghetto, took them to the banks of the Danube, then shot them. Their bodies were thrown into the river. 'The Budapest orgy of blood has no equal in the black pages of Nazidom', stated Philip Friedman. He quoted the Christian scholar Istvan Bibo and the Hungarian Jewish writer Robert Major on the callous indifference of the Christian populace. Both of them agree that the attitude of the Christians at large toward the ordeal of the Jews was one of total indifference. Among officials and the officer corps many participated in the anti-Jewish excesses. Notwithstanding, the crude savagery displayed by the Arrow Cross horrified and alienated many.[5]

After the war, Szálasi and other Arrow Cross leaders were tried as war criminals by Soviet courts; he was executed.

---

[1] Cymet, David. *History vs. Apologetics: The Holocaust, the Third Reich, and the Catholic Church.* p358
[2] Refer to 'The Nazi Holocaust and the Church' at page 245 et seq for additional details.
[3] Cymet, David. *History vs. Apologetics: The Holocaust, the Third Reich, and the Catholic Church.* p358
[4] Quoted in: Ibid. p367
[5] Cymet, David. *History vs. Apologetics: The Holocaust, the Third Reich, and the Catholic Church.* p367

At the height of the massacre, the nuncio in Budapest, Monsignor Angelo Rotta,[1] helped to save *converts* by issuing at least 15,000 letters of protection and providing them with baptismal certificates.

The Budapest Ghetto

The Budapest Ghetto consisted of several blocks of the old Jewish quarter of the city around the main synagogue. It was surrounded by a high fence and stone wall that was guarded. The ghetto was established in November 1944, and lasted for less than three months, until the liberation of Budapest on 17 January 1945 by the Soviet Army during the Battle of Budapest.

The ghetto area was completely cut off from the outside world: no food was allowed in, rubbish and waste were not collected, the dead lay on the streets and piled up in the bombed-out store fronts, and the buildings were overcrowded, leading to the spread of diseases such as typhoid.

More than half of those who were forced into the ghetto in 1944 were almost immediately sent to concentration camps.[2]

Anti-Semitism during the War in Germany

Only a very brief mention is made in this chapter of the tragic events in Germany.

Additional to concentration camps, in 1942 the SS built a network of extermination camps to systematically kill millions of prisoners by gassing. The extermination camps (Vernichtungslager) and death camps (Todeslager) were camps whose primary function was genocide.

A wide range of citizens was incarcerated, including many Jews.

Many of the prisoners died in the camps through deliberate maltreatment, disease, starvation, and overwork, or were executed as unfit for labour.

Dachau Concentration Camp

Dachau was the first Nazi concentration camp opened in Germany. It was located on the grounds of an abandoned munitions factory near the town of Dachau, in the state of Bavaria. Opened 22 March 1933, it was the first regular concentration camp established by the coalition government of the National Socialist Party (Nazi Party) and the German Nationalist People's Party. It served as a prototype and model for the other Nazi concentration camps. Heinrich Himmler officially described the camp as 'the first concentration camp for political prisoners.'

By the first of May 1933 there were 1200 inmates in the camp; mostly political prisoners from Munich. They comprised 'many Jewish doctors and lawyers.'[3]

Guards began murdering inmates from the very first days of the camp's existence.

---

[1] Also, as Dean of the Diplomatic Corps, Msgr Rotta vehemently protested several times to the Hungarian Governments against the Jewish Deportations. He retired from diplomacy in 1957 and was recognised as Righteous among the Nations by Yad Vashem in 1997. (*Wikipedia*)

[2] http://en.wikipedia.org/wiki/Budapest_Ghetto (2012)

[3] *The Dachau Gas Chambers* – an essay by Harry W Mazal, OBE

In his book *By Train to Dachau*, Ernst Raubitschek, a survivor, has a vivid chapter heading:

> In Dachau gibt es nur Gesunde und Tote (In Dachau there are only Healthy Men or Corpses)[1]

206,206 prisoners had been registered by 1945. The total number of dead may never be known.[2]

In his essay *The Dachau Gas Chambers*, Harry W Mazal recorded:

> The first crematorium was erected in 1940, on the North-West corner of the camp, and can only be reached over a small footbridge. The ovens are housed in a wooden shed surrounded by a grove of trees. The well-concealed site was carefully chosen, and further isolated from the main camp by a large drainage ditch, the camp wall, a barbed wire fence, and a large ditch with running water. It is quite impossible even today to see the old crematorium from the camp, and many visitors miss it altogether even when walking within a few yards of it on the path to the new crematorium.[3]

Buchenwald Concentration Camp

Buchenwald Concentration Camp was established on the Ettersberg, near Weimar, in July 1937. It was one of the first and the largest of the concentration camps on German soil.

Although Buchenwald was technically not an extermination camp, it was a site of an extraordinary number of deaths. A primary cause of death was illness due to harsh camp conditions and starvation. Malnourished and suffering from disease, many were literally 'worked to death' under the 'Vernichtung durch Arbeit' ('extermination through labour') policy, because inmates had only the one choice between slave labour and inevitable execution. Many inmates died as a result of human experimentation or fell victim to arbitrary acts perpetrated by the SS guards. Other prisoners were simply murdered, primarily by shooting and hanging.[4]

Well-known Jewish inmates included:

Jacob Avigdor, Chief Rabbi of Drohobych;

Léon Blum, French politician;[5]

Marian Filar, Polish concert pianist and virtuoso;

Yisrael Meir Lau, Ashkenazi Rabbi.

Anti-Semitism during the War in Catholic Austria

According to political science academic David Art, Austrians played a central role in the Nazi's crimes. Although they comprised only 8 percent of the population of the Third Reich, over 13 percent of the members of the SS were Austrian. Many of the key

---

[1] Raubitschek, Ernst. *By Train to Dachau*. p52
[2] Vivid photos of dead and dying victims may be seen at http://www.dachau.oskarschindler.dk/
[3] *The Dachau Gas Chambers* – an essay by Harry W Mazal, OBE
[4] http://en.wikipedia.org/wiki/Buchenwald_concentration_camp (2012)
[5] The kibbutz of Kfar Blum in northern Israel is named after him.

figures in the exterminations were Austrian, as were more than 75 percent of commanders and 40 percent of the staff at Nazi death camps. Simon Wiesenthal estimates that Austrians were directly responsible for the deaths of 3 million Jews.[1]

Mauthausen-Gusen Concentration Camp Complex

Mauthausen is a small market town in Austria. During World War II, it became the site of the Mauthausen-Gusen Concentration Camp complex.

In early 1940 a large number of Polish Jews were transferred to Mauthausen – an estimated 30,000 of them died there. Inmates were subjected to barbaric conditions, the most infamous of which was being forced to carry heavy stone blocks up 186 steps from the camp quarry. The steps became known as 'the Stairway of Death.'[2]

Anti-Semitism during the War in Catholic Italy

Italian Jews were subjected to inimical legal impositions, forced labour, arrest and deportation.

After Italy entered the war in 1940, Jewish refugees living in Italy were interned in concentration camps such as the Campagna Concentration Camp and the concentration camp at Ferramonti di Tarsia.

The deportations of Italian Jews to Nazi death camps began after September 1943, when Italy capitulated to the Allies and, in response, the German troops invaded Italy from the North.

In October 1943 Nazis raided the ghetto in Rome; characteristically and significantly Pius XII remained silent even when the Nazis rounded up nearly 2000 Jews of these Jews, many of whom, mostly women and children, were then transported to Auschwitz.

A month later, the Jews of Genoa and Florence were deported to Auschwitz. Jews of Friuli were deported to Auschwitz via Risiera di San Sabba Concentration Camp. It is estimated that 7500 Italian Jews became victims of the Holocaust.[3]

Historian Meir Michaelis wrote in *Mussolini and the Jews*, although Mussolini 'was too much of an Italian to approve of the "final solution," … he and his henchmen helped to create the conditions in which the Holocaust became possible.' While Mussolini did not put Italian forces to work to implement the "Final Solution," he had legally isolated Italian Jews to strengthen the Rome-Berlin Axis.[4]

Historical research has contradicted the conventional belief that Italians began to enforce anti-Semitic laws only after German troops occupied the country in 1943, and then with reluctance. A spate of studies, many of them based on a little-publicised Italian government report commissioned in 1999, 'have revealed a vast wartime record detailing a systematic disenfranchisement of Italy's Jews, beginning in the summer of 1938, shortly before the Kristallnacht attacks in November.'

[1] Art, David. *The Politics of the Nazi Past in Germany and Austria* p43

[2] http://en.wikipedia.org/wiki/Mauthausen (2012)

[3] http://en.wikipedia.org/wiki/History_of_the_Jews_in_Italy#Jews_during_the_Fascist_era (2014)

[4] Brownfeld, Peter Egill. 'The Italian Holocaust: The Story of an Assimilated Jewish Community'. *Issues* (Fall 2003). Source: http://www.acjna.org/acjna/articles_detail.aspx?id=300 (2014)

That same year, Mussolini's fascist government forbade Jewish children from attending any schools, 'ordered the dismissal of Jews from professorships in all universities, and banned Jews from the civil service and military as well as the banking and insurance industries.'

A series of incrementally more onerous laws in 1939 and 1940 revoked peddlers' permits and shopkeepers' licenses, and required Jewish owners of businesses, as well as stock or bond holders, to sell those assets to 'Aryans'. Bank accounts were ordered to be transferred to government authorities.[1]

While there were several important bishops who worked hard to save Jewish lives, some prelates refused to do anything to help the Jews in their dioceses. Such was the case of: Adeodato Cardinal Piazza, the patriarch of Venice; the Bishop of Modena, who insisted on the removal of dozens of orphaned Jewish children from their hiding place in a diocesan seminary; and the Bishop of Mantua, who was a known fascist sympathizer. Others actually tried to obstruct the rescue of Jews.[2]

Generally, historians agree with the assessment of Yehuda Bauer that 'after the summer of 1943, when the south of the country had fallen to the Allies and an Italian Fascist Republic was established in the north under the direct rule of the Nazis, the attitude of the population at large to the Jews was one of commiseration and, very often, of active help.[3]

Nevertheless, some historians have tried to absolve Italians from their role in the Holocaust, claiming that while Italy did institute racial laws, the annihilation campaign was solely a German invention. They fail to take account of the effect of Italy's 1938 racial laws that brought in harsher restrictions than Germany's first anti-Semitic legislation. They also ignore the impact of Italy's anti-Semitic campaign that worked to isolate Jews from Italian society and remove their wealth.[4]

Professor David Kertzer provides an overview of the political role of the Church:

> The Vatican played a central role in both making the Fascist regime possible and in keeping it in power. Italian Catholic Action worked closely with the Fascist Authorities to increase the repressive reach of the police. Far from opposing the treatment of Jews as second-class citizens, the Church provided Mussolini with his most potent arguments for adopting such harsh measures against them. ... the Vatican made a secret deal with Mussolini to refrain from any criticism of Italy's infamous anti-Semitic 'racial laws' in exchange for better treatment of Catholic organizations.[5]

Cardinal Eugenio Pacelli, an acknowledged anti-Semite, was the central player in

---

[1] http://www.nytimes.com/2010/11/05/nyregion/05italians.html?_r=1 (2015)

[2] http://www.shc.edu/theolibrary/resources/09Western.htm (2014)

[3] Yehuda Bauer, 'Christian Behavior During the Holocaust', *Jewish Spectator* 43:3 (1978) p17. Source: http://www.shc.edu/theolibrary/resources/09Western.htm (2014)

[4] Brownfeld, Peter Egill. 'The Italian Holocaust: The Story of an Assimilated Jewish Community'. *Issues* (Fall 2003). Source: http://www.acjna.org/acjna/articles_detail.aspx?id=300 (2014)

[5] Kertzer, David I. *The Pope and Mussolini: The Secret History of Pius XI and the Rise of Fascism in ...* p389

ameliorating Pius XI's increasing doubts about Mussolini and Hitler.[1]

Anti-Semitism during the War in Catholic France

The capture of France by the Nazis resulted in the country's division into an occupied northern half governed by the Germans, and an unoccupied southern half under a French government located in the city of Vichy, headed by Philippe Pétain. 'Catholic authorities welcomed the Vichy government because it seemed to represent a repudiation of certain liberal values against which the Church had long fought in France.'[2] Pierre-Marie Cardinal Gerlier said:

> No one supports more zealously than I the policies of Marshal Pétain.

When, in October 1940, French Jews were deprived of their rights, and foreign Jews were deprived of their liberty, there was no response at all from the Church. In June 1941 when the Vichy government promulgated the second anti-Jewish law, the Church was again silent, and its silence continued after the occupation authorities required Jews living in the southern part of the country to wear the yellow star.[3]

In July 1942, 13,300 Jewish men, women and children were arrested by the Paris police and placed in camps. There was no reaction from the Church. However, several southern bishops issued declarations condemning the anti-Jewish measures – their cumulative effect was powerful. They encouraged many Catholics to take extraordinary risks in saving Jews.[4]

Yehuda Bauer commented that 'the Catholic clergy, by and large, and with a few honorable exceptions, echoed antisemitic sentiments.'[5]

In helping the Jews, the courageous member of the Résistance, Catholic Germaine Ribière, was opposed at every turn by Catholic priests and hierarchs. *One priest refused her Communion,*[6] and another commented that he had more important things than the welfare of the Jews. Professor Robert Michael found that 'Centuries of anti-Jewish Catholic teachings diminished the value of the Jews as human beings and put them beyond the realm of humane treatment.[7]

Anti-Semitism during the War in Serbia

The Serbian genocide of Jews and Roma during World War II occurred in the 'Territory of the Military Commander in Serbia' supported by the puppet government led by Milan Nedić.[8]

On 25 March 1941, Prince Paul of Yugoslavia signed the *Tripartite Pact*, allying the

---

[1] Ibid. pp405-6
[2] http://www.shc.edu/theolibrary/resources/09Western.htm (2014)
[3] Ibid.
[4] http://www.shc.edu/theolibrary/resources/09Western.htm (2014)
[5] Bauer, Yehuda. *A History of the Holocaust.* p305
[6] Nonetheless, Germaine Ribière was recognised as a 'Righteous Among the Nations' by Yad Vashem.
[7] Michael, Robert. *A History of Catholic Antisemitism: The Dark Side of the Church.* p144
[8] Much of this material has been taken from https://en.wikipedia.org/wiki/The_Holocaust_in_Serbia (2015)

Kingdom of Yugoslavia with the Axis powers. He was overthrown, and a new anti-German government under King Peter II[1] and Dušan Simović[2] took power. The new government withdrew its support for the Axis, but failed to repudiate the Tripartite Pact. Notwithstanding, Axis forces led by Nazi Germany invaded Yugoslavia a month later.

The puppet government of Milan Nedić was given responsibility for many Holocaust activities, including the registration and arrest of Jews, and joint control over the Banjica Concentration Camp in Belgrade.[3]

On 29 April, the Chief of the German Military Administration in Serbia, SS commander and Staatsrat, Harald Turner, issued the order to register all Jews and Gypsies throughout Serbia. This prescribed the wearing of yellow armbands, introduced forced labour and curfew, limited access to food and other provisions, and banned the use of public transport. The main racial laws in Serbia were adopted a day later – the *Legal Decree on Racial Origins* (*Zakonska odredba o rasnoj pripadnosti*).

The destruction of Serbian Jews was carried out in two distinct phases. The first involved the murder of Jewish men, who were shot as part of retaliatory executions carried out by German forces in response to the rising anti-Nazi partisan insurgency in Serbia. In October 1941 General, Franz Böhme ordered the execution of 100 civilians for every German soldier killed and 50 for every wounded. In all, some 30,000 people were executed during the first two months of this policy.

Additionally, in late August 1941 the Germans ordered the mass internment of Jewish men in the concentration camps of Topovske šupe and in the city of Šabac.[4]

The second genocide, between December 1941 and May 1942, involved the incarceration of the women and children at the Semlin Judenlager (Semlin Jewish camp) in Belgrade and their gassing in a mobile gas van. Another concentration camp, Sajmište, was established across the Sava River from Belgrade, on the territory of the Roman Catholic Independent State of Croatia to process and eliminate captured Jews, Serbs, Roma, and others. Some 7000 to 10,000 Jews are estimated to have been exterminated there, plus more than 10,600 other Serbs and uncounted Roma. Harald Turner[5] described how the Nazis carried out the genocide of Serbian Jews:

> Already some months ago, I shot dead all the Jews I could get my hands on in this area, concentrated all the Jewish women and children in a camp and with the help of the SD[6] got my hands on a 'delousing van', that in about 14 days to 4 weeks will have brought about the definitive clearing out of the camp ...[7]

---

[1] Peter II Karađorđević was the third and last King of Yugoslavia, and the last reigning member of the Karađorđević dynasty.

[2] Dušan Simović was a Serbian general who served as Chief of the General Staff of the Royal Yugoslav Army and as the Prime Minister of Yugoslavia.

[3] Refer to https://en.wikipedia.org/wiki/Banjica_concentration_camp for further details.

[4] https://www.open.ac.uk/socialsciences/semlin/en/holocaust-in-serbia.php (2015)

[5] After the war, Turner was executed by hanging.

[6] SD – Sicherheitsdienst – Nazi Security Services.

[7] Dr Harald Turner's letter to Karl Wolff dated April 11, 1942.

- While the Nazis were exclusively responsible for attempted total extermination of the Jews of Serbia proper, they were assisted by local quislings in the Nedić government and others. Dimitrije Ljotić, who was a leading Serbian Nazi ideologist founded a pan-Serbian, pro-Nazi and fascist party, Zbor. It was very active, and published a large amount of extreme anti-Semitic literature. The military arm of Zbor renowned as the Serbian Voluntary Guard was a reliable ally of the Gestapo in the elimination of Jews.

- Accordingly, in August 1942 Serbia was the first state to be declared judenfrei (Jew free). SS-Oberführer Emanuel Schäfer, commander of the Security Police and Gestapo in Serbia, infamously cabled Berlin:

> Serbien ist judenfrei.

- Similarly, Harald Turner stated that:

> Serbia is the only country in which the Jewish question and the Gypsy question has been solved.

- By the time Serbia was liberated in 1944, most of its 16,000 Jews had been murdered. Summing up, historian Christopher Browning stated:

> Serbia was the only country outside Poland and the Soviet Union where all Jewish victims were killed on the spot without deportation, and was the first country after Estonia to be declared 'Judenfrei' ...[1]

Vojvodina

The occupation of Vojvodina (a province of modern Serbia) from 1941 to 1944 was carried out by Nazi Germany and its puppet regimes of Horthy's Hungary and Pavelić's Croatia.

In 1941, Nazi Germany, Italy and Hungary invaded and occupied the Kingdom of Yugoslavia. Control of Vojvodina was divided between Hungary (Bačka), local German Volksdeutsche authorities (Banat), and the Independent State of Croatia (Syrmia) (Srem), all of whom assisted in the genocide.

In January 1942 Hungarian military units shot 600 Jews and 2500 Serbs in Novi Sad.

After the Germans occupied Hungary in 1944, Hungarian gendarmerie units rounded up some 16,000 Jews from Bačka and nearby Baranja, and deported them to the German police, who had them transported to Auschwitz where the majority died in the gas chambers.

In total, Axis (German, Croatian, and Hungarian) occupational authorities killed about 50,000 citizens of Vojvodina (mostly Serbs, Jews and Roma) while more than 280,000 people were interned, arrested, violated, or tortured.[2]

Anti-Semitism during the War in the Netherlands

There were about 140,000 Dutch Jews at the start of the War. They were well

---

[1] https://en.wikipedia.org/wiki/The_Holocaust_in_Serbia (2015)
[2] https://en.wikipedia.org/wiki/Vojvodina#Period_after_1918 (2015)

integrated into a society that exhibited very little anti-Semitism. Nonetheless, various segments of Dutch society, including the thirty percent of the population who were Catholic, sought accommodation with the Germans.

When the Reichkommissar ordered the registration of all people who had at least one Jewish grandparent, there was no protest from the Catholic hierarchy. Protests against anti-Jewish measures came earlier from Protestants than from Catholics, and they came more from pastors, priests and laity than from church leaders.[1]

Deportations of Jews from Holland began in July 1942, and continued for over a year, until there were very few left.

A 1995 statement by the Dutch bishops acknowledged the role played in the Holocaust by 'a tradition of theological and ecclesiastical anti-Judaism', and rejected 'this tradition of ecclesiastical anti-Judaism and deeply regret its horrible results.'[2]

Anti-Semitism during the War in Catholic Belgium

The Germans occupied Belgium in May 1940. The deportations of Jews took place in 1942 and 1943. Nevertheless, about half of Belgium's Jews survived the Holocaust. Many Catholics were involved in the rescue of Jews, but most were not.

The leading historian of the Shoah in Belgium, Dr Maxime Steinberg, has stated:

> In this Catholic country where the word of the Church counted and where it never failed to make itself heard, the hierarchy did nothing to express popular feeling about the Jewish question.[3]

There were several courageous efforts on behalf of the Jews, but 'it is simply not true to state that "the Church saved 70% of Belgium Jews." '[4]

Anti-Semitism during the War in Denmark

There is no other Holocaust story similar to that of the rescue of Danish Jews. Most of the country's 8000 Jews were saved by being ferried in boats to neutral Sweden.

Leon Stein summed up the efforts of the Danish Lutheran Church:

> In Denmark the overwhelming majority of Lutheran laymen and pastors and the official institutional church opposed the Nazi persecution of the Jews and ... joined the Danish resistance and rallied to help save the Jews of that country.[5]

Anti-Semitism during the War in Catholic Lithuania – the Lithuanian Holocaust

Lithuania was generally an independent country between the two world wars. However, in 1940 the Soviets occupied the country and incorporated it into the Soviet Union. When the Germans invaded the Soviet Union in 1941, they quickly overran Lithuania and systematically annihilated the Jewish community. Additionally:

---

[1] http://www.shc.edu/theolibrary/resources/09Western.htm (2014)
[2] Ibid.
[3] Steinberg, Maxime. 'Faced with the Final Solution in Occupied Belgium: The Church's Silence and Christian Action'. In: Bauer, Yehuda. *Remembering for the Future: Working Papers and Addenda*. Vol 3. p2746
[4] Boyle, Stephen. 'Pius XII and the Jews: Greatness Dishonored', in: *Homiletic and Pastoral Review* (April 1999) p29
[5] Stein, Leon. 'A Parting at the Cross: The Contrasting National Cultures of Lutheranism in Germany and Denmark during the Holocaust', in: *Remembering for the Future: The Holocaust in an age ...* Vol 2. p618

Lithuanians, 95 percent of whom were Catholics, welcomed the Germans as liberators and more often than not were willing collaborators in gathering and killing Jews. In fact, *Lithuanian Catholics tortured and killed Jews in at least forty communities even before the German army arrived.*[1]

Of approximately 208,000-210,000 Jews, an estimated 190,000-195,000 were murdered by the end of the War. Yet the Catholic Church, which had considerable power in that country, never spoke out on behalf of the Jews or in opposition to Catholic and German anti-Jewish activities.[2]

The Jews in Bulgaria during the War

The Jews who were living in Bulgaria at the beginning of the War survived the Holocaust, and their numbers actually increased. This happy situation was the consequence of the Bulgarian Orthodox Church's playing a major role in saving Bulgarian Jews. The resistance by Orthodox Church leaders was forceful and effective.[3]

The Attitude of the Catholic Church

An example – In 1941 in *Operational Situation Report USSR No. 54*, the German 'Einsatzgruppen A' reported from Kaunas: 'The attitude of the Church regarding the Jewish question is, in general, clear. In addition, Bishop Brizgys has forbidden all clergymen to help Jews in any form whatsoever. He rejected several Jewish delegations who approached him personally and asked for his intervention with the German authorities. In the future he will not meet any Jews at all.'[4]

- In 1938 Catholic Justice Herbert O'Brien of New York praised Hitler's early conquests as 'a natural re-adjustment in Europe'. He applauded Hitler's success in destroying Protestant British dominance in central Europe and in procuring a return to the political and social union of states in a revived Holy Roman confederation.[5]

Synopsis

Adolf Hitler's Holocaust was the worst military genocide in history. Its object was the systematic elimination of all European Jews.

During World War II, under a Catholic majority, the Jews of Poland suffered extreme intolerance – more than 3 million of them were liquidated. Nevertheless, the Catholic Church in Poland stated that the Nazis had been proven to possess a realistic attitude in 'liberating Polish society from the Jewish plague.'

Some of the most horrific Holocaust atrocities against Jews were perpetrated in the Catholic State of Croatia. 'The tragic history of the Jewish communities in that country has yet to be told because there are literally no survivors.'

Catholic Hungary was home to a significant Jewish community. Most Hungarian

---

[1] http://www.shc.edu/theolibrary/resources/06Eastern.htm (2014)
[2] Ibid. https://en.wikipedia.org/wiki/The_Holocaust_in_Lithuania (2016)
[3] Ibid.
[4] http://www.sullivan-county.com/id2/timeline.htm (2007)
[5] Lehmann, L H. *Behind the Dictators: A Factual Analysis of the Relationship of Nazi-Fascism and Roman Catholicism.* p23

Jews were either deported to concentration camps, from which the majority did not return, or were murdered by the Hungarian Arrow Cross Catholic fascists.

In Germany, a wide range of citizens died in concentration camps. Additionally, the SS built a network of extermination camps to systematically kill millions.

Catholic Austria played a key role in the Nazi crimes. Many of the key figures in the extermination project of the Third Reich were Austrian, as were over 75% of commanders and 40% of the staff at Nazi death camps. It has been estimated that Austrians were directly responsible for the deaths of 3 million Jews.

Half the population of Hitler's Greater Reich was Catholic.

Conclusion

Leon Stein summed up the valiant efforts of the Danish Lutheran Church:

> In Denmark the overwhelming majority of Lutheran laymen and pastors and the official institutional church opposed the Nazi persecution of the Jews and, when Denmark was occupied by the Nazis, joined the Danish resistance and rallied to help save the Jews of that country.[1]

Of which, Professor Gerald Darring wrote 'To my knowledge, *no one* has said that about the Catholic Church in *any* country.'[2]

The Final Count

1,500,000 children were killed in the Holocaust. In total, 6,000,000 Jews, one third of all the Jews then in the world, were obliterated.

During the entire War, the Holy See *never* condemned the diabolical atrocities of the Einsatzgruppen or the other killers and torturers.

———

[1] Stein, Leon. In: *Remembering for the Future: The Holocaust in an Age of Genocide.* Vol 2. p618
[2] http://www.shc.edu/theolibrary/resources/09Western.htm (2014)

16 – Adolf Hitler – a Confirmed Catholic

It is obvious that the war which Hitler and his accomplices waged was a war not only against Jewish men, women, and children, but also against Jewish religion, Jewish culture, Jewish tradition, therefore Jewish memory. Elie Wiesel

Adolf Hitler, a Confirmed 'Soldier of Christ'

Adolf Hitler was a devout Roman Catholic. In a speech at Hamburg in 1936, he is reported to have said:

> Providence has caused me to be Catholic ... In standing guard against the Jew I am defending the handiwork of the Lord.[1]

Hitler was born in Austria, the western country most influenced by the chronic anti-Semitism of the Church. 'Catholic antisemitism conditioned Hitler's ideas and behaviour towards Jews.'[2] In the final election of the Habsburg Empire, more than two-thirds of German Austrians voted for candidates who were extreme anti-Semites. After World War I, Austrian Catholics established many anti-Semitic paramilitary groups, often led and supported by priests.

Nevertheless, apologists have regularly promoted the fiction that Adolf Hitler was an atheist.[3] The fact is that Hitler was the product of the Christian anti-Semitism that he imbibed from the Church. He was born into a devout Catholic family, he was baptised in a Catholic Church in 1889,[4] lived in predominantly Catholic Austria, and went to Catholic schools and churches as a child.

His father regarded the Catholic priesthood as the highest state to which anyone could aspire; and to Adolf as a child the priest appeared to be the ideal human being. In his autobiography, Hitler says that he was deeply impressed with the religious ceremonies of the Catholic Church and was a member of the choir in his parish church. For two years he attended classes at the Benedictine monastery at Lambach. There, he sang in the choir.[5] 'This,' he said, 'supplied me with the best opportunity to steep myself in the solemn magnificence of the brilliant feasts of the Church.'[6]

'The only teacher he admired was an antisemitic historian and politician.'[7]

Hitler did well in monastery school (St Michael's, in Leonding, Austria), sang in the choir, found High Mass and other Church ceremonies intoxicating, and idolised priests.[8]

---

[1] http://historum.com/war-military-history/14094-were-nazis-atheists-3.html (2015)

[2] Michael, Robert. *A History of Catholic Antisemitism: The Dark Side of the Church.* p113

[3] Dawkins, Richard. *The God Delusion.* p273

[4] http://atheism.about.com/od/isatheismdangerous/a/HitlerAtheist.htm (2007)

[5] Shirer, William L. *The Rise and Fall of the Third Reich.* p24. Source: http://www.freewebs.com/nexxcentral/conspiracyihistory.htm (2008)

[6] Lehmann, L H. *Behind the Dictators: A Factual Analysis of the Relationship* ... p26

[7] Michael, Robert. *A History of Catholic Antisemitism: The Dark Side of the Church.* p114

[8] Paul, Gregory S. *The Great Scandal: Christianity's Role in the Rise of the Nazis.* Source: http://www.secularhumanism.org/library/fi/paul_23_4.html (2007)

He was a communicant and an altar boy of the Catholic Church, and was confirmed as a 'soldier of Christ'.[1]

In 1920 when Hitler was thirty-one, his comrade Rudolf Hess wrote a letter to the Prime Minister of Bavaria: 'I know Herr Hitler very well personally and am quite close to him. He has an unusually honourable character, full of profound kindness, is religious, a good Catholic.'

In a speech of 12 April 1922, and in his unpublished book *Zweites Buch* (*Second Book*), Hitler explained his perspective on Jesus:

> My feelings as a Christian point me to my Lord and Saviour as a fighter. It points me to the man who once in loneliness, surrounded by a few followers, recognized these Jews for what they were and summoned men to fight against them and who, God's truth! was greatest not as a sufferer but as a fighter.

> In boundless love as a Christian and as a man I read through the passage which tells us how the Lord at last rose in His might and seized the scourge to drive out of the Temple the brood of vipers and adders. How terrific was his fight against the Jewish poison. Today, after two thousand years, with deepest emotion I recognize more profoundly than ever before the fact that it was for this that He had to shed his blood upon the Cross.[2]

Hitler never renounced the religious doctrines nor condemned the political aims and aspirations of the Church.[3] He published his hate-filled book *Mein Kampf* (*My Struggle*) in 1925. It was edited by the Jesuit Bernhard Staempfle.

In *Mein Kampf*, Hitler approved the indisputability of Church dogmas, the intolerant attitude of Catholic education, the necessity of blind faith, the infallibility of the pope, and the compulsory celibacy of the clergy. He wrote that his plan for a triumphant Nazism was modelled on the Church's traditional 'tenacious adherence to dogma' and its 'fanatical intolerance'. Particularly was this so in the Church's past when in building 'its own altar', Christianity had not hesitated to 'destroy the altars of the heathen.'[4]

In *Mein Kampf* Hitler also wrote:

> Since in my free time I received singing lessons in the cloister at Lambach, I had excellent opportunity to intoxicate myself with the solemn splendour of the brilliant church festivals. As was only natural, the abbot seemed to me, as the village priest had once seemed to my father, the highest and most desirable ideal.[5]

And, in admiration of the Church, Hitler stated:

> Thus the Catholic Church is more secure than ever. It can be predicted that, as

[1] Murphy, John Patrick Michael. *The Religion of Hitler* (1998). 'Confirmation makes us "Soldiers of Christ".' https://www.ewtn.com/library/CATECHSM/CONFIRM1.HTM (2015)

[2] http://infidels.org/library/modern/mathew/sn-hitler.html (2015)

[3] Lehmann, L H. *Behind the Dictators: A Factual Analysis of the Relationship of Nazi-Fascism and ...* p26

[4] Stannard, David. *American Holocaust*. p150. Source: http://www.thirdworldtraveler.com/History/Sex_Race_AH.html (2010).

[5] Hitler, Adolf. *Mein Kampf*. Vol One. Ch I: 'In the House of my Parents'. Source: http://www.hitler.org/writings/Mein_Kampf/mkv1ch01.html (2014)

passing phenomena vanish away, she will remain as a beacon light amid these vanishing elements, attracting blind adherents in ever-increasing numbers.[1]

He wrote of his enthusiasm:

> Even today I am not ashamed to say that, overpowered by stormy enthusiasm, I fell down on my knees and thanked Heaven from an overflowing heart for granting me the good fortune of being permitted to live at this time.

> I had so often sung 'Deutschland über Alles' and shouted 'Heil' at the top of my lungs, that it seemed to me almost a belated act of grace to be allowed to stand as a witness in the divine court of the eternal judge and proclaim the sincerity of this conviction.[2]

Hitler also wrote of his years of study and suffering in Vienna:

> In this period my eyes were opened to two menaces of which I had previously scarcely known the names, and whose terrible importance for the existence of the German people I certainly did not understand: Marxism and Jewry ...

> Only a knowledge of the Jews provides the key with which to comprehend the inner, and consequently real, aims of Social Democracy ...

> Not until my fourteenth or fifteenth year did I begin to come across the word 'Jew,' with any frequency, partly in connection with political discussions. This filled me with a mild distaste ...[3]

In 1928, aged 39, Hitler certainly went to confession and communion. In 1933 he let it be officially announced:

> Reich Chancellor Hitler still belongs to the Catholic Church and has no intention of leaving it.

As late as 1941 Hitler told his adjutant, General Gerhard Engel, 'I shall remain a Catholic for ever.'[4] He also stated 'I believe today that my conduct is in accordance with the will of the Almighty Creator.'[5]

· Hitler never left the Church. The Church *never* criticised his diabolical operations during their relentless progress.[6] He was *never* excommunicated. (As examples of the double standards of the Catholic Church, Martin Luther was excommunicated for simply translating the Bible into German, and President Juan Domingo Perón of Argentina was excommunicated in 1955 because of the enactment of the divorce law and the expulsion of two Catholic priests from the country.)

[1] Lehmann, L H. *Behind the Dictators: A Factual Analysis of the Relationship of Nazi-Fascism and ...* p26

[2] http://www.nobeliefs.com/hitler.htm (2012)

[3] Hitler, Adolf. *Mein Kampf.* Vol One. Ch II: 'Years of Study and Suffering in Vienna'. Source: http://www.hitler.org/writings/Mein_Kampf/mkv1ch01.html (2014)

[4] Dawkins, Richard. *The God Delusion.* pp273-77

[5] http://www.brainyquote.com/quotes/authors/a/adolf_hitler.html#6wZXtE1SdpuldWDo.99 (2015)

[6] Boettner, Loraine. *Roman Catholicism.* Ch 18. Source: http://www.acts2.com/thebibletruth/Intolerance.htm (2005)

In *Mein Kampf* Hitler expressed his imbibed Christian beliefs that included the view that the Jews were godless and were corrupting Christendom; he also expressed his racist ideology, making the Aryans the 'genius' race and Jews the 'parasites'. His main thesis of 'The Jewish peril' alleged a Jewish conspiracy to gain world leadership. 'Therefore I am convinced that I am acting as the agent of our Creator. By fighting off the Jews, I am doing the Lord's work.' he wrote. Years later, when in power, he quoted those same words in a speech in the Reichstag.

 Mein Kampf was never placed on the Church's *Index of Forbidden Books*. By contrast, the fictional work *Robinson Crusoe* by Daniel Defoe was placed on the *Index*.[1] *Mein Kampf* was studied for three years by the Congregation of the Index, but according to the Roman Catholic doctrine of the state, Hitler was deemed to have come to power legally. So, the Congregation conveniently and self-righteously applied Paul's *Epistle to the Romans* (13:1-2), which, it is claimed, says that all state authority derives from God and must be obeyed:

> Let every soul be subject unto the higher powers. For there is no power but of God: the powers that be are ordained of God. Whosoever therefore resisteth the power, resisteth the ordinance of God: and they that resist shall receive to themselves damnation.[2]

'Who says I am not under the special protection of God?' asked Adolf. He never formally renounced his Catholicism.

In the Nationalsozialistiche Deutsche Arbeiter Partei Programm, written by Adolf Hitler and Anton Drexler, and publicly presented on 24 February 1920, are included the statements:

> We demand freedom for all religious denominations in the State, provided they do not threaten its existence nor offend the moral feelings of the German race.

> The Party, as such, stands for positive Christianity, but does not commit itself to any particular denomination. It combats the Jewish materialistic spirit within and without us, and is convinced that our nation can achieve permanent health only from within on the basis of the principle: The common interest before self-interest.[3]

Hitler stated in a speech in 1922:

> It is a battle which began nearly 120 years ago, at the moment when the Jew was granted citizen rights in the European States. The political emancipation of the Jews was the beginning of an attack of delirium. For thereby they were given full citizen rights and equality to a people which was much more clearly and definitely a race

---

[1] Notwithstanding the negative efforts of the Church, Defoe gained enduring fame for his novel *Robinson Crusoe*. He is notable for being one of the earliest practitioners of the novel, and helped popularise the genre in Britain. In some texts he is even referred to as one of the founders, if not the founder, of the English novel.

[2] Heneghan, Tom 'Secrets Behind the Forbidden Books', *America*, February 7, 2005. http://www.america magazine.org/content/article.cfm?article_id= 3998

[3] http://richarddawkins.net/articles/3730-german-bishop-atheism-responsible-for-nazis-and-mass-murder/comments?page=3 (2011)

apart from all others, that has always formed and will form a State within the State...

Parallel with this was a gradual 'moneyfication' of the whole of the nation's labour-strength. 'Share-capital' was in the ascendant, and thus bit by bit the Stock Exchange came to control the whole national economy.

The directors of these institutions were, and are without exception, Jews. [They kept] up the appearance that these institutions were after all founded as a natural outcome of the needs and the economic life of all peoples alike, and were not, as was the fact, institutions which correspond only with the essential characteristics of the Jewish people and are the outcome of those characteristics.[1]

A year later, Hitler declared his Judenhass (anti-Semitism) in a speech in Munich:

The first thing to do is to rescue [Germany] from the Jew who is ruining our country ... We want to prevent our Germany from suffering, as Another did, the death upon the Cross.

In a speech to Polish Catholics, Hitler declared: 'I as a German Catholic, ask only what is permitted to Polish Catholics. To be anti-Semitic is not to be un-Catholic. The Church used every weapon against the Jews, even the Inquisition. Christ himself was a pioneer in the fight against Judaism.'[2] In a 1933 speech Hitler said that 'To do justice to God and our own conscience, we have turned once more to the German Volk.'[3]

In the same year, he said in a speech:

We were convinced that the people need and require this faith. We have therefore undertaken the fight against the atheistic movement, and that not merely with a few theoretical declarations: we have stamped it out.[4]

Hitler compared the methods of the Catholic Church to those of his own:

I have followed [the Church] in giving our party programme the character of unalterable finality, like the Creed. The Church has never allowed the Creed to be interfered with. It is fifteen hundred years since it was formulated, but every suggestion for its amendment, every logical criticism, or attack on it, has been rejected. The Church has realised that anything and everything can be built up on a document of that sort, no matter how contradictory or irreconcilable with it. *The faithful will swallow it whole, so long as logical reasoning is never allowed to be brought to bear on it.*[5]

In a speech at Koblenz in 1934 Hitler said:

National Socialism neither opposes the Church nor is it anti-religious, but on the

---

[1] http://www.hitler.org/speeches/07-28-22.html (2015)
[2] *Dictionary of Antisemitism*, p146. Source: Golding, Shmuel. 'Anti-Semitism in the New Testament'. http://www.jdstone.org/cr/files/antisemitisminthenewtestament.html (2007)
[3] http://atheism.about.com/od/isatheismdangerous/a/HitlerAtheist.htm (2007)
[4] http://englishatheist.org/indexz22.shtml (2008)
[5] Rauschning, Hermann. *The Voice of Destruction.* pp239-40. Source: http://liberalslikechrist.org/Catholic/HitlersFaith.html (2007)

contrary it stands on the ground of a real Christianity ... For their interests cannot fail to coincide with ours alike in our fight against the symptoms of degeneracy in the world of today, in our fight against a Bolshevist culture, against atheistic movement, against criminality, and in our struggle for a consciousness of a community in our national life ... These are not anti-Christian, these are Christian principles![1]

In a 1944 speech Hitler declared:

I may not be a light of the church, a pulpiteer, but deep down I am a pious man, and believe that whoever fights bravely in defence of a natural law framed by God and never capitulates will never be deserted by the lawgiver, but will, in the end, receive the blessings of Providence.[2]

In the 1960s a prominent Viennese theologian, Friedrich Heer, described Hitler as a misguided 'Austrian Catholic' – a man whose faith was sincere. A man, who as a nine-year-old choirboy caught his first glimpse of a swastika in the coat of arms at the Lambach monastery[3]; whose beer-hall speeches resounded with biblical allusions; who as the Führer re-created the grandeur of the Catholic mass at the annual Nuremberg Rally. Even Hitler's virulent anti-Semitism found nourishment in those Christian roots.

In his book *Hitler: Diagnosis of a Destructive Prophet*, Fritz Redlich, an eminent Yale psychiatrist, maintained that Hitler acted from a profound belief in God. He noted Hitler's own words 'Man kommt um den Gottesbegriff nicht um' ('You cannot get around the concept of God').[4]

In his *Adolf Hitler: The Definitive Biography*, historian John Toland, Hitler's acclaimed biographer, wrote of Hitler's religious situation at the time of the Final Solution. He recorded that Hitler was still a member in good standing of the Roman Church despite his detestation of its hierarchy, and still believed in the Catholic Church's teaching that the Jew was God's killer[5] – consequently, the extermination of Jews could be undertaken without a twinge of conscience.[6]

Hitler found in mediaeval Catholic anti-Jewish legislation a model for his own.

He claimed, as he chronicled his sixteen steps to Nazi policy, 'I am only doing the work of the Catholic Church.'[7]

Based on Catholic legal precedent, Hitler wrote his *Nuremberg Laws* in 1935 which led to his 'Final Solution of the Jewish Question in Europe'. He described the Jews as 'untermenschen', and promoted the idea, which the Church had fostered for millennia,

---

[1] http://englishatheist.org/indexz22.shtml (2008)

[2] http://catholicarrogance.org/NaziLeadership.html (2007). History witnesses that the use of so called natural law is one of the Church's means of imposing its will in relation to almost any act that it chooses to perform.

[3] Hitler attended the primary school run by Benedictines at Lambach monastery.

[4] *The Unknown Hitler: Nazi Roots in the Occult.* http://www.crystalinks.com/hitleroccult.html (2007)

[5] Quoted in: Murphy, John Patrick Michael. *Murphy's Law: The Religion of Hitler*

[6] Dawkins, Richard. *The God Delusion.* p274

[7] Sister Pista. Evangelical Sisterhood of Mary, Darmstadt. http://www.cdn-friends-icej.ca/antiholo/guilt.html (2007)

that Jesus was not a Jew, but an Aryan.[1]

A Rhenish[2] group of German Christians in April 1937 passed the resolution: 'Hitler's word is God's law, the decrees and laws which represent it possess divine authority.'[3]

Adolf Eichmann testified at his trial in Jerusalem that Reinhard Heydrich informed him around two to three months before the invasion of Russia that the Führer had ordered the physical annihilation of all the Jews in Europe.[4,5] This annihilation was no different in essence to the persistent extermination of the Jews in Europe throughout the previous millennia by Catholics conforming to the Church's overt anti-Semitism. Hitler was merely pursuing, albeit on a larger scale, the same Catholic philosophy. Accordingly, the size of Hitler's operations was consistent with that exhorted by Pope Martin V (1417-31), who commanded the King of Poland to kill all Christian Hussites:

> Know that *the interests of the Holy See*, and those of your crown, make it a duty to exterminate the Hussites [who] dare proclaim principles of equality ... Turn your forces against Bohemia; burn, massacre ... nothing could be more agreeable to God, or more useful to the cause of kings, than the extermination of the Hussites.[6]

The anti-Semitism that Hitler had imbibed from the Church persisted to the end. Even when he made his farewell speech to the German nation from his Berlin bunker where he committed suicide, he did not refer to the glories of Germany, nor did he express regrets for having implemented the Second World War, instead, he stressed that the Jews had not been totally defeated and implored the Germans to continue the struggle against their 'eternal enemy'.[7]

Even after his death, Hitler was supported by the Church. Sister Pascalina Lehnert, Pius XII's housekeeper and confidante, recorded that 'When His Holiness was told of their [Hitler's and Mussolini's] demise, he said nothing, holding to the Catholic teaching that one does not speak unkindly of the deceased ... Yet, he went to the Papal Chapel on both occasions and said silent prayers for the repose of the souls of Mussolini and Hitler.[8]

---

[1] Sister Pista. Evangelical Sisterhood of Mary, Darmstadt. http://www.cdn-friends-icej.ca/antiholo/guilt.html (2007)

[2] Rhenish – of, or relating to the Rhine River and the lands adjacent to it.

[3] http://www.cassiopaea.org/cass/hitler.htm (2007)

[4] Cymet, David. *History vs. Apologetics: The Holocaust, the Third Reich, and the Catholic Church.* p201

[5] Consequently Auschwitz became the greatest killing institution in history.

[6] Alexis, John E. *In the Name of Education: How Weird Ideologies Corrupt ...* p182

[7] http://www.zionism-israel.com/his/judeophobia.htm (2007)

[8] Adolf Hitler committed suicide. The *Catholic Encyclopedia* states: 'The teaching of the Catholic Church concerning the morality of suicide ... [is]: Positive and direct suicide perpetrated without God's consent always constitutes a grave injustice towards Him. To destroy a thing is to dispose of it as an absolute master and to act as one having full and independent dominion over it; but man does not possess this full and independent dominion over his life, since to be an owner one must be superior to his property. God has reserved to himself direct dominion over life ...

'That suicide is unlawful is the teaching of Holy Scripture and of the Church, which condemns the act as a most atrocious crime and, in hatred of the sin and to arouse the horror of its children, denies the suicide Christian burial.'

Spanish dictator Francisco Franco (Knight of the Order of Christ) published a statement on 3 May 1945, three days after Hitler's death:

> Adolf Hitler, son of the Catholic Church, died while defending Christianity. It is therefore understandable that words cannot be found to lament over his death, when so many were found to exalt his life. Over his mortal remains stands his victorious moral figure. With the palm of the martyr, God gives Hitler the laurels of Victory.[1]

Terminus

Not only did Hitler commit suicide, so also did Göring. Other Nazi criminals, who were hanged, included Frank, Frick, Kaltenbrunner, Keitel, Rosenberg, Streicher, and von Ribbentrop. After cremation, the ashes of Göring and these other men were fittingly dumped into a muddy drain in the Bavarian countryside.[2]

Synopsis

Adolf Hitler was the product of the Christian anti-Semitism that he imbibed from the Church. He was born into a devout Catholic family, was baptised in a Catholic Church, lived in predominantly Catholic Austria, and went to Catholic schools and churches as a child.

Hitler was deeply impressed with the religious ceremonies of the Church, and was a member of the choir in his parish church. He did well in monastery school, found High Mass and other Church ceremonies intoxicating, and idolised priests. Hitler was a communicant, an altar boy, and confirmed as a 'soldier of Christ'.

Hitler never renounced the religious doctrines nor condemned the political aims and aspirations of the Church. In *Mein Kampf* he approved the indisputability of Church dogmas, the intolerant attitude of Catholic education, the necessity of blind faith, and the infallibility of the pope. His plan for a triumphant Nazism was modelled on the Church's traditional 'tenacious adherence to dogma' and its 'fanatical intolerance.' Particularly was this so in the Church's past when in building 'its own altar,' it had not hesitated to 'destroy the altars of the heathen.'

Adolf Hitler's *Mein Kampf* was *never* placed on the Church's 'Index of Forbidden Books'. Hitler *never* left the Church. The Church *never* criticised his diabolical operations during their relentless progress. It *never* refused him the sacraments. He was *never* excommunicated.

Adolf Hitler, the Faithful Catholic

As late as 1941, Adolf Hitler, a confirmed Catholic, then aged 52, stated:

> I am now, as before, a Christian and will always remain so.

------

[1] *Reforme*, 21 July 1945. Source: http://forum.davidicke.com/showthread.php?t=38403 (2015)
[2] Read, Anthony. *The Devil's Disciples: Hitler's Inner Circle*. p913

17 – Other Major Catholic Nazis and Fascists

When I was very young, I remember my mother telling me about a friend of hers in Germany, a pianist who played a symphony that wasn't permitted, and the Germans came up on stage and broke every finger on her hands. I grew up with stories of Nazis breaking the fingers of Jews. Steven Spielberg

Most of the major participants in the planning and implementation of the Holocaust were born and bred Catholics. A quarter of the members of the Nazi Schutzstaffel (SS), a large security and military organisation of the Nazi Party in Germany, were Catholics. David Cymet has noted that the principal perpetrators of the Final Solution (Hitler, Himmler, Heydrich and Höss) were born into Catholic families, received a strict Catholic education, and *never* severed their connection to the Roman Catholic Church.[1] Gordon C Zahn recorded that German Catholics exhibited an almost unanimous support for Hitler's war.[2] Indeed, despite repeated enquiries of chancery officials and Catholics who had been active in the pre-Hitler peace movement, he was able to learn of no more than seven Catholics who openly refused to serve in Hitler's armed services. In fact, several of these conscientious objectors, which included at least one priest, were denied the sacraments because their refusal to cooperate with the Nazis was deemed to be proof that they were bad Catholics.

Zahn's research, led him to conclude that the members of the Catholic laity, notwith-standing other reasons, supported Adolf Hitler's wars because:

> Church leaders formally required them to do so; the Catholic press and Church organisations gave their total commitment to the Nazi cause; the Church and its values encouraged them to act in the defence of the people and the fatherland; in looking to the religious hierarchy for spiritual guidance and direction with respect to war service with the Nazis they received almost the same answers that they would have received from Hitler himself.[3]

CV

'Cartellverband der katholischen deutschen Studentenverbindungen' (CV) was, and is, a German umbrella organisation of Catholic male student fraternities. Following the signing of the 1933 *Reichskonkordat*, members of the CV wore uniforms of the SA and the SS. In that year, a process of Gleichschaltung (alignment) developed whereby the fraternities developed a principle of leadership similar to that of the Nazi Party, with connection to the National Socialist student community.[4]

Nikolaus 'Klaus' Barbie

Nikolaus Barbie was born to Catholic school teachers. In September 1935 he joined

---

[1] Cymet, David. *History vs. Apologetics: The Holocaust, the Third Reich, and the Catholic Church.* p15
[2] Zahn, Gordon C. *German Catholics & Hitler's Wars: A Study in Social Control.* p265
[3] Ibid. pp17, 56
[4] See, for example: http://en.wikipedia.org/wiki/Cartellverband#National_Socialism_and_WWII (2010)

the Sicherheitsdienst (Security Service), a special branch of the SS. In 1940 he went to The Hague to gather information about the Jewish 'situation' there. Then he went to Amsterdam, where he was responsible for rounding up and deporting that city's Jewish population. There, he earned a reputation for excessive brutality, even by the Gestapo's standards. He was awarded his first Iron Cross for bludgeoning to death a Jewish ice cream peddler (an 'enemy of the Reich') in public view, because the man refused to salute him properly. Barbie was promoted for his adeptness in combating resistance cells and rooting out hidden Jews in Amsterdam.[1]

In 1942 Barbie was sent to Lyon, France, where he became the head of the Gestapo. It was during this time that he earned the title 'the Butcher of Lyon'. He was responsible for the torture and death of more than 26,000 people. In April 1944 Barbie ordered the deportation to Auschwitz of a group of 44 Jewish children from an orphanage. He is best known for one of his 'cases', the arrest, torture and death of Jean Moulin, one of the highest-ranking members of the French Resistance.[2]

After the end of World War II, Barbie was protected and employed by the American Counter Intelligence Corps (CIC) because of his 'police skills'.

In 1951 he fled to Argentina with the help of the notorious Catholic priest Krunoslav Draganović.[3] Later he was extradited to France, tried, and sentenced to life imprisonment for crimes against humanity.[4] He died in prison in 1991.

Alois Brunner

Alois Brunner was a Hungarian Catholic who became Adolf Eichmann's assistant (his 'best man') and a former commander of a mobile killing squad in Russia.[5]

Brunner worked in Berlin from late 1942 to January 1943, deporting Jews from the Reich's capital. The following month he was in Salonika, Greece, whence Jews were deported to Auschwitz and Treblinka.

From July 1943 until August 1944, Brunner served in France, where he commanded the Drancy Internment Camp, near Paris. As commander of Drancy, Brunner is held responsible for sending some 140,000 European Jews to the gas chambers. At Drancy also, Brunner sought by all means to terrorise the detainees. From the first days there were beatings. For example there was a rather special torture which in the camps was called 'the torture of the spinning top'.[6]

Brunner was then transferred for the deportation of Slovakian Jews from the Sered' labour camp.[7]

After the war Brunner was sentenced to death in absentia by a French court, but he fled to Damascus, where he was granted asylum. Whilst there, Brunner lost an eye and

---

[1] http://members.aol.com/voyl/barbie/kbbio.htm (2007)

[2] http://en.wikipedia.org/wiki/Klaus_Barbie (2007)

[3] Refer to Chapter 23 for details of Fr Draganović and the Vatican's ratlines for escaping Nazi war criminals.

[4] http://en.wikipedia.org/wiki/Klaus_Barbie (2007)

[5] http://en.wikipedia.org/wiki/Drancy_deportation_camp (2007)

[6] http://www.HolocaustResearchProject.org (2012)

[7] Refer to Chapter14 – Croatian and Slovakian Holocausts, for details of this and other fascist camps.

several fingers as a result of a letter bomb sent to him by Mossad, the Israeli Secret Service.

In 1987, in a telephone interview, he told the *Chicago Sun-Times*:

> The Jews deserved to die. They were garbage, I have no regrets. If I had the chance I would do it again.[1]

In 2003 *The Guardian* newspaper described Brunner as 'the world's highest-ranking Nazi fugitive believed still alive.'

Dietrich Eckart

Dietrich Eckart was the son of royal notary and lawyer Christian Eckart and his wife Anna, a devout Catholic. He became a journalist and politician, and together with Adolf Hitler, was one of the early key members of the Nazi Party and a participant of the 1923 Nazi Party's failed Beer Hall Putsch.

After World War I, Eckart edited the anti-Semitic periodical *Auf gut Deutsch* (*In plain German*), working with Alfred Rosenberg and Gottfried Feder. He vehemently opposed the Treaty of Versailles, which he viewed as treason, and was a proponent of the so-called stab-in-the-back legend (Dolchstoßlegende), according to which the Social Democrats and Jews were to blame for Germany's defeat in the war.

Hitler dedicated the second volume of *Mein Kampf* to Eckart. In 1925 Eckart's unfinished fictional essay *Der Bolschewismus von Moses bis Lenin: Zwiegespräch zwischen Hitler und mir* (*Bolshevism from Moses to Lenin: Dialogues Between Hitler and Me*) was published posthumously.[2]

Hans Michael Frank

Hans Frank embraced Catholicism during his childhood. He went on to study law, and rose to become the personal legal advisor to Hitler. When Hitler became Chancellor in 1933 he appointed Frank Minister of Justice in Bavaria.

In 1929 Hitler appointed Frank director of the headquarter's legal department of the Nazi Party. He won an election to the Reichstag (German parliament) as a National Socialist representative in 1930. In 1931 Hitler designating him as a Reichsleiter (high Party official). By 1933, when the National Socialists came to power, Frank was a leading protagonist of the New Order. In 1939 Hitler made him president of the German Academy of Law.

Following the invasion of Poland, Frank became the Governor-General of the Generalgouvernement for the occupied Polish territories, that is, those areas of Poland that had not been directly incorporated into Germany. He was given the SS rank of Obergruppenführer and tasked to oversee the segregation of the Jews into ghettos, and the use of Polish civilians as 'forced and compulsory' labour.

Governor Frank published in the *Warschauer Zeitung* an edict ordering compulsory

---

[1] http://www.HolocaustResearchProject.org (2012)
[2] http://en.wikipedia.org/wiki/Dietrich_Eckart (2012)

labour for all Jewish males between the ages of 14 and 60. By the spring of the following year, 437 of these forced-labour camps were in operation. The ultimate aim was to kill the Jews by overwork, physical torture, sickness, and starvation. The death toll was extremely high.[1]

The ghettos, also, were not only used for isolating the Jews, using them as slave labourers, or gathering them for deportation, but they were also places of annihilation. Ghetto dwellers were denied external work opportunities and confined in severely cramped conditions. Starvation, inadequate sanitation, heavy work, and lack of medical care took their toll. 'Typhus, dysentery, and tuberculosis, brought death to many inhabitants. Starvation reached the borderline of death. After the critically meagre ghetto rations were cut in half, Frank said in August 1942 to his officials:

> It must be done in cold blood and without pity; the fact that in this way we condemn 1,200,000 Jews to death by hunger is only of indirect importance. If the Jews should not starve I sincerely hope that it will inspire further anti-Jewish regulations.'[2]

Frank's famous thirty-eight volume diary contains countless passages designed to impress by their brutality.[3]

Frank was found guilty of war crimes and crimes against humanity, and executed in 1946. During his trial he renewed his Catholic faith.[4]

Kurt Hubert Franz

Kurt Franz's mother was an observant Catholic. He was an SS officer and one of the commanders of the Treblinka extermination camp. He became the most feared man at Treblinka for the cruelty that he visited upon the prisoners.

He was one of the major perpetrators of genocide during the Holocaust.

Following the war, Franz was arrested in December 1959. A search of his home found a photo album of the Treblinka horrors with the title 'Beautiful Years'.

At the Treblinka Trials in 1965, he denied ever having killed a person, ever having set his dog on a Jew, and claimed to have only beaten a prisoner once. He was found guilty of the collective murder of at least 300,000 people, 35 counts of murder involving at least 139 people, and for attempted murder. He was sentenced to life imprisonment.[5]

Hans Globke

Dr Hans Globke, the legal advisor of the Minister of the Interior who drafted the *Ermächtigungsgesetz* (*Enabling Act*)[6] in 1933, wrote the commentary to the *Reichsbürgergesetz* (*Reich Citizenship Law*), which became the standard reference of the *Nuremberg Laws* that made German Jews pariahs.

In 1938 Globke, a practising Catholic, a former prominent member of the Catholic

---

[1] Cymet, David. *History vs. Apologetics: The Holocaust, the Third Reich, and the Catholic Church.* p184
[2] Ibid. pp184-85
[3] http://www.holocaustresearchproject.org/ar/frank.html (2012)
[4] http://en.wikipedia.org/wiki/Hans_Frank (2010)
[5] http://en.wikipedia.org/wiki/Kurt_Franz (2012)
[6] See below.

Centre Party, and a close friend and confidant of Cardinal Faulhaber, was responsible for the addition of the names 'Israel' and 'Sara' in the documents of every German Jew and Jewess. He also assisted Himmler in promoting the adoption of anti-Semitic legislation similar to the *Nuremberg Laws* in the various countries allied with Germany.[1]

Odilo Lotario Globocnik

Globocnik was a baptised Catholic.

In November 1939, Himmler appointed him SS and Police Leader in the Lublin district of the Generalgouvernement. In the years that followed, Globocnik was responsible for:

> implementing and supervising the Lublin reservation, to which 95,000 Jews were deported, with its adjacent network of forced labour camps in the Lublin district. He was also in charge of over 45,000 Jewish labourers;

> liquidating the Bialystok Ghetto, which stood out for its strong resistance to German occupation;

> liquidating the Warsaw Ghetto that contained about 500,000 Jews, the largest Jewish community in Europe and the second largest in the world after New York;

> resettling a large number of Poles under the premise of ethnic cleansing.

In October 1941 Globocnik received a verbal order from Himmler to start immediate construction work on Bełżec Extermination Camp, the first labour camp in the Generalgouvernement. The construction of three more camps, Sobibór and Majdanek in the Lublin district, and Treblinka at Małkinia Górna, followed in 1942. Globocnik was complicit in the extermination of more than 1.5 million Polish, Czech, Dutch, French, Russian, Slovak, German, and Austrian Jews and non-Jews in the death camps that he organised and supervised.[2]

Globocnik was also put in charge of plundering the wealth of the victims. Aktion Reinhard was a financial windfall for the Nazis in general and Globocnik in particular – the Reinhard camps netted nearly 180 million Reichsmarks.

In 1943 Globocnik was put in charge of the Trawniki Concentration Camp, where SS guards were trained and where Aktion Erntefest[3] took the lives of 10,000 Jews. Before finally leaving the Generalgouvernement, Globocnik was instrumental in the liquidations of the ghettoes in Białystok and Warsaw.[4]

Globocnik was captured in May 1945. He committed suicide – a major Catholic sin.

Paul Joseph Goebbels

Goebbels was German Minister for Public Enlightenment and Propaganda during

---

[1] Cymet, David. *History vs. Apologetics: The Holocaust, the Third Reich, and the Catholic Church.* pp82-83

[2] http://en.wikipedia.org/wiki/Odilo_Globocnik (2012)

[3] Aktion Erntefest (Operation Harvest Festival) was a programme of concentrated large scale mass executions to liquidate all Jews in the remaining work camps in the Lublin district of Poland.

[4] http://www.holocaust-history.org/short-essays/globocnik.shtml (2007)

the Nazi regime. He was a baptised Catholic, was brought up in a devoutly Catholic home, and was never excommunicated.

He was one of Hitler's closest associates and most devout followers. He was so close to Hitler that the Führer served as first witness at his Catholic marriage.[1]

In a radio broadcast in 1936, Goebbels said:

> We have a feeling that Germany has been transformed into a great house of God, including all classes, professions and creeds, where the Führer as our mediator stood before the throne of the Almighty.[2]

Goebbels was known for his zealous, energetic oratory and virulent anti-Semitism.[3] He stated:

> A Jew is for me an object of disgust. I feel like vomiting when I see one. Christ could not possibly have been a Jew. It is not necessary to prove that scientifically – it is a fact.[4]

He was responsible for the 'Kristallnacht' pogrom.[5]

On 12 December 1941, Goebbels noted in his diary: 'As concerns the Jewish question, [Hitler] is determined to make a clean sweep. He had prophesied to the Jews that if they once again brought about a world war they would experience their own extermination. This was not just an empty phrase. The World War is there, the extermination of Jewry must be the necessary consequence.'

Goebbels committed suicide on 1 May 1945.

Juan Carlos Goyeneche

The Argentinian Nationalist leader Juan Goyeneche went to Europe to organise a conference of pro-Axis Catholic delegates from Vichy France, Hungary, Romania, Slovenia, Italy, Spain and Portugal, who met in Rome 'to integrate the Christian order in the New Order'. After the War, he told American interrogators that the sole purpose of his trip was to 'reconcile Hitlerism with Catholicism'.[6]

Reinhard Tristan Eugen Heydrich

Reinhard Heydrich was born and baptised a Catholic.

He was one of the main architects of the Holocaust, and was the founding head of the Sicherheitsdienst (SD), an intelligence organisation charged with seeking out and neutralising resistance to the Nazi Party through arrests, deportations, and murders.

The Gestapo (Geheime Staatspolizei) was the official secret police of Nazi Germany, and was under the overall administration of the SS. The Einsatzgruppen were formed under the direction of SS-Obergruppenführer Reinhard Heydrich.

---

[1] Source: http://liberalslikechrist.org/Catholic/HitlersFaith.html (2007)
[2] http://www.jews-for-allah.org/messianic-jews/christianhistorywithjews/henchmen.htm (2007)
[3] http://en.wikipedia.org/wiki/Joseph_Goebbels (2007)
[4] http://www.liberalslikechrist.org/Catholic/NaziLeadership.html (2007)
[5] Ibid.
[6] Goñi, Uki. *The Real ODESSA: How Perón Brought the Nazi War Criminals to Argentina.* p14

As SS General in the Nazi organisation Heydrich was the chief of the:

Reich Security Main Office (Reichssicherheitshauptamt; RSHA);

Security Service of the Reichsführer-SS (Sicherheitsdienst; SD) from 1931 until 1942;

German Secret State Police (Gestapo) from 1934 to 1936;

German Security Police (Sicherheitspolizei; SiPo), which consisted of the Gestapo and the criminal police detective forces (Kriminalpolizei; Kripo), from 1936 until 1942.

After September 1939, the Security Police and SD were formally unified under Heydrich's command in the RSHA. The RSHA was the agency most directly concerned with implementing 'the Final Solution'.[1]

In 1941 Heydrich signed *Polizeiverordnung über die Kennzeichnung der Juden (Police Regulation in Regard to the Marking of Jews)*.[2] On 20 January 1942, a meeting of high-ranking Nazi officials was convened, known as the Wannsee Conference. Heydrich told the conference that Jews unfit for work were to be killed and that any Jews who survived forced labour were also to be killed. The Wannsee Conference was particularly important because it was there that the participants were instructed to co-ordinate efforts for the liquidation of the Jews.

Heydrich died in 1942, aged 38, of sepsis from wounds received in an ambush by two Czech ex-patriots.

Heinrich Luitpold Himmler

Himmler was one of the most powerful men in Nazi Germany, being second only to Hitler. He was one of the persons most directly responsible for the Holocaust.

He purposely constructed the black-clad Nazi SS on Jesuit principles by carefully copying the service statutes and spiritual exercises introduced by Íñigo Oñaz López de Loyola (Ignatius Loyola),[3] the founder of the infamous Jesuit Order.[4] Adolf Hitler said of Himmler having modelled the SS on the Jesuit Order:

I can see Himmler as our Ignatius of Loyola.

As Reichsführer-SS he controlled both the SS and the Gestapo. In 1941 Himmler issued an order to SS units preparing to comb the Pripet Marshes in Belarus: 'All male Jews must be shot. Drive the female Jews into the swamp.'

As founder and officer-in-charge of the Nazi concentration camps and the Einsatz-gruppen death squads, Himmler held final command responsibility for the annihilation

---

[1] http://www.ushmm.org/wlc/article.php?lang=en&ModuleId=10007406 (2007)

[2] *Adolf Eichmann: The Travelling Salesman of Genocide.* Source: http://www.pep-web.org/document.php?id=irp.003.0111a (2007)

[3] The very dark Ignatius appears in several places in this book. He has been named one of the 25 most evil people of all time (http://one-evil.org/content/people_16c_loyola.html (2013))

[4] Toland, John. *Adolf Hitler.* Vol 2. p869. Source: http://www.mosquitonet.com/~prewett/ hag1016.html (2010)

of millions who were deemed unworthy to live. He has been described as 'a man often seen as the very personification of evil'.[1]

Himmler was the son of pious Catholic parents, he was baptised and brought up a Catholic, attended mass regularly, and was never excommunicated. In his diaries he claimed to be a devout Catholic, and wrote that he would never turn away from the Church.[2] He declared that:

> By and large ... we have performed this task in love of our people, and we have suffered no damage from it, in our inner self, in our soul, in our character.[3]

> True wars, wars between races, are merciless and fought to the last man, until one side or the other is eliminated without trace.

In a speech to the SS guards Himmler stated: 'Man must defend himself against bedbugs and rats – against vermin.'

Rudolf Franz Ferdinand Höss (Hoess)

Rudolf Höss has been described as one of history's greatest mass murderers, being responsible for exterminating 2.5 million people.

He was the architect and SS Commandant of the death camp at Auschwitz-Birkenau (Oświęcim), the largest killing centre ever created, and the site where more people were murdered than any other in recorded human history. He testified during the War Crimes Trials after the War that at peak efficiency Auschwitz had the capacity to 'get rid of ten thousand people in 24 hours.' He had a view of the crematoria chimneys from his bed-room window.

He was brought up in a rigorous Catholic tradition. In his youth, his pious Catholic parents often took him on pilgrimages to Lourdes and Einsiedeln. His father took a religious oath dedicating him to God and the priesthood. When asked if his father ever beat him, Höss replied that he was only punished by prayer.[4]

Höss was captured in March 1946.

In his Nuremberg cell, Höss told psychologist G M Gilbert how he was brought up in a rigorous Catholic tradition:

> My father was really a bigot. He was very strict and fanatical. I learned that my father took a religious oath at the time of the birth of my younger sister, dedicating me to God and the priesthood, and after that leading a Joseph married life. He direct-ed my entire youthful education toward the goal of making me a priest.[5]

Höss' affidavit at Nuremberg on 5 April 1946 reads:

> I commanded Auschwitz until 1 December 1943, and estimate that at least 2,500,000 victims were executed and exterminated there by gassing and burning,

---

[1] http://www.auschwitz.dk/Himmler.htm (2012)

[2] http://en.wikipedia.org/wiki/Heinrich_Himmler (2007)

[3] Cohn-Sherbok, D. *The Crucified Jew: Twenty Centuries of Christian Anti-Semitism.* pp208-9

[4] http://www.liberalslikechrist.org/Catholic/NaziLeadership.html (2007)

[5] Snyder, Louis Leo. *Hitler's Elite: Shocking Profiles of the Reich's Most Notorious Henchmen*

and at least another half million succumbed to starvation and disease, making a total dead of about 3,000,000. This figure represents about 70% or 80% of all persons sent to Auschwitz as prisoners, the remainder having been selected and used for slave labour in the concentration camp industries. Included among the executed and burnt were approximately 20,000 Russian prisoners of war who were delivered at Auschwitz in Wehrmacht transports operated by regular Wehrmacht officers and men. The remainder of the total number of victims included about 100,000 German Jews, and great numbers of citizens (mostly Jewish) from Holland, France, Belgium, Poland, Hungary, Czechoslovakia, Greece, or other countries. We executed about 400,000 Hungarian Jews alone at Auschwitz in the summer of 1944.[1]

Höss was hanged at Auschwitz-Birkenau on 16 April 1947.

Ernst Kaltenbrunner

Ernst Kaltenbrunner was a Catholic Nazi official who rose through the ranks to become General of the Waffen-SS. He was responsible for heading Operation Long Jump, the attempt to assassinate Stalin, Churchill and Roosevelt.

At the Nuremberg Trials, Kaltenbrunner was found guilty of war crimes and crimes against humanity, and was executed.

Heinrich Müller (Mueller)

Heinrich Müller (aka 'Gestapo Müller') was born in Munich, the son of working-class Catholic parents.[2] He joined the Bavarian police in 1919, and was involved in the suppression of the communist risings in the early post-war years. Duty and discipline were paramount for him, and he was determined to serve the German state, irrespective of what political form it took. He was an able organiser, utterly ruthless, and lived for his work.

He joined the SS in 1934 and quickly rose through its ranks – by 1939 he was a Gruppenführer (general). When the Gestapo and other police organisations were consolidated into the Reich Main Security Office (RSHA), Müller was made chief of the RSHA 'Office 4', the Gestapo. As Gestapo chief, Müller was involved in the regime's policy towards the Jews.[3]

According to Robert Wistrich, in his book *Who's Who in Nazi Germany*, Müller had a central role in the extermination of European Jewry. For him, mass murder became an automatic administrative procedure.[4]

His fate after the War is not known.

Benito Mussolini

Mussolini was raised by a devoutly Catholic mother. She had him baptised into the

[1] http://en.wikipedia.org/wiki/Rudolf_Franz_Ferdinand_H%C3%B6ss (2012)
[2] Makow, Henry. *Hitler's Gestapo Chief became Top Truman Advisor.* http://educate-yourself.org/cn/makow gestapochiefandtruman20aug06.shtml (2007)
[3] http://en.wikipedia.org/wiki/Heinrich_Müller (2007)
[4] Wistrich, Robert S. *Who's Who in Nazi Germany.* p174

Catholic Church and took him to services every Sunday. Later, he declared himself to be an atheist. He became the dictator of Italy, who, nonetheless, in the 1920s enacted a law stating that all courtrooms and schools in Italy must display the Christian Cross, and who created the fascist environment later adopted by the Nazis. In 1929 Mussolini signed a concordat with the Holy See whereby the Catholic Church officially endorsed the fascist regime. Both Italy and Germany became allies during World War II, and their leaders regularly met Pius XII.

Henri Philippe Pétain

After the German defeat of France in 1940, the town of Vichy was made the seat of the quisling French government under military and political leader Marshal Pétain and his aide Pierre Laval. Vichy was a personal government that revolved around Pétain.

Pétain was brought up in the Catholic faith, and consequently the national revolution that he intended to lead emphasised traditional Catholic values, such as religion and the importance of the family. Consequently, divorce was made more difficult, abortion was severely repressed, and the parents of large families were decorated with state honours.[1]

Kobert Sencourt, Special Diplomatic correspondent of the *Catholic Herald*[2] praised Pétain:

> When Paris fell, the Nazis may well have thought that they saw the final ruin of a country which had been laid low by three mortal diseases: freemasonry, demo-plutocracy and Bolshevism ... The new men who form the present French Government have always sought a reasonable, dignified and honest understanding with both Franco and Mussolini. A new France could be a true friend to Italy and Spain ... At any rate, this much is clear: all that is vital in the soul of France, purified and glorified in heroic suffering can look out once more on Europe with a clear Christian purpose.[3]

Pétain signed Vichy's first *Statut des Juifs* (Statute on the Jews), under which Jews were banned from teaching, journalism, radio, film, theatre, and the civil service, to prevent them from influencing the French people. This was followed by a second decree for which Pétain, 'as a loyal Catholic, sought the approval of the Holy See.'[4] The *Statuts* were widely accepted in Catholic circles.[5]

The reply from the Holy See to Pétain's enquiry 'is one of the most explicit and important documents that throws light on Vatican policy during World War II.' The text of the extensive answer informed Pétain that Pius XII's Holy See found no objections to the legislation from a doctrinal viewpoint. Referring to historical precedent, it found that 'appropriate measures be taken to limit the action of the Jews and to restrict their influence.' Even the requirement to wear the yellow star was well established in

---

[1] *Encarta Encyclopedia* 'Vichy Government'
[2] The *Catholic Herald* is a London-based Roman Catholic newspaper.
[3] Moore, Edith. *No Friend of Democracy: A study of Roman Catholic politics – their influence on the ...*
[4] Cymet, David. *History vs. Apologetics: The Holocaust, the Third Reich, and the Catholic Church.* p345
[5] Michael, Robert. *A History of Catholic Antisemitism: The Dark Side of the Church.* p140

ecclesiastical law. No conflict, censure, or objections to the *Statut des Juifs* came from the Church.[1,2] Specifically, the Holy See stated:

> In principle, there is nothing in these measures which the Holy See would find to criticise.[3] The Holy Father [Pius XII] does not disapprove of the recent anti-Jewish measures.[4]

Pétain told the Ecuadorian ambassador in Vichy that he was at peace, because the Pope approved his policy of deporting Jews.[5]

The *Statuts* permitted the préfets of provincial France to collect all foreign Jews and place them in internment/deportation camps or to impose forced labour on them. This made life perilous for Jews everywhere. Later General Huntziger removed all Jews from the army.[6]

Internment camps were established in Les Milles and Le Vernet, Rivesaltes and St Cyprien, Compiègne, Pithiviers, Beaune-la-Rolande, Gurs, and Drancy.

Drancy Internment camp was the infamous temporary prison camp in the city of Drancy, north of Paris, which was used to hold Jews, homosexuals, and other 'undesirables', who were later deported to the Nazi extermination camps. 65,000 Jews were deported from Drancy – of these, 63,000 were murdered, including 6000 children.

Throughout the German Occupation, the French Catholic Church provided indispensable support for Pétain and Vichy.[7] Pétain obtained this support immediately and without restrictions. In February 1944, Cardinal Gerlier confirmed: 'Pétain is France, and France is Pétain!'

The French Press was also supportive:

> *La Croix*: 'The teachings of the Head of State are similar to those of the Sovereign Pontiff.'

> The brochure *Frenchmen! Your Bishops address You*: 'In the social and civic domain we profess complete loyalty to the power established by the Government of France, and we urge our faithful to enter into this spirit.'[8]

In return for the Church's favours, Pétain gave extensive concessions to the Church. From the very beginning, Pétain, in concert with the Church, attacked the laïcité[9] of the school and that of the State. His industrial measures conformed closely with both papal encyclicals and Catholic-Fascist ideology. Extraordinary legislative measures were

---

[1] Cymet, David. *History vs. Apologetics: The Holocaust, the Third Reich, and the Catholic Church.* pp345-46
[2] Michael, Robert. *A History of Catholic Antisemitism: The Dark Side of the Church.* p140
[3] Cohn-Sherbok, D. *The Crucified Jew: Twenty Centuries of Christian Anti-Semitism.* pp208-9
[4] Callil, Carmen. *Bad Faith: A Forgotten History of Family & Fatherland.* pp238-40
[5] Cymet, David. *History vs. Apologetics: The Holocaust, the Third Reich, and the Catholic Church.* pp345-46
[6] Callil, Carmen. *Bad Faith: A Forgotten History of Family & Fatherland.* p225
[7] See, for example: Ibid. pp238-40
[8] http://www.concordatwatch.eu/showkb.php?kb_id=1527 (2014)
[9] The conception of laïcité is based on the respect of freedom of thought and of freedom of religion. Thus, the absence of a state religion and the subsequent separation of the state and Church is considered a prerequisite of such freedom of thought.

introduced between 1940 and 1944, and their essence is still maintained on the statute books. The intentions of the 1905 law have been subverted as follows:

1940: Cardinals wrote to Pétain to reintroduce teaching of religion in Public Schools.

1940: The prestigious Écoles Normales,[1] established in 1794 after the French Revolution, were abolished.

1940: The French state decided that 'Duties towards God' should be taught in Public Schools.

1941: The optional teaching of religion was introduced in Public Schools.

1941: Religious buildings were restored to the Church by the Pétain regime, thereby undoing the work of the Third Republic and the provisions of the 1905 law.

1941: The archbishops wrote to Pétain, seeking a new concordat with the Holy See.

1941: A law was promulgated, allowing private Catholic schools to be subsidised by public funds. Later, public (state) school budgets were allowed to finance private schools.

1942: The July 1904 law on Congregations was abrogated and they were allowed back. Even after the Liberation of France, the 1904 law remained abrogated.

1942: Catholic cultural associations were accorded civil and testamentary rights. The 1905 law prohibited prelates from visiting and extracting donations from dying persons – this constraint was removed.

1943: A law rendered communes responsible for the maintenance costs of churches.[2]

Oswald Pohl

Oswald Pohl was a Catholic who became a Nazi official and SS-Obergruppenführer in charge of the SS-Wirtschafts-Verwaltungshauptamt (SS-WVHA) ('SS main bureau for economic administration'). Among other things, the SS-WVHA was responsible for the organisation of the concentration camps, deciding on the distribution of detainees to the various camps and the 'rental' of detainees for slave labour.

Captured in 1946, Pohl was sentenced to death by an American military tribunal after the Nuremberg Trials for crimes against humanity, war crimes and membership in a criminal organisation, as well as for mass murders and crimes committed in the concentration camps administered by the SS-WVHA.

---

[1] École Normale Supérieure – a French institution of higher education, founded 'to give the Nation teachers of quality'.
[2] Marshal Pétain's marriage of convenience with the Church. http://www.concordatwatch.eu/showkb.php?org_id=867&kb_header_id=850&kb_id=1527&order=kb_rank%20ASC (2007)

When it 'suited him best' during the trials, Pohl started to see a Catholic priest again. In 1950 his book *Credo. Mein Weg zu Gott* (*Credo. My way to God*) was published with permission from the Catholic Church, which Pohl had re-joined.[1]

Pohl was hanged in 1951.

Arthur Seyss-Inquart

Arthur Seyss-Inquart was a Chancellor of Austria, lawyer, and later Nazi official in pre-Anschluss Austria, the Third Reich, and for wartime Germany in Poland and the Netherlands. He drafted the legislative act reducing Austria to a province of Germany and signed it into law.

Following the capitulation of the Low Countries, Seyss-Inquart was appointed Reichskommissar for the Occupied Netherlands. He was an unwavering anti-Semite. Within a few months of his arrival in the Netherlands, he took measures to remove Jews from the government, the press and leading positions in industry. Anti-Jewish measures intensified after 1941: approximately 140,000 Jews were registered, a ghetto was created in Amsterdam, and a transit camp was set up at Westerbork. Subsequently, 600 Jews were sent to Buchenwald and Mauthausen Concentration Camps. Later, the Dutch Jews were sent to Auschwitz. As Allied forces approached in September 1944, the remaining Jews at Westerbork were removed to Theresienstadt. Of 140,000 registered, only 30,000 Dutch Jews survived the war.

At the Nuremberg Trials, Seyss-Inquart was found guilty of planning, initiating and waging wars of aggression; war crimes; and crimes against humanity. He was sentenced to death. Before his execution, Seyss-Inquart, having returned to Catholicism, received absolution in the Sacrament of Confession from prison chaplain Fr Bruno Spitzl.[2]

Franz Paul Stangl

Franz Stangl was raised a Catholic. He became known as 'The White Death'.

After the Anschluss, he was quickly promoted through the ranks, and in 1940, through a direct order from Himmler, Stangl became superintendent of the 'T4 Euthanasia Programme' at the Euthanasia Institute at Schloss Hartheim, where between 75,000 and 250,000 mentally and physically handicapped people were sent to be killed.

In 1942 Stangl was transferred to Poland where he became Commandant of the Sobibór camp. He was told by the former Commandant, Globocnik, that if the Jews 'were not working hard enough' he was fully permitted to kill them; and he, Globocnik, would send replacements. While Stangl was the administrator, around 100,000 Jews are believed to have been killed there. Later that year, Stangl began his role at Treblinka.

In her book *Into That Darkness*, Gitta Sereny quotes Stangl:

> The killings were organized systematically to achieve the maximum humiliation and dehumanization of the victims before they died. This pattern was dictated by a

---

[1] http://en.wikipedia.org/wiki/Oswald_Pohl (2012)
[2] http://en.wikipedia.org/wiki/Arthur_Seyss-Inquart (2012)

distinct and careful purpose, not by 'mere' cruelty or indifference – the crammed airless freight trains without sanitary provisions, food or drink, far worse than any cattle transport; the whipped-up (literally so) hysteria of arrival; the immediate and always violent separation of men, women and children; the public undressing; the incredibly crude internal physical examinations for hidden valuables; the hair cutting and shaving of the women; and finally the naked run to the gas chambers, under the lash of the whips.[1]

During his time at Treblinka, Stangl conceded that he grew accustomed to the killings – even eventually regarding the Jewish prisoners as 'baggage'. He is quoted as saying, 'I remember Wirth[2] standing there, next to the pits full of black-blue corpses ... Wirth said "what shall we do with this garbage?".'[3]

After the War, Stangl was handed over to the Austrians and transferred to an open, civilian prison in Linz in connection with his involvement in the Euthanasia programme at Schloss Hartheim. There, he simply walked out of the prison with his ex-colleague at Sobibór death camp, Gustav Wagner, and managed to escape to Italy with the help of Bishop Hudal and his Vatican 'Ratline' network.[4] Thence he escaped via Rome on a Red Cross passport with an entrance visa for Syria. In 1948 he arrived in Damascus.

Eventually tracked down by Nazi-hunter Simon Wiesenthal, Stangl was arrested in Brazil in 1967. After extradition to West Germany he was tried for co-responsibility in the mass murder of 900,000 Jews at Treblinka and sentenced to life imprisonment.

He died of heart failure in Dusseldorf prison on 28 June 1971.[5]

Julius Streicher

Julius Streicher was the product of a very devout Bavarian Catholic family. He was one of the earliest members of the Nazi party, and was one of Hitler's most loyal supporters. He was editor (1923-1945) of *Der Stürmer* (*The Stormer*), a Nazi newspaper notorious for its fanatical anti-Semitism. In his grotesque attacks on Jews, Streicher claimed the discovery that 'Christ was not a Jew but an Aryan.' His solutions to the Jewish problem: 'If the danger of the reproduction of that curse of God in the Jewish blood is finally to come to an end, then there is only one way – the extermination of that people whose father is the devil ...',[6] and 'Germans must fight Jews, that organised body of world criminals against whom Christ, the greatest anti-Semite of all time, had fought.'[7] When Hitler became chancellor in 1933, he appointed Streicher as Gauleiter (district leader) for Franconia.[8]

---

[1] Quoted in: Cymet, David. *History vs. Apologetics: The Holocaust, the Third Reich, and the* ... pp266-67
[2] Christian Wirth was a senior SS officer during the programme of extermination of the Jews of Poland known as Operation Reinhard.
[3] http://en.wikipedia.org/wiki/Franz_Stangl (2007)
[4] For details of the Vatican's 'ratlines' refer to Chapter 23 – Catholic Assistance to War Criminals.
[5] http://www.holocaustresearchproject.org/ar/stangl.html (2012)
[6] Paraphrasing *John* 8:44 as his justification for Jewish extermination. *Trial of The Major War Criminals before the International Military Tribunal.* Vol 12
[7] http://www.liberalslikechrist.org/Catholic/NaziLeadership.html (2007)
[8] Franconia (German: Franken) – a duchy in mediaeval Germany. The territory comprising the old Franconia

Like the Church, Streicher fully believed allegations that the Jews murdered non-Jews in order to obtain blood for the feast of Passover, that Jews were of the Devil, and that Jews hated Christianity and mankind in general. His highly visible placards indoctrinated the Germans everywhere:

Ohne Lösung der Judenfrage keine Erlösung des deutschen Volkes! (Without a solution of the Jewish question there is no salvation for the German people!)

Streicher was found guilty of crimes against humanity at the Nuremberg War Crimes Trial and sentenced to death on 1 October 1946. The judgment against him read:

For his 25 years of speaking, writing and preaching hatred of the Jews, Streicher was widely known as 'Jew-Baiter Number One.' In his speeches and articles, week after week, month after month, he infected the German mind with the virus of anti-Semitism, and incited the German people to active persecution ... Streicher's incitement to murder and extermination at the time when Jews in the East were being killed under the most horrible conditions clearly constitutes persecution on political and racial grounds in connection with war crimes, as defined by the Charter, and constitutes a crime against humanity.'[1]

Paul Touvier

Paul Touvier was a Nazi collaborator. He was the first Frenchman convicted of crimes against humanity for his actions in Vichy France.

His family was devoutly Catholic – his mother was raised by nuns, was very religious, and went to mass every day. His father was also piously Catholic. Paul was an altar boy and spent one year in a seminary, intending to become a priest. He graduated from the Institut Saint-François de Sales in Chambéry at the age of sixteen.

The 'Milice française' ('French Militia') was a paramilitary force created in 1943 by the Vichy Regime, with German aid, to help fight the French Resistance. It participated in summary executions, assassinations, and helped round up the Jews and résistants in France for deportation. Touvier joined the Milice, and was eventually appointed head of its intelligence department in Chambéry, under the direction of Klaus Barbie. In January 1944 he became second regional head.

In September 1946 Touvier was sentenced to death in absentia for treason and collusion with the Nazis. In May 1989, he was arrested at the Society of Saint Pius X Priory in Nice. The Society stated at the time that: Touvier had been allowed to live in the Priory as 'an act of charity to a homeless man.'[2]

After his arrest, further allegations appeared in print, stating that he had been aided by the Church for years – being hidden in convents and monasteries[3] by the Catholic hierarchy in Lyon and later by members of the Traditionalist Catholic movement.

---

is now included in the German states of Baden-Württemberg, Hesse, and Bavaria.

[1] http://en.wikipedia.org/wiki/Julius_Streicher (2010)
[2] http://en.wikipedia.org/wiki/Paul_Touvier (2011)
[3] Callil, Carmen. *Bad Faith: A Forgotten History of Family & Fatherland.* p435

In 1994 Touvier was defended in court by the lawyer Jacques Tremollet de Villers, who later became president of the Traditionalist Catholic[1] organisation La Cité Catholique. A Traditionalist Catholic priest of the Society of Saint Pius X sat beside him at the defence table. On 20 April, Touvier was found guilty and was sentenced to life imprisonment.[2] He died in 1996 in prison. A Tridentine Requiem Mass was offered for the repose of his soul by Fr Philippe Laguérie at St Nicolas du Chardonnet in Paris.[3]

Eduard Wirths

Eduard Wirths was born in Bavaria to a Catholic family. He became an ardent Nazi while studying medicine at the University of Würzburg. He joined the Nazi Party and the SA in June 1933 and applied for admission into the SS in 1934. He entered the Waffen SS in 1939. He was the Chief SS doctor (SS-Standortarzt) at the Auschwitz Concentration Camp. Thus Wirths had formal responsibility for everything undertaken by the nearly twenty SS doctors who worked in the medical sections of Auschwitz between 1942 and 1945. He was involved in ordering arbitrary and pseudo-scientific medical experimentation that directly led to prisoner fatalities.

He was captured by the allies, and while awaiting trial, committed suicide.[4]

Karl Friedrich Otto Wolff

Wolff was educated at a Catholic school. He rose to the rank of SS-Obergruppenführer, and became General of the Waffen-SS. He was subsequently indicted for war crimes of genocide, including the deportation of 300,000 Jews to Treblinka. He received an apostolic blessing from Pius XII.

Synopsis

Half the population of Hitler's Greater Reich was Catholic.

A quarter of the members of the Nazi Schutzstaffel (SS) were Catholics.

Most of the major participants in the planning and implementation of the Holocaust were born and bred Catholics.

The main perpetrators of the Final Solution – Hitler, Himmler, Heydrich and Höss – were born into Catholic families, received a strict Catholic education, and *never* severed their connection to the Catholic Church.

---

[1] Traditionalist Catholics are Roman Catholics who believe that there should be a restoration of many or all of the liturgical forms, public and private devotions and presentations of Roman Catholic teachings that prevailed in the Church before the Second Vatican Council (1962–65). They are most commonly associated with an attachment to the Mass liturgy in general use in that time period, often called the Tridentine Mass.
[2] http://en.wikipedia.org/wiki/Paul_Touvier (2011)
[3] Ibid.
[4] http://en.wikipedia.org/wiki/Eduard_Wirths (2012). Currently: 'What the Church teaches is that anyone who commits a mortal sin and does not repent before death goes to hell … Only someone who freely chooses to commit suicide with full knowledge of the gravity of the sinfulness would commit mortal sin by his suicide.'

18 – Hitler's Catholic Partners, European Fascist Dictators

I have always thought the actions of men the best interpreters of their thoughts. John Locke

Born and Bred Catholics

Most of the major participants in the planning and implementation of the Holocaust were born and bred Catholics. For example:

Klaus Barbie – 'the Butcher of Lyon'.

Alois Brunner – responsible for sending some 140,000 European Jews to the gas chambers.

Odilo Globocnik – in charge of the administration of all three Operation Reinhard camps where 1.7 million people were liquidated.

Joseph Goebbels – a Jesuit, known for his virulent anti-Semitism. 'A Jew is for me an object of disgust. I feel like vomiting when I see one.'

Reinhard Heydrich – 'the Butcher of Prague'. Chief of the Reich Security Main Office – the agency most directly concerned with implementing 'the Final Solution'.

Heinrich Himmler –'a man often seen as the very personification of evil.'

Rudolf Höss (Hoess) – one of history's greatest mass murderers.

Heinrich Müller – utterly ruthless.

Franz Stangl – 'Commandant of Sobibór. At least 250,000 people were killed there.

Julius Streicher – His solutions to the Jewish problem was: 'the extermination of that people whose father is the devil ...'

Karl Friedrich Otto Wolff – indicted for war crimes of genocide.

The Society of Jesus (Jesuits) was a model for Hitler's Nazi organisation and particularly for the SS.

Hitler's Catholic Anti-Semitic Partners

Hitler's entire political career was based on his original notion of cementing his political and military alliances by means of anti-Semitism. Even in 1922, Hitler, 'paraphrasing Marx's call to the workers of the world to unite against their exploiters, called all the anti-Semites and Aryans from the world to unite against the Jewish race.'[1]

For example, in 1939 František Chvalkovský, the Czech Foreign Minister, was greatly impressed to learn from Hitler himself that anti-Semitism was the adhesive that held together his international alliances:

---

[1] Cymet, David. *History vs. Apologetics: The Holocaust, the Third Reich, and the Catholic Church.* p147

What appears to have most impressed him [Chvalkovský] was the importance that Herr Hitler and Herr von Ribbentrop attached to the Jewish Question – absolutely out of proportion to the importance assigned to other questions dealt with.

Germany will seek to form a bloc of anti-Semitic states, for she could not adopt a friendly attitude towards states in which the Jews either by their economic activity or as result of their high positions could exercise any kind of influence.[1]

Hitler also used anti-Semitism as a means to internally weaken the resistance of the countries he wished to conquer or control. He used it to create a fifth column within them to subvert their strength by attacking and destroying their Jews.

He had no trouble looking for partners. 'The soil of Christian Europe had been well prepared in modern times by the Catholic press and politicians all over Europe and Hitler saw the opportunity to harvest the hatred they had so diligently sown to create his bloc of anti-Semitic states.'[2]

The clerico-fascist[3] parties of Europe were willing and ready to join Hitler in a coordinated attack on the Jews: the Rexists in Belgium, Ante Pavelić's Ustaša in Croatia, the Laval collaborationists in France, the Arrow Cross in Hungary, Mussolini's fascists in Italy, and Monsignor Jozef Tiso's Hlinka Party in Slovakia, all combined their clericalism and Fascism with rabid anti-Semitism.

Thus, in his negotiations with the heads of these states, Hitler found a commonality in anti-Semitism. These men often pre-empted Hitler and 'proudly displayed what they had already achieved in this respect on their own in their countries.'[4]

The anti-Semitic campaign in the Catholic press of European fascist Christian countries was not only concerned with defamation, but was aimed at promoting anti-Jewish legislation during the late 1930s. This legislation intended stripping the civic and political rights of Jews that had existed for many centuries in Catholic countries before emancipation.

'The Catholic clergy and Catholic political parties were among the most vocal and politically active promoters of these infamous laws, which prepared the public for the Final Solution of the Jewish Question that the Nazis were preparing to carry out.' They were active participants and promoters in the adoption of anti-Semitic laws.[5]

In his work *Moral Purity and Persecution in History*, Barrington Moore, Jr found that the reason why humans kill and torture each other is because they see 'them' ('the

---

[1] Dwork, Deborah and Robert Jan Van Pelt. *Holocaust: A History.* pp140-41. Quoted in: Cymet, David. *History vs. Apologetics: The Holocaust, the Third Reich, and the Catholic Church.* p147

[2] Cymet, David. *History vs. Apologetics: The Holocaust, the Third Reich, and the Catholic Church.* p148

[3] Clerico-fascism is distinguishable from pure Fascism. In a purely Fascist state the clergy exist separately from the fascist political party. In clerico-fascism the clergy are more or less identical with a fascist element.

[4] Cymet, David. *History vs. Apologetics: The Holocaust, the Third Reich, and the Catholic Church.* p148

[5] Cymet, David. *History vs. Apologetics: The Holocaust, the Third Reich, and the Catholic Church.*

other') as polluting, due to their impure religious, political or economic ideas.[1] Consequently, the prior, long-term promotion of anti-Semitism by the Church enabled the promulgation of the anti-Jewish laws that placed the Jews beyond humanity in the eyes of society.[2] 'They conditioned the public to view the crimes against Jews as legal, normal, and acceptable.' Accordingly, when the Jews were finally deported to an unknown destiny in the east, a conditioned, morally-immunised population, 'expecting short-term and long-term windfalls from the elimination of the Jews, greeted their disappearance with delight.'[3]

David Cymet has confirmed that the clerico-fascist governments consulted both their own Church authorities and the Holy See regarding these laws. The ecclesiastic moral sanction was needed to justify their actions before their people. 'Canonical law specialists in the Vatican responded approvingly. They did not find Nazi persecution of the Jews radically different from historical precedent in canon law and took a tolerant view toward their evil actions.'[4,5]

As a consequence, both the Church and Nazi Germany agreed on the fundamental principle of placing Jews outside society. The Church welcomed the laws as 'a defense of Christian society against Jewish influence in the religious, cultural, social and economic spheres.' 'They became part of the process that culminated in the gas chambers and killing fields of Eastern Europe.'

The anti-Semitic legislation that the Church supported and promoted was the crucial preparation for the Final Solution. The adoption of this vicious legislation 'stands out as a heinous crime against a defenseless people according to any standard of justice and morality.'[6]

In 1933, after becoming Chancellor of Germany, Adolf Hitler informed Bishop Berning of Osnabrück that he was going to eliminate the Jews, which was exactly what the Church had been trying to do for 1500 years.[7] He assured a group of bishops that he had been 'attacked for my way of dealing with the Jewish question. For 1500 years the Church has considered the Jews to be harmful, exiling them to the ghetto ... I am furnishing Christianity with the greatest service.'[8]

Religious Affiliations of the European Nazi and Fascist Dictators, Puppets, and Quislings

- Most European Nazi and fascist dictators, puppets, and quislings were Catholics.

[1] Moore, Barrington Jr. *Moral Purity and Persecution in History.* dust cover
[2] This demonisation of 'the other' is examined in various places within this encyclopaedia.
[3] Cymet, David. *History vs. Apologetics: The Holocaust, the Third Reich, and the Catholic Church.* p148
[4] Ibid.
[5] Particularly so, Pius XII. Refer to Stockwell, Antony. *Pius XII: The Dark Side* for further details.
[6] Cymet, David. *History vs. Apologetics: The Holocaust, the Third Reich, and the Catholic Church.* p149
[7] Phayer, Michael. *The Catholic Church and the Holocaust, 1930-1965.* p17
[8] Kertzer, David I. *The Pope and Mussolini: The Secret History of Pius XI and the Rise of Fascism in Europe.* p208

Table 9. Religious Affiliations of the European Nazi and Fascist Dictators, Puppets and Quislings

Léon M Degrelle	Belgian Rexist Leader	Catholic
Francisco Franco	Spanish Caudillo[1]	Catholic
Konrad Henlein	'Quisling' of Sudetenland	Catholic
Adolf Hitler	Nazi Führer	Catholic
Pierre Laval	Vichy Chief of Government	Catholic
Anton A Mussert	'Quisling' of Occupied Holland	Protestant
Benito Mussolini	Italian Duce	See footnote[2]
Milan Nedić	Prime Minister of Serbia	Orthodox
Ante Pavelić	Croatian Poglavnik (Headman)	Catholic
Henri P Pétain	Vichy Chief of State	Catholic
Vidkun Quisling	Premier of Occupied Norway	Protestant
Antonio Salazar	Portuguese Dictator	Catholic
Ferenc Szálasi	Hungarian Head of State & Prime Minister	Catholic
Jozef Tiso	Slovakian Chief of State	Catholic
Vojtech Tuka	Prime Minister of Slovakia	Catholic
Milovan Žanić	President of Croatian Legislative Council	Catholic[3]

A Comparison between the Anti-Jewish Measures of the Church and Those of the Nazis

The *Nuremberg Laws* (*Nürnberger Gesetze*) of 1935 comprised anti-Jewish legislation that was introduced by the Nazi Party at the annual Nuremberg Rally, and proclaimed at a special session of the Reichstag in Nuremberg.

The first, *Reich Citizenship Law*, stated that only Germans or people with related blood could be citizens of the Reich. German Jews lost their political rights and became Staatsangehörige (state subjects), while Aryan Germans were Reichsbürger (citizens of the Reich).

---

[1] As head of state, Franco used the title 'Caudillo de España, por la gracia de Dios', meaning 'Leader of Spain, by the grace of God'.

[2] Mussolini was raised by a devoutly Catholic mother and an anti-clerical father. His mother had him baptised into the Catholic Church and took her children to services every Sunday. Later, Benito declared himself to be an atheist.

[3] Source: Mannanberg, Leopold. *A Vital Condition for Lasting Peace.* Appendix to: Lehmann, L H. *Behind the Dictators: A Factual Analysis of the Relationship of Nazi-Fascism and Roman ...* pp90-91

The second, *Law for the Protection of German Blood and Honour*, prohibited: marriage and extramarital intercourse between Jews and Germans; the employment of German maids less than 45 years of age in Jewish households; and the raising of the German flag by Jews.[1]

The Conference of Dutch Bishops of 1995 stated very bluntly that there is a direct road that leads from the New Testament theology, and its application via canon law, to Auschwitz.[2] One of the first historians of the Holocaust, Raul Hilberg, was able to compile a chart in which he showed that each of the principal *Nuremberg Laws* had their precedent in Catholic ecclesiastic legislation. Similarly, William Nichols, in his book *Christian Antisemitism: A History of Hate*,[3] compiled a list comparing measures taken by the Church against the Jews, with those introduced by the Nazis. In the table below, RGB is an abbreviation of *Reichsgesetzblatt* (*Reich law Gazette*):

Table 10. The Similarity of Nazi Measures against the Jews to Catholic Canon Laws[4] against the Jews

Nazi Measures	Catholic Canon Laws
Law for the Re-establishment of the Professional Civil Service, 7 April 1933 (RGB I, 175)	Jews not allowed to hold public office (Synod of Clermont, 535)
Law against overcrowding of German schools and universities, 25 April 1933 (RGB I, 225)	Jews not permitted to obtain academic degrees (Council of Basel, 1434, Session XIX)
Burning of books in Nazi Germany, 10 May 1933	Burning of the *Talmud* and other books (12th Synod of Toledo, 681)
Law for the Protection of German Blood and Honour, 15 September 1935 (RGB I, 1146)	Prohibition of intermarriage and of sexual intercourse between Christians and Jews (Synod of Elvira, 306)
Law for the Protection of German Blood and Honour, 15 September 1935 (RGB I, 1146)	Jews not allowed to employ Christian servants or possess Christian slaves (3rd Synod of Orléans, 538)
Decree providing for the liquidation of Jewish real estate agencies, brokerage agencies, and marriage agencies, 6 July 1938 (RGB I, 823)	Jews not permitted to act as agents in the conclusion of contracts between Christians (Council of Basel, 1434, Session XIX)

[1] http://motlc.learningcenter.wiesenthal.org/text/x23/xm2310.html (2007)
[2] http://www.zionism-israel.com/his/judeophobia6.htm (2010)
[3] Nichols, William. *Christian Antisemitism: A History of Hate*. pp204-6. Source: http://englishatheist.org/indexz22.shtml (2008)
[4] The *Catholic Encyclopedia* records that 'The ultimate source of canon law is God'.

Decree of 25 July 1938 (RGB I, 969)	Christians not permitted to patronise Jewish doctors (Quinisext Council, 692)
Decree empowering the Justice Ministry to void wills offending the 'sound judgment of the people', 31 July 1938 (RGB I, 937)	Jews not permitted to withhold inheritance from descendants who had accepted Christianity (Third Lateran Council, 1179, Canon 26)
Destruction of synagogues in the entire Reich, 10 November 1938 (Heydrich to Göring, 11 November 1938 (PS-3058)	Construction of new synagogues prohibited (Council of Oxford, 1222)
Decree authorising the banning by local authorities of Jews from the streets on certain days (e.g., Nazi holidays), 3 December 1938 (RGB I, 1676)	Jews not permitted to show themselves in the streets during Passion Week (3rd Synod of Orléans, 538)
Decree providing for compulsory sale of Jewish real estate, 3 December 1938 (RGB I, 1709)	Christians not permitted to sell or rent real estate to Jews (Synod of Ofen, 1279)
Directive by Hermann Göring providing for concentration of Jews in houses, 28 December 1938 (Bormann to Rosenberg, 17 January 1939) (PS-69)	Christians not permitted to live in Jewish homes (Synod of Narbonne, 1050)
Order by Heydrich, 21 September 1939 (PS-3363)	Compulsory ghettos (Synod of Ofen, 1279)
Jews barred from dining cars (Transport Minister to Interior Minister, 30 December 1939 (Document NG-3995)	Jews and Christians not permitted to eat together (Synod of Elvira, 306)
The 'Sozialausgleichsabgabe' required that Jews pay a special income tax in lieu of donations for Party Purposes, 24 December 1940 (RGB I, 1666)	Jews required to pay taxes for the support of the Church to the same extent as Christians (Synod of Gerona, 1078)
Decree of 1 September 1941 forcing all Jews to wear the yellow star (RGB I, 547)	The marking of Jewish clothes with a badge (Fourth Lateran Council, 1215, Canon 68)
Friendly relations with Jews prohibited, 24 October 1941 (Gestapo directive, L-15)	Christians not permitted to attend Jewish ceremonies (Synod of Vienna, 1267)

Adoption by a Christian of Judaism placed him in jeopardy of being treated as a Jew (Decision by Oberlandesgericht Königsberg, 4th Zivilsenat, 26 June 1942)	Adoption by a Christian of the Jewish religion or the return by a baptised Jew to the Jewish religion defined as a heresy (Synod of Mainz, 1310)
Proposal by the Party Chancellery that Jews not be permitted to institute civil suits, 9 September 1942 (Bormann to Justice Ministry, 9 September 1942, NG-151)	Jews not permitted to be plaintiffs, or witnesses against Christians in the Courts (Third Lateran Council, 1179, Canon 26)

- In 1592 the Jesuits introduced a rule prohibiting the admission to the Order of men of Jewish origin, calculating ancestry back to the fifth generation. This rule was often cited by the Nazis to show that their own racial policies simply reflected those of this most respected religious order.

In his favourably reviewed book *History vs. Apologetics: The Holocaust, the Third Reich, and the Catholic Church*, David Cymet concluded that the Nuremberg Racial Laws posed no problem for the Catholic Church.[1]

- In Catholic Austria the *Nuremberg laws* were declared to be effective on 23 May 1938, long before Reich legislation in general became the law in that country.

- In London, American Ambassador Joseph 'Joe' Kennedy, a Catholic, expressed his full understanding of the German policy to the German ambassador. He only objected to the excessive noise that accompanied its implementation. In his telegram to Berlin the German ambassador summarised Kennedy's position:

> He said Germany was hurting her own cause, not so much because we want to get rid of the Jews but rather by the way we set out to accomplish this purpose with such a lot of noise. At home in Boston, for instance, Kennedy said there were clubs to which no Jews have been admitted in fifty years ... people simply avoided making a fuss about it. He himself understood our policy on Jews completely.[2]

Synopsis

Adolf Hitler's Holocaust was the worst military genocide in history. Its object was the systematic elimination of all European Jews.

Hitler's entire political career was based on his original notion of cementing his alliances by means of anti-Semitism. Hitler had no trouble finding partners. 'The soil of Christian Europe had been well prepared in modern times by the Catholic press and politicians all over Europe and Hitler saw the opportunity to harvest the hatred they had so diligently sown to create his bloc of anti-Semitic states.'

---

[1] Cymet, David. *History vs. Apologetics: The Holocaust, the Third Reich, and the Catholic Church.* p10
[2] Ibid. p115

A catalogue of the religious affiliations of the European Nazi and fascist dictators, puppets and quislings during World War II discloses that 12 out of the 16 were Catholics.

Most of the major participants in the planning and implementation of the Holocaust were born and bred Catholics.

Each of the principal *Nuremberg Laws* and other anti-Semitism regulations and restrictions had their precedents in Catholic anti-Semitic ecclesiastic legislation.

———

19 – The Mid- and Low-Level Catholic Hierarchy during the War

Treat the other man's faith gently; it is all he has to believe with. His mind was created for his own thoughts, not yours or mine. Henry S Haskin

The Cardinalate

Cardinal Bertram

Shortly after the *Reichskonkordat* was signed in 1933 between the Holy See and Germany, Adolf Cardinal Bertram, Archbishop of Breslau and the senior cardinal of Germany wrote to Hitler as follows:

> The Episcopate of all the German dioceses, as is shown by its statements to the public, was glad to express, as soon as it was possible after the recent change in the political situation through the declarations of Your Excellency, its sincere readiness to cooperate to the best of its ability with the new government which has proclaimed as its goal to promote Christian education, to wage war against Godlessness and immorality, to strengthen the spirit of sacrifice for the common good, and to protect the rights of the Church.[1]

Bertram publicly expressed his appreciation of the new regime in the name of the Fulda Bishops' Conference. After the signing of the *Reichskonkordat* he identified the Catholic clergy with the Hitler Reich: 'No one should any longer doubt the sincerity of the Church in accepting and standing up for the new order.'[2]

Following the Anschluss, Bertram sent Hitler an effusive telegram, published on 2 November 1938 in the Nazi newspaper *Völkischer Beobachter:*

> The great deed of safeguarding peace among the nations moves the German episcopate acting in the name of the Catholics of all the German dioceses, respectfully to extend congratulations and thanks and to order a festive ringing of bells on Sunday.[3]

From 1939 onwards, every 20th of April, Hitler's birthday, Cardinal Bertram sent 'warmest congratulations to the Führer in the name of the bishops and the dioceses in Germany,' to which he added 'fervent prayers which the Catholics in Germany are sending to heaven on their altars.'[4]

As Archbishop of Breslau and head of the German Bishops' Conference, Bertram was opposed to all public protest against the deportation and massacre of the Jews. Indeed, in August 1943, Archbishop Konrad von Preysing of Berlin proposed making a public protest against the Jewish exterminations. It was rejected by his fellow bishops

---

[1] *Catholic Universe* (London: 18 August 1933). Source: http://www.liberalslikechrist.org/Catholic/1933 Concordat.html (2010)

[2] Cymet, David. *History vs. Apologetics: The Holocaust, the Third Reich, and the Catholic Church.* p67

[3] Cornwell, John. *Hitler's Pope: The Secret History of Pius XII* (2nd edn) p202

[4] Cornwell, John. *Hitler's Pope: The Secret History of Pius XII.* p209. Source: Jim Walker. 'Christianity in Europe during World War II'. http://www.nobeliefs.com/ChurchesWWII.htm#anchor2b (2012)

on the instigation of Cardinal Bertram It was also ignored by Pius XII.[1]

Bertram, who was then Cardinal Archbishop of Berlin, maintained a cordial relationship with Adolf Hitler. In May 1945, following Hitler's suicide on 30 April, in his own handwriting, Bertram ordered all the parish priests of his archdiocese to hold a Mass, not only for the man who has been described as 'the supreme embodiment of evil in human history',[2] but also for those who died for him:

> To hold a solemn requiem in memory of the Führer[3] and all those members of the Wehrmacht who have fallen in the struggle for our German Fatherland, along with the sincerest prayers for Volk and Fatherland and for the future of the Catholic Church in Germany.[4,5]

Cardinal-Priest Baudrillart

Alfred-Henri-Marie Baudrillart, Cardinal-Priest, and later Auxiliary Bishop of Paris, supported militarism and the Nazis:

> as a priest and a Frenchman ... should I refuse to approve this noble common enterprise, in which Germany is taking the lead?[6]

> In the skies over France in 1940, skies full of tempests, a beneficial light has been manifested and has revived all our hopes! This light is, of course, the Marshal [Pétain] ... Against the powers of the demons, Archangel Gabriel wields his avenging sword, shining and invisible. With him march the Christian and civilised peoples who defend their Fatherland, their future, beside the German armies.[7]

Cardinal Copello

Cardinal Primate Santiago Luis Copello of Argentina was a sympathiser of the Vichy regime, as well as being a supporter of Francisco Franco, and a regular visitor at the German embassy in Buenos Aires during the war.[8]

Cardinal von Faulhaber

Michael von Faulhaber, Archbishop of Munich, was a key figure in the rapprochement between the Church and the Nazis. On 1 April 1933 there was a violent boycott of Jewish businesses and a week later Jews were banned from the German civil service. Yet, at a meeting of the Bavarian Council of Ministers three weeks later, the Premier reported that Cardinal Faulhaber had issued an order to the clergy to support the new

[1] *Crimes of War: Guilt and Denial in the Twentieth Century.* p25

[2] Cymet, David. *History vs. Apologetics: The Holocaust, the Third Reich, and the Catholic Church.* p411

[3] This Requiem Mass for Hitler was celebrated in spite of the fact that the Roman Church condemns the act of suicide 'as a most atrocious crime and, in hatred of the sin and to arouse the horror of its children, denies the suicide Christian burial.' *Catholic Encyclopedia.* 'Suicide'. See also, above.

[4] Cornwell, John. *Hitler's Pope: The Secret History of Pius XII.* p317

[5] Cymet, David. *History vs. Apologetics: The Holocaust, the Third Reich, and the Catholic Church.* p411

[6] Callil, Carmen. *Bad Faith: A Forgotten History of Family & Fatherland.* pp238-40

[7] http://www.concordatwatch.eu/showkb.php?org_id=867&kb_header_id=850&kb_id=1527&full=full& edit= (2012)

[8] Goñi, Uki. *The Real ODESSA: How Perón Brought the Nazi War Criminals ...* p177

regime in which he, Faulhaber, had confidence.[1]

After the conclusion of the *Reichskonkordat*, von Faulhaber sent a handwritten note to Adolf Hitler stating:

> What the old parliaments and parties did not accomplish in 60 years, your states-manlike foresight has achieved in six months. For Germany's prestige in East and West ... this handshake with the papacy, *the greatest moral power in the history of the world*,[2] is a feat of immeasurable blessing.[3]

In the same year, he sent another hand-written letter to Adolf Hitler: 'May God protect our Chancellor for our people.' Four years later, he appraised the *Reichskonkordat*'s international impact in a 1937 sermon:

> At a time when the heads of the major nations in the world faced the new Germany with cool reserve and considerable suspicion, the Catholic Church, *the greatest moral power on earth*, through the Concordat, expressed its confidence in the new German government. This was a deed of immeasurable significance for the reputation of the new [Nazi] government abroad.[4]

In a letter addressed to Cardinal Pacelli, von Faulhaber wrote:

> We bishops are being asked why the Catholic Church, as often in its history, does not intervene on behalf of the Jews. This is not possible at this time because the struggle against the Jews would then, at the same time, become a struggle against the Catholics, and because the Jews can help themselves, as the sudden end of the boycott shows.[5]

In 1939 when Hitler narrowly escaped assassination in Munich, von Faulhaber ordered that a *Te Deum* be said in the cathedral, 'To thank Divine Providence in the name of the archdiocese for the Führer's fortunate escape.'[6]

At the height of the Nazi's deportations of the Jews during November 1941, Cardinal Faulhaber wrote to Cardinal Bertram saying that he was being asked by lay people whether the bishops could not do something about the 'brutal deportation of non-Aryans to Poland under inhuman conditions paralleled only in the African slave trade.' Bertram's answer was a replica of that given several years earlier by von Faulhaber himself when Oskar Wasserman appealed to him for beleaguered German Jewry and he had then answered pompously that:

---

[1] Lewy, Guenter. *The Catholic Church and Nazi Germany*. p41. Source: http://en.wikipedia.org/wiki/Michael_von_Faulhaber (2007)

[2] An oft repeated phrase of the Catholic Church. History reveals the converse to be true.

[3] http://www.geocities.com/inthedevilsgarden/pig.html (2007)

[4] Lewy, Guenter. *The Catholic Church and Nazi Germany.* p90

[5] Friedlaender, Saul. *Nazi Germany and the Jews*. Vol I. 'The Years of Persecution 1933-1939'. Source: http://en.wikipedia.org/wiki/Michael_von_Faulhaber (2007)

[6] Dawkins, Richard. *The God Delusion.* pp273-77

for the higher ecclesiastical authorities there are immediate issues of much greater importance.

This time, Bertram responded:

> The Bishops must concentrate on other concerns which are more important for the Church and more far reaching; in particular, the ever more urgent question of how best to prevent anti-Christian and anti-Church influences on the education of Catholic youth.[1]

After World War II, the West German Federal Republic honoured Michael Cardinal von Faulhaber with its highest award, the Grand Cross of the Order of Merit of the Federal Republic of Germany.[2]

Cardinal Gerlier

On 24 October 1940, Marshal Pétain met Hitler and issued a call to the French to follow him down the path of collaboration with Nazi Germany. Archbishop of Lyon and Catholic Primate of France, Pierre-Marie Cardinal Gerlier declared:

> Pétain is France and France is Pétain! In one of the most tragic hours of our history, Providence has given France a leader around whom we can be proud to gather. Marshal! You gave yourself to France. And now France has replied by giving herself to you. We pray God to bless you and bestow wisdom on your ministers.[3]

Gerlier likened Pétain to General Franco as a magnificent leader, and, 'speaking on behalf of the Church in France', stated that 'France needed a leader to guide her towards her eternal destiny. God permitted that you should be there.'[4] He condoned the Nazi's horrific acts without protest.[5]

Cardinal Hlond

In Poland, the attitude of Church authorities towards Jews exacerbated their life. Church leaders, including August Cardinal Hlond, believed that Jews should emigrate, or, failing this, that their influence on domestic life be strictly limited by law.[6] A pastoral letter was read from the Catholic pulpits of Poland as part of an official Church endorsement of a Nazi boycott of Jewish businesses:

> There will be the Jewish problem as long as the Jews remain. It is a fact that the Jews are fighting against the Catholic Church, *persisting in free-thinking*, and are the vanguard of godlessness, Bolshevism and subversion. It is a fact that the Jewish influence on morality is pernicious and that their publishing houses disseminate pornography. It is a fact that the Jews deceive, levy interest, and are pimps. It is a

---

[1] Cymet, David. *History vs. Apologetics: The Holocaust, the Third Reich, and the Catholic Church.* pp314-15
[2] Ibid. p134
[3] Ibid. p191
[4] After the War, Pétain was tried, and found guilty of treason. He was condemned to life imprisonment.
[5] See, for example: Callil, Carmen. *Bad Faith: A Forgotten History of Family & Fatherland.* pp238-40
[6] Phayer, Michael. *The Catholic Church and the Holocaust, 1930-1965.* p14

fact that the religious and ethical influence of the Jewish young people on Polish young people is a negative one.[1]

› *Cardinal Innitzer*

The 'Heil Hitler Cardinal'[2] Theodor Innitzer, Archbishop of Vienna and leader of the Church in Austria, was active in the late 1930s in Austrian politics, leaning heavily towards Fascism. He was a paid-up member of the controversial Catholic movement 'Cartellverband'.

Cardinal Innitzer offered whole-heartedly his blind support of the future aims of the Anschluss, thereby aligning himself and the Church with Hitler's National Socialism. Innitzer also coerced his fellow bishops to sanction the plebiscite. He sent a message to Cardinal Bertram on 1 April 1938 expressing his wish that the German bishops would similarly urge the Germans to vote 'yes' to the Anschluss. Preceding his signature Innitzer added in his own handwriting 'Und Heil Hitler!'[3]

With the implementation of the Anschluss, Innitzer ordered Nazi flags to fly from country and town churches as well as from his own cathedral, St Stephens, in Vienna.[4] He warmly received Hitler in Vienna after his triumphal march through the capital where he expressed public satisfaction with Hitler's regime.[5]

In 1938 Innitzer met Hitler: 'Those who are entrusted with souls and the faithful will unconditionally support the great German state and the Führer ... for the power and honour of the Reich and for the unity of the German nation, is obviously accompanied by the blessing of Providence.'[6]

Cardinal Liénart

Achille Cardinal Liénart, Bishop of Lille, greeted the installation of Pétain with fervour. He condoned the Nazi's horrific acts without protest.[7]

Cardinal Maglione

Luigi Maglione was an Italian Cardinal who served as the Vatican Secretary of State under Pius XII.

Maglione never criticised the basic injustice of the Nazi anti-Semitic regulations, nor did he evidence any particular concern about the sufferings of the Jews.[8]

The Allied governments issued a declaration of condemnation of the *German Policy of Extermination of the Jewish Race*. When Maglione was asked if Pius XII would issue a similar proclamation, Maglione replied that the papacy was 'unable to denounce

---

[1] Carroll, James. *Constantine's Sword: The Church and the Jews.* pp271-72
[2] http://en.wikipedia.org/wiki/Theodor_Innitzer (2010)
[3] Cymet, David. *History vs. Apologetics: The Holocaust, the Third Reich, and the Catholic Church.* p112
[4] http://www.excatholicsforchrist.com/articles.php?PageURL=innitzer.htm (2010)
[5] Cornwell, John. *Hitler's Pope: The Secret History of Pius XII.* p201. Source: Jim Walker. 'Christianity in Europe during World War II'. http://www.nobeliefs.com/ChurchesWWII.htm# anchor2b (2012)
[6] Kertzer, David I. *The Pope and Mussolini: The Secret History of Pius XI and the Rise of Fascism in ...* p276
[7] See, for example: Callil, Carmen. *Bad Faith: A Forgotten History of Family & Fatherland.* pp238-40
[8] Morley, John F. *Vatican Diplomacy and the Jews during the Holocaust 1939-43.* pp196-202

publicly particular atrocities.' He made a similar comment when a complaint was made that Pius had failed to condemn the wave of atrocities in Poland.

Cardinal Serédi

A round of harsh anti-Jewish legislation was approved by the Hungarian Parliament on 8 August 1941. Differences between Nazis and Catholics surfaced relating to mixed marriages between Hungarian Christians and baptised Jewish converts. The primate of Hungary, Jusztinián György Cardinal Serédi,[1] while fully supporting the main body of the new anti-Semitic law, objected to the mixed marriages aspect:

> Had this bill prohibited marriages between Jews and Christians, I too would have supported it. But the bill does not distinguish between real Jews and those Jews who had already become Christians. This bill harms mainly Christians of Jewish origin. This bill will drive them back to Judaism forever – them, their children and their posterity – and in so doing will increase to a considerable degree the number of Jews in our midst ... My opposition to the proposed bill does *not* stem from my interest in Jewish welfare.[2]

On 19 March 1944, after the German occupation, 'Hungarian Jewry was subjected to the most ruthless and concentrated destruction process of the war.'[3] Apart from Budapest, Hungary became free of Jews within less than four months. Notwithstanding, on 29 June 1944, Cardinal Serédi issued a pastoral letter defaming Hungarian Jewry at that most tragic time and expressing his support for anti-Jewish laws; 'the letter will forever remain a stain on Christian Hungary ... The document is a sad reminder of what made the Holocaust of Hungarian Jewry possible.' The letter stated:

> We do not deny that many Jews had a wicked, destructive influence on the economic, social and moral life of Hungary. It is also true that the others did not protest against the actions of their co-religionists. We do not doubt that the Jewish question must be settled in a legal and just manner. And so, we do not voice any opposition to the measures taken against them until now in the economic field in the interests of the state. We do not protest either against the elimination of their noxious influence. On the contrary, we wish it to disappear. But it would be neglect of our and Episcopal duty if we did not raise a warning voice against suffering inflicted on our Hungarian compatriots and devout members of our Catholic Church, who are being harmed only because of their racial origin ... We therefore solemnly reject all responsibility for the consequences ... Pray and work for our Catholic brethren, our Catholic Church and our beloved Hungary.[4]

Cardinal Suhard

Emmanuel Célestin Cardinal Suhard was Archbishop of Paris during the Nazi

---

[1] Cardinal Serédi appears elsewhere in this book.
[2] Cymet, David. *History vs. Apologetics: The Holocaust, the Third Reich, and the Catholic Church.* pp355-56
[3] Braham, Randolph L. *The Politics of Genocide: The Holocaust in Hungary.* p13
[4] Quoted in: Cymet, David. *History vs. Apologetics: The Holocaust, the Third Reich, and the ...* p363

occupation. He joined Pétain's Council of Ministers, and appeared with Pétain in public well into 1944.

At the time that trains were deporting Jews to the East, no protest was expressed by Suhard. In fact, David Cymet records that at that time 'Cardinals Gerlier and Suhard even went personally to express their loyalty to Petain ... and to discuss government subsidies for religious education, Petain showed his generosity and increased the subsidies for Catholic schools.'[1]

Suhard was so despised by the French Resistance, that when Paris was liberated, General de Gaulle refused to enter Notre Dame Cathedral until Suhard was gone.[2]

Valerio Valeri, later, Cardinal

Nuncio Valeri did not protest against the deportations of French Jews when they were disappearing without trace. 'Neither did he stand up to Pétain to let him know the moral abyss in which he was descending. In the words of Father Morley:

> Valeri, as far as it can be ascertained, never made known to Pétain the moral horror involved in the 1942 and 1943 actions taken against the Jews.'[3]

After researching the correspondence between Valeri and Cardinal Maglione, Father Morley concluded that the nuncio had little concern for the Jews of France. This, despite his being well informed. 'His orientation was totally diplomatic and his interest in human suffering minimal.'[4]

Valeri also justified Pius XII's lack of response to the Jewish situation as a result of his inclination 'toward prudent delay and enlightened reserve.'[5]

The Millenari, a concerned group within the Vatican, have recorded of Monsignor Valeri and the political Holy See that:

> In Paris during the years, Charles de Gaulle was at odds with the apostolic delegate, Monsignor Valerio Valeri, over the thirty French bishops who de Gaulle claimed had collaborated with the government of Pétain, and for which he was demanding Valeri's resignation. The Vatican would never agree to such a proposal, and it instructed Valeri to firmly oppose it. Relations between the two sides reached a breaking point, and de Gaulle demanded and succeeded in obtaining the removal of Valeri, who, when he was recalled to Rome, was immediately made a cardinal.[6,7]

Cardinal Joseph-Emest van Roey

Cardinal van Roey, Archbishop of Mechelen, never made a public protest against the persecution and deportation of the Jews. In Catholic Belgium, where the clergy were

---

[1] Cymet, David. *History vs. Apologetics: The Holocaust, the Third Reich, and the Catholic Church.* p349
[2] http://hist.academic.claremontmckenna.edu/jpetropoulos/church/CardinalEmmanuelCelestineSuhard.htm (2007)
[3] Cymet, David. *History vs. Apologetics: The Holocaust, the Third Reich, and the Catholic Church.* p348
[4] Quoted in: Ibid. p349
[5] Ibid. p348
[6] Millenari, The. *Shroud of Secrecy. The Story of Corruption Within the Vatican.* p59
[7] Yet another example of papal ethics and politics.

very influential, helpful exhortations would have assisted the Jews. Cardinal van Roey disbanded the Katholiek Bureau voor Israel, an Antwerp Catholic organisation that tried to help Jewish refugees.[1]

The Archbishops

Archbishop Gröber

Monsignor Konrad Gröber was nicknamed 'Konrad the Brown' because of his policy of cooperation with the Nazis.

In 1933 the Archdiocese of Freiburg published in its official newspaper, under Gröber's direction, an instruction of the Baden Ministry for Culture and Education which officially sanctioned the Hitler Salute. In that year also, at a large Catholic event in Karlsruhe, Gröber stated 'I also believe that I will not be betraying a secret, either to you or to the German people, if I say that I place myself unreservedly behind the new government and the new Reich.'[2]

During the course of the subordination of provincial governments to the Nazi central government, Gröber sent a congratulatory telegram to a National Socialist politician: 'At the mighty task which lies before you, I place myself as the chief shepherd of Catholics in Baden unreservedly at your side.'[3]

Archbishop Gröber commented on the 1935 *Nuremberg Laws*:

> Every people bears responsibility for the success of its existence, and the absorption of entirely alien blood will always constitute a risk for a nation that has proven its historic worth. Consequently, the right to safeguard the purity of the race, and to devise measures necessary to that end, can be denied to no one.[4]

Hitler denounced the Versailles Treaty in early 1935. 'The episcopate was overjoyed with the denunciation of the Versailles Treaty and the rearmament program.' In his 1936 New Year's sermon, Gröber addressed Catholics in support of Hitler's military actions:

> The strength of the German people has blossomed forth manifold and unemploy-ment has decreased to a surprising degree. Newly rearmed, the Reich again now takes its place in the family of nations and in place of the dishonour that since the Versailles Treaty has besmirched the German name the world is faced by a united, upward-striving and *power-conscious state.*[5]

Gröber stressed his general loyalty to the Nazi Government and his support of the War when he spoke of the 'glorious brotherhood of arms at the front.' His Pastoral Letter was quoted in *The Catholic Times* (4 April 1941):

---

[1] Cymet, David. *History vs. Apologetics: The Holocaust, the Third Reich, and the Catholic Church.* p353
[2] http://en.wikipedia.org/wiki/Conrad_Gr%C3%B6ber (2007)
[3] Ibid. (2012)
[4] Cymet, David. *History vs. Apologetics: The Holocaust, the Third Reich, and the Catholic Church.* p83
[5] Ibid. p79

Far be it for me in this terrible struggle to say anything that would turn aside the energies of the people or prejudice their devotion to their country. Everyone who thinks as a German desires to secure for his country a lasting peace with honour.[1]

On Good Friday in 1941 he gave a sermon:

As a driving force behind the Jewish legal power stood the aggressive toadyism and malevolent perfidy of the Pharisees. They unmasked themselves more than ever as Christ's arch-enemies, deadly enemies ... Their eyes were blindfolded by their prejudice and blinded by their Jewish lust for worldly dominion ...

All the sympathy of the Jews is hidden under barbaric rawness. The beast has smelled human blood and wants to slake its wild-burning thirst with it ... At the same time the insane but truthful self-curse of the Jews screams: 'His blood come upon us and our children!' The curse has been frightfully fulfilled. Unto this present day ...[2,3]

Archbishop Orsenigo

Hitler had greeted Archbishop Cesare Vincenzo Orsenigo in 1935. On 20 April 1939, at Eugenio Pacelli's express wish, Archbishop Orsenigo, the nuncio in Berlin, opened a gala reception for Hitler's birthday. The birthday greetings thus initiated by Pacelli immediately became a tradition.

Orsenigo 'had strong sympathies for the Nazis.' His attitude to pleas for clemency for non-Aryan spouses was that:

Charity is well and good but the greatest charity is not to make problems for the Church.[4]

Father John F Morley, in his thoroughly researched book *Vatican Diplomacy and the Jews during the Holocaust 1939-43*, characterised the role of Cardinal Orsenigo during his long tenure in Germany (1930-1946): 'His acts of defense, however, were never extended to the Jews.' Apart from some concern for Jews married to Christians, 'he said nothing ... he apparently felt no similar sympathy for the 100,000 Jews deported.'[5]

Archbishop Karol Kmet'ko

Archbishop Karol Kmet'ko, Bishop of Nitra, Slovakia, was approached in 1942 by his old acquaintance Rabbi Michael Dov-Ber Weissmandel, a leader of the Jewish underground, who begged him to intervene with the latter's former personal secretary, President Monsignor Jozef Tiso, in the expulsion of the Jews from Slovakia. The archbishop replied:

This is no mere expulsion. There, you will not die of hunger and pestilence; there,

---

[1] Edith Moore. *No Friend of Democracy: A study of Roman Catholic politics – their influence on the course ...*
[2] http://en.wikipedia.org/wiki/Conrad_Gr%C3%B6ber (2007)
[3] See also: Goldhagen, Daniel Jonah. *Hitler's Willing Executioners: Ordinary Germans and ...* p109
[4] Quoted in: Cymet, David. *History vs. Apologetics: The Holocaust, the Third Reich, and the Catholic Church. The Holocaust, the Third Reich, and the Catholic Church. The Holocaust, the Third Reich, and the Catholic Church.* p317
[5] Quoted in: Ibid.

they will slaughter you all, young and old, women and children, in one day. This is your punishment for the death of our Redeemer. There is only one hope for you, to convert to our religion. Then I shall effect the annulling of this decree.[1]

Archbishop Ivan Šarić

In 1941, the diocesan newspaper of Archbishop Šarić of Sarajevo ('the Hangman of the Serbs') declared that:

> Jewish greed increases. The Jews have led Europe and the world towards disaster, moral and economic disaster. Their appetite grows till only domination of the whole world will satisfy it.

> There exists limits to love. The movement for ridding the world of Jews is a movement for restoring human dignity. Almighty God stands behind this movement.[2]

> [it would be] stupid and unworthy of Christ's disciples to think that the struggle against evil could be waged in a noble way and with gloves on.[3]

Archbishop Alojzije (Aloysius) Viktor Stepinac, Primate of Croatia

From the time of the revival of the Ustaša terrorist organisation in the late twenties, the closest ties had existed between the Ustaše and sections of both the lower and higher Catholic clergy. The plot against Yugoslavia had been thoroughly prepared over a long period by Hitler and Mussolini, by their Ustaša agents, and by influential representatives of the Catholic hierarchy in Yugoslavia. The whole plot was directed by responsible members of the Catholic hierarchy. 'The presidents and members of the directing bodies of these organizations were appointed by Archbishop Stepinac of Zagreb. They were in most cases well-known priests or secretly sworn members of the Ustashi ... This propaganda persuaded the faithful that it would be a good deed, in the highest interests of Croatia and the Catholic Church, to kill or convert the Serbs and to exterminate the Jews.'[4]

Catholic publications such as *Katolički List* (*Catholic Letter*) – the official organ of Stepinac's archbishopric of Zagreb – frequently published condemnations of Jews during the 1930s as being the source of Communism, Freemasonry, abortions and immorality.[5]

For most of the War, Alojzije Stepinac showed not a trace of concern for the fate of the Jews. Indeed, in a letter to Andrija Artuković[6] he showed his agreement with the

---

[1] Berkovits, Eliezer. *Faith After the Holocaust.* pp16-17. Source: http://www.geocities.com/pharsea/Perfidy.html (2007)

[2] Lituchy, Barry. *What Is The Vatican Hiding? The Vatican's Complicity in Genocide in Fascist Croatia:...* http://www.holocaustrevealed.org/_domain/holocaustrevealed.org/Main.htm (2012)

[3] http://strangeside.com/holocaust-yugoslavia/ (2015)

[4] *The Case of Archbishop Stepinac*

[5] Manhattan, Avro. *The Vatican's Holocaust: The Sensational Account of the Most Horrifying Religious ...* p62

[6] Andrija Artuković was a Croatian politician and lawyer, Ustaše intellectual, and minister in the Government of the Independent State of Croatia (NDH). Artuković was eventually convicted of war crimes committed against minorities in the NDH during World War II.

racial policies: 'Everyone approves the efforts to place the economy in the hands of the people, and to forbid foreign and anti-national elements to accumulate capital...'[1] Stepinac never spontaneously reacted against the persecutions of Serbs and Jews.[2]

Stepinac was also an observer in the Croatian Sabor (parliament). He could therefore have not been unaware of the despotic legislation that was passed against the Serbs, Roma and Jews.

Israeli historian M Shelah has written that:

> It was not until the middle of 1943 that Aloysius Stepinac, the archbishop of Zagreb, publicly came out against the murder of Croatian Jews (most of whom had been killed by that time) ...[3]

The Bishops

The German Bishops, the Enabling Act, the Fulda Bishops' Conferences

Guenter Lewy, professor emeritus of political science at the University of Massachusetts, recorded in his book *The Catholic Church & Nazi Germany* that the policy of the German Catholic episcopate, of accommodation to and support of the Nazi regime, provides the most recent outstanding example of the Church's inability to surpass its institutional interests and to be a custodian of human morality.[4] For instance:

> Catholics were told in 1937 that resistance to the Nazi state was sinful.

> Catholics serving in both of the warring factions were assured that they were fighting a just war.[5,6]

> There is no evidence that either the pope or any bishop excommunicated or refused the sacraments to either Hitler or any other Catholic in the Nazi leadership.

> When the Rhineland was occupied by Nazi troops, Services of Thanksgiving were held in all Catholic Churches throughout Germany, and hymns of praise were sung for the Führer and the Great German Nation.[7]

In defence, a recent apologist has stated that the bishops 'were not entitled to take a position or participate in the legal and political arena.' Ergo, no one could have expected them to have opposed the National Socialist regime from the beginning.[8] They were completely blameless.

---

[1] Source: Kostich, Lazo M. *The Holocaust in the 'Independent State of Croatia'.* p237

[2] Ibid. p218

[3] *Encyclopedia of the Holocaust,* Vol 1, p328. Source: http://en.wikipedia.org/wiki/Involvement_of_Croatian_Catholic_clergy_with_the_Usta%C5%A1a_regime (2009)

[4] Lewy, Guenter. *The Catholic Church and Nazi Germany.* pp338-41

[5] Ibid. p339. Source: http://www.mosquitonet.com/~prewett/lewy337341.html (2007)

[6] In 1962, Professor Emeritus Gordon C Zahn published his book *German Catholics and Hitler's Wars: A Study in Social Control.* It has been said of it that 'There is no better documentation of the hollowness and dangerousness of 'just war,' than this courageous book ...' (*Cistercian Studies Quarterly*)

[7] Moore, Edith. *No Friend of Democracy: A study of Roman Catholic politics – their influence on the ...*

[8] Refer: Lewy, Guenter. *The Catholic Church and Nazi Germany.* p338. Source: http://www.mosquitonet.com/~prewett/lewy337341.html (2007)

In his book *The Vatican's Holocaust: The Sensational Account of the Most Horrifying Religious Massacre of the 20th Century*, Avro Manhattan has a picture of the Pope's nuncio addressing Hitler: 'I have not understood you for a long time. But I have worried for a long time. Today I understand you.' Afterwards, this slogan was repeated for many years by the Vatican.[1]

The general attitude of the German bishopric may be gauged by the statements of Maximilian Kaller, Bishop of Ermland: 'As believing Christians, inspired by God's love, we faithfully stand behind our Führer', and by Bishop Clemens August von Galen of Münster cabling the supreme commander of the German Army: 'In the name of the staunchly German Catholics of the diocese of Münster and especially of the lower Rhine, I welcome the German armed forces, which from today on will again shield the German Rhine, as protection and symbol of German honour and German justice.'[2]

A diplomatic correspondent of the *Manchester Guardian* (24 May 1940) wrote:

> Among the higher ranks of the Catholic clergy a decisive majority desire to see the victory of the Reich or at least a peace that will leave Germany's political and military strength unimpaired. At the same time they still look to an eventual Catholic-Conservative restoration. The National Socialist State has, it seems, been able to reach an understanding with the Catholic leaders ... In spite of the persecution of laymen and priests by the Nazis, in spite of all the attacks upon the Christian religion, new hopes have been raised among the German Catholics as a result of these negotiations.[3]

The diocesan chancelleries assisted the Nazi state in detecting people of Jewish descent by supplying information from Church records on the religious background of their parishioners. This cooperation continued throughout the war years. The public reaction of Catholic bishops to the mass murder of Jews in the death camps consisted of vague pronouncements that had no mention of the word Jew.[4]

On Hitler's birthday, 20 April 1933, Monsignor Ludwig Kaas sent a congratulatory telegram from the Vatican, which was widely publicised in the German press. For many German Catholics this was a signal to join the Nazi Party:

> For today's birthday sincere good wishes and the assurance of unflinching cooperation in the great enterprise of creating a Germany internally united, enjoying social peace and externally free.[5]

James Carroll, in his work *Constantine's Sword: The Church and the Jews*, recorded that in 1933, two weeks after Eugenio Pacelli offered his overture to Hitler, the Fulda

[1] Manhattan, Avro. *The Vatican's Holocaust: The Sensational Account of the Most Horrifying Religious Massacre of the 20th Century.* Chapter 15 'The Vatican Saves The Catholic War Criminals Of Croatia – Roman Monasteries As Their Asylums – The Croatian Holocaust Minimized'. Source: http://www.reformation.org/holoc15.html (2008)
[2] http://www.shc.edu/theolibrary/resources/04German.htm (2014)
[3] http://clc-library-org.tripod.com/world2.html (2015)
[4] http://www.zionism-israel.com/his/judeophobia6.htm (2007)
[5] Cymet, David. *History vs. Apologetics: The Holocaust, the Third Reich, and the Catholic Church.* p55

Episcopal Conference, representing the Catholic hierarchy of Germany, voted to lift the ban on Catholic membership in the Nazi Party. The bishops expressed 'a certain confidence in the new government, subject to reservations concerning some religious and moral lapses.' Bearers of the swastika were now welcomed at the communion rail. This was in complete contrast to the 1932 Conference, which banned membership in the Nazi Party and forbade priests from offering communion to anyone wearing the swastika.[1]

The Enabling Act

Ermächtigungsgesetz (*Enabling Act*) was a 1933 amendment to the Weimar Constitution giving the German Cabinet (in effect, Chancellor Adolf Hitler) the power to enact laws without the involvement of the Reichstag.[2,3]

In September 1928, Ludwig Kaas was elected chairman of the German Catholic Centre Party (CCP). From 15 March 1933, he was the main advocate supporting the *Enabling Act*. A considerable group of parliamentarians opposed Kaas' course.

Der Angriff (*The Attack*) was a newspaper founded in 1927 by the Berlin chapter of the Nazi party. It was set up by Joseph Goebbels. The paper mentioned openly that Kaas had the CCP's approval of the *Enabling Act* dependent on the willingness of the Reichstag to negotiate with the Holy See for a Reich concordat, and to respect the rights of the Church.[4] In the end, all 92 parliamentary members of the CCP voted to support it. Thereby, the *Enabling Act* was passed by the Reichstag and signed by President von Hindenburg on 23 March 1933. The Act granted the cabinet, under Chancellor Adolf Hitler, the authority to enact laws without the participation of the Reichstag. 'From that moment on, Hitler's Third Reich was born; his word became the law in Germany, and legislation fundamentally took the form of Führer edicts.'[5]

Heinrich Brüning, the former Chancellor, called the *Act* the 'most monstrous resolution ever demanded of a parliament'.

A year later, Kaas was rewarded by the Holy See by being appointed papal protonotary, and a year later again, canon of the Basilica of Saint Peter, Vatican City.[6]

The *Enabling Act* became a corner stone of Adolf Hitler's seizure of power, by delegating to him virtually dictatorial powers. It enabled the government not only to create decrees, but even laws and treaties with other countries; these laws could even deviate from the constitution; there were no thematic limits; neither any house committee nor the Reichsrat (the common organ of the German regional states) had the right to control, or to abolish these laws.

Joseph Goebbels wrote shortly after the passage of the *Act*:

---

[1] Source: *The Scandal of Roman Catholicism*. http://liberalslikechrist.org/Catholic/RC_scandal-2.html (2007)
[2] http://en.wikipedia.org/wiki/Enabling_Act_of_1933 (2008)
[3] Midlarsky, Manus I. *The Killing Trap: Genocide in the Twentieth Century*. p222
[4] Cymet, David. *History vs. Apologetics: The Holocaust, the Third Reich, and the Catholic Church*. p45
[5] Ibid. p47
[6] Ibid.

The authority of the Führer has now been wholly established. Votes are no longer taken. The Führer decides. All this is going much faster than we had dared to hope.[1]

The Fulda Bishops' Conference and the Enabling Act

The highest body of the Catholic Church in Germany, the Fulda Bishops' Conference, convened five days after the *Enabling Act* was passed on 23 March 1933. It issued a public declaration expressing the bishops' trust in the promises that Hitler made before the Reichstag.

> Without revoking the condemnation contained in our previous statements of certain religious and ethical errors, the Episcopate nevertheless believes it can cherish the hope that those general warnings and prohibitions need no longer be regarded as necessary ... Members in uniform may now be admitted to the divine services and to the sacraments even if they appear in large numbers.[2]

The Catholic vote for the *Enabling Act* and the bishops' declaration were perceived by German Catholics as a signal to join the Nazis and to rally behind Adolf Hitler. Most German Catholic newspapers called for support of the new Reich. The custodians of Catholic education in Germany, the Catholic Teachers' Association, considered its independent existence superfluous and voluntarily disbanded itself and joined the Nazi Teachers League.[3]

The Fulda Bishops' Conference acted on the proposal of Cardinal Faulhaber to congratulate the Führer:

> The great deed of safeguarding international peace moves the German episcopate, acting in the name of the Catholics of all the German dioceses, respectfully to tender congratulations and thanks and to order a festive peal of bells on Sunday. In the name of the Cardinals of Germany. *Archbishop Cardinal Bertram.*[4]

On 26 April 1933, Hitler received an official delegation from the Fulda Bishops' Conference. Bishop Wilhelm Berning of Osnabrück and Vicar-General of Berlin, Johannes Steinmann, conveyed the congratulations of the Conference on his becoming Chancellor. The bishop's secretary recorded their conversation in a protocol:

> Hitler welcomed the opportunity to explain himself to a Catholic bishop for he had been accused of being an enemy of Christianity and this charge hurt him deeply. He was convinced that without Christianity one could neither run a personal life nor a state, and Germany in particular needed the kind of religious and moral foundation only Christianity could provide.[5]

Their conversation included Hitler's stating that he would take no steps against the

---

[1] http://en.wikipedia.org/wiki/Ludwig_Kaas (2008)
[2] Cymet, David. *History vs. Apologetics: The Holocaust, the Third Reich, and the Catholic Church.* p47
[3] Ibid.
[4] Ibid. p134
[5] Ibid. p51

Jews that the Church had not already taken in the previous 1500 years. There was no opposition by the prelates. And Hitler did exactly that.

The historian of the Centre Party, Karl Bachem, defended the Catholic vote and emphasised the unity of purpose that had been created between the Nazis and the Catholics:

> The bishops have voted unanimously for the recognition of the new government, such resistance, no longer morally defensible, would have been impossible for us ... It is true that parliamentarism and with it the democratic idea have come to a dead end ... So was it justified to try a new way? Certainly, Hitler had inserted several points in his speech that meet our wishes to a far greater extent than would have been thought possible, and give us a certain security ... It is certain that even Catholics loyal to the Church will now join the National Socialists formations in great numbers just as in Italy.[1]

Bishop Bornewasser addressed a Catholic gathering in the cathedral of Trier:

> With raised heads and firm step we have entered the new Reich and we are prepared to serve it with all the might of our body and soul.[2]

Oskar Wasserman, the president of the Committee for Inter-confessional Peace approached the Catholic bishops' conference seeking intervention with the Nazi government to stop the Nazi boycott against the Jews. The bishops firmly refused the request. Cardinal Faulhaber explained to clergyman Alois Wurm, the editor of the periodical *Seele* (*Spirit*), that the bishops had more important concerns than the fate of the Jews:

> For the higher ecclesiastical authorities there are immediate issues of much greater importance: Schools, the maintaining of Catholic associations, sterilization, are more important for Christianity in our homeland. One must assume that the Jews are capable of helping themselves.[3]

The Fulda Bishops' Conference, the Annexation of the Sudetenland, and Subsequent Catholic-Nazi Cooperation

The German bishops were elated at the annexation of the Sudetenland to the Third Reich in 1938 – not only with the expansion of the German Lebensraum, but also with the increase in the proportion of Catholics in the Reich by ten percent.

The Tablet (21 September 1940) viewed the Bishops' Fulda Conference as a definite step forward in Catholic-Nazi cooperation. It pointed out that all the Bishops of the Greater German Reich were present. It also stressed that the final address was delivered by Monsignor Berning, Bishop of Osnabrück, who occupied an exclusive position because of his appointment in 1933 by Hermann Göring as the representative of the Catholic Church to the Council of the Prussian State. *The Tablet* concluded:

---

[1] Cymet, David. *History vs. Apologetics: The Holocaust, the Third Reich, and the Catholic Church.* p48
[2] Ibid. p59
[3] Ibid. p50

The fact that this bishop was chosen to give the final word at the end of the Conference must be regarded as an indication of a new and positive evolution in the future relations between the German State and the Catholic Church ... well-informed circles believe that very important and positive decisions have been reached, which will result in a much closer rapprochement between the Church and the Reich.[1]

German Catholic Bishops

Enthusiasm for the Nazis ran high among the Catholic hierarchy. The first German bishop to take the oath of allegiance prescribed by the *Reichskonkordat* was the Bishop of Münster, Clement August von Galen, on 23 October 1933. Others followed.

Until the very end, Hitler remained for the German bishops the legitimate authority of Germany to whom they had sworn loyalty. They publicly praised his achievements, and many of the highest members, such as Berning, Gröber, and Wolker, publicly eulogised the new regime in inflated terms.

The most prominent Catholic theologians and historians, such as Joseph Lortz, Karl Adam of Tübingen, Michael Schmaus of Münster, and Theodor Bratter of Cologne, emphasised similarities between Roman Catholicism and the Nazi Weltanschauung.[2]

Bishop Wilhelm Berning of Osnabrück – In 1933 Hitler met Berning, the representative of the German Bishops' Conference, who held favourable views of the Führer. Hitler declared:

> I have been attacked because of my handling of the Jewish question. *The Catholic Church considered the Jews pestilent for fifteen hundred years*, put them in ghettos, etc., because it recognised the Jews for what they were. In the epoch of liberalism the danger was no longer recognised. I am moving back toward the time in which a fifteen-hundred-year-long tradition was implemented. I do not set race over religion, but I recognise the representatives of this race as pestilent for the state and for the Church, and perhaps I am thereby doing Christianity a great service by pushing them out of schools and public functions.[3]

Military Bishop (Feldbischof) Franz-Justus Rarkowski – This Catholic spiritual leader of priests assigned to the Wehrmacht was a particularly blatant proponent of Nazism.[4] A pastoral letter that he addressed to Catholic members of the Wehrmacht read:

> As so often in history, many European states know that the war against Russia is a European crusade ... This strong and obligatory experience of mission in the East will let you know how unspeakably great and fortunate we are as Germans.[5]

Bishop Buchberger of Regensburg called Nazi racism directed at Jews 'justified self-

---

[1] Moore, Edith. *No Friend of Democracy: A study of Roman Catholic politics – their influence on the ...*
[2] See, for example: Cymet, David. *History vs. Apologetics: The Holocaust, the Third Reich, and the Catholic Church.* p67
[3] http://en.wikipedia.org/wiki/Catholic_Church_and_Nazi_Germany (2012)
[4] *In God's Name: Genocide & Religion in the Twentieth Century*
[5] Frank, Ewald. *The Roman Empire & Its Significance in the End Time.* From 'Traditional Christianity - Truth or Deception?'. Source: http://www.biblebelievers.org.au/bb931015.htm (2007)

defence' in the face of 'overly powerful Jewish capital.'[1]

Bishop Hilfrich of Limburg said that the true Christian religion 'made its way not from the Jews but in spite of them.'[2]

On 19 August 1936, the German bishops issued a collective pastoral endorsing Adolf Hitler's support for General Franco.

The bishops stated in their pastoral letter from Fulda on 30 August 1936:

> There is no need to speak at length of the task which our people and our country are called upon to undertake. May our Führer, with the help of God, succeed in this extraordinary difficult work ... What we desire is that belief in God, as taught by Christianity, will not be overcome, but that it be universally recognized that this faith constitutes the only sure foundation upon which can be built the powerful and victorious bulwark destined to hold back the forces of Bolshevism ...[3]

At their 1941 annual conference in Fulda, the bishops recommended the introduction of a special 'war prayer' that was to be read at the beginning and end of all divine services. The prayer beseeched God's blessing on German arms, with victory and the granting of protection to the lives and health of all soldiers.[4]

Bishop von Galen – David Cymet commented: 'When the Holocaust came to light in all its horror after the war, it could have been expected that the Church would have welcomed or at least accepted the efforts made by the Allies to bring the genocide perpetrators to justice to reestablish in some measure the moral order that had been shattered. Things turned out differently.' In 1946 Bishop von Galen published a slanderous attack on the Nuremberg Tribunals:

> The trials were not about justice but about the defamation of the German people.[5]

In 1948 the German bishops issued a collective statement denying the moral and legal grounds of the Nuremberg Trials and accusing the tribunal of putting on trial people for breaking 'laws hitherto unknown in Germany,' that is, for murdering Jews.[6]

Austrian Catholic Bishops

David Cymet has recorded that 'The proclamation of the Austrian Bishops is one of the most eloquent expressions of the identification of the Austrian Church with the Third Reich.' The proclamation stated:

> We joyfully acknowledge the eminent work that the National Socialist movement has done and is still doing in the domain of national construction and economy as well as in the domain of social welfare, for the benefit of the Reich and the German

---

[1] http://en.wikipedia.org/wiki/Catholic_Church_and_Nazi_Germany (2012)

[2] Ibid.

[3] Lehmann, L H. *Behind the Dictators: A Factual Analysis of the Relationship of Nazi-Fascism and Roman Catholicism.* p33. So reflective of Eugenio Pacelli's disastrous paranoia of Bolshevism.

[4] *The New York Times*, 7 December 1941. Source: http://liberalslikechrist.org/Catholic/RC_scandal-2.html (2007)

[5] Cymet, David. *History vs. Apologetics: The Holocaust, the Third Reich, and the Catholic Church.* p427

[6] http://www2.dsu.nodak.edu/users/dmeier/23461117-The-Catholic-Church-and-the-Holocaust.pdf (2014)

nation, and notably for the poorest strata of the population. We are also convinced that the activity of the National Socialist movement has averted the danger of an all-destroying atheistic Bolshevism. For the future, the bishops confer their heartiest blessings on this activity, and they will instruct the faithful to this effect.

On the day of the plebiscite, it goes without saying that it is for us a national duty, as Germans, to vote for the German Reich, and we also expect all believing Christians to demonstrate that they know what they owe to their nation.[1]

A day before the plebiscite, all the churches in Austria and Germany complied with the request of the Nazi government to toll their bells as a sign of 'overwhelming expression of confidence of the entire nation in the Führer and his work.'[2]

Accordingly, the resistance of the Catholics of Austria to the Anschluss, and thereby to becoming part of the German Reich, ended in a submissive acceptance of, and identification with the Nazis.

In this case again, the Catholic Church rendered invaluable help to Hitler at the crossroads of history.[3]

French Catholic Bishops

Bishop Dutoit of Arras – 'The duty is simple, yet of utmost gravity: to follow, and support with our confidence, Marshal Pétain.'

Bishop of Marseille, Jean Delay

We are not ignoring the fact that the Jewish question poses difficult problems, nationally and internationally. We well recognise that our country has the right to take all necessary measures to defend us against those who, especially in recent years, have done it so much harm, and that it has the duty to severely punish those who abuse the hospitality which is so liberally accorded them.[4]

Bishop Lusaunier, Director of the seminary of the Carmelites – 'The French should obey Pétain, not De Gaulle.'

Archbishop Salièges – 'The legitimate government of France is headed by a man who has given France the gift of his person. A magnificent example of the renunciation of all egotism and of a noble love of the fatherland.'

Archbishop of Aix – 'Without hesitation we should all group ourselves around the illustrious Marshal.'

The Annual Assembly of the French Episcopate – The largest deportation of Jews from France, known as La Grande Rafle (the Big Raid), took place on 15-16 July 1942, in Paris. Approximately 13,300 men, women, and children were rounded up by French police and marched to the Velodrome D'Hiver, where they were held without food or water until they were taken to Drancy Deportation Camp, and thence deported to

---

[1] Cymet, David. *History vs. Apologetics: The Holocaust, the Third Reich, and the Catholic Church.* p112
[2] Ibid. p113
[3] Ibid. p111
[4] Ibid. p346

Sobibór Extermination Camp. At the annual assembly of the French episcopate on 22 July, the cardinals and bishops voted to abstain from any public protest against the deportations on grounds that their protest might bring about the banning of Catholic Action.[1]

Another major roundup occurred on 15 August, when 7000 foreign Jews were arrested and handed over to the Germans. Cardinal Maglione was informed.

Post-War Declaration – At Drancy, on 30 September 1997, the French Catholic bishops issued a *Declaration of Repentance*:

> The anti-Semitic legislation enacted by the French government – beginning with the October 1940 law on Jews and that of June 1941, which deprived a whole sector of the French people of their rights as citizens, which hounded them out and treated them as inferior beings within the nation – and given the decision to put into internment camps foreign Jews who thought they could rely on the rights of asylum and hospitality in France, we are obliged to admit that the bishops of France made no public statements, thereby *acquiescing by their silence* in the flagrant violation of human rights and leaving the way open to a death-bearing chain of events ... we must recognize that silence was the rule in face of the multifarious laws enacted by the Vichy government, whereas speaking out in favor of the victims was the exception.[2]

Belgian Catholic Bishops

While the Jews without citizenship were being hunted down and dispatched to death camps, the bishops of Belgium were silent.

Polish Catholic Bishops

Poland was chosen as the site of the death camps to carry out the Final Solution in Europe, not only because of Poland's geographic position as the centre of European Jewry, but also because of the fierce eliminative anti-Semitism that prevailed there.

The courageous Polish courier Ian Karski wrote in a report from occupied Poland to France in 1940:

> Nazi Jewish policy posed a grave danger to the Polish resistance because a large proportion of Polish society appreciated Nazi anti-Jewish policies and a narrow bridge was thus created between Germans and Poles.[3]

None of the three Polish Bishops' Councils during the German occupation mentioned the mass murder of the Jews nor expressed any protest about it. Even during the synod that took place on 1 June 1943, days after the merciless liquidation of the Warsaw ghetto, the bishops were silent.[4] Pius XII never apologised.[5]

---

[1] Cymet, David. *History vs. Apologetics: The Holocaust, the Third Reich, and the Catholic Church.* pp347-48
[2] Ibid. p350
[3] Ibid. p256
[4] Ibid.
[5] Phayer, Michael. *Pius XII, the Holocaust, and the Cold War*. pp39-41

· *Hungarian Catholic Bishops*

Ecclesiastics, such as *Cardinal Justinian Serédi* and *Bishop Gyula Glattfelder*, who served in Hungary's Parliament, voted in favour of the anti-Semitic legislation first passed in 1938. These laws commenced with economic and social restrictions on Jews, and ended, during World War II, with an initiative to expel Jews from Hungary.[1]

Archbishop Gyula Czapik wrote to Cardinal Serédi advising him against helping the Jews in any manner:

> While it is true that everyone is aware of the horrors, and everyone knows what happens to them at their final station, it would not be right to put this before the public in writing; what is happening to the Jews at the present time is nothing but appropriate punishment for their misdeeds in the past.[2]

From this perspective, it is evident how it was possible for Eichmann and his small team to send, in a few weeks, more than half a million Hungarian Jews to their death in Auschwitz. The assistance of the Hungarian police, the bishops, and the Hungarian laity was made possible by the approvals of almost all the Hungarian episcopate following the lead of Cardinal Serédi.

Several priests, such as *Ignác László* and *András Kun*, exulted in the deportations, and publicly called for the obliteration of the Jews. When all the Jews of Veszprém were deported, a *Te Deum* was held in the Franciscan[3] Church there. It was overflowing with people celebrating the town's absence of Jews. Notwithstanding, Cardinal Serédi and the Hungarian episcopate, the principal advocates of the anti-Jewish laws in Hungary, are now 'presented as charitable Samaritans who stood up in defense of Hungarian Jewry in their most tragic hour.'[4]

·   When the fate of the Hungarian Jews became known worldwide, appeals were again issued by Jewish organisations to Pius XII and other authoritative persons to use his influence to stop the annihilation of Hungarian Jewry. Placed in an embarrassing situation, Pius sent an open cable to Admiral Horthy, the regent of Hungary, on 25 June 1944, in which he avoided identifying the Jews as such 'and requested in his typical elliptic style' that the suffering of 'numerous unfortunate people' in Hungary be not prolonged. Avoiding all reference to their annihilation, Pius wrote:

> We have been requested from several sides to do everything possible to ensure that the suffering that *had to be borne* for so long by numerous unfortunate people in the bosom of this noble and chivalrous nation because of the nationality or racial origin not be prolonged and made worse.[5]

/   Rather than issuing a warning of excommunication against the perpetrators of genocide, Pius XII praised the 'chivalrous and noble Hungarian nation' which was sending

---

[1] Phayer, Michael. *The Catholic Church and the Holocaust, 1930-1965.* pp13-14
[2] Quoted in: Cymet, David. *History vs. Apologetics: The Holocaust, the Third Reich, and the Catholic ...* p364
[3] Once again, the iniquitous Franciscans appear on the pages of history.
[4] Cymet, David. *History vs. Apologetics: The Holocaust, the Third Reich, and the Catholic Church.* p364
[5] Ibid. p365

them to annihilation. Nor did he make any mention of religion. His evasive stance was 'in stark contrast to his excommunication of Italian Catholics who voted for the Communist Party in 1948 and those joining that party in 1949.'[1]

‘ *Ukrainian Catholic Bishops*

Nazi troops arrived in Lvov (Lviv) the capital of Western Ukraine on 30 June 1941. Crowds greeted them enthusiastically.

The Ukrainians had already begun rioting against the Jewish population there and in surrounding towns.

Archbishop Andrei Sheptyts'kyi of Lvov – Sheptyts'kyi was the highest authority of the Ukrainian Greek Catholic Church, which recognised the authority of the Roman Pope. In desperation, the chief rabbi of Lvov, Dr Yehezkel Levin, went to the residence of Archbishop Sheptyts'kyi on 2 July in the company of two representatives of the Jewish council to plead for his help in stopping the attacks on the Jews. Sheptyts'kyi promised to issue a pastoral letter to his parish, in which he would warn the Ukrainians against murder and plundering, but refused to intervene with the Germans. He offered asylum in his home to the rabbi, which was declined.[2]

On 25 July 1941, a second pogrom occurred. Numerous Ukrainian youths appeared in the streets of Lvov and dragged Jews from their homes. Around 2000 Jews were murdered, mostly by civilian collaborators.[3]

During the Nazi occupation Sheptyts'kyi's behaviour was contradictory.

On the one hand, he wrote to Pius XII and described the atrocities and mass murder being carried out against the Jews and the local population. Typically, Pius XII had no other advice to offer Sheptyts'kyi than to 'bear adversity with serene patience' – in other words, to stand aside quietly while the Jews were annihilated.[4] Sheptyts'kyi also protested to Himmler himself. He issued a pastoral letter entitled 'Thou Shalt not Murder', in which he publicly threatened 'with Divine punishment' any who 'shed innocent blood'.[5]

On the other hand, Sheptyts'kyi's correspondence in December 1939 with Pius XII reveals his antagonism to the Jews. He complained about the mass of Jewish refugees who fled in haste from the Germans to the Soviet side, swelling the Jewish population of Lvov to a record high of 135,000. 'His remarks maligning the fleeing refugees in classical anti-Semitic terms as unethical and avaricious belong in the same class as the defamatory reports of Vatican representatives in Bolivia and Chile to Pius XII, intended to stop the small flow of Jewish refugees from Nazi Germany to South America.'[6]

Additionally, Sheptyts'kyi issued a proclamation welcoming the German troops, and calling for collaboration with the Germans. He supported the creation of a Ukrainian

---

[1] Cymet, David. *History vs. Apologetics: The Holocaust, the Third Reich, and the Catholic Church.* p365
[2] Gitelman, Zvi Y. *Bitter legacy: confronting the Holocaust in the USSR.* pp279-80
[3] Cymet, David. *History vs. Apologetics: The Holocaust, the Third Reich, and ...* p232
[4] Ibid.
[5] http://www.lvov.us/famous-people/andrey-sheptytsky (2012)
[6] Cymet, David. *History vs. Apologetics: The Holocaust, the Third Reich, and the Catholic Church.* p232

division within the Waffen SS and ordered that a Solemn Mass be officiated in the Lvov cathedral to celebrate the formation of the division.[1] He linked the future of his country to the Third Reich and its Führer at the same time that his followers were annihilating Jews everywhere: 'they helped to round up Lvov's Jews and marched virtually every Jew in Lvov, around 140,000, to their death.'[2] Sheptyts'kyi was also one of several Ukrainian leaders who signed a letter to Hitler pledging support for the 'New Order' in Europe; and he blessed the Waffen-SS Galicia as it set out to do battle in 1943.[3]

Lithuanian Catholic Bishops

Bishop Vincentas Brizgys – In 1939 when Russia occupied the Baltic countries, Lithuanian Jews asked Bishop Brizgys to issue a pastoral letter forbidding Catholics from participating in pogroms. The bishop replied: 'The church cannot help you, I personally can only weep and pray.'[4,5]

Archbishop Juozapas Skvireckas and Bishop Vincentas Brizgys – Kaunas (Kovno), the capital of Lithuania, fell to the Axis on 24 June 1941. During the occupation of the Baltic States by the Nazis, the Archbishop of Kaunas, Juozapas Skvireckas and his assistant, Bishop Vincentas Brizgys, publicly welcomed the Nazis and expressed their gratitude to Hitler. Skvireckas provided chaplains for Lithuanian-manned Nazi auxiliary units.[6] Church authorities held solemn mass ceremonies in the cathedrals.

The bishops promised to fight with the Germans, and strongly supported the formation of Lithuanian Waffen SS divisions and SS police. Many Catholics volunteered in the SS Einsatzgruppen formations, which participated directly in the annihilation of the Jews. Catholic priests from the Baltics also served in these death squads.[7]

In one of the most brutal pogroms in memory, the Lithuanians then attacked the Jews of Kaunas. The killings lasted three days. 1500 defenceless Jewish men and women were dragged into the town square and mercilessly beaten to death with clubs by the laity, while synagogues and many homes were destroyed by fire.

The Nazis eventually established the Kaunas Ghetto, which at its peak held 40,000 people, most of whom were later sent to concentration and extermination camps, or were shot.[8]

In Slobodka,[9] a suburb of Kaunas, 'its venerable rabbi R Zalman Osovsky was bound hand and foot to a chair and his head sawed off.[10] His decapitated body was found still sitting at his desk ... His head was displayed at the window with a sign:

---

[1] Cymet, David. *History vs. Apologetics: The Holocaust, the Third Reich, and the Catholic Church.* p231
[2] Ibid. p232
[3] http://www.lvov.us/famous-people/andrey-sheptytsky (2012)
[4] Ibid.
[5] So similar to the phraseology of Pius XII.
[6] http://en.wikipedia.org/wiki/Juozapas_Skvireckas (2011)
[7] Cymet, David. *History vs. Apologetics: The Holocaust, the Third Reich, and the Catholic Church.* p223
[8] http://en.wikipedia.org/wiki/Kaunas_Ghetto (2012)
[9] Slobodka is now known as Vilijampolė.
[10] This was also a practice of the Catholic Ustaše in Croatia at that time.

This is what we will do to all the Jews![1]

When the Nazis ordered the Jews to move to a ghetto in Slobodka, a delegation headed by Rabbi Samuel Snieg appealed to Bishop Brizgys to intervene with the German commander. Brizgys replied:

> With all my regrets, I cannot do it. This may endanger the position of the Catholic Church in Lithuania. Such a responsibility I cannot take upon myself.[2]

Not a single word was heard coming from the episcopate to their flock on behalf of the Jews. The following excerpt from the 1941 report of 'Einsatzgruppen A' reveals Bishop Brisgys' instructions that he issued as acting head of the Catholic Church in Lithuania and his refusal to help the Jews in any way:

> The attitude of the Church regarding the Jewish question is, in general, clear. In addition, Bishop Brisgys has forbidden all clergymen to help Jews in any form whatsoever. He rejected several Jewish delegations that approached him personally and asked for his intervention with the German authorities. In the future he will not meet any Jews at all.[3]

. Most of the Lithuanian Jews had been murdered by the end of the war.[4] Historians have emphasised that no other Jewish community in Nazi-occupied Europe suffered such proportionately high losses as those in Lithuania.[5]

Latvian Catholic Bishops

SS Obergruppenführer Friedrich Jeckeln, one of the bloodiest mass murderers of all times, was dispatched to Riga to liquidate Latvian Jewry. In the smaller towns and villages, from June to the end of September 1941, the Einsatzgruppen, with the active participation of Latvian collaborators, murdered approximately 30,000 Jews – one third of the total Jewish population. The annihilation of Jews in the larger cities followed soon after.

Jeckeln turned the Riga massacre into a public spectacle with specially invited guests. In search of optimum efficiency and order he developed an original mass murder and burial system that became famous among the SS as the 'Jeckeln Sardinenpackung' (sardine-packing) method. The first group of victims was forced to undress, descend into the pit, and lie face down to be shot in the back of the head. Layer after layer of the victims was executed until the pit was full. The shooting of approximately 27,000 people included the Chief Rabbi of Riga, M M Zak.[6]

It has justifiably been asked: 'While this was happening, where were the Christian bishops?'

---

[1] Cymet, David. *History vs. Apologetics: The Holocaust, the Third Reich, and the Catholic Church.* p223
[2] Ibid. p224. The ever self-serving Church.
[3] Ibid.
[4] http://en.wikipedia.org/wiki/Kaunas#Kaunas.27_Jews.27_fate (2012)
[5] Cymet, David. *History vs. Apologetics: The Holocaust, the Third Reich, and the Catholic Church.* p226
[6] Ibid. pp225-26

Slovakian Catholic Bishops

The Slovakian Catholic Holocaust is described in detail in Chapter 14.

President Monsignor Jozef Tiso promulgated the first anti-Semitic legislation in 1939 and 1940. It placed race before religion by declaring that those who were baptised after 1918 were to be treated as Jews. Pius XII extended an apostolic blessing to President Tiso.[1] Tiso was captured on 8 June 1945. The next day, Cardinal Faulhaber protested his arrest:

> I feel duty bound to notify the Holy Father of your arrest of Dr Tiso, since as a prelate in good standing he is a member of the papal family.[2]

Tiso was convicted of war crimes. Impenitent to the end, he declared before his execution:

> If God allowed me to carry out my policy again under similar circumstances, I would do exactly as I have done.[3]

When Tiso's death was announced, the Slovak bishops ordered Church bells to be tolled throughout the country as a sign of mourning. 'The Slovak episcopate, anti-Semitic as ever, issued a letter on January 8, 1946, eulogising the remorseless persecutor of Slovak Jewry:'

> Dr Tiso was always a zealous priest of exemplary life. In his extensive activity he worked and labored for the common good ... The majority of the Slovak people agree with us that the intentions of Dr Tiso in the execution of his public activity were always the best.[4]

Croatian Catholic Bishops

The Croatian Catholic Holocaust is introduced in Chapter 14.

Bishop Antun Akšamović of Đakovo praised Hitler and taught that 'today it is the sacred duty of every citizen to prove his Aryan origins.'[5,6]

Slovenian Catholic Bishops

Gregorij Rožman was a Slovenian Roman Catholic clergyman and theologian. Between 1930 and 1959, he served as bishop of the Diocese of Ljubljana. He is best known for his role during World War II, when he collaborated with the fascist Italian and Nazi German occupying forces. He has also been accused of having abused his authority to actively promote military collaboration with these forces to fight against the resistance.[7]

---

[1] Phayer, Michael. *The Catholic Church and the Holocaust, 1930-1965.* p14
[2] Cymet, David. *History vs. Apologetics: The Holocaust, the Third Reich, and the Catholic Church.* p428
[3] Ibid. p429
[4] Ibid.
[5] http://www.sullivan-county.com/id2/timeline.htm (2007)
[6] http://www.jasenovac-info.com/cd/biblioteka/pavelicpapers/vatican/va0013.html (2007)
[7] http://en.wikipedia.org/wiki/Gregorij_Ro%C5%BEman (2012)

Rožman supported the Nazis. His anti-Semitism is evident in a pastoral letter published in 1943, in which he wrote:

> only by this courageous fighting and industrious work for God, for the people and the Fatherland will we, under the leadership of Germany, assure our existence and better future in the fight against the Jewish conspiracy.[1]

The Argentinian Church

Anti-Semitism in the Argentinian Church was based on the anti-Jewish theological position held by priests and Catholic intellectuals close to the Church hierarchy. Influential Catholic writers and the clergy gave credence to the fictitious *The Protocols of the Elders of Zion*, and lower ecclesiastics used the terms 'Jew' and 'communist' synonymously. After the June 1943 coup d'état, the similar aims of the army and the Church produced a 'Catholic Argentina'. The Church opposed Jewish immigration to the country, which would have upset the country's homogeneity. During the 1930s and 1940s, the anti-Semitism of the lower clergy was conveyed in parochial bulletins, while intellectual Catholics, through their contributions to Catholic newspapers and journals, had a strong influence on society in general.[2]

Confirmation of Catholic Bishops' Support for Militancy

Several sites on the internet show photographs of Catholic ecclesiastics supporting National Socialism. For example: 'Hitler greets a Catholic Cardinal'; 'Priests giving the Hitler salute at a Catholic youth rally in the Berlin-Neukolln Stadium in August 1933'; 'Cardinal Michael Faulhaber marches between rows of SA men at a Nazi rally in Munich'; 'Spanish Bishops giving the fascist salute'; 'Catholic Bishops giving the Nazi salute in honour of Hitler'.[3]

Daniel J Goldhagen, in his book *Hitler's Willing Executioners: Ordinary Germans and the Holocaust*, reminds his readers that thousands of Catholic priests cared for the spiritual needs of the millions of Germans serving in the institutions of killing. He then asked the salient question: why, so far as is known, did virtually none of these men of God ever raise a voice against the slaughter of the Jews?[4]

In the Vichy Zone of France, less than half the prelates, and not a single one in the Occupied Zone, objected to the deportation of the Jews.[5]

Gordon C Zahn is a former Professor of Sociology at Loyola University of Chicago, professor emeritus at the University of Massachusetts, Boston, former national director for the US Center on Conscience and War, and 1968 President of the American Catholic Sociological Society. He went to Germany in the 1950s to search for evidence of resistance on the part of the Catholic Church to the Nazi regime.

---

[1] Friedländer, Saul. *Pius XII and the Third Reich: A Documentation.* p106
[2] Review of: Ben-Dror, Graciela. *The Catholic Church and the Jews – Argentina 1933–1945.*
[3] http://www.nobeliefs.com/nazis.htm (2007)
[4] Goldhagen, Daniel Jonah. *Hitler's Willing Executioners: Ordinary Germans and the Holocaust.* p597
[5] Callil, Carmen. *Bad Faith: A Forgotten History of Family & Fatherland.* p299

His classic investigations, reported in his book *German Catholics & Hitler's Wars*,[1] provided empirical validation of the generalisation of the Catholic man of peace, E I Watkin, that historical fact reveals that bishops have systematically supported all wars waged by the government of their country.[2]

The Lower Catholic Echelons

Uncharitable Catholic priests appear frequently in these chapters. Only a few additional comments are offered here.

, The implementation of the *Nuremberg Laws* depended on information contained in the birth and marriage certificates kept by the churches in their archives. These archives were the only source of birth records before 1875. Both Catholic and Protestant churches willingly cooperated with the Nazi regime and provided it with the information necessary to identify Jews. Their enthusiasm did not wane even during the war years when identification meant deportation and death. The question, whether the Church should help the Nazi state in classing people of Jewish descent, was never debated.[3]

A 'brown priest' was a Catholic priest who was a member or public supporter of the Nazi Party. In his book *Hitler's Priests: Catholic Clergy and National Socialism*, Professor Kevin P Spicer lists 138 of these men.[4]

A few examples of actively murderous priests include:

> Catholic priests from the Baltics served in the murderous Einsatzgruppen formations.[5]

During the Croatian Holocaust:

> There were more than 1000 Roman Catholic priests who were war criminals and who served under archbishop Stepinac in Zagreb. Their service to Roman Catholic Christianity will remain a stain on the Christian faith.[6]

Additionally, in Croatia, Diana Johnstone, the widely-published essayist and columnist, wrote of:

> the extraordinary involvement of Roman Catholic clergy in the massacre of the Serbs.[7]

, *German Catholic Military Chaplains*

The Catholic chaplains serving in the German army were the eyes and ears of their

---

[1] The book has been praised by both *Cistercian Studies Quarterly* and *The Catholic Worker*.

[2] Watkin, E I. 'Unjustifiable War'. p57. Quoted in: Zahn, Gordon C. *German Catholics & Hitler's Wars: A Study in Social Control*. p261

[3] Cymet, David. *History vs. Apologetics: The Holocaust, the Third Reich, and the Catholic Church*. p83

[4] Spicer, Kevin P. *Hitler's Priests: Catholic Clergy and National Socialism*. Source: http://en.wikipedia.org/wiki/Brown_priest (2012)

[5] Cymet, David. *History vs. Apologetics: The Holocaust, the Third Reich, and the Catholic Church*. p223

[6] http://www.orthodoxchristianity.net/forum/index.php?topic=3556.0;all (2009)

[7] Johnstone, Diana. *Fools' Crusade: Yugoslavia, NATO and Western Delusions*. p149

ecclesiastic superiors. They witnessed the extermination of the Jews by the Einsatzgruppen. Their reports reached the highest Church authorities.

One letter quoted by historian Klaus Scholder, a Catholic chaplain of the Second Panzer Division, described the mass execution of the whole Ukrainian Jewish population of Berdychiv (men, women, and children) which he witnessed in 1941 after they were forced to undress and dig their own collective grave.[1] According to *Wikipedia* 'Most civilians from areas near the border did not have a chance to evacuate when the Nazis began their invasion on June 22, 1941. An "extermination" unit was established in Berdychiv in early July 1941 and a Jewish ghetto was set up. It was liquidated on October 5, 1941, after all the inhabitants were murdered.' The Nazis killed about 20,000 to 30,000 Jews who had not evacuated Berdychiv.[2]

Historian Doris Bergen has gathered conclusive evidence that the great majority of German military chaplains were not only eye witnesses to genocidal crimes, but they 'normalized' the brutality in which the men in their care were involved, and often supported them, condoning and blessing their crimes through words, actions, and silence. One of the most obvious manifestations of this iniquitous function was the provision of group absolution[3] for these soldiers.[4]

Hungarian Priesthood

The Minister of the Interior, Andor Jaross, declared after the War:

The leaders of the priesthood made declarations on behalf of the converts only.[5]

Austrian Priesthood

Albert Hartl was a former Catholic priest who totally embraced the Nazi movement. He initially sought support for the T4 Euthanasia programme. Later, he became a commander of the Einsatzgruppen SS paramilitary death squads.[6,7]

Catholic Moral Theology

Dr Joseph Mayer – During his preparations for war, Hitler also began to develop his plan for the elimination of the mentally and physically disabled. Josef Bühler, a Catholic, the head of Hitler's chancellery, stated at the Wannsee Conference the importance of solving 'the Jewish Question in the General Government as quickly as possible'. Bühler commissioned Albert Hartl to look for support for euthanasia among Catholic

---

[1] Cymet, David. *History vs. Apologetics: The Holocaust, the Third Reich, and the Catholic Church.* p315
[2] http://en.wikipedia.org/wiki/Berditchev (2012)
[3] In the Catholic Church 'Absolution proper is that act of the priest whereby ... he frees man from sin.' *Catholic Encyclopedia* ('Absolution'). In this instance, the soldiers killed the Jews, they were then absolved of the crime. Accordingly, in the words of Michael Cardinal Faulhaber, the Catholic Church is 'the greatest moral power on earth'.
[4] Cymet, David. *History vs. Apologetics: The Holocaust, the Third Reich, and the Catholic Church.* p315
[5] Ibid. p362
[6] Ibid. p214
[7] See also a review of: Denzler, Georg. *Widerstand ist nicht das richtige Wort: Katholische Priester und Theologen im Dritten Reich,* by Kevin P Spicer, Department of History, Stonehill College.

theologians. Dr Joseph Mayer, a professor of moral theology at the Catholic University of Paderborn, a long-term defender within the Catholic Church of sterilisation and abortion of the mentally ill, was consulted by Hartl in early 1939. After six months, Professor Mayer presented his conclusions to the chancellery. He suggested, that in his opinion, the Church would not oppose such a programme if it were seen to be in the national interest.[1]

The Jesuits

In January 1933 Ludwig Kaas, a Jesuit priest and an intimate of Eugenio Pacelli, sent a letter to German Chancellor Kurt von Schleicher, with a copy to President Paul von Hindenburg, suggesting that, as he, von Schleicher, did not have parliamentary backing, he should be dismissed, and his place taken over by Adolf Hitler, who controlled the largest party in the Reichstag. With decreasing support, von Schleicher resigned in February 1934. Seventeen months after his resignation, in the Night of the Long Knives, he was assassinated by order of his successor, Adolf Hitler.

The text of the *Reichskonkordat* was finalised on 1 July 1933. The next day, from the Vatican, Monsignor Kaas telephoned Joseph Joos of the Centre Party and hurled at him the dreadful words: "What! Haven't you dissolved yourselves yet?" Two days later, Brüning,[2] having been denied options, made the terrible decision to voluntarily dissolve the Centre Party. With its expiration, democracy disappeared from Germany. As a consequence, millions of people died terrible, violent deaths.[3]

In their monthly *Stimmen der Zeit*, the Jesuits expressed in their summary of 1933 the singleness of purpose between the Cross and the Hakenkreuz (swastika):

> The speedy conclusion of the concordat has demonstrated that hostility need not prevail between the swastika and the Christian cross. On the contrary: the symbol of nature only finds its fulfilment and consummation in the symbol of grace.[4]

Hitler and Himmler were greatly influenced by the Jesuits, as was Mussolini, whose father confessor was a Jesuit.

Dr L H Lehmann pointed out in his book *Behind the Dictators* that Jesuit Father Staempfle was the ghost writer for Hitler of *Mein Kampf*. In it, Staempfle argued in favour of the indisputability of Catholic dogmas and of the intolerant attitude of Catholic education, as well as the necessity of blind faith and of the personal infallibility of the Pope.[5]

In *The Vatican Against Europe*, Edmond Paris related that Hitler's associate, Hermann Rauschning, recalled Hitler as saying that he learned most of all from the Jesuit

---

[1] Cymet, David. *History vs. Apologetics: The Holocaust, the Third Reich, and the Catholic Church.* p252

[2] Dr Heinrich Brüning was a German politician during the Weimar Republic. In 1929, he was elected chairman of the Centre Party's faction in the Reichstag. He served as Chancellor of Germany from 1930 to 1932.

[3] Noel, Gerard. *Pius XII: The Hound of Hitler.* p72

[4] Cymet, David. *History vs. Apologetics: The Holocaust, the Third Reich, and the Catholic Church.* p68

[5] Hilton, Adrian. *The Principality and Power of Europe.* Source: http://www.freewebs.com/nexxcentral/conspiracyihistory.htm (2008)

order: 'So far there has been nothing more imposing on earth than the hierarchical organisation of the Roman Catholic Church. A good part of that organisation I have transported to my own party. I will tell you a secret. I am founding an order.'[1] Hitler was also quoted as saying of Heinrich Himmler: 'In Himmler I see our Ignatius de Loyola.'

In world politics, much of the murky machinations of the Jesuits ("Rome's caterpillars") is yet to be fully revealed.

Synopsis

The German and Austrian cardinalates were most supportive of Adolf Hitler and his 'genocidal state'.[2]

Cardinal Bertram congratulated Hitler on the signing of the *Reichskonkordat*. Every April 20th (Hitler's birthday), Bertram sent 'warmest congratulations to the Führer in the name of the bishops and the dioceses in Germany ...'

The 'Heil Hitler Cardinal', Theodor Innitzer, Archbishop of Vienna, was active in Austrian politics, leaned heavily towards Fascism, and offered whole-heartedly his blind support of the future aims of the Anschluss.

Michael von Faulhaber, Archbishop of Munich, was a key figure in the rapprochement between the Church and the Nazis.

The diocesan chancelleries assisted the Nazis in detecting people of Jewish descent. This cooperation continued throughout the war years.

The public reaction of Catholic bishops to the mass murder of Jews in the death camps consisted of vague pronouncements that had no mention of the word Jew.

Prelate Ludwig Kaas was the main advocate supporting the *Enabling Act,* through which Chancellor Adolf Hitler legally established his dictatorship. Kaas was later elevated by the Holy See for his efforts.

Archbishop Orsenigo, the nuncio in Berlin, was supportive of Hitler and his top associates.

Monsignor Konrad Gröber was nicknamed 'Konrad the Brown' because of his policy of cooperation with the Nazis.

Archbishop Ivan Šarić of Sarajevo was known as 'The Hangman of the Serbs' and was also strongly anti-Semitic. He stated: 'The movement for ridding the world of Jews is a movement for restoring human dignity.'

Bishop Antun Akšamović of Đakovo praised Hitler and taught that 'today it is the sacred duty of every citizen to prove his Aryan origins.'

---

[1] Hilton, Adrian. *The Principality and Power of Europe.* Source: http://www.freewebs.com/nexxcentral/conspiracyinhistory.htm (2008)

[2] Berenbaum, Michael. *The World Must Know.* p103

Alfred-Henri-Marie Baudrillart, Cardinal-Priest, and later Auxiliary Bishop of Paris, supported the Nazis.

The annual German Bishops' Conferences at Fulda regularly supported Hitler and the Nazis. For example, 'May our Führer, with the help of God, succeed in this extraordinary difficult work ...'

Monsignor Berning, Bishop of Osnabrück, was the representative of the Catholic Church to the Council of the Prussian State. He conveyed to Hitler the congratulations by the 1933 Fulda Bishops' Conference on his becoming Chancellor.

Military Bishop Franz-Justus Rarkowski, a particularly blatant proponent of Nazism, was the Catholic spiritual leader of priests assigned to the Wehrmacht.

The Catholic bishops of Poland were strongly anti-Semitic.

Slovakian President Monsignor Jozef Tiso promulgated the first anti-Semitic legislation in 1939 and 1940. Slovakia was the only country to pay Germany to take its Jews.

Archbishop Karol Kmet'ko of Slovakia was extremely anti-Semitic. He said of the war effort: 'This is your punishment for the death of our Redeemer. There is only one hope for you, to convert to our religion.'

Catholic Moral Theology[1] sanctioned sterilisation and abortion of the mentally ill.

The Catholic press was supportive of Hitler and National Socialism.

The Jesuit Order assisted the rise of Adolf Hitler, and was a model for his Nazi organisation.

————

---

[1] In the words of Cardinal Faulhaber, the Catholic Church is 'the greatest moral power in the history of the world.'

20 – The Popes pre-War, Eugenio Pacelli

> *The world is a dangerous place to live; not because of the people who are evil, but because of the people who don't do anything about it.* Albert Einstein

> *Our lives begin to end the day we become silent about things that matter.* Martin Luther King, Jr

Pope Gregory XVI (1831-1846)

Gregory 'treated the Jews of the Roman ghetto so atrociously that the most conservative head of state in Europe, Austria's Chancellor Metternich, begged him to lighten up'.[1]

Pius IX (1846-1878)

Pius IX sought a loan from the Jewish Rothschild Bank, which he was granted only after he promised to improve the living conditions of the Roman Ghetto. This promise he broke.[2]

Leo XIII (1878-1903)

For centuries, the political Holy See had hoped to restore its dominion over the states of Europe. Its policy was aimed at a strong, martial Germany which would erase British Protestant influence from the West, and especially safeguard it from Russo-Slavic invasion from the East. To achieve this, a Greater Germany had to be again made the centre of a revived Holy Roman Empire.[3] Kaiser Wilhelm II ruled both the German Empire and Prussia from 1888 to 1918. During his last visit to the Vatican, Leo XIII urged this very policy upon him. In his *The Kaiser's Memoirs*, Wilhelm II described the solemn circumstance in which the interview took place, and recorded that he had noted what was said for future reference. The salient point was Leo's insistence that the Holy Roman Empire should be restored, by war, if necessary; and to achieve this 'Germany must become the Sword of the Catholic Church.' The Kaiser wrote:

> It was of interest to me that the Pope said to me on this occasion that Germany must become the sword of the Catholic Church. I remarked that the old Roman Empire of the German nation no longer existed, and that conditions had changed. But he stuck to his words.[4]

Referring to such an insistence of the Pope, an editorial in *The New York Times* of 14 February 1887 was headed: 'the German political fight; papal influence directly exerted in favor of the septennate'. The article included a forceful indictment of the Church:

> All is grist that comes to the mills of Rome. The collision between the spirit of

[1] Phayer, Michael. *Pius XII, the Holocaust, and the Cold War*. p97
[2] Ibid.
[3] Lehmann, L H. *Behind the Dictators: A Factual Analysis of the Relationship ...* p22
[4] Wilhelm II. *The Kaiser's Memoirs*. p172

military absolutism and the spirit of Parliamentary liberty in Germany, a contest watched with the deepest interest all over the world, and whose issue will be potent in molding the history of Europe for years to come, *is viewed by the Pope merely as a welcome opportunity to improve the condition of the Roman Catholic Church in Germany.*

The party of the Centre in the Reichstag is the Catholic party. Dr Windthorst, who has been its leader throughout the long struggle against the May laws, is its leader now. He led the successful opposition to Bismarck's bill increasing the army and providing for its support for a period of seven years, commonly called the Septennate bill.

When the Reichstag had rejected the bill and Bismarck had dissolved that body and a new general election had been ordered, Baron Frankenstein sent to Koine, through the Papal Nuncio at Munich, an inquiry as to the views and wishes of the Pope concerning the conduct of Catholics in the struggle. The Pope's reply is made in a letter written by Cardinal Jacobini: 'That the Septennate question embraces religious and moral considerations which justify him in expressing the opinion that he may expect from the Centre party's conciliation towards the measure *a beneficial effect* in the final revision of the May laws.' The Pope desires, moreover, 'to meet the views of Emperor William and Bismarck, and thereby *induce the powerful German Empire to improve the position of the Papacy.*'

It summarised the Church's sole interest – itself:

One sentence of Dr Windthorst's address reveals with pitiless and perhaps unintentional frankness *the profound immorality of the temporal policy of the Church of Rome.* 'The Pope's advocacy of the Septennate bill,' said Dr Windthorst, 'was independent of the merits of the measure, and arose from reasons of expediency and from political considerations.' It would be difficult to frame a more accurate analysis of the Papal motives while at the same time indicating a more sweeping denunciation of the Papal policy. Liberal principles, the right of popular government, the German constitution and its guarantee of Parliamentary institutions, says the Pope, may go to the dogs if we can secure some further modification of the laws which relate to the Church, and *so improve the condition of the Papacy in Germany.*[1]

Pius X (1903-1914)

Pope St Pius X is known for vigorously opposing modernist interpretations of Catholic doctrine, and promoting traditional devotional practices and orthodox theology.

He was sympathetic with Charles Maurras' Action Française. For Pius X, the Jewish faith was 'superseded by the teachings of Christ … we cannot admit that it still enjoys any validity.'

Unashamedly, Pius used some of the 'offerings of the faithful poor' (Peter's Pence)

---

[1] Mannanberg, Leopold. 'A Vital Condition for Lasting Peace'. Appendix to: Lehmann, L H. *Behind the Dictators: A Factual Analysis of the Relationship of Nazi-Fascism and Roman Catholicism.* pp107-8

'to bail out bankrupt members of the Roman Catholic aristocracy, including members of his own family.'[1]

In 1894 Father Henri Delassus wrote 'antisemitism and Catholicism are one and the same thing.' Pius appointed him Apostolic Prothonotary and made him a monsignor.

During the First World War, Pius refused to condemn the German invasion of neutral Belgium.[2]

Benedict XV (1914-1922)

In 1916 during World War I, American Jews petitioned Benedict on behalf of Polish Jews. The Pope responded with a letter that condemned everything that violated 'the natural law'.[3] The letter had asked Benedict to exert his authority to stop the mistreatment of Jews throughout the world, in particular the pogroms on the Russian front. Benedict declined, since, he said, he had no way of confirming the facts claimed in the letter.[4] His reply said nothing about equality in civil rights nor any rejection of social, political, or legal restrictions on Jews. Martin Rhonheimer, in his article 'The Holocaust: What Was Not Said', concludes that it is fair to assume that the people responsible for the pogroms never learned of the papal letter.[5]

On the positive side, during Benedict's pontificate, 'the anti-Jewish campaign in the *Civiltà Cattolica* and the *Osservatore Romano* was curtailed.'[6]

By contrast, Benedict made a point of praising the work of Father Ernest Jouin, who wrote during the 1920s: 'From the triple viewpoint of race, of nationality, and of religion, the Jew has become the enemy of humanity.'[7]

Pius XI (1922-1939)

Monsignor Achille Ratti, the future Pius XI, was sent in 1918 on a special diplomatic mission by Benedict XV to assess the chaotic situation in Poland. Specifically, he was to investigate the killings of Jews. 'Ratti did no such thing.' He falsely reported that Jews were an 'extremist [party] bent on disorder,' and that 'one of the most evil and strongest influences that is felt here ... is that of the Jews.'[8]

Pius XI and Benito Mussolini were alike in many ways, and 'had many things in common. They shared a distrust of democracy ... Each relied on the other to consolidate his power and achieve his political goals.' Neither could have real friends, because that would imply equality. Both required obedience.[9]

[1] Phayer, Michael. *Pius XII, the Holocaust, and the Cold War*. p98

[2] Michael, Robert. *A History of Catholic Antisemitism: The Dark Side of the Church*. pp163-66

[3] The Natural Law – a favoured concept of the Church, which has been adapted to almost any situation.

[4] Similar to the excuse of the Holy See with respect to World War II atrocities.

[5] Rhonheimer, Martin. The Holocaust: What Was Not Said', *First Things Magazine*, November 2003. Source: http://en.wikipedia.org/wiki/Pope_Benedict_XV_and_Judaism (2014)

[6] Coppa, Frank J. *The Papacy, the Jews, and the Holocaust*. p133

[7] Review of: Kertzer, David I. *The Popes Against the Jews: The Vatican's Role in the Rise of Modern Anti-Semitism*. http://atheism.about.com/library/books/full/aafprPopesJews.htm (2014)

[8] Michael, Robert. *A History of Catholic Antisemitism: The Dark Side of the Church*. p148-49

[9] Kertzer, David I. *The Pope and Mussolini: The Secret History of Pius XI and the Rise of ...* dust cover, p68

Pius was conscious of his status, and 'thought it undignified to be photographed with visitors, royal or not.'[1]

'Pius XI played a crucial role in making Mussolini's dictatorship possible and keeping him in power.'[2] Thus in September 1923 the Holy See initiated a programme of collaboration of Catholics with Mussolini's Government.[3] This it did, by concluding that 'In every respect the constitution by Catholics of a mass support for the Honourable Mussolini's government seems to be the most dependable and reassuring combination imaginable in Italy.'[4]

Under Pius, 'the Catholic clergy played a crucial role in lending the Duce cult a religious flavor, promoting a heady mix of fascist and Catholic ritual.'[5] As a consequence, the Italian fascist revolution became a clerico-fascist revolution. In this context it is noteworthy that Pius 'was careful to distinguish between good Fascism – that which recognized the Church's rights and followed its precepts – and bad Fascism, which did not.'[6]

In 1925 Pius declared a Holy Year. He closed it by issuing the Encyclical *Quas primas*, in which he declared that humanity could only be saved if it embraced the one true religion, Roman Catholicism.[7]

In 1926 an assassination attempt was made on Benito Mussolini. Pius told Il Duce of his 'immense joy' that he was 'safe and sound thanks to Jesus Christ's special protection.'[8]

In 1929 Pius XI chose anti-Semitic Archbishop Francesco Duca as nuncio to the Kingdom of Italy. In 1930 he selected Cesare Orsenigo as nuncio to Germany. Orsenigo informed the German Foreign Office in June 1940 of his pleasure at the German victories, that he could not wait for Italy to enter the War, and that he hoped the Germans would march into Paris by way of Versailles. Pius neither replaced Orsenigo, nor chided those German bishops who exhibited anti-Semitism, nor informed German bishops of the particulars he knew about the early Holocaust, nor did he urge them to oppose the Final Solution on moral or any other grounds.[9]

Pius XI was also anti-Protestant. He acknowledged that the Protestants in Italy were few, but argued that the threat of their proselytising was great;[10] and he kept pushing Mussolini's government to restrict Protestants' rights there. Nor was Pius happy to learn that the government planned to allow high schools with sufficient non-Catholics to offer

---

[1] Kertzer, David I. *The Pope and Mussolini: The Secret History of Pius XI and the Rise of Fascism in Europe.* p137

[2] Ibid.

[3] Ibid. p61

[4] Ibid. p64

[5] Ibid. p178

[6] Ibid. p161

[7] Ibid. p84

[8] Ibid. p87

[9] Michael, Robert. *A History of Catholic Antisemitism: The Dark Side of the Church.* p172

[10] Kertzer, David I. *The Pope and Mussolini: The Secret History of Pius XI and the Rise of Fascism ...* p185

them instruction in their own religion.[1]

During the 1930s, Pius XI said nothing about Polish anti-Semitism. During his tenure, Judaism was generally seen in Poland as a direct threat to a Polish Catholic identity. The Church encouraged discrimination, economic boycotts, and the branding of Jews as spiritual and political enemies. The Catholic press and education were generally anti-Semitic.[2]

For most of his papacy 'Pius XI accepted antisemitism without objection.' He admired the anti-Semitic saints: St Ambrose, St Augustine, St John Chrysostom, St Thomas Aquinas, and St Ignatius Loyola. He modelled himself on another Catholic saint: the eleventh-century pope St Gregory VII, who referred to the Jews as 'the synagogue of Satan.'[3]

Pius XI had the reputation of being 'the Pope of Catholic Action.'[4]

During the inter-war years, when Germany was a democratic republic, many of the clergy and some of the religious orders favoured the liberal, secularising spirit. They formed the mainstay of the Deutsche Zentrumspartei (Catholic Centre Party) (CCP), which was to become the last impediment to Hitler's rise to power. In the Reichstag, the CCP had the potential support of around 27 million German Catholics. Between 1919 and 1933, five CCP members served as chancellors in ten ruling cabinets of the Weimar Republic.

Concordats (diplomatic treaties) between the Holy See and the different governments became the favourite modus operandi of Pius XI to guarantee Church rights. He sought accommodation with the one-party fascist dictatorships of Europe. These dictators, delighted with this new policy that gave their politics clear reign, lined up to sign concordats with the Holy See. Eugenio Pacelli, the Holy See's main diplomatic negotiator of concordats, signed a total of eighteen concordats in rapid succession 'with such reactionary regimes as Poland, Portugal, and Italy, among others.'[5]

'The Night of the Long Knives' ('Nacht der langen Messer'), or more commonly 'the blood purge', was a purge that took place in Nazi Germany in June-July 1934, during which the Nazi regime carried out a series of political executions. The leader of the CCP, Erich Klausener, was assassinated.[6]

Karl Boka, a fervent supporter of Catholic restoration, wrote in his book *Staat und Parteien*:

> At this decisive moment the Pope [Pius XI] seized the reins and took into his hands the unified control of all fields of endeavour in which his predecessors had distinguished themselves. This was the beginning of Catholic Action of far-reaching importance, of the entrance of the church into the fight, into the battle for moral and

---

[1] Kertzer, David I. *The Pope and Mussolini: The Secret History of Pius XI and the Rise of Fascism...* p197-98
[2] Michael, Robert. *A History of Catholic Antisemitism: The Dark Side of the Church.* p148-49
[3] Ibid. p171
[4] Kertzer, David I. *The Pope and Mussolini: The Secret History of Pius XI and the Rise of Fascism...* pp55-56
[5] Cymet, David. *History vs. Apologetics: The Holocaust, the Third Reich, and the Catholic Church.* p55
[6] Lehmann, L H. *Behind the Dictators: A Factual Analysis of the Relationship ...* p28

religious renovation, and for the reform of social institutions. And this intervention *had for its end the destruction of the liberal spirit of the 19th century* and the triumph of the Christian Idea.[1]

Catholic Action was the crusade for Jesuit-Catholic reforming action. Pius XI's encyclical *Quadragesimo anno* established that its direction was explicitly entrusted to the Society of Jesus, and that its aims were the:

> extermination of the liberal spirit of the 19th century; formation of a world crusade against socialism and Communism; success of the counter-Reformation.

The most suitable political regime to assure the success of this crusade was the hierarchical, authoritarian fascist state.[2]

An outstanding Roman Catholic historian, Josef Schmidlin (1876-1944), stated in the *History of the Popes of Modern Times*:

> This conservative heritage appears not only by the fact that the Pope (Pius XI) allied the church to the fascist state, but also by the fact that he seeks to deprive the clergy and Catholicism of all political activity and strongly supports Catholic Action, which is based upon the principle of an absolute hierarchy.[3]

Bishop Dr Alois Hudal wrote at Rome on 2 September 1944:

> I was most profoundly convinced that this movement [National Socialism – NS] should it make war on Christianity, *would drag the German people into an unheard-of tragedy.*

> I may add that, as the first theologian and bishop of the whole world, I handed to Pope Pius XI on his request a *Pro Memoria* on the fundamentals of NS already in November 1934 (!), after I had returned from a tour of lectures in Germany. Especially at Trier I had spoken on 'Rome and the German People'. My proposal to the Holy Father was the following: 'to condemn by a Papal statement issued in Rome the following heresies as dangerous for our epoch: Radical nationalism, racism and *state totalitarianism.*'

The Bishop's proposal was rejected by Pius XI. Later, Hudal commented:

> I am sorry that my proposal could not be carried out ... I am sure that the German people, Austria and other nations that had to feel the cruel consequences of these false doctrines, could have spared much, had the ban as I proposed, in time been thrown against these doctrines which to whole Europe have brought so much disaster. The salvation of mankind lies in the courage to fight ruthlessly against the error even at the cost of present sacrifices.[4]

* Recently a draft has come to light of an encyclical that Pius XI himself commissioned

[1] Boka, Karl. *Staat und Parteien.* p75. Quoted in: Lehmann, L H. *Behind the Dictators* ... p39
[2] Ibid. p56
[3] Ibid. p49
[4] http://www.isracast.com/link_page.asp?link=http://web.archive.org/web/20030415213347/ (2010)

in 1938 on Nazi anti-Semitism. It is entitled *Humani generis unitas* (*The Unity of the Human Race*). It notes that 'the Church is only interested in upholding her legacy of Truth ... *The purely worldly problems in which the Jewish people may see themselves involved, are of no interest to her.*'[1] It condemned the Jews as being 'blinded by vision of material domination and gain [and therefore] spiritually blind', as failing to recognise Christ, as being guilty of the death of Jesus, and as being cursed to perpetually wander.[2]

✝ Eugenio Pacelli (Pius XII, 1939-1958)

Eugenio Pacelli led a protected life. At age 41 he left his mother and his parental home. He was undeveloped psychologically, and spoiled. For example, when he first left for Munich to take up the new role of nuncio to Bavaria, he occupied two compartments on the train, 'one for himself, and a second for the sixty cases of food he brought with him.'[3]

Pacelli was trained as a canon lawyer.[4] He was an intellectual Church official who possessed a theological-bureaucratic constriction with which he conceived relations between the Church and the World.[5]

Essentially, Pacelli was a diplomat and a politician. His politics had disastrous consequences for the world.

He was also interested in money. 'For Pope Pius, money mattered.'[6,7] At this time, 'Rome rewarded those who rewarded it with cash.'[8] Evidence confirms that the dollar power of the US Church was a good investment 'for career-minded prelates.'[9]

During World War II, under Pius XII, the Vatican transferred large sums in gold from Europe to the United States. Significantly, that from the UK coincided with the Battle of Britain.[10] Reprehensibly, the Vatican even supplied money to Japan via Switzerland.[11]

Pius XII shared in the long-standing Catholic culture of anti-Semitism which viewed the Jews as God killers and the authors of their own deserved history of misfortunes.[12,13]

A measure of Pius' strong anti-Semitism may be gauged from the following. Under Mussolini,[14] Italy promulgated its anti-Semitic laws. These contradicted the Lateran Agreement between the Holy See and the Italian State. Pius XI did not like this at all.

---

[1] Noel, Gerard. *Pius XII: The Hound of Hitler.* p90
[2] Michael, Robert. *A History of Catholic Antisemitism: The Dark Side of the Church.* p178
[3] Kertzer, David I. *The Pope and Mussolini: The Secret History of Pius XI and the Rise of Fascism...* p150
[4] Further information on the attitudes and activities of Eugenio Pacelli is given in *'A Corrupt Tree'*, Chapter II-7 of this encyclopaedia, and in Stockwell, Antony. *Pius XII: The Dark Side.*
[5] See, for example: Falconi, Carlo. *The Silence of Pius XII.* p105
[6] Phayer, Michael. *Pius XII, the Holocaust, and the Cold War.* p102
[7] See also: Pollard, John. *Money and the Rise of the Modern Papacy*
[8] Phayer, Michael. *Pius XII, the Holocaust, and the Cold War.* p41
[9] Ibid. p102
[10] Ibid. p103
[11] Ibid. p107
[12] See, for example: Atkin, Nicholas & Frank Tallet. *Priests, Prelates & People.* p256
[13] See also, Phayer, Michael. *Pius XII, the Holocaust, and the Cold War.* p120
[14] Mussolini had recognised the benefit that dealing with the Holy See would have for his political aspirations. Refer to: Kertzer, David I. *The Pope and Mussolini: The Secret History of Pius XI and the Rise of ...* p xx

'The standoff between dictator and pope escalated until Pius XI's death.' Pius XII, however, 'let the matter drop,'[1] and made no social or economic objections to the anti-Semitic policies of Mussolini.[2]

As Cardinal Secretary of State, Eugenio Pacelli's 'political skills and ambition made him Mussolini's most powerful ally inside the Vatican.'[3] And approval by the Holy See played a major role in legitimising Mussolini's new regime.[4]

The American Jewish Joint Distribution Committee (JDC) is a worldwide Jewish relief organization headquartered in New York. It was established in 1914 and is active in more than 70 countries. It offers aid to Jewish communities around the world through a network of social and community assistance programs.

During the War, Reuben Resnik, an American Jew, worked for the JDC in Italy, and became its director there after the War. In 1988 he was profuse in his praise of Italian Catholics for their efforts to save Jews, but not so for Pius XII:

> I was not a great admirer of top Vatican policy with respect to the Holocaust. During its height there was constant apologizing by the Vatican for its inability to do anything about it when as a matter of fact *no effort* was made to do anything about it.[5]

He believed that an audience that he had with Pius XII was just a publicity stunt.

Michael Phayer concluded that Resnik's statement reflects accurately the absence of concentrated concern by Pius for Roman Jews during the Nazi occupation.

Pacelli was also an unassailable Germanophile. Of this there is no doubt.[6] Shortly after his consecration as bishop, he was appointed in 1920 to Munich as the first Papal Nuncio to Germany. His main task was to impose, through the *1917 Code of Canon Law*, the supreme papal authority over the Catholic bishops, clergy and laity.

'From the day he came to Germany as nuncio in 1917 until his death in 1958, Pius identified himself so thoroughly with Germany,' as if he were a member of the German episcopate. The Church's differences with Nazism did not prevent it from supporting Hitler in all his aggressive enterprises, although it meant endorsing a regime of extreme evil. Except where it directly affected the interests of the Church, 'the bishops kept their peace.' With their silence they rendered a service of incalculable value to Hitler by leaving the field completely free to Pacelli.[7]

Pacelli had a penchant for concordats. Consequently, to fulfil his task, he began re-negotiating the existing concordats with the separate German states. He negotiated concordats between the Holy See and the German states of Bavaria and Prussia in 1924 and 1929.

---

[1] Phayer, Michael. *Pius XII, the Holocaust, and the Cold War*. pp114-15
[2] Ibid. p121
[3] Kertzer, David I. *The Secret History of Pius XI and the Rise of Fascism in Europe. The Secret History of Pius XI and the Rise of Fascism in Europe* … dust cover
[4] Ibid. p51
[5] Quoted in: Phayer, Michael. *The Catholic Church and the Holocaust, 1930-1965*. p125
[6] Ibid. p55
[7] Cymet, David. *History vs. Apologetics: The Holocaust, the Third Reich, and the Catholic Church*. p166

Pacelli acquired a reputation as an able diplomat. During his career, he acquired impeccable skills in using veiled language. He assessed every word he spoke or wrote with caution. His utterances were outstanding achievements of circumspection, cast in a web of elegantly ambiguous periphrasis. He never lost either these skills or this habit.[1]

In 1939 Cardinal Pacelli became Pius XII.

The actions and inactions of Pius XII during the Holocaust remain controversial. During most of the war, while German atrocities were committed, he presented a public face of indifference and remained silent. On the grounds of neutrality, he refused supplications for help, yet made statements condemning injustices in general. Privately, he sheltered a relatively minor number of Jews and spoke to a few select officials, encouraging them to help the Jews.[2]

In his book *History vs. Apologetics: The Holocaust, the Third Reich, and the Catholic Church,* David Cymet concluded that the signing by Pacelli of the *Reichskonkordat* and his subsequent behaviour enabled the fruits of the millennial Catholic background of anti-Semitism and pro-German prejudice to reinforce each other in enticing the Holy See 'to enter into a Faustian pact with Hitler by which the Church was turned into an accomplice of the Nazi crimes against the Jewish people.' The Holy See supported a transaction 'in which the lives of the Jews of Europe were the prize requested by Hitler.'[3]

Pacelli's Introduction to, and Support of Adolf Hitler

Włodzimierz Ledóchowski was the 26th Superior-General ('the Black Pope') of the Society of Jesus (the Jesuits). In 1917 he invited Mathias Erzberger, a deputy of the German Catholic Centre Party, for a secret meeting. There, Ledóchowski persuaded Erzberger to support a strategy of destroying the unified Reich under the Protestant Kaiser Wilhelm II, in order to bring the Catholic nations of central and eastern Europe together in a pan-Germanic federation under a 'charismatic dictator'.[4]

The German writer Dr Hans Carossa observed that 'Every political manoeuvre that Erzberger has engaged in since his discussion with the Jesuit General has only served to advance this Jesuit political strategy.'[5]

Accordingly, one blustery night during the winter of 1919, this 'charismatic dictator' arrived at Briennerstrasse 15, Munich, Bavaria – the nunciature of the Holy See. This building housed three significant players in world politics: Eugenio Pacelli (Archbishop of Sardi, nuncio to Bavaria, and administrator of the Vatican's foreign affairs); his

---

[1] Noel, Gerard. *Pius XII: The Hound of Hitler.* p16
[2] Schoenberg, Shira. *Pope Pius XII and the Holocaust.* http://www.jewishvirtuallibrary.org/jsource/anti-semitism/pius.html (2007)
[3] Cymet, David. *History vs. Apologetics: The Holocaust, the Third Reich, and the Catholic Church.* p404
[4] http://www.tuppersaussy.com/museum/html/writings/articles/15brienner.html (2008)
[5] Barthel, Manfred. *The Jesuits.* pp 254-55. Source: http://www.tuppersaussy.com/museum/html/writings/articles/15brienner.html (2008)

housekeeper and confidant, Pascalina Lehnert, a Holy Cross nun; and his Jesuit speech-writer Robert Leiber.[1,2]

Sister Pascalina recalled the moment of the arrival of this 'charismatic dictator' at the nunciature. She heard a knock at the door, and opening it saw a young Austrian soldier – a Catholic corporal bearing a letter of introduction from General Ludendorff. Pascalina ushered the young man into the sitting room and informed Archbishop Pacelli. Their meeting went well. Pascalina heard Pacelli say: 'Munich has been good to me, so has Germany. I pray Almighty God that this land remain a holy land, in the hands of Our Lord, and free of communism.' She then witnessed Pacelli giving the soldier 'a large cache of Church money to aid the rising revolutionary and his small, struggling band of anti-communists.' This 'charismatic dictator' was Adolf Hitler.[3,4,5]

Significantly, the Nationalsozialistische Deutsche Arbeiterpartei (National Socialist German Workers' Party) (NSDAP), the Nazi Party, was formed one year later.

Pacelli's stay in Germany lasted more than twelve years. He was in Munich under the short-lived Bavarian Soviet Republic which he fought, and at the time of the Beer Hall Putsch[6] in 1923. When France occupied the industrial Ruhr Valley because Germany refused to continue reparation payments resulting from World War I, Pacelli, though not accredited to Prussia, ostentatiously flew to Düsseldorf in the Prussian Rhineland and induced Pius XI to publish an open condemnation of the 'Ruhr adventure'.

Pacelli had Franz von Papen, an influential publisher in Germany and a Catholic Centre Party member, persuade President Hindenburg to appoint Hitler as German Chancellor. Von Papen became vice-chancellor to Hitler.

Pacelli negotiated a concordat between the Holy See and Bavaria in 1925, a concordat with Prussia in 1929 after his appointment as nuncio in Berlin, and in 1933 the infamous *Reichskonkordat* with Adolf Hitler's Germany. Kees van Hoek, his official Catholic biographer wrote in 1939 that:

> Cardinal Pacelli has always been known for his strong German leanings.[7]

Fritz Thyssen was the most important single financial and industrial supporter of Adolf Hitler until 1939. He gave up all his properties in Germany in 1939 when his conscience moved him to renounce Hitler and flee the country. He wrote an article in the Swiss *Arbeiter-Zeitung* (*Workers' Paper*) entitled, 'Pius XII, as Nuncio, brought

---

[1] http://www.tuppersaussy.com/museum/html/writings/articles/15brienner.html (2010)

[2] See also: Cymet, David. *History vs. Apologetics: The Holocaust, the Third Reich, and the Catholic Church.* p21

[3] Ibid.

[4] Murphy, Paul I and R Rene Arlington. *La Popessa.* p68

[5] Noel, Gerard. *Pius XII: The Hound of Hitler.* pp65,103

[6] The 'Beer Hall Putsch' was a failed coup that occurred between November 8 and 9, 1923, when the Nazi party's leader Adolf Hitler, World War I General Erich Ludendorff, and other leaders of the Kampfbund, unsuccessfully tried to gain power in Munich, Bavaria, and Germany. (The Kampfbund was a league of 'patriotic' fighting societies and the German National Socialist party in Bavaria).

[7] van Hoek, Kees. Source: Lehmann, L H. *Behind the Dictators: A Factual Analysis of the Relationship ...* p72

Hitler to Power.'[1,2] In this article he reported that Pacelli commissioned a meeting without the knowledge of the CPP:

> that brought about the fall of the final legal German government of Brüning, and meant the beginning of that epoch of German and European politics for which we thank the Second World War.

Thyssen referred to 'the diplomatic mastery of Nuncio Pacelli' that 'left its stamp on the whole politics of the last years of the Weimar Republic'.[3]

He also plainly stated what the aim of the Hitler-Vatican plan was:

> The idea was to have a sort of Christian Corporate State organised according to the classes, which would be supported by the Churches – in the West by the Catholic, and in the East by the Protestant – and by the Army.[4]

Confirming, Mr A Raven Thompson wrote in *The Catholic Gazette*, April, 1937:

> One can no longer deny that the Corporate State is so far the nearest thing to the ideals of the Popes that the modern world can offer.[5]

Pacelli was disposed to a pragmatic alliance with not only totalitarian Nazism but also with the fascist regimes in Italy, Spain, and Portugal. During his papacy the Holy See pressured Austria, Czechoslovakia, Poland, Belgium and France to surrender to Germany in World War II.[6]

Pacelli and the Holy See dissolved an Italian Catholic party, endorsed fascist Benito Mussolini and urged voters to support him and his party,[7] signed the *Lateran Treaty* (drafted by Pacelli's brother and Pietro Gasparri) with Italy and the Axis powers in 1929, and never renounced its aggression.[8] Hitler took note of the Lateran Treaty and hoped for an identical agreement for his future regime.[9]

Foreign Relations of the Holy See

The Church has a history of pacts with criminal states – the Holy See having signed treaties with monarchs and governments regardless of slavery, inhumanity, or the infliction of torture.

Mussolini's attack on Ethiopia on 3 October 1935 was not condemned by the Holy See. Nor did Pius XI restrain the Italian ecclesiastic hierarchy from belligerent

---

[1] http://www.liberalslikechrist.org/Catholic/NaziLeadership.html (2007)

[2] Bible Students Congregation of New Brunswick. *Can We Identify Antichrist?* http://www.bible411.com/identifyantichrist/chapter1.htm (2007)

[3] http://www.weltkrieg.cc/articles/browse-Hitler-8.html (2015)

[4] See: Fritz Thyssen's memoirs, *I Paid Hitler.* Source: http://en.wikipedia.org/wiki/Fritz_Thyssen

[5] http://www.iterasi.net/openviewer.aspx?sqrlitid=z3mvttwmhk61bd_zubmgqq (2010)

[6] Bible Students Congregation of New Brunswick. *Can We Identify Antic*hrist? http:// http://www.bible411.com/identifyantichrist/chapter1.htm (2007)

[7] Cornwell, John. *Hitler's Pope: The Secret History of Pius XII.* p116. Quoted in: Ibid.

[8] http://www.bibletoday.com/archive/popeapology_text.htm (2004)

[9] Cornwell, John. *Hitler's Pope: The Secret History of Pius XII*

ebullience: 'O Duce!' declared the bishop of Terracina, 'today Italy is Fascist and the hearts of all Italians beat together with yours.'[1]

Francisco Franco entered the Military Academy in Toledo in 1907 to take up a military career. The army was his great formative and brutalising experience. In 1936 the Holy See and Mussolini together backed General Franco's civil war against the Spanish Republic and further supported his ruthless dictatorial fascist regime.

The involvement of Pacelli in world politics was summarised by Joseph McCabe, a former professor of Catholic philosophy:

> Pius XII strongly supported right wing dictatorships. He cooperated with the Japanese from their invasion of Manchuria onward, consecrated Fascism in Italy, Nazism in Germany, and Phalangism[2] in Spain, inspired the sordid dictatorships in South America, was intimately associated with the Germans, Italians and Japanese in setting the world aflame in the Second World War.[3,4]

Two key components of great influence in Pacelli's international career were:

1. that he cultivated an extreme hatred and paranoid fear of Communism that deeply influenced his political Weltanschauung. In 1919, in Munich, he witnessed at first hand the abortive communist coup; and

2. the fact that some of these revolutionaries were Jews, established a strong association in Pacelli's mind between Jews and Communism that boded ill for his later policies during the Holocaust. For example, a 1919 letter signed by Pacelli described the meeting between representatives of the nunciature and the revolutionaries:

> An army of employees were dashing to and fro, giving out orders, waving bits of paper, and in the midst of all this, a gang of young women, of dubious appearance, Jews like all the rest of them, hanging around in all the offices with lecherous demeanour and suggestive smiles. The boss of this female rabble was [the chief revolutionary's] mistress, a young Russian woman, a Jew and a divorcee ... [Her lover] is a young man, of about 30 or 35, also Russian and a Jew. Pale, dirty, with drugged eyes, hoarse voice, vulgar, repulsive ...[5]

Avro Manhattan was, at that time, the world's foremost authority on the role of Catholicism in politics. He described Pius as a cunning politician and a brilliant diplomat, who, more than anyone else outside Germany helped Hitler to power. He did this by steering the German Catholic Party and top Catholic leaders to support Hitler,[6] even though Catholic associations and the Catholic media were steadfastly opposed to

---

[1] Cornwell, John. *Hitler's Pope: The Secret History of Pius XII.*

[2] Phalangism (Falangism) – Dictator Franco's political party system.

[3] McCabe, Joseph. *The Columbia Encyclopedia's Crimes against the Truth ...*

[4] See also: McCabe, Joseph. *How the Pope of Peace Traded in Blood* ('The Red Pope', Ch 1).

[5] See, for example: Midlarsky, Manus I. *The Killing Trap: Genocide in the Twentieth ...* pp220-21

[6] Manhattan, Avro. *The Vatican's Holocaust: The Sensational Account of the Most Horrifying ...*

National Socialism.[1] Ultimately, therefore, Pacelli, by his influence over the German Catholic Party and by putting his signature to the Holy See's concordat with Nazi Germany, greatly assisted Hitler to power.[2,3]

In 1939, with the fall of Czechoslovakia the Holy See and Hitler set up a Catholic fascist State in Slovakia headed by Monsignor Tiso. His barbarous regime tortured and massacred Jews and others. After the war Tiso was executed for war crimes.

Ante Pavelić was the Head (Poglavnik) and founding member of the murderous Croatian Ustaša. Pius XII showed special deference towards Pavelić, receiving him in a private audience in 1941 when the Ustaša's atrocities were already well under way.[4]

Pierre Daye was a Belgian collaborator and war criminal. After the War, with the help of President Perón, Daye assisted in setting up the Nazi rescue organisation 'Society in Argentina for the Reception of Europeans' (SARE). In Uki Goñi's book *The Real ODESSA: How Perón Brought the Nazi War Criminals to Argentina* there is a photograph of a memento from the Vatican of the reception of Pierre Daye by Pius XII on 6 January 1943.[5]

Pacelli and the Vatican-Serbian Concordat

In the autumn of 1912 Eugenio Pacelli began to negotiate in secret a concordat with the Serbian government which was to subvert and eliminate the Austro-Hungarian protectorate. This *Serbian Concordat* was aimed at increasing Papal power over Balkan Catholics.

Documents show that for more than a year Pacelli disregarded all the warnings about the potentially calamitous consequences of his policies. The papal nuncio in Vienna wrote to him on 13 February 1913:

> Austria appears determined to deal harshly with Serbia, and it is widely believed that there could be a war ... Would it not be better to leave the negotiations for now rather than take risks in an uncertain and perilous set of circumstances?[6]

But Pacelli persisted. Accordingly, on 24 June 1914, four days before Archduke Franz Ferdinand of Austria was assassinated in Sarajevo, representatives of the Holy See and the government of Serbia sat down in the Vatican Secretariat of State and signed the *Serbian Concordat*.[7] It dealt with the 'Protectorate' of Catholics in the Balkans. It seriously antagonised Austria – the Italian ambassador in Vienna reported that 'The Austrian press and people consider the Serbian Concordat a major diplomatic defeat for their Government.' Under the headline 'New defeat', *Die Zeit*, the Viennese paper,

---

[1] Noel, Gerard. *Pius XII: The Hound of Hitler.* p67

[2] Lehmann, L H. *Out of the Labyrinth*

[3] Manhattan, Avro. *The Vatican's Holocaust: The Sensational Account of the Most Horrifying Religious Massacre of the ...* Ch 15 'The Vatican saves the catholic war criminals of Croatia – Roman monasteries as their asylums – the Croatian holocaust minimized'. Source: http://www.reformation.org/holoc15.html (2008)

[4] Goñi, Uki. *The Real ODESSA: How Perón Brought the Nazi War Criminals ...* p207

[5] Ibid.

[6] Cornwell, John. *Hitler's Pope: The Secret History of Pius XII*

[7] Ibid.

proclaimed: 'Now Serbian prestige will be inflated, and its bishops and priests will become an important factor in pan-Slav agitation.' There is no indication that Pacelli ever questioned the dangerous implications of the *Serbian Concordat*.

~ The concordat undoubtedly contributed to the uncompromising terms that the Austro-Hungarian Empire pressed on Serbia, making war inevitable. Consequently, most historians agree that the First World War – 'the bloodiest war which has ever been fought'[1] – was triggered by Pacelli's concordat.[2]

~ John Cornwell, in his book *Hitler's Pope: The Secret History of Pope Pius XII*, found that this event marked the beginning of Pacelli's 'myopic aloofness' from the eventful consequences of his diplomatic actions in his quest for increased papal power.[3]

Pacelli and the Reichskonkordat

Under the new Weimar government (1919), Eugenio Pacelli became the first diplomat to the Reich, and the most senior diplomat in Berlin. He stated: 'For my part, I will devote my entire strength to cultivating and strengthening the relations between the Holy See and Germany.'[4]

The *Reichskonkordat* was an integral part of four concordats that Pacelli concluded on behalf of the Holy See with German states. The state concordats were necessary because the German federalist Weimar Constitution gave the German states authority in the areas of education and culture and thus diminished the authority of the churches in these areas. This diminution of church authority was a primary concern of Pacelli and the Holy See.

As Bavarian Nuncio, Pacelli negotiated successfully with the Bavarian authorities in 1925. The State of Bavaria, with its large Catholic population, was a logical place for his first state concordat.[5] This concordat 'achieved ... recognition, protection, and advancement of the Catholic Church and all its associations and institutions for all time.'[6]

Pacelli expected the concordat with Catholic Bavaria to be the model for the rest of Germany. Prussia showed interest in negotiations only after the *Bavarian Concordat* was signed. However, Pacelli obtained less favourable conditions for the Church in the *Prussian Concordat* of 1929, which excluded educational issues.

A concordat with the Austrian state of Baden was completed by Pacelli in 1932 after he had moved to Rome. There, he also negotiated a concordat with Austria in 1933.

With his zest for hierarchical control, a total of sixteen concordats and treaties with European states had been concluded in the ten year period 1922–1932.

Pacelli's predilection for concordats was now fully established, and Hitler well knew

[1] Rhodes, Anthony. *The Power of Rome in the Twentieth Century.* pp223-25

[2] Saussy, F Tupper. http://www.tuppersaussy.com/museum/html/writings/articles/15brienner. html (2008)

[3] Cornwell, John. *Hitler's Pope: The Secret History of Pius XII.* Source: http://www.ianpaisley.org/ article.asp? ArtKey= hitler_2 (2008)

[4] Noel, Gerard. *Pius XII: The Hound of Hitler.* p47

[5] Cornwell, John. *Hitler's Pope: The Secret History of Pius XII* (2nd edn) p85

[6] Ibid. p100

of his obsession with obtaining a Reich concordat.[1] Furthermore, Hitler knew that he could use such a concordat to silence Catholic protests against National Socialism. Additionally, he could use the agreement to legitimise his dictatorship, while rendering his political enemies impotent. That was the great prize.[2]

Pacelli 'believed that Stalin, Russian Bolshevism, and its offshoots in Europe represented the real devil at work. By contrast, no mention was made at the time [in his notes, etc.] of demonizing, let alone challenging, Hitler. Although Pacelli remained sceptical of Hitler's attitude to the Church and Catholicism, his anti-Communism went a long way toward neutralizing these concerns.'[3]

Consequently, the principal condition imposed by Hitler in 1933 was nothing less than the voluntary withdrawal of Germany's Catholics from social and political activity as Catholics, including the voluntary disbanding of the Centre Party, which was then the only surviving viable democratic party in Germany.[4]

The transcripts of Hitler's cabinet deliberations concerning the signing of the *Reichskonkordat* were published for the first time in 1957. It is abundantly clear that Hitler considered the Catholic Church to be a natural ally in a global war against Jewry. He declared unambiguously at the cabinet meeting that this was his main reason for accepting the treaty. The signing of the concordat was essential for creating an 'area of trust' with the Church which was critical to the struggle (fostered for so long by the Church's extensive anti-Semitic propaganda) against 'International Jewry'.[5]

In Rome, priest and politician Monsignor Ludwig Kaas[6] and Eugenio Pacelli were working on the concordat with Adolf Hitler. Knowing that the Catholic Church was going to give formal acknowledgement to National Socialism prompted the German Protestant churches to make their own acceptance. Two days later, the German Catholic bishops issued a statement declaring that 'the designated general prohibitions and warnings [against National Socialism] need no longer be considered necessary'.[7]

The Catholic Bishops and Priests

On 28 March 1933, the Catholic bishops published a devastating conciliatory statement with respect to Nazism:

> Without revoking the judgement made in our previous declarations in respect to certain religious-ethical errors, the episcopate believes it can cherish the confidence that the designated general prohibitions and warnings need no longer be considered necessary. For Catholic Christians, to whom the voice of the Church is sacred, it is not necessary at the present moment to make special admonition to be loyal to the

[1] Noel, Gerard. *Pius XII: The Hound of Hitler.* p67
[2] Ibid. pp67-68
[3] Wolf, Hubert. *Pope and Devil: The Vatican's Archives and the Third Reich.* pp157-58
[4] Cornwell, John. *Hitler's Pope: The Secret History of Pius XII* (2nd edn) p85
[5] Cymet, David. *History vs. Apologetics: The Holocaust, the Third Reich, and the Catholic Church.* p61
[6] Monsignor Kaas, *a Jesuit* and the leader of the German Centre Party, whose role in making the party vote in favour of Hitler's *Enabling Act* of March 1933 is still one of the most controversial acts of German history.
[7] Noel, Gerard. *Pius XII: The Hound of Hitler.* p68

lawful government and to fulfil conscientiously the duties of citizenship, rejecting on principle all illegal or subversive behaviour.[1]

Eventually, around 150 Catholic priests became members of the Nazi Party: they saw no conflict between their membership in the NSDAP and the teachings of the Catholic Church. After Hitler's seizure of power, National Socialist priests acted as open protagonists of the Party, and there were several friends of Hitler in priestly robes. After the War, in true Catholic fashion, this history was quickly hushed up.

Dissolution of the CCP and the End of German Democracy

During the inter-war years, when Germany was a democratic republic, many of the clergy and some of the religious orders favoured the liberal, secularising spirit. They formed the mainstay of the Deutsche Zentrumspartei (Catholic Centre Party) (CCP), which was to become the last impediment to Hitler's rise to power. In the Reichstag the CCP had the potential support of around 27 million German Catholics. Between 1919 and 1933, five CCP members served as chancellors in ten ruling cabinets of the Weimar Republic.

- As Cardinal Secretary of State, Eugenio Pacelli had the opportunity to formulate the foreign policy of the Holy See. Pacelli 'detested Catholic democratic parties as inimical to papal authority.'[2]

, Accordingly, Monsignor Ludwig Kaas, a Jesuit and an intimate of Eugenio Pacelli, telephoned Joseph Joos of the CCP from the Vatican, and hurled at him the dreadful words: "What! Haven't you dissolved yourselves yet?" 'Joos was to remember for the rest of his life the order from the Vatican insisting on the sacrifice of the Center Party to ensure the success of Pacelli's diplomacy.'[3]

/ Heinrich Brüning, the former German Chancellor,[4] then having been denied options, made the terrible decision to voluntarily dissolve the CCP.

⁙ Consequently, during the negotiations for the *Reichskonkordat*, and following his 'urgent prompting', Pacelli 'acquiesced' to the dissolution of the CCP – the last element of German liberalism. With its expiration, democracy disappeared from Germany and Pacelli's immorality rose even further.

, This dissolution removed the final obstacle to Hitler's ascension to power, and also deprived the Catholic laity and clergy in Germany of any voice in political matters.[5] As a consequence, millions of people died.[6]

⁙ That the CCP dissolved itself voluntarily rather than mandatorily also 'conveyed an impression of Catholic endorsement of Hitler in the eyes of the world.'[7]

---

[1] Cornwell, John. *Hitler's Pope: The Secret History of Pius XII* (2nd edn) p138

[2] Cornwell, John. *Hitler's Pope: The Secret History of Pius XII* (2nd edn)

[3] Cornwell, John. *Hitler's Pope: The Secret History of Pius XII.* p148

[4] Dr Heinrich Brüning was a German politician during the Weimar Republic. In 1929, he was elected chairman of the Centre Party's faction in the Reichstag.

[5] Lehmann, L H. *Behind the Dictators: A Factual Analysis of the Relationship of Nazi-Fascism and ...* p54

[6] Noel, Gerard. *Pius XII: The Hound of Hitler.* p72

[7] Cornwell, John. *Hitler's Pope: The Secret History of Pius XII* (2nd edn) p xiii

Pacelli then steered the top Catholic leaders to support Hitler.[1] In this way Pacelli became 'the doyen of the diplomatic corps in Bonn.'[2]

These political machinations of Pacelli reveal 'a colluding appeasement that dignified the Nazi regime in the eyes of the world.'[3]

The fate of German Catholics and their Church was being made entirely by Pacelli in the Vatican.[4] Accordingly, Heinrich Brüning (Chancellor of Germany from 1930 to 1932) has been quoted as saying:

> Behind the agreement with Hitler stood not the Pope [Pius XI], but the Vatican bureaucracy and its leader, Pacelli. He visualised an authoritarian state and an authoritarian Church directed by the Vatican bureaucracy, the two to conclude an eternal league with one another. For that reason Catholic parliamentary parties, like the Centre, in Germany, were inconvenient to Pacelli and his men, and were dropped without regret in various countries. The Pope did not share these ideas.[5]

Thus it further came about that Pacelli ignored the misgivings of his German bishops, and on 4 July 1933 disbanded the Bayerische Volkspartei (BVP), the Bavarian branch of the Zentrumspartei (Centre Party). All the Catholic organisations with any political function, including Catholic labour unions, were also dissolved in the process. Consequently, Reichstag members of both parties were incorporated into the Nazi block in the parliament.[6]

By Pacelli's disbanding of the CCP in exchange for the acceptance of the *Reichskonkordat*, Heinrich Brüning realised that:

> [Pacelli] had already silenced and surrendered German Catholics to the power and designs of Adolf Hitler.'[7]

In his memoirs Brüning recorded that Eugenio Pacelli had 'never correctly understood the fundamentals of German politics nor the particular position of the Centre Party.'[8]

Pacelli's Deception

In Rome, priest and politician Monsignor Ludwig Kaas and Eugenio Pacelli were working on the concordat (*Reichskonkordat*) with Adolf Hitler.

After Hitler's accession to power, Brüning desperately argued against a concordat that would have depoliticised German Catholicism.[9] He wrote that Pacelli believed that:

---

[1] Manhattan, Avro. *The Vatican's Holocaust: The Sensational Account of the Most Horrifying Religious Massacre of the 20th Century*

[2] Phayer, Michael. *Pius XII, the Holocaust, and the Cold War.* p219

[3] Cornwell, John. *Hitler's Pope: The Secret History of Pius XII* (2nd edn) p xviii

[4] See, for example: Ibid. p129

[5] Ibid. p150

[6] Cymet, David. *History vs. Apologetics: The Holocaust, the Third Reich, and the Catholic Church.* p61

[7] Cornwell, John. *Hitler's Pope: The Secret History of Pius XII* (2nd edn) p218

[8] Wolf, Hubert. *Pope and Devil: The Vatican's Archives and the Third Reich.* p66

[9] Midlarsky, Manus I. *The Killing Trap: Genocide in the Twentieth Century.* pp221-23

All successes could only be attained by papal diplomacy. The system of concordats led him and the Holy See to despise democracy and the parliamentary system ... Rigid governments, rigid centralisation, and rigid treaties were supposed to introduce an era of stable order, an era of peace and quiet.'[1]

At the end of April 1933 Pacelli informed Cardinal von Faulhaber[2] that nothing concrete had been done with respect to a concordat. At the end of May, at a meeting of the German bishops, they were abruptly told that work on the concordat was virtually complete and that Pacelli wanted their support – and speed was of the essence. Thus, Pacelli revealed himself as 'a shamelessly amoral negotiator' by delaying his reply to Cardinal Bertram (archbishop of Breslau) in April, then telling Cardinal von Faulhaber an outright lie, and finally presenting the concordat as a virtual fait accompli with a 'time is of the essence' argument to force its adoption.[3]

In the words of John Cornwell, 'Pacelli kept Germany's bishops and lay politicians in the dark throughout.'[4]

Pacelli later insisted that the *Reichskonkordat* was 'a last ditch attempt to protect Germany's Catholics from Nazi persecution.' This is not in accord with recorded history.[5] In fact, Pacelli indicated to Chancellor Brüning that:

if the price of a Reich concordat was the inclusion of Hitler into his [Brüning's] cabinet, then he should do it without delay.[6]

Hitler said: 'They (the Church) will swallow anything in order to keep their material advantages.'[7] And indeed it was so. The *Reichskonkordat* was negotiated in record time, and Pacelli initialled the concordat with Nazi Germany in July 1933.[8]

Signing of the Reichskonkordat

Pacelli said the *Reichskonkordat* had been entered into solely for the purposes of regulating the so call *res mixtae*, matters of equal concern to the state and the Church.[9] Notwithstanding, it was well known that 'the Church was well informed of the Nazi's attempts, particularly in their work with youths, to replace Jesus Christ with Adolf Hitler and to pass him off as a messiah.'[10]

The *Reichskonkordat*[11] was signed by Eugenio Pacelli on 20 July – four months after

---

[1] Midlarsky, Manus I. *The Killing Trap: Genocide in the Twentieth Century.* p221
[2] Michael von Faulhaber was archbishop of Munich for 35 years, from 1917 to his death in 1952.
[3] Noel, Gerard. *Pius XII: The Hound of Hitler.* p70
[4] Cornwell, John. *Hitler's Pope: The Secret History of Pius XII* (2nd edn) p xvi
[5] Ibid.
[6] Ibid.
[7] Cymet, David. *History vs. Apologetics: The Holocaust, the Third Reich, and the Catholic Church.* p61. This emphasis on materialism by the Catholic Church is evident throughout its history.
[8] Lehmann, L H. *Out of the Labyrinth*
[9] Wolf, Hubert. *Pope and Devi: The Vatican's Archives and the Third Reich.* p223
[10] Ibid. p227
[11] The full text of the *Reichskonkordat* (with Supplementary Protocol and Secret Supplement) is available at http://www.concordatwatch.eu/kb-1211.834

the Nazis opened the Oranienburg Concentration Camp (Konzentrationslager Oranien-burg), which maltreated political prisoners, homosexual men, and 'undesirables'.

The Centre Party having been disbanded, Hitler expressed the frightening opinion that the *Reichskonkordat* would be 'especially significant in the urgent struggle against international Jewry.' Pacelli had effectively silenced the only potential large-scale opposition to Hitler's virulent anti-Semitic programme.[1] The result was, in the words of John Cornwell, 'the moral abyss into which Pacelli the future Pontiff had led the once great and proud German Catholic Church.'[2]

Pacelli's signing of the *Reichskonkordat* was made to avoid, in his stated opinion, the virtual elimination of the Catholic Church in Germany. Supporting this statement, the Vatican's *L'Osservatore Romano* expressed Pacelli's contention that the concordat had been a triumph of canon law, a victory for the Holy See.[3]

By contrast, in the words of Professor Hubert Wolf, 'The Reichskonkordat was a pact with the devil,'[4] because its signing 'marked the formal beginning of German Catholicism's acceptance of its obligations … to obey the Nazi rulers.'[5]

The concordat was, and still is, binding under international law.[6]

The Catholic Church's Celebration of the Signing of the Reichskonkordat

The final ratification of the *Reichskonkordat* took place on 10 September 1933 in Rome. A celebratory Mass amid great pomp and circumstance[7] was held in Rome, and the bells of St Peter's rang out in joy, even though there was in reality nothing to celebrate in this formalisation of what historians have called 'shaking hands with the Devil'.

Shortly afterwards, the ratification was celebrated by a service of thanksgiving held in St Hedwig's Cathedral[8] in Berlin. Nazi flags hung alongside Catholic banners.[9] The *Horst Wessel*, which became the Nazi Party's anthem and Germany's official co-national anthem from 1933 to 1945, was sung inside the cathedral and relayed by loudspeakers to the thousands of celebrants outside.[10] A more powerful symbol would be hard to imagine of the Church's endorsement of Nazism.

Hitler was overjoyed. He authorised the following announcement:

---

[1] Midlarsky, Manus I. *The Killing Trap: Genocide in the Twentieth Century.* pp222-23

[2] Cornwell, John. *Hitler's Pope: The Secret History of Pius XII* (2nd edn) p154

[3] Ibid. p155. Confirming Martin Luther's conclusion that the Church's Canon Law has nothing to do with Christ.

[4] Wolf, Hubert. *Pope and Devil: The Vatican's Archives and the Third Reich.* p177

[5] As defined in *Article 16* and *Article 30* of the concordat. Cornwell, John. *Hitler's Pope: The Secret History of Pius XII* (2nd edn) p157

[6] Wolf, Hubert. *Pope and Devil: The Vatican's Archives and the Third Reich.* p223

[7] Reflecting Pacelli's 'love of pomp and circumstance.' Murphy, Paul I with R René Arlington. *La Popessa.* p204. But, compare with Lehnert, Pascalina. *Ich Durfte Ihm Dienen: Erinnerungen an Papst Pius XII.*

[8] St Hedwig's Cathedral is the see of the Archbishop of Berlin.

[9] Paul, Gregory S. *The Great Scandal: Christianity's Role in the Rise of the Nazis*

[10] Noel, Gerard. *Pius XII: The Hound of Hitler.* p74

The conclusion of the concordat seems to me to give sufficient guarantee that the Reich members of the Roman Catholic confession will, from now on, put themselves, without reservation, at the service of the new National Socialist state.[1]

The French Catholic journal *La Croix* expressed satisfaction that 'the German concordat of 20 July is the most important religious event since the Reformation'; *La Croix* 'rejoices that the new German education regulations require the complete exclusion of secularism from the school.'[2] Pius XII extended his blessing to *La Croix* in 1942, and described it as 'an organ of pontifical thought'.[3]

The Fulda Bishops' Conference of 1935 continued taking pride in the fact that the *Reichskonkordat* was the first international treaty signed by Hitler that opened for him the doors of international recognition and trust. In their congratulations to the Führer they reminded him of this fact:

Pope Pius XI exchanged the handshake of trust with you through the Concordat – the first foreign sovereign to do so ... Pope Pius XI spoke high praise of you ... Millions in foreign countries, Catholics and non-Catholics alike, have overcome their original mistrust because of *this expression of papal trust*, and have placed their trust in your regime.[4]

Before the concordat, the German Catholic Church had opposed the rise of Nazism and generally barred party members from receiving Holy Communion. The concordat effectively reversed all this and prevented the Church from any continued opposition to Hitler.[5]

When the Nazis came to full power, Hitler became Europe's most popular leader[6] due to this recognition of his regime by the Catholic Church.

Accordingly, the *Reichskonkordat* was one of the most immoral, corrupt, duplicitous, and parlous agreements ever formulated between two authoritarian powers. It integrated the Catholics, their episcopate, and their clergy into the Nazi system.[7]

When Pacelli realised his folly, he retreated into silence throughout the War.[8]

The Reichskonkordat was seen as a Catholic Success

The *Reichskonkordat* was initially seen as an indescribable success for Catholicism. Even a year before, the Holy See had only been able to dream of the concessions that

[1] http://atheism.about.com/library/weekly/aa111799n.htm (2014)

[2] http://www.concordatwatch.eu/showkb.php?org_id=867&kb_header_id=850&kb_id=1527&order=kb _rank%20ASC (2007)

[3] Ibid.

[4] Cymet, David. *History vs. Apologetics: The Holocaust, the Third Reich, and the Catholic Church.* p97

[5] http://www.theatlantic.com/issues/99oct/9910pope.htm

[6] Paul, Gregory S. *The Great Scandal: Christianity's Role in the Rise of the Nazis.* Source: Source: http://www. secularhumanism.org/index.php?section=library&page=paul_23_4 (2007)

[7] See, for example: Küng, Hans. *The Catholic Church: a short history.* pp177-78

[8] 'A holy fool for the Führer'; review by Peter Stanford of: Noel, Gerard. *Pius XII: The Hound of Hitler.* http:// www.independent.co.uk/arts-entertainment/books/reviews/pius-xii-the-hound-of-hitler-by-gerard-noel-887846.html (2009)

the concordat gave. Consequently, it was described as nothing short of a 'masterpiece.'[1]

Thereafter, Hitler's portrait was placed on all walls of Catholic churches and Sunday schools.

The Imposition of Vatican Legal Authority and Bias

Pacelli saw the concordat 'as the successful imposition of Vatican legal authority ... over the German Church.' Thus, it was another step in furthering his 'Great Design'.[2]

A measure of his religious bias is reflected in the fact that 'Pacelli grew angry when Brüning insisted that in Germany, Protestants and Catholics should be treated equally, especially in education.'[3]

The Reichskonkordat neutralised Germany's Catholics

The *Reichskonkordat* imposed a moral duty on Catholics to obey the Nazi rulers.[4] *Article 16* of Pacelli's compact required the Catholic bishops to swear to honour the Nazi government, to make their subordinates honour it, and to shun acts that would endanger it. It read:

> Before bishops take possession of their dioceses they are to take an oath of fealty either to the Reich Representative of the State concerned, or to the President of the Reich, according to the following formula:
>
> Before God and on the Holy Gospels I swear and promise as becomes a bishop, loyalty to the German Reich and to the [regional] State of ... I swear and promise to honour the legally constituted Government and to cause the clergy of my diocese to honour it. In the performance of my spiritual office and in my solicitude for the welfare and the interests of the German Reich, I will endeavour to avoid all detrimental acts which might endanger it.'[5,6]

Article 30 stipulated that a special prayer would be said at the end of every High Mass for the welfare of the German Reich and its people.[7]

One of the disastrous aspects of this concordat was that it neutralised the potential of Germany's 23 million Catholics 'to protest and resist'[8] the machinations of Adolf Hitler. In the words of John Cornwell:

> The abdication of German political Catholicism in 1933, negotiated and imposed from the Vatican by Pacelli with the agreement of Pope Pius XI, ensured that

---

[1] Scholder, Klaus. *The Churches and the Third Reich.* p405. Source: http://www.secularhumanism.org/library/fi/paul_23_4.html (2007)

[2] See below.

[3] Cornwell, John. *Hitler's Pope: The Secret History of Pius XII* (2nd edn) pp xvi, xvii

[4] Ibid. p157

[5] http://www.bytwerk.com/gpa/hitler2.htm (2007)

[6] Moore, Edith. *No Friend of Democracy: A study of Roman Catholic politics – their influence on the course of the present War and the growth of Fascism* Source: http://www.iterasi.net/openviewer.aspx?sqrlitid=z3mvttwmhk61bd_zubmgqq (2009)

[7] Vidmar, John. *The Catholic Church through the Ages: A History.* p323

[8] Ibid. p4

Nazism could rise unopposed by the most powerful Catholic community in the world.[1]

Pacelli's concordat effectively prevented potential Catholic protest in defence of the Jews, whether they were converts to Christianity or not, as constituting 'outside' interference. The concordat's potential for sanctioning the killing of the Jews was acknowledged by Hitler in his cabinet meeting of 14 July 1933.[2] Gerard Noel summarised the situation: the Holy See and all German Catholics were complicit in anti-Semitic and racist legislation, and the German Church was 'led into a moral abyss' by Pacelli's act.[3]

Later, Pacelli told François Charles-Roux that he had no regrets about signing the *Reichskonkordat*.[4] His stance was that the Catholic Church must be protected by the state in Germany, irrespective of human rights abuses or the fate of other religious groups or Churches.[5]

The Benefits for Hitler

Adolf Hitler stated, in wording agreed to by Pacelli, that the *Reichskonkordat* gave:

> sufficient guarantee that the Reich members of the Catholic confession will from now on put themselves without reservation at the service of the new National Socialist state.[6]

Ominously, in signing the concordat the Vatican became the first national government to acknowledge Hitler as the leader of Germany and to recognise officially the Nazi regime, on which it thereby conferred international credence and legitimacy.[7] Accordingly, it is generally agreed that the *Reichskonkordat* substantially increased the prestige of Hitler and the acceptance of his regime around the world.[8,9] For example, on 24 July 1933, the official Nazi organ *Völkischer Beobachter* emphasised the import of the signing of the concordat:

> This fact signifies a tremendous moral strengthening of the National Socialist government of the Reich and its reputation.[10]

This belief was endorsed when Hitler wrote to the Nazi Party in 1933:

> The fact that the Vatican is concluding a treaty with the new Germany means the acknowledgement of the National Socialist state by the Catholic Church. This treaty

---

[1] Vidmar, John. *The Catholic Church through the Ages: A History.* p7

[2] Cornwell, John. *Hitler's Pope: The Secret History of Pius XII.* p296

[3] Noel, Gerard. *Pius XII: The Hound of Hitler.* p73

[4] Ibid. p74

[5] Ibid. p75

[6] Callil, Carmen. *Bad Faith: A Forgotten History of Family & Fatherland.* p534

[7] See, for example: http://blogs.setonhill.edu/ncche/015098.php (2008)

[8] Lewy, Guenter. *The Catholic Church and Nazi Germany.* p90. Source: http://en.wikipedia.org/wiki/Michael_von_Faulhaber (2007)

[9] Vidmar, John. *The Catholic Church through the Ages: A History.* p324

[10] Cymet, David. *History vs. Apologetics: The Holocaust, the Third Reich, and the Catholic Church.* p63

shows the whole world clearly and unequivocally that the assertion that National Socialism is hostile to religion is a lie.[1]

The concordat definitely contributed to the outbreak of World War II, and, by Hitler's own admission, sealed the fate of not only the Jews in Europe, but also that of Europe itself.[2,3]

The Reichskonkordat and the Jews

Following the signing of the concordat, Hitler declared:

The concordat gives Germany an opportunity and creates an area of trust that is particularly significant in the developing struggle against international Jewry.[4]

Thus, Pacelli effectively silenced the only potential large-scale opposition to Hitler's virulent anti-Semitic programme.[5]

On 14 August 1933, James G McDonald, the League of Nations' High Commissioner for Refugees, visited Eugenio Pacelli and discussed the situation of the Jews in Germany. He left with the distressing impression that the Jews could expect no help from the Holy See. He wrote to his friend Felix Warburg:

Deeply disappointed by the Cardinal ... Pacelli was non-committal but left me with definite impression that no vigorous cooperation could be expected from that direction.[6]

The Immorality of the Reichskonkordat

The *Reichskonkordat* was modelled on the mutually advantageous concordat of 1929 between the fascist dictator Benito Mussolini and the Holy See.

To the certain knowledge of the Church, Hitler had already promulgated his notorious decree that mandated sterilisation and castration of the disabled and mentally sick, and which violated hallowed moral and religious standards. This 'is tangible proof of how little the Church cared about moral principles when it concerned its interests.'[7] Additionally, the infamous burning of books under the Nazis had occurred on 10 May 1933.

In negotiating the concordat, Pacelli was not concerned about the fate of parallel faiths, religious communities, or institutions, or about human rights and social ethics. Nothing could have been better designed to deliver the powerful institution of the Catholic Church in Germany into the hands of Hitler.[8]

There was also a secret *Supplement* to the concordat. It reveals that by 1933 Pacelli

---

[1] Quoted in: Cornwell, John. *Hitler's Pope: The Secret History of Pius XII.* Source: http://liberalslikechrist.org/Catholic/HitlersFaith.html (2007)

[2] See, for example: http://www.bibliotecapleyades.net/sociopolitica/esp_sociopol_rothschild05.htm (2014)

[3] See, also: Cornwell, John. *Hitler's Pope: The Secret History of Pius XII* (2nd edn) p7

[4] Cornwell, John. *Hitler's Pope: The Secret History of Pius XII* (2nd edn) p xiv

[5] *Midlarsky, Manus I. The Killing Trap: Genocide in the Twentieth Century.* pp222-23

[6] Cymet, David. *History vs. Apologetics: The Holocaust, the Third Reich, and the Catholic Church.* p64

[7] Ibid. p62

[8] Cornwell, John. *Hitler's Pope: The Secret History of Pius XII* (2nd edn) p85

and the Holy See knew that Hitler was going to re-arm Germany in defiance of the Treaty of Versailles[1], and they wanted to help him keep this secret.[2]

Later, the *Reichskonkordat* had the dire effect, as mentioned above, of conditioning the German bishops from speaking out about the Holocaust.[3] In his book *History vs. Apologetics: The Holocaust, the Third Reich, and the Catholic Church*, David Cymet concluded that the signing by Pacelli of the *Reichskonkordat*, and his subsequent behaviour, enabled the fruits of pro-German prejudice and the millennial Catholic background of anti-Semitism to reinforce each other in enticing the Holy See:

> to enter into a Faustian pact with Hitler by which the Church was turned into an accomplice of the Nazi crimes against the Jewish people.

In this way, the Holy See supported a transaction 'in which the lives of the Jews of Europe were the prize requested by Hitler.'[4]

Pacelli's acceptance of Hitler's deal with respect to the *Reichskonkordat* 'poisoned the wells of Catholic moral and social integrity from the very outset of the Hitler regime.' It 'imposed a moral duty on Catholics to obey the Nazi rulers ... A great Church, which might have formed the basis of an opposition, confined itself to the sacristy.'[5]

As part of the *Reichskonkordat*, religious instruction and prayer in school were reinstated. Criticism of the Church was forbidden. On the other hand, nothing in the concordat protected the rights of non-Catholics. Critics allege that the concordat under-mined the separation of church and state.[6]

At the same time that Hitler offered more funding for Catholic schools, 'he was withdrawing wide ranging educational benefit for the Jews.' The acceptance of this by Pacelli 'signaled an eloquent collusion with ... Jewish persecution.' It was a measure of Pacelli's hypocrisy, whereby he 'ostensibly remained aloof from Hitler's ideology while accepting his beneficence.'[7]

Just before the ratification of the concordat, the German bishops pleaded with Pacelli:

> Would it be possible for the Holy See to say a heartfelt word for those Christians who have converted from Judaism?[8]

The Jews themselves appear not to have been mentioned.

Pacelli did make such an entreaty to the Reich on behalf of these converts. 'This very

---

[1] The *Treaty of Versailles* was the peace treaty signed at the end of World War I between Germany and the Allies. Its military restrictions on Germany included the following: Manufacturing, importing and exporting of weapons were prohibited. Possession of artillery, tanks, submarines and military aircraft were also prohibited.

[2] http://www.concordatwatch.eu/showkb.php?org_id=858&kb_header_id=752&order=kb_rank%20ASC&kb_id=1211 (2007)

[3] Phayer, Michael. *Pius XII, the Holocaust, and the Cold War.* p74

[4] Cymet, David. *History vs. Apologetics: The Holocaust, the Third Reich, and the Catholic Church.* p404

[5] Cornwell, John. *Hitler's Pope: The Secret History of Pius XII* (2nd edn) p157

[6] Paul, Gregory S. *The Great Scandal: Christianity's Role in the Rise of the Nazis*

[7] Cornwell, John. *Hitler's Pope: The Secret History of Pius XII* (2nd edn) pp xii-xiii

[8] Ibid. p158

fact of such a distinction revealed Pacelli's diplomatic collusion with the overall anti-Semitic policy of the Reich.'[1]

On 4 October 1933, Cardinal Bertram brought to Pacelli a catalogue of protests against the Nazi regime. It included: restrictions on the Catholic press, the sacking of Catholic public servants, and the widespread discrimination against Jewish converts to Catholicism. There was, again, no mention of the Jews themselves.[2]

The Financial Benefits to the Church

As part of the *Reichskonkordat*, the Church received enormous subsidies, and protection of its property, wealth and ecclesiastic privileges. While religious instruction and prayer in school were reinstated, nothing in the concordat protected the rights of non-Catholics.

In his book, *How the Cross Courted the Swastika for Eight Years*, Joseph McCabe called attention to the fact that:

> The German government has always subsidized the Churches but Hitler had more than trebled the subsidy. Between 1933, when he took office, and 1938 it rose from 150,000,000 Marks to 500,000,000 a year. What was your subsidy to the Churches, he asked of France, Britain, and America? He had never closed a church, and he left the Roman Church the richest land-owner in south and west Germany.[3]

The Reichskonkordat was Pacelli's Most Catastrophic Mistake

The general consensus of the results of historical research is that in pushing the *Reichskonkordat* Pacelli made a catastrophic political miscalculation. Hitler brilliantly utilised it to persuade a potentially deadly enemy, the Catholic Church, to render itself impotent – because the concordat imposed a moral duty on 23 million German Catholics to obey the Nazi rulers. Additionally, Pacelli legitimised the Nazi party in the eyes of the world. After the ratification of the concordat, Catholics flocked to the Nazi Party, and thence, ultimately, they comprised a quarter of the membership of the SS.[4]

In his rash impulsiveness, Pacelli failed to heed the old Curial adage: 'Historia concordatorum, historia dolorum Ecclesiae' ('The history of concordats is one of sadness of the Church').[5,6]

Pacelli's constricted over-riding ideology of centralised papal power 'proved disastrous' for the Jews, for Europe, and for the world.[7] The resulting World War caused an estimated 50 million to 85 million fatalities – it was the deadliest conflict in human

---

[1] Cornwell, John. *Hitler's Pope: The Secret History of Pius XII* (2nd edn) p159

[2] Ibid. pp160-61

[3] McCabe, Joseph. *How the Cross Courted the Swastika for Eight Years.* Ch V. Source: http://www.infidels. org/library/historical/joseph_mccabe/big_blue_books/book_03.html#4 (2007)

[4] Paul, Gregory S. *The Great Scandal: Christianity's Role in the Rise of the Nazis*

[5] Noel, Gerard. *Pius XII: The Hound of Hitler.* p76

[6] Setton, Kenneth M. *The Papacy and the Levant, 1204-1571.* Vol 1: 'The Thirteenth and Fourteenth Centuries'. p41

[7] See, for example: Cornwell, John. *Hitler's Pope: The Secret History of Pius XII* (2nd edn) p8

history. It was the result of the damage caused by the extreme ambition of two deeply flawed key characters.

The Consequences of the Reichskonkordat

Following the signing of the concordat, Monsignor Kaas, the ancient chief of the Catholic Party, who had left Germany and gone to Rome, said 'Hitler knows well how to guide the ship. This man, bearer of high ideals, will do all that is necessary to save the nation from catastrophe ...'[1]

Pacelli's *Reichskonkordat* gave the Nazi regime the legitimacy to depict itself as being, in the words of Pacelli himself on 30 April 1937, 'a state power on the side of order'.[2]

Nazi officials throughout Germany felt they were not bound by the spirit of the concordat, since, through Pacelli's impetuosity in pushing it through, it was incomplete in relation to the definition of 'political' associations.[3] Thus, in Bavaria in particular, bans and aggression against Catholic groups, especially the Catholic press, were frequent.[4]

The Church never made any attempt to rescind the concordat and its loyalty clause during the Nazi regime. Reflecting the self-serving orientation of the Catholic Church, *it is the only diplomatic treaty negotiated with the Nazi regime that is still in force anywhere in the world.*[5,6]

The Church's political manipulations continue. Not only did the *Reichskonkordat* survive Hitler's defeat without so much as a scratch, its scope was extended by Catholic Chancellor Konrad Adenauer's Subsidiarity Legislation. This gave church organisations preference over public bodies in the running of hospitals and nursery schools. This is tantamount to a professional ban for non-denominational doctors, nurses and kindergarten workers as soon as church organisations run the majority of hospitals and nursery schools. Under the same pretence, Christian employees can be sacked if their marriage should end in divorce.'[7] In 1949, Adenauer, a member of the parliamentary council, told a fifty-five-year-old:

> You, young man, must learn how to despise people.[8]

Synopsis

Leo XIII's advocacy of the Septennate Bill of 1887 revealed 'the profound

---

[1] Edith Moore. *No Friend of Democracy: A study of Roman Catholic politics – their influence on the course ...* Source: http://inpursuitofhappiness.wordpress.com/2008/04/04/ vatican-always-backs-fascist-regimes/ (2010)

[2] Quoted in: Deschner, Karlheinz. *God and the Fascists: The Vatican Alliance with Mussolini, Franco, Hitler, and Pavelić.* p95

[3] Cornwell, John. *Hitler's Pope: The Secret History of Pius XII* (2nd edn) p157

[4] Cornwell, John. *Hitler's Pope: The Secret History of Pius XII* (2nd edn)

[5] http://en.wikipedia.org/wiki/Reichskonkordat (2007)

[6] Paul, Gregory S. *The Great Scandal: Christianity's Role in the Rise of the Nazis.*

[7] Dr Peter Gorenflos. http://www.jewishmag.com/133mag/vatican_nazi/vatican_nazi.htm (2015)

[8] Bundestag protocol, 11 June 1949. Quoted in: Deschner, Karlheinz. *God and the Fascists: The Vatican Alliance with Mussolini, Franco, Hitler, and Pavelić.* p93

immorality of the temporal policy of the Church of Rome.'

Pius XI took into his hands the unified control of all fields of endeavour in which his predecessors had distinguished themselves. This was the beginning of Catholic Action of far-reaching importance, which 'had for its end the destruction of the liberal spirit of the 19th century'.

Under Pius XI, the Church had a history of pacts with criminal states – the Holy See signed treaties with monarchs and governments regardless of slavery, inhumanity, or the infliction of torture.

A draft of an encyclical that Pius XI commissioned in 1938 concerning Nazi anti-Semitism notes that 'The purely worldly problems in which the Jewish people may see themselves involved, are of no interest to her.'

Eugenio Pacelli acquired a reputation as an able diplomat. Early in his career, he showed a definite aversion to the Jews. His increasing ambition for power and control conflicted with, and ultimately separated, authority from true Christian love.

In 1919 Pacelli gave the young Adolph Hitler 'a large cache of Church money to aid the rising revolutionary ...'

Pacelli, who became Pius XII, was a deeply flawed, political individual. He had a penchant for concordats, which he believed would centralise the power and prestige of European politics within the Holy See. In pushing the *Reichskonkordat*, Pacelli made a catastrophic miscalculation. It imposed a moral duty on all German Catholics to obey the Nazi rulers. Additionally, Pacelli legitimised the Nazi party in the eyes of the world. After its ratification Catholics flocked to the Nazi Party.

The *Reichskonkordat*'s potential for sanctioning the killing of the Jews was acknowledged by Hitler.

The Holy See and all German Catholics were complicit in racist and anti-Semitic legislation, and the German Church was 'led into a moral abyss' by Pacelli.

Pacelli said that he had no regrets about signing the *Reichskonkordat*, because the Catholic Church had to be protected by the state in Germany, irrespective of the fate of other Churches or human rights abuses.

---

21 – The Pope during the War

Silence – the sin of evasion.

The Church's complicity in face of the annihilation of the Jewish people during the long twelve years of the Third Reich. David Cymet

Pacelli as Pope

Eugenio Pacelli became Pope Pius XII on 12 March 1939. He made it clear that he would handle all German affairs personally. He proposed the following affirmation of Hitler:

> To the Illustrious Herr Adolf Hitler, Führer and Chancellor of the German Reich! Here at the beginning of Our Pontificate We wish to assure you that We remain devoted to the spiritual welfare of the German people entrusted to your leadership ... During the many years we spent in Germany, We did all in Our power to establish harmonious relations between Church and State. Now that the responsibilities of Our pastoral function have increased Our opportunities, how much more ardently do We pray to reach that goal. May the prosperity of the German people and their progress in every domain come, with God's help, to fruition![1]

World War II commenced six months later.

Pius was heir to a long-standing Catholic anti-Judaism that still enjoyed a respectability as late as the 1930s.[2]

Pius' Knowledge of the Massacres

When the French Vichy puppet government of Marshal Pétain introduced 'Jewish statutes', the Vichy ambassador to the Holy See informed Pétain that the Holy See did not consider the legislation in conflict with Catholic teachings, provided it was implemented with 'charity' and 'justice'.[3,4] These Jews were later exterminated by the Nazis.

The Holy See was an active agent between Italy and France at the time when Marshal Pétain allied France with the Nazis. Pius XII sent a personal message to Pétain asking that his country accept the situation 'with fortitude and realism.' He also sent a letter to the French Bishops containing these disingenuous words:

> These very misfortunes with which God has today visited your people, give assurance, we feel certain, of conditions for greater spiritual labour, favourable to bringing about a reawakening of the entire nation.[5]

---

[1] Walker, Jim. *Christianity in Europe during World War II.* http://www.nobeliefs.com/ChurchesWWII.htm#anchor2b (2012)

[2] Atkin, Nicholas & Frank Tallet. *Priests, Prelates & People.* p260

[3] Schoenberg, Shira. *Pope Pius XII and the Holocaust.* http://www.jewishvirtuallibrary.org/jsource/antisemitism/pius.html (2007)

[4] This was typical of Pacelli's acquired impeccable skills in veiled language, in which he assessed every word he spoke or wrote with caution, and from which his utterances were outstanding achievements of circumspection.

[5] Moore, Edith. *No Friend of Democracy: A study of Roman Catholic politics – their influence on the course of the present War and the growth of Fascism*

ˎ   In 1940 Isaac Herzog, the Chief Rabbi of Palestine, asked Cardinal Luigi Maglione, the Papal Secretary of State, to intercede to prevent Jews in Spain from being deported to Germany. Later, he made a similar request for Jews in Lithuania. Pius did nothing.[1]

'The barbaric round-up actions and deportation of Jews in cattle trains headed to the East was a daily public spectacle witnessed by the population all over Europe. The deportation was a public spectacle not a secret operation. Hundreds of thousands of Jews from every European country, Slovakia, the Netherlands, France, Belgium, Luxembourg, Norway, Italy, Yugoslavia, Romania, Hungary, Greece, even as far as Rhodes and Corfu offshore, were deported to extermination centers.'

Pius and the Holy See were well informed of the deportations by their own representatives all over Europe and by the desperate calls for help from the Jewish communities. Ecclesiastics 'in every country were spectators and often actors involved in a variety of ways in the cruel drama that led directly to the killing sites in the East and were deaf to these tragic calls of help. The deportation of Jews from Rome to Auschwitz[2] ... is a paradigm of that callous attitude.'[3]

In 1941 Harold Tittman, Assistant Chief of the United States delegation to the Holy See, asked Pius to condemn the Nazi atrocities. The reply was invariably that the Pope had already condemned crimes against morality in war and that the Holy See wanted to remain 'neutral', and that any condemnation of the atrocities would have a negative influence on Catholics in Nazi occupied lands. Notwithstanding, the Allied governments issued a declaration of condemnation – the *German Policy of Extermination of the Jewish Race*.[4] When Tittman asked Secretary of State, Cardinal Luigi Maglione, if Pius would issue a similar proclamation, Maglione replied that the papacy was 'unable to denounce publicly particular atrocities.'

In the same year Theodor Cardinal Innitzer of Vienna informed Pius of Jewish deportations.[5] The British Envoy Extraordinary and Minister Plenipotentiary to the Holy See, Sir D'Arcy Osborne, the Duke of Leeds, brought additional confirmatory information to the Pope's notice.[6] Pius still did nothing.

These refusals by Pius cannot, therefore, be attributed to ignorance of the facts. Carlo Falconi, in *The Silence of Pius XII*, has recorded that 'The Holy See was extremely well informed of the situation in Poland', from the country's invasion to the end of the occupation. With the help of many channels, Pius was able to know about every sector of the country's life under the Nazis.[7]

---

[1] Schoenberg, Shira. *Pope Pius XII and the Holocaust*
[2] With the certain knowledge of Pius XII.
[3] Cymet, David. *History vs. Apologetics: The Holocaust, the Third Reich, and the Catholic Church.* p313
[4] See, for example: http://avalon.law.yale.edu/imt/jack01.asp (2014)
[5] Schoenberg, Shira. *Pope Pius XII and the Holocaust.*
[6] Atkin, Nicholas & Frank Tallet. *Priests, Prelates & People.* pp256-57
[7] Ibid. p198

In November 1942 Jan Karski, a courier for the Polish underground, carried a message from the Polish Jews to Pius asking him to excommunicate the perpetrators of the atrocities.[1] Pius never did.

In that same year, after the Holy See's ten years of immoral misdirected work, Pius XII, who had helped Adolf Hitler to power, and who had supported Benito Mussolini's right-wing state, was 'left holding a withered fascist flower.'[2] Realisation began to dawn.

It has been noted by historians that Pius only supported the Jews after 1942, when it became likely that the allies would achieve victory. The conclusion, that any intervention by Pius was based on practical advantage rather than moral inclination, is supported by the fact that in late 1942 he began advising the German and Hungarian bishops that it would be *politically* advantageous to denounce the massacre of the Jews.[3]

The known documents of Pius' private correspondence confirm that he was continually bearing witness to his awareness of the conditions in the countries he was addressing – yet doing little or nothing. For example, his letter of 30 April 1943 to Monsignor Konrad von Preysing, Bishop of Berlin, admits:

> Day after day We hear of inhuman acts which have nothing to do with the real necessities of war, and they fill us with stupefaction and bitterness. *Only a recourse to prayer...*[4]

Pius never condemned the Atrocities

Hitler received support from the Church in many ways, particularly from Pius XII's continuous refusal to take an overt stand against Nazism. Pius had an obsessive aversion to Bolshevism. In his attempts to destroy it, although he nominally condemned Nazism, German Catholics were never excommunicated for belonging to the Nazi Party or for supporting Hitler. By contrast, those who became communists were automatically excommunicated. When the Berlin correspondent of *L'Osservatore Romano*, Eduardo Senatro, asked Pius if he would protest against the extermination of Jews, the pope was reported as replying:

> Dear friend, do not forget that millions of Catholics serve in the German armies. Shall I bring them into conflicts of conscience?[5]

Regardless of pleadings throughout the world, Pius XII *never* publicly condemned Nazi war crimes or Nazi Germany to the end. US President Roosevelt, through his 'peace ambassador' to the Holy See, requested that Pius condemn Hitler's invasion of Protestant Denmark and Norway. Pius definitely refused this request.[6] Nicholas Atkin and Frank Tallet, in their book *Priests, Prelates & People*, confirmed that the fact that

---

[1] Phayer, Michael. *Pius XI, the Holocaust, and the Cold War*. p50

[2] Ibid. p52

[3] Schoenberg, Shira. *Pope Pius XII and the Holocaust*

[4] Falconi, Carlo. *The Silence of Pius XII*. p62

[5] Cohn-Sherbok, D. *The Crucified Jew: Twenty Centuries of Christian Anti-Semitism*. pp208-9

[6] Lehmann, L H. *Behind the Dictators: A Factual Analysis of the Relationship of Nazi-Fascism and Roman Catholicism*. p29

Pius never explicitly condemned the Holocaust must stand to his eternal discredit.[1] His silence was an abandonment of moral guidance on an appalling scale.[2]

The horrendous, organised genocide had only a fragmentary or generalised mention in Papal documents. Not a single one among the hundreds of pages of Pius' allocutions, messages and writings addressed it explicitly or exclusively, and only rare and limited hints were made in summary allusions. Moreover, instead of being in a language of outrage, they were consistently phrased in a cold and judicial style.[3]

Pius waited until the end of the Holocaust and the death of Hitler in 1945 before issuing a condemnation of Nazism as a blasphemous aberration.[4]

Pius' Complicity in Atrocities

Dr Jonathan Levy, co-counsel for the Plaintiffs in *Alperin v. Vatican Bank and Franciscan Order* United States District Court for Northern California, Case No C-99-04941 MMC, has recorded:

> With the 50th Anniversary of the death of Pius XII, the Vatican is again pushing for his sainthood. While Pius can be legitimately criticized for his tepid condemnations of the Nazi Holocaust there is no question he was complicit in the deaths of at least 500,000 Orthodox Christian Serbs, Jews and Roma murdered in Croatia, Bosnia, and Krajina during the Second World War by the Axis allied Croatian regime.[5]

Pius' 'Neutrality'

Pius' oft repeated claim for his need to remain neutral between the Axis and the Allies, and during the horrors of the Holocaust, was a measure of his strong positive feelings towards Germany. This self-imposed 'neutrality' has been refuted. A report by Monsignor Giovanni Battista Montini, Pius XII's Secretary of State, described and denounced several abuses committed by the Soviet Army against *German* inhabitants of the Soviet Union. This report was widely viewed as demonstrating the Holy See's bias towards Germany and its non-neutral selectivity in speaking out against atrocities.

Furthermore, Pius' neutrality was totally contrary to the embedded teachings of the Catholic Church with respect to a 'Just War'. *Catholic Answers*[6] provides relevant information on this doctrine. It explains that 'the most authoritative and up-to-date expression of just war doctrine is found in paragraph 2309 of the *Catechism of the Catholic Church*:

> *The strict conditions for legitimate defense by military force require rigorous consideration. The gravity of such a decision makes it subject to rigorous conditions of*

[1] Atkin, Nicholas & Frank Tallet. *Priests, Prelates & People.* pp259-60
[2] Notwithstanding that a *New York Catechism* grandiloquently stated: 'The pope takes the place of Jesus Christ on earth. ... By divine right the pope has supreme and full power in faith and morals over each and every pastor and his flock.'
[3] Falconi, Carlo. *The Silence of Pius XII.* p39
[4] Gerard Noel. *Pius XII: The Hound of Hitler.* pp4,130
[5] http://www.remnantofgod.org/ustashe.htm (2015).
[6] http://www.catholic.com/documents/just-war-doctrine (2015)

moral legitimacy. At one and the same time:

> *the damage inflicted by the aggressor on the nation or community of nations must be lasting, grave, and certain;*

> *all other means of putting an end to it must have been shown to be impractical or ineffective;*

> *there must be serious prospects of success; ...*

These are the traditional elements enumerated in what is called the 'just war' doctrine. The evaluation of these conditions for moral legitimacy belongs to the prudential judgment of those who have responsibility for the common good.'

Catholic Answers continues:

Justice in War

Once the decision to go to war has been reached, a new set of issues is placed in focus. These have to do with how the war is conducted ...

A particular danger in wartime is brutality toward those not engaged in combat. Frequently in the history of warfare, soldiers have maimed, raped, and even killed those who did not pose a physical threat to them. Sometimes this has escalated into genocide. The Catechism is at pains to stress the moral illegitimacy of all of these:

> *Non-combatants, wounded soldiers, and prisoners must be respected and treated humanely. Actions deliberately contrary to the law of nations and to its universal principles are crimes, as are the orders that command such actions. Blind obedience does not suffice to excuse those who carry them out. Thus <u>the extermination of a people, nation, or ethnic minority must be condemned as a mortal sin.</u> One is morally bound to resist orders that command genocide (CCC 2313).*

> *Every act of war directed to the <u>indiscriminate destruction of whole cities</u> or vast areas with their inhabitants is a crime against God and man, which <u>merits firm and unequivocal condemnation</u>.... (CCC 2314).* [Original italics]

The war waged by the Allies against the evils of Nazism and the Axis Powers fell within the ambit of a Just War. Its moral legitimacy belonged to the prudential judgment of those who had responsibility for the common good.

Consequently, Pius' ongoing pursuit of his alleged neutrality was totally at odds with the accepted moral ethos of the Catholic Church. By his failure to issue an explicit condemnation of the genocides, he was, effectively, condoning the mortal sins of millions of Nazi exterminators. By allowing these annihilations to continue without disapprobation, it can justifiably be asked: "did Pius' icy silence constitute a mortal sin on his part?"

Furthermore, the bombings of London, Coventry, Warsaw, Rotterdam, Belgrade, Manila, Pearl Harbor, and various towns in the South Pacific constituted crimes against

God and man, which merited firm and unequivocal condemnation. Pius *never* condemned these wholesale destructions.

Pius' Involvement with, and Jubilation over Hitler's Invasion of Russia via Operation Barbarossa

'Operation Barbarossa', commencing 22 June 1941, was the code name for Nazi Germany's invasion of the Soviet Union.

Over the course of the operation, seven armies comprising about 3,500,000 soldiers invaded the USSR along a 2900 kilometre front. In addition, it employed more than 3000 tanks, 2700 aircraft, 7184 artillery pieces, 600,000 motor vehicles and 650,000 horses.[1] It was the greatest invasion in the history of warfare, opening the largest and bloodiest theatre of combat ever. It resulted in the greatest case of mass murder in human history.

Riga, the Latvian capital was taken by the Nazis on 1 July 1941; Kiev, the capital of Ukraine, fell on 19 September; the Germans reached the gates of Leningrad in early September, and the suburbs of Moscow on 25 November.

'Barbarossa' resulted in an extremely high rate of Axis losses – more than 1,000,000 men – particularly, 95% of all German Army casualties that occurred from 1941 to 1944, and 65% of all Allied military casualties from the entire war. Approximately 2.8 million Soviet prisoners were killed in just eight months of 1941-1942.[2]

In his 'Declaration of War on the Soviet Union' speech to the German people on the day of the invasion, Catholic Adolf Hitler explained his reasons for the invasion, and ended it with the words: 'May God help us especially in this fight!'[3]

While Pius XII encouraged Catholics to volunteer to join the Nazi forces for military participation in the Russian front,[4] so also, Hitler ordered Himmler to exterminate the Soviet Union's Jews. Accordingly, as the Wehrmacht spread across the land, four Einsatzgruppen killing units followed. They rounded up and murdered the Jews, then buried them in mass graves.

Not only did Pius encourage this voluntary pro-Nazi militancy, he and his confidante, Sister Pascalina Lehnert, showed great jubilation as Hitler's armies crossed the Russian frontier. 'They both joined in joyful prayers. Even in defiance of world opinion, Pius and Pascalina said novenas for the Nazis and *asked God to intercede for their total victory* in Russia ...'[5]

---

[1] https://www.jewishvirtuallibrary.org/jsource/ww2/barbarossa.html (2015)
[2] http://en.wikipedia.org/wiki/Operation_Barbarossa (2014). See also: Read, Anthony. *The Devil's Disciples: Hitler's Inner Circle.* pp710, 741
[3] https://www.jewishvirtuallibrary.org/jsource/ww2/hitlersoviet.htm (2015)
[4] Manhattan, Avro. *Vietnam: Why did we go? The Religious Beginnings of an Unholy War* ... Ch 3
[5] Murphy, Paul I with Rene R Arlington. *La Popessa.* p252. In complete contrast to the record in this book, the article 'Sacro Vergente' in *Wikipedia* states categorically 'despite strong pressures, he [Pius XII] never approved a war against communism or Russia in 1941.' http://en.wikipedia.org/wiki/Sacro_Vergente (August 2015). See also: Lehnert, Maria Pascalina. *Ich durfte ihm dienen, Erinnerungen an Papst Pius XII.*

Pius' Silence

Pius was silent about the notorious Nazi war crimes all over Europe and was silent about the Holocaust even though he was consistently besieged with pleas for help on behalf of the Jews.[1] He *never* declared it a sin for Catholics to participate in the slaughter.

1938

Susan Zuccotti has charted the near-total silence of both Pius XI and Pius XII in the face of the Italian anti-Jewish laws of 1938, underlining how the Vatican intervened only on specific issues such as interracial marriages and converts to Catholicism.[2]

Pius was silent over Kristallnacht in 1938.

At the end of 1938, when anti-Semitism was increasingly evident, when Jews were being brutally murdered and others sent to concentration camps, and Jewish rights were being steadily eroded, Pacelli, in his usual manner, declaimed at Budapest:

> *We love our times*, despite their danger and their anguish ... precisely because of that danger, and because of the difficult tasks that the age imposes on us; we are ready to dedicate ourselves wholly and unconditionally, regardless of ourselves; otherwise nothing great and decisive can result.[3]

1939

Pius was silent over Mussolini's fascist attacks on Ethiopia and Albania.

Soon after Pius XII's accession, seasoned Vatican observers quickly noted a warmer tone in the Pope's dialogue with Germany. *L'Osservatore Romano* and Vatican Radio were prohibited from indulging in polemics against the Nazis. One of Pius' immediate initiatives was a letter he was planning to address to Hitler, in which he stressed his love for the German people; by contrast, his predecessor, Pius XI, had been composing a letter announcing the withdrawal of the papal nuncio from Berlin. Accordingly, there was no papal condemnation of the German occupation of Prague that March.

The Free French ambassador François Charles-Roux pressured Pius to make it clear that if Europe were to go to war then the responsibility lay at the door of Germany. But Pius continued to declare his neutrality while appearing indulgent of Hitler's increasingly belligerent behaviour.[4] To the astonishment of the British and French, he exerted pressure on the beleaguered Poles during the summer of 1939 to make yet more concessions to the German Reich. Nor did Pius protest against the attack on Poland in September 1939 that triggered World War II. The recent work by Professor José M Sánchez, *Pius XII and the Holocaust: Understanding the Controversy*, confirms the deafening silence of the Vatican in the case of Catholic Poland throughout the war.[5]

---

[1] Küng, Hans. *The Catholic Church: a short history.* pp177-80
[2] https://www.nytimes.com/books/01/02/04/reviews/010204.04duggant.html (2015)
[3] Noel, Gerard. *Pius XII: The Hound of Hitler.* p90
[4] Sir Francis d'Arcy Osborne commented: 'Is there not a moral issue at stake which does not admit of neutrality?'. Phayer, Michael. *Pius XII, the Holocaust, and the Cold War.* p49
[5] Atkin, Nicholas & Frank Tallet. *Priests, Prelates & People.* p246

1940

Early1940, the Chief Rabbi of Palestine, Isaac Herzog, asked the papal Secretary of State, Cardinal Maglione to intercede to prevent Jews in Spain from being deported to Germany. He later made a similar request for Jews in Lithuania. Pius did nothing.[1]

'In a September 1940 broadcast, the Vatican called its policy "neutrality," but stated in the same broadcast that where morality was involved, no neutrality was possible. This could only imply that mass murder was not a moral issue.'[2]

1941

Pius' Christmas broadcast of 1941 confirmed his intransigent non-involvement and his persistent refusal to condemn Nazism:

> As God is Our witness, We love all peoples without exception with equal affection; and up till now We have imposed the maximum reserve on Ourselves so as to avoid even the appearance of being contaminated by the Party spirit ...[3]

1942

In March 1942 Pius received, via Monsignor Filippe Bernadini the apostolic nuncio in Berne, a lengthy document compiled by the World Jewish Congress and the Swiss Israelite community registering the atrocities being perpetrated in Germany, Vichy France, Slovakia, Croatia, and Hungary – all countries in which it was believed that Pius could exert some restraining influence; particularly in the latter three countries, which had strong ties between their governments and the Church. Concerning the Roman Catholic Independent State of Croatia, the document reads:

> Several thousand families were either deported to desert islands on the Dalmatian coast or incarcerated in concentration camps ... all the male Jews were sent to labour camps ... where they perished in great number ... At the same time, their wives and children were sent to another camp where they, too, are enduring dire privations.

Additional information relative to Pius XII' silence appeared in an article in *Civiltà Cattolica* of 30 June 1961. Jesuit Father Fiorello Cavalli wrote concerning the spring of 1942:

> In those days anguished appeals for help reached the Vatican from the Jews and their governments in many countries, through the British Minister to the Holy See, President Roosevelt's personal representative to Pius XII, the Apostolic Delegations in Great Britain, the United States and Turkey, and the Nunciatures in Rumania, Hungary and Switzerland.[4]

Gerhart Riegner, a signatory to the above Swiss document, revealed in his 1998

[1] Gutman, Israel, *Encyclopedia of the Holocaust.* p1136
[2] https://www.jewishvirtuallibrary.org/jsource/anti-semitism/pius.html (2015)
[3] Carlo Falconi. *The Silence of Pius XII.* p36
[4] Falconi, Carlo. *The Silence of Pius XII.* p52

memoirs that this document was excluded by the Vatican from its *Actes et Documents du Saint Siege relatifs a la Seconde Guerre Mondiale* of released wartime documents.[1]

Pius was definitely informed about the atrocities in the Soviet Union. Archbishop Antonijs Springovics wrote to him on 12 December 1942 stating that most of the Jews of Riga, Latvia, had been killed.[2]

The Holy See was constantly besieged by reports and appeals from organisations of all kinds, especially Jewish. In his article on the Holy See and the Romanian Jews, Father Angelo Martini quoted examples in the year 1942:

> In June 1942 Pope Pius XII received a pressing appeal written in Latin from a group of Jews in Cernauti imploring his protection so as to avoid deportation across the Dniester and the Bug and gain mitigation of the punishments in the ghetto; and drew his special attention to the thousands of orphaned children who were deprived of all aid.

> In October the nuncio in Switzerland, Mgr Bernardini, sent to the Holy See a report by the president of the Israelite Communities in Switzerland asking for a speedy intervention of the Holy Father not only on behalf of the Rumanian Jews across the Dniester but also on behalf of the others threatened with mass-deportation to those regions.

> A similar memorandum was presented at that time on behalf of the Jews of the Banat who were also threatened with deportation.[3]

In 1942 the United States, Great Britain, Belgium, Brazil, Uruguay and Poland presented Pius simultaneously with démarches that warned him of the loss of papal moral authority: 'A policy of silence in regard to such offences[4] against the conscience of the world must necessarily involve a renunciation of moral leadership and a consequent atrophy of the influence and authority of the Vatican.'[5]

In September 1942, US President Roosevelt sent a personal representative, Myron Taylor, to plead with Pius to condemn the extermination of the Jews. His task was to urge Pius to issue an unequivocal denunciation of Nazi barbarities. He brought yet further distressing news of Nazi atrocities, and later Pius XII was presented with evidential documentation compiled by the allies.[6] He warned the Pope that his silence was endangering his moral prestige. The Vatican Secretary of State responded on behalf of Pius that it was impossible to verify rumours about crimes committed against the Jews.[7] It is also reported that Pius actually made the lame hypocritical excuse that he must 'rise above the belligerent parties'.[8]

[1] Midlarsky, Manus I. *The Killing Trap: Genocide in the Twentieth Century.* p225
[2] Phayer, Michael. *The Catholic Church and the Holocaust, 1930-1965.* p48
[3] Falconi, Carlo. *The Silence of Pius XII.* p61
[4] The Nazis' attacks on the Polish people.
[5] Phayer, Michael. *The Catholic Church and the Holocaust, 1930-1965.* p28
[6] Atkin, Nicholas & Frank Tallet. *Priests, Prelates & People.* pp256-57
[7] Schoenberg, Shira. *Pope Pius XI and the Holocaust*
[8] http://www.xanga.com/home.aspx?user=ReligionStinks&nextdate=8%2f30%2f2002+8%3a22%3a57.0

Pius even remained silent during the Nazis' massive atrocities in Poland against Catholic Poles.[1] Dr Kazimierz Papée, the Polish ambassador to the Holy See, met Pius in September 1940, but left disappointed when the pope declined to condemn the double invasion of Poland, because he did not want the Holy See 'to become a platform for Polish objections against Germany'.[2] In May 1942 Papée complained again that Pius had failed to condemn the wave of atrocities in Poland, to which the Cardinal Secretary of State Maglione fell back on the Holy See's recurrent theme that it could not document individual atrocities. Papée retorted 'when something becomes notorious, proof is not required.'[3] Papée never accepted Pius XII's proposal to accept the Nazi annexation of a portion of Poland.

The vast majority of Nazi Holocaust victims were western Russian, Baltic, and Polish Jews, who were either shot, or gassed and cremated in the killing centres. All of these victims were murdered without any papal protest other than the veiled ineffectual reference of Pius' 1942 Christmas address.[4] This speech is his most famous one, where, during several tens of thousands of words, he spoke twenty seven words, from twenty six pages of text, on what could possibly be interpreted as a condemnation of the Nazi Holocaust.[5] His exact words were:

> hundreds of thousands who, without any fault of their own, sometimes only by reason of their nationality or race, are marked down for death or gradual extinction.

This was the greatest extent of Pacelli's condemnation of the Final Solution. Nothing more. The actual millions who had been and were being annihilated he scaled down to 'hundreds of thousands'; his 'by reason of their nationality or race,' excluded any mention of religion. Nowhere did he mention the word 'Jews', and nowhere did he mention the terms 'Nazi' or 'National Socialism'.[6] It was, say Michael Phayer, 'both his first and his last pronouncement on genocide.'[7]

Michael Phayer also commented 'no one, certainly not the Germans, took it as a protest against their slaughter of the Jews.'[8] And, the editorial of the lay Catholic journal *Commonweal* stated that it is 'difficult to realize that certain sections [of the broadcast] are issued in the very midst of a world cataclysm.'[9]

In 1942 during the implementation of the Final Solution, when, in Poland alone, 700,000 innocent Jews were murdered, as an offset to his silence, Pius consecrated the

(2009)

[1] *'Et Papa tacet': the Genocide of Polish Catholics.* http://www.thefreelibrary.com/'Et+Papa+ tacet'%3a+the+ genocide+of+Polish+Catholics-a0131753946

[2] http://en.wikipedia.org/wiki/Kazimierz_Pap%C3%A9e (2010)

[3] http://www.astrotheme.fr/en/portraits/HD5ErVtDrzha.htm (2008)

[4] Phayer, Michael. *The Catholic Church and the Holocaust, 1930-1965.* p72

[5] http://www.abc.net.au/rn/religionreport/stories/2008/2378841.htm#transcript (2008)

[6] See, for example: Noble, Arthur. *Hitler's Pope: Vicar of Christ or Instrument of the Devil?* Part III: 'The Conspiracy against the Serbs'. Source: http://www.ianpaisley.org/article.asp?hitler_3.htm (2008)

[7] Phayer, Michael. *Pius XII, the Holocaust, and the Cold War.* p65

[8] Source: Michael, Robert. *A History of Catholic Antisemitism: The Dark Side of the Church.* p179

[9] Phayer, Michael. *Pius XII, the Holocaust, and the Cold War.* p58

whole human race to the 'Immaculate Heart of Mary', the 'Queen of the World'.[1]

1943

From 1939, Władysław Raczkiewicz, President of the Polish government-in-exile, was the internationally recognised Polish head of state, and this government was recognised as the continuum to the Polish government of 1939. In 1943 Raczkiewicz appealed to Pius to publicly denounce Nazi violence.[2] Bishop Preysing of Berlin did the same, at least twice. Pius refused.[3]

For five long years Pacelli was pope as the tragic figures of people killed and property destroyed in Poland steadily accumulated. Yet he never spoke. Never. His lips were sealed from the moment of the German aggression, and only became unsealed on rare occasions when he made laments of a generalised kind. Never, never, did he issue a cry of protest.

On 6 March 1943, Bishop Preysing wrote to Pius XII about the Berlin round-ups, informing him that many baptised converts were being deported. He appealed to the Pope to intercede for them:

> Among the deportees are also many Catholics. Is it not possible for Your Holiness again to intervene for the many unfortunate innocents? It is the last hope for many and the profound wish of all decent people.

Pius was not moved to action. He replied more than one month later that this was a matter that should be dealt by the local bishops. Preysing himself should be the one to intervene, if he considered it appropriate. Pius' actual pharisaic words were:

> In the present situation we can unfortunately not offer them any effective help outside *Our prayers*. We are, however, determined to raise Our voice anew on their behalf as circumstances indicate and permit.[4]

The evidence is conclusive. However much Pius may, or may not, have agonised over the fate of the Jews and other victims of the Nazis, he chose to put their fate second to that of the Catholic Church.[5]

His silence, ensuring the collusion of the large community of German Catholics in the Nazis' persecution and extermination of Jews and others, can never be condoned.[6] Had Pius condemned Hitler's atrocities, his influence would have been significant. In the words of historian J P Stern:[7]

---

[1] See, for example: http://www.rosary-center.org/consecrt.htm (2015); https://en.wikipedia.org/wiki/Pope_Pius_XII_Consecration_to_the_Immaculate_Heart_of_Mary (2015)

[2] See, for example: Phayer, Michael. *The Catholic Church and the Holocaust* ... p49

[3] Schoenberg, Shira. *Pope Pius XII and the Holocaust*

[4] Cymet, David. *History vs. Apologetics: The Holocaust, the Third Reich, and the Catholic Church.* pp317-18. This is one of many examples of Pius' political reliance on his ineffectual prayers.

[5] See, for example: Gerard Noel. *Pius XII: The Hound of Hitler.* p197

[6] See, for example: Callil, Carmen. *Bad Faith: A Forgotten History of Family* ... pp238-40

[7] Joseph Peter Stern (1920-1991), was an authority on German literature. He was a professor at University College, London, from 1972 to 1986.

It seems beyond any doubt, that, if the churches had opposed the killing and the persecution of the Jews, as they opposed the killing of the congenitally insane and the sick, there would have been no Final Solution.[1]

Pius XII even decided not to speak out against the Nazis' moral outrages perpetrated against Roman Catholics in Poland in the hope of avoiding moral outrages that he believed communists would perpetrate against the entire Church if they prevailed against Nazi Germany. 'This was a flawed and mistaken political judgement.'[2] Post-War, East European communist regimes did not commit genocide; but during the War the Nazis did in Poland and elsewhere, and the Catholics did in Croatia and Slovakia.

Condemnations of the Silence of Pius XII and the Church

In 1960 Julius August Cardinal Döpfner of Munich, spoke of regrettable decisions that had been made by Church leaders during the Nazi era.[3] On 8 March 1964, in St Michael's Church in Munich, Cardinal Döpfner, former Archbishop of Munich and Freising, did not hesitate to pronounce in a sermon commemorating Pius XII:

> The retrospective judgment of history provides every ground for the view that Pius XII should have protested with greater firmness.[4]

David Cymet finds that there was no neutrality in the anti-Semitic campaign from the Catholic pulpits and press in the pre-war years; nor in the Catholic forefront role in the promotion of anti-Jewish legislation in the Catholic countries of Europe; nor in the Catholic agreements signed or verbally established with Hitler's regime; nor in the role played by the Church in the consolidation of that regime. He concludes that 'it is only against the general background of its record of coincidence and collaboration with the Nazis and their helpers that the silence of the Church during the Holocaust acquires its full significance.'[5]

On 27 January 1998, Yehuda Bauer, Professor of Holocaust Studies at the Avraham Harman Institute of Contemporary Jewry at the Hebrew University of Jerusalem, delivered a speech to the German Bundestag in which he said:

> I come from a people who gave the Ten Commandments to the world. Time has come to strengthen them by three additional ones, which we ought to adopt and commit ourselves to: thou shall not be a perpetrator; thou shall not be a victim; and thou shall never, but never, be a bystander.

The following is the caption that Yad Vashem affixes in English and Hebrew to two photographs of Pius XII in its Jerusalem Memorial:

---

[1] Source: Noel, Gerard. *Pius XII: The Hound of Hitler.* p131
[2] Phayer, Michael. *Pius XII, the Holocaust, and the Cold War.* p41
[3] Ibid. In: *Holocaust and Genocide Studies,* Vol 12, No 2, Fall 1998. pp 233-56
[4] Carlo Falconi. *The Silence of Pius XII.* p14
[5] Cymet, David. *History vs. Apologetics: The Holocaust, the Third Reich, and the Catholic Church.* Preface, p xiv

In 1933, when he was Secretary of the Vatican State, he was active in obtaining a Concordat with the German regime to preserve the Church's rights in Germany, even if this meant recognizing the Nazi racist regime. When he was elected Pope in 1939, he shelved a letter against racism and anti-Semitism that his predecessor had prepared. Even when reports about the murder of Jews reached the Vatican, the Pope did not protest either verbally or in writing. In December 1942, he abstained from signing the Allied declaration condemning the extermination of the Jews. When Jews were deported from Rome to Auschwitz, the Pope did not intervene. The Pope maintained his neutral position throughout the war, with the exception of appeals to the rulers of Hungary and Slovakia towards its end. His silence and the absence of guidelines obliged Churchmen throughout Europe to decide on their own how to react.[1]

It appears never to have occurred to Pius XII that 'preserving a Church that had not had its finest hour in the service of humanity would leave it indelibly stained'.[2]

Polish reactions to Pius' silence may be gauged from the following extract of an article 'Does Independent Poland need Union with the Vatican?' in *Chlopski boj* (*The Peasants' Struggle*), n.35, 30 November 1941:

> For centuries one of the Church's most important duties has been the moral education of mankind. Christ's ethical teaching had a revolutionary value, given the moral laws and customs of the time ... Today this ethic is the exact opposite of reality as it was then ...
>
> As for Catholicism, it seems to have failed completely when confronted with the judgment of history. A great Catholic country – Italy – is on the Axis side, among the butchers of mankind. Another great Catholic country, and the eldest daughter of the Church – France – has provided the largest number of traitors. With the exception of Poland, which is saving the reputation of Catholicism, it is countries of other confessions (England, Holland, Norway, Greece, Yugoslavia) that have shown lively sentiments of honour and justice ...
>
> It has been shown in our times that Catholicism has gone into shameful and dishonourable bankruptcy. In saying this we are thinking above all of moral bankruptcy ...
>
> The Pope's defenders are saying, as we have heard more than once, that he *'could not expose the possessions and organization of the Church' [to destruction]*. Thus we can see that the Christian ideal is dying. The Church today is a material and administrative power and a political force, but, alas, it has ceased to be a moral force.
>
> *In the person of the Pope we have found neither a great apostle nor a father.* The evil goes deeper ... In measures taken by ecclesiastical authority the Christian ideal is relegated to the last place, *politics and diplomacy coming first.* Thus we wonder whether, when the Third Republic comes to birth, we shall need union with Rome

[1] http://en.wikipedia.org/wiki/Pope_Pius_XII_and_Yad_Vashem (2012)
[2] Phayer, Michael. *Pius XII, the Holocaust, and the Cold War.* p94

and whether such a union will have any significance. And whether, by regaining our independence from the papal State, we shall experience political, ideological or moral loss. Perhaps this will not be the same as putting aside and breaking political and material links? And, finally, apart from the other important problems, we wonder whether the uninterrupted stream of our gold should continue to flow towards Rome to increase the wealth of the Sacred Palaces and the power of *the man who was supposed to be the Vicar of Christ*.[1]

The Jews of Rome

Pius remained silent even when the Nazis rounded up nearly 2000 Jews of Rome on 16 October 1943,[2] mostly women and children, and who were then transported to Auschwitz.[3] The Apostolic Palace (Papal Palace) contains over 1000 rooms. This would have been more than sufficient to hide every one of these Jews. In her book *Under His Very Windows: The Vatican and the Holocaust in Italy*, Dr Susan Zuccotti concluded that Pius did not welcome Jews in the Vatican, and that he appears to have made no contacts and no appeal to either the Italians or any German officials on behalf of the Roman Jews.[4]

Historian John Cornwell has recorded that Pius refused to intervene on behalf of the Jews of Rome even though the leaders of the German occupation themselves urged him to protest publicly and register his objections with Berlin. Significantly, the trucks that carted the Jews to their deaths were driven past St Peter's square to enable the Catholic soldiers on them to see this famous centre of their faith.[5] It has been claimed that the Jews called out for the Pope to help them as they passed along the perimeter of the square. Eyewitnesses described the scene. An Italian journalist reported: 'The eyes of the children were dilated and unseeing. It seemed as if they were asking for an explanation for such terror and suffering.' In one street, several trucks came to a halt. The Marquise Fulvia Ripa di Meana was passing down the street. She stated: 'I saw in their terror-stricken eyes, in the faces grown pale as if with pain, and in their little quivering hands that clung to the sides of the truck, the maddening fear that had overtaken them.'[6]

Five days later, the entry in the meticulously kept log at Auschwitz recorded:

> After the selection 149 men (registered with numbers 158451-158639) and 47 women (registered with numbers 66172-66218) have been admitted to the detention camp. The rest have been gassed.[7]

Paul O'Shea is a member of the New South Wales Council for Christians and Jews, a former Carmelite, and has completed his doctoral research on Pius XII and the Jews.

[1] Falconi, Carlo. *The Silence of Pius XII.* pp225-26
[2] Phayer, Michael. *The Catholic Church and the Holocaust, 1930-1965.* p50
[3] http://www.zionism-israel.com/his/judeophobia6.htm (2007)
[4] Zuccotti, Susan. *Under His Very Windows: The Vatican and the Holocaust in Italy.* pp253, 294
[5] *The Scandal of Roman Catholicism.* http://www.liberalslikechrist.org/Catholic/RC_scandal-2.html (2007)
[6] Source: Cornwell, John. *Hitler's Pope: The Secret History of Pius XII.* p304
[7] Zuccotti, Susan. *The Italians and the Holocaust: Persecution, Rescue, and Survival*

He teaches at St Patrick's College, Sydney. He has degrees in theology, education and history. When asked in a radio interview about the removal of the Roman Jews, Dr O'Shea replied that Pius XII had more than ample information from many sources of what was happening to the Jews of Europe. Nevertheless, Pius held to his 'fiction of papal neutrality', even to the point where the Roman Jews were rounded up and incarcerated in the military college that is adjacent to the Vatican wall.

'I think it becomes a moral failure on his part,' said Dr O'Shea – 'because all the major religious traditions say that one cannot be mute, one cannot be silent in the face of overwhelming evil. One has a moral duty to speak out for one's neighbour.'[1] Dr O'Shea confirmed that: 'There is no doubt that Pius never spoke out explicitly against the massacre of the Jews of Europe.'[2]

In his book *A Cross too Heavy: Eugenio Pacelli, Politics and the Jews of Europe 1917 – 1943*, Dr O'Shea 'comes to the conclusion that the diplomatic expertise of Pius the XII may well have been the tragic flaw that relegated the Jews to be "lesser victims" in the time of World War.' The Pope's blinkered diplomacy led to official silence from the Holy See as the Holocaust was taking place and as the Jews of Rome were rounded up under the Pope's very windows.[3]

A week after Pius' Christmas broadcast, at which time most of the Roman Jews were already dead, *L'Osservatore Romano* stated unequivocally that the Holy Father's charity was universal and extended to all races.[4] By contrast, a researcher has concluded that Pius' silence was 'the canonical example of collusion and collaboration.'[5]

Pius' Motivation for His Silence

Ultimately, Pius' silence was motivated by his fear that were he to speak out against the atrocities it would fatally jeopardise his 'Great Design'.[6,7] Furthermore, his elimination of Catholic politics in Germany – another aspect of his Great Design – removed the very mechanisms by which protest against the Nazi's atrocities might have been amplified.[8]

Pius' motives were opportunism and restraint, in which he followed a secret ecclesiastic realpolitik. His policy with respect to the Jews varied little from that followed by nearly all the previous ninety popes who spoke or acted on the Jewish situation.[9]

Guenter Lewy summarised Pius XII's muteness. He pointed out that when thousands of German anti-Nazis were being tortured to death in Hitler's concentration camps,

---

[1] 'Pope Pius XII – Was He the Nazi Pope or Not?' http://www.abc.net.au/rn/ark/stories/2008/2365876.htm# transcript (2008)

[2] http://www.abc.net.au/rn/religionreport/stories/2008/2378841.htm#transcript (2008)

[3] http://www.abc.net.au/sundaynights/stories/s2376372.htm (2012)

[4] Phayer, Michael. *Pius XII, the Holocaust, and the Cold War*. p78

[5] Michael, Robert. *A History of Catholic Antisemitism: The Dark Side of the Church*. p190

[6] See, for example: Noel, Gerard. *Pius XII: The Hound of Hitler*. p4

[7] Great Design, see below.

[8] Noel, Gerard. *Pius XII: The Hound of Hitler*. p130

[9] Michael, Robert. *A History of Catholic Antisemitism: The Dark Side of the Church*. p181

when the intelligentsia in Poland were being massacred, when hundreds of thousands of Russians were slaughtered as 'Untermenschen', and when six million 'non-Aryans' were murdered, Pius XII, the spiritual and moral leader of the Catholic Church, remained silent – his utterances were heard in only vague generalities.[1,2]

> What is troubling about Pius's preoccupation with diplomacy is that Jews would continue to be murdered as peace negotiations were underway ... The difficulty with Pius's inadvertence to the Holocaust lies in the fact that Catholics in high and low stations kept reminding him of it. ... it was not the fate of the Jews but *the fate of Christendom and of the Church that preoccupied him.*

Six million Jews were allowed to die in order to satisfy Pius' gentile priorities.

Post-War, the Holy See showed great interest in getting the perpetrators of the Holocaust freed, 'it showed little or no interest in the question of restitution for survivors of the Holocaust.'[3] Pius' world vision remained fixated on his Church and his paranoid perception of the Marxist danger.

Pius' Principal Diplomatic Concerns

Avoiding a communist uprising in Rome. In 1943 the Vatican's guard was increased by 1000 men; and 60,000 cartridges and automatic rifles were ordered.

Communism in Italy, which Pius perceived as threatening the *financial* foundation of the Holy See,[4] that financial-politico centre of the Catholic Church.

Guarding Rome from artillery battles, by its being considered an open city.

Preventing the Nazis from seizing Vatican City and the person of the Pope. Hence the abandonment of the Roman Jews to the Nazis.

Protection of Rome from aerial bombing. The US National Archives contain page after page of entreaties from the Holy See. No such appeal was made on behalf of the Roman Jews or of the dozens of European cities that suffered under the blitzkrieg.[5]

Positively, Pius did support some of the Jews

There are publications and websites that claim that Pius was, in fact, a friend and helper of the Jews.[6] Several affirmative comments have been made about Pius' efforts to save many Jews and others from the Nazis. A recent book, edited by Gary Krupp,

---

[1] Lewy, Guenter. *The Catholic Church and Nazi Germany.* p341. Source: http://www.mosquitonet.com/~prewett/lewy337341.html (2007)

[2] It was noted above that during his career Pacelli acquired impeccable skills in veiled circuitous language.

[3] Phayer, Michael. 'Pope Pius XII, the Holocaust, and the Holy War' In: *Holocaust and Genocide Studies*, Vol 12, No 2, Fall 1998. pp233-56

[4] Noel, Gerard. *Pius XII: The Hound of Hitler.* pp80-87, 89

[5] See, for example: Phayer, Michael. *Pius XII, the Holocaust, and the Cold War.* p95

[6] See, for example: 'How Pius XII Protected Jews' by Jimmy Akin in *Catholic Answers* at: http://www.catholic.com/library/HOW_Pius_XII_PROTECTED_JEWS.asp

himself a Jew, entitled *Pope Pius XII and World War II: The Documented Truth*, presents a very favourable picture of the Pope. A reviewer comments that there are revealed documents in the book about the bona fide heroism and courage of Pius and Catholic authorities during these dark times.[1]

A Summary of Pius' Actions and Inactions during the War

In his book *The Silence of Pius XII*, Carlo Falconi, the well-known Italian writer on religious affairs, found that an objective examination of the known documents, as at December 1964, enabled three irrefutable observations. Pius XII:

> *never* promulgated an explicit and direct condemnation of the war of aggression and the abominable acts of violence carried out by the Axis;

> had *full knowledge* of the gravity of the facts from the earliest stages – possibly greater than that of any other head of state;

> continued to *remain silent* even though he received ceaseless appeals from victims and governments alike asking him to speak out.[2]

Pius' Post War Assistance to Nazi Criminals

Details of Pius' involvement in these matters are described in Chapter 23.

The International Catholic-Jewish Historical Commission (ICJHC)

The ICJHC comprised three Jewish and three Roman Catholic scholars. It was appointed in 1999 by the Holy See's 'Commission for Religious Relations with the Jews'. It was given the task of trying to evaluate the role of Pius XII and the rest of the Holy See during the Holocaust.

The panel was able to search eleven published volumes of wartime Vatican documents. It found that the Holy See had received reports of Nazi atrocities as early as January 1941. However, 'the pope's responses to reports of atrocities were missing from the sources they examined.'[3]

In October 2000 the group finished its review of those Vatican's archives that had been made available, and submitted its preliminary findings to the Commission's President, Edward Cardinal Cassidy. The report, entitled *The Vatican and the Holocaust*, nullified several of the Church's conventional defences of Pius XII:[4]

> The often-espoused view that the Pontiff was unaware of the seriousness of the situation of European Jewry during the war was definitively found to be inaccurate. Numerous documents demonstrated that the Pope was well-informed about the full extent of the Nazi's anti-Semitic practices ... The commission also revealed several

---

[1] http://www.amazon.com/POPE-PIUS-WORLD-International-ebook/dp/B00A5LQGB6#reader_ B00A5LQGB6 (2013). See also *Wikipedia* 'The Myth of Hitler's Pope'.

[2] Carlo Falconi. *The Silence of Pius XI*. p29

[3] http://www.religioustolerance.org/vat_hol12.htm (2008)

[4] *The Vatican & the Holocaust: Pope Pius XII and the Holocaust.* http://www.jewishvirtuallibrary.org/jsource/ anti-semitism/pius.html (2015)

documents that cast a negative light on the claim that the Vatican did all it could to facilitate emigration of the Jews out of Europe … Similarly, the attempts of Jews to escape from Europe to South America were sometimes thwarted by the Vatican representatives …

. The Commission asked 47 questions that could only be answered by consulting the unreleased Vatican files from that era. The Commissioners unanimously asked for access to the records. In June 2001 the Holy See refused. Walter Cardinal Kasper wrote to the group that they would be welcome to speak with the scholar who was heading the campaign for the beatification of Pius, but that post-1923 Vatican archives were not available for 'technical reasons.'[1] Consequently, the Commission suspended its study in July 2001 without issuing a final report. Dr Michael Marrus, a professor of history at the University of Toronto, explained that the Commission 'ran up against a brick wall ... It would have been really helpful to have had support from the Holy See on this issue.'[2]

Dr Efraim Zuroff, director of the Simon Wiesenthal Center in Jerusalem, said: 'We're very disappointed ... but I can't say I'm surprised ... There is no transparency in the Vatican and as a result we don't know the answers to a lot of serious questions.'[3]

. Father Peter Gumpel is a German Jesuit who is assembling documentation to support the beatification of Pius XII. On 7 August 2001, he issued a statement accusing some of the Jewish historians on the Commission of 'clearly incorrect behavior' and of having helped launch a 'slanderous campaign' against the Catholic Church. He said that he had met the group and had answered some of their questions, and offered to answer the rest at a later time. He declared that 'some Jewish members in the group had systematically affirmed that they never received answers to their questions', and accused them of having 'publicly spread the suspicion' that the Vatican was trying to hide documents 'that in their judgment could be compromising.'[4]

. Nevertheless, the Commission found that the view, often presented, that Pius was unaware of the dire straits of European Jewry during the war, was found to be unequivocally inaccurate. Many documents revealed that the Pope was well-informed of the full extent of the Nazi's anti-Semitic practices. The Commission particularly noted a letter of appeal directed to Pius himself from Konrad von Preysing, Bishop of Berlin, that proved that Pius was au fait with the situation as early as January 1941:

> Your Holiness is certainly informed about the situation of the Jews in Germany and the neighbouring countries. I wish to mention that I have been asked both from the

---

[1] *The Wall Street Journal* reported that some documents in the Archive are still being kept secret. Those dating from 1939 (the year Pius XII took office) 'are locked behind metal fences.' (Reported in *The Australian*, 2 March 2012)

[2] *The Vatican & the Holocaust: Pope Pius XII and the Holocaust.* http://www.jewishvirtuallibrary.org/jsource/anti-semitism/pius.html (2015)

[3] http://www.religioustolerance.org/vat_hol12.htm (2008)

[4] Ibid.

Catholic and Protestant side if the Holy See could not do something on this subject ... in favour of these unfortunates.[1]

▸ The ICJHC revealed several documents that negated the claim that the Holy See fully facilitated the emigration of the Jews from Europe. Internal notes, intended only for Vatican representatives, revealed the opposition of the Holy See to Jewish emigration to Palestine:

> The Holy See has never approved of the project of making Palestine a Jewish home ... [because] Palestine is by now holier for Catholics than for Jews.[2]

Additionally, attempts by Jews to escape from Europe to South America were sometimes thwarted by the Holy See. The Commission concluded that derogatory correspondence from Vatican representatives in Bolivia and Chile probably biased Pius against assisting more European Jews in emigrating.[3]

Pius' Inhumanity

In August 1942 Ukrainian Metropolitan Andrei Sheptyts'kyi notified the Holy See from Lwów (Lvov) that over 100,000 Jews had been killed in the Ukraine alone. He appealed to the Pope, referring to the German Nazi government as a regime of terror and corruption, more diabolical than that of the Bolsheviks. Pius replied by quoting verses from *The Book of Psalms* and advising Sheptyts'kyi to 'bear adversity with serene patience.'[4]

▾ Pius XII's anti-Semitism extended beyond World War II, because it forbad the post-War reunification of many Jewish families whose children sheltered from the Holocaust in Catholic institutions. In 2005 the Italian newspaper *Corriere della Sera* discovered a letter dated 20 November 1946, showing that Pius directed that Jewish babies baptised, *with or without* parental consent, by Catholics during the Holocaust not be returned to their parents.[5]

The Vatican Archives

⌐ In February 2002 in the hope of ending the controversy surrounding the Church's role in the Holocaust, John Paul II announced the opening of Vatican archives containing Nazi-related documents from 1922 to 1939. Researchers are particularly interested in the inner workings of Pius XII's pontificate during that period. With knowledge of the dissimulation of the Church, Michael Phayer, the well respected professor of history at

---

[1] Schoenberg, Shira. *Pope Pius XII and the Holocaust*. http://www.jewishvirtuallibrary.org/jsource/anti-semitism/pius.html (2010)

[2] Refer also to Chapter 23 – Catholic Assistance to War Criminals.

[3] But note the Church's post-War assistance to war criminals emigrating to South America.

[4] Hilberg, Raul, *Perpetrators Victims Bystanders*. p267. Source: https://www.jewishvirtuallibrary.org/jsource/anti-semitism/pius.html (2015)

[5] Midlarsky, Manus I. *The Killing Trap: Genocide in the Twentieth Century*. pp225-26

Marquette University, commented 'The Vatican is not going to release all the archives. They will only open those that shed a good light on Pius XII.'[1,2]

The Church's Apologetics concerning Pius XII

Finding themselves confronted with such an array of indicting evidence, the official defenders of Pius' silence fall back to a final explanation. They argue that the news that reached the Vatican might seem substantial as a whole because it was spread over many years; but in fact, they say, it was inadequate in quantity or quality to justify a solemn protest. They allege that detailed descriptions were often lacking, the information was generalised and vague, and came from suspect sources such as the Nazi's political and military enemies or victims. Furthermore, the information was unverifiable.[3]

Jesuit Robert Leiber, who had been Pacelli's secretary for thirty-four years (from 1924 until Pius' death), was asked by the *Frankfurter Allgemeine Zeitung* to comment on Hochhuth's play *The Representative*,[4] which had been put on in Berlin in 1963. Leiber answered with a long article in which he stated:

> Pius XII did not know what was really happening. Nor did the allies. It was not until after the war that they were able to realize the extent of the Nazi crimes.[5]

Yet, as one example among many that have been described above, at the height of the Nazi's deportations of the Jews during November 1941, Cardinal Faulhaber wrote to Cardinal Bertram that he was being asked by lay people whether the bishops could not do something about the 'brutal deportation of non-Aryans to Poland under inhuman conditions paralleled only in the African slave trade.'[6]

At about the same time, the Holy See mobilised its official historian, Monsignor Alberto Giovannetti, author of *Il Vaticano e la Guerra, 1939-1940* (*The Vatican and the War, 1939-1940*) and *Roma Città Aperta* (*Rome, Open City*). He compiled and wrote a commentary on the Pacellian documentation.

L'Osservatore Romano of 5 April 1963 published a substantial article entitled 'Storia, Teatro e Storie' ('History, Theatre and Gossip') by the permanent representative of the Holy See at the United Nations. It maintained the following thesis:

> With the conflict there began the systematic deportation and the scientifically or-ganized extermination of Jews and other categories of citizens ... but its immense dimensions, and the monstrous cruelties that accompanied it, appeared in all their sinister light only after the war was over. Even the great majority of the German

---

[1] http://www.highbeam.com/doc/1P1-51071337.html (2009)

[2] Also, refer above to the reception by Pius in 1942 of a document of atrocities against the Jews. Gerhart Riegner, a signatory to the document, revealed in his 1998 memoirs that this document was excluded by the Vatican from the eleven volumes of released wartime documents.

[3] Falconi, Carlo. *The Silence of Pius XII.* p64

[4] *The Deputy, a Christian tragedy* (*Der Stellvertreter. Ein christliches Trauerspiel*), also known as *The Representative*, is a controversial 1963 drama by Rolf Hochhuth that indicts Pope Pius XII for his failure to take action or speak out against the Holocaust. It has been translated into more than twenty languages.

[5] Falconi, Carlo. *The Silence of Pius XII.* p46

[6] Cymet, David. *History vs. Apologetics: The Holocaust, the Third Reich, and the Catholic Church.* pp314-15

population only knew of these appalling crimes after the war ...

Information about these crimes reaching the Vatican itself was scarce and vague. For the most part it originated from one belligerent side (the Allied powers) and was based on revelations and news whose certainty could not be guaranteed even by those who divulged them ... The absence of Vatican representatives in German-occupied countries, the isolation and inactivity to which the nuncio in Berlin was condemned, the answers he received when he dared refer to various rumours, the general lack of accurate detail about the information available, suggested that it was inadvisable to adopt a public position which might give the Nazis an excuse for accusing the Holy See of violating its neutrality.[1]

Finally, Father Peter Gumpel, SJ, the relator in the cause of Pius XII's canonisation, stated:

The cause of the beatification and canonisation of Pope Pius XII, who is rightly venerated by many millions of Catholics, will not be stopped or delayed by the unjustifiable and calumnious attacks against this great and saintly man.[2]

By contrast, the magazine *The Atlantic*, stated in its October 1999 issue:

Some in the Vatican want to make Pius XII a saint. If they succeed, 'the Church will have sealed its second millennium with a lie.'[3]

In October 2015, *The Times of Israel* reported: 'Pope Francis remained firm in his refusal to allow the beatification of Pope Pius XII, the World War II-era pope accused by some Jews of not speaking out enough against the Holocaust, because he doesn't have enough miracles in his record.'[4]

Quotations about, and Criticisms of Pacelli

Heinrich Brüning, the German Chancellor from 1930 to 1932, wrote of Pacelli:

All successes could only be attained by papal diplomacy. The system of concordats led him and the Vatican to despise democracy and the parliamentary system ... Rigid governments, rigid centralisation, and rigid treaties were supposed to introduce an era of stable order ...[5]

Rabbi Louis Finkelstein, chancellor of the Jewish Theological Seminary of America stated in 1940:

No rebuke has come to Nazism from Pope Pius XI and his successor, Pope Pius XII.

Carlo Falconi, in his book *The Silence of Pius XII*:

---

[1] Falconi, Carlo. *The Silence of Pius XII.* pp46-47
[2] Quoted in: Cornwell, John. *Hitler's Pope: The Secret History of Pius XII*
[3] http://www.theatlantic.com/magazine/archive/1999/10/the-holocaust-and-the-catholic-church/305061/ (2015)
[4] http://www.timesofisrael.com/pope-francis-says-pius-xiis-beatification-wont-go-ahead/ (2015)
[5] Quoted in: Cornwell, John. *Hitler's Pope: The Secret History of Pius XII*

his unconscious professional deformation explains the final victory of the diplomat over the man of God.[1]

Paul I Murphy:

Pacelli's 'love of pomp and adulation'.[2]

Stanisław Musiał, secretary from 1986 to 1994 of the Commission of the Polish Episcopate for Dialogue with Judaism, and editor of the Catholic weekly *Tygodnik Powszechny (General Weekly)*:

We [Catholics] were in silence during the Shoa. Maybe Pope Pius XII was a good man, but he did not lead as a shepherd, or help form a consciousness of 'Thou shall not kill.' And for this reason we should not falsify the historical perspective.[3]

Rabbi Eric H Yoffie, president of Union of American Hebrew Congregations (2000):

I simply cannot understand the failure of the Pope to speak out.

Yisrael Meir Lau, Israeli Chief Rabbi, 2000:

Pius XII, did nothing to either condemn it [the Holocaust] or protest against it; his standing by while blood was being shed deserves full condemnation, on behalf of future generations as well. At Yad Vashem in Jerusalem, there is an avenue on which every tree is dedicated to the memory of a Righteous Gentile. Had Pius XII fulfilled his basic duty, this avenue would be much longer and the lives of many more Jews would have been saved during those horrible days.

Elan Steinberg, executive director of the World Jewish Congress 2001, speaking on the discovery of a report by Archbishop Montini on the Soviet occupation of Berlin:

In a sense, it's an indictment of the dual standard of morality practiced by Pius XII. They [Holy See] have no hesitation in properly charging the Soviets with atrocities but tragically failed to do so when it came to the murder of the Jews in the Holocaust.

Rabbi Marvin Hier, Dean of the Simon Wiesenthal Center:

The facts are that Pius XII was the best informed leader on what was happening in Europe during the Holocaust. Yet unlike many priests and bishops who risked their lives and showed great courage in defying Hitler, the Pope sat in stony silence as millions of Jews were murdered in the death camps.[4]

Giuseppe Roncalli – In 2006, correspondence was discovered between Haim Barlas, an emissary of the Jewish Agency sent to Europe to save Jews in the 1940s, and Giuseppe Roncalli, who later became Pope John XXIII. Roncalli expressed criticism of the Vatican's silence during the war.[5]

[1] Carlo Falconi. *The Silence of Pius XII.* p97
[2] Murphy, Paul I and R Rene Arlington. *La Popessa.* p401
[3] Michael, Robert. *A History of Catholic Antisemitism: The Dark Side of the Church.* p181
[4] http://en.wikiquote.org/wiki/Pope_Pius_XII (2014)
[5] Schoenberg, Shira. *Pope Pius XII and the Holocaust.* http://www.jewishvirtuallibrary.org/jsource/anti-

› Yehuda Bauer, Professor of Holocaust Studies at the Avraham Harman Institute of Contemporary Jewry at the Hebrew University of Jerusalem, delivered a speech to the German Bundestag on 27 January 1998, in which he said:

> I come from a people who gave the Ten Commandments to the world. Time has come to strengthen them by three additional ones, which we ought to adopt and commit ourselves to: thou shall not be a perpetrator; thou shall not be a victim; and thou shall never, but never, be a bystander.

· Rabbi Richard L Rubenstein, Professor Emeritus of the University of Bridgeport:

> Over time I have become convinced that during World War II Pope Pius XII and the vast majority of European Christian leaders regarded the elimination of the Jews as no less beneficial than the destruction of Bolshevism.[1]

Schmuley Boteach, Orthodox Rabbi:

> Yet, if the Roman Catholic Church pursues its plans to canonize Pope Pius XII, it will be more damaging to its reputation than another huge explosion of pedophile priest scandals. For even child molestation – evil and sinister as it is – remains a step below complicity in the extermination of millions of people and ordering mass kidnapping, two great sins among many by which Pius XII disgraced himself.

Emil Carlebach, Jewish survivor of Buchenwald:

> With an unequalled cynicism the Vatican 'suada' [art of persuasion] refers to a few Catholics who took a firm stand against the fascistic atrocities – and omits the fact that the Pope and his bishops did not support these courageous priests at all.[2]

Michael Lerner, progressive Rabbi and editor of *Tikkun*:

> We can't help but notice that under Cardinal Ratzinger's tutelage, the Church began moves to elevate the infamous Pope Pius XII to the status of saint. Instead of repenting for the failure of the Church to give unequivocal messages telling all Catholics that they would be prevented from receiving communion for collaborating or cooperating in any way with Nazi rule, or for failing to hide and protect Jews who were marked for extermination, Ratzinger has sought to whitewash this disgraceful moment in Church history.[3]

Rev Dr John F Morley found that Vatican diplomacy failed the Jews during the Holocaust because it did not do all that it would have been possible to do on their behalf; it neglected the needs of the Jews; it exhibited reserve rather than humanitarian sympathy; it abandoned its own ideals.[4]

͏ Rolf Hochhuth, in *Sidelights on History*, effectively stated that Pius XII must have

---

semitism/pius.html (2007)

[1] *Pope Pius XII and the Holocaust.* Quoted in: http://en.wikiquote.org/wiki/Pope_Pius_XII (2008)

[2] http://en.wikiquote.org/wiki/Pope_Pius_XII (2014)

[3] Ibid.

[4] Quoted in: *Pope Pius XII & the Holocaust*

realised, had he given any thought to the matter, that a protest by him against the Nazis would have elevated the Church in the eyes of the world; cannot have been anguished by the extended suffering of defenceless people; was a fence-sitter; was an overambitious careerist; left a legacy of 22 volumes of discourses that reveal that he was occupied by trivialities during the period of the Holocaust.[1]

Settimia Spizzichino, the sole Roman Jewish woman survivor from the death camps:

> I came back from Auschwitz on my own. I lost my mother, two sisters and one brother. Pius XII could have warned us about what was going to happen. We might have escaped from Rome and joined the partisans. He played right into the Germans' hands. It all happened right under his nose. But he was an anti-Semitic pope, a pro-German pope. He didn't take a single risk. And when they say the Pope is like Jesus Christ, it is not true. He did not save a single child.[2]

Conclusions about Pius XII

Pius' reaction to the Holocaust was complex and inconsistent. Some have praised his efforts. However, it is difficult to escape the conclusion that he could have done much, much more to save the Jews.[3]

Pius featured in a self-promoting film, *Pastor Angelicus* (*Angelic pastor*) that was released on 17 December 1942.[4] At one stage the camera pointedly focused on the statue of the good shepherd in the Vatican gardens – the good shepherd of the gospel:

> I am the good shepherd: the good shepherd giveth his life for the sheep. But he that is an hireling, and not the shepherd, whose own the sheep are not, seeth the wolf coming, and leaveth the sheep, and fleeth: and the wolf catcheth them, and scattereth the sheep. *John* 10:11-12

The *Catholic Encyclopedia* refers to the Pope as the chief pastor of the entire Church, yet Pius XII generally abandoned the Jews of Rome, disregarding them as members of his Roman flock. Effectively, he was 'an hireling', and was far from being 'the good shepherd'.[5]

There is no record of Pius XII ever having offered a single public prayer, or psalm, or lamentation, or celebrated a Mass for the Jews of Rome, either during their terrible ordeals or after their deaths.[6]

  John Cornwell, during archival research for his book *Hitler's Pope: The Secret History of Pius XII*, found that in 1933 the Church's ambitions for unprecedented papal power drew it into complicity with the dark forces of Nazism. He found that from early in his career, Pacelli showed a definite aversion to the Jews, and that his diplomacy

---

[1] Quoted in: *Pope Pius XII & the Holocaust*
[2] http://emperors-clothes.com/analysis/hitlerspope.htm (2014)
[3] See, for example: Schoenberg, Shira. *Pope Pius XII and the Holocaust.* http://www.jewishvirtuallibrary.org /jsource/anti-semitism/pius.html (2007)
[4] The film may be seen in its entirety at http://www.youtube.com/watch?v=l9pVFRSa3QI (2014)
[5] Cornwell, John. *Hitler's Pope: The Secret History of Pius XII.* p318
[6] Ibid. p316

silenced Catholic political associations that might have challenged Hitler's programme. His increasing ambition for power and control conflicted with, and ultimately separated, authority from true Christian love.[1] Pacelli, he found, was a narcissistic, power-aspiring manipulator who was disposed to lie, appease, and collaborate to protect and advance the power of the papacy.[2]

Pius' failure to respond to the immensity of the Holocaust was more than a personal failure, it was not only a failure of the papacy, but it was also the prevalent ethos of the Catholic Church.

Pius' 'Great Design' had two major components. His determination not to protest directly against Nazi policies during the War, stifled Catholic protests at the lower level; while his elimination of Catholic politics in Germany removed the mechanisms that would have amplified protest.[3]

Carlo Falconi described Pius as an intellectual who was interested in systems and abstract ideas.[4]

Nicholas Atkin and Frank Tallet, historians, summarised the man by referring to Pius' 'pusillanimous response' to the Holocaust.[5]

Many more Catholics would have spoken out and would have protected the Jews if they had been given the details of the death camps and the mass gassings. This information, which the Holy See knew about, it withheld.[6]

Peter Hayes, Theodore Z Weiss Professor of Holocaust Studies, summarised:

> Pius XII's anti-communism warped his moral judgement during the 1940s. As a result, he behaved more like a Metternich or the CEO of a self-interested corporation than the Vicar of Christ on earth.

Johannes Fleischer, in *Das Andere Deutschland*, recorded 'Under the leadership of this Pope it now looks so gloomy in the Catholic Church that it only remains to say with resignation, as an honest Catholic: The situation is hopeless!'[7]

Hans Küng, Catholic priest and theologian, in *Kleine Geschichte der katholischen Kirche* (*The Catholic Church: a short history*), impeached Pius and his successors over their silence about the Holocaust. He confirmed that from the beginning Pius resisted public condemnation of National Socialism and anti-Semitism. Küng found that the Pope was always more concerned with the freedom and power of the institutional church than he was with human rights and democracy – these latter ideals remaining alien to him all his life.[8]

---

[1] Cornwell, John. *Hitler's Pope: The Secret History of Pius XII*. pp x-xi
[2] http://www.theatlantic.com/issues/99oct/9910pope.htm
[3] See, for example: Noel, Gerard. *Pius XII: The Hound of Hitler*. p131
[4] Quoted in: Ibid. p189
[5] Atkin, Nicholas & Frank Tallet. *Priests, Prelates & People*. p333
[6] See, for example: Michael, Robert. *A History of Catholic Antisemitism: The Dark Side of the Church*. p110
[7] Quoted in: Deschner, Karlheinz. *God and the Fascists: The Vatican Alliance with Mussolini, Franco, Hitler, and Pavelić*. p155
[8] Küng, Hans. *The Catholic Church: a short history* ... pp177-78

Over all, history reveals Pacelli to have been a significantly flawed person.[1,2] Pius' papacy during this critical period comprised:

a long, sad record of delusion and deceit.[3]

Monsignor Giovanni Montini (Pope Paul VI, 1963-1978)

At the time that the Einsatzgruppen were murdering Jews in Russia, Marshal Pétain was about to adopt his second *Statut des Juifs* (*Statute on Jews*). To obtain the sanction of the Church, he turned to his ambassador to the Holy See, Léon Bérard, on 7 August 1941. The response was written by Monsignori Giovanni Battista Montini and Domenico Tardini. The reply that has been published in recent years is an explicit document that illuminates the 'Holy See's policy on anti-Jewish legislation during World War II.'[4]

The text of the extensive reply informed Pétain that these prelates found no objections to the legislation from a doctrinal viewpoint. They found, based on the Church's historical precedent, that the requirement to wear the yellow star was well established in ecclesiastical law, and that Jews should not hold any position of authority over Christians, and that their access to universities and the professions should be minimised.

Bérard was given the strongest assurances that no conflict, censure, or even objections from the Church to the *Statut des Juifs* would follow. Rev John F Morley, Professor Emeritus, has commented on the significance of the Bérard report:

> The importance of the document rests on the implication that it removed from Pétain's mind any doubts he might have had about the Christian reaction to the racial legislation.[5]

The Truth

After at least five years' operations of the diabolical horrors of the Nazi Holocaust, Pius XII, 'the Architect of Peace', cordially welcomed and gave his apostolic blessing[6] to Karl Friedrich Otto Wolff. Wolff was an SS-Obergruppenführer, a General of the Waffen-SS, and Chief of Personal Staff to the Reichsführer. Wolff was subsequently indicted for war crimes of genocide, including the deportation of 300,000 Jews to Treblinka. He later recorded:

---

[1] See, for example: Cornwell, John. *Hitler's Pope: The Secret History of Pius XII*. p384
[2] See, for example: Noel, Gerard. *Pius XII: The Hound of Hitler*.
[3] Phayer, Michael. *Pius XII, the Holocaust, and the Cold War*. back cover
[4] Cymet, David. *History vs. Apologetics: The Holocaust, the Third Reich, and the Catholic Church*. p162
[5] Morley, John F. *Vatican Diplomacy and the Jews During the Holocaust 1939-1943*. Quoted in: Cymet, David. *History vs. Apologetics: The Holocaust, the Third Reich, and the Catholic Church*. p163
[6] In the words of the *Catholic Encyclopedia*: 'The Apostolic blessing is a sacramental with which is granted a plenary indulgence ...' 'An indulgence is the extra-sacramental remission of the temporal punishment due, in God's justice, to sin that has been forgiven, which remission is granted by the Church in the exercise of the power of the keys, through the application of the superabundant merits of Christ and of the saints, and *for some just and reasonable motive*.' (emphasis added)

From the Pope's own words I could sense the sincerity of his sympathy and how much he loved the German people.[1,2]

Pius' 'sympathy' has been stated to have been occasioned by his realisation that, at that stage, the Germans and the Nazis were going to lose the War.

A Summary of Pius XII

Pius/Pacelli:

gave the young Adolf Hitler 'a large cache of Church money to aid the rising revolutionary and his small, struggling band';

legitimised Hitler and the Nazi party in the eyes of the world;

became, through his driving ambition, 'Hitler's pawn',[3] Hitler's cardinal, 'Hitler's pope',[4] and the 'Hound of Hitler';[5]

never excommunicated German Catholics for belonging to the Nazi Party or for supporting Hitler;

never excommunicated Adolf Hitler or any of the major Nazis, except one;

never placed 'Mein Kampf' on the 'Index of Forbidden Books';

never publicly uttered the word 'Jew';

never expressed a candid public word on behalf of the millions of Jews who were suffering during the Holocaust;

allowed the Jews of Rome to be sent for annihilation, without a word of protest;

never declared it a sin for Catholics to participate in the Nazi's slaughter;

never 'spoke out explicitly against the massacre of the Jews of Europe';

never explicitly condemned the Holocaust during the entire War.

Throughout the entire Holocaust, Pius XII *never* condemned Nazi war crimes nor did he decry Nazi Germany.

---

[1] See also: Katz, Robert. *The Battle for Rome: The Germans, the Allies, the Partisans, and the Pope, September 1943-June 1944*

[2] Cymet, David. *History vs. Apologetics: The Holocaust, the Third Reich, and the Catholic Church.* p403

[3] Ibid.

[4] Cornwell, John. *Hitler's Pope: The Secret History of Pius XII* (2nd edn) p297

[5] Noel, Gerard. *Pius XII: The Hound of Hitler*

22 – The Catholic Church and the Holocausts – Summation and Conclusions

The following table gives a perspective of the enormity of the Nazi's and others' twentieth-century anti-Semitic atrocities, and of the vastness of Catholic involvement.[1]

Table 11. Estimated Number of Jews Murdered in the 20th Century Holocausts, by Country

Country	Pre-war Jewish Population	Estimated Number Murdered	Percentage Murdered
Finland	2,000	7	0.35
Denmark	8,000	60	0.75
Norway	1,700	762	45
Luxembourg	3,500	1,000	29
Estonia	4,500	2,000	44
Italy	44,500	7,500	17
Serbia	16,000	14,500	91
Belgium	66,000	25,000	38
Croatia[2]	46,000	32,000	70
Austria	185,000	50,000	27
Yugoslavia	78,000	60,000	77
Greece	75,000	65,000	87
Latvia	91,500	70,000	77
France	350,000	77,000	22
Bohemia/Moravia	118,000	78,000	66
Netherlands	140,000	100,000	71
Slovakia[3]	137,000	112,000	82
Germany	565,000	142,000	25
Lithuania[4]	209,000	193,000	92
Romania	609,000	270,000	44
Hungary	825,000	550,000	67
Soviet Union[5]	3,020,000	>1,500,000	>50
Poland	3,300,000	3,000,000	91
Total	**9,894,700**	**c.6,349,800**	**c.64**

[1] The table is adapted from: http://history1900s.about.com/library/holocaust/bldied.htm. For additional estimates, reference may be made to: Lucy Dawidowicz's *The War Against the Jews, 1933-1945*; Abraham and Hershel Edelheit's *History of the Holocaust: A Handbook and Dictionary*; the *Encyclopedia of the Holocaust*; and to *Destruction of European Jews* by Raul Hilberg. The Simon Wiesenthal Center is also a useful source, as is *Holocaust Facts* (http://history1900s.about.com/od/holocaust/a/holocaustfacts.htm).
[2] Catholic Holocaust in Croatia under dictator Ante Pavelić.
[3] Catholic Holocaust in Slovakia under Monsignor Jozef Tiso.
[4] Lithuanian Holocaust. Large numbers of Jews were murdered by Catholics before the arrival of the Nazis.
[5] Estimates of the number of Jews murdered in the Soviet Union vary from one to three million.

The following table gives a limited perspective of the extent of Catholic involvement in the extreme physical and emotional sufferings of the Jews over the centuries.

Table 12. Some of the Genocides inflicted by Catholics on the Jews

Year	Place / Event / Person	Outcome	Numbers
613	Spain – King Sisebut's decree	converted	90,000
1096-1453	The Major Crusades[1]	slaughtered	3,500,000
1182	France – King Philippe II	expelled	all in his demesne
1290	Bohemia	slaughtered	10,000
1298	Germany – Rintfleisch Pogrom	slaughtered	20,000
1306	France – King Philippe IV	expelled	100,000
1347-1351	Reactions to the Black Death[1]	slaughtered	>20,000
1355-1369	Judería of Toledo	slaughtered	12,000
14th Century	Germany – pogroms[1]	slaughtered	100,000
1391	Guerra Sacra Contra Los Judios	slaughtered	10,000
1481+	Spanish Inquisition	incinerated	30,000
1492+	*Alhambra Decree* – 'Los Reyes Católicos' [1]	expelled, many died	130,000-800,000
1492+	*Alhambra Decree*	converted	50,000-70,000
1560-1812	Portuguese Inquisition in Goa	annihilated[2]	c.10,000
1724	Poland	annihilated	20,000
1939-1945	Slovakia – Msgr Jozef Tiso[1]	annihilated	c.60,000
1941-1945	Croatia – Ante Pavelić[1]	annihilated	32,000
1939-1945	'The Final Solution'[3]	annihilated	c.6,300,000
		Total	**c.11,000,000**

The Catholic 'Butchers' and Murderers

The following table lists the various Catholic 'Butchers' and murderers who were prominent in the Final Solution and in other twentieth-century genocides. Not one of the top Nazi leaders was raised in a Catholic-maligned liberal or atheistic family.[4]

---

[1] The Catholic Holocausts.

[2] The figure is an estimate. Most of this brutal Inquisition's records were destroyed. It is known that its activities led to a massive depopulation of Jews in the region.

[3] Of Adolf Hitler, a confirmed Catholic.

[4] http://www.catholicarrogance.org/Catholic/NaziLeadership.html (2015). The *Catechism of the Catholic Church* identifies atheism as a violation of the First Commandment, calling it 'a sin against the virtue of religion'. This 'virtue of religion' is contradicted by the widespread evidence in this encyclopaedia.

Table 13. Notable Catholic 'Butchers' and Murderers

Andrija Artuković	'The Himmler of the Balkans'
Klaus Barbie	'The Butcher of Lyon'
Josef Bühler	'Crimes against humanity'
Hans Kurt Eisele	'The Exterminator'
Miroslav Filipović (Friar)	'Father Satan'
Francisco Franco	*Knight of the Order of Christ*
Hans Michael Frank	'The Terminator in the Generalgouvernement'
Odilo Lotario Globocnik	'The Liquidator of the Warsaw Ghetto'
Josef Goebbels	'A Virulent propagandist'
Amon Leopold Göth	'The Butcher of Płaszów'
Aribert Heim	'Dr Death'
Reinhard Heydrich	'The Butcher of Prague'
Heinrich Himmler	'The very personification of evil'
Adolf Hitler	'The supreme embodiment of evil in human history'
Rudolf Höss	'One of history's greatest mass murderers'
Alexander Mach	'A sort of Himmler'
Josef Mengele	'The Angel of Death'
Heinrich Müller	'Utterly ruthless' 'Gestapo Müller'
Ante Pavelić[1]	'The Butcher of the Balkans'
Oswald Pohl	'The Exterminator of Hungarian Jews'
Erich Priebke	'The Ardeatine Caves Murderer'
Walter Rauff	'The Gas Van Man' 'Totally ruthless'
Eduard Roschmann	'The Butcher of Riga'
Dinko Šakić	'The Ogre of Jasenovac'
Ivan Šarić (Archbishop)	'The Hangman of the Serbs'
Franz Stangl	'The White Death'
Julius Streicher	'Jew-Baiter Number One'
Jozef Tiso (Monsignor)	'The Jew Vendor'
Otto Gustav von Wächter	'The Butcher of the Jews of Lvov'

A Conspectus

In 1995 Johann Neumann, a German emeritus professor of sociology of law and religion at the University of Tübingen, addressed the issue of the appalling record of the German church with respect to the Jews. He posed the rhetorical question: 'Where was the obedience to the word of God that the churches normally swore to uphold? Was the commandment 'Thou shall not kill' no longer the word of God in the Third Reich?'

Both Christians as individuals, and the churches as institutions, failed morally. The churches set no standard for moral behaviour. On the contrary, their directives on the authority sanctioned by God 'soothed the troubled consciences of many Germans, and indeed they discredited and often criminalized the voice of individual conscience.'[1] Society, in turn, reflected the churches and their amoral values.

In particular, the affinity between the Catholic Church, the Nazis, the Slovakian hierarchy, and the Croatian governance, and its failure to oppose them, was rooted, not only in its long ongoing, anti-Semitism, but also in the Church's self-serving active passivity.

Gerald Darring, in his article *The Holocaust and the Teaching of Contempt*, answered the question: 'Did the history of Christian antisemitism contribute anything to the Holocaust?' His answer was, unfortunately, yes. The centuries of Christian 'teaching of contempt' gave the Nazis (and Tiso and Pavelić) something even more fundamental than precedents to follow: they passed on to them a propagandised contempt for everything Jewish. 'This deep-seated aversion to Jewish culture and Jewish religion and the Jewish people helped create not only the perpetrators but also the collaborators and the bystanders to the Holocaust.' He pointed out that discussions of Christian contributions to the Holocaust usually focus on the perpetrators alone. 'But something more than perpetrators were needed for there to be a Holocaust; there had to be collaborators, many thousands of them, and there had to be bystanders, many millions of them, and all these collaborators and bystanders were, for the most part, Christian, and their actions can only be explained by the Christian history that preceded them.'

Professor Darring concluded:

> So what did Christianity contribute to the Holocaust? Three things: precedents in aggression towards Jews, profound contempt for Jews, and tens of thousands of collaborators plus scores of millions of bystanders. By any account, those are major contributions.[2]

Final Summation

Over the centuries, the Catholic Church, which 'is the society of the faithful collected into one and the same body,'[3] introduced slander, contempt, denigration, invective, demonic perception, control, repression, persecution, torture, expulsion, and extermination of the Jew. The Church is therefore ultimately responsible for the evil thoughts, words and deeds described throughout this book. It is particularly responsible for what happened in the Shoah. In the words of Rabbi Eliezer Berkovits:

> In terms of the Jewish experience in the lands of Christendom, the final result of that age is bankruptcy – the moral bankruptcy of Christian civilization and the spiritual bankruptcy of Christian religion. After nineteen centuries of Christianity the extermination of six million Jews, among them one-and-a-half million children, carried out in cold blood in the very heart of Christian Europe, encouraged by the *criminal*

---

[1] Quoted in: Cymet, David. *History vs. Apologetics: The Holocaust, the Third Reich, and the ...* pp318-19
[2] http://www.shc.edu/theolibrary/resources/03Connection.htm (2014)
[3] de la Salle, Jean-Baptiste. *Les Devoirs du Chrétien ...*, x

silence of virtually all Christendom, including that of an infallible Holy Father in Rome, was the natural culmination of this bankruptcy.

Rabbi Berkovits continued:

> A straight line leads from the first act of oppression against the Jews and Judaism in the fourth century to the holocaust in the twentieth. In order to pacify the Christian conscience it is said that the Nazis were not Christians. But they were all the children of Christians. They were the fruit of nineteen centuries of Christianity – the logical fruit of violence and militancy, oppression and intolerance, hatred and persecution, which dominated European history for the sixteen centuries since Constantine the Great.

He concluded:

> Without the contempt and the hatred for the Jew planted by Christianity in the hearts of the multitude of its followers, Nazism's crime against the Jewish people could *never* have even been conceived, much less executed.[1]

A Temporal Overview

The Holocausts followed three successive Christian anti-Jewish evolutions:[2]

Catholic missionaries and inquisitors said in effect:

'You have no right to live among us as Jews.'

Catholic secular rulers proclaimed:

'You have no right to live among us.'

Catholics Hitler, Pavelić and Tiso decreed:

'You have no right to live.'

Catholic Pius XII said:

nothing

The Essence

That which was formalised at the First Church Council at Nicaea in 325 CE was:

continued over the centuries in the many Christian denigrations, oppressions, ghettos, pogroms, expulsions, tortures, and deaths of the Jews;

supported by a multitude of anti-Semitic and anti-Judaic denunciations in the nineteenth- and twentieth-century Catholic press;

---

[1] Berkovits, Eliezer. 'Judaism in the Post-Christian Era', *Judaism* 15 (Winter 1966) p77. See also: the response by Jacob Neusner, 'The Jewish-Christian Encounter: To the Editor of Judaism', *Judaism* 15 (Spring 1966) p223, and 'Rabbi Berkovits Replies', *Judaism* 15 (Spring 1966) p225. Source: http://www.shc.edu/theo library/resources/03Connection.htm (2014). See also: http://www.newspapers.com/newspage/30614749/ (2014)

[2] See, for example: http://www.shc.edu/theolibrary/resources/03Connection.htm (2014)

encouraged by the donation of a large cache of Church funds by Eugenio Pacelli (later, Pius XII) to a young aspiring Adolf Hitler;

strengthened by the *Reichskonkordat* between the Holy See and Hitler's Nazi Germany;

facilitated by the actions of Eugenio Pacelli in effectively dissolving the CCP – the last element of German liberalism – thereby removing the last obstacle to Hitler's ascension to power, and also depriving the Catholic laity and clergy in Germany of any voice in political matters;

assisted by the significant number of SS officers who were Catholics;

encouraged by the failure of Pius XII and the Holy See to clearly and explicitly condemn Hitler, the Nazis, Tiso, Pavelić, or the atrocities;

completed in the concentration camps, extermination camps, killing fields, mass graves, gas chambers and crematoria of the *never-excommunicated* Catholics Adolf Hitler, Jozef Tiso, Ante Pavelić, and their Catholic henchmen, where 6,000,000 of the world's Jews were exterminated.[1]

The Importance of the Nazi and Catholic Holocausts to the Present and the Future of Humanity

These Holocausts reveal the Catholic Church's and the Holy See's:

perpetrating injustice by assisting war criminals in escaping justice;

ceaseless pursuit of their ambitions for religious dominance;

chronic involvement in international politics;

expediently callous indifference to, and absence of remorse for human suffering;

failure to acknowledge the role of the *institutional* Church in these evil events;

mendacity and hypocrisy;

pervasive practice of generally denying their involvement in atrocities;

persistent denial of their moral obligations resulting from their involvement in evil;

relentless habit of propagating the false notion of their moral purity;

self-serving propaganda;

two millennial hatred of Judaism.

---

[1] See, for example: Bazes, Moses. *Jesus the Jew, the Historical Jesus.* Quoted in: Golding, Shmuel. *Anti-Semitism in the New Testament.* http://www.jdstone.org/cr/files/anti-Semitisminthenewtestament.html (2007)

By Contrast – Genuine Catholic Acknowledgements of the Consequences of the Church's Teachings against the Jews

In 1997 the French Catholic Bishops issued a *Declaration of Repentance* at the commune of Drancy, seeking forgiveness for the failings of their Church during the Holocaust period:

> The end result is that the attempt to exterminate the Jewish people, instead of being perceived as a central question in human and spiritual terms, remained a secondary consideration. In the face of so great and utter a tragedy, too many of the Church's pastors committed an offense, by their silence, against the Church itself and its mission. Today we confess that *such a silence was a sin*. In so doing, we recognise that the Church of France failed in her mission as teacher of consciences.[1]

In the same year, the Swiss Catholic Bishops' Conference published a document on the role of Switzerland during the Second World War:

> For centuries, Christians and ecclesiastical teachings were guilty of persecuting and marginalizing Jews, thus giving rise to antisemitic sentiments ... It is in reference to these past acts of churches for which we proclaim ourselves culpable and ask pardon of the descendants of the victims.[2]

The conclusion of the 2001 United States National Conference of Catholic Bishops' 'Catholic Teaching on the Shoah: Implementing the Holy See's *We Remember, a Reflection on the Shoah*' was that:

> Christian anti Judaism did lay the groundwork for racial, genocidal antisemitism by stigmatizing not only Judaism but Jews themselves for opprobrium and contempt. So the Nazi theories tragically found fertile soil in which to plant the horror of an unprecedented attempt at genocide.[3]

There is the need both to know 'the tragic connection between our theological teachings of anti-Judaism and the perpetuation of antisemitic behaviors,'[4] and to embrace the Church's past 'teaching of contempt'.[5]

Daniel C Napolitano of the National Catholic Center for Holocaust Education at Seton Hill University has stated that an excellent way to help his students understand and care about the world is by teaching about the Holocaust. He believes that it is among the most important and most valuable aspects of the curricula. He acknowledges that

---

[1] http://www.sullivan-county.com/id2/timeline.htm (2007)

[2] Ibid.

[3] See, for example: http://www.bc.edu/research/cjl/meta-elements/texts/cjrelations/resources/documents/catholic/NCCB_Shoah_teaching.htm#A%20Word%20on%20the%20Present%20Document (2007)

[4] Nowak, Susan. 'To Stand Before the World as the Church Repentant.' *Holocaust Scholars Write to the Vatican*. p71. Source: http://blogs.setonhill.edu/ncche/015098.php (2008)

[5] See, for example the description of *Holocaust Scholars Write to the Vatican*: 'The Holocaust was a Christian as well as a Jewish tragedy; nonetheless, the Roman Catholic hierarchy has offered very little official discourse on the Church's role in it ...' http://www.amazon.com/Holocaust-Scholars-Vatican-Contributions-Religion/dp/0313304874 (2015)

Catholicism's portrayal of Jews throughout history has had a devastating effect on their lives and culture. Thus, 'the wrongs of the past may in some way be rectified.'[1]

Conclusions

- It has been reliably estimated that over the centuries at least as many Jews were exterminated by Christians (predominantly Roman Catholics) as were annihilated in the Nazi Holocaust.

Pius XII stated that '[The Church is] that authority established by God to see to a just order and to direct the consciences and actions of men along the path to their true and final destiny ...'

By contrast, unbiased history reveals, with respect to Nazism and the Holocausts, that the Church saw an unjust order, but it allowed to be directed, and itself directed the consciences and actions of men along the path in opposition to their true and final destiny.

David Cymet found that the Church had a 'key role in Hitler's rise to power, in the consolidation of his regime, and his later Lebensraum claims and conquest of Europe.'[2]

Thus the Catholic Church, which 'should exemplify the human face of God', did fail to live out its founder's highest ideals, and did fail, to a very large extent, to recognise the human face of God in the persecuted victims.[3]

Lest We Forget

In the words of Ronald Reagan at the site of the future United States Holocaust Memorial Museum, 5 October 1988:

> We who did not go their way owe them this. We must make sure that their deaths have posthumous meaning. We must make sure that from now until the end of days all humankind stares this evil in the face ... and only then can we be sure it will never arise again.

In staring this evil in the face, humankind also needs to be fully aware that the long, vicious history of Catholic anti-Semitism and the resulting Nazi and Catholic Holocausts reveal that the Holy See, and the institutional Catholic Church, its popes, its prelates, its priests, its press, and its protagonists, lacked, above all, compassion, humanity, morality, and true Christianity. In failing to recognise the human face of God in the persecuted victims they *all* betrayed Christ.

———

[1] Napolitano, Daniel C. *Why should Catholic Schools Teach About the Holocaust?* http://blogs.setonhill.edu/ncche/015098.php (2010)

[2] Cymet, David. *History vs. Apologetics: The Holocaust, the Third Reich, and the Catholic ...* Preface, p28

[3] Waller, James E. 'Genocide in the Christian World'. In: *Christianity and Human Rights: Christians and the Struggle for Global Justice.* p4

23 – Catholic Assistance to War Criminals

The crematorium could not burn the bodies fast enough – so after we dug long trenches, we pulled and dragged the bodies to the edges and threw them in. You'll not believe it, but the SS forced the prisoners' band to play music as we lugged the corpses ... Mary Ann Shaffer

Robert Graham, SJ, who was one of the editors of the Holy See's documents, collected additional material about the Vatican's affairs during the War and eventually took these to California in his retirement. After his death, the Holy See insisted on the return of all the material to the Vatican. Professor Michael Phayer concludes that the Holy See 'has a problem with the conduct of its affairs during the war, a problem it wishes to conceal.'[1]

It also has a major problem with its conduct after the War.

The Church's Post-War Escape Routes for Nazi Criminals

The Catholic Church's culpability did not end with the conclusion of World War II. It played a major role in abetting the escape of war criminals through Church-organised 'ratlines'.

Ratlines were systems of escape routes for Nazis and other fascists fleeing Europe at the end of World War II. These routes mainly led towards safe havens in South America, particularly Argentina, Paraguay, Brazil and Chile, all of which were predominantly of the Catholic faith. Vatican representatives provided the escapees with the assistance necessary to avoid justice, including hiding places, false identity papers, visas, and travel tickets. The criminals then found their way to Rome or to the Port of Genoa where Bishop Hudal and Father Draganović (see below) assisted them in escaping.[2]

Each of the Nazi groups among the refugees established effective clandestine networks to protect fugitives and aid their escape. They were greatly aided by the Holy See, which under Pius XII's direction established a vast network of underground assistance, supposedly 'in the name of Christian charity.'[3]

As early as 1942, Monsignor Luigi Maglione contacted Ambassador Llobet, inquiring as to the 'willingness of the government of the Argentine Republic to apply its immigration law generously, in order to encourage at the opportune moment European Catholic immigrants to seek the necessary land and capital in your country'. Afterwards, a German priest, Anton Weber, the head of the Rome-based Society of Saint Raphael, travelled to Portugal, then to Argentina, to lay the groundwork for future Roman Catholic immigration.[4]

Spain, not Rome, was the first centre of ratline activity that facilitated the escape of Nazi fascists, although the exodus itself was planned within the Vatican. Charles Lescat,

---

[1] Phayer, Michael. *Pius XII, The Holocaust, and the Cold War*. p xiv
[2] Cymet, David. *History vs. Apologetics: The Holocaust, the Third Reich, and the Catholic Church*. pp420-21
[3] Aarons, Mark. *War Criminals Welcome: Australia, a Sanctuary for Fugitive War* ... p134
[4] http://en.wikipedia.org/wiki/Ratlines_(history)#Early_Spanish_ratlines (2009)

a member of Action Française, and Pierre Daye,[1] a Belgian, were among the primary organisers. Lescat and Daye were the first able to flee Europe, with the help of French Eugene Cardinal Tisserant and Argentinian Antonio Cardinal Caggiano.[2]

By 1946, there were probably hundreds of war criminals in Spain, and thousands of former Nazis and fascists. According to US Secretary of State James F Byrnes, Vatican cooperation, in turning over asylum-seekers to justice was 'negligible'.[3]

Michael Phayer, in his book *The Catholic Church and the Holocaust, 1930-1965*, found that Pius XII 'preferred to see fascist war criminals on board ships sailing to the New World rather than seeing them rotting in POW camps in zonal Germany.'[4,5]

Graham Parsons, US State Department adviser, stated that anyone could secure a letter of recommendation to any Welfare Group under the protection of the Vatican, stating that his name is so, and his nationality is such, and that he desires an International Red Cross Identity Document:

> He may be directed to Father Gallov, [the] Hungarian Catholic priest, in temporary control of welfare units operating under the protection of the Vatican. Father Gallov will either direct subject by letter to his personal contact in the International Red Cross or to Dr Vida ... stating in effect that he has known subject for some time and assistance will be appreciated ... to enable him to secure an IRC Identity document. This letter will bear the S an official stamp of the Vatican. UFFICIO ASSISTENZA RELIGIOSA PER UNGAREAL IN URBO.[6]

Father Anton Weber admitted, in connection with the Spanish ratlines, that he helped members of the Nazi SS emigrate when they applied to his St Raphael Society's office in Rome. Father Weber said that funds of the Holy See were used for this service.[7]

Werner Brockdorff (Alfred Jarschel), a leader of the Hitler Youth, described in his book *Flucht vor Nürnberg. Plane und Organisation der Fluchtwege der NS-Priminenz in 'Römischen Weg'* (*Flight from Nuremberg*) how Catholic priests helped former SS members by taking them to Rome, disguising them as Catholic priests, and finally providing them with passports and money to reach Latin America.[8]

Catholic Argentina offered the warmest welcome to the Nazi escapees. Researcher Uki Goñi accessed the country's archives to show that Argentinian diplomats and intelligence officers had vigorously encouraged Nazi and fascist war criminals to make their home there. The Argentinians also collaborated with Draganović's ratline (see below), and also set up their own ratlines.[9]

---

[1] Pierre Daye was a Nazi collaborator. He was sentenced to death in 1946 by the Brussels War Council.
[2] http://en.wikipedia.org/wiki/Ratlines_(history)#Early_Spanish_ratlines (2009)
[3] Ibid.
[4] http://en.wikipedia.org/wiki/Ratlines_%28World_War_II_aftermath%29 (2014)
[5] The dark actions of Pius XII feature prominently in various parts of this encyclopaedia.
[6] 'Ungareal' is said to be the Latin for Hungary. http://world-news-research.com/nvatican6.html (2015)
[7] http://en.wikipedia.org/wiki/Ratlines_%28World_War_II_aftermath%29 (2014)
[8] Cymet, David. *History vs. Apologetics: The Holocaust, the Third Reich, and the Catholic Church.* p423
[9] Goñi, Uki. *The Real ODESSA: How Perón Brought the Nazi War Criminals to Argentina*

. More than 30,000 Catholic Croatian Ustaše and a similar number of Slovak Hlinkas escaped to Argentina. 'The entire Croatian wartime government ended up in Argentina with part of the loot they brought out from Croatia.'[1]

Towards the end of World War II, SS members formed a well-financed organisation with the sole purpose of helping Nazis escape from justice. It was called the 'Organization Der Ehemaligen SS-Angehörigen' ('The Organisation of former SS members') – better known as ODESSA.[2] Recent research shows that this organisation played at most a minor part in the organised smuggling of some tens of thousands of Nazi war-criminals. A far more significant role was played by the Catholic Church.

' Some war criminals took on new identities and then were smuggled out of Germany to freedom by an underground network called 'Die Spiner' ('The Spider'). It supplied false papers and passports, safe houses, and contacts that moved these criminals across un-patrolled Swiss borders. From there, they travelled quickly to Italy, using what has become known as 'The Monastery Route'. Catholic priests, especially Franciscans,[3] helped move these fugitives from one monastery to the next until they reached Rome. By way of example, in a monastery in Genoa, a Franciscan monk provided Adolf Eichmann with a refugee passport bearing the name Ricardo Klement.[4]

It has been estimated that there were as many as 150,000 war criminals registered in the lists of the War Crimes Commission, of which only 50,000 were apprehended. Many of the fugitives were directed by their Catholic protectors to Argentina and other countries. Thus, according to this estimate, 100,000 criminals evaded international justice in the postwar period. David Cymet concluded that 'in a sad travesty of justice, the SS guards at Auschwitz were the ones to come out best.' Nearly 90 percent of the members of the SS in Auschwitz were never prosecuted, and ended up in Perón's Argentina with the help of Pius XII's Holy See's ratlines.[5]

Catholic Organisations, Ecclesiastics and Laity Assisting the Criminal Escapees

The Argentine Catholic Church

French Nazi collaborators were the first to be relocated when the Argentine Catholic Church, in league with President Perón and the Holy See, arranged their escape during secret talks in Rome in 1946.[6]

Caritas International (Caritas Internationalis)

Dr Hans Hefelmann, one of the main Nazi leaders associated with the Aktion T4 euthanasia programme, escaped initially to Austria, where the Catholic group Caritas

---

[1] Cymet, David. *History vs. Apologetics: The Holocaust, the Third Reich, and the Catholic Church.* p422
[2] Recent claims are that ODESSA was a myth. Refer, for example, to the article by Professor David Cesarani in the *New Statesman* http://www.newstatesman.com/books/2011/06/war-criminals-german-nazis
[3] The Franciscans – so nefariously prominent in many contexts within this encyclopaedia.
[4] http://www.remember.org/eichmann/timeline.htm (2007)
[5] Cymet, David. *History vs. Apologetics: The Holocaust, the Third Reich, and the Catholic Church.* pp425-26
[6] Goñi, Uki. *The Real ODESSA: How Perón Brought the Nazi War Criminals to Argentina.* p322

International formalised the paperwork for his migration to Argentina.[1] Thence he went to Genoa via the monastery route, being sponsored by the Bishop of Innsbruck, Henrich Winker. He emigrated successfully. Monsignor Karl Bayer, the Rome Director of Caritas International, also cooperated in the escape system.[2]

Delegation for Argentine Immigration in Europe (DAIE)

Delegación Argentina de Inmigración en Europa (DAIE) was opened by President Juan Domingo Perón of Argentina in 1946. This immigration service, which had its main office in Rome and another in Genoa, was set up by José Clemente Silva of the Salesian brotherhood. It worked closely with the Church in Italy, by sending both bona fide emigrants and rescuing Nazi war criminals.[3]

  · Once in Argentina, Franciscan priests led by Fr Blas Stefanic of the Bari Basilica[4] in Buenos Aires, helped the fugitives establish themselves in the new country. Stefanic operated a collective in Buenos Aires on behalf of the Croatian Caritas Immigration Act. Almost the entire leadership of the Ustaša state was smuggled in this way to Argentina: ministers, concentration camp commandants, plunderers, and mass murderers.[5]

  · 'Perón's great interest in the escapees was not so much due to his sympathies for Hitler and Mussolini from his years as military attaché in fascist Italy, but to his expectations of putting their looted wealth and technical skills to the service of Argentina's armament and aeronautical industry.'[6]

Father Krunoslav Stjepan Draganović

Fr Draganović was a Croatian Catholic priest known as one of the main organisers of the ratlines. He is believed to have been instrumental in the escape to Argentina of the Croatian wartime dictator, war criminal, and mass murderer, Ante Pavelić.

  In 1935 Draganović returned to Bosnia, initially as secretary to Catholic Bishop Ivan Šarić (known as 'the Hangman of the Serbs' for his gruesome wartime activities). In August 1943 Draganović returned to Rome, where he became secretary of the Croatian 'Confraternity of San Girolamo', based at the Croatian monastery of San Girolamo degli Illirici, also known as San Girolamo dei Croati (Saint Jerome of the Croats) which is the national Catholic church of Croatia in the Campus Martius, at Via Tomacelli 132, just outside Vatican City. As documented by CIA surveillance files, this monastery became the centre of operations for the Croatian ratlines which also aided the escape of Nazi war criminals from Europe after the War.[7] Draganović was known to be one of the main

---

[1] 'The deep moral and spiritual principles of dignity, justice, solidarity and stewardship still guide Caritas today.' http://www.caritas.org/who-we-are/ (2015)
[2] Sereny, Gitta. *Into that Darkness*. p289. Source: http://en.wikipedia.org/wiki/Alois_Hudal (2008)
[3] Ibid. pp237-38
[4] Cymet, David. *History vs. Apologetics: The Holocaust, the Third Reich, and the Catholic Church*. p421
[5] See, for example: Buike, Bruno A. *Principles of Power in 20th Century*
[6] Cymet, David. *History vs. Apologetics: The Holocaust, the Third Reich, and the Catholic Church*. p421
[7] http://en.wikipedia.org/wiki/Krunoslav_Draganovi%C4%87 (2007)

organisers of these ratlines.[1]

Monsignor Giovanni Battista Enrico Antonio Maria Montini

Monsignor Montini (the future Pope Paul VI) knew Draganović from his close association with the Croatian Archbishop Alojzije Stepinac, and also through his close connection with Bishop Ivan Šarić. Draganović reported regularly to Montini in his position as a representative of the Pontifical Commission of Assistance (PCA)[2] (see below). Montini gave frequent extensive reports to Pius XII.

In their book *Unholy Trinity: How the Vatican's Nazi Networks betrayed Western Intelligence to the Soviets*, John Loftus and Mark Aarons report that some of the priests who assisted Draganović in smuggling Nazis confirmed that both Pius XII and Montini supported Draganović's work. Indeed, 'it was Montini who, as head of the Vatican's Pontifical Commission of Assistance, chose Draganovic as his liaison with the Croatian prisoners of war held in Allied detention camps. In a 1988 interview, William Gowen, a CIC agent in Rome, said that he knew "Draganovic reported regularly to Montini" in his capacity as a representative of the PCA.'[3]

Monsignor Simčić, who worked with Draganović in his people smuggling activities, asserted that 'Draganovic and Montini were together many times' and that Draganović sought Montini's aid in many cases including interceding with foreign diplomats to obtain visas for felonious fugitives from San Girolamo.[4]

Notwithstanding his unrighteous ratline activities, Montini was given the title of 'Servant of God' in 2012. Benedict XVI declared that he had lived a life of heroic virtue, hence he could be called 'Venerable'. A miracle attributed to him was approved by Pope Francis whence he can now be called 'Blessed'.

Bishop Alois Hudal ('the Brown Bishop')

Many escape arrangements were made possible by Austrian Bishop Hudal, Rector of the Pontificio Istituto Teutonico Santa Maria dell'Anima in Rome.

A report of the German Agency Nord Press reported that by the end of 1949 Hudal was receiving from 60 to 100 Germans daily in Rome who were helped with tickets and visas to escape to Latin America.[5]

During the War, Hudal had been both Commissioner of the Episcopate for German speaking Catholics in Italy, and Father Confessor to the German community of Rome. He had strong anti-Semitic feelings and was well known for his pro-Nazi perspective. He often spoke about the unity between the Catholic Church and Hitler's government.[6] His and others' activities were widely known around the Vatican.

After the liberation of Rome, Hudal made a secret deal with the Italian Carabinieri

---

[1] http://en.wikipedia.org/wiki/Klaus_Barbie (2007)
[2] Goñi, Uki. *The Real ODESSA: How Perón Brought the Nazi War Criminals to Argentina.* pp347-48
[3] Ibid.
[4] Ibid. p261
[5] Cymet, David. *History vs. Apologetics: The Holocaust, the Third Reich, and the Catholic Church.* p423
[6] http://hist.academic.claremontmckenna.edu/jpetropoulos/holocaust/aftermathintro.htm (2007)

whereby they directed wanted Nazis to specified churches, convents and monasteries. Over all, Hudal became 'the greatest and best friend' of the fleeing Nazis, being associated with the escape of the most infamous Nazi criminals.[1]

Pius XII was obsessed with Communism. At the end of the war, he appointed Hudal to the position of the Holy See's official Spiritual Director of the German People, and ordered him to visit all of the German POW camps to find worthy anti-communists and to give them special assistance.[2] Hudal used this position to aid the escape of wanted Nazi war criminals through the 'Nazi grapevine'. In his memoirs[3] he wrote:

> I thank God that He [allowed me] to visit and comfort many victims in their prisons and concentration camps and to help them escape with false identity papers.

He explained, that in his eyes:

> The Allies' War against Germany was not a crusade, but the rivalry of economic complexes for whose victory they had been fighting. This so-called business ... used catchwords like democracy, race, religious liberty and Christianity as a bait for the masses. All these experiences were the reason why I felt duty bound after 1945 to devote my whole charitable work mainly to former National Socialists and Fascists, especially to so-called 'war criminals'.[4]

According to Mark Aarons and John Loftus, Hudal was the first, and one of the principal Catholic priest to dedicate himself to establishing escape routes. There is evidence that Hudal provided the escapees with money and false papers including identity documents issued by the PCA. These documents were used to obtain a displaced person passport from the International Committee of the Red Cross, which in turn was used to apply for visas.[5]

Researcher Uki Goñi recorded that Hudal organised the escape of Treblinka[6] commandant Franz Stangl.[7] Stangl had been captured by the Americans in 1945, but 'escaped' from prison camp two years later. When he was finally met by Hudal, the Bishop greeted him with both hands extended. Stangl later reported that Hudal had arranged 'quarters in Rome where I was to stay till my papers came through.'[8] Other war criminals aided by Hudal included Eduard Roschmann, 'the Butcher of Riga', and the SS officer Friedolin Guth, who was assigned to kill partisans in France.

With great pride, Hudal wrote about the help that Catholic religious orders gave to

---

[1] Goñi, Uki. *The Real ODESSA: How Perón Brought the Nazi War Criminals to Argentina.*. pp230-32
[2] Aarons, Mark and John Loftus. *Unholy Trinity: How the Vatican's Nazi Networks* ... p37
[3] After the war, the Italian press attacked Hudal for the help he had given to Nazis. The Holy See under pressure finally forced Hudal to retire in 1953. In his embittered retirement he wrote *Römische Tagebücher: Lebensbeichte Eines Alten Bischofs jetzt kaufen* (*Roman Dairy: The Life Confessions of an Old Bishop*).
Source: http://www.podles.org/case-studies/Canon-N-Case-Study-page1.htm (2012)
[4] http://en.wikipedia.org/wiki/Ratlines_(World_War_II) (2012)
[5] Aarons, Mark and John Loftus. *Unholy Trinity: How the Vatican's Nazi Networks* ... p56ff
[6] Treblinka – where some 900,000 people are estimated to have been murdered.
[7] Goñi, Uki. *The Real ODESSA: How Perón Brought the Nazi War Criminals to Argentina.* pp xi-xv
[8] Ibid. p261

such major perpetrators as Otto Gustav von Wächter, an indicted war criminal, who was in charge of the Galician Ukrainian SS Division that was responsible, among other crimes, for the murder of 100,000 Jews in the ghetto of Lvov. Wächter[1] died allegedly from poisoning in the arms of Hudal in a Roman hospital in 1949:

> In Rome's Spital Santo Spirito, the vice-military governor of Poland, Lieutenant General and SS-Lieutenant Colonel Baron Otto von Wächter, who was wanted by the Allies and Jewish groups everywhere, died in my arms, loyal to me until his end. Although his boss Hans Frank was hanged at Nürnberg, Wächter succeeded, not least of all thanks to the stirring selfless aid of Italian members of the Orders, in living under an assumed name, until his death by poisoning.

Franz Stangl, the commander of Sobibór and Treblinka, confirmed in his trial:

> During the time we were in the internment camps we knew that we should go to Rome ... Catholics should go to Bishop Hudal who would give us an International Red Cross Identity card and then a visa.[2]

Pius XII's use of Hudal 'in the immediate postwar era is a comment on the ineptness of pontifical governance and its flawed judgement.'[3] It was a measure of Pius' hypocrisy.

Bishop Antonio Caggiano, Bishop Agustín Barrére, Cardinal Eugène Tisserant

The Argentinians' ratlines began in 1946 when Bishop Caggiano (leader of the Argentine chapter of Catholic Action, and later made a Cardinal) and Bishop Agustín Barrére (a political being obsessed with the fear that a 'Masonic-Communist plot' might undermine the Church's authority in Argentina)[4] met French Cardinal Eugène Tisserant in Rome. It is recorded in Argentina's diplomatic archives that while in Rome, they passed on a message that 'the Government of the Argentine Republic was willing to receive French persons, whose political attitude during the recent war would expose them, should they return to France, to harsh measures and private revenge.' Several French war criminals and collaborators grouped around Charles Lescat and Pierre Daye in Spain and other undesirables escaped to Argentina in the same way with the assistance of Cardinal Caggiano and the Argentine Catholic Church.[5,6]

A number of French war criminals, including Marcel Boucher, Fernand de Menou and Robert Pincemín, were issued visas stamped on Red Cross passports by the Argentine Consul in Rome. The normal requirements were dispensed with: these included 'health certificates and other required documents bearing in mind the special recommendation of His Excellency Cardinal Antonio Caggiano'. Shortly after, many more of these 'special recommendations' for 'French gentlemen' were received by the

---

[1] His wife became a devout Catholic. Of her 22 grandchildren 'four started their professional life as catholic nuns or monks, and others joined militant religious groups.' *Wikipedia*. There is no mention of his crimes.

[2] Cymet, David. *History vs. Apologetics: The Holocaust, the Third Reich, and the Catholic ...* p419

[3] Phayer, Michael. *Pius XII, the Holocaust, and the Cold War.* p207

[4] Cymet, David. *History vs. Apologetics: The Holocaust, the Third Reich, and the Catholic Church.* p93

[5] http://en.wikipedia.org/wiki/Ratlines_%28history%29 (2007)

[6] Goñi, Uki. *The Real ODESSA: How Perón Brought the Nazi War Criminals to Argentina.* p93

consul from Caggiano and Barrére.[1] Another preferential treatment was issued following the recommendation by 'high Vatican authorities and at the personal request of His Excellency Reverend Monsignor Agustin Barrére'.[2]

The Pontifical Commission of Assistance (Commissione Pontificia d'Assistenza)

The PCA, at Villa San Francesco, provided documents that helped a large number of Nazi fugitives to escape to Argentina.[3]

The Holy See, under Pius XII, appointed Hudal, 'the most notorious pro-Nazi bishop in the entire Catholic Church' to the head of the Austrian branch of the PCA.[4]

For fleeing Nazis, the port of departure for Argentina was Genoa. The PCA had an office conveniently located at the city's main railway station.[5]

One Nazi who had his passport application endorsed by the PCA was the SS mass murderer Gerhard Bohne.[6,7] Another was SS officer Hauptsturmführer Erich Priebke, who was eventually condemned of war crimes in Italy in 1998 for the Ardeatine Caves massacre. Priebke recorded:

> The problem was that I couldn't travel under my own passport and that is why Bishop Alois Hudal in the Vatican helped me, handing me a blank passport with the Red Cross insignia.[8]

Priebke was initially sentenced to life imprisonment, but thanks to the efforts of the Catholic Church, he finally ended up living in a monastery outside Rome. He died of natural causes at the age of 100.[9]

Don Florian Abrahamowicz, a former SSPX priest, told Italy's Radio 24: 'Priebke was a friend of mine, a Christian, a faithful soldier.'[10]

Pope Pius XII

When Monsignor Bayer was interviewed in the 1970s by Gitta Sereny, he recalled how he and Hudal had helped Nazis to Southern America with the support of the Vatican: 'The Pope [Pius XII] did provide money for this; in driblets sometimes, but it did come.'[11]

Uki Goñi reported how examination of dossiers at the Public Record Office in London proved that not only was Pius XII fully aware of the sanctuary provided by Roman ecclesiastical institutions to war criminals, that Pius also personally liaised with

---

[1] Goñi, Uki. *The Real ODESSA: How Perón Brought the Nazi War Criminals to Argentina.* pp96-99
[2] Ibid.
[3] Ibid. p95
[4] Phayer, Michael. *Pius XII, the Holocaust, and the Cold War.* p206
[5] Ibid. p235
[6] Ibid. pp249-51
[7] Bohne was director of the administrative office of the T4 Euthanasia programme.
[8] Goñi, Uki. *The Real ODESSA: How Perón Brought the Nazi War Criminals to Argentina.* p261
[9] Silva, Daniel. *A Death in Vienna.* Author's Notes. p399
[10] http://en.wikipedia.org/wiki/Erich_Priebke (2015)
[11] Sereny, Gitta. *Into that Darkness ...* p289. Source: http://en.wikipedia.org/wiki/Alois_Hudal (2008)

the Nazi-smuggling operation at the Croatian Confraternity of San Girolamo, and also that he secretly appealed to Washington and London on behalf of notorious Nazi criminals and collaborators.[1]

• In this regard, in 1946, Pius himself launched an attack on the war crimes trials. His opposition was due to both his being a long-time stalwart Germanophile and to his paranoia of Communism. He believed that the trials would only serve to further weaken Germany and thereby lessen the European opposition to Soviet Communism. In this way, Pius was prepared to, and did, betray both his alleged neutrality and his morality by subverting the course of justice to further his political aims.

~ The ecclesiastical hierarchy took up Pius' cue. Cardinal von Galen proclaimed that the Nuremberg Trials were about defamation of the German people – not about justice. Josef Cardinal Frings voiced his objection with a view to dismantling all the trials. He claimed the allies had followed a 'pagan and naïve' approach in making judgements of innocence or guilt. US Senator Joseph McCarthy, 'a good Catholic', brought serious damage to the war crimes programme. The total effect of this Catholic barrage was to downgrade the effectiveness of the whole system of war crimes justice.[2]

Pius also sought individual pardons for some of the major Nazis convicted at the Nuremberg and other post-war trials. For example, he wanted the death sentences commuted for the following criminals:

Arthur Greiser – who committed torture, persecution, injury, and the murder of civilians, POWs, and 100,000 Jews.

Otto Ohlendorf – the murderer of some 90,000 people as commander of the mobile killing squad Einsatzgruppe D.

Oswald Pohl – head of the SS-Wirtschafts-Verwaltungshauptamt (SS-WHVA), the vast SS agency that ran the Nazi concentration camps, supervising a slave force of 500,000 prisoners.[3]

Franz von Papen – leader of the Catholic Party of Germany. When Chancellor of Germany, von Papen tried to set up a Catholic-Nazi Coalition. He persuaded von Hindenburg to ask Hitler to form a Government. He helped Hitler to power. When Hitler became Chancellor of Germany, he made von Papen Vice-Chancellor – second in command in Nazi Germany only to Hitler himself. Later, the Vatican honoured *von Papen* by making him a Chamberlain of the Pope.[4] Von Papen was an official war criminal.[5]

---

[1] Goñi, Uki. *The Real ODESSA: How Perón Brought the Nazi War Criminals to Argentina.* pp327-28
[2] Phayer, Michael. *Pius XII, the Holocaust, and the Cold War.* p164
[3] Goñi, Uki. *The Real ODESSA: How Perón Brought the Nazi War Criminals to Argentina.* p346
[4] Cymet, David. *History vs. Apologetics: The Holocaust, the Third Reich, and the Catholic Church.* p110
[5] Manhattan, Avro. *The Vatican's Holocaust: The Sensational Account of the Most Horrifying Religious Massacre of the 20th Century.* Ch 15. 'The Vatican saves the catholic war criminals of Croatia – Roman monasteries as their asylums – the Croatian holocaust minimized'. Source: http://www.reformation.org/holoc15.html (2008)

Pius XII also had an interest in arranging the emigration of Nazi officers imprisoned in Italy's POW camps. He considered Argentina the only country where these men could find, in his oblique way, 'a satisfactory solution to their needs.' He was willing for 'the Vatican's experts to get in touch with the Argentine experts to arrange a plan of action.'[1]

In 1947, an American intelligence report stated:

> In those Latin American countries where the Church is a controlling or dominating factor, the Vatican has brought pressure to bear which has resulted in the foreign missions of those countries taking an attitude almost favouring the entry into their country of former Nazi and former Fascists or other political groups, so long as they are anti-Communist.[2]

Father Edoardo Dömöter

Father Dömöter was a Hungarian priest who headed the Franciscan parish of San Antonio in Genoa. He worked with Bishop Hudal in aiding Nazi escapes to Argentina. He was responsible for obtaining a Red Cross passport for Adolf Eichmann.[3]

Father Vilim Cecelja

Father Cecelja was former Deputy Military Vicar to the Croatian Ustaša. He passed fugitives from Austria to Draganović, and 'was fully empowered by the Holy See and was in charge not only for Croatians, but for everybody', that is, for Nazis.[4]

Father Dominic Mandić

Father Mandić was an official Holy See representative at San Girolamo, and treasurer of the Franciscan order. He used his position to put the Franciscan press at the disposal of the ratlines.[5]

Monsignor Heinemann and Monsignor Karl Bayer

These monsignori also assisted fugitive Nazis. Heinemann operated at Pontificio Istituto Teutonico Santa Maria dell'Anima in Rome, while Bayer was at Via Piave 23. Bayer was in charge of 'the German refugee action of the Vatican'. He was in:

> close contact with the elements who have been using the former German Embassy to the Vatican at Via Piave 21 as a lodging or forwarding address. He has further been most useful in supplying food and letters from the Holy See which has been of tremendous help in this chain.[6]

Dr Willy Nix

Dr Willy Nix was a German double agent whose overt work for the Vatican was a cover for his actual work for the Soviet Union. His operations enjoyed Pius' support and

---

[1] Goñi, Uki. *The Real ODESSA: How Perón Brought the Nazi War Criminals to Argentina.* pp96-99
[2] Ibid. pp249-51
[3] Ibid. pp xi-xv
[4] Ibid. pp347-48
[5] Yet another immoral Franciscan. http://en.wikipedia.org/wiki/Ratlines_(history) (2008)
[6] Goñi, Uki. *The Real ODESSA: How Perón Brought the Nazi War Criminals to Argentina.* pp233-35

protection. Escaping Nazis were assisted by Nix's furnishing them with false ID papers; they then made contact with others, including Monsignor Bayer, who made arrangements for their hiding until their departure for safe havens. When Nix eventually got in to trouble, the Vatican opened its doors to him and he conveniently disappeared.[1]

Father Filiberto

At a gigantic religious palace at Via dei Monti Parioli 64, Fr Filiberto provided 'food, lodging and contacts with German and Vatican officials' for escapees.[2]

Padre Don Carlos

Don Carlos of the Vatican provided jobs for the escapees in South America.[3]

Archbishop Giuseppe Siri

Archbishop Siri of Genoa was the founder of the 'National Committee for Emigration to Argentina' and the diocesan committee 'Auxilium', both of which aided fugitives. He headed:

> an international organization whose purpose is to arrange for the emigration of anti-Communist Europeans to South America ... This general classification of anti-Communists would obviously cover all persons politically compromised with the Communists, namely Fascists and Ustashi and other similar groups.[4]

Monsignor Ferene Luttor

Monsignor Luttor, a Hungarian diplomat, had been posted to the Hungarian embassy at the Vatican during the war. Postwar, he organised false papers for Hungarian criminal fugitives in Rome. Later he went to Argentina and became a founding member of the Nazi rescue organisation 'Society in Argentina for the Reception of Europeans' (SARE).[5] This organisation established its headquarters in a building owned by the archbishopric of Buenos Aires.

Cardinal Ildebrando Schuster

CIA archives appear to implicate Cardinal Ildebrando Schuster, Archbishop of Milan, suggesting that he was involved in the transfer of large sums of money from Milan to Rome by Nazi agents at the War's end.[6,7]

Other clerics who were active in the ratline chain included:

> *Monsignor Karlo Petranović*, based in Genoa; and

> *Father Dragutin Kamber*, based at San Girolamo.

[1] http://soc.world-journal.net/nvatican6.html (2008)
[2] Goñi, Uki. *The Real ODESSA: How Perón Brought the Nazi War Criminals to Argentina.* pp233-35
[3] Ibid.
[4] Ibid.
[5] Ibid. pp xi-xv
[6] http://www.telusplanet.net/public/dgarneau/euro75.htm (2009)
[7] *The Guardian,* International News, 3 July 2000. http://www.guardianunlimited.co.uk/international/story/0,3604,339155,00.html (2009)

Via Sicilia

Via Sicilia was a Franciscan[1] monastery in Rome – it was effectively a transit station for Nazis. War criminals such as Klaus Barbie, Adolf Eichmann, Heinrich Müller, and Franz Stangl escaped through this system. From Rome, many of the fugitives dispersed around the globe.[2] Catholic Argentina was particularly welcoming of these criminals.

The American National Catholic Welfare Conference (NCWC)

The NCWC, through its Italian delegate, provided Bishop Hudal with significant funds for his 'humanitarian' work. Father Draganović participated in the NCWC's meetings in Rome.[3]

Spanish Commission of Charity and Aid for Refugees

The Roman Catholic Church and Spanish security forces had an 'elaborately contrived escape plan' that involved the Spanish Commission of Charity and Aid for Refugees and Jesuit Father Juan Guim of Sevilla.[4]

The German Bishops

At the War Crimes trials of Nazi camp doctors accused of abominable crimes, Pius' Holy See and the bishops worked for their acquittal or pardon. 'What the Vatican denied to their victims during the war, it generously granted to their victimizers after the war in the name of Christian charity.'[5]

For example, the German bishops defended the death camp physician Dr Hans Kurt Eisele who was an SS camp doctor at Buchenwald, Dachau, Mauthausen, and Natzweiler. Eisele murdered on average sixty Jewish 'patients' per week, injecting evipannatrium directly into their hearts to produce instantaneous death. Eisele was saved from the gallows by the director of Caritas, Heinrich Auer, who mobilised the German bishops and Pius XII's envoy Aloysius Muench in favour of Eisele. Eisele went back to a successful medical practice in Munich with funds provided by the German government.[6]

Nazi and Other Criminal Escapees Assisted by the Catholic Church

Infamous Nazis and criminals assisted by the Roman Catholic Church to escape justice include:[7]

Klaus Barbie – 'the Butcher of Lyon'.

Alois Brunner – Adolf Eichmann's assistant, a commander of a mobile killing squad in Russia, and director of the Drancy Internment camp.

---

[1] The Franciscans, yet again.
[2] http://www.jewishvirtuallibrary.org/jsource/Holocaust/odessa.html (2007)
[3] Goñi, Uki. *The Real ODESSA: How Perón Brought the Nazi War Criminals to Argentina.* pp230-32
[4] Ibid. p99
[5] Cymet, David. *History vs. Apologetics: The Holocaust, the Third Reich, and the Catholic Church.* p429
[6] Ibid. p430
[7] http://en.wikipedia.org/wiki/Ratlines_(history) (2008)

Adolf Eichmann – responsible, inter alia, for organising the deportation and transport of Jews from German-occupied Europe to ghettos, concentration camps, and extermination camps; he also personally led an SS task force that carried out the deportation of some 400,000 Hungarian Jews to Auschwitz Concentration Camp.[1,2]

Hans Kurt Eisele (see above).

French war criminals *Marcel Boucher*, *Fernand de Menou* and *Robert Pincemín*.

Hans Hefelmann – one of the main leaders associated with the Aktion T4 euthanasia programme.

Aribert Heim – an SS doctor in a Nazi concentration camp in Mauthausen, who was accused of killing and attacking many inmates by various methods, such as direct injections of toxic compounds into the heart.

Josef Mengele – German SS officer and a physician in the Nazi Concentration Camp Auschwitz-Birkenau. He supervised the selection of arriving transports of prisoners, determining who was to be killed and who was to become a forced labourer. He performed human experiments on camp inmates, and was known as 'The Angel of Death'.

Erich Priebke – a former Hauptsturmführer in the Waffen SS, who committed war crimes in Italy by participating in the massacre at the Ardeatine Caves in Rome.

Walter Rauff – the SS officer who oversaw the development of the Nazi's mobile gas vans known as the 'Black Ravens'.

Eduard Roschmann – a Hauptsturmführer SS commander; one of the heads of the concentration camp at Riga; infamous as 'The Butcher of Riga'.

Franz Stangl – superintendent of the T4 Euthanasia Programme at the Euthanasia Institute at Schloss Hartheim, where mentally and physically handicapped people were sent to be killed; also commandant of the Sobibór extermination camp; also commandant of the Treblinka Extermination Camp.

Otto Gustav von Wächter – responsible for the persecution of Jews in Austria, and for mass murders in Poland and Ukraine. He died in a Roman hospital 'in the arms' of Bishop Hudal.[3]

Gustav Franz Wagner – an SS officer and deputy commandant of the German Sobibór death camp.

---

[1] See, for example: Mauri. *Vatican Ratline: The Vatican, the Nazis, and the New World Order.* p34

[2] See also: Steinacher, Gerald. *Nazis on the Run: How Hitler's Henchmen Fled Justice*

[3] Klee, Ernst, *Das Personenlexikon zum Dritten Reich. Wer war was vor und nach 1945*

Additional names of escapees assisted by the Church are provided in Uki Goñi's well-researched book *The Real ODESSA: How Perón Brought the Nazi War Criminals to Argentine.*

A Criminal's Appreciation of the Catholic Church for his Escape

The efforts of Bishop Hudal and the other Roman Catholic ecclesiastics were greatly appreciated. For example, Adolf Eichmann who had been head of the 'Final Solution' programme, and has been called 'the Travelling Salesman of Genocide', after landing safely in Argentina, described himself in his newly minted passport as a Catholic even though he was a Protestant. He explained 'I recall with deep gratitude the aid given to me by Catholic priests in my flight from Europe and decided to honour the Catholic faith by becoming an honorary member.'[1]

Synopsis

At the end of World War II, the Church established 'Ratlines', which were systems of escape routes for Nazi war criminals and other fascists fleeing Europe.

The Holy See used its credentials to obtain International Red Cross identity documents for these escapees. The Pontifical Commission of Assistance was particularly prominent in these activities.

These escape routes mainly led towards safe havens in South America; especially Argentina, Paraguay, Brazil and Chile, all of which were predominantly of Roman Catholic faith.

Many prominent Catholic ecclesiastics including Pius XII and the future Pope Paul VI circumvented the processes of international justice.

Many prominent criminals were assisted by the Church in this way, including:

'The Angel of Death'; 'Dr Death'; 'The Hangman of the Serbs'; 'The Butcher of Lyon'; 'The Butcher of Riga'; and 'The Butcher of the Balkans'.

Pius XII launched an attack on the war crimes trials for his own political ends.

The ecclesiastic hierarchy took up Pius' cue. Cardinal von Galen proclaimed the Nuremberg Trials to be about defamation of the German people – not about justice. Josef Cardinal Frings voiced his objection with a view to dismantling the all the trials.

The Holy See was directly involved in these illegal post-War activities.

———

[1] Goldhagen, Daniel. *Hitler's Willing Executioners: Ordinary Germans and the Holocaust.* pp175-76. Source: http://liberalslikechrist.org/Catholic/RC_ scandal-3.html (2007)

24 – Catholic Apologetics and Evasion concerning the Holocaust

The judge is condemned when the criminal is absolved. Publilius Syrus

- *Nostra aetate*

In 1965 Paul VI issued the *Declaration on the Relation of the Church to Non-Christian Religions. Nostra Aetate (In Our Time)*. The document was announced as a significant change in Jewish-Christian relations. However, critics claimed it was 'much too little and much too late' and pointed out its lack of acknowledgement of the Holocaust as a reference point. In fact, the document makes no mention of Holocaust, Nazi, genocide, or Catholic participation in such matters. Rabbi David Polish called the statement a 'unilateral pronouncement by one party which presumes to redress on its own terms a wrong which it does not admit.'[1]

In a radio address, Benedict XVI expressed reservations about *Nostra Aetate*, and even criticised it:

> in a precise and extraordinarily dense document, a theme is opened up whose importance could not be foreseen at the time. The task that it involves and the efforts that are still necessary in order to distinguish, clarify and understand, are appearing ever more clearly. In the process of active reception, a weakness of this otherwise extraordinary text has gradually emerged: it speaks of religion solely in a positive way and *it disregards the sick and distorted forms of religion which, from the historical and theological viewpoints, are of far-reaching importance ...*[2]

Papal Apology an Empty Gesture

In 1997 Shimon Samuels, the head of international relations at the Simon Wiesenthal Center attacked the plans by John Paul II to make a historic 'apology to the Jews' as a 'cosmetic exercise' that would leave the facts about help given to Nazi criminals by the Catholic Church hidden in the Vatican archives.

He said that Pius XII had 'sold the soul of the Church to the Nazi Devil'. He found the seminar on Judaism to be an 'incestuous exercise' behind closed doors to which 'not a single Jew has been invited'.

The only way for the Church to 'come to terms with the past' was for the Vatican archives to be opened up to shed true light on what really happened during the World War. Dr Samuels said that he had asked the Pope to open the files, but Vatican officials had told him there were 'no plans to do so'.[3]

Accordingly, Jews made it clear that Benedict XVI was not welcome to visit Israel unless he offered an unqualified apology for the role of the Church and particularly of Pius XII's role in the Holocaust, and made public documents of that period which are

---

[1] Wills, Garry. *Papal Sin: Structures of Deceit.* p26
[2] http://unamsanctamcatholicam.blogspot.com.au/2012/10/pope-on-nostra-aetates-weakness.html (2015)
[3] Owen, Richard. "Pope's Apology to Jews Attacked as Empty Gesture" (*The Times,* 30 October 1997) Source: http://www.jerusalim.org/cd/biblioteka/pavelicpapers/vatican/va0009.html (2009)

now stored in the Vatican's archives. 'The Vatican may have eliminated the phrase "perfidious Jews" from its liturgy and John Paul II may have made it fashionable for the Pontiff to refer to Jews as "older brothers", these are seen as no more than meaningless, insincere gestures.'[1]

Commission for Religious Relations with the Jews

Consequent to these criticisms, to examine the role that the Church had played in the Holocaust, *Nostra Aetate* was followed in 1975 by *Religious Relations with the Jews: Guidelines for Implementing Nostra Aetate*, and in 1986 with *Notes on the Correct Ways to Present Jews and Judaism in Preaching and Catechesis in the Roman Catholic Church* by the Commission for Religious Relations with the Jews. Further dissatisfaction resulted from the Church's issuing in 1998 the same Commission's *We Remember: A Reflection on the Shoah*.[2]

A letter from John Paul II to Cardinal Cassidy, President of the Commission, stated that the Church 'encourages her sons and daughters[3] to purify their hearts, through repentance of past errors and infidelities.' In imposing responsibility on its 'sons and daughters' the Commission evaded the need for the institutional Church, with its heavy burden of responsibility in these events, to engage in such repentance.[4]

The Commission asserted that the Holy See could accept responsibility for the historically evident mediaeval and pre-mediaeval *religious* anti-Semitism, but insisted that such practices were generally overcome by 1800. It reported that a study of the Church of the nineteenth century showed that it had *no* role in the development of the Holocaust.

In avoiding any reference to the institutional Church's involvement, the report devolved blame onto individual Christians by posing two questions and then providing an exemplary model of Roman Catholic apologetics:

> But it may be asked whether the Nazi persecution of the Jews was not made easier by the anti-Jewish prejudices imbedded in some Christian minds and hearts. Did anti-Jewish sentiment among Christians make them less sensitive, or even indifferent, to the persecutions launched against the Jews by National Socialism when it reached power? ... *A response would need to be given case by case*. To do this, however, it is necessary to know what precisely motivated people in a particular situation.[5]

---

[1] http://www.dailypioneer.com/134662/Vatican-owes-us-an-apology.html (2011)

[2] The term 'Shoa' refers to the Nazi Holocaust. It is derived from the Hebrew word 'Ha-Shoah' meaning 'catastrophe' or 'total destruction'.

[3] John Paul II had a propensity for employing the expression 'sons and daughters' rather than referring to the institutional Church. He used it in the encyclicals: *Redemptor Hominis*, *Dives in Misericordia*, *Laborens Exercens*, and *Centesimus Annus*.

[4] In like manner, during the reign of John Paul II, Roger Cardinal Etchegaray, opening a symposium on the Inquisition as part of the Church's countdown to the year 2000, passed the burden of blame from the institutional Church to its 'children': 'The church cannot cross the threshold of the new millennium without pressing its children to purify themselves in repentance for their errors, infidelity, incoherence.'

[5] Commission for Religious Relations with the Jews. *We Remember: A Reflection on the Shoah*. http://www.

The report then went on to blame other nations for not opening their borders to the Jews, but conveniently 'forgot' that the Holy See did not intervene to prevent the Jews of Rome from being sent to Auschwitz by the Nazis. This supreme example of 'national selfishness' did not evidence 'a heavy burden of conscience' on Pius XII or his Curia:

> At first the leaders of the Third Reich sought to expel the Jews. Unfortunately, the governments of some Western countries of Christian tradition, including some in North and South America, were more than hesitant to open their borders to the persecuted Jews. Although they could not foresee how far the Nazi hierarchs would go in their criminal intentions, the leaders of those nations were aware of the hardships and dangers to which Jews living in the territories of the Third Reich were exposed. The closing of borders to Jewish emigration in those circumstances, whether due to anti-Jewish hostility or suspicion, political cowardice or shortsightedness, or national selfishness, lays a heavy burden of conscience on the authorities in question.

Circumventing the fact that Pius XII and the institutional Church did not give 'every possible assistance to the Jews', the report asked:

> Did Christians give every possible assistance to those being persecuted, and in particular to the persecuted Jews?

> Many did, but others did not.

> the spiritual resistance and concrete action of other Christians was not that which might have been expected from Christ's followers.

However, the dominant thesis of the report centred on the rise of modern anti-Judaism:

> By the end of the eighteenth century and the beginning of the nineteenth century, Jews generally had achieved an equal standing with other citizens in most states[1] and a certain number of them held influential positions in society. But in that same historical context, notably in the nineteenth century, a false and exacerbated nationalism took hold. In a climate of eventful social change, Jews were often accused of exercising an influence disproportionate to their numbers. Thus there began to spread in varying degrees throughout most of Europe *an anti-Judaism that was essentially more sociological and political than religious* ...

> Thus we cannot ignore the difference which exists between anti-Semitism, based on theories contrary to *the constant teaching of the Church* on the unity of the human race and on the equal dignity of all races and peoples,[2] and the long-standing sentiments of mistrust and hostility that we call anti-Judaism ...

The report goes on to say that the anti-Jewishness of the Nazi regime was the product

---

vatican.va/roman_curia/pontifical_councils/chrstuni/documents/rc_pc_chrstuni_doc_16031998_shoah_en.html (2015)

[1] But not in the Papal States.

[2] So typical of the prevalent hypocrisy of the institutional Church.

of this new social and political form of anti-Judaism, which was *alien* to the Church, and which contained new *racial* ideas that were also *contrary* to the Church's doctrine. It insisted that the Church had only objected to Jews on religious, not on *racial* grounds – a stance that it had insisted on for decades. It declared that:

> The Shoah was the work of a thoroughly modern neo-pagan regime. Its anti-Semitism had its roots outside of Christianity.[1]

Refutation of the Conclusions of the Commission for Religious Relations with the Jews – particularly with Respect to Race

Many critics complained that this document, *We Remember*, again, failed to acknowledge the complicity of the institutional Church in the Holocaust; while others criticised the tributes to Pius XII.[2]

In fact, the anti-Semitic and anti-Judaic sentiments developed and propagated by the church Catholic included every one of the following. They are central to this modern anti-Semitism and anti-Judaism, and had the support of the highest Church authorities including the popes. The Jews:

are a race;

are by nature immoral, evil, demonic;

are dirty, thieves, liars, malodorous;[3]

are totally money-oriented and will stop at nothing to acquire it;

control the banks, and hold untold numbers of Christians in thrall;

are unpatriotic, and always ready to sell their country to the enemy;

control the press;

founded and furthered Communism;

intend to conquer the world;

murder defenceless Christian children and use their blood for religious purposes;

seek to destroy the Christian religion;

must be segregated from the larger society.[4]

Consider, for example, the 1569 Bull of Pius V – *Hebraeorum gens* (*The Jewish Race*). It states:

---

[1] http://liberalslikechrist.org/Catholic/RC_scandal-4.html (2007)

[2] *Journal of Religion & Science*. Supplement Series. 'The Contexts of Religion and Violence'. Waller, James E. 'Deliver Us From Evil. Genocide and the Christian World'. http://moses.creighton.edu/JRS/2007/2007-10.html (2008)

[3] The Catholic publication *La Croix du Nord*, for example, used the Jewish odour, hooked nose and nasal voice as pretexts for the vilification of the Jews.

[4] See, for example: Kertzer, David I. *The Popes Against the Jews: The Vatican's Role in the Rise of ...* p206

> This *people* … odious, bedecked with every infamy and vice, they exercise all descriptions of nefarious and scandalous acts by which they may satisfy their hunger … they are accomplices of robbers and thieves …[1]

As another example, Cardinal Bertram told the clergy in a synod in Breslau in 1935 that many National Socialist ideas were already contained in Catholicism and that the Church had always admitted the significance of *race*, soil, and blood, which it consecrated through Christianity.[2]

Significantly, the Commission's report failed to acknowledge the institutional Church's primary responsibility for the persuasions that were instrumental in moulding the attitudes and values (both religious and racial) of this 'neo-pagan regime'. Professor David I Kertzer, in his book *The Popes Against the Jews: the Vatican's Role in the Rise of Modern Anti-Semitism*, concluded that the Commission's report is the product of a Church that evades confronting its historical record.[3]

Rabbi A James Rudin refers to 'the document's most surprising, even astonishing statement,'[4] namely, that: 'The Shoah was the work of a thoroughly modern neo-pagan regime. Its anti-Semitism had its roots outside of Christianity.' What made this assertion even more startling was that it came after the bishops of both France and Germany had already confessed to the guilt of 'the Church as such' in those countries.[5]

This evasion follows the institutional Church's recurrent theme 'Mea non culpa'. The Church's claimed distinction between firstly, its older religious hatred, and secondly, the more modern racial and social prejudices, is a denial of historical truth. Both actions are distinctly anti-Jew, and both were actively promoted by the institutional Church.

The Institutional Church and its Antagonism to the Jewish Race

Any equality of civil rights acquired by European Jews in the eighteenth and nineteenth centuries were gained against the vibrant antagonism of the Church. For example, immediately after his election, Pius VI (1775-1799) issued an edict that returned the status of the Jews of the Papal States to those of the 1500s. He ordered its rigorous enforcement through the supervision of Inquisitors. To this end, Jews were no longer to 'infect' the Christian population, and were, once again, to be confined to ghettos. They were prohibited from owning any real estate, and from pursuing any occupation other than selling rags.

Later, under Pius VII, the Jewish ghettos were reinstated in Rome in 1814. The city's

---

[1] Wraxall, Sir C F Lascelles. *Historic Bye-ways: In Two Volumes*. Vol 2. p96
[2] Cymet, David. *History vs. Apologetics: The Holocaust, the Third Reich, and the Catholic Church.* p97
[3] See, for example: Kertzer, David I. *The Pope Against the Jews: The Vatican's Role in the Rise of Modern …*
[4] Rudin, A James. 'Reaction of a Jewish Theologian to the Vatican's We Remember Document', in: *The Vatican and the Holocaust: The Catholic Church and the Jews during the Nazi Era*. pp89-98. See also Rudin, A James. 'Reflections on the Vatican's "Reflection on the Shoah" '. *CrossCurrents* 48 (Winter 1998) p518. Source: http://www.shc.edu/theolibrary/resources/03Connection.htm (2014)
[5] *Catholics Remember the Holocaust*. This book contains the statements made by the Hungarian, German, Polish, American, Dutch, Swiss, French, and Italian bishops between 1994 and 1998. Source: http://www.shc.edu/theolibrary/resources/03Connection.htm (2014)

rabbis were once again compelled to make their demeaning appearance at Carnival time. They were required to dress in grotesque black outfits, with short pants and a small cloak. As part of the festivities they were then forced to march through the streets where they were targets for unsavoury missiles hurled by the jeering crowds.[1]

Pre-World War II, the Catholic Church was incessantly warning the population of the emerging 'Jewish peril'. The Jews, as a *race*:

constituted a foreign body in the society of their residence;

had already a voracious grasp on many of the major European cities;

were predatory and merciless, striving to acquire the world's gold;

were trying to take over the world;

were unpatriotic;

should be isolated and restricted.[2]

The Nazis' 1930s *Nuremberg Laws* and the Italian fascists' racial laws, which removed the rights of citizenship from the Jews, were modelled on measures that the Church had imposed for as long as it was able to do so. The Papal States provide prime examples of the Church's social anti-Semitism. For example, even as late as the nineteenth century, Jews there were still required to wear the yellow badge on their clothes. This practice was prescribed by Church councils for more than six hundred years. At the same time, the pope was forcing Jews, in the lands that he controlled, to live in or near ghettos. Other anti-Judaic restrictions were imposed including exclusion from public office.

In 1933 by way of example, Counsellor of the German Embassy, Eugen Klee, reminded Monsignor Giuseppe Pizzardo that:

racial purity had been pursued by the Church itself even to a greater degree than by Nazi Germany and was applied by the Church to baptized converts and their descendants over the centuries.

He quoted the *Statute of Blood Purity* adopted by the Jesuit Order since its founding in the sixteenth century that required anyone entering its ranks to prove that he had no Jewish blood in the previous five generations.[3]

The German, Austrian and Polish Catholic populations had been conditioned by the Church for so long, that the anti-Jew basis of the Holocaust was, in fact, nothing new. The Church had taught for centuries that the Jew was a demonic threat to society.[4]

Historical evidence reveals that fascist anti-Semitism and anti-Judaism in the twentieth century was a direct ideological outgrowth of the Roman Catholic anti-Jew

---

[1] Refer also to *'A Corrupt Tree'* 'Volume 1: II-9 – Rome and the Papal States – Dominions of Papal Unholiness'.

[2] Refer to the section '19th and 20th Century Precursors of the World War II Holocausts' in this volume.

[3] Cymet, David. *History vs. Apologetics: The Holocaust, the Third Reich, and the Catholic Church.* p65

[4] See, for example: Ibid. pp10-11

practices of the nineteenth century. The connection is so strong that many of these fascist policies and programmes were direct inheritances of policies of the Holy See. For example, the papal nuncio Monsignor Antonio Agliardi enthusiastically supported the aggressively anti-Semitic political leader Karl Lueger, who was head of the nationalist Christian Socialist Party.[1] The late nineteenth- and early twentieth-century also were especially important in Austria, and particularly Vienna, because it was there that Adolf Hitler, a Catholic, developed his political and social attitudes towards the Jews.

 Post-War, 'Holocaust amnesia set in'. Throughout the 1950s the German bishops retreated from the issue of restitution, busying themselves instead with defending Nazi perpetrators and ignoring growing anti-Semitism in German society. In the following years, the German bishops followed the lead of Pius XII, who had mendaciously stated that German Catholics were martyrs and that most Catholics had opposed Nazism. They portrayed the Church as victim rather than as bystander and participant, and they seldom showed any ability to express sadness or grief over the Jewish tragedy.[2]

 The Austrian bishops went even further than the Germans in declaring that 'no group had to make greater sacrifice in terms of property and wealth, of freedom and health, of life and blood as Christ's church.'[3]

 In 1967 in an interview with a Los Angeles rabbi, Cardinal Frings of Cologne stated that the Jews (as a *race*) had been economically too powerful in the 1920s, and he doubted if six million Jews had actually been killed under Hitler.[4]

Subsequently, the Catholic Church has largely eliminated its anti-Semitic teachings and prayers, but it has not pursued any substantial consideration of how it engendered anti-Semitism and anti-Judaism, and it has made little effort in informing Christians of the role that Christianity, and particularly Catholicism, played in generating such hatred.[5]

 John Paul II called for an enquiry into the culpability of the Church during the Nazi Holocaust. In 1999 the panel was finally convoked by the 'Vatican's Commission for Religious Relations with the Jews' and the 'International Jewish Committee on Inter-religious Consultations'. The panel comprised: Professors Robert Wistrich (Hebrew University, Jerusalem), Michael Marrus (University of Toronto), and Bernard Sucheky (University of Brussels), and three Roman Catholic researchers. The panel released a report asking forty-seven 'significant' questions concerning the policies and actions of Pius XII. This was not what the Holy See wanted the world to know, so it immediately cancelled the enquiry.[6]

The Church's argument that its anti-Judaism was never *racial* is demonstrably false. Statements of biological and social differences between Jews and Christians have a long

---

[1] A résumé of: Cymet, David. *History vs. Apologetics: The Holocaust, the Third Reich, and the Catholic Church.* Source: http:// atheism.about.com/library/books/full/aafprPopesJews.htm (2007)
[2] http://www.shc.edu/theolibrary/resources/04German.htm (2014)
[3] Ibid.
[4] http://www.sullivan-county.com/id2/timeline.htm (2007)
[5] See, for example: http://www.zionism-israel.com/his/judeophobia14.htm (2007)
[6] 'The Popes Against the Jews: The Vatican's Role in the Rise of Modern Anti-Semitism'. Reviewed by Steven K Baum, Book Review Editor for the *Journal of Hate Studies* (2007)

history in the church.

Another example: in 1798, after the gates of the Roman Ghetto had been demolished, the prelate Giuseppe Sala wrote of the Jews of Rome:

> This wretched *race* is insolent beyond belief, and now that it has left the walls of the ghetto, it can live where it pleases and so it is beginning to infest the neighborhoods of the city.[1]

This history helped prepare Roman Catholics in the late nineteenth century and into the twentieth for further developments in racial intolerance.

The Catholic Press – a Strongly Anti-Semitic Institution

The Catholic press has been a major contributor to the racial hatred of the Jews.

Anti-Semitism and anti-Judaism in Catholic literature increased during the nineteenth and early twentieth century. It became a vital component in forming Roman Catholic identity during that time because it was the easiest way to transmit the Church's ideology of social anti-Modernism, which was pushed so forcefully by, for example, Saint Pius X in his syllabus *Lamentabili Sane Exitu* ('with truly lamentable results').

La Civiltà Cattolica – From the 1880s, this paper's articles had to be approved by either the Pope himself or the Papal Secretary of State. It commenced its extended campaign against the Jews in December 1880 with a series of thirty-six savage articles drafted by Father Giuseppe Oreglia di Santo Stefano, one of the journal's founders. In one of these early features the author wrote that societies had to protect themselves from the Jews, and consequently governments would be well advised to introduce 'exceptional laws for a *race* that is so exceptionally and profoundly perverse.'[2]

Oreglia wrote thousands of words against the Jews. A recurrent theme was that the Jews had always been seen as a foreign people, 'and never considered to have the right of either native-born or naturalised citizens.' He declared 'if this foreign Jewish *race* is left too free, it immediately becomes the persecutor, oppressor, tyrant, thief, and devastator of the countries where it lives.' Additionally, as a *race*:

> The Jews – eternal insolent children, obstinate, dirty, thieves, liars, ignoramuses, pests and the scourge of those near and far ... They managed to lay their hands on ... all public wealth ... and virtually alone they took control not only of all the money ... but of the law itself in those countries where they have been allowed to hold public offices.

And:

> Oh how wrong and deluded are those who think that Judaism is just a religion, like Catholicism, Paganism, Protestantism, and not in fact a *race, a people, and a nation*! While it is certain that others can be, for example, both Catholic and either Italian, French or English ... or Protestant and a member of whatever country or nation ... it

---

[1] Kertzer, David I. *The Popes Against the Jews: The Vatican's Role in the Rise of Modern Anti-Semitism.* p208
[2] Ibid. pp134-35

is a great error to believe that the same is true of the Jews. For the Jews are not only Jews because of their religion ... they are Jews also and especially because of their *race*.

But all of them, having been moved not by God's spirit but by the devil's, have done so to further their material interests ... Even if we presume that they are no longer Jews in religion, neither do they become members of the Italian or French race, or of any other country. Because they are born Jews they must remain Jews.[1]

In 1890 Father Ballerini wrote three long articles in *La Civiltà Cattolica* on 'the Jewish Question in Europe', which were later made into a book. The Jews, it stated, only pretended patriotism, in reality they wanted to destroy the very nations that had given them citizenship.

In 1893 in an article entitled 'Jewish Morality', Jesuit Father Saverio Rondina enumerated all the recent accusations against the Jews in Europe – from fraudulent banking to murder.[2]

Father Enrico Rosa, writing in the late 1920s in *La Civiltà Cattolica*, declared that the Jews, having been given equal rights, had established their:

hegemony in many sectors of public life, especially in the economy and industry, as well as in high finance, where they are indeed said to have dictatorial power. They can dictate laws to States and Governments, in political as well as financial matters, without fear of having any rivals.[3]

La Croix – The Assumptionist Fathers' daily newspaper, *La Croix*, was 'the most anti-Jewish newspaper in France'.[4] It differed from other Roman Catholic papers in becoming involved more directly in mass politics. It was strongly against the Jews as a *race*. Its 1882 article 'Who governs France?' asked: 'Germany, it is said, is governed by the Jews. Will the French Republic also become the servant of the Jews – whether baptised or unbaptised – of the Stock Exchange?' The head of the Assumptionist Order, Father François Picard, wrote of the Jews:

To whom do the treasuries of Prussia, of Austria, of the German provinces belong? To the Jewish bankers of Frankfurt, Vienna, and Berlin ... [As the] influence of the synagogue rises, so too do the financial disasters that befall so many families ... showing us the all-powerful Jew atop his golden throne and modern societies under the yoke of this gutless king. What do the collapse of nations, the destruction of families, people's desperation, and the raft of suicides matter to him? The Jew ... seeks financial monopoly. He stops at nothing to obtain it. ... The Jew is everywhere a Jew and nothing but a Jew.[5]

The director of *La Croix*, Father Vincent Bailly, wrote an article entitled 'The

[1] Kertzer, David I. *The Popes Against the Jews: The Vatican's Role in the Rise of Modern Anti-Semitism.* p137
[2] Ibid. p143ff
[3] Ibid. p272
[4] Callil, Carmen. *Bad Faith: A Forgotten History of Family & Fatherland.* p15
[5] Kertzer, David I. *The Popes Against the Jews: The Vatican's Role in the Rise of Modern ...* pp171-72

Enemy'. In it he claimed that the Jews are agents of Satan, the murderers of Christ. 'The Jew is the enemy!' he declared. He also wrote: 'The Jew Freemason governs the world.'[1]

La Croix restated the Roman Catholic theme that the Jews sought 'universal domination and stop at nothing to obtain their end.' Looking at Russia as an example, the paper wrote that the peasants, 'having been ruined ... have struck back en masse against the cursed *race*, the cause of all their problems.'[2] These anti-Semitic effusions of *La Croix* were reflections of not only the Pope and the Cardinal Secretary of State but also their Parisian representative.[3]

L'Osservatore Romano – this, the Holy See's own newspaper, declared in 1898 that the emancipation of the Jew had led to his:

> abandoning himself recklessly and heedlessly to that innate passion of his *race*, which is essentially usurious and pushy. This, in turn, aroused and magnified a thousandfold the natural aversion that the Christian peoples have for the deicide people.[4]

The paper also formulated the notion, which was regularly repeated in the Church's publications during subsequent decades, that there are two kinds of anti-Semitism – the good kind and the bad kind.

The good 'Anti-Semitism ought to be the natural, sober, thoughtful, Christian reaction against Jewish predominance.' It 'is and can be in substance nothing other than Christianity, completed and perfected in Catholicism.'[5]

The bad kind, was a non-Christian form. It had lately become the most dominant one, and imperilled the good, Christian anti-Semitism. It was 'nothing but an artificial form of Judaism itself, which has introduced and maintained it so that it will be impossible for the true anti-Semitism to be organized, to be put into action, and to succeed.'[6]

In the early 1890s, although anti-Semitism was gaining strength in Europe, there was also a consequent increasing sympathy for the Jews. This was of concern to *L'Osservatore Romano*. Might not the cunning Jews, asked the paper, provoke 'hostile demonstrations ... so that people sympathise with the victims and forget who their true persecutors are.'? It therefore reasoned that a lot of the Austrian, French and Russian anti-Jewish movements were the work of 'cosmopolitan Judaism'.[7]

Additionally, *L'Osservatore Romano* reported that the Jews were urgently trying to avoid 'the reaction that is everywhere about to explode against their rapacious tyranny.' Ominously, the paper warned the Jews:

> As we have said on other occasions, take care what you are doing. Don't play with fire. The people's ire, although at the moment somewhat dampened by sentiments

---

[1] Kertzer, David I. *The Popes Against the Jews: The Vatican's Role in the Rise of Modern Anti-Semitism.* pp172-73

[2] Ibid. pp174-75

[3] Ibid. p177

[4] Ibid. p211

[5] Ibid. p147

[6] Ibid.

[7] Kertzer, David I. *The Popes Against the Jews: The Vatican's Role in the Rise of Modern Anti-Semitism.*

of Christian charity and by the tender influence of the Catholic clergy, may at any moment erupt like a volcano and strike like a thunderbolt.[1]

By 1898 the paper, again menacingly, reported with satisfaction that:

> Masonry and Judaism, sprung up together to combat and to destroy Christianity in the world, must now together defend themselves against the Christian awakening and against the people's wrath.[2]

L'Osservatore Cattolico – This anti-Liberalism paper was established in 1864. By the 1870s it had achieved high standing among Italian Catholics. The views of the Jews which it promoted during the next thirty years were the same as those in the other Vatican papers. An 1885 article by the paper's sarcastic director Davide Albertario was entitled 'The World's Jews'. It referred to:

> This fine *race* of people ... our masters, that is, the masters of thirty million souls, as they are the masters in Austria-Hungary, in Germany, in France, and almost everywhere else.... and so the Jew is the ruler of the world.[3]

L'Unità Cattolica – this paper also was published by ecclesiastics close to the pope. It printed articles similar to those in the other papers. The Jews and the Masons were responsible for all the recent ills in Italy and other countries. In a lead article in 1892, the paper recorded that the Jews personify 'the most odious form of degradation that one could imagine in the human species.'[4] The same year, the paper claimed that it was *secular* Jews, rather than the religious Jews, who were taking over the world.

In all these publications the battle against the Jews was equated with the battle by the Church against Modernism, Liberalism, and democracy.

Professor David Kertzer quotes the esteemed Church historian and Jesuit priest, Giuseppe De Rosa, who referred to the pre-1965, century-long, campaign against the Jews by *La Civiltà Cattolica* and by many major Catholic publications. This campaign included charges that, above all, the Jews exerted considerable anti-Christian economic influence through their great wealth, which had been acquired through usury. De Rosa also presented examples which clearly demonstrated that much of the Church's campaign involved condemnations of Jews as both enemies of the Church and enemies of the state; as threats to both Christianity and to Christian people. Additionally, De Rosa cited some of *La Civiltà Cattolica*'s passages written by Fathers Rondina and Ballerini in the 1890s. These reiterated the Jews' hunger for gold and their lust for world domination, and, by transposition of the Church's long-held fabrications, stated that the Jews perceive Christians as being no better than animals. These fathers claimed that wherever the Jews live they 'form a foreign nation, and sworn enemy of well-being' of the people. The answer to this situation was clearly presented in *Civiltà Cattolica*: the 'civil equality'

---

[1] Kertzer, David I. *The Popes Against the Jews: The Vatican's Role in the Rise of Modern Anti-Semitism.* p148
[2] Ibid.
[3] Ibid. pp149-50
[4] Ibid. p150

of the Jews had to be immediately rescinded as 'they have no right to it,' for they remain eternally 'foreigners in every country, enemies of the people of every country that puts up with them.'[1]

La Croix du Nord (*The Northern Cross*) stated in 1898 that the Jews are:

> a foreign *race*, camped among us, a *race* that has neither our blood, nor our instincts, nor our ideals; a *race* that is cosmopolitan by its nature, a *race* without a country, an intransigent, usurious *race*, lacking a moral sense, a *race* capable of selling and buying anything.[2]

Le Bloc Catholique, eight years later, argued that the Freemasons were:

> inspired and directed by the Jewish *race*, that parasitical and vampire *race*, always and everywhere scorned and shunned, that wandering *race*, witness over the centuries of the curse which weighs upon it ... The Church of Satan is incarnated in the Jewish *race* ... [3]

The French Priest Ernest Jouin

Father Jouin wrote during the 1920s: 'From the triple viewpoint of *race*, of nationality, and of religion, the Jew has become the enemy of humanity.' Jouin was never criticised by the Church for his anti-Judaic diatribes. In fact, Benedict XV (1914-22) made a point of praising Jouin's work, and Pius XI (1922-39) complimented him in a private audience because he was 'combating our mortal enemy.'[4] Pius XI also, in a report of his that examined the situation in Poland following World War I, stated:

> One of the most evil and strongest influences that is felt here, perhaps the strongest and the most evil, is that of the Jews.

Conclusions about *We Remember*

The indisputable conclusion of these above instances, is that the central exoneration of the Church in *We Remember* is not supported by an unbiased examination of history.

In his book *Papal Sin: The Structures of Deceit*, Professor Garry Wills records that an examination of *We Remember* reveals that it is not an honest confrontation with a complicated history. Far from being useful to the cause of understanding, which would prevent another Holocaust, it 'is useful only to the fictions that the Vatican wants to maintain about itself.'[5] It is 'a sad repetition of the kind of muted and aborted justice that was undertaken at the very time when the Holocaust was about to occur.'[6]

Israel's Chief Rabbi, Meir Lau, was candid in his condemnation of *We Remember,*

---

[1] De Rosa, Giuseppe. *La Civiltà Cattolica: 150 anni al servizio della Chiesa 1850-1999*. Quoted in: Kertzer, David I. *The Popes Against the Jews: The Vatican's Role in the Rise of Modern Anti-Semitism*. p8
[2] Kertzer, David I. *The Popes Against the Jews: The Vatican's Role in the Rise of Modern Anti-Semitism*. p210
[3] Ibid. p211
[4] A résumé of ibid. Source: http://atheism.about.com/library/books/full/aafprPopesJews.htm (2007)
[5] Wills, Garry. *Papal Sin: The Structures of Deceit*. From a review in: http://atheism.about.com/od/book reviews/fr/PapalSin.htm (2011)
[6] Wills, Garry. *Papal Sin: Structures of Deceit*. p26

and focused attention on the revealed historical role of Pius XII, whom he called 'an accomplice to Nazi murderers.'[1]

Conclusively, the historical evidence reveals that it is impossible to exonerate the institutional Catholic Church of having nourished the development of the anti-Semitic ideology behind the Holocaust.

Committee for Ecumenical and Interreligious Affairs

In August 2002, the US Bishops' Committee for Ecumenical and Interreligious Affairs, under the direction of William Cardinal Keeler, together with the US National Council of Synagogues issued a paper entitled *Reflections on Covenant and Mission* that claimed that:

> A deepening Catholic appreciation of the eternal covenant between God and the Jewish people, together with a recognition of a divinely given mission to the Jews to be witness to God's faithful love, lead to the conclusion that campaigns that target Jews for conversion to Christianity are no longer theologically acceptable in the Catholic Church.

When it became apparent that this statement did not conform to the Church's ethos, the Cardinal went into damage control mode by claiming that the announcement did not constitute any kind of formal position by the bishops, but rather it merely represented 'the state of thought among participants' in their dialogue 'between Catholics and Jews.'

It became clearly evident that the Holy See did not support the paper's claim because it was never promulgated as an official document of the Conference.[2]

Commission for Religious Relations with the Jews

Rabbi David Rosen, a participant in the Commission for Religious Relations with the Jews, stated on 27 October 2005:

> Some Catholic scholars have suggested that the very reason that there has not been more theological reflection exploring the meaning and power of *Nostra Aetate* on the part of the Church, is precisely because the document obliges Christian theologians to rethink their Christology and ecclesiology in keeping with the idea of God's abiding covenant with the Jews. Indeed there are *some recent signs not only of a reluctance to do so, but even of attempts to minimize this very idea* and the significance of *Nostra Aetate* itself. For example in May 2003 an interview with an Italian theologian (Illana Morelli) was published by the Zenit News Service expressing the position that as *Nostra Aetate* is a pastoral document *it has no doctrinal authority* and that to attribute such to it would be 'greatly ingenuous' and a 'historical error' ...

[1] 'The Vatican Releases Document on Church's Role During the Holocaust,' CNN transcript of programme aired 16 March 1998. Source: Lituchy, Barry. *What Is The Vatican Hiding? The Vatican's Complicity in Genocide in Fascist Croatia: The Suppressed Chapter of Holocaust History.* Source: http://www.ccg.org/_domain/holocaustrevealed.org/Church/Vatican_Hiding.htm (2009)

[2] Jones, E Michael. *The Jewish Revolutionary Spirit and its Impact on World History (Selections)*

Rabbi Rosen continued:

> Moreover Cardinal Avery Dulles, who criticized the aforementioned USCCB Reflections on Covenant and Mission, stated at the Nostra Aetate 40th anniversary conference in Washington last March that it is 'an open question whether the Old Covenant remains in force today' and has opined that *it is still a Catholic duty to invite Jews to receive the Christian faith ...*[1]

Bishop Bernard Fellay, Superior General and one of the bishops of the Society of St Pius X, said the relationship between Jews and Christians is a fundamentally antagonistic one. Jews, he said, were at fault for the Holocaust. He did not attribute such an attitude to 'every Jew, as a people,' but to 'the religion, Judaism, which is something different.'[2]

The Holy See – Self-Exculpation at all Costs

In his analytical book *History vs. Apologetics: The Holocaust, the Third Reich, and the Catholic Church*, David Cymet recorded that after the War, 'A veil of silence was drawn over the role of institutional Catholicism in the Holocaust ...'[3]

As late as 1942, the Holy See said that 'rumours' about mass murder by the Nazis could not be verified. Later, when this evasion could no longer be maintained, it stated that the crimes of one World War II combatant could not be condemned without condemning the crimes of another.[4]

Instead of a self-critical analysis of its institutional role in the Holocaust – which has often been described as 'complicity' – the Church's principal response was to appropriate the suffering of the Jews by quickly ensuring that the Nuremberg Trials also included the persecution of the Catholic Church under Nazism. Accordingly, while choosing (on the grounds that the 'universal religious mission of the Church would be compromised') not only not to cooperate with the Nuremberg Tribunal in preparing a list of war criminals, but also advocating that war criminals be given clemency, the Holy See readily supplied the tribunal with 'an important collection of documents dealing with the persecution of the Church by the Nazi regime'.[5]

Later, notwithstanding its well-publicised dialogues with certain sectors of Judaism, Catholic anti-Semitism has been evinced in a more subtle and covert manner. In particular, the Holy See's active passivity, propaganda, whitewashing the past, and self-exculpation continue in the face of overt contemporary antagonism by laity, ecclesiastics and papacy alike.

Therefore, for the sake of those who will follow, humanity should be conscious of the statement of journalist and writer Martin Pollack:

---

[1] http://www.vatican.va/roman_curia/pontifical_councils/chrstuni/relations-jews-docs/rc_pc_chrstuni_doc_20051027_rabbi-rosen_en.html (2015)

[2] http://jstandard.com/content/item/cardinal_reaffirms_nostra_aetates_centrality_in_catholic-jewish_relations/23347 (2015)

[3] Cymet, David. *History vs. Apologetics: The Holocaust, the Third Reich, and the Catholic ...* Preface, p xi

[4] Phayer, Michael. *The Catholic Church and the Holocaust, 1930-1965.* p43

[5] Rychlak, Ronald J. *Hitler, the war, and the pope.* p424

We can only meet the ghosts of the past with openness. Any attempt to expel them, to make them disappear by remaining silent, by closing our eyes or blocking our ears, is inevitably doomed to failure.[1]

Accordingly, the words of Antonio Cardinal Bacci are highly significant:

Vatican diplomacy was born one sad evening in Jerusalem, in the atrium of the highest priest, when Peter the apostle, warming himself by the fire, came across a young maid who, with finger pointed, asked, 'Are you not also a follower of the Galilean?' and Peter gave a start and responded, 'No, I don't know what you are talking about.' This was a diplomatic answer with which neither faith nor spirit was compromised.[2]

Finally, it behoves humankind to be mindful that the long history of the church Catholic reveals it to be principally a self-exculpating, self-serving corporation.[3]

Never, it seems, has the institutional Church publicly admitted its significant role in the lead up to, and the implementation of the Shoah. Indeed, the recent record of the Church is that of continually attempting to disengage itself from its appalling history of anti-Semitism by pursuing political diplomacy, propaganda,[4] dialogue, or otherwise. For example, it has recently issued such publications as *Nostra Aetate* and *We Remember*; by blaming its 'sons and daughters' for its own iniquities; by other ecclesiastic sleights of hand; and by expressing its task 'of promoting ... love among men' and 'the boldness of brotherhood'. Accordingly, it is pertinent that the words of Benjamin Disraeli be remembered:

The Jews are a nervous people. Nineteen centuries of Christian love have taken a toll.

––––––

[1] Pollack, Martin. 'Was ist es, das den Menschen den Mund verschliesst? – Das Massaker im österreichischen Rechnitz im März 1945. Mutmassungen über ein Verbrechen. *Nueu Zürcher Zeitung* (20 June 2009) http://www.nzz.ch/mutmassungen-ueber-ein-verbrechen-1.2776199 (2015)

[2] Millenari, The. *Shroud of Secrecy: The Story of Corruption within the Vatican.* p20

[3] 'The Church is a worldwide corporation'. *Catholic Encyclopedia* ('The Church')

[4] The English word 'propaganda' is derived from the New Latin 'Congregatio de Propaganda Fide' ('Congregation for the Propagation of the Faith') – a committee of cardinals established in 1622 by Gregory XV.

25 – Catholic Anti-Semitism Today

I swore never to be silent whenever and wherever human beings endure suffering and humiliation. We must take sides. Neutrality helps the oppressor, never the victim. Silence encourages the tormentor, never the tormented. Elie Wiesel

It's discouraging to think how many people are shocked by honesty and how few by deceit. Noël Coward

Post-War and Contemporary Anti-Semitism
Poland

'The Polish Church has followed a tortured path since the Holocaust.' Nazi occupation and the witnessing of the annihilation of Jews left the Polish people traumatised – a condition exacerbated by 'the guilt brought on by their relief at the disappearance of the Jews from their land and their taking over the land and possessions of former Jewish owners.'[1,2]

• Even after the end of World War II, there were still isolated pogroms, the most notable being the Kielce[3] Pogrom of 1946, in which 40 Jews were killed.[4] This pogrom was a major factor in the flight of Jews from Eastern Europe.[5,6]

⌐ In 1968 the Polish government launched a campaign on radio and television against 'Polish Zionists'.[7] The radio station Radio Maryja (Radio Mary), 'The Catholic Voice in Your Home', is owned by the Warsaw Province of the Congregation of the Most Holy Redeemer (Congregatio Sanctissimi Redemptoris) (CSsR).[8] Critics agree that the station propagates extreme anti-Semitism. Due to a concordat with the Holy See, Radio Maryja is not bound by any accounting rules. It therefore does not disclose the exact sources of its financing, nor of any of its enterprises, nor does it pay taxes. It is generously supported by Jan Kobylański, a Uruguay-based millionaire, who was reportedly prevented from entering the United States because of his alleged wartime collaboration with the Nazis. The station was also sponsored by Edward Moskal, the anti-Semitic chairman of the American Polish Congress.[9] Its manager is a Catholic priest.[10]

---

[1] http://www.shc.edu/theolibrary/resources/05Polish.htm (2014)
[2] In Catholic moral theology wrongful possession of another's goods has always required restitution. In the light of the history of this stolen property it is valid to ask, where is the Catholic theological morality of the Catholic Poles?
[3] Kielce is a city in central Poland. Roman Catholicism is the religion of at least 90 percent of Poles – it maintains an important influence on many aspects of Polish life.
[4] http://astro.temple.edu/~hfreiden/Antisemitism/timeline.htm (2007)
[5] http://en.wikipedia.org/wiki/Pogroms (2007)
[6] Further details of the anti-Semitic actions of both the laity and ecclesiastics are given in: David Cymet. *History vs. Apologetics: The Holocaust, the Third Reich, and the Catholic Church*, Ch 12.
[7] http://www.zionism-israel.com/his/judeophobia.htm (2007)
[8] CSsR is a Roman Catholic missionary congregation founded by St Alphonsus Liguori in 1749.
[9] http://en.wikipedia.org/wiki/Radio_Maryja#Ownership_and_finances (2007)
[10] Michael, Robert. *A History of Catholic Antisemitism: The Dark Side of the Church.* p160

◆ Radio Maryja has spread anti-Semitism, including concepts such as żydokomuna, the conspiracy theory blaming Jews for the rise of Communism in Poland. In January 2000 it aired an interview between Ryszard Bender, a historian from the Catholic University of Lublin, and Dariusz Ratajczak, a convicted Holocaust disputant who claimed that Auschwitz was a labour camp rather than an extermination camp.

In July 2007, over 700 Poles signed a public letter of protest condemning Radio Maryja's anti-Semitic comments. Poland's Media Ethics Council decried the station's 'weakly documented accusations' against Jews. According to a US State Department report of 2008:

> ◆ Radio Maryja is one of Europe's most blatantly anti-Semitic media venues.

A report of the Council of Europe stated that Radio Maryja has been 'openly inciting to antisemitism for several years'. And, in 2011 the Polish Broadcasting Authority Commission reprimanded the station for its anti-Semitic statements and 'nationalistic racism'.[1]

In 1979 John Paul II performed Mass over train tracks leading to the Auschwitz Concentration and Extermination Camp. John Paul II again came to Poland in 1983. He spoke of the murder of 'six million Poles', which included the three million Polish Jews under the rubric of 'Poles'. 'The pope thus confirmed Polish ideas about the equal fate of Jews and Poles and about the absence, or near absence, of anti-Semitism in pre-war Poland.'[2]

Two major events took place in the late 1980s.

The first was a 1987 article in a respected Catholic magazine, *Tygodnik Powszechny* (*General Weekly*), by a distinguished Polish author, Jan Błoński. His controversial essay 'Biedni Polacy patrzą na getto' ('The Poor Poles look at the ghetto') explored historic relations between Catholic and Jewish Poles, and the experiences of the Holocaust.[3] He wrote that Poles must stop defending themselves and must start admitting:

> yes, we are guilty. We accepted Jews into our house, but told them to live in the basement. When they wanted to enter the rooms, we promised them admission if they ceased to be Jews ... In a word, instead of bargaining and justifying ourselves we must first reflect on our own sin or weakness.

Błoński's article sparked a major controversy, 'and the reactions to it left no doubt that anti-Semitism was alive and well in Poland.'[4]

◆ The second event was the eruption of a major controversy over the establishment of a Carmelite convent and the erection of a large Cross on the grounds of the Auschwitz Concentration and Extermination Camp. For Jews and for most of the rest of the world, Auschwitz represents the Nazis' attempt to annihilate every Jewish man, woman and

---

[1] https://en.wikipedia.org/wiki/Radio_Maryja#Allegations_of_antisemitism (2015)
[2] Irwin-Zarecka, Iwona. 'Catholics and Jews in Poland Today', in: *Holocaust and Genocide Studies* 4:1 (1989) pp27-40
[3] http://en.wikipedia.org/wiki/Tygodnik_Powszechny (2015)
[4] http://www.shc.edu/theolibrary/resources/05Polish.htm (2014)

child. But, as Iwona Irwin-Zarecka[1] has pointed out, Auschwitz 'is not, for Poles, a symbol of Jewish suffering. Rather, it is a general symbol of 'man's inhumanity to man'.' Therefore, it never occurred to Poles to consult Jews before going ahead with the construction.[2]

On the one hand, there was extensive criticism of this appallingly inconsiderate action, on the other hand, over a thousand inhabitants of the town of Oświęcim (Auschwitz) protested 'the illegal demands of the Jews to ruthlessly carry out an unwarranted eviction of the nuns', and other anti-Jewish reactions were reported from elsewhere in Poland.[3] Eventually, the nuns moved out of the building.

The large Cross remained – a symbol of chronic Catholic insensitivity.

Even in the 1990s, Catholics were still being taught that the Jews killed Christ and that they continued to murder Christian children. Anti-Semitic graffiti was still being produced; such as 'Żydzi do gazu!' ('Jews to the gas!').[4]

The parliamentary and presidential elections held in Poland on 25 September 2005 resulted in a nationalist right-wing victory and boosted the influence of Radio Maryja, which continued to promote anti-Semitic views, including a denial of the facts of the Jedwabne pogrom[5] in 1941. This, despite the paucity of Jews then living in Poland. These elections radically changed the political situation in Poland. In particular, they increased the influence of Radio Maryja, together with its associated television and print outlets (such as the newspaper *Nasz Dziennik* (*Our Daily*), as well as that of its founder, and founder of Telewizja Trwam,[6] Father Tadeusz Rydzyk, CSsR.[7]

Former President and Nobel Prize Laureate, Lech Wałęsa, wrote an open letter to the bishops and faithful of the Catholic Church accusing Radio Maryja of provoking anti-Semitism. Archbishop Sławoj Leszek Głódź, head of the Church's Mass Media Council, replied that Wałęsa was emotional.

President Lech Aleksander Kaczyński has stated in the major weekly news magazine *Polityka*, 'I believe in the need for cooperation with people of national Catholic views in one political party.' Nationalist activists in the ruling party include the Parliamentary Speaker Marek Jurek who has been known for years for his fundamentalist Catholic views. In 1998 he made a trip to London to meet his hero, Chilean dictator Augusto Pinochet,[8] while the latter was under arrest in Britain.

There have also been protests in Poland against a proposed monument at the grave of the famous Rabbi Akiba Eger in Poznan. There were shouts of 'This is a Catholic

[1] Professor Iwona Irwin-Zarecka is the author of *Neutralizing Memory: The Jew in Contemporary Poland.*
[2] http://www.shc.edu/theolibrary/resources/05Polish.htm (2014)
[3] http://www.jewishvirtuallibrary.org/jsource/judaica/ejud_0002_0002_0_01611.html (2014)
[4] Michael, Robert. A *History of Catholic Antisemitism: The Dark Side of the Church.* p159
[5] See above.
[6] Telewizja Trwam is a Polish TV channel located in Toruń, Poland. It belongs to the Lux Veritatis Foundation.
[7] https://pl.wikipedia.org/wiki/Tadeusz_Rydzyk (2015)
[8] From the beginning, under Pinochet, the Chilean government implemented harsh measures against its political opponents. According to various reports and investigations 1200–3200 people were killed, up to 80,000 were interned, and up to 30,000 were tortured by his regime including women and children.

land and we don't want a Jewish cemetery here.' In 2004 the notorious anti-Semitic Father Henryk Jankowski, who was accused and investigated for paedophilia, said in a speech: 'anti-Catholic Masons, Jewish bankers and hell-born atheist socialists' are imposing their agenda on the laws of Poland.[1,2]

Throughout the September 2005 Polish election, Radio Maryja continued to promote anti-Semitic views, including denial of the facts of the Jedwabne Pogrom. Its support of the right-wing conservative Law and Justice Party is considered a major factor in its electoral victory.[3]

In April 2006, well-known essayist Stanisław Michalkiewicz, a significant personality on Telewizja Trwam, was reported in *Gazeta Wyborcza* (*Electoral Gazette*) as stating that 'men from Judea ... are trying to surprise us from behind', and referring to the World Jewish Congress as 'a main firm in the Holocaust Industry'.[4]

Spain

Spain has a history of deep and intense anti-Judaism. This results from a national obsession with unity and homogeneity, which, in turn, relates to the frequency with which Blood Libels were fabricated and incorporated in law.[5] Judeophobia is rampant in some areas, and in some traditional fiestas and rituals the effigy of a Jew is derided and beaten or even symbolically murdered. In 1999 a newspaper published an article about an Easter tradition in the province of León, where cafeterias offered special lemonade in bottles that 'will be used to kill Jews'. Gustavo D Perednik has drawn attention to the fact that 'Spaniards' vocabulary includes many striking examples of Judeophobic expressions, which in other languages have been eroded by modern political correctness.'[6]

England

Bishop Richard Williamson of the Society of Saint Pius X (SSPX) has denied the Holocaust. He recently wrote 'The fact is that the 6 million people who were supposedly gassed represent a huge lie ... a completely new world order was built.' The Jews 'became ersatz saviours thanks to the concentration camps.'[7]

The Vatican

In 2007, Benedict XVI, through the apostolic letter *Summorum Pontificum*, officially revived the Tridentine mass, which contains a Good Friday prayer asking for the

[1] http://www.antisemitism.tau.ac.il/asw2004/poland.htm (2007)
[2] http://www.tau.ac.il/Anti-Semitism/asw2005/poland.htm (2007)
[3] http://en.wikipedia.org/wiki/Timeline_of_antisemitism (2015)
[4] https://en.wikipedia.org/wiki/Radio_Maryja#Allegations_of_antisemitism (2015)
[5] http://www.jcpa.org/phas/phas-perednik-f03.htm (2007)
[6] Perednik, Gustavo D. 'Naive Spanish Judeophobia'. *Jewish Political Studies Review* 15:3-4 (Fall 2003) http://www.jcpa.org/phas/phas-perednik-f03.htm (2007)
[7] http://abcnews.go.com/International/catholic-bishop-williamson-unrepentent-holocaust-denial/story?id= 9717252 (2012)

conversion of the Jews. This led to criticism from Jewish leaders, charging that the prayer is anti-Semitic.[1]

Republic of Lithuania

The Baltic Times has reported that 'The Lithuanian Jewish Community has recently noticed an increased threat of anti-Semitism in Lithuania, some members going so far as to worry that another holocaust may happen.'[2]

The State of Israel

The Catholic Church's vehement opposition to the aspirations and efforts of the Jewish people to return to their ancient homeland cannot be ignored in the context of its modern anti-Semitism and anti-Judaism. The Church considered it legitimate for every other nation on earth to have a homeland (including itself), but denied that right to the Jews. Accordingly, strong opposition to rescue Jews, even children, to Mandate Palestine emanated from the Church 'at the most tragic moment of the Jews' need and abandonment.'[3]

In 1943 when most of the Slovakian Jews had already been deported to Auschwitz, Monsignor Angelo Roncalli (who became Pope John XXIII) was approached by the representative of the Jewish Agency in Istanbul asking the Holy See to request the Catholic government of Slovakia to allow the exit of one thousand Jewish children whom the British government had agreed to grant visas to Palestine. Monsignor Federico Tardini, the Vatican Under-Secretary of State became alarmed that this request might help Jews to convert Palestine into a Jewish national home. Accordingly, he wrote in his notes:

> The Holy See has never approved the project of making Palestine a Jewish home ... But unfortunately England does not yield ... And the question of the Holy places? Palestine is by this time more sacred for Catholics than for Jews.[4]

In 1943 also, the Vatican Secretary of State, Luigi Maglione, replied to a similar appeal channelled through Monsignor Godfrey from England, concerning the rescue of Jewish children from Europe to Palestine:

> The Vatican had long opposed the notion of a Jewish homeland in Palestine. The land of Palestine was sacred to Catholics because it was the land of Christ, and Catholics would justifiably fear for their rights if that land were occupied by a majority of Jews.[5]

Also that year, the Vatican Secretariat of State instructed its apostolic delegate in Washington, Monsignor Amleto Cicognani, to actively encourage this anti-policy with President Roosevelt's representative to the Holy See, Myron Taylor, and to advise the

---

[1] http://en.wikipedia.org/wiki/Timeline_of_antisemitism (2015)

[2] http://www.baltictimes.com/news/articles/22748/ (2015)

[3] Cymet, David. *History vs. Apologetics: The Holocaust, the Third Reich, and the Catholic Church.* p11

[4] Cymet, David. *History vs. Apologetics: The Holocaust, the Third Reich, and the Catholic Church*

[5] Ibid. p11

American bishops to be alert to any change in public policy concerning Palestine. In a letter to Myron Taylor, Monsignor Cicognani stated:

> It is true that at one time Palestine was inhabited by Jews; but how can the principle of bringing back people to this land where they were until nineteen centuries ago, be historically accepted?

In another contemporary document, the Vatican Secretary of State wrote that

> Palestine, under a Jewish majority, would give rise to new and grave international problems, would displease Catholics throughout the entire world, would provoke the justifiable protest of the Holy See, and would badly correspond to the charitable concern [sic] that the same Holy See has had and continues to have for the Jews.[1]

Dr David Cymet wrote:

> That such a desperate request to save one-thousand Jewish children from extermination at Auschwitz should have elicited such a harsh reception from the highest authorities of the Church is in itself a most powerful indicator of the deeper roots of the Holocaust.[2]

Notwithstanding, the State of Israel was declared in May 1948, but there was a sharp contrast between the Church's hasty recognition of the Nazi regime of Adolf Hitler and the forty-five years' resistance to its official acknowledgement of the State of Israel.[3]

The Cardinal Secretary of State adduced the Church's 'highest principles' in rejecting Jewish requests:

> I do not quite see how we can take any initiative in this matter. As long as the Jews deny the divinity of Christ, we certainly cannot make a declaration in their favour. Not that we have any ill will toward them ... The history of Israel is our own heritage, it is our foundation. But in order for us to come out for the Jewish people in the way you desire, they would first have to be converted.[4]

L'Osservatore Romano imperiously announced to the world:

> Modern Israel is not the true heir of Biblical Israel, but a secular state ... Therefore the Holy Land and its sacred sites belong to Christianity, the True Israel.

Behind all this sanctimony was Pius XII. He 'was the one who refused to recognize Israel upon its rebirth.'[5]

For decades the Holy See declined to articulate the country's name. In 1964 for instance, Paul VI spent a day in Jerusalem without pronouncing the word 'Israel'. During that period the Holy See recognised almost every other country in the world

[1] Lewy, Guenter. *The Catholic Church & Nazi Germany.* p xxiv
[2] Cymet, David. *History vs. Apologetics: The Holocaust, the Third Reich, and the Catholic Church.* p12
[3] 'Israel is the world's only Jewish State and is the Middle East's *only* liberal democracy.' https://www.jewishvirtuallibrary.org/jsource/israel.html (2015)
[4] Goldhagen, Daniel Jonah. *Hitler's Willing Executioners: Ordinary Germans and the Holocaust.* Source: http://liberals likechrist.org/Catholic/RC_scandal-3.html (2007)
[5] Honig, Sarah. 'The Holy See's Unholy Sanctimony'. *The Jerusalem Post.* 20 May 2015

including atheistic Communist states and many tyrannical regimes, such as those in Central and South America during the 1970s and 1980s.

⌐ Eventually, the Church's continuing denial of the legitimacy of the state of Israel became too embarrassing and too great a political liability. The Holy See therefore agreed, in December 1993, to formally recognise the State of Israel.[1]

⌐ Nevertheless, in April 2007 the Holy See's ambassador to Israel, Antonio Franco, threatened to boycott that year's observances at Yad Vashem.[2] Following bitter criticism, the Holy See backed down, and Ambassador Franco attended the observances. In March 2009, Franco announced that Benedict XVI would visit Yad Vashem during his forthcoming Middle East trip, but would definitely not enter the Yad Vashem museum, thus contradicting standard protocol for visiting dignitaries. In May, Benedict XVI did indeed boycott the museum.[3,4]

⌐ On 29 November 2012, the United Nations General Assembly passed *Resolution 67/19*, upgrading Palestine from an 'observer entity' to a 'non-member observer state' within the United Nations system. Palestine's new status is equivalent to that of the Holy See. On 13 May 2015, the Holy See recognised the State of Palestine – far quicker than its 45 years' delay in recognising the State of Israel.

Sarah Honig, senior editorial writer of *The Jerusalem Post*, commented:

> The adjective which most immediately comes to mind to describe the Vatican's blatant bias is sanctimonious. Its dictionary definitions are 'affecting piety, making a display of holiness, showing false righteousness, marked by hypocritical virtue.' All the above fit the Holy See to a tee …

> the Vatican's organizational zeitgeist, its officialdom's inbuilt bias, remains unaltered. The Holy See's unholy sanctimony of yesteryear callously lives on.[5]

Pius XII's Holy See post-Nazi Holocaust

Pius XII's post-war approach to the Jews was set in 1945. On 2 June, with the war in Europe over, Pius addressed the College of Cardinals. His talk was to report on the condition of the Church after the Nazi experience. Its significance lies in the fact that Pius presented the Church as victim, with particular focus on Poland. He never mentioned the Jews, nor the murder of millions of Jews that had taken place on Polish soil.[6]

In 1947 the Holy See began discussions with the Polish Communist regime, this had the effect of putting 'a good face on Pius XII's lack of help for Poland during the war.'[7]

The Director of the Center of Contemporary Jewish Documentation at Tel Aviv,

---

[1] http://www.cfr.org/holy-seevatican/vatican-israel-relations/p19344 (2014)
[2] Yad Vashem is the "Holocaust Martyrs' and Heroes' Remembrance Authority". It is Israel's official memorial to the Jewish victims of the Holocaust.
[3] Agence France Presse, 10 March 2009
[4] http://guardian.co.uk/world/2007/apr/13/religion.catholicism (2010)
[5] Honig, Sarah. 'The Holy See's Unholy Sanctimony'. *The Jerusalem Post*. 20 May 2015
[6] http://www.shc.edu/theolibrary/resources/08Vatican.htm (2014)
[7] Phayer, Michael. *Pius XII, the Holocaust, and the Cold War*. p168

Dr Aryeh Kubovy, met Pius XII in September 1945 and suggested that the Pope issue an encyclical on how Christians should view Jews and Judaism. Pius said he would consider it, but it came to nothing. Pius completed the last thirteen years of his papacy fixated on the Cold War, with no concern about the Jews, but rather about the status of Christian sites in the new State of Israel.[1]

The *Universal Declaration of Human Rights* was adopted by the United Nations in 1948. The respected teacher Gerald Darring wrote:

> as far as I can tell, Pius XII never acknowledged it and certainly did not refer to it as a significant source document. Human rights, taken in whole as an issue of social justice, was not a concern of Pius XII, and the story of the Catholic Church and human rights begins after Pius XII died.

Michael Phayer has charged the Holy See with defending war criminals and helping fugitives from justice to escape.[2] Under Pius XII, the Holy See 'sought clemency for convicted war criminals; was uncooperative in extraditing potential German war criminals; may have accepted funds from the criminal Ustasha regime … abetted the escape of fugitives by appointing Nazi and Ustasha sympathizers (Hudal and Draganović) to key positions … By allowing the Vatican to become engaged in providing refuge for Holocaust perpetrators, Pius XII committed the greatest impropriety of his pontificate.'[3]

Professor Darring summarised Pius' continuing silence:

> How do we defend the total silence of Pius XII after the war? The defenders of Pius do not deal with this issue; they stop with the end of the war. Read such books as … Margherita Marchione's Pope Pius XII: Architect for Peace, and you will find nothing about the last thirteen years of Pius' papacy.

> Pius XII never condemned the Holocaust, and the important word here is *never* … I have looked in vain for a statement of condemnation by the post-war pope liberated from his self-imposed restraint of impartiality.[4]

Additionally, there was the silence of Pius XI after Kristallnacht, Paul VI's silence after the Six-Day War, and the silence of John Paul II after Bashar al-Assad's anti-Israeli tirade in the Pope's presence.

Synopsis

There has been an extensive post-War resumption of anti-Semitism in several European countries. Catholic Poland particularly so.

Even after the Holocaust, Pius XII continued to display overt anti-Semitism.

The Church's hasty recognition of Adolf Hitler's Nazi regime contrasted with its 45 years' resistance to its official acknowledgement of the State of Israel.

————

[1] http://www.shc.edu/theolibrary/resources/08Vatican.htm (2014)
[2] Phayer, Michael. *The Catholic Church and the Holocaust, 1930-1965.* pp162-75
[3] http://www.shc.edu/theolibrary/resources/08Vatican.htm (2014)
[4] Ibid.

26 – Final Conclusions and Verdict

... the hour is coming, in the which ... they that have done evil, unto the resurrection of damnation. John 5:29-29[1]

For what is the hope of the hypocrite, though he hath gained, when God taketh away his soul? Job 27:8

- In the words of John Adams, the second president of the United States:

  [T]he Hebrews have done more to civilize men than any other nation. If I were an atheist, and believed blind eternal fate, I should still believe that fate had ordained the Jews to be the most essential instrument for civilizing the nations.'[2]

- Neither Islam, nor Christianity generally, nor Roman Catholicism in particular merited his commendation. In confirmation, it is worthy of note that the proportion of Muslims having been awarded a Nobel Prize is 0.006 per million of the world's Islamic population. The comparable figures are, for Christians 0.23, and for Jews 9.21.

The Magnitude of Catholicism's Crimes against the Jews, the Route to Auschwitz

As evidence paralleling this conclusion of John Adams, there are no known better summaries of the world's longest hatred and the world's greatest extended genocide (*both* by the Catholic Church) and of Judaism's survival from the Church's enduring soulless bigotry, than that of G W Foote and J M Wheeler in their *Crimes of Christianity* and that of Professor Henry Charles Lea's *History of the Inquisition of Spain*.

Foote and Wheeler concluded:

The story of the crimes of Christianity against the people from whom it is derived, and to whom it owes its God and Savior, is one which *lasts from the time when it first obtained civil power until the present day*. Like an unnatural child, Christianity has turned against and pursued its parent with relentless malice. Pious Christians have fulfilled the prophecies by making the name of Jew a byword and a reproach, and have plundered and persecuted the chosen race until their lives became a curse. Yet, hounded from country to country, like beasts of the chase, visited with such atrocities that to escape them mothers have destroyed the children to whom they gave suck, they have not ceased to make their mute but unanswerable protest against the errors of Christianity. Their very persecution has preserved them from merging their individuality in that of other races, and *they remain to this day a monument of Christian ingratitude, falsity, and impotence.*[3]

---

[1] 'they that have done evil' is quoted in Denzinger, *Enchiridion symbolorum, definitionum et declarationum de rebus fidei et morum* (10th edn) 1908, n.40 – it is incorporated in Catholic dogma, in somewhat similar wording in the Athanasian Creed, and was repeated in like terms by the Fourth Lateran Council.

[2] Nowlan, Robert A. *The American Presidents, Washington to Tyler: What They Did, What They Said, What Was Said About Them, with Full Source Notes.* p82

[3] Foote, G W & J M Wheeler. *Crimes of Christianity.* Vol I. Ch VIII. 'Persecution of the Jews'

Lea presented a more detailed picture:

> It would be superfluous to recount in detail the dreary catalogue of wholesale slaughters which for centuries disgraced Europe, whenever fanaticism or the disappearance of a child gave rise to stories of the murder rite, or a blood-stained host suggested sacrilege committed on the sacrament, or some passing evil, such as an epidemic, aroused the populace to bloodshed and rapine. The medieval chronicles are full of such terrible scenes, in which *cruelty and greed assumed the cloak of zeal to avenge God* ...[1]

He then expanded on the plight of the Jews:

> The vicissitudes endured by the Jewish race, from the period when Christianity became dominant, may well be a subject of pride to the Hebrew and of shame to the Christian. The annals of mankind afford no more brilliant instance of steadfastness under adversity, of unconquerable strength through centuries of hopeless oppression, of inexhaustible elasticity in recuperating from apparent destruction, and of conscientious adherence to a faith whose only portion in this life was contempt and suffering.

Specifically, the role of the Catholic Church in this hatred was laid bare:

> Nor does the long record of human perversity present a more damning illustration of the facility with which the evil passions of man can justify themselves with the pretext of duty, than the manner in which the Church, *assuming* to represent Him who died to redeem mankind, *deliberately planted the seeds of intolerance and persecution* and assiduously cultivated the harvest for nearly fifteen hundred years.

Christlessness prevailed within the professed 'Church of Christ':[2]

> It was in vain that Jesus on the cross had said 'Father, forgive them, for they know not what they do': it was in vain that St Peter was recorded as urging, in excuse for the Crucifixion, 'And now, brethren, I wot that through ignorance ye did it, as did also your rulers'; the Church taught that, short of murder, no punishment, no suffering, no obloquy was too severe ... Under the canon law *the Jew was a being who had scarce the right to existence* and could only enjoy it under conditions of virtual slavery.

This ecclesiastic bigotry was also embodied in civil law:

> Gregory XIII [1581] declared that the guilt of the race in rejecting and crucifying Christ *only grows deeper with successive generations*, entailing on its members perpetual servitude, and this authoritative assertion was embodied in an appendix to the Corpus Juris.

---

[1] Lea, Henry Charles. *History of the Inquisition of Spain*. Vol I. p83
[2] http://www.vatican.va/archive/hist_councils/ii_vatican_council/documents/vat-ii_decl_19651028_nostra-aetate_en.html (2015)

Lea concluded: [1]

> It is not too much to say that for the infinite wrongs committed on the Jews during the Middle Ages, and for the prejudices that are even yet rife in many quarters, *the Church is mainly if not wholly responsible*. It is true that occasionally she lifted her voice in mild remonstrance when some massacre occurred more atrocious than usual, but these massacres were the direct outcome of the hatred and contempt which she so zealously inculcated, and she never took steps by punishment to prevent their repetition.

History reveals unequivocally that subsequent to Lea's writing, the exclusive Roman Catholic Church (the 'corporate' image of 'the new people of God', 'remaining one and only one')[2] has continued to express in diverse ways its aversion to the Jews, to the memory of their sufferings, to Judaism, and to the State of Israel.

During the period of the Holocausts this antipathy was all-pervasive.

Accordingly, Professor Robert Michael of the University of Chicago concluded:

> Catholic theological and Catholic racist antisemitism prepared, conditioned, and encouraged Catholic antisemites and others to collaborate actively or passively with individual and institutional antisemitic behaviors – avoidance, discrimination, expropriation, antilocution, physical assault and torture, murder and mass murder. This Catholic antisemitism paved the long via dolorosa that led to Auschwitz and beyond.[3]

Catholic Faith, Doctrine, and the Deicide

'The light of faith is a gift supernaturally bestowed upon the understanding', objectively, 'it stands for the sum of truths revealed by God in Scripture *and tradition* and which the Church presents to us in a brief form in her creeds', so states the *Catholic Encyclopedia* – doctrine 'is synonymous with catechesis and catechism.'

Joseph Rebhun, in his book *Crisis of Morality and Reaction to the Holocaust*, stated that 'the theological anti-Judaism of Christianity did not hesitate to silence opposing arguments … The ideas of deicide … became imprinted in Christian minds.'[4] Likewise, Ignaz Maybaum confirmed in his chapter entitled 'The Medieval Passion Play' that the branding of Jewish deicide 'is a doctrine for which the Church is fully responsible.'[5]

Amici Israel (Friends of Israel) came into existence in 1926 – 'it sought to promote a new and loving attitude to Israel and the Jews, to leave off speaking of the people of

---

[1] Lea, Henry Charles. *History of the Inquisition of Spain*. Vol I. pp35-36

[2] Refer to: *Catechism of the Catholic Church* with respect to 'the new people of God', etc. at http://www. vatican.va/archive/ccc_css/archive/catechism/p123a9p2.htm (2015), and also to *Dogmatic Constitution on the Church: Lumen Gentium* at http://www.vatican.va/archive/hist_councils/ii_vatican_council/documents/ vat-ii_const_19641121_lumen-gentium_en.html (2015). See also: *Catholic Heritage Vatican II: The Church as the 'people of God'* at http://www.cam.org.au/News-and-Events/Features/Catholic-Heritage/Article/ 4533/vatican-ii-the-church-as-the-people-of-god (2015)

[3] Michael, Robert. *A History of Catholic Antisemitism: The Dark Side of the ...* pp7-8. See also p22, above.

[4] Rebhun, Joseph. *Crisis of Morality and Reaction to the Holocaust*. p19

[5] Maybaum, Ignaz. *Ignaz Maybaum: A Reader*. p91

the deicide.' In March 1928 the Holy Office issued a decree ordering the suppression of this association following its proposal to revise the Good Friday prayer by eliminating the term 'perfidus' that was applied to the Jews, having been accused of deicide. His Eminence Merry del Val,[1] a 'Servant of God' and Secretary of the Holy Office, registered his Votum:

> We are dealing with ancient prayers and rites of the liturgy of the Church, a liturgy inspired and consecrated for centuries that includes condemnation of the rebellion and betrayal perpetrated by the chosen people who were at once unfaithful and deicide ...[2]

These doctrines, teachings and rites were embraced within the ambit of Catholic faith. For example, the mystic Juliana of Norwich (1342-1423), declared, 'I knew in my faith that the Jews were accursed and condemned without end, except those who were converted.'[3]

In 1965, the Church partially abandoned its historical stance towards Jews and Judaism. It rejected its earlier doctrines that: all of the Jews in Palestine circa 30 CE were responsible for the execution of Jesus; all Jews who are currently living are also responsible for Jesus' death; God has rejected Jews because they murdered Jesus.[4]

Catholic Faith, Mendacity and Hypocrisy

The US National Conference of Catholic Bishops, 1975, and the Catholic Bishops' Committee for Ecumenical and Interreligious Affairs, 1988, reaffirmed that any pre-sentation of the Passion that seeks to shift responsibility from human sin (equivocal, and nebulous) onto the Jews, can only be said to obscure a core gospel truth. Evading the two millennial Church's own human sin of the accusation of the collective guilt of the Jews (embedded in Catholic doctrine, Passion plays, rites of the liturgy, and faith) the Committee mendaciously stated:

> Correctly viewed, the disappearance of the charge of collective guilt of Jews pertains as much to the *purity of the Catholic faith* as it does to the defense of Judaism.[5]

This assertion is a prime example of the Church's inherent, pervasive: mendacity, dishonesty, hypocrisy, pious dissimulation, specious propaganda, and 'unholy sancti-mony'.[6] These attributes constitute the Church's 'essential characteristics', which are evident throughout its history, and are likewise manifest throughout this encyclopaedia.

---

[1] Rafael María José Pedro Francisco Borja Domingo Gerardo de la Santíssima Trinidad Merry del Val y Zulueta was born within the Spanish Embassy in London to a Spanish diplomat. He was a theologian. Emphasising a key role of theology in the evils recorded herein, there are 108 occurrences of the words 'theology', 'theological', 'theologically', 'theologian' in this book.

[2] Fattorini, Emma. *Hitler, Mussolini and the Vatican: Pope Pius XI and the Speech That was Never* ... p109

[3] *Sixteen Revelations of Divine Love.* http://www.romancatholicism.org/accursed-race.html (2013)

[4] http://www.religioustolerance.org/jud_jesu5.htm (2015)

[5] https://www.bc.edu/content/dam/files/research_sites/cjl/texts/cjrelations/resources/documents/catholic/NCCB_Statement.htm (2015)

[6] Honig, Sarah. 'The Holy See's Unholy Sanctimony'. *The Jerusalem Post.* 20 May 2015

The similarity is clear between the Bishops' statement and the document *We Remember: A Reflection on the Shoah*[1] published in 1998 by the Catholic Commission for Religious Relations with the Jews. Both are hypocritical, sanctimonious attempts by the institutional Church to exonerate itself of its diabolical history against the Jews.

From the evidence provided in this book, the opportunistic, rapid post-Holocaust disappearance of the Church's previous charge of Jewish guilt pertains to the *impurity* of much of the Catholic faith. That which was once doctrine is no longer so. That which was once faith is no longer so. That which for centuries was propagandised as pure is now revealed to have been grossly impure.

The folios of history bear witness to the multitude of situations in which articles of 'supernaturally bestowed' pure Catholic faith have been amended, deleted, denied, or abandoned to suit the changing political, social, territorial, controlling, or financial ambitions of the Catholic Church.

As noted above, the Church 'will preserve unimpaired its essential characteristics.' The unimpaired chameleon has merely changed its colours once again.

The Truth

Accountability cannot be disowned. Father Edward Flannery, 'one of this century's spiritual giants', emphasised: 'There can be no quarter conceded to pious dissimulation or defensive minimizing of the magnitude of the crime committed against the Jews ...'[2]

From the broad canvas of Christian history, from the narrower context of the Holocausts, and from contemporary anti-Semitic events, the unequivocal conclusion to be drawn may be expressed by paraphrasing the above words of Henry Charles Lea:

> It is a fact that for the infinite wrongs committed on the Jews during the Middle Ages, for the diabolical acts inflicted on them during the Catholic and Nazi Holocausts, and for the anti-Semitic prejudices and practices that are even yet rife in many quarters, the Catholic Church is mainly if not totally responsible.

Jesus said:

> You shall love the Lord your God with your whole heart and with your whole soul and with your whole mind. This is the greatest and the first commandment. And the second is like to this: You shall love your neighbour as yourself. *On these two commandments depends the whole law and the prophets.* (Matthew 22:37-40)

The *Catholic Encyclopedia* ('Truth') explains that 'To judge that things are what they are is to judge truly.' 'The object about which we judge is reality itself ...'

Accordingly, by committing horrendous crimes against the Jews, the Latin Church, a claimed 'perfect society', has consistently broken both of these fundamental commandments of Christ – it has broken the eternal law. This is the unfettered truth.

---

[1] Refer to page 49, and Chapter 24, above.
[2] Flannery, Edward H. *The Anguish of the Jews*. p294. Throughout his career, Father Flannery fought against anti-Semitism at all levels.

A single example serves to emphasise this point, namely, that around the time of the Black Death, more Jews were murdered by Catholics in an 'epidemic of extermination' during a single year in Germany, mostly by being burned alive, than all the Christians who were persecuted by the Romans over a period of 200 years.

The Catholic apostle wrote 'He that loveth not knoweth not God; for *God is love*. So, the ultimate truth is that the Church, having not loved the Jews, has not known God.[1]

The Verdict

'Sin is a moral evil', so states the *Catholic Encyclopedia*. Mortal sin is defined by the Church as 'something said, done or desired contrary to the eternal law, or a thought, word, or deed contrary to the eternal law.' It is 'an aversion from God'.

'A straight line leads from the first act of oppression against the Jews and Judaism in the fourth century to the holocaust in the twentieth.'[2] Furthermore, historical evidence suggests that the Catholic Church has been responsible for the annihilation of at least as many Jews as were killed by the Nazis.

But:

> God did not make death, and he does not delight in the death of the living. For he has created all things that they might exist ... but through the devil's envy death entered the world ...

And:

> the souls of the just are in the hand of God ... because God hath tried them, and found them worthy of himself. As gold in the furnace, he hath proved them, and as a victim of a holocaust, he hath received them ...[3]

Cognisant of these irrefutable facts and the above truths, the verdict of impartial history is that the countless unholy anti-Semitic acts based in Catholic faith, and executed by the Roman Church and its 'central ecclesiastical government' the Holy See, have been contrary to the eternal law. They have therefore been associations of the devil's envy, moral evils, and mortal sins – gross aversions from both love and God.

Irrevocably, from the Holy See down, the *institutional* Church is guilty. And yet it has never apologised, nor made reparation, nor been punished for its key role in these horrendous sins. This allegedly holy institution continues to deny its unholy darkness.

Contemporary sanctimonious words of opportunistic theological accommodation and hypocritical self-exculpation and self-promotion cannot erase these facts. The truth is ineradicable. Contrary to the Catholic Church's incessant claims to holiness, for two millennia it has not only not known God, it has been an aversion to God.

---

[1] The reference to 'the Catholic apostle' (*1 John* 4:8) derives from the description of the Epistles of the apostles in the Catholic *Douay-Rheims Bible*. The Epistles of the New Testament are described as 'Catholic Epistles' in the *Catholic Encyclopedia*.

[2] Berkovits, Eliezer. 'Judaism in the Post-Christian Era', *Judaism* 15 (Winter 1966) p77.

[3] 'God did not make death' is from the *Douay-Rheims Bible*, *Wisdom* 1:13-14; 2:23-25, and 'the souls of the just' is likewise from *Wisdom* 3:1-6.

The *Catholic Encyclopedia* states:

> The direct killing of an innocent person is, of course, to be reckoned among the most grievous of sins. It is said to happen directly when the death of the person is viewed either as an end attractive in itself, or at any rate is chosen as a means to an end. The malice discernible in the sin is primarily chargeable to *the violation of the supreme ownership of God over the lives of His creatures*.

By their hatreds and their resultant killings, direct and indirect, the institutional Catholic Church, its popes, its hierarchy, and its members have irrefutably violated God's supreme ownership over the lives of millions of Jews.

And yet the Church has never apologised, nor made reparation, nor been punished for its multitude of horrendous sins against these people. This professed holy institution continues to deny its unholy darkness.

——:——

Bibliography

A Dictionary of Jewish-Christian Relations (eds Edward Kessler & Neil Wenborn) (Cambridge University Press, 2005)

A Handbook of Living Religions (ed John R Hinnels) (London: Penguin, 1991)

A History of the Catholic Inquisition, compiled from various authors (Boston: Perkins, Marvin, & Co)

A.S. *'A Corrupt Tree': An Encyclopaedia of Crimes committed by the Church of Rome against Humanity and the Human Spirit. Volume 1 – The Unholy Popes and the Debasement of Western Civilisation* (Bloomington: Xlibris, 2013)

Actes et Documents du Saint Siege relatifs a la Seconde Guerre Mondiale (Holy See, 1972)

Agrippa, Henry Cornelius. *The Philosophy of Natural Magic* (Secaucus: University Books, 1974)

Albertus Magnus. *De animalibus*

Allen, Stewart Lee. *In the Devil's Garden: A Sinful History of Forbidden Food.*

Anti-Semitism (Jerusalem: Keter Publishing House, 1974).

Armstrong, Karen. *A History of God* (London: Mandarin, 1994)

——. *Holy War: The Crusades and their Impact on Today's World* (2nd edn) (New York: Anchor Books, 2001)

'Arnoume', D Christie Sinton. *Christian Terrorism.* http://www.antichrist.com.au/crimeline.html

Art, David. *The Politics of the Nazi Past in Germany and Austria* (Cambridge University Press, 2006)

Arthur, Joseph, Comte de Gobineau. *Essai sur l'inégalité des races humaines* (1854)

Atkin, Nicholas & Frank Tallet. *Priests, Prelates & People: A History of European Catholicism since 1750* (Oxford University Press, 2003)

Barthel, Manfred. *The Jesuits* (William Morrow)

Bauer, Yehuda. *A History of the Holocaust* (New York: Franklin Watts, 2001).

——. *Remembering for the Future: Working Papers and Addenda* (Oxford: Pergamon, 1989)

Bazes, Moses. *Jesus the Jew, the Historical Jesus* (Jerusalem: Alpha Press, 1979)

Bécquer, Gustavo Adolfo. *La Rosa de Pasión* (1862)

Ben-Dror, Graciela. *The Catholic Church and the Jews – Argentina 1933–1945.* (Zalman Shazar Center for Jewish History/Vidal Sassoon International Center for the Study of Antisemitism, The Hebrew University of Jerusalem, 2000)

Berenbaum, Michael. *The World Must Know* (United States Holocaust Memorial Museum, 2006)

Berkovits, Eliezer. *Faith after the Holocaust* (Brooklyn: KTAV Publishing House, 1973)

Betrayal: German Churches and the Holocaust (eds Robert P Ericksen, Susannah Heschel) (Minneapolis: Fortress Press, 1999)

Blet, Pierre. 'The Church in Occupied Poland'. *Pius XII and the Second World War: According to the Archives of the Vatican* (Mahwah: Paulist Press, 1999)

Blum, Howard. *Wanted: The Search for Nazis in America* (Greenwich: Fawcett Books, 1977)

Boettner, Loraine. *Roman Catholicism* (Phillipsburg: Presbyterian & Reformed Publishing Co, 1962)

Boka, Karl. *Staat und Parteien* (Zurich & Leipzig: Max Niehams Verlag)

Bonhoeffer, Dietrich. *The Cost of Discipleship* (various publishers)

Braham, Randolph L. *The Politics of Genocide: The Holocaust in Hungary* (condensed edn) (Detroit: Wayne State University Press, 2000)

Brockdorff, Werner. *Flucht vor Nürnberg. Pläne und Organisation der Fluchtwege der NS-Priminenz in 'Römischen Weg'* (München-Wels: Verlag Welsermühl, 1969)

Brown, Michael L. *Our Hands are Stained with Blood: The Tragic Story of the 'Church' and the Jewish People* (Shippensburg: Destiny Image Publishers, 1992)

Buike, Bruno Antonio. *Principles of Power in 20th Century* (Neuss, 2009)

Bukey, Evan Burr. *Hitler's Austria* (The University of North Carolina Press, 2000)

Burl, Aubrey. *God's Heretics: The Albigensian Crusade* (Stroud: Sutton Publishing, 2002)

Callil, Carmen. *Bad Faith: A Forgotten History of Family & Fatherland* (London: Jonathan Cape, 2006)

Carroll, James. *Constantine's Sword: The Church & the Jews* (Boston: Houghton Mifflin, 2001)

Catholic Encyclopedia (original version: New York: Robert Appleton Co) (CD Version 2.1)

Catholics Remember the Holocaust. (Washington, DC: United States Catholic Conference, 1998)

Chabauty, E - A. *Les Juifs, nos maitres!* (Paris: Société Générale de Librairie Catholique, 1882)

Cheyne, Edward P. *A Short History of England* (Ginn & Co, 1927)

Christianity and Human Rights: Christians and the Struggle for Global Justice (ed F M Shepherd) (Lexington Books, 2009)

Cohn-Sherbok. D. *The Crucified Jew: Twenty Centuries of Christian Anti-Semitism* (London: Harper-Collins, 1992)

Collins, Paul. *From Inquisition to Freedom* (Continuum International, 2001)

Constant, Julien P. *Les Juifs devant L'Église et l'Histoire* (Paris: Gaume & Cie, 1896)

Coppa, Frank J. *The Papacy, the Jews, and the Holocaust* (The Catholic University of America Press, 2006)

Cornwell, John. *Hitler's Pope: The Secret History of Pius XII* (London: Viking, 1999)

——. *Hitler's Pope: The Secret History of Pius XII* (2nd edn) (London: Penguin, 2008)

Crimes of War: Guilt and Denial in the Twentieth Century (eds O Bartov, A Grossman, M Nolan) (New York: The New Press, 2002)

Cymet, David. *History vs. Apologetics: The Holocaust, the Third Reich, and the Catholic Church* (Lanham: Lexington Books, 2010)

Darring, Gerald. *'Central European Churches and the Holocaust'*. http://www.shc.edu/theolibrary/resources/07Central.htm#_edn5 (2009)

Dawidowicz, Lucy. *The War Against the Jews, 1933-1945* (Bantam, 1986)

Dawkins, Richard. *The God Delusion* (London: Transworld Publishers, 2006)

de Cañizares y Suárez, José. *La imagen de Cristo*

de la Salle, Jean-Baptiste. *Les devoirs du chrétien envers Dieu, et les moyens de pouvoir bien s'en aquitter* (1703)

de Mello, Alfredo. *'The Jews in Portugal'*. http://www.saudades.org/chapivjewsinport.htm (2007)

De Rosa, Gabriele. *I tempi della 'Rerum Novara'* (Roma: Istituto Luigi Sturzo, 2002)

De Rosa, Giuseppe. *La Civiltà Cattolica: 150 anni al servizio della Chiesa 1850-1999* (Roma: *La Civiltà Cattolica*, 1999)

de Rosa, Peter. *Vicars of Christ: The Dark Side of the Papacy* (London: Bantam Press, 1988)

Dedijer, Vladimir. *The Yugoslav Auschwitz and the Vatican: The Croatian Massacre of the Serbs during World War II* (trans H L Kendall) (Buffalo: Prometheus Books, 1992)

Denzinger, Heinrich Joseph Dominicus. *Enchiridion symbolorum, definitionum et declarationum de rebus fidei et morum* (10th edn) (1908)

Deschner, Karlheinz. *Kriminalgeschichte des Christentums* (Vols 1-10) (various publishers)

——. *God and the Fascists: The Vatican Alliance with Mussolini, Franco, Hitler, and Pavelić* (ed Peter Gorenflos) (trans Richard Pepper) (New York: Prometheus Books, 2013)

Denzler, Georg. *Widerstand ist nicht das richtige Wort: Katholische Priester und Theologen im Dritten Reich* (Zürich, 2003)

Dietrich, Donald J. *God & Humanity in Auschwitz* (London: Transaction Publishers, 1995)

Discoveries, Missionary Expansion and Asian Cultures (ed, T R de Souza) (New Delhi: Ashok Kumar Mittal, 1994)

Doobov, Arieh. *The Vatican and the Shoah: Purified Memory or Reincarnated Responsibility?* (Jerusalem: Institute of the World Jewish Congress, 1998)

Douay-Rheims Bible (http://www.newadvent.org)

Dowe, Dieter. *Europe in 1848: revolution and reform* (trans D Higgins) (Berghahn Books, 2001)

Drumont, Édouard Adolphe. *Testament d'un antisémite* (Paris: Libraire de la Sociétés des Gens de Lettres, 1891)

Durant, Will. *The Age of Faith* (New York: Simon and Schuster, 1972)

Dwork, Deborah and Robert Jan Van Pelt. *Holocaust: A History* (New York: W W Norton, 2002)

Dworkin, Andrea. *The Jews, Israel, and Women's Liberation* (New York: The Free Press, 2000)

Eckart, Dietrich. *Der Bolschewismus von Moses bis Lenin: Zwiegespräch zwischen Hitler und mir* (München, 1925)

Edelheit, Abraham & Hershel Edelheit. *History of the Holocaust: A Handbook and Dictionary* (Westview Press, 1995)

Eisenmenger, Johann Andreas. *Entdecktes Judenthum* (Scan, Fraktur: Erster Theil, 1711)

Encarta Encyclopedia (Microsoft, CD, 2005)

Encyclopedia Britannica (CD, Standard Edition, 2001)

Encyclopedia of the Holocaust (eds Robert Rozett and Shmuel Spector) (Jerusalem: Yad Vashem, and New York: Facts on File, 2000)

Evangelical Sisterhood of Mary. *The Guilt of Christianity towards the Jewish People* (1997)

Exterminate the Jews. Originally published in a pamphlet by the Yugoslav Government.

Falconi, Carlo. *The Silence of Pius XII* (Boston: Little, Brown, 1970)

Fattorini, Emma. *Hitler, Mussolini and the Vatican: Pope Pius XI and the Speech That was Never Made* (Trans Carl Ipsen) (Cambridge: Polity Press, 2011)

Flannery, Edward H. *The Anguish of the Jews: Twenty-Three Centuries of Antisemitism* (2nd edn) (New York: Paulist Press, 1985)

Fleischer, Johannes. *Das Andere Deutschland*

Flornoy, E. *Le Bienheureux Bernardin de Feltre* (Tours: Mame, 1902-1903)

Foote, G W & J M Wheeler. *Crimes of Christianity* (London: Progressive Publishing Co, 1887)

France, Anatole. *The Garden of Epicurus* (trans A Allinson) (London: The Bodley Head, 1923)

Friedländer, Saul. *Nazi Germany and the Jews, Vol I - The Years of Persecution 1933-1939* (New York: 1997)

———. *Pius XII and the Third Reich: A Documentation* (New York: Alfred A Knopf, 1966)

Friedman, Saul S. *Jews and the American Slave Trade* (New Brunswick: Transaction Publishers, 2000)

Giovannetti, Alberto. *Il Vaticano e la Guerra, 1939-1940* (Città del Vaticano: Libreria Editrice Vaticana, 1960)

———. *Roma Città Aperta* (Milano: Editrice Ancora, 1962)

Gitelman, Zvi Y. *Bitter legacy: confronting the Holocaust in the USSR* (Indiana University Press, 1997)

Goldhagen, Daniel J. *A Moral Reckoning* (New York: Alfred A Knopf, 2002)

———. *Hitler's Willing Executioners: Ordinary Germans and the Holocaust* (New York: Alfred A Knopf, 1996)

Golding, Shmuel. 'Anti-Semitism in the New Testament'. *Biblical Polemics*. 1 (May 1988)

Goñi, Uki. *The Real ODESSA: How Perón Brought the Nazi War Criminals to Argentina* (rev edn) (London: Granta Books, 2003)

———. *The Real Odessa: Smuggling the Nazis to Perón's Argentina* (Granta Books, 2002)

Haas, Peter J. *Morality after Auschwitz: The Radical Challenge of the Nazi Ethic* (Philadelphia: Fortress Press, 1988).

Hardy, Rob. *What Role did the Vatican Play in Fostering Anti-Semitism?*

Herczl, Moshe Y. *Christianity and the Holocaust of Hungarian Jews* (trans Joel J Lerner) (New York University Press, 1995)

Hilberg, Raul. *The Destruction of the European Jews* (New York: Holmes & Meier, 1985)

———. *Perpetrators Victims Bystanders: The Jewish Catastrophe 1933-1945* (New York: Aaron Asher Books)

Hilton, Adrian. *The Principality and Power of Europe* (Rickmansworth: Dorchester House, 1997)

Historisch-Politische Blätter für das katholische Deutschland (München: In Commission der Literarisch-artistischen Anstalt, 1860)

Hitchens, Christopher. *God is not Great: How religion poisons everything* (Crows Nest: Allen & Unwin, 2008)

Hitler, Adolf. *Mein Kampf* (trans, reprinted) (Boston, 1971)

———. *Zweites Buch* (unpublished)

Hochhuth, Rolf. *Der Stellvertreter. Ein christliches Trauerspiel* (Reinbek, 1963)

———. *The Deputy. Sidelights on History* (New York: Grove Press, 1964)

Holocaust and Genocide Studies (Oxford University Press in Association with the United States Holocaust Memorial Museum)

Holocaust Facts (http://history1900s.about.com/od/holocaust/a/holocaustfacts.htm)

Holocaust Scholars Write to the Vatican (ed Harry James Cargas) (Praeger, 1998)

Holokaust na Slovensku, Vols 1-5. (eds Niznansky, E, et al) (Bratislava: NMS/ZNO, 2001-2004)

Hory, Ladislaus & Martin Broszat. *Der Kroatische Ustascha-Staat, 1941-1945* (Stuttgart: Deutsche Verlags-Anstalt, 1964)

Hudal, Alois. *Römische Tagebücher: Lebensbeichte Eines Alten Bischofs* (Graz: Leopold Stocker Verlag, 1976)

——. *Die Grundlagen des Nationalsozialismus: Eine ideengeschichtliche Untersuchung* (Leipzig & Vienna, 1936–37)

I Documenti della conquista ebraica del Mondo (Firenze-Roma: Fede e Ragione, 1921)

In God's Name: Genocide & Religion in the Twentieth Century (eds Omer Bartov & Phyllis Mack) (Oxford: Berghan Books, 2001)

Irwin-Zarecka, Iwona. *Neutralizing Memory: The Jew in Contemporary Poland* (New Brunswick, NJ: Transaction Publishers, 1989)

Isaac, Jules. *Jésus et Israël* (various publishers, 1948-2000)

James, Alexander. *The Myth of Christianity* (Perth: Premier Publishers, 2001)

Johnstone, Diana. *Fools' Crusade: Yugoslavia, NATO and Western Delusions* (New York: Monthly Review Press, 2000)

Jones, E Michael. *The Jewish Revolutionary Spirit and its Impact on World History* (Fidelity Press, 2008)

Kahl, Joachim. *The Misery of Christianity: A Plea for a Humanity without God* (trans N D Smith) (Harmondsworth: Penguin, 1971)

Kamen, Henry. *The Spanish Inquisition: An Historical Revision* (London: Weidenfeld & Nicolson, 1997)

Katz, Robert. *The Battle for Rome: The Germans, the Allies, the Partisans, and the Pope, September 1943-June 1944* (New York: Simon & Schuster, 2003)

Kertzer, David I. *The Kidnapping of Edgardo Mortara* (New York: Alfred A Knopf, 1997)

——. *The Pope and Mussolini: The Secret History of Pius XI and the Rise of Fascism in Europe* (New York: Random House, 2014)

——. *The Popes Against the Jews: The Vatican's Role in the Rise of Modern Anti-Semitism* (New York: Vintage Books, 2002)

Klee, Ernst. *Das Personenlexikon zum Dritten Reich. Wer war was vor und nach 1945* (Frankfurt am Main: S Fischer Verlag, 2003)

Kostich, Lazo M. *The Holocaust in the 'Independent State of Croatia': an account based on German, Italian and the other sources* (Chicago: 'Liberty', 1981)

Krupp, Gary. *Pope Pius XII and World War II: The Documented Truth* (Xlibris, 2012)

Kühner, Hans. *Der Antisemitismus der Kirche: Genese, Geschichte und Gefahr* (Zurich: Verlag Die Waage, 1976)

Küng, Hans. *On Being a Christian* (Garden City: Doubleday, 1976)

——. *The Catholic Church: a short history* (trans John Bowden) (London: Weidenfeld & Nicolson, 2001)

Landau-Czajka, Anna. *The Image of the Jew in the Catholic Press during the Second Republic* (*Polin: Studies in Polish Jewry*, 8 (1994)

Lea, Henry Charles. *A History of the Inquisition of the Middle Ages* (reprint: Cosimo, 2005)

——. *History of the Inquisition of Spain* (New York: AMS Press, 1966)

Lehmann, L H. *Behind the Dictators: A Factual Analysis of the Relationship of Nazi-Fascism and Roman Catholicism* (2nd edn) (New York: Agora Publishing, 1944)

——. *Out of the Labyrinth* (New York: Agora Publishing, 1947)

Lehnert, Pascalina. *Ich Durfte Ihm Dienen: Erinnerungen an Papst Pius XII* (Würzburg: Naumann, 1985)

Lessons and Legacies: The Meaning of the Holocaust in a Changing World (ed Peter Hayes) (Northwestern University Press, 1999)

Lewy, Guenter. *The Catholic Church & Nazi Germany* (London: Weidenfeld & Nicolson, 1964)

Lituchy, Barry. *What Is The Vatican Hiding? The Vatican's Complicity in Genocide in Fascist Croatia: The Suppressed Chapter of Holocaust History* (May 1998).

Lockhart, Douglas. *The Dark Side of God: A Quest for the Lost Heart of Christianity* (Shaftesbury, Dorset: Element Books, 1999)

Lope de Vega y Carpio, Félix Arturo. *El niño inocente de La Guardia* (Madrid, 1617)

Lortz, Joseph. *Geschichte der Kirche: in ideengeschichtlicher Betrachtung* (Münster: Aschendorff, 1929-1930)

Los judios en la literatura espanola (ed Rafael Cansinos Assens) (Valencia: Pre-Textos, 2002)

Makow, Henry. *Hitler's Gestapo Chief became Top Truman Advisor*. http://www. henrymakow.com/ 001699.html (2016)

Manhattan, Avro. *The Vatican's Holocaust: The Sensational Account of the Most Horrifying Religious Massacre of the 20th Century* (5th edn) (Springfield: Ozark Books)

Markman, Sidney David. *Jewish Remnants in Spain: Wanderings in a Lost World* (Mesa: Scribe, 2003)

Mauri. *Vatican Ratline: The Vatican, the Nazis, and the New World Order* (BookSurge, 2007)

Maybaum, Ignaz. *Ignaz Maybaum: A Reader* (ed. de Lange) (New York: Berghahn Books, 2001)

Mazal, Harry W. *The Dachau Gas Chambers*. http://www.phdn.org/archives/www.mazal.org/archive/ documents/Dachau-article.htm

McCabe, Joseph. *A Biographical Dictionary of Ancient, Medieval, and Modern Freethinkers* (Girard, Kansas: Haldeman-Julius Publications)

——. *How the Cross Courted the Swastika for Eight Years* (ed E Haldeman-Julius) (The Black International No. 3)

——. *How the Pope of Peace Traded in Blood: The Red Pope* (ed E Haldeman-Julius)

——. *The Columbia Encyclopedia's Crimes against the Truth: How a Popular Reference Work is Being Used as a Weapon against Free Culture and Twisted to Fit the Purposes of Lying Obscurantists* (Girard, Kansas: Haldeman-Julius Publications)

——. *The Myth of Catholic Scholarship: The Absurdities, Falsehoods and Distortions of the Catholic Encyclopedia* (Girard, Kansas: Haldeman-Julius Publications, 1950)

——. *The Story of Religious Controversy* (Boston: The Stratford Co, 1929)

Mešťan, Pavel and Alexander Rehák. *Catholic Church of Slovakia involved in attempts to exculpate Fascism.* Unpublished MS, 2004. Source: http://www.humanizm.net.pl/rehak.html (2016)

Michael, Robert. *A Concise history of American anti-Semitism* (Roman & Littlefield, 2005)

——. *A History of Catholic Antisemitism: The Dark Side of the Church* (New York: Palgrave Macmillan, 2008)

——. *Holy Hatred: Christianity, Antisemitism, and the Holocaust* (New York: Palgrave Macmillan, 2006)

Michaelis, Meir. *Mussolini and the Jews: German-Italian Relations and the Jewish Question in Italy, 1922-1945* (Oxford: Clarendon Press, 1978)

Midlarsky, Manus I. *The Killing Trap: Genocide in the Twentieth Century* (Cambridge University Press, 2005)

Millenari, The. *Shroud of Secrecy: The Story of Corruption within the Vatican* (trans Ian Martin) (Toronto: Key Porter, 2000)

Mitchell, Ruth. *The Serbs choose war* (New York: Garden City, 1943)

Modras, Ronald. *Catholic Church and Antisemitism: Poland, 1933-1939* (Chur: Harwood Academic Publishers, 1994)

Moore, Barrington, Jr. *Moral Purity and Persecution in History* (Princeton University, 2000)

Moore, Edith. *No Friend of Democracy: A study of Roman Catholic politics – their influence on the course of the present War and the growth of Fascism* (London: International Publishing Co, 1941)

Morley, John F. *Vatican Diplomacy and the Jews during the Holocaust 1939-43* (Brooklyn: KTAV Publishing House, 1980)

Murphy, John Patrick M. *Murphy's Law: The Religion of Hitler* (essay, 1998). Source: http://infidels.org/library/modern/john_murphy/religionofhitler.html (2016)

Murphy, Paul I and R Rene Arlington. *La Popessa* (New York: Warner, 1985)

Napolitano, Daniel C. *Why should Catholic Schools Teach About the Holocaust?* (National Catholic Center for Holocaust Education: Seton Hill University, 2006)

Neumann, Johann. *'The churches in Germany before and after 1945'.* Lecture at the University of Tübingen, 1995 (trans & edited). http://www.secularism.org.uk/thechurchesingermanybefore andaft.html (2016)

Noel, Gerard. *Pius XII: The Hound of Hitler* (London: Continuum, 2008)

Nowlan, Robert A. *The American Presidents, Washington to Tyler: What They Did, What They Said, What Was Said About Them, with Full Source Notes* (Jefferson: McFarland & Company, 2012)

O'Shea, Paul. *A Cross too Heavy: Eugenio Pacelli, Politics and the Jews of Europe 1917 – 1943* (Kenthurst: Rosenberg Publishing, 2008)

Pagnossin, Joseph. *The Calvary of Padre Pio* (Padua, 1978).

Paldiel, Mordecai. *Churches and the Holocaust: Unholy Teaching, Good Samaritans, and Reconciliation* (Brooklyn: KTAV Publishing House, 2006)

Paris, Edmond. *The Vatican Against Europe* (trans A Robson) (London: Macmillan, 1961)

Parkes, James. *Prelude to Dialogue* (New York: Schocken Books, 1969)

Paskuly, Steven (editor). *Death Dealer: The Memoirs of the SS Kommandant at Auschwitz* (New York: Prometheus Books, 1996)

Pauley, Bruce F. *From Prejudice to Persecution: A History of Austrian Anti-Semitism* (University of North Carolina Press, 1992)

Phayer, Michael. *Pius XII, the Holocaust, and the Cold War* (Indiana University Press, 2008)

——. *The Catholic Church and the Holocaust, 1930-1965* (Indiana University Press, 2000)

Pius XI and the Second World War: According to the Archives of the Vatican (Mahwah: Paulist Press, 1999)

Pinay, Maurice (pseudonym) (authored anonymously by a group of Catholic priests). *The Plot Against the Church* (trans) (St Anthony Press, 1967)

Pohl, Oswald. *Credo. Mein Weg zu Gott* (Landshut: Alois Girnth Verlag, 1950)

Poliakov, Léon. *The History of Anti-Semitism* (trans Richard Howard) (London: Elek, 1966)

Pollard, John. *Money and the Rise of the Modern Papacy: Financing the Vatican, 1850-1950* (Cambridge University Press, 2005)

Protocols of the Elders of Zion (*Протоколы сионских мудрецов*) (Russia: Знамя, 1903)

Raubitschek, Ernst. *By Train to Dachau* (trans and intro Renate Yates) (Sydney Jewish Museum)

Rausch, David. *A Legacy of Hatred: Why Christians must not Forget the Holocaust* (Grand Rapids: Baker, 1990)

Rauschning, Hermann. *The Voice of Destruction* (New York: G P Putnam's Sons, 1940)

Read, Anthony. *The Devil's Disciples: Hitler's Inner Circle* (New York: W W Norton & Co, 2004)

Rebhun, Joseph. *Crisis of Morality and Reaction to the Holocaust* (Borgo Press, 1998)

Redlich, Fritz. *Hitler: Diagnosis of a Destructive Prophet* (Oxford University Press, 1998)

Reitlinger, Gerald. *The Final Solution* (New York: Beechhurst Press, 1953)

Remembering for the Future: The Holocaust in an Age of Genocide (eds John K Roth and Elisabeth Maxwell) (Houndmills: Palgrave, 2001)

Remembering for the Future: Working Papers and Addenda (ed Yehuda Bauer) (Oxford: Pergamon Press, 1989)

Reves, Emery. *I Paid Hitler* (based on memoirs dictated by Fritz Thyssen) (1941)

Rhodes, Anthony R E. *The Power of Rome in the Twentieth Century: The Vatican in the Age of Liberal Democracies, 1870-1922* (London: Sidgwick & Jackson, 1983)

Ritter, Emil. *Katholisch-konservatives Erbgut: eine Auslese für die Gegenwart* (Freiburg im Breisgau: Herder, 1934)

Robertson, John Mackinnon. *A Short History of Christianity* (London: Watts & Co, 1902)

Roman Martyrology: The Complete Martyrology in English for Daily Reflection. http://www. boston-catholic-journal.com/roman-martyrology-complete-in-english-for-daily-reflection.htm (2015)

Russell, J B. *Witchcraft in the Middle Ages* (Cornell University Press, 1972)

Rychlak, Ronald J. *Hitler, the war, and the pope* (Our Sunday Visitor Publishing Division, Our Sunday Visitor, Inc, 2010)

Sánchez, José M. *Pius XII and the Holocaust: Understanding the Controversy* (The Catholic University of America Press, 2002)

Schmidlin, Josef. *History of the Popes of Modern Times*

Schoenberg, Shira. *Pope Pius XII and the Holocaust*. http://www.Jewishvirtuallibrary.org/jsource/anti-semitism/pius.html (2007)

Scholder, Klaus. *The Churches and the Third Reich* (Philadelphia: Fortress Press, 1979) (English version, 1988)

Segni, L. *L'Esprit du Fascisme*

Sereny, Gitta. *Into That Darkness: from Mercy Killing to Mass Murder, a study of Franz Stangl, the commandant of Treblinka* (London: 1974)

Setton, Kenneth Meyer. *The Papacy and the Levant, 1204-1571* (Philadelphia: American Philosophical Society, 1984)

Shirer, William L. *The Rise and Fall of the Third Reich* (New York: Simon and Schuster)

Silva, Daniel. *A Death in Vienna* (London: Penguin, 2004)

Sinclair, Upton. *The Profits of Religion: An Essay in Economic Interpretation* (Pasadena: Upton Sinclair, 1917)

Singh, Simon. *The Code Book* (London: Fourth Estate, 1999)

Sister Pista. Evangelical Sisterhood of Mary, Darmstadt. http://www.cdn-friends-icej.ca/antiholo/guilt.html (2007)

Snyder, Louis Leo. *Hitler's Elite: Shocking Profiles of the Reich's Most Notorious Henchmen* (Berkley Books, 1990)

Sparks, Thomas. *The Curse of Cain and Theologically Correct Social Policy toward the Jews* https://www.stormfront.org/posterity/ci/curseofcain.html (2016)

Spong, John Shelby. *Living In Sin?* (New York: Harper Collins, 1990)

——. *Liberating the Gospels: Reading the Bible with Jewish Eyes* (New York: HarperCollins Publishers, 1996)

Stannard, David. *American Holocaust* (Oxford University Press, 1992)

Steinacher, Gerald. *Nazis on the Run: How Hitler's Henchmen Fled Justice* (Oxford, 2011)

Stockwell, Antony. *Pius XII: The Dark Side* (Brisbane: Book Pal, 2015)

Tatarka, Dominik. *Farská Republika* (Published 1955 by Slovak writer. First published 1948)

The Case of Archbishop Stepinac (Washington: The Embassy of the Federal Peoples Republic of Yugoslavia, 1947)

The Einsatzgruppen Reports: Selections from the Dispatches of the Nazi Death Squads' Campaign Against the Jews July 1941-January 1943 (eds, Yitzhak Arad, Shmuel Krakowski and Shmuel Spektor) (New York: Holocaust Library, 1989)

The Holocaust and the Christian World: Reflections on the Past, Challenges for the Future (eds Carol Rittner, Stephen D Smith and Irena Steinfeldt) (London: Kuperard for the Beth Shalom Holocaust Memorial Centre and the Yad Vashem International School for Holocaust Studies, 2000)

The Nazi Holocaust (ed Michael R Marrus) (Wesport: Meckler, 1989)

The Roman Martyrology, March 24. http://www.breviary.net/martyrology/mart03/mart0324.htm (2007). See also: http://www.statemaster.com/encyclopedia/Simon-of-Trent (2016)

The Scandal of Roman Catholicism. http://www.liberalslikechrist.org/Catholic/RCscandal-1.html (2016)

The Vatican and the Holocaust: The Catholic Church and the Jews during the Nazi Era (ed Randolph L Braham) (New York: Rosenthal Institute for Holocaust Studies, distributed by Columbia University Press, 2000)

The Vatican & the Holocaust: Pope Pius XII and the Holocaust. http://www.jewishvirtuallibrary. org/jsource/anti-semitism/pius.html (2015)

Toland, John. *Adolf Hitler: The Definitive Biography* (New York: Anchor Books, 1992)

Trachtenberg, Joshua. *The Devil and the Jews: The Medieval Conception of the Jew and its Relation to Modern Anti-Semitism* (Philadelphia: The Jewish Publication Society, 1983)

Trial of the Major War Criminals before the International Military Tribunal (Nuremberg, 1945)

Tuchman, Barbara. *A Distant Mirror* (New York: Alfred A Knopf, 1978)

Universal Declaration of Human Rights (Paris, 1948)

US Department of State. *'Slovak Republic Human Rights Practices, 1995'*, March 1966.

Verdès-Leroux, Jeannine. *Scandale financier et antisémitisme Catholique* (Paris: Centurion, 1969)

Voltaire. *Dictionnaire Philosophique*

Vrba, Rudolf. *Escape from Auschwitz: I cannot forgive.* (First published as *I Cannot Forgive* by Sidgwick and Jackson, Grove Press, London, 1963)

Waagenaar, Sam. *The Pope's Jews* (Chicago: Open Court Publishing Co, 1974)

Walls, Andrew. 'Christianity'. *A Handbook of Living Religions* (ed John R Hinnells) (London: Penguin, 1991)

Watkin, E I. 'Unjustifiable War'. *Morals & Missiles* (London: 1959)

Weitzman, Mark. *Antisemitism: A Historical Survey.*

Why Didn't the Press Shout?: American and International Journalism During the Holocaust (ed Robert Moses Shapiro) (Brooklyn: KTAV Publishing House, 2003)

Wilhelm II. *The Kaiser's Memoirs I* (trans Thomas R Ybarra) (Harper & Bros, 1922)

Wills, Garry. *Papal Sin: Structures of Deceit* (New York: Image Books, 2000)

———. *Why Priests?: A Failed Tradition* (New York: Penguin Books, 2013)

Wistrich, Robert S. *Anti-Semitism: The Longest Hatred* (London: Methuen London, 1991)

———. *Who's Who in Nazi Germany* (New York: Macmillan, 1982)

Wraxall, C F Lascelles. *Historic Bye-ways: In Two Volumes.* Vol 2 (London: John Maxwell, 1864)

Yad Vashem Studies, Vol 6 (Jerusalem: Yad Vashem, 1967)

Yepes, Rodrigo de. *Historia de la muerte y glorioso martirio del santo inocente que llaman de Laguardia* (1583)

Zacharia, Fareed. *The Future of Freedom: Illiberal Democracy at Home and Abroad* (New York: W W Norton & Co, 2003, 2007)

Zahn, Gordon C. *German Catholics & Hitler's Wars: A Study in Social Control* (London: Sheed & Ward, 1963)

Zola, Émile. *J'accuse!* (1898)

Zuccotti, Susan. *The Italians and the Holocaust: Persecution, Rescue, and Survival* (New York: Basic Books, 1987)

——. *Under His Very Windows: The Vatican and the Holocaust in Italy* (Yale University Press, 2002)

Papal Allocutions, Bulls, Constitutions, Declarations, Encyclicals, and Such

Benedict XIII. *Etsi doctoribus genium*

Benedict XIV. *A Quo Primum*

——. *Beatus Andrea*

Benedict XVI. *Summorum Pontificum*

Callixtus III. *Si ad reprimendos*

Catechism of the Catholic Church (1993)

Clement IV. *Turbato corde (1267)*

Clement VIII. *Bull of 1591*

——. *Caeca et Obdurata Hebraeorum pefidia*

——. *Christiana pietas*

——. *Cum Hebraeorum malitia*

——. *Cum saepe accidere*

CRRJ. *Notes on the Correct Ways to Present Jews and Judaism in Preaching and Catechesis in the Roman Catholic Church*

——. *Religious Relations with the Jews: Guidelines for Implementing Nostra Aetate*

——. *We Remember: A Reflection on the Shoah*

Eugene IV. *Dudum ad nostram audientiam*

——. *Super Gregem Dominicum*

Gregory I. *Sicut judaeis non*

Gregory IX. *Bul. Rom. Pont., III, 497*

——. *Bul. Rom. Pont., IV, 509*

——. *Si vera sunt*

——. *Sufficere debuerat perfidioe judeorum perida*

Gregory X. *Turbato corde (1274)*

Gregory XIII. *Antiqua judaeorum improbitas allias piae*

Gregory XIII. *Multos adhuc ex Christianis*

——. *Sancta mater ecclesia*

——. *Vices eius nos*

Honorius III. *In generali concilio*

Innocent III. *Etsi non displiceat*

——. *Post miserabile*

Innocent IV. *Ad extirpanda*

——. *Impia gens*

——. *Impia judaeorum perfidia*

Martin V. *Etsi doctoribus genium*

——. *Sedes apostolica*

Nicholas III. *Vineam sorce*

Nicholas IV. *Turbato corde (1288)*

Nicholas V. *Super Gregem Dominicum*

Paul IV. *Cum nimis absurdum*

Paul VI. *Lumen Gentium*

Pius V. *Cum nos nuper*

——. *Hebraeorum gens sola*

Pius VI. *Editto sopra gli Ebrei*

Pius X. *Lamentabili Sane Exitu*

Pius XI. *Humani generis unitas*

——. *Quadragesimo Anno*

——. *Quas primas*

Pius XII. *Ad Apostolorum Principis*

Second Vatican Council. *Nostra Aetate*

Sixtus IV. *Numquam dubitavimus*

Urban VIII. *Cum allias piae*

Letters, Treatises and other Publications by Popes, Saints, Church Fathers, and the Like

Abélard, Pierre. *Dialogus inter Philosophum, Judaeum, et Christianum*

Agobard, St. *Letter to the Bishop of Narbonne*

——. *Epistola de baptizandis Hebraeis*

Albertus Magnus, St. *De animalibus*

Alexander III, Pope. *Ad Haec de Judaeis*

——. *Etsi Judaeos*

Amphilocius of Iconium, St. *Oration 5*

Aquinas, Thomas, St. *De regimine Iudaeorum ad Ducissam Brabantae*

Athanasius, St. *Letter 6 (Easter 334)*

Augustine, St. *Contra Judaeos*

——. *De Civitate Dei*

——. *Reply to Faustinus the Manichaean*

Barnabas. *Letter*

Basil ('Basil the Great'), St. *On Prayer*

Chrysostom, John, St. *Adversus Judaeos*

——. *Eight Orations (Homilies) against the Jews*

Clement VIII. *Caeca et obdurata*

Cyprian of Carthage, St. *The Lord's Prayer*

——. *Three Books of Testimonies against the Jews*

de Espina, Alonso, Friar. *Fortalitium fidei contra Judaeos*

Eisenmenger, Johann Andreas. *Entdecktes Judenthum*

Ephraem (Ephraim) the Syriac, St. *Rhythm against the Jews*

Eusebius of Caesarea. *Church History*

Fulgentius of Ruspe, St. *Writings*
Fumo, Bartolomeo, Fra. *De Judaeis*
Gregory IX. *de Judaeis*
—. *Epistle to the Hierarchy of Germany*
Gregory of Nyssa, St. *Oration on the Resurrection of Christ*
Hilary of Poitiers, St. *Tractus Mysteriorum*
Hippolytus of Rome. *Against the Jews*
Innocent III. *Epistle to the archbishops of Sens and Paris*
Irenaeus, St. *Against the Heresies*
Isidore. *De fide catholica contra Iudaeos*
Justin the Martyr, St. *Dialogue with the Jew Trypho*

Liguori, Alphonsus Maria. *The Passion and Death of Jesus Christ*
Maximus of Turin, St. *Christ our Leaven*
Melito of Sardis. *Peri Pascha*
Origen. *Contra Celsum*
Prudentius. *Apotheosis*
Stephen III, Pope. *Epistle to the Bishop of Narbonne*
Sulpicius Severus. *The Chronicle*
Tertullian. *Adversus Judaeos*
—. *Apologeticus*
Thomas de Chantimpré. *The Accursed Talmud*

Statutes, Edicts, Bills, Regulations, Resolutions, Oaths, and the Like

Arierparagraph
Aryan Law (Croatia)
Canons of the Councils of Elvira
Canons of the Councils of Toledo
Codex Gregorianus
Codex Hermogenianus
Codex Judaicus (Slovakia)
Codex Theodosianus
Constitutional Law 210 (Slovakia)
Corpus Juris Canonici
Corpus Juris Civilis
Decretum Gratiani
Decreto de la Alhambra
Edict of Expulsion (France)
Edict on the Jews (Bologna)
edicto al Ghetto judío
Első zsidótörvény 'a társadalmi és a gazdasági élet egyensúlyának hatályosabb biztosításáról'
Ermächtigungsgesetz
fuero de Cuenca
Ghetto Edict (Castilian)
Juramentum Judaeorum

Law to Limit the Expansion of Jews in the Public and Economic Domain (Hungary)
Ordenamiento de doña Catalina
Nürnberger Gesetze
Polizeiverordnung über die Kennzeichnung der Juden
Provvidimenti nei confronti degli ebrei stranieri. RDL 1381
Provvidimenti per la difesa della razza nella scuola fascita. RDL 1390
Reichsbürgergesetz
Resolution 67/19
Sentencia-Estatuto
Siete Partidas
Statut des Juifs
Statute of Blood Purity (Jesuit)
Statute of Jewry
Statutum Judeismo
Universal Declaration of Human Rights
Wiener Gesera
Zakonska odredba o rasnoj pripadnosti
Zidovsky kodex

The Press, Periodicals, Magazines, Documents, Declarations, and the Like

America
Auf gut Deutsch
Biblical Polemics
Bollettino antisemita
Catholic Standard
Catholic Universe
Central Europe Review
Chicago Sun-Times
Cistercian Studies Quarterly

Chronicle (of Konrad Justinger)
Common Knowledge
Commonweal
Corriere della Sera
CrossCurrents
Das Vaterland
Der Bauernbündler
Ebrei-Cristianesimo-Fascismo
Fede e Ragione

First Things Magazine
Frankfurter Allgemeine Zeitung
Free Inquiry
Frenchmen! Your Bishops address You
Gazeta Wyborcza
German Policy of Extermination of the Jewish Race
Giornale d'Italia
Glasnik Sv. Ante
Grazer Volksblatt
Gränzbote
Historisch-Politische Blätter für das katholische
    Deutschland
Holocaust and Genocide Studies
Homiletic and Pastoral Review
Hrvatska Straža
I Documenti della conquista ebraica del Mondo
Il Regime Fascista
Il Tevere
International Humanist News
Jewish Political Studies Review
Jewish Spectator
Journal of Hate Studies
Journal of Religion & Society
Judaism
Katholisches Kirchenblatt
Katolički Tjednik
Kikiriki
Kleines Kirchenblatt
Klerus Zeitschrift für soziale Arbeit
Klerusblatt
Kultura
L'Osservatore Cattolico
L'Osservatore Romano
L'Unità Cattolica
L'Univers
La Civiltà Cattolica
La Corrispondenza
La Croix
La Croix du Nord
La Cruz
La Défense
La Difesa della razza
La Libre Parole
La Semaine religieuse de Cambrai
Le Bloc Catholique
Le Flambeau
Le Pèlerin
Mały Dziennik

Manchester Guardian
Matičné zvesti
Narodne Novine
Nasz Dziennik
National Catholic Reporter
National Journal (Hungary)
New Britain
New Generation (Hungary)
Nueu Zürcher Zeitung
Occasional Papers on Religion in Eastern Europe
Operational Situation Report USSR No. 54
Perche siamo antisemiti
Piccolo Monitore delle Associazioni cattoliche
    dell'Umbria
POLIN. Studies in Polish Jewry
Polityka
Pro Christo
Reflections on Covenant and Mission
Reforme
Reichsport
Report of the Inter-Allied Information Committee in
    London
Revue du Monde Catholique
Revue Internationale des Sociétés Secrètes
Ruch Katolicki
Salzburger Volksblatt
Schönere Zukunft
Seele
Slovák
Sme
Sodalis Marianus
South-East Europe Review
St Heinricksblatt
Stimmen aus Maria Laach
Stimmen der Zeit
The Atlantic
The Australian
The Baltic Times
The Catholic Times
The Catholic Worker
The Churchman's Monthly Review
The Independent
The Jerusalem Post
The Jewish Magazine
The Jewish Quarterly Review
The Jewish Standard
The Point
The Slovak Spectator

The Tablet   Warschauer Zeitung
The Times of Israel   Why Jews are Persecuted in Germany
The Wall Street Journal   Wiener Kirchenzeitung
Tikkun   Yad Vashem Studies
Tygodnik Powszechny   ZENIT. 'The world seen from Rome'
Völkischer Beobachter

Index

Lightning Source UK Ltd.
Milton Keynes UK
UKHW011226290319
340144UK00001B/123/P